Property and Trust Law in Singapore

Property and Trust Law in Singapore

Alvin See
Yip Man
Goh Yihan

This book was originally published as a monograph in the International Encyclopaedia of Laws/Property and Trust Law.

Founding Editor: Roger Blanpain
General Editor: Frank Hendrickx
Volume Editors: Alain Verbeke & Vincent Sagaert

Wolters Kluwer

Published by:
Kluwer Law International B.V.
PO Box 316
2400 AH Alphen aan den Rijn
The Netherlands
E-mail: international-sales@wolterskluwer.com
Website: lrus.wolterskluwer.com

Sold and distributed in North, Central and South America by:
Wolters Kluwer Legal & Regulatory U.S.
7201 McKinney Circle
Frederick, MD 21704
United States of America
Email: customer.service@wolterskluwer.com

Sold and distributed in all other countries by:
Air Business Subscriptions
Rockwood House
Haywards Heath
West Sussex
RH16 3DH
United Kingdom
Email: international-customerservice@wolterskluwer.com

ISBN 978-94-035-0884-9

e-Book: ISBN 978-94-035-0885-6
web-PDF: ISBN 978-94-035-0890-0

This title is available on www.kluwerlawonline.com

The Authors

Alvin See is Assistant Professor of Law (Education) in the School of Law, Singapore Management University. He teaches Property Law, the Law of Equity and Trusts and Business Law. His research focuses mainly on property, unjust enrichment and civil remedies, but he also dabbles in animal law. He has published in reputable international peer-reviewed journals, including *Lloyd's Maritime Commercial Law Quarterly*, *Conveyancer and Property Lawyer*, *Law Quarterly Review*, *Journal of Business Law*, *Restitution Law Review* and *Journal of Contract Law*. He is also the Co-section Editor (Singapore & Hong Kong) for the *Property Law Review* (2017–present). His articles have been cited by courts in Singapore and Malaysia as well as leading works on private law. In recognition of his teaching excellence, he was the recipient of the School of Law's Dean's Teaching Excellence award (2015, 2016, 2018) and Most Outstanding Teacher award (2017) as well as the university-level Excellent Teacher award (2018) and Most Promising Teacher award (2015).

Yip Man is Associate Professor of Law in the School of Law at the Singapore Management University. Her principal research interests are in equity and trusts, private international law, contract law and restitution. She has published in leading international and local peer-reviewed journals, including *International and Comparative Law Quarterly*, *Cambridge Law Journal*, *Law Quarterly Review*, *Legal Studies*, *Lloyd's Maritime Commercial Law Quarterly*, *Journal of Equity*, *Restitution Law Review*, *Conveyancer and Property Lawyer*, *Journal of Private International Law*, *Trusts and Trustees*, *Journal of Business Law*, *Singapore Academy of Law Journal* and *Singapore Journal of Legal Studies*. In recognition of her research, she has been awarded the DS Lee Foundation Fellowship in 2016 and the Lee Kong Chian Fellowship in 2018. Her works have been cited by the Singapore Court of Appeal, the Singapore High Court, the High Court of England and Wales as well as leading treaties on private law. She has acted as an expert on Singapore commercial law and private international law in a recent arbitration matter. She is presently the Deputy Director of Centre for Cross-Border Commercial Law in Asia (SMU) and the Private Law Cluster Coordinator at the SMU School of Law. She is an editor of *Trust Law International* and the Asia-Pacific Digest Editor of *Restitution Law Review*.

Associate Professor Goh Yihan is the Dean of the School of Law, Singapore Management University. His research focuses primarily on the law of contract and torts, with a secondary interest in the principles of statutory interpretation and the legal process. In recognition of his contributions to the development and advancement of Singapore law, he became the youngest recipient of the pentennial Singapore Academy of Law Singapore Law Merit Award in 2013. Apart from his academic activities, Yihan is also active in the Singapore legal profession. Amongst his appointments, he is a board member of the Singapore Institute of Legal Education and the Singapore Judicial College. He has been appointed amicus curiae before the Singapore Court of Appeal and the Singapore High Court. He is also a Visiting Academic at Rajah & Tann Singapore LLP and a Professorial Fellow at the AGC Academy. He is periodically consulted by law firms in his areas of expertise and has appeared as instructed counsel and an expert witness. Before entering academia, Yihan was an Assistant Registrar, the Senior Justices' Law Clerk and a Justices' Law Clerk between 2006 and 2008 at the Singapore Supreme Court.

Table of Contents

List of Abbreviations

AELA	Application of English Law Act
AVA	Agri-Food & Veterinary Authority of Singapore
BCA	Building and Construction Authority
BMSMA	Building Maintenance and Strata Management Act
BSA	Bills of Sale Act
CA	Companies Act
CLA	Civil Law Act
CLO	Crown Lands Ordinance
CLPA	Conveyancing and Law of Property Act
CRTPA	Contracts (Rights of Third Parties) Act
HDB	Housing and Development Board
LAA	Land Acquisition Act
LTA	Land Titles Act
LTO	Land Titles Ordinance
LTSA	Land Titles (Strata) Act
MCST	Management Corporation Strata Title
MRTC	Mass Rail Transit Corporation
OCBC	Oversea-Chinese Banking Corporation
OTP	Option to Purchase
OUE	Overseas Union Enterprise
PC	Privy Council
RHB	RHB Bank
SCB	Standard Chartered Bank
SCDF	Singapore Civil Defence Force
SGCA	Singapore Court of Appeal
SGDC	Singapore District Court
SGHC	Singapore High Court
SHD	Singapore Height Datum

List of Abbreviations

SLA	Singapore Land Authority
SLR	Singapore Law Reports
SSLR	Straits Settlement Law Reports
STB	Strata Titles Boards
UOB	United Overseas Bank
UOF	United Overseas Finance
URA	Urban Redevelopment Authority
URAA	Urban Redevelopment Authority Act

Preface

Land law, personal property law and trust law are more often than not taught in different courses as though they are discrete topics. The Property and Trusts monograph series of the International Encyclopaedia of Laws departs from this conventional approach by placing all three topics into a single collection. While this makes writing the book more challenging, we hope that this style of presentation enables readers to better appreciate the connections, interplay and independence between the topics, which we find to be important in the study of land law, the personal property law and the law of trusts.

This book is written as a general introduction to the laws of property and trusts in Singapore. The topics are examined against the country's history, societal conditions and policies to highlight trends and aspects of property and trust laws that are unique to Singapore.

Originally written with our students in mind, we have attempted to strike a good balance between accessibility and depth. With an emphasis on the practical application of the law, the legal principles are discussed by reference to the facts of decided cases and real-life examples. By also weighing in on controversial aspects of the law, we hope that this book will appeal not only to students but also to scholars and practitioners.

It merits mentioning that the completion of this project would have been impossible without the support of Singapore Management University, School of Law and our colleagues with whom we have had the benefit and joys of teaching The Law of Property, The Law of Equity & Trusts and Contract Law. We are also grateful for the able research assistance rendered by Chan Ming Jie, Choo Kwok Meang, Ho Wei Yang, Daniel Lim, Pesdy Tay and Andrea Seet. Their meticulous proofreading, in particular, has helped us in delivering the content as accurately as possible.

Above all, we thank our families for their unrelenting love, encouragement and support.

Although we were able to accommodate some later developments during the editorial process, our aim is to state the law as of 1 March 2018.

AS, YM & GYH

ce

Contributions

Alvin See
Part I (Land) Chapters 1–13,
Part II (Personal Property) Chapters 1–2
Part III (Acquisition of Property Rights) Chapters 1–7
Part IV (Trusts) Chapter 3
Yip Man
Part IV (Trusts) Chapters 2, 5–8
Goh Yihan
General Introduction
Part IV (Trusts) Chapters 1–2 & 4

General Introduction

§1. General Background of the Country

I. Geography

1. Singapore is an independent city-nation situated at the southern tip of the Malay Peninsula. It used to be a British colony from 1819 until its independence in 1965. Apart from its main island, Singapore also consists of several other much smaller islands. The main island is extremely small: it is approximately 42 km in length and 23 km in breadth, making for a total land area of approximately 712.4 km^2.[1] Reclamation work has added to the existing land area.[2] The main island comprises mainly flat land, with the greater part of the island within 15 m of sea level, the highest point being Bukit Timah peak that is only 163.36 m high.[3]

II. Population and Cultural Composition

2. The population of the island presently exceeds 5 million and continues to grow.[4] Out of this total population, over 3 million are residents in Singapore. There are three main ethnic groups (*viz*, Chinese, Malay and Indian), with the Chinese population constituting over 70% of the total population.[5] This multiracial nature of the population is further nuanced: for example, there are many dialect groups within the Chinese and Malay communities, although there are only four official languages (Malay, Mandarin, Tamil and English). Uniquely among multiracial countries, Singapore continues to grow in both strength and unity and does not suffer from ethnic and other divisiveness and consequent violence.

---

1. 'Statistics Singapore: Key Annual Indicators' <http://www.singstat.gov.sg/stats/keyind.html #popnarea> 25 March 2011.
2. There are, of course, limitations, not least of which would be territorial limits under international law.
3. 'Singapore at a Glance' <http://app.www.sg/who/1/Singapore-at-a-Glance.aspx> 25 March 2011.
4. 'Statistics Singapore: Key Annual Indicators' <http://www.singstat.gov.sg/stats/keyind.html #popnarea> 25 March 2011.
5. 'Census of Population 2010 Statistical Release 1: Demographic Characteristics, Education, Language and Religion' (Singapore: Singapore Department of Statistics, 2011) at 35.

III. Political System

3. The Singapore political system is based on the Westminster system, with three different and coequal branches of government: (1) the executive, (2) the legislature and (3) the judiciary. We will elaborate on this when we discuss this division in the context of the Singapore legal system.

§2. The Singapore Legal System: A Brief Overview

I. The Legal Framework

A. The Executive, Legislature and Judiciary

4. Singapore is a republic with a parliamentary system of government based on the Westminster model.[6] This model, which in Singapore is created by the Constitution, comprises three branches: the Executive, Legislature and Judiciary. The three branches play different, if at times overlapping, roles within the Singapore legal system.

5. The Executive includes the Elected President, the Cabinet and the Attorney-General.[7] Each performs various vital roles in the Singapore legal system. For instance, if the President does not agree with the advice given to him/her by the Prime Minister, he has the power to refuse to make an appointment, or refuse to revoke an appointment, to a number of key offices in the legal system, including the Chief Justice, Judges and Judicial Commissioners of the Supreme Court and the Attorney-General.[8] This power was meant to avoid an irresponsible government making such key appointments based on considerations other than merit.[9] However, this power is not untrammelled in practice. The President must, for one, consult with the Council of Presidential Advisers in the exercise of such power.[10] While the President is not directly bound by the Council's recommendation, an amendment to the Constitution[11] provides that the President's refusal to make or revoke an appointment may be overruled by a resolution passed by at least two-thirds of all elected Members of Parliament, if his refusal was contrary to such recommendation.[12]

---

6. 'Our Legal System', Ministry of Law <http://www.mlaw.gov.sg/content/minlaw/en/our-legal-system.html> 13 May 2014.
7. 'Our Legal System', Ministry of Law <http://www.mlaw.gov.sg/content/minlaw/en/our-legal-system.html> 13 May 2014.
8. Article 22(1), Constitution of the Republic of Singapore (1999 Rev. Ed.).
9. 'Constitutional amendments to safeguard financial assets and the integrity of the public services', Cmd 10 of 1988 para 11.
10. Article 21(3), Constitution of the Republic of Singapore (1999 Rev. Ed.).
11. Constitution of the Republic of Singapore (Amendment) Act 1998 (No. 41 of 1996)
12. Article 22(2), Constitution of the Republic of Singapore (1999 Rev. Ed.).

6. The Cabinet, which comprises the Prime Minister and Ministers appointed from the Members of Parliament, is responsible for the general direction and control of the Government.[13] In particular, a Minister on behalf of the Government usually introduces drafts of laws, also known as 'Bills' before they are passed by Parliament.[14] While the Bill must go through three readings in Parliament and receive the President's assent before it becomes law, the Minister's initial draft sets the initial direction of the law. Thus, subject to Parliament's passage and the President's assent, the Cabinet has considerable latitude in shaping the laws of the Singapore and, through that, developing the legal system.

7. Last, the Attorney-General is the principal legal advisor to the Government.[15] In that capacity, he may influence the drafting of Bills and other written laws. In conjunction with the various departments of the Attorney-General's Chambers, he may also reform the laws of Singapore. The Attorney-General is also the Public Prosecutor and possesses the sole discretion to 'institute, conduct or discontinue any proceedings for any offence'.[16]

8. The Legislature comprises the President and Parliament. Together, they are responsible for enacting statutory laws.[17] Apart from elected Members of Parliament, Parliament also consists of non-elected Members, who sit in debates but with restricted voting rights. After a Bill has been introduced by a Minister (or a Member), it is given a First Reading without any debate. If the Minister proposes that the Bill be read a second time, Members of Parliament then debate the Bill and vote on whether the Bill should be given a Second Reading. If the Bill is read a second time, it goes to the Committee of the Whole Parliament or a Select Committee, which will then examine the Bill clause by clause. Following the Committee's report back to Parliament, the Bill will be given its Third Reading and then passed. The Bill then goes to the Presidential Council for Minority Rights, which considers if the Bill has any differentiating measure that affects any racial or religious community. Once approved by the Council, the Bill will be assented to by the President and gazetted in the Government Gazette to become law.[18]

9. The Judiciary, which is headed by the Chief Justice, consists of the judges and judicial officers of the Supreme Court and State Courts. Singapore has a two-tier court system. The first tier comprises the State Courts, which consist of the District Courts, the Magistrates' Courts and various specialised courts. Collectively, these

13. 'Our Legal System', Ministry of Law <http://www.mlaw.gov.sg/content/minlaw/en/our-legal-system.html> 13 May 2014.
14. 'What we do', Parliament of Singapore <http://www.parliament.gov.sg/what-we-do> 4 May 2014. However, any Member of Parliament may introduce a Private Member's Bill as well.
15. Article 35(7), Constitution of the Republic of Singapore (1999 Rev. Ed.).
16. Article 35(8), Constitution of the Republic of Singapore (1999 Rev. Ed.).
17. 'Our Legal System', Ministry of Law <http://www.mlaw.gov.sg/content/minlaw/en/our-legal-system.html> 13 May 2014.
18. 'What we do', Parliament of Singapore <http://www.parliament.gov.sg/what-we-do> 4 May 2014.

courts are responsible for more than 95% of the Judiciary's caseload.[19] These courts' authority to hear civil and criminal cases is limited to prescribed monetary amounts or criminal sanctions. The second tier of the Singapore court system is the Supreme Court, which comprises the Court of Appeal and the High Court. Both courts can hear criminal and civil cases in excess of the State Courts' authority. The Court of Appeal is the highest court of the land and its decisions are not subject to any further appeal.

10. Apart from these judicial functions, the Judiciary, mainly through the Singapore Academy of Law, also engages in the governance and reform of the Singapore legal system. For example, the Chief Justice chairs a committee that appoints Senior Counsel from amongst the outstanding lawyers in Singapore. The Academy, separately from the Attorney-General's Chambers, also engages in the reform of various laws in Singapore.

B. A Common Law System

11. The Singapore legal system is a common law system. Judges rely on the doctrine of precedent, by which they are bound by the law as stated in cases decided by higher courts. Courts, especially higher courts, can develop the law incrementally, in accordance with the principles of stare decisis, in response to changing social and economic conditions.

12. The principles relating to stare decisis are well established in Singapore. Insofar as its vertical aspect is concerned, decisions of the highest court, the Court of Appeal, bind all lower courts. The issue of horizontal stare decisis is, however, complicated by the problem that a number of courts would constitute predecessor courts of co-ordinate jurisdiction and thus result in their decisions being binding on the present Singapore High Court, which is subject to the doctrine of horizontal stare decisis (following the 'rule' in *Young v. Bristol Aeroplane Co Ltd*).[20]

13. However, the Singapore Court of Appeal is not completely bound by its own previous decisions. In a Practice Statement (Judicial Precedent),[21] the court declared that it would not, in exceptional circumstances, consider itself bound by its own previous decisions:

> We recognise the vital role that the doctrine of stare decisis plays in giving certainty to the law and predictability in its application to similar cases. However, we also recognise that the political, social and economic circumstances of Singapore have changed enormously since Singapore became an independent and

19. 'Overview', State Courts of Singapore <https://app.statecourts.gov.sg//subcourts/page.aspx?pageid=4393> 28 April 2011.
20. [1944] KB 718.
21. [1994] 2 SLR 689.

sovereign republic. The development of our law should reflect these changes and the fundamental values of Singapore society.

Accordingly, it is proper that the Court of Appeal should not hold itself bound by any previous decisions of its own or of the Privy Council, which by the rules of precedent prevailing prior to 8 April 1994 were binding on it, in any case where adherence to such prior decisions would cause injustice in a particular case or constrain the development of the law in conformity with the circumstances of Singapore.

Therefore, while this court will continue to treat such prior decisions as normally binding, this court will, whenever it appears right to do so, depart from such prior decisions. Bearing in mind the danger of retrospectively disturbing contractual, proprietary and other legal rights, this power will be exercised sparingly.

This statement is not intended to affect the use of precedent in the High Court or in any subordinate courts.[22]

14. The principles of stare decisis do not bind the Singapore courts to the decisions of the English courts, despite the fact that Singapore used to be a British colony. This is now beyond all doubt with the enactment of the Application of English Law Act (AELA) in 1993 and the issuance of the Practice Statement (Judicial Precedent).[23]

II. Development of an Autochthonous Singapore Legal System

15. The development of an autochthonous Singapore legal system only took off in the 1990s.[24] The courts, particularly in the decades shortly after independence, generally accepted English decisions without question. Indeed, while the earliest decisions favoured giving the local population the full benefit of their own laws, religions and customs,[25] such modifications were rarely forthcoming in cases concerning land law and commercial law, where the greater commercial interests of the British empire (as given effect by a uniform application of English law) prevailed.[26]

16. The passage of the AELA in 1993 set off a series of events that led to the development and spread of an autochthonous body of Singapore law. It enabled the courts to develop a uniquely Singapore jurisprudence. It did so by providing that English law no longer bound the Singapore courts thereby freeing the courts to make laws suitable for the local conditions. It heralded a renewed sense that the Singapore courts are independent from foreign oversight and must develop its own jurisprudence. Indeed, driven perhaps by the effects of the AELA, Chief Justice

22. [1994] 2 SLR 689.
23. [1994] 2 SLR 689.
24. *See* Goh Yihan, 'Tort Law in the Face of Land Scarcity in Singapore' (2009) 26 Arizona J Intl & Comp L 335 at 351–353.
25. *See* Helena H.M. Chan, *An Introduction to the Singapore Legal System* (Malayan Law Journal, 1986) at 8.
26. *See ibid.*, at 9–10.

Yong Pung How said in 1995 that Singapore 'must develop its own legal system, and where necessary, part company with the English'.[27] He highlighted that the courts' approach to the law 'must reflect our own Asian values, such as consensus and respect for authority'.[28]

17. Today, the Singapore courts are actively developing an autochthonous Singapore legal system with decisions that reflect national social and economic values. Nevertheless, it must be emphasised that, notwithstanding the desirability of developing an autochthonous Singapore legal system, legal autochthony is not to be pursued for its own sake.[29]

III. Sources of Singapore Law

A. *The Reception of English Law*

18. The foundation of the Singapore legal system is clear, *viz*, English law. This is not surprising in view of the fact that the nation state began its modern history as a British colony in 1819. Although the British left behind workable legal and judicial structures and institutions, there was considerable confusion as the extent to which English law was received in Singapore after the British left. This was largely a result of the interaction between English law and local conditions.

19. The interaction between English and Singapore law began with Raffles' 1823 Code. Although the Code established that English law would apply to all,[30] it also catered for local conditions so long as they did not offend English legal principles.[31] Indeed, Raffles acknowledged that it would be 'repugnant to natural justice' to apply the law of Europe directly to a settlement whose population was nine-tenth natives of China and the Malay archipelago.[32] Raffles proclaimed that the principles of English law should apply, but with mildness, kindness and 'indulgent consideration for the prejudices of each tribes [sic] as far as substantial justice will allow'.[33] However, the reality was quite different: English law was still predominantly applied because the colonial judges who administered law were familiar with it and regarded it as 'superior' to the local conditions.[34]

27. 'S'pore must develop its own legal system', *Straits Times*, 13 September 1995 at 27; see also 'Distinctively S'porean', *The Business Times*, 9 November 1995 at 6; 'Courts' role to develop the law', *Straits Times* 15 September 2000 at 59.
28. 'S'pore must develop its own legal system', *Straits Times*, 13 September 1995 at 27.
29. *See* Andrew Phang, *From Foundation to Legacy – The Second Charter of Justice* (Singapore Academy of Law, 2006) at 60.
30. 'Report by the Lieutenant-Governor on the Magistracy and Administration of Justice' in *The Singapore Local Laws and Institutions, 1823* (London: Cox and Baylis, 1824) at 37.
31. *Ibid.*
32. 'Proclamation respecting the Administration of Justice', in *The Singapore Local Laws and Institutions, 1823* (London: Cox and Baylis, 1824) at 40.
33. *Ibid.*, at 47.
34. Andrew Phang Boon Leong, *The Development of Singapore Law* (Singapore: Butterworths, 1990) at 55–61.

20. Such interaction between English law and local conditions continued with the Second Charter of Justice in 1826. The Charter created a single legal system for all, with established laws and institutions that were able to 'give and pass Judgment and Sentence according to Justice and Right'. Although the Charter did not mention that English law applied, the landmark case of *Regina v. Willans*[35] decided that it did introduce English law into the Straits Settlements of Penang, Malacca and Singapore. However, English law was to be applied subject to modifications to suit the circumstances of the place and the customs, religions, usages and manners of the native inhabitants.[36]

21. The problem of how far English law applied became more serious after Singapore became independent, since there was now a conflict between two independent bodies of laws. The problems generated by this conflict can be demonstrated by the specific reception of English law by section 5 of the Civil Law Act.[37] Section 5 provides for the continuous reception of English commercial law. However, the first difficulty was whether the provision entailed the reception of the common law as well.[38] The second difficulty was the problem of characterisation. It was unclear how a local court was to ascertain whether an issue had arisen that called for the application of section 5. The problems with section 5, as well as the extent to which English law applied in Singapore, was only to be solved many years after Singapore's independence.

22. The specific problems surrounding section 5 are far too complex to render in detail here. Indeed, there is copious literature that examines the historical background as well as the intractable difficulties associated with this provision.[39] More importantly, section 5 has since been repealed. There is therefore no need to delve into technical detail in order to understand the historical roots just referred to.

B. The Application of English Law Act

23. After almost 175 years since the founding of modern Singapore by the British in 1819, the Singapore legislature passed the extremely important AELA[40] that

35. (1858) 3 Ky 16.
36. *Yeap Cheah Neo v. Ong Cheng Neo* (1875) LR 6 PC 381 at 393.
37. (Cap. 43, 1988 Rev. Ed.).
38. The original purpose of section 5 can be inferred from part of a report on the original Civil Law Ordinance by Thomas Braddell which was enclosed in the then Governor's (William C.F. Robinson) submission of, among others, the Civil Law Ordinance to the then Secretary of State, M.E. Hicks Beach, Bart, for the Queen's Confirmation and Allowance.
39. *See*, e.g., Andrew Phang, 'Theoretical Conundrums and Practical Solutions in Singapore Commercial Law: A Review and Application of Section 5 of the Civil Law Act' (1988) 17 *Anglo-American L Rev* 251, and the literature cited therein, as well as Soon Choo Hock and Andrew Phang Boon Leong, 'Reception of English Commercial Law in Singapore – A Century of Uncertainty' in Andrew Harding (ed.), *The Common Law in Singapore and Malaysia* (Butterworths, 1985) Chapter 2.
40. No. 35 of 1993. The date of coming into operation of the Act is 12 November 1993: see Art. 58(2) of the Constitution of the Republic of Singapore (1999 Rev. Ed.) and section 10(b) of the Interpretation Act (Cap. 1, 2002 Rev. Ed.). And see generally Andrew Phang, 'Cementing the Foundations:

clarifies the application of English law in the island republic. The Act purports (save for certain exceptions[41]) to be exhaustive,[42] and the discussion of the sources of Singapore law must now be read in the light of the provisions of this Act which settle many of the problems hitherto existing, especially with regard to section 5 of the Civil Law Act.[43]

24. Constraints of space preclude an extended discussion of the AELA. What may be stated shortly is that the AELA has done away with many of the problems and consequent uncertainty that existed previously. The Minister of Law has therefore justifiably described it as 'one of the most significant law reform measures since Singapore's independence'.[44] Indeed, the AELA was also viewed by the Minister as being consistent with the development of an autochthonous Singapore legal system. In particular, the Minister stated that the Government would be taking further steps to amend the local law in order to free it from dependence on English law. He further stated that '[w]e must have certainty in our laws and move away from reliance on English law, because we do not know what the conditions are that shape the UK decisions'.[45] In a similar vein, the Minister also observed earlier that 'it makes our commercial law independent of future legislative changes in the [UK] – changes which we have in fact no control'.[46] The Minister was, in this last-mentioned regard, probably referring to the very real problems centring on the UK's entry into the European Community, which problems were in fact perceived as far back as 1979 when the Civil Law Act was amended.

25. The basic structure of the AELA itself may be worth noting briefly. The AELA attempts to encompass (as far as is possible) all applicable English laws within its four corners. In this regard, section 5 of the AELA is instructive, as it provides that:

> **Other enactments not part of law of Singapore**
>
> 5. (1) Except as provided in this Act, no English enactment[47] shall be part of the law of Singapore.

The *Singapore Application of English Law Act 1993*' (1994) 28 *U British Columbia L Rev* 205 and, by the same author, *Cheshire, Fifoot and Furmston's Law of Contract*, 2nd Singapore and Malaysian edn (Butterworths Asia, 1998) at 19–31.

41. These principally centre on various specific reception provisions, but shall not be discussed here; and see section 4(1)(b) of the AELA. There are clear problems which tend to militate against the certainty achieved by the present Act (see e.g., G.W. Bartholomew, 'The Singapore Statute Book' (1984) 26 *Malayan L Rev* 1 at 15.
42. And see section 5(1) which states that '[e]xcept as provided in this Act, no English enactment shall be part of the law of Singapore'.
43. (Cap. 43, 1999 Rev. Ed.).
44. *See Singapore Parliamentary Debates, Official Report*, vol. 61, col. 616 (12 October 1993) (Prof. S. Jayakumar, Minister for Law, during the Second Reading stage of the Bill).
45. *See ibid.*
46. *See ibid.*; see also vol. 61, cols 611 and 613.
47. 'English enactment' is defined in section 2 of the Application of English Law Act (Cap. 7A, 1994 Rev. Ed.) as meaning 'an enactment of the Parliament of England, the Parliament of Great Britain

(2) Where any English enactment ceases by virtue of this Act to be part of the law of Singapore, the Interpretation Act[48] shall apply as it would apply on the repeal of an Act of the Parliament of Singapore.

26. Second, section 4 of the AELA deals with English statute law. The net effect of this particular provision is to list English enactments that are considered to be part of Singapore law. However, where a local statute in fact provides expressly for the reception of an English enactment(s), such an (English) enactment will be part of Singapore law;[49] in this specific regard, specific reception of English law is, therefore, alive and well, although its chief 'protagonist', *viz*, section 5 of the Civil Law Act, has been laid to rest. Indeed, section 5 of the Civil Law Act is repealed, although some saving is provided for in transitional situations. This is to be found in sections 6(1) and 6(2), respectively, of the AELA, which read as follows:

Repeal

6. (1) Subject to subsection (2), section 5 of the Civil Law Act is repealed.
(2) In respect of any proceedings instituted or any cause of action accruing before 12th November 1993,[50] section 5 of the Civil Law Act shall continue to apply as if it had not been repealed by this Act.

27. Section 7 read with the Second Schedule details specific amendments to be made to specific local Acts. These amendments are primarily based on specific provisions of English legislation (principally in the fields of real property, trusts, succession, insurance and piracy) and have been inserted in the relevant local Acts. All archaic language has been done away with, in many cases by way of adoption of the latest restatement of the original statutory provision.[51] Some of these amendments (as at the time of the enactment of the AELA) that may be of potentially more interest to commercial lawyers may be briefly mentioned here: these include the new section 6 of the Civil Law Act[52] which is based on section 4 of the UK Statute of Frauds 1677[53] which was itself replaced by section 40 of the Law of Property

or the Parliament of the United Kingdom'. This is, of course, subject to the usual caveat embodied in the phrase 'unless the context otherwise requires', which is also to be found in section 2.

48. Interpretation Act (Cap. 1, 2002 Rev. Ed.): see section 16.
49. *See* section 4(1)(b) of the Application of English Law Act (Cap. 7A, 1994 Rev. Ed.).
50. The date of coming into force of the Application of English Law Act 1993 (Act 35 of 1993).
51. A good example is the adoption of the relevant provisions of the UK Law of Property Act 1925 instead of the older statutory counterparts in, e.g., the Statute of Frauds 1677 or the Accumulations Act 1800.
52. (Cap. 43, 1999 Rev. Ed.).
53. *Cf* also the new section 7 of the Civil Law Act which is based on sections 7, 8 and 9 of the 1677 Act which was, in turn, replaced by section 53 of the Law of Property Act 1925.

Act 1925[54] and the new sections 64 and 65 of the Insurance Act[55] which are based on the UK Life Assurance Act 1774 and section 86 of the Fire Prevention (Metropolis) Act 1774, respectively.[56]

C. Common Law and Equity

28. As discussed above, it is clear that the common law forms part of Singapore law. In addition to the common law, another important source of law in Singapore is equity. As the Singapore Court of Appeal stated in *Lau Siew Kim v. Yeo Guan Chye Terence*,[57] equity 'is the body of principles that has evolved progressively to mitigate the severity sometimes occasioned by the rigid application of the rules of the common law'.[58] Thus, in Singapore, as in other Commonwealth jurisdictions, equity forms a distinct body of law with unique characteristics that distinguish it from the common law. Many of equity's unique characteristics can be explained by its historical genesis.

1. Historical Development of Equity and Its Relationship with Common Law

29. In medieval England, the common law developed rapidly. However, rules of the common law were inflexible. Judges interpreted and applied the law strictly, and not before long, the common law was a web of complex rules. What made the common law especially inflexible was that claimants had to bring their cases within clearly established forms of action. Each form of action prescribed precise elements, all of which must be satisfied, failing which the claimant would not succeed. Claimants were also bound by strict rules of pleading and proof. Collectively, these made the common law emphasise form over substance, and the instances of injustice were plentiful. Thus, Loughlan has described one of the perceived sources of inadequacy and injustice in the common law being found in the generality of its rules and the ability of the rules to fit the circumstances of the particular case.[59]

54. Though *c.* now the change wrought by the UK Law of Property (Miscellaneous Provisions) Act 1989.
55. (Cap. 142, 1994 Rev. Ed.).
56. Reference may also be made to the new sections 73A, 73B and 73C of the Conveyancing and Law of Property (Cap. 61, 1985 Rev. Ed.) which deal with a joint tenant or tenant in common being liable to account to his co-owner for receiving more than his share or proportion of any rents or profits arising from the property; voluntary conveyances to defraud creditors; and voluntary dispositions of land, respectively. These three new sections are based (respectively) on the (UK) Administration of Justice Act 1705, the statute 13 Eliz., c. 5 (1571), and the statute 27 Eliz., c. 4 (1585), the latter two of which have been rendered into modern form in sections 172 and 173 of the Law of Property Act 1925, respectively.
57. [2007] SGCA 54; [2008] 2 SLR(R) 108.
58. *Ibid.*, [24].
59. Patricia Loughlan, 'The Historical Role of the Equitable Jurisdiction' in Patrick Parkinson (ed.), *The Principles of Equity*, 2nd edn (Lawbook Co, 2003) 3 at 6.

30. The slender stream of redress was the possibility of a petition being made to the King to seek justice. The King's approach, much like a non-lawyer would view the law today, was to concentrate on the substantive justice of the case, rather than whether every legal requirement was met. The approach, in contrast to the strict forms of action adopted by the common law, was flexible. Thus laid the early foundations of equity. Eventually, the sheer number of petitions meant that the King had to delegate the hearing of petitions to his chief minister, the Lord Chancellor. The Lord Chancellor, who might have been influenced by biblical notions of fairness and justice, as well as Greek and Roman authors, was ultimately moved by his own conscience.[60] A system based on a person's conscience was inherently discretionary and flexible and gave rise to the notion that equity is a 'roguish' thing, with no standard form of measure save for what John Selden famously called the chancellor's foot.[61]

31. Ultimately, both the King and his Lord Chancellor were unable to deal with the number of petitions. A separate court, known as the Court of Chancery, was established for the purpose of hearing these petitions. Thus was born the system that administered a body of law that we know today as equity. At its inception, the law administered by the Court of Chancery was very different from that meted out by the common law courts. Because of its origins, it was much more discretionary and flexible. Early decisions did not follow any abstract methodology and any strict notion of precedent, and there was, accordingly, no commitment to the values of continuity, consistency, uniformity and predictability, in stark contrast to the common law.[62] This manifested not only in establishing whether a claim had been made out but also extended to the powers and remedies that could be exercised and given. For example, whereas monetary compensation was the primary remedy in the common law courts, the Court of Chancery fashioned the injunction, which allowed the court to order that a party do or desist from doing a certain thing. In some cases, this was far more effective than monetary compensation, for it compelled the performance or non-performance of an act for which failure to do so amounted to contempt of court.

32. As equity developed in its own distinct manner alongside the common law, it soon became unclear which one prevailed in certain cases. In the *Earl of Oxford's case*,[63] Lord Chancellor Ellesmere decided that equity should prevail over the common law, given that its function was 'to soften and mollify the extremity of the law'. In the subsequent case of *Lord Dudley v. Lady Dudley*, Lord Chancellor Cowper said that 'equity is no part of the law, but a moral virtue which qualifies, moderates and reforms the rigour, hardness and edge of the law'.[64] And thus was formalised the modern view that equity exists to moderate the harshness of the common law, which was the very purpose of equity to begin with.

60. *See* Graham Virgo, *The Principles of Equity and Trusts* (OUP, 2012) at 6.
61. Frederick Pollock (ed.), *Table Talk of John Selden* (Selden Society, 1927) at 43.
62. Patricia Loughlan, 'The Historical Role of the Equitable Jurisdiction' in Patrick Parkinson (ed.), *The Principles of Equity*, 2nd edn (Lawbook Co, 2003) 3 at 6.
63. (1615) 1 Ch Rep 1.
64. (1705) Prec Ch 241 at 244.

33. While equity started out as ad hoc petitions made to the Court of Chancery, which brought with it a measure of discretion that was marred by unsystematic development, it became much better organised from the seventeenth century. This was a natural judicial reaction to the arbitrariness of early instances where the chancery courts 'attempted to make a virtue out of inconsistency'.[65] For example, Lord Eldon consolidated many rules of equity to make it a much better-principled body of law.[66] Thus, in *Campbell Discount Co Ltd v. Bridge*,[67] Harman LJ remarked that:

> Equitable principles are, I think, perhaps too often bandied about in common law courts as though the Chancellor still had only the length of his own foot to measure when coming to a conclusion. Since the time of Lord Eldon the system of equity for good or evil has been a very precise one, and equitable jurisdiction is exercised only on well-known principles.[68]

Many of these principles still apply today, alongside the common law.

34. However, the conflict between the common law and equity was undesirable. While it was largely accepted that equity performed a moderating function over the common law, it remained the case that different courts administered common law and equity respectively. This meant that a claimant had to choose the correct court to begin his or her action; failure to do so meant starting over again in the correct court or, worse still, no recourse. The complexity occasioned by the claimant having to select the correct court replicated in some measure the injustice caused by the inflexibility of the common law that resulted in the development of equity in the first place. The difference was that the problem here laid in the administrative of law, rather than its substantive content. This problem was largely solved by the enactment of the English Supreme Court of Judicature Acts of 1873 and 1875, which replaced the separate chancery and common law courts with a single unified court, known as the High Court. The High Court was to have many divisions, including the Chancery Division, which tended to equity business, and the Queen's Bench Division, which dealt with contract and tort issues. This structure saved a claimant from having to choose the correct court, since the (English) Supreme Court of Judicature Act 1873 provided that any division could apply equity. Equity thus continued to exist as a separate body of law that was concurrently administered by the same court. The result is the development of a body of law that is flexible yet systematic, which complements the common law to the present day.

35. The development of equity in Singapore is very much derived from its initial development in England as recounted above. Equity was introduced into Singapore by the Second Charter of Justice in 1826. By this time, equity was already

---

65. *See Lau Siew Kim v. Yeo Guan Chye Terence*, [2007] SGCA 54; [2008] 2 SLR(R) 108 at [25].
66. *See* Graham Virgo, *The Principles of Equity and Trusts* (Oxford: OUP, 2012) at 7.
67. [1961] 1 QB 445.
68. [1961] 1 QB 445 at 459.

a proper system of law, quite unlike its early development in medieval England.[69] The reported equity cases from the Straits Settlements courts generally show that English equity law was being applied in local cases. One important difference between the Straits Settlements courts and the English courts was that the former was already administering both common law and equity before the Judicature Acts of 1873 and 1875 led to the same result in England. However, the formal fusion of common law and equity came about only in 1878, via section 10 of the Civil Law Ordinance. This section conferred on the Supreme Court of the Straits Settlements the same jurisdiction and authority as that of the High Court in England that administered both common law and equity concurrently.

36. The passage of the AELA in 1993 clarified the application of equity in post-independence Singapore. Section 3 of the AELA deals with the application of common law and equity, subject to the concepts of modification and suitability thus:

> **Application of common law and equity**
> 3. (1) The common law of England (including the principles and rules[70] of equity), so far as it was part of the law of Singapore immediately before the commencement of this Act, shall continue to be part of the law of Singapore.(2) The common law shall continue to be in force in Singapore, as provided in subsection (1), so far as it is applicable to the circumstances of Singapore and its inhabitants and subject to such modifications as those circumstances may require.

37. It is not immediately clear whether section 3(1) actually effects a 'cut-off' date for the common law and equity and, if so, what the date is. Constraints of space, again, preclude a lengthy analysis, although it is submitted that whether or not the reception of the common law and equity is subject to a 'cut-off' date is, in the practical sphere, probably immaterial since in either event, the local courts would be free to either accept or reject[71] the common law and equity. This may be done on the basis that it was not part of the corpus of Singapore law in the first place[72] (thus giving rise to the aforementioned freedom of choice) or that even if it were so part of the law of Singapore,[73] section 3(2) furnished the necessary flexibility in any event.

---

69. Yip Man, 'Trusts and Equity: Dreaming and Building a Singapore Equitable Jurisdiction' in Goh Yihan & Paul Tan (eds), *Singapore Law: 50 Years in the Making* (Academy Publishing, 2015) Chapter 12.
70. This appears to be a Dworkinian distinction: see, e.g., Ronald Dworkin, *Taking Rights Seriously* (Harvard University Press, 1978) Chapter 2.
71. And, of course, modify.
72. That is, if a 'cut-off' date exists and the case concerned was decided after this date.
73. That is, under an assumed regime of continuous reception or where a 'cut-off' date were thought to exist, that the case concerned was in fact decided prior to the 'cut-off' date.

2. Jurisdiction and Influence of Equity on Singapore Law

a. Jurisdiction

38. The jurisdiction of equity in Singapore may be divided into its concurrent, auxiliary and exclusive forms. In *Yong Kheng Leong v. Panweld Trading*,[74] the Singapore Court of Appeal accepted Swadling's explanation of these three forms of jurisdictions as being applicable in Singapore.[75] According to Swadling, the concurrent jurisdiction comprises equity's response to common law claims. For example, in a common law action for breach of contract, common law recognises the underlying cause of action but it may be equity that gives substantive relief such as specific performance. In this case, equity is said to be exercised concurrently with the common law.[76]

39. Equity's auxiliary jurisdiction is said to be exercised with regard to matters of procedure. For example, where discovery is ordered by a court of equity, that is done pursuant to equity's auxiliary jurisdiction. Finally, equity's exclusive jurisdiction concerns claim that the common law does not recognise at all, such as the claim of a beneficiary to enforce a trust.[77]

40. In Singapore, equity's concurrent jurisdiction is clearly spelt out by sections 3 and 4 of the Civil Law Act.[78] Section 3 provides that:

> Law and equity to be administered concurrently
> 3. In every civil cause or matter commenced in the court, law and equity shall be administered by the court in its original jurisdiction and by the Court of Appeal according to the rules following …

This section thereby mirrors the substantive effects of the English Supreme Court of Judicature Acts of 1873 and 1875, which provided for the concurrent administration of equity with the common law. Rules (a) to (h) of section 3 give effect to this concurrent administration. For example, rule (a) states plainly that the courts shall accord to a plaintiff equitable rights or remedies that could only be granted by the court 'on its equity side' before 1 January 1879. Similarly, rule (b) provides that the defendant shall be the same before the court, whether a common law or equitable defence is being asserted. Finally, rule (h) provides that the High Court and the Court of Appeal shall grant all remedies, whether arising out of the common law or equity, in cases brought before them so as to avoid multiplicity of legal proceedings.

74. [2012] SGCA 59; [2013] 1 SLR 173.
75. *Ibid.*, at [76].
76. William Swadling, 'Limitation' in Peter Birks and Arianna Pretto (eds) *Breach of Trust* (Hart Publishing, 2002) 319 at 323.
77. *Ibid.*
78. (Cap. 43, 1999 Rev. Ed.).

41. Various subsections of section 4 of the Civil Law Act further elaborate on equity's concurrent jurisdiction, especially what happens if it conflicts with the common law. For example, section 4(12) provides that in questions relating to the custody and education of minors, the rules of equity shall prevail. A more significant example is section 4(9), which provides that stipulations as to time in contracts shall be construed as they would before a court of equity. The history behind this provision was ably summarised by the House of Lords in *United Scientific Holdings Ltd v. Burnley Borough Council*,[79] which had to consider the English equivalent of the section found in section 25(7) of the (English) Supreme Court of Judicature Act 1873, later replaced by section 41 of the (English) Law of Property Act 1925. According to the House, before the administrative fusion of the common law and equity, the courts of common law regarded stipulations as to time as presumptively to be of the essence of a contract, while the Court of Chancery regarded such stipulations as presumptively not essential. The effect of section 25(7) of the (English) Supreme Court of Judicature Act 1873 was therefore to provide that the rules of equity prevailed in this regard.

42. Because there might be other aspects not within Parliament's contemplation where the common law and equity diverged, section 25(11) of the (English) Supreme Court of Judicature Act 1873 provided more generally the outcome where the common law and equity conflicted. This finds expression in Singapore in section 4(13) of the Civil Law Act, which provides that:

> Cases of conflict not enumerated, equity to prevail
> 4(13) Generally in all matters not particularly mentioned in this section, in which there is any conflict or variance between the rules of equity and the rules of the common law with reference to the same matter, the rules of equity shall prevail.

Section 4(13) thereby provides that equity is to prevail over the common law where there is any conflict or variance between the two bodies of law, save as otherwise mentioned in section 4. In this regard, section 4 does not appear to have reserved areas where the common law is to prevail over equity, but that does not prevent the section from being amended in the future to do this.

43. The concurrent jurisdiction of equity is also more provided for by other statutes in Singapore. For example, section 18 of the Supreme Court of Judicature Act[80] provides that the High Court shall have powers including those set out in the First Schedule to the Act. The First Schedule in turn provides under section 14 that the court shall have the power to 'grant all reliefs and remedies at law and in equity, including damages in addition to, or in substitution for, an injunction or specific performance'.

---

79. [1978] AC 904.
80. (Cap. 322, 2007 Rev. Ed.).

44. Similarly, the power of the lower courts to grant equitable remedies is also set out in the State Courts Act.[81] Section 31(1)(a) of that Act provides that the District Court shall in any proceedings before it 'grant such relief, redress or remedy or a combination of remedies, either absolute or conditional ... as ought to be granted or given in the like action by the High Court and in as full and ample a manner'. Because the High Court is given the power to grant all reliefs and remedies in equity, this would likewise apply to the District Court by way of section 31(1)(a). To put the matter beyond doubt insofar as the equitable remedy of injunction is concerned, section 31(2)(a) expressly confers on the District Court the power 'to grant an injunction whether or not any other relief is or could be claimed'. Section 52(1B)(a)(i) provides the same for the Magistrates' Court.

45. Statutes also provide for equity's auxiliary jurisdiction in Singapore. For example, section 12 of the First Schedule of the Supreme Court of Judicature Act provides that the High Court shall have the power to order discovery of facts or documents by any party to the proceedings before it. Equity's exclusive jurisdiction is undoubtedly recognised by the Singapore courts, which, for example, recognise the concept of a trust just as the English courts do.

b. Influence on Singapore Law

46. Equity has had a discernible influence on Singapore law since its introduction here. Generally, there has been an upward trend in the number of equity cases before the Singapore courts, as shown by a study of all reported Singapore cases decided between 1965 and 2013.[82] This can be seen in Figure 1 below.

81. (Cap. 213, 2007 Rev. Ed.).

82. Yip Man, 'Trusts and Equity: Dreaming and Building a Singapore Equitable Jurisdiction' in Goh Yihan & Paul Tan (eds), *Singapore Law: 50 Years in the Making* (Academy Publishing, 2015) Ch 12.

Figure 1 Total Number of Reported Equity Cases from 1965 to 2013 (Broken Down per Level of Court)

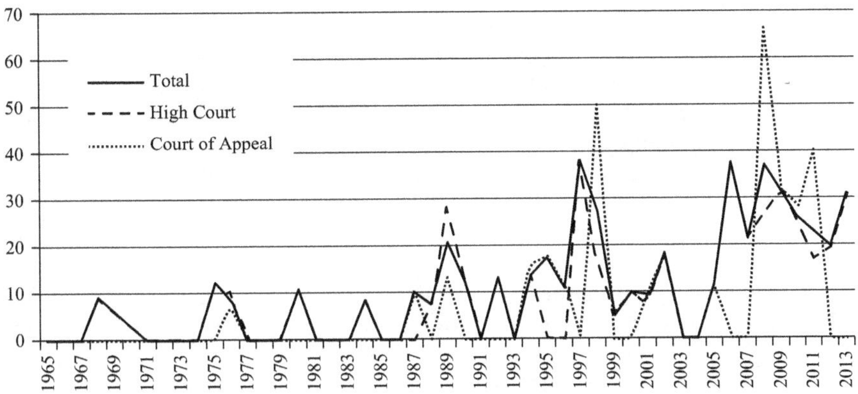

47. The length of judgments in equity cases has also similarly increased over the years, as seen in Figure 2. This can be seen as an approximation to the increasing sophistication by which the Singapore courts approach equity cases. Indeed, as we shall see in this book, the Singapore courts have fashioned principles of equity that, while English in origin, certainly bear a distinctly Singaporean favour.

Figure 2 Average Number of Pages per Judgment for Reported Equity Cases from 1965 to 2013 (Broken Down per Level of Court)

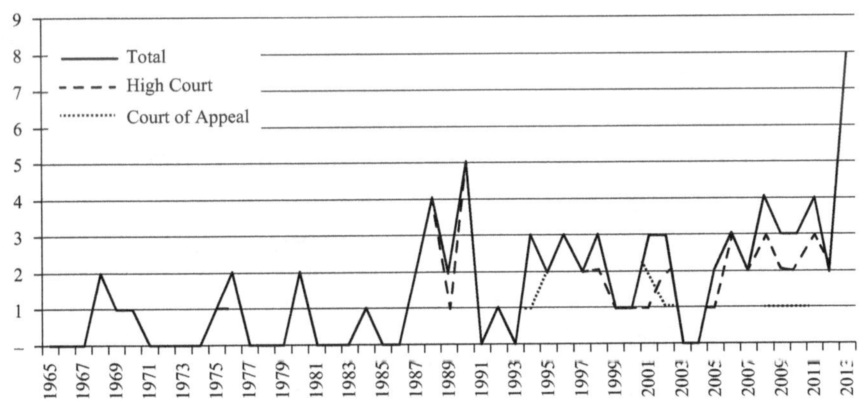

48. More specifically, the influence of equity on Singapore law is evident by a simple survey of various legal areas, such as contract, tort, commercial law and remedies.

3. Characteristics of Equity

49. Equity is often associated with maxims, which are simply broad guidelines designed to simplify a complex body of law. However, it would be a mistake to regard these guidelines as representing rigid rules, for that is antithetical to the purposes of equity. Instead, the guidelines should be applied with regard to the specific circumstances of each case. In this regard, equity has traditionally recognised 12 maxims, although some are no longer applicable today. We will only go through three maxims or characteristics of equity that are foundational to its operation.

a. Creativity

50. Compared to the common law, which is rigid and unimaginative, equity is usually seen as flexible and creative. An example of equity's creativity is seen in the remedy of rescission. Whereas the common law will not allow for rescission where the claimant has received benefits from the defendant and the law is unable to value those benefits, equity can allow for rescission even in such a case. It does so valuing the benefit in kind and making it a condition of rescission that the claimant repays this value.[83]

51. However, as we have seen above, equity today is based on precise rules that, paradoxically, may have stifled its creativity in supplying substantive justice according to the circumstances of the case. Indeed, there are some who are of the view that the creativity of equity has become 'progressively circumscribed and, to some extent, calcified'.[84] Martin, for instance, complains that the rules of equity have become so fixed that a 'rigor aequitatis' has developed and 'equity itself displayed the very defect that it was designed to remedy'.[85] Lord Denning has similarly remarked extrajudicially that the chancery courts are today 'no longer courts of equity' and that 'they are as fixed and immutable as the courts of law ever were'.[86]

52. Yet, while equity's capacity to develop new rights and remedies has been stifled in recent times, it has not been completely surrendered. For example, the traditional concepts of resulting and constructive trusts have been developed and refined to deal with the joint acquisition of residential property by married and cohabiting couples, a relationship which was unknown in the past. Thus, as the Singapore Court of Appeal said in *Lau Siew Kim v. Yeo Guan Chye Terence*,[87] an apparent balance has been struck between 'uncertainty and judicial law-making by way of "palm tree" justice on the one hand, and the continuing need for equity's creativity to mitigate the rigours of the law on the other.'[88] Where that balance has been struck appears to be predicated on the need for equity to be capable of flexible

83. *See* Graham Virgo, *The Principles of Equity and Trusts* (OUP, 2012) at 36.
84. *See Lau Siew Kim v. Yeo Guan Chye Terence* [2007] SGCA 54; [2008] 2 SLR(R) 108 at [26].
85. J.E. Martin, *Modern Equity*, 17th edn (London: Sweet & Maxwell, 2005) at [1-002].
86. Lord Denning, 'The Need for a New Equity' (1950) 5 CLP 1.
87. [2007] SGCA 54; [2008] 2 SLR(R) 108.
88. *Ibid.*, at [28].

development to address new circumstances. Thus, as Glass JA said in the Australian case of *Allen v. Snyder*,[89] it is inevitable that judge-made law will alter to meet the changing conditions of society. However, this must be done with consideration of existing principles and precedents rather than plucked seemingly out of thin air.[90]

53. In Singapore, the present approach to equity's creativity appears to be well summarised in *Lau Siew Kim v. Yeo Guan Chye Terence* as follows:[91]

> In our view, this balance governs the manner in which equitable principles and doctrines ought to be developed and applied in the modern context. The courts should be principled and pragmatic when resolving the tension of applying an unguided and untrammelled discretion as an antidote to the blind acceptance of inflexible hard and fast rules.

According to the court, four primary perspectives laid down by Watt[92] should guide the court in the development of equitable principles in Singapore,[93] namely, precedent, principle, policy and pragmatism. Thus, the Singapore courts, when confronted with a legal problem founded in equity, should turn first to judicial precedent for a solution, but if that fails, then they should seek to produce a solution consistent with principles derived from precedent, with a consideration as to policy and pragmatism. It is therefore with 'principled pragmatism'[94] that equity retains its creativity in Singapore, but not at the expense of certainty and consistency.

b. Unconscionability

54. That equity is triggered by unconscionability is unsurprising, given that it is historically based on the Lord Chancellor's conscience. In *Westdeutsche Landesbank Girozentrale v. Islington LBC*, Lord Browne-Wilkinson recognised that 'equity operates on the conscience of the owner of the legal interest'.[95] Similarly, the Singapore Court of Appeal in *Anna Wee Chiaw Sek v. Ng Li-Ann Genevive*[96] accepted that unconscionability is 'often used as an overarching justification or rationale undergirding the whole of equity'.[97]

55. While it is accepted that equity is triggered by unconscionability, what is less clear is the meaning of unconscionability. It is important to understand what unconscionability encapsulates; indeed, as Lord Nicholls noted in the Privy Council decision of *Royal Brunei Airlines Sdn Bhd v. Philip Tan Kok Ming*,[98] while

89. [1977] 2 NSWLR 685.
90. [2007] SGCA 54; [2008] 2 SLR(R) 108 at [30].
91. *Ibid.*, at [28].
92. Gary Watt, *Trusts and Equity*, 2nd edn (OUP, 2006) at 47–48.
93. [2007] SGCA 54; [2008] 2 SLR(R) 108 at [32].
94. *Ibid.*, at [33].
95. [1996] AC 669 at 705.
96. [2013] SGCA 36; [2013] 3 SLR 801.
97. *Ibid.*, at [101].
98. [1995] 2 AC 378.

unconscionability 'is a word of immediate appeal to an equity lawyer', 'if it is to be the touchstone for liability as an accessory, it is essential to be clear on what, in this context, unconscionable means'.[99] A failure to appreciate this is apt to give rise to confusion and uncertainty.

56. In Singapore, the courts have treated unconscionability to be a guiding principle, rather than a substantive rule that must be satisfied.[100] As the Singapore Court of Appeal stated in *Anna Wee Chiaw Sek v. Ng Li-Ann Genevive*, unconscionability applies once the relevant equitable doctrine has been applied and not before.[101] This thereby shows that unconscionability does not operate as a free-standing doctrine on which liability is found, but expresses the rationale that underpins the doctrine or test being applied.[102] Put another way, unconscionability characterises the result, rather than identify the reasoning that leads to the application of that description.[103] One reason for the Singapore courts' treating unconscionability as a rationale rather than a test is due to its uncertain definition.

c. Discretion

57. It is often said that equity is discretionary, but it is important to consider what that means exactly. As we have already seen, this certainly does not mean that the courts are at liberty to fashion out a cause of action where there is none. Thus, whereas at its genesis, equity allowed the courts considerable latitude to develop causes of action to supplement the common law, equity today is a well-established body of law and rules that imbue it with certainty and predictability.[104] Therefore, the courts must be able to find a cause of action within equity, without which the action does not even take off; as the English Court of Appeal said in *Re Diplock*:[105]

> If a claim in equity exists, it must be shown to have an ancestry founded in history and in the practice and precedents of courts administering equity jurisdiction. It is not sufficient that because we may think that the 'justice' in the present case requires it, we should invent such a jurisdiction for the first time.

58. Similarly, in *Cowcher v. Cowcher*,[106] where the English High Court had to decide whether the wife had a beneficial interest in the matrimonial home upon divorce, Bagnall J, having set out the relevant principles in law and equity, said:[107]

> In any individual case the application of these propositions may produce a result which appears unfair. So be it; in my view, that is not an injustice. I am

99. *Ibid.*, at 392.
100. *See* Graham Virgo, *The Principles of Equity and Trusts* (OUP, 2012) at 30.
101. [2013] SGCA 36; [2013] 3 SLR 801 at [101].
102. *Ibid.*.
103. *Ibid.*.
104. *See* Graham Virgo, *The Principles of Equity and Trusts* (OUP, 2012) at 28.
105. [1948] Ch 465 at 481–482.
106. [1972] 1 WLR 425.
107. *Ibid.*, at 430.

> convinced that in determining rights, particularly property rights, the only justice that can be attained by mortals, who are fallible and are not omniscient, is justice according to law; the justice which flows from the application of sure and settled principles to proved or admitted facts. So in the field of equity the length of the Chancellor's foot has been measured or is capable of measurement. This does not mean that equity is past childbearing; simply that its progeny must be legitimate – by precedent out of principle. It is well that this should be so; otherwise, no lawyer could safely advise on his client's title and every quarrel would lead to a law suit.

In saying that in the field of equity 'the Chancellor's foot has been measured or is capable of measurement', Bagnall J makes it clear that the discretion in equity does not extend to judges fashioning out actions where there is none. Indeed, the learned judge also said that equity's progeny must be legitimate, by precedent out of principle, so as to ensure certainty in future cases.

59. However, once a cause of action is engaged, then the courts do have discretion within that cause of action. Indeed, as Virgo notes, the award of equitable remedies 'lies in the discretion of the court, and it is entirely appropriate that questions of justice and fairness arise at that stage'.[108] For example, once the elements of common mistake in equity are made out, the Singapore courts retain discretion in fashioning the appropriate remedy in the circumstances. It is in that light that equity is said to be discretionary.

60. It ought, however, still be noted that such discretion is still exercised in accordance with established principles. For example, the Singapore Court of Appeal in *Lee Chee Wei v. Tan Hor Peow Victor*[109] clearly said that the discretion to grant the equitable remedy of specific performance must be exercised 'in accordance with fixed rules and principles'.[110] Indeed, in the English High Court decision of *Vercoe v. Rutland Fund Management Ltd*,[111] Sales J, in discussing how the courts award damages for the equitable wrong of breach of confidence, said that while the courts' decision in this regard might be described as 'discretionary', the courts are in truth 'seeking to articulate underlying principles which will govern the choices to be made as to the remedy or remedies available in any given case'.[112] This emphasises the point that the courts' discretion, even where available, is to be exercised in accordance with established principles that are constantly being refined by the courts.

108. *See* Graham Virgo, *The Principles of Equity and Trusts* (OUP, 2012) at 28.
109. [2007] SGCA 22; [2007] 3 SLR(R) 537.
110. *Ibid.*.
111. [2010] EWHC 424 (Ch); [2010] All ER (D) 79.
112. *Ibid.*, at [340].

4. Fusion of Equity and Common Law?

61. Although there are fundamental differences between equity and the common law, the profound influence that equity has had on the latter has led some to suggest that it should be assimilated into the common law. It is important to note at this juncture that while the administration of common law and equity is now concurrently done, that does not mean that the bodies of law are fused. In considering the fusion of equity and common law substantively, one needs to consider a few questions. First, as Virgo suggests, whether common law and equity are already fused; secondly, whether they are in the process of being fused; and thirdly, whether they should be, if they have not already been fused.[113]

a. Have Common Law and Equity Been Already Fused?

62. According to Virgo, it is clear that common law and equity are not already fused.[114] He points out that it remains a fundamental principle of English law that equitable proprietary interests and legal interests are distinct. Thus, common law does not recognise the trust, which is a distinct creation of equity. Therefore, proprietary rights will differ depending on whether they are legal (that is, derived from the common law) or equitable. The same is undoubtedly the case in Singapore as well, where the concept of the trust remains a fundamental part of the law, along with the recognition of both legal and equitable proprietary rights. Indeed, another clear example is the Singapore courts' continuing recognition of their equitable jurisdiction in mistake, such that different consequences follow depending on whether a mistake has been pleaded at common law or in equity.

b. Are Common Law and Equity in the Process of Being Fused?

63. As for whether common law and equity are in the process of being fused, there have been judicial pronouncements that this is the case. In United Scientific *Holdings Ltd v. Burnley Borough Council,*[115] the House of Lords, in considering the effect of stipulations as to time in contracts, had occasion to consider the extent to which common law and equity were being fused. This was due to section 25(7) of the (English) Supreme Court of Judicature Act 1873, which provided that stipulations in contracts as to time were to be construed as they would have been in a court of equity. The House had to consider if section 25(7) superceded the common law. In this regard, Lord Diplock said that:[116]

> My Lords, if by 'rules of equity' is meant that body of substantive and adjectival law that, prior to 1875, was administered by the Court of Chancery but not by courts of common law, to speak of the rules of equity as being part of the law of England in 1977 is about as meaningful as to speak similarly of the

113. *See* Graham Virgo, *The Principles of Equity and Trusts* (OUP, 2012) at 22.
114. *See ibid.* at 22–23.
115. [1978] AC 904.
116. *Ibid.*, at 924–925.

> Statutes of Uses or of Quia Emptores. Historically all three have in their time played an important part in the development of the corpus juris into what it is today; but to perpetuate a dichotomy between rules of equity and rules of common law which it was a major purpose of the Supreme Court of Judicature Act 1873 to do away with, is, in my view, conducive to erroneous conclusions as to the ways in which the law of England has developed in the last hundred years ... the waters of the confluent streams of law and equity have surely mingled now.

Similarly, Lord Simon of Glaisdale in the same case suggested that there would come a time when the intermixing between common law and equity would be complete.[117] Lord Fraser of Tullybelton also accepted that the legal and equitable streams of English jurisdiction 'have now merged into a single stream' and that rules of equity 'are now simply part of the corpus of English law and as such they are free to develop like other parts of that law'.[118]

64. Despite some of the more definitive statements in *United Scientific Holdings Ltd v. Burnley Borough Council*, it is clear that the fusion of the common law and equity is still in progress and certainly has not been completed. Virgo suggests that there is 'growing evidence' of this happening.[119] For example, whereas common law pecuniary remedies are compensatory, the House of Lords in *Attorney-General v. Blake*[120] has suggested that the remedy of an account of profits – a gain-based remedy – may be exceptionally available for the common law action of breach of contract. Although no Singapore case has awarded damages on this basis, the Court of Appeal in *MFM Restaurants Pte Ltd v. Fish & Co Restaurants Pte Ltd*[121] did recognise this possibility, although it did qualify that such damages would only be awarded exceptionally. Another example can be found in *Seager v. Copydex (No. 2),*[122] where compensatory damages were awarded for the equitable wrong of breach of confidence. This was in contrast to the usual remedies, which were equitable in nature, including an injunction and account of profits.

c. Should Common Law and Equity Be Fused?

65. Given that there is some evidence of the fusion of equity and common law, the next nineteen question is whether this should be the case. Burrows has argued that having two separate systems of law is illogical and unprincipled.[123] He argues that a harmonised rule or principle that has features of both common law and equity is at the very least acceptable and may represent the best way for the law to develop in a particular area. He suggests that, insofar as fusion is concerned, the private law can be divided into three categories, namely, first, where common law and equity

117. *Ibid.*, at 945.
118. *Ibid.*, at 957.
119. *See* Graham Virgo, *The Principles of Equity and Trusts* (OUP, 2012) at 23.
120. [2000] UKHL 45; [2001] 1 AC 268.
121. [2010] SGCA 36; [2011] 1 SLR 150.
122. [1969] 1 WLR 809.
123. Andrew Burrows, 'We Do This at Common Law But That in Equity' (2002) 22 OJLS 1.

coexist coherently and where the historical labels of common law and equity remain useful terminology; second, where common law and equity coexist coherently but there is nothing to be gained by adherence to the historical labels; and thirdly, where common law and equity do not coexist coherently. In his view, fusion is not needed for the first category. In relation to the second category, the historical labels are not useful and should therefore be excised. But because the law is already divided, and not in an inconsistent manner, there is no need for fusion. It is in relation to the third category that fusion is needed to erase the inconsistencies between common law and equity.

66. In contrast, Lord Millett does not think that there is a problem with having two systems. He argues that the three greatest systems of jurisprudence in the Western world, including English law, have all been dual systems. In each system, a rigid body of law, which provides certainty, is supplemented by a more flexible body, which provides the necessary flexibility and adaptability to enable justice to be done.[124] Virgo supports the view that equity and common law should not be fused, since any fusion would result in the subtleties and nuances of the law to be lost.[125]

67. To be fair though, Burrows is not advocating total fusion; indeed, his approach would address both Lord Millett and Virgo's concerns that the flexibility of equity is not lost. Burrows' approach would still preserve the flexibility that equity provides, albeit not by such a label, and also keep the unique creations of equity, such as the trust, alongside the common law. All that Burrows seeks is for fusion where there is an inconsistency between common law and equity.

68. Courts appear to straddle both arguments for and against fusion in favour of gradual assimilation. For example, in Australia, the New South Wales Court of Appeal decision of *Harris v. Digital Pulse Pty Ltd*[126] contains a detailed discussion of the desirability of fusion. The case raised the issue of whether exemplary damages should be awarded for breach of fiduciary duty. In rejecting the award of exemplary damages, the majority also rejected 'automatic fusion' of common law and equity, which refers to the view that the joint administration of both common law and equity meant that the doctrines of one were applicable to the other.[127] However, Mason P, who dissented, appears to have accepted 'fusion by analogy', which refers to the process by which common law and equity are fused to eradicate inconsistencies in like cases.[128] Mason P considered that there was an analogy to be drawn between common law torts and breaches of fiduciary duty, since the rationale of exemplary damages, which are awarded under torts, likewise underpinned breaches of fiduciary duty. While Heydon JA disagreed that this particular analogy could be drawn, he did not disagree that the development of equity by analogy with the common law was possible. Spigelman CJ, in contrast, thought that analogical reasoning

124. Lord Millett, 'Proprietary Restitution' in Simone Degeling and James Edelman (eds) *Equity in Commercial Law* (Law Book Co, 2005) 309.
125. *See* Graham Virgo, *The Principles of Equity and Trusts* (OUP, 2012) at 25.
126. [2003] NSWCA 10.
127. James Edelman, 'A "Fusion Fallacy" Fallacy?' (2003) 119 LQR 375 at 377.
128. *Ibid.*

at this level of generality was inappropriate. In his view, equitable rights and remedies are fundamentally different from those at common law. If this view is correct, it would make 'fusion by analogy' very unlikely.

69. The Singapore courts have not considered whether common law and equity should be fused, but have in many decisions recognised that the two exist concurrently. For example, in *Chwee Kin Keong v. Digilandmall.com Pte Ltd*,[129] the Singapore Court of Appeal recognised that there was a concurrent equitable jurisdiction with regard to unilateral mistake, notwithstanding the fact that it may be difficult to delineate the scope or extent of that jurisdiction.[130] Indeed, the Court resisted the simplistic option of reducing unilateral mistake to the common law jurisdiction, which would eradicate the problems of deciding exactly when equity should intervene.[131] This shows that in Singapore, the courts are against the fusion of common law and equity to iron out inconsistencies, at least in relation to the legal difficulties of deciding when equity should apply.

§3. Introduction to the Law of Property and Trust in Singapore

I. Historical Origin and Evolution

70. Like most other areas of the law, Singapore inherits a significant portion of its property law from English law. However, the two broad categories of property law – land law and personal property law – developed at difference paces and in different directions. Singapore land law became more closely aligned with Australian land law since the 1960s, following the enactment of the Land Titles Ordinance in 1956.[132] Drafted by John Baalman, the statute introduced into Singapore the Torrens system of land titles registration modelled after the South Australian version. Thereafter, the effect of registration (and non-registration) has to be borne in mind in examining every aspect of land law. In contrast, the law of personal property has seen far less development except in the area of trust law, which has been shaped by much judicial creativity.

71. We will, in the following parts of this book, deal with some introductory and general rules pertaining to the law of property and trusts in Singapore. Indeed, in the pages that follow, we shall have occasion to observe, through the discussion of various doctrines of the law of property and trusts, that Singapore law in this regard has, at its core, a uniquely Singaporean character.

129. [2005] SGCA 2; [2005] 1 SLR(R) 502.
130. *Ibid.*, at [74].
131. *Ibid.*, at [76].
132. Ordinance 21 of 1956.

II. The Concept of Ownership

A. *Land*

72. Singapore adopts a system of title by registration.[133] In simple words, title in land is acquired only by registration, upon which the ownership of the land is reflected in the land register. Supplementing the mirror principle is the principle of indefeasibility, which ensures that a registered owner enjoys a certain degree of security against an adverse claim based on a prior title. However, the development of trust law is accounted for under the trust exception to the principle of indefeasibility. In other words, the law recognises that the registered owner is not always the absolute owner.

B. *Personal Property*

73. There is no unified concept of ownership in personal property law given that personal property exists in many forms. Personal property may be broadly divided into choses in possession and choses in action.[134] For the first category, title is closely linked with possession, subject to exceptions.[135] For the second category, much depends on the nature of the property. For shares and trademarks, ownership is based on registration. For copyrights, ownership is automatically conferred by the relevant legislation based on a predetermined set of criteria. For money in bank account, much depends on the terms of the relevant contract.

C. *Trust: Splitting of Legal and Equitable Interests*

74. The law of trust is premised on the idea that a single property can be owned both at law and in equity by different persons.[136] This is traditionally understood to involve a splitting of the legal and equitable interests in the trust property. As the legal owner holds it on trust for the equitable owner, the latter is recognised as the true owner of the property.

75. The development of trust law is closely linked to the development of the law of equity, which has been discussed earlier. While initially Singapore law closely aligned with English law, the conscious effort to develop Singapore's own trust law and the courts' willingness to look to other Commonwealth jurisdictions (such as Australia, Canada and New Zealand) for inspiration have resulted in various points

---

133. *See* Part I (Land) Chapter 4 (Torrens System).
134. *See* Part II (Personal Property) Chapter 1 (General Classifications).
135. *See* Part III (Acquisition of Property Rights) Chapters 2 (Contract for the Sale of Goods), 4 (Possession and Appropriation) and 5 (Accession and Specification).
136. *See* Part IV (Trusts and Fiduciary Law).

of departure. With an eye on principle, precedent, pragmatism and policy, the courts have strived to develop a law of trust that best suits local conditions.[137]

D. Unity and Fragmentation

76. Unlike the civilian system of property law, which emphasises the unitary nature of ownership, the common law concept of ownership is more receptive to fragmentation. Three examples sufficiently illustrate this unique characteristic of ownership under the common law. First, concurrent ownerships in land is recognised through the doctrine of estates, under which each owner has exclusive possession of the land for a specific duration.[138] Second, any person who takes possession of a chattel acquires such a title that is enforceable against all but a person having a better title.[139] Any title dispute between the concurrent owners is resolved by the doctrine of relativity of title, under which the title of an earlier possessor is superior to the title of a subsequent possessor.

---

137. *See* Part IV (Trusts and Fiduciary Law).
138. *See* Part I (Land) Chapter 13 (Comparative Property Law).
139. *See* Part III (Acquisition) Chapter 4 (Possession and Appropriation).

Part I. Land

Chapter 1. Meaning of Land

§1. Definitions

77. In its ordinary sense, land consists of the solid surface of the earth on which most human activities take place. The common law definition of land is wider. It includes also vegetation that grows on, or structures that are substantially affixed to, the earth's surface so as to become part of the land, as well as certain airspace above and subterranean space below the earth's surface. This broad definition emphasises the three-dimensional nature of land.

78. Definitions of land can also be found in various legislations. A notable example is in the Land Titles Act (LTA), section 4 of which provides:[140]

> 'land' means –
>
> (a) the surface of any defined parcel of the earth, all substances thereunder and so much of the column of airspace above the surface whether or not held apart from the surface as is reasonably necessary for the proprietor's use and enjoyment, and includes any estate or interest therein and all vegetation growing thereon and structures affixed thereto; or
>
> (b) any parcel of airspace or any subterranean space held apart from the surface of the earth and described with certainty by reference to a plan approved by the Chief Surveyor and filed in the Survey Department, and includes any estate or interest therein and all vegetation growing thereon and structures affixed thereto,
>
> and where the context so permits, the proprietorship of land includes natural rights to air, light, water and support and the right of access to any highway on which the land abuts;[141]

140. (Cap. 157, 2004 Rev. Ed.).
141. The same definition is also used by the Land Titles (Strata) Act (Cap. 158, 2009 Rev. Ed.) (LTSA).

79. While this statutory definition mirrors the common law definition to a great degree, the former is wider as it also includes natural rights, which are ordinary incidence of land –ownership rather than a reference to physical land.[142] This is unsurprising once it is understood that the various statutory definitions were never meant to accurately describe land per se but instead to serve the purposes of the particular legislations, e.g., for the facilitation of the practice of conveyancing and the registration of interests in land. It is therefore helpful in this introductory chapter to focus on the common law definition while keeping in mind that the extent to which land may be dealt with is largely regulated by legislation.

§2. Extent to Which Land Can Be Owned

80. Of greater practical importance is the extent to which land can be legally owned,[143] which also sheds light on the meaning of land. Traditionally, land is delineated by the vertical boundaries surrounding it. Most certificates of title (or title deeds) do not specify the extent to which the landowner owns the space above and below the surface of the earth. Reflecting the broad definition of land, it was once assumed that a landowner owns everything below to the centre of the earth and above to the heaven.[144] This assumption has long been regarded as untenable in the modern world.[145] Today it is well established that the landowner's right is limited to such height or depth that is necessary for his ordinary use of the land.[146]

81. Where a person acquires a clearly defined airspace or subterranean space, he does not own anything more, either above or below that defined space.[147] The best example is a person who has acquired a subsidiary strata certificate of title of a clearly defined unit in a multistorey building.[148]

I. Airspace

82. A landowner's right to airspace above his land is reflected by his freedom to erect structures as high as he likes, subject to him/her obtaining the required planning permission.[149] A proposed development is likely to be granted so long as it is

142. *See also* the definition of land in the Conveyancing and Law of Property Act (Cap 61, 1994 Rev Ed) (CLPA), s. 2, which refers also to the different kinds of estates in land and hereditaments, corporeal or incorporeal (e.g., easements).
143. *See generally* Kevin Gray, 'Property in Thin Air' (1991) 50 CLJ 252.
144. *Bury v. Pope* (1856) Cro Eliz 118.
145. *Bocardo SA v. Star Energy UK Onshore Ltd and another (Secretary of State for Energy and Climate Change intervening)* [2010] UKSC 35; [2011] 1 AC 380 at 395; *Willoughby Hills v. Corrigan* (1972) 278 NE 2d 658 at 664; *Chance v. BP Chemicals Inc* (1996) 670 NE 2d 985.
146. *Bernstein of Leigh (Baron) v. Skyviews & General Ltd* [1978] 1 QB 479, cited with approval in *Kim Beng Lee Construction Ltd v. Kosion Enterprise (S) Pte Ltd* [1993] SGHC 312; [1993] 3 SLR(R) 909.
147. *See e.g., Reilly v. Booth* (1890) LR 44 Ch D 12 at 23.
148. *See* Teo Keang Sood, *Strata Title in Singapore and Malaysia*, 5th edn. (LexisNexis, 2015).
149. *See* Planning Act (Cap. 232, Rev Ed 1998) Part III (PA).

in conformity with the Master Plan.[150] More debatable is the extent to which a landowner owns the airspace beyond those structures which he does not directly utilise.

83. Where the airspace immediately above a parcel of land is intruded by an overhanging structure from a neighbouring land, a claim in trespass or nuisance is likely to succeed. In *Nasrat Lucas Muzayyin v. Shi Ka Yee*, the branches of a huge rain tree growing on the defendant's land overhung the plaintiffs' land.[151] Dead branches from the tree were found on the plaintiff's land and there was a real possibility of the plaintiff's house being damaged by falling branches. In light of such evidence, Chiah DJ held that the intrusion amounted to a nuisance. It shall only be added that had the plaintiff brought a claim in trespass instead, there would have been no need to prove that the intrusion had interfered with the plaintiff's enjoyment of his land. Unlike nuisance, trespass is a strict liability tort.

84. In *Kim Beng Lee Construction Ltd v. Kosion Enterprise (S) Pte Ltd*, the defendant contracted to sell its land to the plaintiff subject to it not being adversely affected by the work of the Mass Rail Transit Corporation (MRTC). In this case the MRTC constructed a airspace high viaduct that intruded into the airspace above a private land.[152] Selvam JC held that the land was adversely affected as the intrusion deprived the landowner of full and uninterrupted enjoyment of the land. The decision impliedly recognises that the landowner's ownership extended to that portion of airspace.

85. A complaint in respect of overflying aircrafts is unlikely to succeed. The idea is that airspace beyond a certain height is a public pathway.[153] In the English case of *Bernstein of Leigh (Baron) v. Skyviews & General Ltd*, where the defendant's employee flew a plane several hundred meters above the plaintiff's land to photograph the plaintiff's farm, it was held that no trespass was committed.[154] Griffith J explained that between the landowner's right and the public's right of passage an appropriate balance is struck by 'by restricting the rights of an owner in the airspace above his land to such height as is necessary for the ordinary use and enjoyment of his land and the structures upon it, and declaring that above that height he has no greater rights in the airspace than any other member of the public'.[155]

86. The height of existing structures on the land is a relevant consideration in determining the extent of the landowner's right to the airspace above. For example, flying an aircraft a kilometre above ground is normally unobjectionable. However, flying an aircraft at the same height over a skyscraper could potentially amount to trespass or nuisance. It is also pertinent to note that the height at which an aircraft

150. PA, section 14(1). The Master Plan, which is reviewed every 5 years, clearly sets out how every parcel of land in Singapore may be used. The most recent Master Plan was published in 2014.
151. [2016] SGMC 26, affirmed by the High Court in *Shi Ka Yee v. Nasrat Lucas Muzayyin* [2016] SGHC 138.
152. [1993] SGHC 312; [1993] 3 SLR(R) 909.
153. *See United States v. Causby* (1946) 328 US 256.
154. [1978] 1 QB 479.
155. [1978] 1 QB 479 at 488.

may fly is regulated by statute. While there is a minimum height below which aircrafts shall not fly, this prohibition is exempted in the case of take-off and landing.[156] Thus, a person who owns land near an air base is unlikely to have any legal recourse against low-flying aircrafts that are taking off from or landing at the air base. This does not necessarily mean that the landowner does not own that column or airspace through which the aircrafts fly. Rather, any infringement is permitted by legislation. In reality, the dispute in *Bernstein* is unlikely to occur in Singapore given the stringent regulation of air traffic. However, the recent rise in popularity of small remote-controlled aircrafts might give rise to disputes that can test the limits of a landowner's right to the airspace above.[157]

87. Once a landowner manages to establish that a defined parcel of airspace belongs to him, he is free to deal with it, e.g. by conveying[158] or leasing[159] it to another person.[160] In reality, airspace is only economically valuable where it is supported by solid ground, e.g. a particular area within a multistorey building, so that common human activity can occur.

II. Subterranean Space

88. In *Bocardo SA v. Star Energy UK Onshore Ltd*,[161] the defendant drilled beneath the claimant's land at depths of between 800 and 2,800 feet to extract petroleum.[162] Although the alleged intrusions occurred at such depths that did not affect the claimant's use and enjoyment of its land, the UK Supreme Court held that the claimant's property right in the land extended to those depths. Lord Hope, who delivered the main judgment on this point, explained:

> The depths to which the wells in question were drilled in this case do not get anywhere near to approaching the point of absurdity. The fact that there were substances at that depth which can be reached and got by human activity is sufficient to raise the question as to who, if anybody, is the owner of the strata where they are to be found. The Crown has asserted ownership of the petroleum, but it does not assert ownership of the strata that surround it. The only plausible candidate is the registered owner of the land above ...[163]

---

156. Air Navigation Order (O. 2, Rev Ed 1990), Eleventh Schedule, rule 3.1.2.
157. For regulation of unmanned aircrafts, see Air Navigation Order (O. 2, Rev Ed 1990) Part XA.
158. *Reilly v. Booth* (1890) LR 44 Ch D 12.
159. *See e.g. Macht v. Department of Assessments of Baltimore City*, 296 A.2d 162, 168 (1972); *Re Trizek Manitoba Ltd and City Assessor for the City of Winnipeg* (1986) 25 D.L.R. (4th) 444.
160. To legally convey or lease a defined airspace, it is necessary to first seek approval for subdivision. *See* Planning Act (Cap. 232, 1998 Rev. Ed.) Part III. However, a dealing of an unpartitioned space may be effective in equity: see e.g. *Golden Village Multiplex Pte Ltd v. Marina Centre Holdings Pte Ltd* [2002] SGCA 6; [2002] 1 SLR(R) 169.
161. *See* John G Sprankling, 'Owning the Center of the Earth' (2008) 55 UCLA L Rev 979.
162. [2010] UKSC 35; [2011] 1 AC 380 at 395.
163. *Ibid.*, at 394.

89. The effect of this test is that a landowner will always win in a dispute concerning intrusion of subterranean space. The fact that physical intrusion occurred at a certain depth necessarily points to the conclusion that that depth does not approach the point of absurdity.

90. The position in Singapore is markedly less generous to landowners.[164] The starting position is that a landowner only owns such subterranean space below his land that is reasonably necessary for his use and enjoyment. This was clarified in section 3B of the State Lands Act (SLA) to mean subterranean space extending to 30 metres below the Singapore Height Datum (SHD).[165]

91. All subterranean space beyond that depth belongs to the State. Besides providing clarity as to what existing landowners own beneath their lands' surface, the practical effect of section 3B is to allow the State to embark on large-scale development of subterranean space for public use without resorting to compulsory acquisition. Importantly, this development is expected to have little impact on the ability of landowners to develop their land underground. A survey shows that the deepest basement in Singapore is only 15 metres below the SHD.[166] Moreover, by virtue of a statutorily implied easement of support, pile foundations may extend beyond 30 metres below the SHD if necessary to support the structure above.[167]

---

164. Elaine Chew, 'Digging Deep into the Ownership of Underground Space – Recent Changes in Respect of Subterranean Land Use' [2017] SJLS 1.
165. (Cap. 314, 1996 Rev. Ed.). According to the Boundaries and Survey Maps Act (Cap. 25, 2006 Rev. Ed.), section 2(1), SHD means 'the fixed datum surface set at 0.000 metres of Singapore's historical mean sea level'.
166. Parliament Reports, 13 March 2015 (Second Reading of the State Lands (Amendment) Bill by Indranee Rajah, Senior Minister of State for Law).
167. SLA, section 3C, read together with State Lands Encroachments Act (Cap. 315, 1985 Rev. Ed.), section 7A.

Chapter 2. General Classifications

92. In Singapore, land and interests in land can be broadly classified into various categories, which serve different purposes.

§1. Registered Land and Unregistered Land

93. The Land Titles Ordinance of 1956, drafted by John Baalman, introduced into Singapore the Torrens system of registered land.[168] Since the statute came into force in 1960, land in Singapore has been consciously and gradually brought under the new system.[169] Today, less than 0.1% of land in Singapore remains unregistered, mostly because their owners could not be identified. The importance of the distinction between registered and unregistered land relates mainly to the manner in which the land may be dealt with.

§2. State Land and Private Land

94. Under English land law, all land is held of the Crown.[170] This system of landholding originated from the feudal doctrine of tenure, under which landholding was granted to servants of the King in exchange for their services. Although landholding today is free from the influence of feudalism, the idea that all land is held of the Crown remains. Following Singapore's independence, all land originally held of the Crown[171] is now held of the State.[172]

95. The term 'state land', however, has a more specific meaning. It refers to all land in Singapore except: (a) land lawfully granted, or contracted to be granted, by or on behalf of the State (private land)[173] and (b) land dedicated as national parks and nature reserves.[174] Land which is the subject of a grant by the State may revert to being state land if it is lawfully forfeited by the State,[175] surrendered to the State

168. Ordinance 21 of 1956.
169. The Land Titles (Amendment) Act 2001 (No. 25 of 2001) gave the Registrar greater ability to convert unregistered land into registered land.
170. *See* Tang Hang Wu and Kelvin F.K. Low, *Tan Sook Yee's Principles of Singapore Land Law*, 3rd edn (LexisNexis, 2009) Chapter 4.
171. *Lim Kien Mok v. B H Kevan* [1963] 1 MLJ 284 (Singapore).
172. Constitution of the Republic of Singapore (1965), Art. 160; Constitution of the State of Singapore (1963), Art. 103. *See also Development Bank of Singapore Ltd v. Eng Keong Realty Pte Ltd* [1990] SGHC 21; [1990] SLR(R) 265 at [13] (In Singapore, all lands ultimately belong to the State).
173. *Cf Koh Ah Kow v. Public Prosecutor* [1995] SGCA 47; [1995] 2 SLR(R) 162.
174. Singapore Land Authority Act (Cap 301, 2002 Rev. Ed.), section 2.
175. For example, where the grant holder has abandoned the state land for more than 3 years. *See* State Lands Encroachments Act (Cap. 315, 1985 Rev. Ed.), sections 9–11. Another example is where there is a breach of condition(s) implied into the state grant. *See* SLA, section 7(1)(e).

by the grantee, or reverted to the State by operation of law.[176] The State may turn privately owned land into state land through lawful acquisition.[177]

96. Since 2015, state land includes all subterranean space deeper than 30 metres below the Singapore Height Datum.[178] In the case of land formed by the reclamation of any part of the foreshore of Singapore, the President may declare the reclaimed land to be state land.[179]

97. State land may be the subject of five kinds of grant: estate in perpetuity;[180] lease;[181] fee simple;[182] and tenancy or licence for temporary occupation.[183] In making any of these grants, the State is likely to impose conditions restricting how the land may be used or developed so as to adhere to the Master Plan.[184]

98. In practice, state land is held and managed on behalf of the State by statutory boards such as the Singapore Land Authority,[185] the Urban Redevelopment Authority,[186] the Housing and Development Board[187] and the JTC Corporation (formerly Jurong Town Corporation).[188]

§3. Types of Property

I. Public Housing: HDB Flats

99. The Housing and Development Board (HDB) was established in 1960 with the aim of providing affordable and quality housing to the public.[189] More than 1 million HDB dwelling units have been built since 1965.[190] Since 1985, the percentage of the Singapore population living in HDB flats has consistently been above 80%.[191]

---

176. For example, where the grant holder has no statutory next of kin. *See* Intestate Succession Act (Cap. 146, 2013 Rev. Ed.), section 7. *See generally* Part III (Acquisition of Property Rights) Chapter 3 (Transfer Upon Death) §1.
177. This includes compulsory acquisition: Land Acquisition Act (Cap. 152, 1985 Rev. Ed.). *See generally* Part III (Acquisition of Property Rights) Chapter 6 (Expropriation) §2.
178. State Lands Act (Cap. 314, 1996 Rev. Ed.), section 3B.
179. Foreshores Act (Cap. 113, 1985 Rev. Ed.), section 5.
180. SLA, Part I.
181. SLA, Part I. *See also* State Land Rules (R.1, 1994 Rev. Ed.) (SLR), rules 5–18.
182. SLA, Part II.
183. SLR, rules 19–31.
184. *See* Planning Act (Cap. 232, Rev Ed 1998), section 6. For a brief description of the Master Plan, see Chapter 11 (Planning Law) §2.II.
185. Singapore Land Authority Act (Cap. 301, 2002 Rev. Ed.), section 6(1)(e).
186. Urban Redevelopment Authority Act (cap. 340, 1990 Rev. Ed.)
187. Housing and Development Act (Cap. 129, 2004 Rev. Ed.).
188. Jurong Town Corporation Act (Cap. 150, 1998 Rev. Ed.).
189. Housing and Development Act (Cap. 129, 2004 Rev. Ed.).
190. Housing Development Board, 'HDB Annual Report 2014/2015: Key Statistics' (2016) at 4.
191. *Ibid.*, at 9.

100. HDB flats are typically leased for a term of 99 years. Ownership of HDB flats is highly regulated. Most HDB eligibility schemes require the flat to be co-owned. Single ownership of a HDB flat is possible only in very limited circumstances and for smaller flats, which form a very small percentage of existing HDB flats. Moreover, an owner of a HDB flat must not own another property and must satisfy other eligibility requirements pertaining to age and income ceiling. The HDB also imposes ethnic quotas for each HDB block to promote ethnic integration and harmony. Foreign ownership is prohibited, except in the case of foreign persons who have obtained permanent residency for at least 3 years.

101. Dealings with HDB flats are also highly regulated. Since 2014, the sale and purchase of HDB flats must proceed by way of an option to purchase prescribed by the HDB. Moreover, section 50 of the Housing and Development Act provides that no HDB flat shall be sold, leased, mortgaged or disposed of without the prior written consent of the HDB Board. Any such dealing without consent may be declared to be void.

II. Private Housing

102. In Singapore, private housing generally consists of two types: (1) condominium (or apartments) and (2) landed property (e.g., terrace, bungalow). Unlike HDB flats, these buildings are owned by private individuals.

A. Condominium: Strata Development

103. Where a multistorey building is intended to be occupied by different persons, the owner of the building (usually a developer) would want to have it subdivided, both vertically and horizontally, into separate lots.[192] This can be achieved by applying to have the building brought within the strata title scheme established under the Land Titles (Strata) Act.[193] Under this scheme, individual lots will be issued separate legal titles known as subsidiary strata certificates of title.[194] The owner of a lot is known as a 'subsidiary proprietor'.[195] He is entitled to deal with his lot in the same manner as the owner of a registered land.[196]

192. *See* Teo Keang Sood, *Strata Title in Singapore and Malaysia*, 5th edn (LexisNexis, 2015); Tang Hang Wu and Kelvin F.K. Low, *Tan Sook Yee's Principles of Singapore Land Law*, 3rd edn (LexisNexis, 2009) Chapter 22; W.J.M. Ricquier, *Land Law*, 5th edn (LexisNexis, 2017) Chapter 9.
193. (Cap. 158, 2009 Rev. Ed.) (LTSA).
194. LTSA, section 10(1)(b).
195. Where a lot is leased, the tenant is a subsidiary proprietor only if the duration of the lease is at least 21 years: LTSA, section 3.
196. LTSA, sections 4 and 9.

104. While the LTSA makes a brief reference to the 'proprietor', i.e. the original owner of the entire parcel of land, nothing was said about him/her retaining a title to the land.[197] This suggests that he is no longer the owner of any part of the land.

105. Such parts of the building that are not comprised in any lot and are capable of being enjoyed by the occupiers of multiple lots are known as common property.[198] Basic examples are corridors, stairways, lifts, car parks, swimming pools, etc. All common properties are owned by the subsidiary proprietors in shares proportional to the share values allocated to their respective lots.[199] Common property may be transferred or leased for a period exceeding 3 years if the relevant authority has given its approval and the required percentage of approval votes (based on share value) is received at a general meeting.[200] A lease not exceeding 1 year may be granted with the approval of the relevant authority.[201]

106. For the purposes of maintaining common property and regulating the use of the building generally, the LTSA provides for the constitution of a management corporation.[202] The duties and powers of the management corporation are set out in the Building Maintenance and Strata Management Act (BMSMA).[203] Subsidiary proprietors are obliged to contribute to the levies imposed by the management corporation.[204] The sum to be levied from each subsidiary proprietor is determined by the share value of his lot.[205]

107. A strata lot may be freely transacted. However, no foreign person is allowed to purchase all the lots in a strata development.[206] Any contravention of this prohibition amounts to a criminal offence.

197. *Ibid.*, section 3(1): 'the person who was the proprietor of the land the subject of the strata title plan immediately before the registration of the strata title application for that plan'.
198. LTSA, section 3; BMSMA, section 2. *See generally Sit Kwong Lam v. Management Corporation Strata Title Plan No 2645* [2018] SGCA 14; *Wu Chiu Lin v. Management Corporation Strata Title Plan No 2874* [2018] SGHC 43; *MCST Plan No 367 v. Lee Siew Yuen* [2014] SGHC 161; [2014] 4 SLR 445; *MCST Plan No 3106 v. Pochuev Vladislav* [2010] SGSTB 1; *MCST Plan No 2504 v. Hyundai Engineering & Construction Co Ltd* [2007] SGHC 63; [2007] 3 SLR(R) 174; *Choo Kok Lin v. MCST Plan No 2405* [2005] SGHC 144; [2005] 4 SLR(R) 175; *Frontfield Investment Holdings (Pte) Ltd v. MCST No 938* [2001] SGHC 161; [2001] 2 SLR(R) 410; *MCST No 473 v. De Beers Jewellery Pte Ltd* [2001] SGHC 207; [2001 2 SLR(R) 669; *Tsui Sai Cheong v. MCST Plan No 1186 (Loyang Valley)* [1995] SGHC 260; [1995] 3 SLR(R) 713; *MCST Plan No 958 v. Tay Soo Seng* [1992] SGHC 311; [1992] 3 SLR(R) 818; *Leong Seow Sum v. MCST Plan No 1047*, STB No 26 of 1992.
199. LTSA, section 13.
200. BMSMA, section 34; LTSA, section 23.
201. BMSMA, section 34(2)(b).
202. LTSA, section 10A.
203. (Cap. 30C, 2008 Rev. Ed.) (BMSMA).
204. BMSMA, section 40(1).
205. *Ibid.*, section 40(2).
206. Residential Property Act (Cap. 274, 2009 Rev. Ed.) (RPA).

B. Landed Housing

108. Like a condominium, a landed housing may be freely transacted. The only exception is the case of foreign ownership, which is regulated by the Residential Property Act. Except with approval from the Minister for Law,[207] no foreign person is allowed to purchase, acquire or retain a landed residential property.[208] Any attempt to do so shall be null and void.[209]

III. Commercial and Industrial Property

109. All other property not used for dwelling is broadly classified as commercial or industrial property. Unlike the case of residential property, there is no restrictions on the ownership of or dealings with commercial or industrial property.

§4. Estates in Land

110. Land has both spatial and temporal elements. The doctrine of estates, which has its roots in the doctrine of tenure, allows the alienation of land for segments of time. Today, in Singapore, there are three kinds of estates: the freehold estate, the leasehold estate and the estate in perpetuity.

I. The Freehold Estate

111. There were originally three kinds of freehold estate: (1) fee simple, (2) fee tail and (3) life estate. In Singapore, the fee tail had been abolished in 1886.[210] Historically, the owner of a freehold estate is entitled to protect it by way of a real action, which entitled him/her to recover the land in the case of intrusion. For this reason, a freehold estate is classified as real property.

112. The fee simple represents the largest segment of time that a person could hold a piece of land. The owner of a fee simple is, for practical purposes, the absolute owner of the land. Historically, the fee simple would last as long as its owner has an heir. The operative words were 'to the grantee and his heirs'. During his lifetime, the owner may alienate his estate, e.g. conveying it to *X*. *X* now becomes a grantee of the fee simple and the estate will last as long as *X* has an heir. If an owner of a fee simple dies leaving an heir, the estate will vest in the heir instead of his personal representative. The fee simple is not available for the purposes of satisfying the deceased owner's debts or for distribution to his next of kin. On the other hand, if the owner of a fee simple dies without leaving an heir, the fee simple will

207. RPA, section 25.
208. *Ibid.*, section 3(1).
209. *Ibid.*, section 3(2).
210. CLPA, section 51.

escheat to the Crown. In Singapore, however, the concept of heir was made redundant since the early 19th century. By virtue of the Indian Act 20 of 1837, all land, for the purposes of transmission on the death of its owner, shall vest in the deceased's personal representative and could be applied for the satisfaction of the deceased's debts. This provision is now found in section 35 of the CLPA. More importantly, the 19th century saw the birth of the practice of distributing the deceased's fee simple to his next of kin rather than to his heir.[211] Although the practice may have arisen from a misconstruction of the Indian Act 20 of 1837,[212] it was subsequently given legal sanction by the Intestate Succession Act, according to whic h the estate of an intestate person shall be distributed to his statutory next of kin, in default of which the estate shall devolve upon the state.[213] As the class of statutory next of kin is very wide, the fee simple is likely to last indefinitely.

113. Since the abolition of the fee tail, the only freehold estate that could be carved out of a fee simple is a life estate. Where a life estate is granted in return for consideration, it is often known as a lease for life.[214] A life estate is not inheritable and will determine upon the life tenant's death. The life tenant may deal with his life estate during his lifetime, e.g. by selling the life estate or leasing the land to someone else, but the interest or any subsequently created interest will automatically determine upon the death of the original life tenant.

II. The Leasehold Estate

114. A leasehold estate entails the grant of exclusive possession of a piece of land for a definite duration, e.g. for 10 years or 99 years.[215] Historically, the leasehold estate was not classified as real property because it was not recoverable by way of a real action. However, because the owner of the leasehold estate was allowed to protect it by an action of trespass, he came to be recognised as having an interest in the land. The leasehold estate was eventually classified as a special type of personalty known as chattel real.

115. As a leasehold estate does not belong to the feudal group of estates, is regarded in law as inferior to a freehold estate. From a fee simple one could carve out unlimited number of leasehold estates.[216] Even a life tenant could grant a 999-year lease. But a 999-year leaseholder cannot grant a life interest. In valuing an

211. *See e.g. In the Goods of Lao Leong An* [1893] 1 SSLR 1; *Syed Ali Bin Mohamed Alsagoff v. Syed Omar Bin Mohamed Alsagoff* (1918) 15 SSLR 103. Whether the doctrine of escheat continues to operate in Singapore, and if so in what circumstances, is a matter of some debate: see Tang Hang Wu and Kelvin F.K. Low, *Tan Sook Yee's Principles of Singapore Land Law*, 3rd edn (LexisNexis, 2009) at 47–50.
212. *See* R Braddell, 'Heirs and the Common Law' (1941) MLJ xlvii.
213. (Cap. 146, 2013 Rev. Ed.), section 7.
214. *See* Barry C. Crown, 'The Lease for Life and the Requirement of Certainty' [2004] SJLS 37.
215. *See* Chapter 6 (Leases).
216. In Singapore, there are even cases of 999,999-year leases: see *Goh Teh Lee v. Lim Li Pheng Maria* [2010] SGCA 18; [2010] 3 SLR 364.

estate, however, one must have regard to commercial reality. There is, in most instances, little practical difference between a 999-year leasehold estate and a fee simple. But a 999-year lease granted by a life tenant is significantly less valuable since it automatically determines upon the death of the life tenant, which is unlikely to live for 999 years.

III. Estate in Perpetuity

116. Only the State can grant an estate in perpetuity. Being entirely a creation of the Crown Lands Ordinance (CLO), it has no common law counterpart.[217] The grant of an estate in perpetuity must be in the prescribed form, which is set out in Schedule A of the CLO. The operative words were 'to the grantee and his heirs and assigns forever'. The CLO was succeeded by the State Lands Act (SLA).[218] Although the SLA continues to provide for the grant of estate in perpetuity, Schedule A was omitted without providing for a substitute definition.[219]

117. In terms of duration, the estate in perpetuity should, as its name suggests, lasts perpetually. Following the demise of the concept of heir, a fee simple and an estate in perpetuity are indistinguishable in terms of duration.[220] When the grantee of an estate in perpetuity dies, the distribution rules as set out in the Intestate Succession Act equally applies.[221] It is only if the grantee dies without leaving any next of kin will the estate devolve upon the state.

118. An estate in perpetuity differs from a fee simple in a number of ways. The fact that it is not of feudal origin has two implications. First, the doctrine of escheat has no application.[222] Second, a life estate cannot be carved out of it.[223] But the same result can be achieved in equity using the device of the trust. A more significant difference is that while a grant of free simple could be in absolute terms, a grant of an estate in perpetuity is subject to various conditions and covenants, such as the reservation by the State of minerals and mining rights, duty of the grantee to repair landmarks, prohibition against using the land for burial, etc.[224] These covenants and conditions can be excluded by agreement, but is unlikely in practice. Due to these

217. (Ordinance 2 of 1886).
218. (Cap. 314, 1996 Rev. Ed.).
219. In *Re Section 16(2)(a) of the Land Titles Act* [1992] SGHC 52; [1992] 1 SLR(R) 493, Chan J held that the following expression sufficiently referred to an estate in perpetuity: 'To hold ... in fee simple subject nevertheless to the payment of the said annual rent reserved by and to the covenants and conditions in the said statutory land grant and the Crown Lands Ordinance ... '
220. *Re Section 16(2)(a) of the Land Titles Act* [1992] SGHC 52; [1992] 1 SLR(R) 493 at [3].
221. (Cap. 146, 2013 Rev. Ed.), section 7.
222. Tang Hang Wu and Kelvin F.K. Low, *Tan Sook Yee's Principles of Singapore Land Law*, 3rd edn (LexisNexis, 2009) at 44, 47.
223. *Ibid.*, at 44.
224. SLA, sections 4, 6 and 7.

differences, a contract purporting to sell an estate in perpetuity as an estate in fee simple is voidable for misrepresentation.[225]

§5. Classification of Things Found on the Surface of Land

I. Classification

119. Physical objects that are found on land may be classified into three kinds: (a) part and parcel of the land; (b) fixture; (c) chattel.[226] Vegetation and buildings are established examples of objects that are part and parcel of the land. While it is not incorrect to say that they are also fixtures attached to the land,[227] the term 'fixture' is more commonly used to refer to objects that are affixed to buildings rather than directly onto the surface of the land.[228] Since both (a) and (b) are regarded as part of the land, there is really no practical distinction between them. The same tests apply to distinguish both (a) and (b) from (c).

120. The issue of classification often arises in two types of disputes. First, where there is a contest over the ownership of the object, e.g. between the person who originally owns the object and the person who owns the land (or building) on which the object is found. Second, where there is a dispute as to whether the object should be taken into account in the assessment of property tax. While this is mostly determined by applying the relevant tax statutes, the common law classification is also often referred to in support of a particular interpretation.

II. The Basic Tests

121. The tests for determining whether something has become part of the land are traditionally rested on the principle of accession, under which a minor object loses its identity when it accedes to a major object.[229] The principle finds expression in the maxim *quicquid plantatur solo, solo cedit*, which is translated to mean whatever is affixed to the soil belongs to the soil. For example, a building becomes part of the land on which it is built. It follows that objects attaching to the building also become part of the land. However, it has come to be accepted that certain objects, although physically attached to the land, are not to be regarded as part of the land. A classic example is the anchor of a vessel firmly attaching to the seabed. Despite the high degree of attachment to the land, it cannot be supposed to have become part of the land.[230]

---

225. *Virginia Developments Pte Ltd v. Behem Investment Pte Ltd* [1988] SGHC 31; [1988] 1 SLR(R) 302.
226. *Elitestone Ltd v. Morris* [1997] 1 WLR 687 at 691.
227. *See e.g. Billing v. Pill* [1954] 1 QB 70 at 75, where Lord Goddard CJ used the term fixture to also refer to a building.
228. *Elitestone Ltd v. Morris* [1997] 1 WLR 687 at 690; *Boswell v. Crucible Steel Co* [1925] 1 KB 119.
229. *See* Part III (Acquisition of Property Rights) Chapter 5 (Accession and Specification).
230. *Holland v. Hodgson* (1872) LR 7 CP 328 at 335.

122. In *Holland v. Hodgson*, Blackburn J conceded that it is very difficult, if not impossible, to lay down any comprehensive test for determining whether something has become part of the land.[231] However, he went on to lay down certain guidelines[232] which have since been accepted as part of Singapore law.[233] Whether something has become part of the land 'must depend on the circumstances of each case, and mainly on two circumstances, as indicating the intention, viz., the degree of annexation and the object of annexation'.[234] Both degree and object of annexation will be discussed below.

123. The reference to intention, specifically whether the object is intended to be part of the land or not, requires some clarification. In *Elitestone Ltd v. Morris*, Lord Lloyd explained that the classification of an object does not depend on what the parties subjectively intended it to be.[235] Instead, 'the intention of the parties is only relevant to the extent that it can be derived from the degree and object of annexation'.[236]

124. In *Holland v. Hodgson*, Blackburn J also suggested the use of presumptions to determine on whom the initial burden of proof lays.[237] Where the object is physically attached to the land or a building, it is presumed to be part of the land. Conversely, where the object is not physically attached to the land or a building, it is presumed to be a chattel. It is for the party claiming otherwise to rebut the presumption. Clearly, these presumptions reflect the traditional emphasis on the degree of annexation. In recent times, however, the emphasis has been gradually shifting towards the object of annexation.[238] This shift in emphasis is apparent from the recent Singapore cases on this topic.[239]

125. Before turning to a detailed discussion of the cases on this topic, readers shall be forewarned that this area of the law is fraught with incoherence and uncertainty. In many cases, a direct appeal to common sense may be required in identifying a workable solution.[240]

---

231. (1872) LR 7 CP 328 at 334–35.
232. *Ibid.*
233. *People's Park Chinatown Development Pte Ltd (in liquidation) v. Schindler Lifts (Singapore) Pte Ltd* [1992] SGCA 69; [1992] 3 SLR(R) 236 at 240; *Gebrueder Buehler AG v. Chi Man Kwong Peter* [1988] SGCA 2; [1998] 1 SLR(R) 185 at 191–92.
234. (1872) LR 7 CP 328 at 334.
235. [1997] 1 WLR 687 at 693. Thus, even if a thing is subject to a retention of title clause, it is not prevented from losing its identity by accession to land: see *Gebrueder Buehler AG v. Chi Man Kwong Peter* [1988] SGCA 2; [1998] 1 SLR(R) 185. On the harshness of this rule, see Tan Sook Yee, 'Of Chattels, Fixtures and Retention of Title' [1988] 3 MLJ xvii; Tang Hang Wu and Kelvin F.K. Low, *Tan Sook Yee's Principles of Singapore Land Law*, 3rd edn (LexisNexis, 2009) at 37–38.
236. [1997] 1 WLR 687 at 693.
237. (1872) LR 7 CP 328 at 335.
238. *Leigh v. Taylor* [1902] AC 157 at 162; *Hamp v. Bygrave* [1983] 266 EG 720 at 724.
239. *See Pan-United Marine Ltd v. Chief Assessor* [2008] SCGA 21; [2008] 3 SLR(R) 569; *Chief Assessor v. Van Ommeren Terminal (S) Pte Ltd* [1993] SGHC 148; [1993] 2 SLR(R) 354.
240. *See e.g. Reid v. Smith* (1906) 3 CLR 656.

A. Degree of Annexation

126. Where an object is attached to the land or a building by way of screws, nails or other similar methods, the courts are likely to find that it has become part of the land. In *Holland v. Hodgson*, looms were attached to the floor of a worsted mill by way of nails.[241] Although the looms could be easily removed without causing any serious damage, the court held that they had become part of the land. Similarly, in *Gebrueder Buehler AG v. Chi Man Kwong Peter*, the Court of Appeal held that machinery that was securely affixed to the factory's floor became part of the land.[242] However, as hinted earlier, the fact that the object is physically affixed to the land is not always conclusive of the issue. The object of annexation may sometimes point to the opposite conclusion.

B. Object of Annexation

127. This inquiry is determined by asking whether the object is brought onto the land merely to be enjoyed temporarily as a chattel or whether it is for the permanent and substantial improvement to the land.[243] While this may seem like a simple inquiry, identifying the right answer is often far from straightforward. Fortunately, at least three useful tests can be derived from the existing cases. However, it shall be noted that, applied independently, each of these tests is overly broad such that there is a risk of overinclusion. Perhaps applying these tests in combination would be a better way of answering the inquiry.[244]

1. The Object Serves the Purpose for Which the Land Is Used

128. The first test focuses on the purpose for which the land (or building) is used and whether the object in question serves that purpose. In *Chief Assessor v. Van Ommeren Terminal (S) Pte Ltd*, the defendant, who was in the business of letting out oil storage facilities, had on its land large oil storage tanks which were resting on their own weight.[245] Chao J held that the storage tanks were part of the land for the purposes of property tax assessment as they were meant to improve the intended use of the land. In *Gebrueder Buehler*, one reason the machinery was held to be a fixture was because its installation enhanced the factory's productivity in the manufacturing of cocoa products.[246] Similarly, in *Material Trading Pte Ltd v. DBS*

241. (1872) LR 7 CP 328.

242. [1988] SGCA 2; [1988] 1 SLR(R) 185 (Wee CJ, Lai and Chua JJ). *See also Van Santen v. Lim Je Ging* (1904) 7 SSLR 1; *Goh Chong Hin v. Consolidated Malay Rubber Estates Ltd* [1924] 5 FMSLR 86.

243. *Elitestone Ltd v. Morris* [1997] 1 WLR 687 at 692; *Hamp v. Bygrave* (1983) 266 EG 720 at 724.

244. *See e.g. Chief Assessor v. Van Ommeren Terminal (S) Pte Ltd* [1993] SGHC 148; [1993] 2 SLR(R) 354.

245. [1993] SGHC 148; [1993] 2 SLR(R) 354.

246. [1988] SGCA 2; [1998] 1 SLR(R) 185.

Finance Ltd, the court held that three overhead cranes which moved along steel runways permanently installed in warehouses were fixtures, for they 'improve the usefulness of the warehouses and enhance their values'.[247] In response to the argument that the steel runways were fixtures while the overhead cranes were not, the court opined that they ought to be treated the same: '[p]lainly, without the steel runways, the cranes are incomplete and cannot operate as overhead cranes'.[248]

129. Similarly, in *People's Park Chinatown Development Pte Ltd (in liquidation) v. Schindler Lifts (Singapore) Pte Ltd* (*Schindler Lifts*), several escalators which were specifically manufactured and designed for the building were hoisted into specially constructed spaces where they rested on their own weight.[249] Although they were not connected to the power supply and the glass panels and handrails were yet to be installed, the Court of Appeal held that they became part of the building and hence part of the land. The court explained that the escalators 'were meant to become integral and permanent features of the building'.[250] Although the court did not explicitly state why this was the case, it is clearly because the lifts were meant to improve accessibility to the different floors of the building, which is essential for a large shopping mall. *Schindler Lifts* is most likely the first local case to implicitly suggest that physical annexation is unnecessary so long as the purpose of bringing the object onto the land is for the permanent improvement of the land.

130. The limits of the first test was explored in a number of cases where the object alleged to be part of the land was located outside the three-dimensional boundaries of the land. In *Pan-United Marine Ltd v. Chief Assessor*, three floating dry docks were berthed above the seabed adjacent to the appellant's land, on which the appellant was operating a shipyard.[251] The floating dry docks were made accessible from the land by a ramp.[252] The Court of Appeal held that the floating dry docks were part of the land for the purposes of property tax assessment because they served the appellant's use of the land. The court said:

> ... it does not matter that these docks were located, strictly and literally, beyond the physical boundary of the property. Put simply, the floating dry docks were clearly intended to be an integral part of the Property – particularly from a functional perspective ... It is also important to note that, as we have seen above, as a point of general legal principle, the purpose of annexation is an extremely important factor (indeed, so it appears, even more so than the degree of annexation ...)[253]

247. [1988] SGHC 17; [1988] 1 SLR(R) 141 at [12].
248. [1988] SGHC 17; [1988] 1 SLR(R) 141 at [6].
249. [1992] SGCA 69; [1992] 3 SLR(R) 236 (Yong CJ, Thean J and Rajendran JJ).
250. *Ibid.*, at [12].
251. [2008] SCGA 21; [2008] 3 SLR(R) 569 (Phang JA, Rajah JA and Ang J).
252. *Ibid.*
253. *Ibid.*, at [55].

131. However, the court went on to add that, in any event, there was sufficient physical annexation between the land and the floating dry docks by way of the ramp. But it may be argued that this basic means of accessing the floating dry docks does not constitute physical annexation in the traditional sense.[254]

2. The Object Is Difficult to Remove from the Land

132. The second test, which has been applied to buildings and large structures resting on their own weight, focuses on whether they could be easily removed from the land. In *Elitestone Ltd v. Morris*, a wooden bungalow was resting on its own weight without any attachment to the land.[255] However, it was constructed in such a way that it could not be removed from the land without being demolished. The House of Lords held that the bungalow became part of the land.

133. Lord Lloyd, who gave the main judgment on this issue, explained:

134. In the case of the house the answer is as much a matter of common sense as precise analysis. A house which is constructed in such a way so as to be removable, whether as a unit, or in sections, may well remain a chattel, even though it is connected temporarily to mains services such as water and electricity. But a house which is constructed in such a way that it cannot be removed at all, save by destruction, cannot have been intended to remain as a chattel. It must have been intended to form part of the realty.[256]

135. In Singapore, a building is accepted to be part of the land simply by virtue of its status. As the Court of Appeal said in *Pan-United Marine*, 'a "building" would, by its very nature and definition, constitute part of the land'.[257] Despite this, the test enunciated by Lord Lloyd in *Elitestone* remains useful in assessing objects or structures which do not fall squarely within the definition of a building. However, some modification is necessary to take into account the advancement in technology which makes it possible to move mega structures while keeping them intact.[258] A possible approach is to regard accession as having occurred if removal of the object from the land would involve significant difficulty. This version of the test was impliedly accepted in *Van Ommeren Terminal*, where Chao J took into account the fact that the storage tanks, each of which having a storage capacity of 6,000 cubic metres, were difficult to remove in coming to the conclusion that they formed part of the land.[259] Applying the same test, a caravan will not be regarded as forming part of the land on which it is resting as it could be readily driven away.

254. *See also Clarke Quay Pte Ltd v. Tan Hun Ling (trading as Sin Lok Cuisine)* [2006] SGCA 22; [2006] 3 SLR(R) 626, although in this case there was clear physical annexation between the object and the building.
255. [1997] 1 WLR 687.
256. *Ibid.*, at 692–93.
257. [2008] SCGA 21; [2008] 3 SLR(R) 569 at [43]. *See also Reid v. Smith* (1906) 3 CLR 656.
258. *See* the television program Mega Movers on The History Channel.
259. [2008] SCGA 21; [2008] 3 SLR(R) 569 at [34].

3. The Object Is Part of the Building's Architectural Design

136. The third test, which is usually applied to determine whether smaller objects have become fixtures to a building, enquires whether they were part of the building's architectural design as opposed to being mere ornaments. In *D'Eyncourt v. Gregory*, the dispute was whether certain articles in a large manor house were fixtures.[260] Lord Romilly MR held that the carved kneeling figures on the staircase in the great hall, the sculptured marble vases in the hall, the lion statues at the head of the flight of steps in the garden, as well as the sixteen stone garden seats in the garden itself, were fixtures as they formed part of the house's architectural design. This was despite the fact that many of these articles could be easily removed. However, the learned judge conceded that the distinction drawn by the third test is extremely thin and may be difficult to apply at times.

III. Tenant's Fixture

137. Where an object is affixed to the land by the landowner, the principle of accession applies in its usual vigour, as the earlier discussion shows. However, where it was a tenant who affixed the object to the land, the principle of accession applies less strictly in the tenant's favour.[261] Initially, the relaxation was applied in cases involving machinery which a tenant uses for his trade. Allowing the tenant to remove his machinery when the lease ends would further the policy of encouraging trade.[262] Soon after, the relaxation was extended to objects which are intended to improve the tenant's enjoyment of the land, including decorative items such as panelling, tapestry, period fireplace, chimney piece etc.[263] The rationale has now been restated more generally: to prevent injustice to the tenant.[264]

138. In principle, the relaxation is justified by reference to the purpose of annexation.[265] The object does not become part of the land if that was not the tenant's intention. This intention is often inferred from the tenant's limited interest in the land as well as the considerable value of the thing.[266]

139. In *Spyer v. Phillipson*, a tenant of a flat for a term of 21 years, after 7 years in occupation, decorated the flat by installing in some rooms expensive antique panelling, ornamental chimneypieces and period fireplaces.[267] These were physically

260. (1866) LR 3 Eq 382.
261. This relaxation could be traced as far back as to the reign of King Henry VII. *See e.g.* (1495) YB. 20 Hen. 7 at 13.
262. *Fisher v. Dixon* (1845) 12 Cl & Fin 312 at 328; *Poole's Case* (1703) 1 Salk 368. Locally, the policy was noted by the Court of Appeal in *Riduan bin Yusof v. Khng Thian Huat* [2005] SGCA 39; [2005] 4 SLR(R) 234 at [26] (Yong CJ, Chao JA and Kan J).
263. *Spyers v. Phillipson* [1931] 2 Ch D 183; *Leigh v. Taylor* [1902] AC 157.
264. *Leigh v. Taylor* [1901] 1 Ch 523 at 539–40.
265. *Riduan bin Yusof v. Khng Thian Huat* [2005] SGCA 39; [2005] 4 SLR(R) 234 at [27].
266. *Spyers v. Phillipson* [1931] 2 Ch D 183; *Leigh v. Taylor* [1902] AC 157.
267. [1931] 2 Ch 183.

attached to the building's structure in various ways. When the tenant died, a dispute arose between his estate and the landlord as to whether those things became the landlord's. Luxmoore J held in favour of the tenant's estate, holding that the things in question were for the tenant's own enjoyment and not for the permanent improvement of the flat. The learned judge explained:

140. It would be a little surprising if this gentleman were to spend 5000*l* in purchasing panelling and have it put in on the footing that he would only enjoy it for eleven or thirteen years, and at the end of that time he would lose all interest in it, and it would belong to a complete stranger, i.e. the landlord of the premises.[268]

141. Unlike the traditional fixture test, in which the parties' subjective intention is irrelevant, in the case of tenant's fixture the parties' intention is given significant emphasis.[269] The landlord and the tenant may agree that certain objects are to be regarded as tenant's fixtures.[270]

142. Neither does difficulty in its removal prevent the object from being regarded as tenant's fixture. In *BP Refinery Singapore Pte Ltd v. Amazon Group Ltd*, Prakash J said:

143. It is accepted that although a particular fixture may not be removable in one piece and has to be dismantled to be removed, it still qualifies as a tenant's fixture if it is capable of reassembly elsewhere. Petrol pumps, sheds of various types and even a glasshouse have been held to be tenant's fixtures.[271]

144. Arguably, the approach adopted for tenant's fixture is to be preferred as it is simpler to apply and infinitely more intuitive.

145. During the continuance of the lease, the tenant is free to remove or dispose of any tenant's fixture from the land.[272] A tenant's fixture is, accurately speaking, the tenant's property. As Prakash J said in *BP Refinery*: '[T]he tenant as the only person with the power to deal with the fixture for the duration of his tenancy must be recognised as having property in the fixture during that time'.[273]

146. If the tenant does not remove the object from the land before expiry of the lease, or within a reasonably time thereafter while remaining in occupation of the land, the object becomes the property of the person who is immediately entitled to

268. *Ibid.*, at 195–96.
269. *See* para. 15 above.
270. *See BP Refinery Singapore Pte Ltd v. Amazon Group Ltd* [1998] SGHC 256; [1998] 3 SLR(R) 4.
271. [1998] SGHC 256; [1998] 3 SLR(R) 4 at [19].
272. *BP Refinery Singapore Pte Ltd v. Amazon Group Ltd* [1998] SGHC 256; [1998] 3 SLR(R) 4; *Official Receiver v. Chi Man Kwong* [1994] SGHC 30; [1994] 1 SLR(R) 277.
273. [1998] SGHC 256; [1998] 3 SLR(R) 4 at [24].

the land (usually the landlord).[274] However, in the event that the lease is subsequently renewed, the tenant's right to the object survives even though it was not removed before the expiry of the prior lease.[275]

274. *BP Refinery Singapore Pte Ltd v. Amazon Group Ltd* [1998] SGHC 256; [1998] 3 SLR(R) 4; *Lyde v. Russell* (1830) 1 B & Ad 394; *Poole's Case* (1703) 1 Salk 368; *Climie v. Wood* (1868–69) LR 4 Ex 328 at 329–30.

275. *Riduan bin Yusof v. Khng Thian Huat* [2005] SGCA 39; [2005] 4 SLR(R) 234; *Leivest International Pte Ltd v. Top Ten Entertainment Pte Ltd* [2006] SGHC 1; [2006] 1 SLR(R) 888.

Chapter 3. Co-ownership

§1. Introduction

147. In the previous chapter, we have examined the doctrine of estates, under which different persons may own a same piece of land for different segments of time. These different estate owners are seldom referred to as co-owners since they do not own concurrent rights to enjoyment of the land. Each is entitled to the enjoyment of the land only during the subsistence of his estate. In such circumstances, there is less opportunity for conflicts to arise. The law of co-ownership is thus concerned mainly with cases where two or more persons together own a piece of land and all are entitled to simultaneous enjoyment of the land.[276]

148. The present topic is particularly important in Singapore due to the high incidence of co-ownership. In *Lau Siew Kim v. Yeo Guan Chye Terence*, the Court of Appeal observed that this phenomenon is attributable to 'a number of factors including rising property prices, joint-income families, gender equality, gender longevity, tax planning and the function of a home both as a residence and an asset'.[277] It is interesting to note that public housing policies significantly contribute to this phenomenon. Since 1985, the percentage of the Singapore population living in Housing and Development Board (HDB) flats has consistently been above 80%.[278] As most HDB eligibility schemes require the flat to be co-occupied, sole ownership of a HDB flat is uncommon and is usually for smaller flats, which form a very small percentage of existing HDB flats.

§2. Two Forms of Co-ownership

149. In Singapore, co-ownership of land can be in the form of joint tenancy or tenancy in common. Identifying the manner in which a particular property is held is important for at least two reasons. First, it affects the manner in which the co-owners can deal with the property. Second, it determines whether a deceased co-owner has any interest to pass to his next of kin.

I. Joint Tenancy

150. In a case of joint tenancy, the co-owners (joint tenants) collectively own a single and identical interest. Between them, the notion of shares does not apply. From this basic description of a joint tenancy, one can see hints of the four unities: unity of interest, unity of title, unity of time and unity of possession. The unity of interest is reflected by the fact that the joint tenants own the very same interest, e.g.

276. *Goh Teh Lee v. Lim Li Pheng Maria* [2010] SGCA 18; [2010] 3 SLR 364 at [9].
277. [2007] SGCA 54; [2008] 2 SLR(R) 108 at [1]. *See also Goh Teh Lee v. Lim Li Pheng Maria* [2010] 3 SLR 364; [2010] 3 SLR 364 at [9].
278. Housing Development Board, 'HDB Annual Report 2014/2015: Key Statistics' (2016) at 9.

fee simple in joint names or a 99-year leasehold in joint names.[279] Unity of interest is necessarily achieved from the unities of title and time. The same interest can only be acquired from the same conveyance, e.g. a fee simple purchased from *X* and conveyed into the joint names of *A* and *B*.[280] Since all joint tenants own the same interest, it follows that all of them have a right to possess the whole property, hence there is unity of possession.

151. The hallmark of a joint tenancy is the rule of survivorship. When one joint tenant dies, the remaining joint tenant(s) becomes fully entitled to the property. Nothing passes to the estate of the deceased joint tenant. Where there are several joint tenants, this process continues until only a single owner remains, in which case the property ceases to be joint-tenanted.

152. As a joint tenant owns nothing by himself/herself, it is incorrect to say that the surviving joint tenants take over the interest of the deceased joint tenant. Rather, the deceased joint tenant simply ceases to have any interest in the property. As the Court of Appeal said in *Shafeeg bin Salim Talib v. Fatimah bte Abud bin Talib*, 'the interest of a deceased joint tenant simply disappears into thin air. Nothing 'passes' or is transmitted to the surviving tenant'.[281] This view finds support from section 114(1) and (2) of the Land Titles Act (LTA),[282] which provides that a surviving joint tenant (or joint tenants) may notify the Registrar of the death of another joint tenant, upon which the Registrar shall make the necessary entry on the land register to indicate that the interest of the deceased joint tenant has determined and the property becomes vested in the surviving joint tenant(s). It is only necessary to add that the rule of survivorship cannot be displaced by a will.[283]

153. Although a joint tenant owns the whole interest in the land, he owns nothing by himself/herself. He owns it together with the other joint tenant(s). Therefore, a joint tenant cannot, by himself/herself, enter into a transaction purporting to bind the entire estate. Unless all joint tenants agree, the property cannot be sold, leased or mortgaged.[284] Neither can a joint tenant, by himself/herself, cast a valid vote for or against a collective sale.[285] However, a joint tenant may deal with his 'own share' in the property, which has the effect of severing the joint tenancy and turning it into a tenancy in common.[286]

---

279. Where, over the same piece of land, *A* has a fee simple and *B* has a life interest, between them there is no unity of interest.
280. Suppose *X*, who owns Redacre, sells a 50% share to *A* and the remaining 50% share to *B*. Although *A* and *B* collectively own the whole of Redacre, they do not own Redacre jointly since their respective interests were acquired through different conveyances at different times. They hold Redacre as tenants in common.
281. [2010] SGCA 11; [2010] 2 SLR 1123 at [35]. *See also* [36], [39]–[43], [45] (Chan CJ, Phang and Rajah JJA).
282. (Cap. 157, 2004 Rev. Ed.).
283. *Neo Hui Ling v. Ang Ah Sew* [2012] SGHC 65; [2012] 2 SLR 831 at [38]. *See also Chan Lung Kien v. Chan Shwe Ching* [2017] SGHC 136 at [22].
284. *Mookka Pillai Rajagopal v. Khushvinder Singh Chopra* [1996] SGCA 58; [1996] 3 SLR(R) 210.
285. *Goh Teh Lee v. Lim Li Pheng Maria* [2010] SGCA 18; [2010] 3 SLR 364.
286. *See* §6.II.B. below.

II. Tenancy in Common

154. In the case of a tenancy in common, each co-owner (tenant in common) owns an undivided share in the title to the property, e.g. *A*, *B* and *C* in the proportion of 10%, 20% and 70% respectively. As these distinct shares can be acquired separately at different times, the unities of title and time are not necessary for the creation of a tenancy in common. The shares of the tenants in common are undivided in the sense that none of them own specific parts of the property. For this reason, there is unity of possession among tenants in common.

155. As each tenant in common owns a distinct share in the property, the rule of survivorship does not apply. The interest of a deceased tenant in common passes to his next of kin. It does not vest in the surviving tenant(s) in common.

156. A tenant in common may assign his own share to another person. For example, if *C* sells his interest to *D*, *D* will simply take *C*'s place as a tenant in common owning a 70% share.

§3. Rights and Duties Between Co-owners

I. Right to Possession

157. As there is unity of possession among co-owners, whether in the case of a joint tenancy or a tenancy in common, no co-owner can exclude another co-owner from possession of the property. In the unfortunate event of this occurring, the hostile co-owner commits an act of ouster. The ousted co-owner is entitled to sue the hostile co-owner for recovery of possession of the property and for occupational rent (also known as *mesne* profit).[287]

158. Normally, an ouster involves a co-owner evicting another co-owner from the property, or a co-owner preventing another co-owner from entering the property. The fact that a co-owner occupies the property by himself/herself does not by itself amount to ouster of the other co-owner. The occupant co-owner could simply be exercising his own right of possession. In *Tan Chwee Chye v. P V RM Kulandayan Chettiar*, Ang J said that for an ouster to occur the occupant co-owner must have 'the necessary intention to possess the property so as to dispossess the other co-owner'.[288] This was a peculiar case where it was the occupant co-owner who argued that he had ousted the other co-owner with the intention of establishing adverse possession. However, the case has lost its relevance since it is no longer possible to acquire title by adverse possession.[289] Perhaps the better view is that ouster is a strict liability wrong, as in the case of trespass.

287. *Dennis v. McDonald* [1981] 1 WLR 810; *Chhokar v. Chhokar* (1984) 5 FLR 313.
288. [2005] SGHC 203; [2006] 1 SLR(R) 229 at [23].
289. LTA, section 50.

159. Besides actual ouster, the law also recognises constructive ouster. This occurs where a co-owner's conduct, although falling short of exclusion, makes it impossible or impracticable for the other co-owner(s) to remain on the property. For example, in *Dennis v. McDonald*, the wife left the co-owned house due to her husband's violent disposition when intoxicated.[290] The English Court of Appeal held that she was ousted from the house for it would be quite unreasonable to expect her to exercise her right of occupation in the circumstances. The threshold for finding constructive ouster, however, appears to be rather high. For example, there is no ouster where one co-owner leaves the property due to feelings of animosity between him/her and the other co-owner(s).[291]

II. Rents and Profits

160. Generally, no rent is payable from one co-owner to the co-owner(s) since each co-owner is entitled to possession of the property.[292] However, where a co-owner receives from a third-party rent or profit generated from the property, he is liable to account to the other co-owner(s).[293] In the case of a joint tenancy, the joint tenants are entitled to the profit in equal shares. In the case of a tenancy in common, the tenants in common are entitled in proportion to their respective shares in the property. If the manner of holding is a joint tenancy at law but tenancy in common in equity, the second measure is to be followed.[294]

§4. Dealings of Co-owned Property

I. Dealings That Bind the Entire Interest

161. Where a property is co-owned, no one co-owner could, by himself/herself, deal with or bind the entire interest in the property. This would require the consent of all co-owners. In the case of a tenancy in common, the logic is simply that a single tenant in common does not own the entire interest. He owns only a share in the interest. A joint tenant, on the other hand, does own the entire interest, but it is also said that by himself/herself he owns nothing.

162. In Goh Teh Lee v. Lim Li Pheng Maria, the Court of Appeal added:

> Since the interest of each joint tenant is the same in extent, nature and duration, a necessary consequence is that each and every joint tenant must partake in any dealings with the whole legal estate before such dealings may effectively bind the entire estate. An action by one joint tenant, or even by some

290. [1981] 1 WLR 810.
291. *Marriott v. Franklin* (1993) 60 SASR 457.
292. *Goodland Ltd v. Lim Ban Toon* [1966] SGHC 9; [1965–67] SLR(R) 264.
293. Conveyancing and Law of Property Act (Cap. 61, 1994 Rev. Ed.) (CLPA), section 73A.
294. *Mariam Khatoon bte Rahim Khan v. Mohamed Saleh* [1999] SGHC 68.

joint tenants but short of all of them collectively, will not suffice to bind the estate, as the whole estate does not reside in the single joint tenant or the select few (as the case may be).[295]

163. In principle, the rule only applies to dealings with the property, i.e. something that binds the estate, such as transferring, leasing or mortgaging the property. Whether other conducts fall within the rule must depend on how they affect the estate. In *Goh Teh Lee*, one joint tenant appended her signature on a document agreeing to a collective sale while the other joint tenant refused. The Court of Appeal said that in such a case the property is regarded as not having agreed or disagreed to the collective sale. The real issue, however, was whether the objecting joint tenant had *locus standi* to file a formal objection before the Strata Titles Board and the courts. The Court of Appeal answered in the negative. However, it could be argued that the act of filing a formal objection does not amount to dealing with the property. It does not bind the property in any way. It merely gives the Strata Titles Board and the courts the opportunity to consider the objection.[296]

164. In *Hammersmith and Fulham LBC v. Monk*, the issue before the House of Lords was whether a periodic tenancy held by two joint tenants could be brought to an end by a notice to quit by one joint tenant without the consent of the other.[297] The court held that it could. Lord Bridge, who delivered the lead judgment, explained that all 'positive dealings' with a tenancy require the concurrence of all joint tenants.[298] These include the exercising of a break clause, surrendering the term, making a disclaimer, exercising an option to renew the term and applying for relief against forfeiture. The act of giving notice to determine a periodic tenancy, while a positive act, is different in substance. Since the omission to give such notice amounts to assent to the extension of the term for a further period, the notice merely serves to withhold the assent.[299] It is merely to prevent the automatic extension of the periodic lease. A contrary but less preferable view is that the giving of the notice amounts to dealing with the interest as it has a direct impact on the continuing existence of the interest. This view was implicit in the judgment of Lord Browne-Wilkinson, who said that allowing the determination of the tenancy by one joint tenant creates an exception to the general rule.[300]

295. [2010] SGCA 18; [2010] 3 SLR 364 at [17] (Chao, Phang and Rajah JJA). *See also Chan Lung Kien v. Chan Shwe Ching* [2017] SGHC 136 at [20]–[21].
296. Barry C. Crown, 'En Bloc Sales and Joint Tenancy' [2011] SJLS 564.
297. [1992] 1 AC 478. *See also Newton Housing Trust v. Alsulaimen* [1999] 1 AC 313; *Harrow LBC v. Johnstone* [1997] 1 WLR 459.
298. [1992] 1 AC 478 at 490.
299. *Ibid.*, at 490–91.
300. *Ibid.*, at 92.

II. Dealing with One's Own Share

165. A tenant in common is, of course, entitled to deal with his own share in the property. He may sell or convey his share to a third party, who will then become a tenant in common in relation to the other co-owner(s). He may also mortgage his share to secure a loan. Whether a tenant in common may grant a lease over the co-owned property is a more difficult question. A lease entails the granting of exclusive possession to the lessee. However, due to the unity of possession, no tenant in common could exclude another tenant in common from the property. No single tenant in common has exclusive possession to the property. However, it is possible that a more limited kind of lease could be created. Suppose *A* and *B* holds a property as tenants in common. *B* grants *C* a 10-year lease of *B*'s own interest. *C* will simply take *B*'s place during those 10 years. Since *B* does not himself/herself have the right to exclude *A*, it follows that *C*, who derives his interest from *B*, has no right to exclude *A*. However, *C* has a right to exclude all other persons including *B*.

166. The question of whether a joint tenant is entitled to deal with his own share is tied to the issue of severance. This will be discussed in more detail below.[301]

§5. Methods of Creation

167. Where a registered land is transferred into the names of more than one person to be co-owned, the form of co-ownership may be indicated in the transfer form.[302] The co-owners may simply state 'joint tenancy' or 'tenancy in common', or use other words that point to whichever form they prefer. As a general rule, in the absence of any words of severance indicating an undivided share, the co-owners will hold the property as joint tenants. Thus, the phrase 'to A and B' is sufficient to create a joint tenancy.[303] On the other hand, the phrase 'to A and B in equal shares' will create a tenancy in common. Where the co-owners clearly indicated that they intend to hold the property as tenants in common but fail to indicate their respective shares, they are presumed to hold in equal shares.[304]

168. In the past, it was mandatory to indicate the form of co-ownership in an instrument of conveyance.[305] The revised edition of the LTA, however, contains no provision that makes such indication mandatory. Instead, where there is no such

301. *See* §6.II.B. below.
302. *See* Form 19 (Transfer) and Form 38 (Lease).
303. Tang Hang Wu and Kelvin F.K. Low, *Tan Sook Yee's Principles of Singapore Land Law*, 3rd edn (LexisNexis, 2009) at 193.
304. LTA, section 53(2).
305. The now repealed section 48(1) of the LTA stated: 'Instruments affecting registered land shall disclose the full name, the address and the occupation or conjugal status of each person claiming thereunder, and, in the case of co-tenants, the manner in which they intend to hold'.

indication, a joint tenancy is presumed,[306] reflecting the common law's fondness for joint tenancy.[307] The presumption of joint tenancy also applies in cases where the wordings used are not sufficiently clear.

§6. Change in the Form of Co-ownership

I. Tenancy in Common to Joint Tenancy

169. Section 53(3) of the LTA provides that tenants in common who are 'entitled in equal shares' may convert the tenancy in common into a joint tenancy by an instrument of declaration in the approved form and have it registered.[308] The declaration may be made by some or all tenants in common, but the declaring tenants in common must own the same percentage of shares. Take the example of a tenancy in common where *A*, *B*, *C* and *D* hold the property in the following proportions: 10%, 10%, 20% and 60%. Only *A* and *B* can make a formal declaration, following which *A* and *B* will become joint tenants in respect of a 20% share in the property.[309] *A* and *B*, now conveniently viewed as a single owner, will continue to be tenants in common with *C* and *D*.[310] If *C* and *D* wishes to join the conversion process, an alternative method is for the property to be conveyed to someone else (*X*) to be held on trust for *A*, *B*, *C* and *D*. When they demand for reconveyance of the property, they may indicate joint tenancy as the preferred manner of holding.

II. Joint Tenancy to Tenancy in Common

A. *Formal Declaration*

170. Section 53(5) of the LTA allows a joint tenant (or joint tenants) to formally sever[311] a joint tenancy by way of an instrument of declaration in the approved form and by serving a copy on the other joint tenant(s).[312] Subsection (6) further provides that upon registration of the instrument of severance, the declarant(s) 'shall be deemed to hold a share that is equal in proportion to each of the remaining joint tenants as if each and every one of them had held the registered land as tenantsin-common in equal shares prior to the severance'.[313]

306. LTA, section 53(1).
307. *See Lau Siew Kim v. Yeo Guan Chye Terence* [2007] SGCA 54; [2008] 2 SLR(R) 108 at [83]–[96].
308. Form 15.
309. LTA, section 53(4)(b)(i).
310. *Ibid.*, section 53(4)(b)(ii).
311. An informal declaration of severance is generally ineffective: see *Chan Lung Kien v. Chan Shwe Ching* [2017] SGHC 136.
312. LTA, section 53(5). Depending on the number of joint tenants who wish to sever, the approved form to be used is different: see Forms 16 (all), 17 (one) and 18 (some).
313. LTA, section 53(6).

171. Take a simple example where a property is jointly held by *A*, *B*, *C* and *D*. If *A* makes a declaration of severance, the interest in the property will now be split into two undivided shares: 25% belonging to *A* and 75% belonging to *B*, *C* and *D*. If *A* dies, his 25% share will pass to his next of kin. As *B*, *C* and *D* did not make a declaration of severance, they will hold the 75% share as joint tenants. The rule of survivorship continues to apply among them.

172. If all the joint tenants make a declaration of severance, it would be a simple case of all of them becoming tenants in common entitled in equal shares, i.e. each owning a 25% share. If some of the joint tenants, e.g. *A* and *B*, make a declaration of severance, they are to choose whether to collectively hold 50% as joint tenants or to each hold a 25% share as tenants in common.[314] In the former case, *A* and *B* jointly own a 50% share while *C* and *D* jointly own the other 50% share.

173. In *Diaz v. Diaz* the Court of Appeal considered the possibility of severing a joint tenancy by an informal declaration.[315] There the house was registered in the joint names of a mother and her elder daughter. A few years later the mother decided to change the manner of co-ownership. She attempted to sever the joint tenancy by executing the required instrument of declaration and served a copy on the elder daughter. The instrument of declaration was stamped but for unknown reason was not registered pursuant to section 53(6). Shortly after, the mother died. In her last will, she left her interest in the house to her younger daughter. The issue, then, was whether the elder took the house entirely by virtue of the rule of survivorship or whether the joint tenancy was severed so that the younger daughter inherits a 50% share in the house. The Court of Appeal held that the mother's conduct was sufficient to effect severance as between herself and her elder daughter.[316]

174. Although the court did not explicitly say so, it is obvious that the severance could only take effect in equity since it was not reflected in the land register. Thus, third parties who have no notice of the severance should be entitled to assume that the house was still joint-tenanted, as reflected in the land register.[317] Suppose in *Diaz v. Diaz* the elder daughter offers to sell the house to a third party. The third party is entitled to regard her as the sole legal and beneficial owner since the other joint tenant had passed away. If the house is sold, the third party takes good title. The younger daughter's interest is restricted to a 50% share in the proceeds of sale.[318] This situation could be prevented by lodging a caveat over the house, as the younger daughter did in this case. The caveat will prevent the elder daughter from selling the house and provide the world with notice of the equitable severance.[319]

314. Form 18 requires the declarants to indicate which mode of holding they prefer.
315. [1997] SGCA 55; [1997] 3 SLR(R) 759 (Yong CJ, Karthigesu and Thean JJA), noted in Barry C. Crown, 'Severance of a Joint Tenancy' [1998] SJLS 166.
316. See also *Ng Kim Chwee v. Chua Chiew Hai* [1998] SGHC 133; [1998] 2 SLR(R) 111.
317. [1996] SGHC 267 at [14].
318. *Ibid.*
319. *Cf* Barry C. Crown, 'Severance of a Joint Tenancy' [1998] SJLS 166 at 169–70.

175. However, the precise basis of the decision in *Diaz v. Diaz* is not entirely clear. The Court of Appeal alluded to the fact that registration of the instrument of severance would require production of the property's duplicate certificate of title and this is not always possible, e.g. where it is withheld by the other joint tenant(s) or by a third party (e.g., a mortgagee).[320] Thus, to insist on fulfilment of the registration requirement would frustrate Parliament's intention to make unilateral severance easier.[321] However, there was nothing in the judgment to suggest that the mother had difficulty producing the duplicate certificate of title. More importantly, this concern has been addressed by Parliament by the addition of section 53(8), which allows the Registrar to dispense with production of the duplicate certificate of title if he is satisfied that the declarant is unable to produce it despite his best efforts.[322]

176. The approach in *Diaz v. Diaz* was recently revisited by the Court of Appeal in *Chan Lung Kien v. Chan Shwe Ching*.[323] In that case, one joint tenant made a declaration of severance in the approved form. However, instead of serving a copy on the other joint tenant, the first joint tenant simply published a notice of severance in the newspaper stating that the form has been deposited with a solicitor. Nor was the form registered pursuant to section 53(6). The Court of Appeal held that the attempted severance was ineffective, overturning its earlier decision in *Diaz v. Diaz*. The court explained that, while the earlier decision was 'well-intentioned',[324] it cannot be supported on plain reading of section 53(6).[325] Therefore, it is now clear that unilateral severance can be effected only by fully complying with the requirements of section 53(5) and (6).

B. Other Acts of Severance

177. Section 53(3) of the LTA, while prescribing a formal mode of severance, also states that it is '[w]ithout prejudice to any rule or principle of law relating to severance of a joint tenancy'. Thus, in *Diaz v. Diaz*, the Court of Appeal confirmed that the common law and equitable modes of severance continue to be available to joint tenants of registered land.[326] In the English case of *Williams v. Hensman*, the court laid down three basic modes of severance: (a) by operating upon one's own share; (b) by mutual agreement; and (c) by any course of dealing sufficient to intimate that the interests of all were mutually treated as constituting a tenancy in common.[327]

320. [1997] SGCA 55; [1997] 3 SLR(R) 759 at [24].
321. *Ibid.*, at [21]–[24].
322. See Barry C. Crown, 'Developments in the Law of Co-Ownership' [2003] SJLS 116 at 120*v.*.
323. [2018] SGCA 24.
324. *Ibid.*, at [64].
325. *Ibid.*, at [65].
326. [1997] SGCA 55; [1997] 3 SLR(R) 759 at [27].
327. (1861) 1 J & H 546 at 557.

178. Mode (a) is the most commonly encountered method of unilaterally severing a joint tenancy. One may find it odd that a joint tenant could deal with his own share although it is said that he has no separate share of his own. However, theory bends to accommodate practice.[328] The joint tenant's act of alienating his own share is taken to be the very same act that severs the joint tenancy and gives rise to that interest of his own.

179. In *Diaz v. Diaz* the Court of Appeal equated mode (a) with a disposal of the joint tenant's own interest by registration.[329] With respect, this is an overly restrictive reading of *Williams v. Hensman*, where disposal of interest was referred to as one example of operating upon one's own share.[330] The common law recognises a far wider range of conducts falling within mode (a), e.g. declaring a trust over one's own share, entering into a contract to sell one's own share, granting a lease over one's own share, etc.[331] However, the Court of Appeal recently held in *Chan Lung Kien v. Chan Shwe Ching* that a unilateral declaration of severance does not amount to an act operating upon one's own share as it does not destroy any of the four unities.[332] It is only necessary to add that where the dealing amounting to an act operating upon one's own share does not change the manner of holding shown in land register, severance necessarily takes effect in equity.[333]

180. The case for finding a severance where a joint tenant grants a lease is based on the desire to protect the lessee's interest. Take the example of a property jointly held by *A* and *B*. *B* grants *C* a five-year lease over the property. What would happen if *B* dies? If *B*'s conduct did not cause a severance, his interest would be extinguished due to the rule of survivorship. It necessarily follows that *C*'s lease, which was carved out of *B*'s interest, would determine. On the other hand, if the joint tenancy was severed by *B*'s conduct, his interest would survive and pass to his next of kin. *C*'s lease will continue to subsist for the agreed duration. However, the severance may be temporary, i.e. it operates only during the subsistence of the lease. Where the lease determines during B's lifetime, the tenancy in common reverts to a joint tenancy.[334]

181. There is also a good reason for regarding the granting of a mortgage over one's own share as giving rise to severance. A tenancy in common better gives effect to the agreement between the mortgagor and the mortgagee. Take the example of a property jointly held by *A* and *B*. *B* then grants *C* a mortgage over his interest in the property. Suppose there is no severance. If *B* dies, his interest in the property would be extinguished due to the rule of survivorship. There would be nothing left for *C*'s mortgage to latch on. On the other hand, if *A* dies, and *B* becomes the sole owner

328. *Wright v. Gibbons* (1949) 78 CLR 313 at 330.
329. [1997] 3 SLR(R) 759 at [27].
330. (1861) 1 J & H 546 at 557.
331. *See* Barry C. Crown, 'Partial Alienation by One Co-Owner of Land' [2000] SJLS 92.
332. [2018] SGCA 24 at [62]. *C.f.* Barry C. Crown, 'Severance of a Joint Tenancy' [1998] SJLS 166 at 171.
333. *See Diaz v. Diaz* [1996] SGHC 267 at [14], discussed at §6(2)(A) above.
334. *Wright v. Gibbons* (1949) 78 CLR 313 at 330.

of the property, *C*'s mortgage would extend to the whole interest in the property. In effect, *C* would gain a stronger security interest than what was initially contemplated. However, just as in the case of a lease, it may be that the tenancy in common would revert to a joint tenancy once the mortgage is discharged.

182. As Crown observed, severance without the other joint tenant(s)'s knowledge could be problematic. Suppose *B* acted upon his own share without *A*'s knowledge. If *B* dies, there is a likelihood that his personal representative might uncover from his personal belongings a document evidencing what *B* did. He could use it to show that there had been a severance and therefore *B*'s estate is entitled to a share in the property. However, if *A* dies, *B* could simply conceal evidence of the dealing so that the rule of survivorship operates in his favour. Thus, Crown suggests that 'the law should strive to avoid any situation which might allow one joint tenant to sever the joint tenancy without the knowledge of the other joint tenants'.[335] In reality, the problem identified by Crown is unlikely to arise where the dealing by *B* is readily discoverable, e.g. it was registered or a caveat had been lodged to protect it. In other cases, it would be necessary to inquire whether *A* actually knows about *B*'s dealing with the property.

183. Severance by way of modes (b) and (c) are best understood as falling within a single category based on the joint tenants' mutual consent to sever. Where there is no explicit agreement to sever, any conduct between the parties intimating such an agreement suffices. A classic example is the case of *Burgess v. Rawnsley*, where one joint tenant agreed to sell his share to the other joint tenant.[336] Another example is where joint tenants agree to execute mutual wills.[337]

C. Resulting Trust and Constructive Trusts

184. For historical reasons, the common law favours a joint tenancy to a tenancy in common.[338] This is reflected in section 53(1) of the LTA, which presumes a joint tenancy where the co-owners are silent as to the manner of holding. Equity, on the other hand, favours a tenancy in common.[339] Where the joint tenants have contributed unequally to the purchase price of the property, a presumption of resulting trust arises, under which they each acquire an equitable share in proportion to their respective contributions. Similarly, the contributions of each joint tenant towards the purchase or maintenance of the property may also give rise to a common intention constructive trust, which usually results in redistribution of the joint tenant's shares in equity. In both instances, the joint tenants become equitable tenants in common.

335. Barry C. Crown, 'Partial Alienation by One Co-Owner of Land' [2000] SJLS 92 at 94.
336. [1975] Ch 429.
337. *Re Wilford's Estate* (1879) LR 11 Ch D 267.
338. *See* Part IV (Trust and Fiduciary Law) Chapters 45 (Resulting Trusts) and 6 (Constructive Trusts).
339. *Lau Siew Kim v. Yeo Guan Chye Terence* [2007] SGCA 54; [2008] 2 SLR(R) 108 at [83]–[96] (Phang JA, Rajah JA and Ang J).

185. Where the co-owners did not indicate the manner of holding and a presumption of joint tenancy arose by virtue of section 53(1) of the LTA, the operation of the equitable doctrines are perfectly justifiable. However, there is some uncertainty as to whether the equitable doctrines will apply if the co-owners have explicitly specified joint tenancy as the preferred manner of co-ownership. In *Lau Siew Kim v. Yeo Guan Chye Terence*, the Court of Appeal said:

> … it is only where the registered co-owners of land had not made a conscious and informed choice to hold as joint tenants at law that equity kicks in to presume a tenancy in common. In contrast, where co-owners had expressly specified their intention to hold land in a legal joint tenancy, there would be no cause for equity not to follow the law; thus, in such instances, legal joint tenants should also be beneficial joint tenants unless it may be shown that the expressly-stated choice should be vitiated for some reason.[340]

186. Despite this qualification to the operation of the equitable doctrines, the courts rarely inquire into whether the co-owners have made an informed decision when they chose joint tenancy as the preferred manner of co-ownership.[341] Based on the existing authorities, the equitable doctrines will apply even in light of clear evidence that the co-owners chose to be registered as joint tenants because they intended the rule of survivorship to apply.[342] In *Neo Hui Ling v. Ang Ah Sew*, Lai J explained that this was because the rule of survivorship says nothing about the co-owners' intention as to their beneficial shares while they are still alive.[343]

D. *Other Events Resulting in Severance*

1. Court Order

187. In *Sivakolunthu Kumarasamy v. Shanmugan Nagaiah*, the Court of Appeal explained that severance could result from the issuance of a court order.[344] In this case it was held that a court order for the joint-tenanted property to be sold pursuant to a decree *nisi* in divorce proceedings had the effect of severing the joint tenancy. The court drew an analogy with an order for partition, which results in severance of the joint tenancy even before it has been carried into effect.[345]

---

340. [2007] SGCA 54; [2008] 2 SLR(R) 108 at [93].
341. A rare exception is *Ishak bin Abdul Kadir v. Khoo Hui Ying* [2015] SGHC 181 at [17].
342. *Mariam Khatoon bte Rahim Khan v. Mohamed Saleh* [1999] SGHC 68; *Neo Hui Ling v. Ang Ah Sew* [2012] 2 SLR 831 at [26]–[43].
343. [2012] SGHC 65; [2012] 2 SLR 831 at [39]–[43].
344. [1987] SGCA 21; [1987] SLR(R) 702 (Lai J, Thean J and Chan JC).
345. *Khoo Seoke Haing v. Cheah Khay Pin* (1885) SSLR 74. *See also* §7 (Termination of co-ownership) below.

2. Bankruptcy

188. Where a joint tenant is adjudicated bankrupt, his interest in the property becomes vested in the Official Assignee.[346] As the automatic vesting breaks the four unities, the Official Assignee will hold the interest as a tenant in common in relation to the other co-owners (who remain as joint tenants among them).[347]

3. Writ of Seizure and Sale

189. There is some uncertainty as to whether a judgment creditor could enforce a judgment debt by way of a writ of seizure and sale in respect of land of which the judgment debtor is a joint tenant.[348] In *Malayan Banking Bhd v. Focal Finance Ltd*, Tay JC held that a writ of seizure and sale can only be used if the interest of the judgment debtor is distinct and identifiable.[349] Absent any severance in other recognised manners, registration of the writ does not by itself cause the severance of the joint tenancy.

190. Later, in *Chan Shwe Ching v. Leong Lai Yee*, Leow JC preferred not to lay down any definitive statement on whether a writ of seizure and sale severs a joint tenancy.[350] However, the learned judge held that a writ of seizure and sale could be used in respect of a joint-tenanted property as severance would occur when the sheriff sells the property. At that point, the joint tenant's interest becomes distinct and identifiable. On this basis, Leow JC made an ex parte order that the 'interest' of one joint tenant in the land be attached and taken in execution under a writ of seizure and sale. This ex parte order was later set aside by Chua J in *Chan Lung Kien v. Chan Shwe Ching*, who preferred the earlier position in *Malayan Banking*.[351] More recently, in *Peter Low LLC v. Higgins, Danial Patrick*, the High Court held that a joint tenant's interest can be the subject of enforcement by way of a writ of seizure and sale.[352] In his detailed judgment, Pang JC explained:

> [T]he severability of the joint tenancy and the ability of a joint tenant to alienate his aliquot share (or potential aliquot share) without the consent of the other joint tenants ought, in principle, lead to the result that any property interest which a debtor-joint tenant is able to alienate on his own should be also saleable in execution by the sheriff on the debtor-joint tenant's behalf.[353]

346. Bankruptcy Act (Cap. 20, 1985 Rev. Ed.), section 46.
347. Tang Hang Wu and Kelvin F.K. Low, *Tan Sook Yee's Principles of Singapore Land Law*, 3rd edn (LexisNexis, 2009) at 207.
348. *See* Tan Sook Yee, 'Execution against Co-Owned Property' [2000] SJLS 52.
349. [1998] SGHC 402; [1998] 3 SLR(R) 1008.
350. [2015] SGHC 210; [2015] 5 SLR 295.
351. [2017] SGHC 136; [2018] 4 SLR 208 at [28]–[43]. *See also One Investment and Consultancy Ltd and another v. Cham Poh Meng (DBS Bank Ltd, garnishee)* [2016] SGHC 208; [2016] 5 SLR 923 at [5]; *Peter Low LLC v. Higgins, Danial Patrick* [2017] SGHCR 18.
352. [2018] SGHC 59.
353. *Ibid.*, at [88].

191. Even if one takes the view that severance is required before a writ of seizure and sale could attach to the interest of the judgment debtor, in the many cases it is likely that severance has already occurred in equity due to the co-owners' unequal contribution to the purchase price.[354]

4. Murder

192. Where a joint tenant murders the other joint tenant and thereby becomes the legal sole owner of the property, the rule of survivorship should not apply. This is due to the strong policy against allowing a wrongdoer to benefit from his own wrong.[355] In equity both co-owners are regarded as tenants in common. The share of the deceased tenant in common will pass to his next of kin. In the meantime, it is held on trust by the wrongdoer.

§7. Termination of Co-ownership

193. Where the entire interest in the property becomes vested in one person, the property ceases to be co-owned. This may occur where one of two joint tenants pass away, where one co-owner sells his interest to the other co-owner(s), where the entire interest in the property is sold to a third party, etc.

194. In cases where the co-owners could not agree on how the property is to be dealt with, the court may make an order: (i) for the property be partitioned; or (ii) for the property to be sold in the open market and for the proceeds to be distributed among the co-owners. Where the property is partitioned and each co-owner becomes the sole owner of each part, the co-ownership comes to an end. The same occurs if the land is sold to a third party, as indicated earlier.

195. The power of the court to make either order is found in paragraph 2 of the First Schedule of the Supreme Court of Judicature Act,[356] which states:

> Power to partition land and to direct a sale instead of partition in any action for partition of land; and in any cause or matter relating to land, where it appears necessary or expedient, to order the land or any part of it to be sold, and to give all necessary and consequential directions.

196. In *Abu Bakar v. Jawahir*, Rajendran J held that a court is 'free to exercise this jurisdiction whenever it appeared necessary or expedient for the court to do

354. *See* §6.II.C. above.
355. *See e.g.*, *Cleaver v. Mutual Reserve Fund Life Association* [1892] 1 QB 147; *In the Estate of Crippen* [1911] P 108; *Riggs v. Palmer*, 115 NY 506 (1889).
356. (Cap. 322, 2007 Rev. Ed.).

so'.[357] This was cited with implicit approval in *Su Emmanuel v. Emmanuel Priya Ethel*,[358] where the Court of Appeal also laid down a number of factors to be taken into account in deciding what order to make:[359]

(a) In deciding whether it is necessary or expedient for a sale to be ordered in lieu of partition, the court conducts a balancing exercise of various factors, including (i) the state of the relationship between the parties (which would be indicative of whether they are likely to be able to co-operate in the future); (ii) the state of the property; and (iii) the prospect of the relationship between the parties deteriorating if a sale was not granted such that a 'clean break' would be preferable.
(b) Regard should be had to the potential prejudice that the various co-owners might face in each of the possible scenarios, namely, if a sale is granted and if it is not granted.
(c) A sale would not generally be ordered if to do so would violate a prior agreement between the co-owners concerning the manner in which the land may be disposed of.

197. To be sure, a court may decline to make either order, thus keeping the co-ownership alive.[360] However, an objection to an application for an order of sale rarely succeeds, especially if the sale would have no serious prejudicial effect on the opposing co-owner. That the objecting co-owner(s) would receive a share in the sale proceeds, thus enabling him/her to seek alternative accommodation, is an important factor that must necessarily be taken into account.

198. In *Tan Bee Hoon v. Quek Hung Heong*, the objecting co-owner argued that he was emotionally attached to the property and that his age and health conditions would make it difficult to find an alternative accommodation.[361] In rejecting these arguments, Abdullah JC said:

199. None of these to my mind were sufficient to bar the sale of the Property. Attachment to a particular plot is not a determining factor. It may be relevant in some circumstances, but it cannot normally be determinative when other co-owners wish to partition or sell. Their property rights, including the rights of disposal,

357. [1993] SGHC 109; [1993] 1 SLR(R) 865 at [17] (Karthigesu JA, Thean JA and Goh J). *See also Chiam Heng Luan v. Chiam Heng Hsien* [2007] SGHC 132; [2007] 4 SLR(R) 305 at [97]; *Wong Kim Wan (alias Wong Loretta) v. Leong Ong Meng Jerome Matthew* [2010] SGHC 318 at [13]; *Toh Tian Sze v. Han Kim Wah* [2012] SGHC 111; [2012] 3 SLR 682 at [12].
358. [2016] SGCA 30; [2016] 3 SLR 1222 (Menon CJ, Chao JA and Chan SJ).
359. *Ibid.*, at [57].
360. *See e.g. Nora Chia v. Muthukrishnan Christopher Pillay* [1998] SGHC 96, where the parties, after divorce, had consented to orders in the decree *nisi* for the matrimonial home to remain in their joint names.
361. [2015] SGHC 229.

would have to be given due weight. Similarly, difficulties in finding alternative property, or health problems, could not normally deprive co-owners of their property rights unless it was of such a significant degree that movement out of the property was near impossible.[362]

200. Earlier, in *Chiam Heng Luan v. Chiam Heng Hsien*, Prakash J suggested that an order for sale would not be made if it would result in serious injustice to the opposing co-owner.[363] The learned judge suggested two examples: 'a case of a wife being evicted from her matrimonial home or an elderly person who may be put to a great disadvantage if asked to leave his home'.[364] With respect, the first example may have been phrased too broadly. This was confirmed in *Su Emmanuel v. Emmanuel Priya Ethel*, where the court found it necessary to consider a range of other factors (see above).[365] In this case the matrimonial property was registered in the joint names of the husband and wife, who subsequently became estranged. Due to financial difficulty, the husband sold 49% of his share to his sister.[366] When the sister encountered financial difficulty and faced bankruptcy proceedings, she applied to the court for the property to be sold so that she could use the sale proceeds to repay her debts. The Court of Appeal decided to order a sale because in this case the prejudice to the sister if the property was not sold significantly outweighed the prejudice to the wife if the property was sold.[367] The sister single-handedly repaid the mortgage loan and she would most certainly be adjudged bankrupt if she could not liquidate her interest in the property. On the other hand, the wife did not contribute at all to the purchase of the property.[368] Moreover, she had four children, two of whom have already started working. Her detriment, if any, would likely to be mitigated by the help from her children.[369]

201. In the case of a commercial property, the courts are likely to order a sale where the parties have previously agreed that the property would be sold to realise the investment,[370] where the parties are in such acrimonious relationship that no cooperation is possible or where the property has not been properly exploited for profit.[371]

---

362. *Ibid.*, at [78].
363. [2007] SGHC 132; [2007] 4 SLR(R) 305 at [97].
364. [2007] SGHC 132; [2007] 4 SLR(R) 305 at [97], cited with approval by Lee J in *Toh Tian Sze v. Han Kim Wah* [2012] SGHC 111; [2012] 3 SLR 682 at [12].
365. [2016] SGCA 30; [2016] 3 SLR 1222.
366. When the husband entered into the agreement to sell his share to his sister, he had operated upon his own share, thus severing the joint tenancy into a tenancy in common under which he and his wife each beneficially held 50% of the property ([2016] SGCA 30; [2016] 3 SLR 1222 at [81]). The 49% sold to the sister was from the husband's share.
367. [2016] SGCA 30; [2016] 3 SLR 1222 at [59]–[60].
368. *See also Gurnam Kaur d/o Sardara Singh v. Harbhajan Singh s/o Jagraj Singh* [2004] SGHC 189; [2004] 4 SLR(R) 420, where Tan J implicitly held that the co-owners' respective contributions to the purchase of the property (if any) were to be taken into account.
369. *See also Neo Hui Ling v. Ang Ah Sew* [2010] SGHC 328, where the mother was offered accommodation by her elder daughter in the event that the property is sold.
370. *Cheong Woon Weng v. Cheong Kok Leong* [2016] SGHC 263.
371. *See Chiam Heng Luan v. Chiam Heng Hsien* [2007] SGHC 132; [2007] 4 SLR(R) 305; *Wong Kim Wan (alias Wong Loretta) v. Leong Ong Meng Jerome Matthew* [2010] SGHC 318.

202. Where a co-owner seeks an order for sale or partition, the viability of an order for partition is an important factor to be taken into consideration. Obviously, a court would not order partition if the relevant authority had refused to approve a subdivision of the property, as in the case of *Toh Tian Sze v. Han Kim Wah.*[372] The same could be said where it is difficult to determine how the land should be partitioned. In *Abu Bakar v. Jawahir*, the property was a single-story house co-owned by four family members and was occupied by two families.[373] One of the co-owners moved out of the house and settled in Malaysia. He persuaded the other co-owners to buy out his share but they could not afford it. Eventually he applied to the court for an order for sale. In deciding to order a sale, Rajendran J took into account the size and nature of the property and noted that it would be difficult to implement an order for partition. Even if the property has a large area, the fact that different parts of the property have unique characteristics may render partition difficult. In *Abdul Razak Valibhoy v. Abdul Rahim Valibhoy*, the land was subject to varying height restrictions and only its eastern part has access to the main road.[374] As these characteristics of the land would make partitioning it difficult, the Court of Appeal decided to order a sale. Similarly, in *Tan Bee Hoon v. Quek Hung Heong*, Abdullah JC decided to order a sale after making the following observation:

203. Partition would also run into difficulties here given the location and shape of the Property: the road frontage for the partitioned plots, as well as the fact that building on the Property straddled the land, would mean that any partition would be awkward. It may be that gerrymandering the Property to preserve the building may yet be topologically possible, but would likely have resulted in a diminished commercial value of the partitioned plots. These difficulties would also probably mean that planning permission would be difficult to obtain.[375]

204. In such cases, partitioning of the land would require 'negotiation, trade-offs and compromise'.[376] This is unlikely to be forthcoming where the parties are in an acrimonious relationship.

---

372. [2012] SGHC 111; [2012] 3 SLR 682.
373. [1993] SGHC 109; [1993] 1 SLR(R) 865 at [18].
374. [1995] SGCA 27; [1995] 1 SLR(R) 441.
375. [2015] SGHC 229 at [77].
376. *Ibid.*

Chapter 4. The Torrens System

§1. Introduction

205. Prior to 1956, land dealings in Singapore were governed entirely by the Conveyancing and Law of Property Act (CLPA),[377] under which a conveyance[378] must be made in the form of a deed.[379] The Registration of Deeds Act (RODA)[380] further provides for the registration of deeds pertaining to such dealings.[381] A title-holder must be prudent in registering his deed, for otherwise it is inadmissible in court as evidence of the title,[382] and even if the deed is subsequently registered, the title loses priority (except in the case of actual fraud) to a subsequently acquired title evidenced by a deed that was registered earlier.[383]

206. It is important to note that what the RODA introduced was neither a system of registered land nor a system of registration of land titles. There is no central land register from which one could obtain necessary information regarding specific parcels of land. The validity of a conveyance also does not depend on registration. All the old system does is to place on public record dealings in land that have already taken place. The purpose is to make land dealings more transparent. In theory, such a system should make the conveyancing process more efficient. For example, a person intending to purchase an interest in land could search the Registry of Deeds for information of past dealings in the land to confirm that there is no anomaly or defect in the seller's title. In reality, however, this goal is hampered by at least two factors. Firstly, as there is no standardised or prescribed form for deeds, extracting the required information from a series of differently drafted deeds, which could be messy or lengthy, becomes a tedious process. Secondly, as the registration of deeds is not compulsory, a search may not reveal all the relevant dealings affecting the land.

207. The Land Titles Ordinance (LTO) of 1956, drafted by John Baalman, introduced into Singapore the Torrens system of registered land.[384] As the ensuing discussion will show, the system is designed to facilitate the purchase of interests in land by allowing the purchaser to deal on the faith of what appears on the land register, thus avoid having to make burdensome and expensive inquiries. Following a number of re-enactments and revisions,[385] the applicable law today is contained mainly in the Land Titles Act (LTA).[386] In the case of strata development, the LTA

377. (Cap. 61, 1994 Rev. Ed.) (originally Ordinance 6 of 1886).
378. Broadly defined in section 2 to include leases and mortgages.
379. CLPA, section 53.
380. (Cap. 269, 1989 Rev. Ed.) (originally Ordinance 13 of 1886).
381. RODA, section 4.
382. *Ibid.*, section 4.
383. *Ibid.*, section 14.
384. Ordinance 21 of 1956.
385. Land Titles Act (Cap. 276, 1970); Land Titles Act (Cap. 157, 1985 Rev. Ed.).
386. (Cap. 157, 2004 Rev. Ed.) (originally No. 27 of 1993).

must be read together with the Land Titles (Strata) Act.[387] Since the LTO came into force in 1960, land in Singapore has been consciously and gradually brought under the new system. Today, less than 0.1% of land in Singapore remains unregistered, mostly because their owners could not be identified.[388] While the old system of deed registration continues to exist and apply to unregistered land, in practice one needs only be concerned about the laws applicable to registered land.

§2. The Land Register

208. The LTA requires the establishment of a land register, which shall comprise records of the following:[389] (a) folios of specific parcels of registered land; (b) instruments of dealings registered under the LTA; and (c) other instruments or documents registered or notified under the LTA.[390] The folio of each registered land (which could be in hard copy or in electronic form) shall contain, among other things, a description of the land itself and of the estate or interest existing over the land, and shall also state the proprietor of the estate or interest.[391] The folio of a parcel of land is also known as its certificate of title. A duplicate certificate of title can be issued upon request to the owner of the estate,[392] a person authorised by the owner to receive it,[393] or such other person which the Registrar considers best entitled to it.[394] With a central registry containing necessary information in standardised forms, land titles search is clearly simplified and more efficient under the new system.

209. The land register is served by two core principles upon which the Torrens system is based: the mirror principle and the principle of indefeasibility.[395] Both principles are concerned with ensuring certainty and finality in the information contained in the land register. Under the mirror principle, the land register sufficiently reflects the true state of land ownership so that it could be confidently relied upon.[396] A printout copy of a folio issued by the Registrar bearing a facsimile of the Registrar's seal shall be conclusive evidence of the information contained therein.[397] The closely related principle of indefeasibility gives validity and priority to a registered title, allowing it to be challenged only on limited grounds.

387. (Cap 158, 2009 Rev. Ed.) (LTSA).
388. The Land Titles (Amendment) Act 2001 (No. 25 of 2001) gave the Registrar greater ability to convert unregistered land into registered land.
389. LTA, section 28(2). In the case of strata development, the LTSA, section 10(1)(a) requires the Registrar to establish and maintain a subsidiary strata land register.
390. Such as caveats.
391. LTA, section 29.
392. *Ibid.*, section 34(5).
393. *Ibid.*, section 35(a).
394. *Ibid.*, section 35(b).
395. *United Overseas Bank Ltd v. Bebe bte Mohammad* [2006] SGCA 30; [2006] 4 SLR(R) 884 at [78].
396. *See Wong Kok Chin v. Mah Ten Kui, Joseph* [1992] SGCA 31; [1992] 1 SLR(R) 894 at 896.
397. LTA, section 36(1)(b).

§3. THE IMPORTANCE AND EFFECT OF REGISTRATION

I. Title by Registration

210. The LTA introduces a system of title by registration.[398] Section 45(1) of the LTA states: 'No instrument until registered as in this Act provided is effectual to pass any estate or interest in land under the provisions of this Act'. In *United Overseas Bank v. Victor Sakayamary*, GP Selvam J explained:

> It is clear therefore that an instrument purporting to create or confer an estate or interest in land is inchoate and does not vest property or security in the purchaser until registration … The important distinction between the making of the instrument and the registration is that the former is an act of parties and the latter is an act of state represented by the Registrar.[399]

211. For example, even if the parties have executed a contract intending a conveyance, there is no valid conveyance under the LTA unless the parties use the prescribed form[400] and have it registered.[401] These two requirements receive particular emphasis in respect of transfers,[402] leases exceeding 7 years,[403] mortgages and charges,[404] and easements.[405] In contrast, under the old system, a deed is sufficient to pass title. The RODA merely provides for the registration of pre-existing title; title was not acquired by registration.

212. It is important to explain at the outset some terminologies used in the present context. Where a particular dealing in land is registered under the LTA, the person who appears from the land register to be the person entitled to the interest dealt with is known as the proprietor.[406] Thus, the word 'proprietor' could be used to describe not only a transferee of title but also a mortgagee, chargee and lessee.[407] The interest acquired by the proprietor from the registered dealing is loosely referred to as 'title' even though the dealing may not involve a transfer of title in the usual sense. For example, it is common to speak of a mortgagee's title although, under the LTA, title in the land remains with the mortgagor.[408] The term 'estate' is sometimes used in the same broad sense.[409]

---

398. The Land Titles (Strata) Act (Cap 158, 2009 Rev. Ed.) (LTSA).
399. [1996] SGHC 98; [1996] 2 SLR(R) 20 at [18].
400. LTA, section 51(1).
401. *Ibid.*, section 45(1) & (2).
402. *Ibid.*, section 63.
403. *Ibid.*, section 87.
404. *Ibid.*, section 68.
405. *Ibid.*, section 97.
406. *Ibid.*, section 4(1).
407. *Ibid.*, section 4(1).
408. *See e.g. United Overseas Bank Ltd v. Bebe bte Mohammad* [2006] 4 SLR(R) 884; *Malayan Banking Bhd v. Sivakolunthu Thirunavukarasu* [2007] SGHC 161; [2008] 1 SLR(R) 149.
409. *See* title of LTA, section 46.

213. Although the LTA introduces a system of title by registration, it is possible to acquire certain interests in land without registration. The Torrens system is designed to accommodate certain unregistered interests. In some instances, registration is explicitly exempted. Restrictive covenants are protected not by registration but by notification on the folio of the relevant land.[410] Similarly, although land could be the subject matter of a trust,[411] particulars of the trust are not to be notified on the folio of that land.[412] A beneficiary of land may enforce the trust by way of an exception to indefeasibility.[413] Furthermore, the LTA sets out a list of overriding interests that are automatically binding without the need for registration or notification.[414] Even more interesting are judicially recognised equitable interests in land such as equitable leases[415] and equitable mortgages.[416] The recognition of these equitable interests tells us that it is possible to deal with land without using the mechanisms provided by the LTA. The downside is that the strong protection afforded to a registered interest is unavailable. Except for overriding interests, which are afforded statutory protection, and restrictive covenants, which are protected by notification, all other unregistered interests are to be protected by the lodgement of caveat. For this reason, the system of caveats is an important pillar of the Torrens system.

II. Indefeasible Title

214. Section 46(1) of the LTA states that a person who becomes a registered proprietor acquires indefeasible title.[417] Indefeasible title simply means a title that is liable to be defeated only on grounds set out in section 46[418] and perhaps certain recognised in personam exceptions.[419]

215. Indefeasible title could be acquired notwithstanding any procedural irregularity under the LTA in respect of the registration,[420] e.g. an erroneous registration by the land registry.[421] Registration confers title even if the proprietor had dealt with

---

410. LTA, section 139.
411. *Ibid.*, section 166(1) & (3). *See also Yeo Kia Yong v. Yeo Kia Hock* [1998] SGHC 203; [1998] 2 SLR(R) 602 at [36].
412. LTA, section 166(2).
413. *Ibid.*, section 46(2)(c).
414. *Ibid.*, section 46(1)(i)–(vii).
415. *Golden Village Multiplex Pte Ltd v. Marina Centre Holdings Ltd* [2002] SGCA 6; [2002] 1 SLR(R) 169.
416. *Société Générale v. Good Property Land Development Pte Ltd* [1989] SGHC 8; [1989] 1 SLR(R) 76; *United Overseas Finance Ltd v. Mutu Jeras* [1989] SGHC 41; [1989] 1 SLR(R) 446.
417. The term 'indefeasible title' is not used in the LTA but has gained wide usage in the academic literatures. The heading of section 46, which reads 'Estate of proprietor paramount', shall be understood to mean the same thing.
418. *See* §5 below.
419. *See* §6 below.
420. LTA, section 46(1)(b).
421. Where an action for ejectment (LTA, section 154) or rectification of land register (LTA, section 160) cannot be sustained, the victim may seek recompense from the insurance fund (LTA, section 155).

a person who was not a proprietor, i.e. a fictitious proprietor[422] or who did not act in good faith.[423] For example, *X* obtains title of Redacre by defrauding *A* and subsequently sells it to *B*. Assuming that *B* is innocent, he acquires indefeasible title by registration. The fact that *X* is fraudulent is irrelevant.[424]

216. Similarly, *B* will acquire indefeasible title even if registration is procured by a defective instrument of dealing, e.g. one that is void for forgery perpetrated by *X*. As the Court of Appeal said in *Alrich Development Pte Ltd v. Rafiq Jumabhoy*, 'a registered proprietor of a property has a good title to the property even if the transfer thereof to him was illegal or void'.[425] Put simply, registration has the effect of validating an otherwise invalid dealing. This is of course assuming that *B* is innocent so that the exceptions to indefeasibility set out in section 46(2)(a) to (e) are not engaged.

217. It is interesting to compare the Torrens system with the old conveyancing system. Take a simple example involving identity fraud. *A* is the registered owner of Blackacre. *X*, pretending to be *A*, entered into an agreement for the sale of Blackacre to *B*. *X* procures the registration of Blackacre in *B*'s name by stealing *A*'s duplicate certificate of title and forging *A*'s signature on the transfer form. Let us assume that *B* is completely innocent. *X* absconds with the purchase money. The contest is now between *A* and *B*, both of whom are victims of *X*'s fraud. Under the Torrens system, *B* gets an indefeasible title. It remains indefeasible as none of the exceptions to indefeasibility are engaged here.[426] In contrast, under the old system, title in Blackacre does not pass to *B* because *X* cannot give what he does not have and there is no provision for registration to perfect the transfer.

218. Put simply, while the old system emphasises protection of the title of an existing owner (*A*), the new system affords more protection to the purchaser of that title (*B*). It may be argued that the result is unfair because *B* was in a better position to prevent the fraud.[427] However, this is simply a trade-off for a system that aims to facilitate conveyancing. Transaction costs are reduced as *B* is freed from embarking on potentially burdensome inquiries to ensure that the transaction was perfectly proper.[428] As the Court of Appeal said in *United Overseas Bank Ltd v. Bebe bte Mohammad* (*Bebe*), 'the courts are constantly struggling to find the right balance

422. LTA, section 46(1). Therefore, the contrary holding of the Privy Council in *Gibbs v. Messer* [1891] AC 248 does not apply in Singapore.
423. LTA, section 46(1)(c). *See also* LTA, section 157(1), which provides that a purchaser who has become a registered proprietor shall not be subject to any action for recovery of land or of money on the plea that the vendor who sold the title may have acted in bad faith.
424. *Assets Co Ltd v. Mere Roihi* [1905] AC 176 at 210: 'Fraud by persons from whom he claims does not affect him unless knowledge of it is brought home to him or his agents.'
425. [1995] SGCA 53; [1995] 2 SLR(R) 340 at [62] (Thean JA, Goh and Rajendran JJ).
426. Negligence is not an exception to indefeasibility: *United Overseas Bank Ltd v. Bebe bte Mohammad* [2006] SCGA 30; [2006] 4 SLR(R) 884.
427. Barry C. Crown, 'Whiter Torrens Title in Singapore?' (2010) 22 SAcLJ 9 at 12–13.
428. *See* LTA, sections 47 and 166.

between the competing considerations of certainty and fairness'.[429] A possible solution is to recognise wider grounds on which the proprietor's title could be defeated.

219. It shall be noticed that the previous examples all involved a *sale* to *B*. Indefeasibility of title is conferred only on a purchaser.[430] Section 4(1) of the LTA defines a purchaser as 'a person who, in good faith and for valuable consideration, acquires an estate or interest in land'. There is a concern that the requirement of good faith may unduly limit the situations in which the principle of indefeasibility applies and cause a reversion to the common law position. However, as the authors of an authoritative textbook suggest:

> In the LTA, 'in good faith' or '*bona fide*' must be construed in the light of the following factors *viz*: (1) one of the stated exceptions is fraud; (2) section 47 of the Act states that actual notice of the existence of a prior unregistered interest is not fraud; (3) case law has defined fraud as dishonesty of some sort; (4) actions for the recovery of land on grounds of fraud can only be brought against the person who has become the registered proprietor by fraud; (5) under section 157 of the Act bad faith on the part of the registered proprietor's predecessor in title shall not affect his title.[431]

In other words, to preserve the general application of the principle of indefeasibility, it is necessary to align the meaning of good faith with the fraud exception to indefeasibility.[432]

§4. Limits to Indefeasibility

I. Prior Registered or Notified Interests

220. An indefeasible title under the LTA does not mean a title that is entirely free from other interests in land. In the first place, section 46(1) makes it clear that the proprietor takes the title subject to interests that are already registered or notified on the land register. This recognises the indefeasibility of prior titles and notified interests and is consistent with section 48(1) which provides that 'interests appearing in the land register shall have priority according to the order of their registration or notification'.

---

429. [2006] SCGA 30; [2006] 4 SLR(R) 884 at [10].
430. LTA, section 46(3). *See also* §3 below.
431. Tang Hang Wu and Kelvin F.K. Low, *Tan Sook Yee's Principles of Singapore Land Law*, 3rd edn (LexisNexis, 2009) at 307.
432. *See e.g. United Overseas Finance Ltd v. Victor Sakayamary* [1996] SGHC 98; [1996] 2 SLR(R) 20 (see §5.V. below).

II. Overriding Interests

A. Overview

221. An indefeasible title is also subject to a list of overriding interests which are set out in section 46(1)(i) to (vii) of the LTA.[433] These overriding interests do not appear on the land register but are automatically binding on registered titles. To be sure, overriding interests are not defects in the title of a particular proprietor. Every successor of title takes subject to them. They are limits to indefeasibility imposed for a variety of policy reasons.

222. For convenience, the list of overriding interests in section 46(1) is set out here:

(i) any subsisting exceptions, reservations, covenants and conditions, contained or implied in the State title thereof;[434]
(ii) any subsisting easement or public right of way which was in existence at the date on which the land was brought under the provisions of this Act and any right on, above or under any land created … in favour of a public authority under any statute and any statutory easement implied under sections 98, 99, 101, 102 and 104 [of the LTA] and section 3C of the State Lands Act (Cap. 314);[435]
(iii) any statutory obligation as defined in section 142;[436]
(iv) the power to correct errors conferred on the Registrar by section 159;
(v) the power to rectify the land-register conferred upon the court by section 160;
(vi) the rights of any person in occupation of the land under a tenancy when the proprietor became registered as such,[437] being a tenancy the term of

433. The term 'overriding interest' was used in *United Overseas Bank Ltd v. Bebe bte Mohammad* [2006] SGCA 30; [2006] 4 SLR 884.
434. For implied reservations, covenants and conditions, see State Lands Act (Cap. 314, 1996 Rev. Ed.), sections 4(2), 4(4), 6 & 7.
435. *See* Chapter 8 (Easements).
436. LTA, section 142(1) states:

For the purposes of this section, 'statutory obligation' means —

(a) any charge on land; and
(b) any order, award, determination, notification, resolution, by-law or proclamation affecting the title to or restricting or otherwise affecting the user of land or prescribing or authorising any act or thing to be done on land,

under the provisions of any written law or regulations made thereunder, and which is intended to bind successive owners of the land.

437. *See Pontiac Land Pte Ltd v. P-Zone Services Pte Ltd* [2010] SGHC 171; [2010] 4 SLR 111.

which does not exceed 7 years and could not have been extended by exercise of the option of renewal to exceed an aggregate of 7 years;[438] and

(vii) the power conferred on the court to make a declaration in respect of any transfer or an order to rectify the land-register and the power conferred on the Registrar to suspend or cancel the registration of the transfer and any related instrument by section 24 of the Residential Property Act (Cap. 274) in respect of any residential property ....[439]

Out of the listed overriding interests, (iv) and (v) warrant brief discussion due to their generality in the application.

B. Power of Rectification by Registrar (Section 159)

223. Section 159(1) empowers the Registrar, either at the request of an aggrieved proprietor or of its own motion, to correct errors and omissions in the land register. Subsection (2) further states that without prejudice to the generality of the power stated in subsection (1), the Registrar may:

(a) correct any folio which is erroneous because of the entry of a mis-spelt name, or of the inclusion of land already included in a prior folio, or of the wrong description of parcels or of the boundaries or dimensions (including the area) of the land;
(b) correct any erroneous entry or endorsement in the land-register;
(c) add to the land-register any matter which has been erroneously omitted; or
(d) where it is not practicable to make corrections to any folio, cancel the folio and create a new folio with the corrections made thereon.

224. Despite the generality in the section's wording, it is intended to confer on the Registrar only limited power to rectify departmental errors.[440] The Registrar does not have the power to alter the substantive errors in the provisions of a registered instrument made by either or both parties to the transaction. Where a departmental error is corrected pursuant to section 159, any person who, having dealt on the faith of an erroneous registration, has suffered loss or damage shall be entitled to compensation from the assurance fund.[441]

---

438. To avoid clogging the land register, the LTA only requires leases exceeding 7 years to be registered. *See* LTA, section 87.

439. These powers are in response to the prohibition of transfer of any residential property or any interest therein to any foreign person. *See* Residential Property Act (Cap. 274, 2009 Rev. Ed.), section 3(1)(a).

440. John Baalman, *The Singapore Torrens system: being a commentary on the Land Titles Ordinance 1956 of the State of Singapore* (Govt. Printer, 1961) at 268, cited in *United Overseas Bank Ltd v. Bebe bte Mohammad* [2006] SGCA 30; [2006] 4 SLR(R) 884 at [41].

441. LTA, section 159(5).

C. Power of Rectification by the Court (Section 160)

225. To supplement the limited power of rectification by the Registrar, section 160 was introduced in 1970 when the LTA was enacted. Section 160(1) allows a court to order rectification of the land register in the following cases:

(a) where 2 or more persons have, by mistake, been registered as proprietors of the same registered estate or interest in the land comprised in a folio;
(b) where the court is satisfied that any registration or notification of an instrument has been obtained through fraud, omission or mistake; or
(c) where the court has declared that any instrument which purports to pass any estate or interest in any residential property within the meaning of the Residential Property Act (Cap. 274) is void under section 24 of that Act.

226. However, section 160(2) disallows rectification in situations (a) and (b) if it would affect a proprietor in possession, 'unless that proprietor is a party or privy to the omission, fraud or mistake in consequence of which the rectification is sought, or has caused that omission, fraud or mistake or substantially contributed thereto by his act, neglect or default'.

227. Unlike in section 159, the power of rectification conferred under section 160 is not concerned with departmental errors. The generality of its wording, particularly in paragraph (b), raises concern that it might dilute the principle of indefeasibility. However, in *Bebe*, the Court of Appeal clarified that paragraph (b) refers to fraud, omission or mistake of the party who presents the instrument of dealing with the registry for registration.[442] In light of the conveyancing practice in Singapore, this refers to the party acquiring the interest in the land, i.e. the proprietor (a transferee, mortgagee, chargee or lessee).[443]

228. Interpreted this way, section 160(1)(b) aligns with the indefeasibility exceptions set out in section 46(2).[444] Interestingly, this restrictive construction of section 160(1)(b) renders the limitation set out in section 160(2) redundant.[445] Section 160(2) allows rectification in respect of a title of a proprietor in possession only if he has caused, is privy or contributed to, the fraud, omission or mistake. The prerequisite to rectification under section 160(1)(b), as construed by the Court of Appeal, is stricter.

229. In *Bebe* the plaintiff (Bebe), a very old lady with Alzheimer's disease executed a mortgage of her property in favour of UOB to secure credit facilities

442. [2006] SGCA 30; [2006] 4 SLR(R) 884 at [47].
443. [2006] SGCA 30; [2006] 4 SLR(R) 884 at [46].
444. [2006] SGCA 30; [2006] 4 SLR(R) 884 at [47]. *See also Harun bin Syed Aljunied v. Abdul Samad bin O K Mohamed Haniffa* [2017] SGHC 248.
445. Tang Hang Wu and Kelvin F.K. Low, *Tan Sook Yee's Principles of Singapore Land Law*, 3rd edn (LexisNexis, 2009) at 295.

granted to a business belonging to her daughter and son-in-law.[446] UOB was handed the executed mortgage and a certificate of title, allowing it to register the mortgage with the land registry. As it transpired, earlier a replacement certificate of title had been applied for and issued presumably because the original one was lost. The replacement certificate of title was with the plaintiff's other daughter. The certificate of title that was presented for registration was therefore an invalid one. The Court of Appeal held that there was no mistake on the part of UOB. It was the registry staff who made a mistake in registering the mortgage. Section 160(1)(b) does not apply in such a case.[447]

230. Although the Court of Appeal said that the plaintiff could claim compensation from the assurance fund for whatever loss she has suffered from the mistake,[448] the court made no mention of possible rectification by the Registrar under section 159, thus reaffirming the very limited application of that section.[449] To illustrate when section 160(1)(b) applies, the Court of Appeal referred to the Malaysian case of *Oh Hiam v. Tham Kong*.[450] Due to common mistake of the vendor and the purchaser, the latter was registered as proprietor of a greater part of the land than was agreed under the contract of sale. Focusing on the purchaser's mistake, rectification pursuant to section 160(1)(b) would have been possible had this been a case under the LTA.[451]

231. It is only necessary to add that section 160(1)(b) does not mandate rectification where there is fraud, omission or mistake. Whether rectification should be ordered, and if so in what form, necessarily depends on the circumstances of the case. For example, where the proprietor's title is declared to be subject to an unregistered interest, obviously no rectification is required.

III. Donee/Volunteer

232. Section 46(3) of the LTA states that a proprietor claiming otherwise than as a purchaser does not acquire any better title than was held by his immediate predecessor, i.e. the donor. In other words, a donee does not automatically acquire indefeasible title upon registration, as a purchaser would pursuant to section 46(1). Instead, it is necessary to inquire into the status of the donor's title. If the donor's title is indefeasible, the donee's title is also indefeasible. Likewise, if the donor's title is defeasible, the donee's title is also defeasible.

233. Take a simple example. *A* is the registered owner of Greenacre. Pursuant to a contract of sale between *A* and *B*, Greenacre was registered in *B*'s name. The sale was procured by a fraudulent misrepresentation made by *B*. Before *A* could bring

446. [2006] SGCA 30; [2006] 4 SLR(R) 884.
447. [2006] SGCA 30; [2006] 4 SLR(R) 884 at [54].
448. LTA, section 155.
449. [2006] SGCA 30; [2006] 4 SLR(R) 884 at [98].
450. [1980] 2 MLJ 159.
451. [2006] SGCA 30; [2006] 4 SLR(R) 884 at [53].

an action against *B*, *B* transferred Greenacre to *C* by registration. While *C* may be completely innocent, his title is only as good as *B*'s. Since *B*'s title was defeasible on the ground of fraud,[452] *C*'s title is also defeasible.[453] It would be different if *C* were an innocent purchaser, in which case he would acquire an indefeasible title pursuant to section 46(1) even though *B*'s title was defeasible.

234. There is only one local case in which section 46(3) was applied. In *Mahidon Nichiar bte Mohd Ali v. Dawood Sultan Kamaldin*, the deceased passed away intestate and the Syariah Court issued a certificate of inheritance naming the widow and her four children as beneficiaries of the deceased's estate.[454] The second son, Dawood, was appointed as the sole administrator of the estate. Dawood asked his three other siblings to sign a deed renouncing their interests in the estate. Dawood then procured registration of the family house in his and his mother's name. The Court of Appeal found that the three siblings had signed the deed of renunciation without understanding its content and set aside the deed on the ground of *non est factum*. Importantly, applying section 46(3), the court held that Dawood, being a mere donee, could not assert indefeasibility of title by virtue of section 46(1).[455] The court ordered that the land register be rectified so as to reflect the distribution mandated by the certificate of inheritance. Although the court did not explicitly say so, the precise reason for Dawood's title being defeasible was that his father's title was subject to a trust, and Dawood's title was no better than his father's.[456]

235. The intent of section 46(3) is followed through in section 154(1)(d) where an action of ejectment or for recovery of land could lie against a donee who has become a registered proprietor. The logic of these provisions is most apparent in the previous example. In most cases *A* would have paid to acquire the property. If *B* were to be allowed to retain the property, *A* would suffer a loss. However, if *A* were to be allowed to recover the property, *B* is not made worse off. *B* merely gives up a windfall. This is unlike where *B* is a purchaser, in which case he would suffer a loss if *A* were allowed to recover the property. Between the two innocent parties with equal interests, the Torrens system prefers the purchaser due to its goal of facilitating conveyancing.

§5. Statutory Exceptions to Indefeasibility

I. Overview

236. The grounds on which a prima facie indefeasible title could be defeated are set out in section 46(2), which reads:

452. LTA, section 46(2)(a).
453. LTA, section 46(3).
454. [2015] SGCA 36; [2015] 5 SLR 62 (Menon CJ, Chao JA and Chan SJ).
455. [2015] SGCA 36; [2015] 5 SLR 62 at [131]–[135].
456. LTA, section 46(2)(d).

> Nothing in this section shall be held to prejudice the rights and remedies of any person –
>
> (a) to have the registered title of a proprietor defeated on the ground of fraud or forgery to which that proprietor or his agent was a party or in which he or his agent colluded;
> (b) to enforce against a proprietor any contract to which that proprietor was a party;
> (c) to enforce against a proprietor who is a trustee the provisions of the trust;
> (d) to recover from a proprietor land acquired by him from a person under a legal disability which was known to the proprietor at the time of dealing; or
> (e) to recover from a proprietor land which has been unlawfully acquired by him in purported exercise of a statutory power or authority.

237. Unlike overriding interests, these exceptions are not automatically binding on the proprietor's title. They are best understood as claims in respect of title against the present registered proprietor. To defeat the title of the present proprietor, it is insufficient to show that the title of his predecessor was defeasible. It is necessary to establish one of the exceptions against the present proprietor.[457]

238. The relationship between sections 46(2) and 160(1)(b) has been briefly noted earlier.[458] Recall that in *Bebe*, the Court of Appeal held that section 160(1)(b) refers to fraud, omission or mistake of the person presenting the document of dealing for registration. This restricts the scope of section 160(1)(b) so that it could be reconciled with section 46(2).[459] Put simply, section 160(1)(b) allows the court to rectify the land register only if one of the indefeasibility exceptions set out in section 46(2) is successfully established.[460]

239. The overlap, however, is not immediately obvious. As shall be explained later, the restricted meaning of omission in section 160(1)(b) does not coincide with the legal disability exception in section 46(2)(d).[461] Even leaving to one side the Court of Appeal's narrow construction of section 160(1)(b), it is obvious that the statutory grounds for rectification is narrower than the list of indefeasibility exceptions set out in section 46(2). The most notable examples are the enforcement of contract and trust under section 46(2)(b) and (c), respectively. It is not immediately clear how such cases fit within the meaning of 'fraud, omission or mistake' in section 160(1)(b). Yet, it would be contrary to the purpose of section 46(2) to withhold rectification of the land register in such cases.

---

457. For a situation where the defeasibility of the predecessor's title is relevant, see §4.III above.
458. *See* §4.II.C. above.
459. [2006] SGCA 30; [2006] 4 SLR(R) 884 at [47].
460. *See also Tien Choon Kuan v. Tien Chwan Hoa* [2016] SGHC 16 at [11].
461. *See* §5.V. below.

240. As noted earlier, section 160 was a subsequent addition to the statute. Prior to its introduction, where a plaintiff is successful in establishing an exception to indefeasibility and in bringing an action for ejectment or recovery of land, the court would order the necessary consequential rectification of the land register.[462] It is likely that the courts retain an inherent power to rectify the land register in respect of exceptions that find no counterpart in section 160(1)(b).

241. The court's statutory power of rectification is superior to its inherent power of rectification. The statutory power has overriding effect on subsequently registered titles.[463] Suppose *A* was tricked into transferring his property to *B*. *A* commences proceedings against *B*. The court finds that *B* acquired his title by way of fraud. At the moment the court makes this finding, the statutory power of rectification arises and exists as an overriding interest.[464] If *B* subsequently sells the property to *C*, *C* takes his title subject to the overriding interest. *C* will have to give up his title to *A*. However, if *B* sells the property to *C* before the court pronounces any finding of fraud, *C* will acquire an indefeasible title. To defeat *C*'s title, *A* must separately establish an indefeasibility exception against *C*. In reality, a transfer during litigation rarely occurs, since the party commencing proceedings will most likely lodge a caveat to prevent dealing with the property.

II. Forgery and Fraud (Section 46(2)(a))

242. While the meaning of forgery is straightforward, the word 'fraud' is obviously capable of encompassing a wider range of conducts. Fraud is not defined in the LTA. However, it is generally accepted by the courts that the hallmark of fraud is dishonesty.[465] It is also said that the fraud must be brought home to the proprietor or his agent.[466] In other words, there must be some realisation that the conduct was dishonest.

243. The most obvious case of fraud is outright cheating. *Waimiha Sawmilling Co Ltd Waione Timber Co Ltd* (*Waimiha*), the Privy Council said: 'If the designed object of a transfer be to cheat a man of a known existing right, that is fraudulent.'[467] The case of *Loke Yew v. Port Swettenham Rubber Co Ltd* (*Loke Yew*) provides a good illustration.[468] Eusope was the registered owner of 322 acres of land.

---

462. John Baalman, *The Singapore Torrens system: being a commentary on the Land Titles Ordinance 1956 of the State of Singapore* (Govt. Printer, 1961) at 255; Tang Hang Wu and Kelvin F.K. Low, *Tan Sook Yee's Principles of Singapore Land Law*, 3rd edn (LexisNexis, 2009) at 292.
463. LTA, section 46(1)(v).
464. *United Overseas Bank Ltd v. Bebe bte Mohammad* [2006] SGCA 30; [2006] 4 SLR(R) 884 at [39]: 'The power of rectification … is exercisable only where the court is satisfied that the underlying condition has been fulfilled.'
465. *United Overseas Bank Ltd v. Bebe bte Mohammad* [2006] SGCA 30; [2006] 4 SLR(R) 884 at [34].
466. *Assets Company, Limited v. Mere Roihi* [1905] AC 176 at 210; *Teo Siew Peng v. Neo Hock Pheng* [1998] SGHC 312; [1998] 3 SLR(R) 472 at [18].
467. [1926] AC 101 at 106.
468. [1913] AC 491.

He subdivided the land into smaller parcels and sub-granted them to various persons in return for yearly rents. Loke Yew purchased a number of these sub-grants, entitling him to possession of 58 acres of the land. Loke Yew did not register his interests in the land. Subsequently Eusope agreed to sell his head grant to PSR. Eusope had earlier repurchased all the sub-grants except for Loke Yew's. But it was agreed that Loke Yew's portion of the land was to be excluded from the sale. The sale price was lowered to take into account this exclusion. To protect Loke Yew's unregistered interests, Eusope requested PSR to sign a written confirmation to this effect before he would execute a transfer. PSR initially refused but eventually complied due to Eusope's insistence. When PSR became registered as the owner of the head grant, however, it sought to eject Loke Yew from his land. The Privy Council held that PSR took the title subject to Loke Yew's unregistered interest (i.e., the title was not indefeasible) because the transfer was procured by deliberate fraud. PSR signed the written confirmation solely for the purpose of inducing Eusope to execute the transfer. PSR had never intended to respect Loke Yew's interests in the land.

244. Although *Loke Yew* has generally been accepted to be a good illustration of the fraud exception, there is some disagreement as to the scope of its application. This is best illustrated by a number of important decisions, two from the Singapore Court of Appeal and one from the High Court of Australia.

245. In *Ho Kon Kim v. Lim Gek Kim Betsy* (*Betsy*), Mdm Ho agreed to sell to Betsy two-thirds of her land.[469] In addition to paying Mdm Ho a purchase price of $4.2m, Betsy was to obtain subdivision of the land into three lots, build three houses on each lot and retransfer one lot with a completed house to Mdm Ho. Based on the proposed subdivision Mdm Ho selected a particular lot to be retransferred to her. After Betsy became the registered owner of the land, she mortgaged the property to OCBC as security for a $4.2m overdraft to be used to finance the development. OCBC agreed to unconditional discharge of the lot earmarked for Mdm Ho upon successful subdivision of the land. Sometime later, unknown to Mdm Ho, Betsy remortgaged the property to RHB to secure facilities granted to a company unrelated to the development. In a regulating agreement entered into along with the mortgage agreement, RHB agreed to an unconditional discharge of the lot earmarked for Mdm Ho for retransfer to her. Subsequently Betsy defaulted on repayment and became bankrupt. RHB claimed that the mortgage was over the whole land and wished to exercise its rights as a mortgagee free of Mdm Ho's interest. On whether RHB's conduct amounted to fraud for the purposes of section 46(2)(a), the Court of Appeal answered in the negative:

> There is no doubt that RHB repudiated the unregistered interest of Mdm Ho and reneged from the agreement made with [Betsy] with regard to Mdm Ho's interest as provided in cl 6(2)(b) of the regulating agreement. However, such repudiation does not amount to fraud, personal dishonesty or moral turpitude

469. [2001] SGCA 62; [2001] 3 SLR(R) 220, noted in Barry C. Crown, 'Equity Trumps the Torrens System' [2002] SJLS 409.

> on their part. The facts in the instant case do not justify a finding of dishonest repudiation of an unregistered interest. In our judgment, what RHB did certainly did not amount to fraud.[470]

However, the Court of Appeal held that RHB's title was defeasible by an in personam claim by Mdm Ho. As the land was not yet subdivided, RHB held an undivided one-third share of the land on trust for Mdm Ho and, upon sale of the land, to account to Mdm Ho one-third of the net proceeds.[471]

246. The Court of Appeal in *Betsy* was strongly influenced by the decision of the Australian High Court in *Bahr v. Nicolay (No.2)*.[472] The Bahrs, who needed funds to develop their land, entered into an agreement to sell it to Nicolay. The agreement further provided that Nicolay shall lease the land back to the Bahrs for three years, at the end of which the Bahrs shall repurchase it at a determined price. The land was transferred into Nicolay's name. Later, Nicolay sold the land to the Thompsons. The sale was subject to a condition that the Thompsons acknowledge Bahrs' right to repurchase the land. After acquiring title to the land, the Thompsons informed the Bahrs that the latter's interest will be recognised. However, when the three-year lease expired, the Thompsons refused to resell the land to the Bahrs. In the High Court of Australia, the majority (Wilson, Toohey and Brennan JJ) held that the Bahrs' interest amounted to an equitable interest and that the Thompsons, by agreeing to take title subject to that interest, held the land on a constructive trust for the former. Essentially, the Bahrs' claim was based on an in personam exception. Importantly, the majority opined that the Thompsons' refusal to resell the land did not amount to fraud. Wilson and Toohey JJ cited *Loke Yew* for the proposition that the fraud exception only applies in the case of 'fraud committed in the act of acquiring a registered title'.[473] They explained:

> Can it be said, using the language of *Waimiha Sawmilling Co. v. Waione Timber Co.*, that the designed object of the transfer to the [Thompsons] was to cheat the [Bahrs] of a known existing right? … [W]e think the evidence falls short of establishing that case. The [Thompsons] agreed to buy [the land] in the hope, even the expectation, that the [Bahrs] would not be able to buy back [the land]. But the evidence does not justify a finding that it was their intention to ensure that the [Bahrs] did not do so.[474]

247. Mason CJ and Dawson J (the minority), on the other hand, did not agree that the previous cases laid down a test that only fraud in procuring a transfer is relevant.[475] In their opinions, the fraud exception is wider. They explained:

470. [2001] SGCA 62; [2001] 3 SLR(R) 220 at [49] (Yong CJ, Thean and Chao JJA).
471. On the right of an equitable co-owner to apply for a sale, see Chapter 3 (Co-ownership) §7.
472. (1988) 164 CLR 604.
473. (1988) 164 CLR 604 at 633.
474. *Ibid.*, at 636–37.
475. *Ibid.*, at 615.

> ... there is no difference between the false undertaking which induced the execution of the transfer in *Loke Yew* and an undertaking honestly given which induces the execution of a transfer and is subsequently repudiated for the purpose of defeating the prior interest. The repudiation is fraudulent because it has as its object the destruction of the unregistered interest notwithstanding that the preservation of the unregistered interest was the foundation or assumption underlying the execution of the transfer. For the same reason the subsequent repudiation by a transferee of property of a limited beneficial interest in that property is fraudulent, when the transferee took the property on terms that the limited beneficial interest would be retained by the transferor.[476]

248. It is submitted that the majority's formulation of the test is to be preferred. Whether the proprietor's title is defeasible must be determined once and for all at the time it was acquired. The question is whether the transfer was procured by fraud. If it was not, the proprietor acquires indefeasible title. Subsequent unconscionability does not amount to fraud for the purposes of section 46(2)(a). It is not even common to speak of such conduct as fraud. As Low explained:

> Fraud does not extend to a situation where [the proprietor] promises to do something, with an honest intention to perform, but then later changes his or her mind. If the elements of a valid contractual promise are present, [the proprietor] may be liable for breach of contract, but even where the contract is intentionally breached, we do not describe it as fraudulent. It seems odd therefore to classify an intentional breach of a promise, where the elements of a valid contractual promise are not present, as fraudulent. It is, of course, a different matter if [the proprietor] made the promise with no intention of keeping it.[477]

249. However, in *Bebe*, the Court of Appeal opined that the facts of *Betsy* would have supported a finding of 'actual fraud' on RHB's part.[478] The Court of Appeal saw *Betsy* as distinguishable from *Bahr v. Nicolay* but indistinguishable from *Loke Yew*.[479] With respect, the facts of *Betsy* are not on all fours with those of *Loke Yew*.[480] There was no finding in *Betsy* that when RHB acquired the mortgage it had no intention to respect Mdm Ho's interest. However, the finding of fraud on RHB's part is arguably justified. No one, except for RHB, could tell whether RHB intended to respect Mdm Ho's interest at the time it acquired the mortgage. In light of RHB's subsequent unconscionability, it is only fair to presume that RHB did not. The burden shifts to RHB to show that it intended to respect Mdm Ho's interest at the time of acquiring the mortgage and only changed its mind later. This approach is not inconsistent with the view of the Court of Appeal in *Bebe*. On a careful reading, the

476. *Ibid.*, at 615–16.
477. Kelvin F.K. Low, 'The Nature of Torrens Indefeasibility: Understanding the Limits of Personal Equities' (2009) 33 Melb U L Rev 205 at 221.
478. [2006] SGCA 30; [2006] 4 SLR(R) 884 at [73], [77], [81] (Chan CJ, Phang JA and Woo J).
479. [2006] SGCA 30; [2006] 4 SLR(R) 884 at [73], [76].
480. *See* Kelvin F.K. Low, 'The Story of "Personal Equities" in Singapore: Thus Far and Beyond' [2009] SJLS 161 at 176.

Court of Appeal did not explicitly endorse the minority's expanded definition of fraud in *Bahr v. Nicolay*. In fact, the Court of Appeal made it clear that any fraud must exist 'at the time of registration of the instrument'.[481]

250. To be sure, it is clear from the wording of section 46(2)(a) that an agent's fraud will be imputed to the principal. In *United Overseas Finance Ltd v. Yew Siew Kien*, a solicitor acted for a father in the transfer of his property to his son.[482] After the transfer was completed, the solicitor retained the certificate of title to that property. Later, pretending to act on behalf of the son, the solicitor applied for a loan from UOF and offered the property as security. When the loan was approved, the solicitor delivered to UOF the certificate of title together with a forged mortgage document for registration. UOF became the registered mortgagee of the property. Goh J found that UOF's mortgage is defeasible on the ground on fraud. As the solicitor was appointed by UOF to act on their behalf, he became their agent and his fraud was attributable to them.

251. The subsequent case of *United Overseas Finance Ltd v. Victor Sakayamary* involved the very same kind of fraud.[483] The solicitor procured the transfer of an estate property from the administrators of the deceased's estate to the deceased's daughter. The solicitor then pretended to act on behalf of the daughter in applying for a loan from UOF. In fact, the loan was for the benefit of the solicitor himself and his associate. After UOF approved the loan, the solicitor delivered to UOF the forged mortgage document along with the certificate of title which the solicitor had retained when he acted for the estate in a prior conveyancing matter. The mortgage was registered in favour of UOF. Selvam J held that the solicitor had committed a fraud and the fraud as attributable to UOF because UOF had appointed the solicitor to also act for them. UOF's mortgage was therefore defeasible.

252. In most other cases where there is no evidence of outright cheating, the more practical question to be asked is what kind of knowledge must the proprietor possess before he could be said to be dishonest. Some hints could be found in section 47, which states:[484]

> (1) Except in the case of fraud, no person dealing with a proprietor or with a person who is entitled to become a proprietor shall be required or in any manner concerned –
> (a) to inquire or ascertain the circumstances in or the consideration for which the current proprietor or any previous proprietor is or was registered;
> (b) to see to the application of the purchase money or any part thereof; or
> (c) to be affected by notice (actual or constructive) of any trust or other unregistered interest, any rule of law or equity to the contrary notwithstanding.

481. [2006] SGCA 30; [2006] 4 SLR(R) 884 at [94].
482. [1993] SGHC 135; [1993] 2 SLR(R) 236.
483. [1996] SGHC 98; [1996] 2 SLR(R) 20.
484. The heading of the section reads: 'Exoneration from effect of notice'.

(2) For the purpose of subsection (1), the knowledge that any unregistered interest is in existence shall not of itself be imputed as fraud.
(3) The protection afforded by this section shall commence at the date of the contract or other instrument evidencing such dealing.

253. Section 47 most likely derives from two important decisions by the Privy Council. The first case is *Assets Company, Limited v. Mere Roihi* where the Privy Council explained:

> The mere fact that he might have found out fraud if he had been more vigilant, and had made further inquiries which he omitted to make, does not of itself prove fraud on his part. But if it be shewn that his suspicions were aroused, and that he abstained from making inquiries for fear of learning the truth, the case is very different, and fraud may be properly ascribed to him.[485]

Thus, the phrase '[e]xcept in the case of fraud' in section 47(1) is best understood to mean 'except where there is a suspicion of fraud'.

254. The second case is *Waimiha* where the Privy Council held that 'dishonesty must not be assumed solely by reason of knowledge of an unregistered interest'.[486] This clearly informs section 47(1)(c) and (2), which has been applied in a number of local cases.[487] Where the unregistered interest is a beneficial interest under a trust, section 166(4) further provides:

> Any purchaser dealing with the registered land which is held in a fiduciary capacity shall not be concerned to enquire whether a dealing of that land is within the powers of the registered proprietor and the purchaser is entitled to assume that the registered proprietor has all the powers of disposition of a beneficial owner and as the absolute proprietor of the estate or interest in question.

255. However, it would be different if the purchaser knew that the vendor had no power to sell the property. In *Yong Koon Chin v. Tong Ki Siang*, the purchasers became aware that the property was subject to a trust and a court approval for the sale was required because the beneficiary was an infant.[488] Since the vendors refused to obtain such approval, Kan J held that the purchasers were not obliged to complete the sale. Had the purchasers had gone on to complete the sale, this would arguably be a good case for invoking the fraud exception.[489]

485. [1905] AC 176 at 210. *See also Waimiha Sawmilling Co Ltd Waione Timber Co Ltd* [1923] NZLR 1137 at 1175.
486. [1926] AC 101 at 106.
487. *Teo Siew Peng v. Neo Hock Pheng* [1998] SGHC 312; [1998] 3 SLR(R) 472 at [30]. *See also United Malayan Banking Corp v. Goodhope Realty* [1989] SGHC 14; [1989] 1 SLR(R) 151 at [17] (the court did not mention fraud). In both cases the courts referred to the predecessor of section 47: Land Titles Act (Cap. 157, 1985 Rev. Ed), section 39.
488. [1991] SGHC 153.
489. This would also be a good case for invoking the legal disability exception in section 46(2)(d). *See* see §5.V. below.

256. Where the suspicion of fraud arises only after a contract has been concluded, the registered proprietor shall not be regarded as fraudulent for proceeding with registration of the dealing. This is the effect of section 47(3).

257. In *Bebe*, the Court of Appeal provided further guidance on what does not amount to fraud. Recall that Bebe had executed a mortgage of her property in favour of UOB to secure a credit facility granted to a business owned by her daughter and son-in-law. The mortgage was registered even though an invalid certificate of title was presented. Earlier, it was noted that Bebe failed to invoke the court's jurisdiction to rectify the land register on the ground of mistake of the registry staff.[490] Bebe's alternative claim was to defeat UOB's registered mortgage on the ground of fraud. The allegation was that UOB's agent, the law firm which procured registration of the mortgage, was a party to the borrowers' fraud. From the title search, the conveyancing clerk became aware that a replacement certificate had been applied for. Yet she presented the invalid certificate of title for registration of the mortgage. Her failure to make further inquiries amounted to wilful blindness akin to fraud. The Court of Appeal disagreed for several reasons.[491] First, the titles search did not show that a replacement certificate of title had been issued. Second, it is impossible to tell by looking at the certificate of title whether it had been cancelled. Third, it was reasonable for the conveyancing clerk to believe that the original certificate of title had been found. In these circumstances, the failure to make further inquiries did not amount to wilful blindness akin to fraud. At most, the conveyancing clerk could be said to be negligent. However, negligence does not amount to fraud. Thus, UOB's mortgage was indefeasible. This aspect of *Bebe* was followed in *Malayan Banking Bhd v. Sivakolunthu Thirunavukarasu*.[492]

258. Finally, it is only necessary to add that should a person be deprived of his land due to fraud of the proprietor, an action for ejectment or to recover the land may be brought by virtue of section 154(1)(d).[493] In such an action, the court may also make an order for the cancellation of any entry in the folio of the land, e.g. a fraudulently procured mortgage.[494]

III. Enforcement of Contract (Section 46(2)(b))

259. An obvious case that comes within this exception is where the proprietor has agreed by contract sell the property to the plaintiff but later reneges on his promise.[495] The proprietor's title would be defeasible if the plaintiff manages to obtain an order for specific performance. The same applies to a contract to grant other interests, e.g. easement, restrictive covenant or lease exceeding 7 years. Whether

---

490. *See* §4.II.C. above.
491. [2006] SGCA 30; [2006] 4 SLR(R) 884 at [20]–[27].
492. [2007] SGHC 161; [2008] 1 SLR(R) 149.
493. LTA, section 154(1)(d) & (4).
494. *Ibid.*, section 154(2).
495. John Baalman, *The Singapore Torrens system: being a commentary on the Land Titles Ordinance 1956 of the State of Singapore* (Govt. Printer, 1961) at 84.

rectification of the land register should be ordered, and if so in what form, necessarily depends on the interest that the proprietor contracted to grant.

260. Recall that in *Bebe* the Court of Appeal cited *Oh Hiam v Tham Kong*[496] as an illustration where rectification under section 160(1)(b) was possible on the ground of the purchaser's mistake.[497] Interestingly, the court saw section 46(2)(b) as setting out the corresponding indefeasibility exception.[498] The court said 'if *Oh Hiam* had been a case under the LTA, it would have been a case of one party enforcing his contractual rights against the registered proprietor to correct a common mistake under s 46(2)(b) of the LTA'.[499] Since the seller was seeking to rectify the mistake so that the true contractual intention of the parties could be given effect to, his claim could be properly characterised as one for the enforcement of the contract.[500]

261. Another example cited by *Bebe* as falling within this exception is *Betsy*,[501] the facts of which have been set out earlier.[502] In *Bebe*, the Court of Appeal said of *Betsy*: 'The facts showed that RHB had induced Betsy to accept the mortgage on the promise that they would release Mdm Ho's plot of land back to her without payment, thus bringing the case within s 46(2)(b) of the LTA'.[503] The obvious problem is that Mdm Ho was not a party to the contract between RHB and Betsy.[504] However, with the enactment of the Contracts (Rights of Third Parties) Act (CRTPA),[505] there is some force in the Court of Appeal's opinion that section 46(2)(b) may accommodate an indirect claim by a person who is not a party to the contract.[506] But whether section 46(2)(b) applies in a particular case must necessarily depend on the nature of the undertaking and whether section 2 of the CRTPA is satisfied.

IV. Enforcement of Trust (Section 46(2)(c))

262. In *Betsy*,[507] the facts of which have been set out earlier,[508] the Court of Appeal held that the agreement between Mdm Ho and Betsy had the effect of creating a trust in favour of the former.[509] As the land was not yet subdivided, Betsy

496. [1980] 2 MLJ 159.
497. [2006] SGCA 30; [2006] 4 SLR(R) 884 at [53].
498. [2006] SGCA 30; [2006] 4 SLR(R) 884 at [53].
499. [2006] SGCA 30; [2006] 4 SLR(R) 884 at [53].
500. Barry C. Crown, 'Whiter Torrens Title in Singapore?' (2010) 22 SAcLJ 9 at 33.
501. [2001] SGCA 62; [2001] 3 SLR(R) 220.
502. *See* §5.II. above.
503. [2006] SGCA 30; [2006] 4 SLR(R) 884 at [73].
504. Kelvin F.K. Low, 'The Story of 'Personal Equities' in Singapore: Thus Far and Beyond' [2009] SJLS 161 at 175.
505. (Cap. 53B, 2002 Rev. Ed.). The CRTPA was not yet in force when *Betsy* was decided.
506. [2006] SGCA 30; [2006] 4 SLR(R) 884 at [80].
507. *See* Teo Keang Sood, 'The Trust Statutory Exception to Indefeasibility in the Singapore Torrens System' [2017] SJLS 151.
508. *See* §5.II. above.
509. [2001] SGCA 62; [2001] 3 SLR(R) 220 at [25].

was to hold an undivided one-third share in the land for Mdm Ho. At this point the matter is straightforward. Betsy's title was defeasible by Mdm Ho's beneficial interest by virtue of section 46(2)(c). But it became more complicated when the land was mortgaged, initially to OCBC and later to RHB. At general law, the simple question is whether RHB was a bona fide purchaser for value. If it was not, then Mdm Ho's beneficial interest persists and RHB will hold the land on trust for her. Under the Torrens system, however, the idea of bona fide purchaser for value gives way to the principle of indefeasibility. Earlier it was noted that the reference to good faith in section 4(1) must be read subject to sections 46(2) and 47.[510] Section 47(1)(c), it shall be recalled, provides that except in the case of fraud the proprietor shall not be affected by notice of any trust. In other words, Mdm Ho's beneficial interest does not persist as it would in equity, unless fraud can be established on RHB's part. As the focus of the inquiry was fraud, the Court of Appeal in *Bebe* was absolutely correct in suggesting that in *Betsy* the focus ought to be on the fraud exception rather than on the trust exception.[511]

263. Interestingly, in *Bebe* the Court of Appeal adopted a restrictive interpretation of the trust exception, observing that its language seems to refer only to express trusts and not constructive trusts.[512] With respect, it is by no means obvious that the exception is meant to apply only to express trusts.[513] Moreover, given the court's hostility towards in personam exceptions, it might make more sense for the trust exception to be interpreted broadly, as in the case of the fraud and contract exceptions. In the subsequent case of *Loo Chay Sit v. Estate of Loo Chay Loo*, the Court of Appeal referred to the doctrine of resulting trust as an exception to indefeasibility but, curiously, did not make an explicit reference to the trust exception under section 46(2)(c).[514]

264. However, even if a court were to concede that the statutory exception covers non-express trusts, it does not necessarily mean that all kinds of trusts are included. The Court of Appeal in *Bebe* expressed the view that the defeasible condition, in this case the trust, must exist before or at the time of the registration.[515] Obvious examples include the resulting trust and the common intention constructive trust.[516] Other possible examples include a constructive trust that arises in response to the *Pallant v. Morgan* equity[517] and proprietary disgorgement by way of a constructive trust in the case of unauthorised fiduciary gain.[518] The position is

510. *See* §3.II. above.
511. [2006] SGCA 30; [2006] 4 SLR(R) 884 at [81].
512. [2006] SGCA 30; [2006] 4 SLR(R) 884 at [81].
513. *Cf Mahidon Nichiar bte Mohd Ali v. Dawood Sultan Kamaldin* [2015] SGCA 36; [2015] 5 SLR 62. *See* §4.III. above.
514. [2010] SGCA 47; [2010] 1 SLR 286 (Chao, Phang and Rajah JJA). In this case a resulting trust was not found as the plaintiff failed to prove that he had contributed to the purchase price.
515. *United Overseas Bank Ltd v. Bebe bte Mohammad* [2006] SGCA 30; [2006] 4 SLR(R) 884 at [94].
516. *See Lau Siew Kim v. Yeo Guan Chye Terence* [2007] SGCA 54; [2008] 2 SLR(R) 108; *Chan Yuen Lan v. See Fong Mun* [2014] SGCA 36; [2014] 3 SLR 1048.
517. Recognised in *Ong Heng Chuan v. Ong Boon Chuan* [2002] SGHC 285; [2003] 2 SLR(R) 469.
518. *Thahir Kartika Ratna v. Pertamina* [1994] SGCA 105; [1994] 3 SLR(R) 312; *Attorney-General for Hong Kong v. Reid* [1994] 1 AC 324.

less clear for other proprietary remedies in the form of trusts that do not arise immediately but imposed at a later time, e.g. in the case of proprietary estoppel. As shall be explained later, however, proprietary remedies in the form of trusts are perhaps better dealt with as personam exceptions.[519]

V. Legal Disability (Section 46(2)(d))

265. A proprietor's title is defeasible if he acquired the property from a person whom he knew was under a legal disability. An illustration of this exception is to be found in *UOF v Victor Sakayamary*.[520] The solicitor caused a transfer of the estate property from the administrators to the deceased's daughter. The solicitor then mortgaged the property to UOF. Selvam J found that the solicitor, who was also appointed by UOF, was fraudulent in causing the transfer and mortgaging the property for his own benefit. This finding was itself sufficient to render UOF's title defeasible.[521] However, the learned judge offered an alternative justification for his conclusion. Since more than 6 years have elapsed from the time of the deceased's death, the administrators had to obtain court approval for the transfer to the deceased's daughter.[522] As no such approval was obtained, there was an omission and section 160(1)(b) allowed the transfer to be set aside.[523] The defeasibility of the daughter's title was relevant to the status of UOF's title because, due to its solicitor's fraud, it was not a purchaser in good faith.[524] Applying section 46(3), UOF had no better title than the daughter.[525]

266. Recall, however, the clarification in *Bebe* that section 160(1)(b) refers to fraud, omission or mistake of the party who presents the instrument of dealing with the registry for registration.[526] The Court of Appeal observed that section 160(1)(b) would apply to the facts of *Victor Sakayamary* because registration of the mortgage was obtained by UOF via its solicitor.[527] With respect, the court's focus on the mortgage was misplaced. The bank had not omitted to do anything which was necessary for the acquisition of the mortgage. Instead, the focus should have been on the transfer of title from the administrators to the daughter. As Selvam J pointed out, it was the administrators who had omitted to obtain the required court order. However, as the administrators were not the party who presented the instrument of transfer for registration, there was no omission for the purposes of invoking section 160(1)(b).

519. Tang Hang Wu and Kelvin F.K. Low, *Tan Sook Yee's Principles of Singapore Land Law*, 3rd edn (LexisNexis, 2009) at 309–12.
520. [1996] SGHC 98; [1996] 2 SLR(R) 20. *See* §5.II. above.
521. *See* §5.II. above.
522. CLPA, section 35(2).
523. [1996] SGHC 98; [1996] 2 SLR(R) 20 at [100].
524. LTA, section 4(1).
525. [1996] SGHC 98; [1996] 2 SLR(R) 20 at [95]. *See also* §3.II. and §4.III. above.
526. [2006] SGCA 30; [2006] 4 SLR(R) 884 at [47]. *See* §4.II.C. above.
527. [2006] SGCA 30; [2006] 4 SLR(R) 884 at [59].

However, as the Court of Appeal rightly recognised, the daughter's title was defeasible on the ground of legal disability on the administrators' part.[528] Applying section 46(3), UOF's title was equally defeasible.

VI. Ultra Vires Acquisition (Section 46(2)(e))

267. This last exception has yet to be invoked in Singapore. As it refers to the acquisition of title by purported exercise of a statutory power or authority,[529] an obviously related topic is compulsory acquisition of land.[530] Where the proprietor's is defeasible under this exception, an action to recover the land may be brought.[531]

§6. In Personam Exceptions to Indefeasibility

268. In *Frazer v. Walker*,[532] the Privy Council said that the principle of indefeasibility 'in no way denies the right of a plaintiff to bring against a registered proprietor a claim in personam, founded in law or in equity, for such relief as a court acting in personam may grant'.[533] Similarly, in *Oh Hiam v. Tham Kong*, the Privy Council referred to 'the ability of the court, exercising its jurisdiction in personam to insist upon proper conduct in accordance with conscience'.[534] In both cases the courts were referring to non-statutory, but judicially recognised, exceptions to the principle of indefeasibility. These are commonly known as 'in personam exceptions' or 'personal equities'. However, it is important not to be misled by these labels. A claim that affects title could hardly be said to be merely personal in nature. It is a proprietary claim. The claim is said to be personal only in the sense that it usually arises from the conduct (e.g., wrongdoing) of the proprietor whose title is being challenged.

269. In Singapore, the possibility that in personam exceptions may exist alongside the statutory exceptions has been accepted in a number of cases. The most notable is *Betsy* where the Court of Appeal held that Mdm Ho's in personam claim

528. [2006] SGCA 30; [2006] 4 SLR(R) 884 at [61].
529. The exception was said to be based on the case of *Caldwell v. Rural Bank of New South Wales* (1951) 53 SR 415.
530. *See* Land Acquisition Act (Cap. 152, 1985 Rev. Ed.).
531. LTA, section 154(1)(d) & (4).
532. *See* Tang Hang Wu and Kelvin F.K. Low, *Tan Sook Yee's Principles of Singapore Land Law*, 3rd edn (LexisNexis, 2009) at 313–22; Tang Hang Wu, 'Beyond the Torrens Mirror: A Framework of the In Personam Exception to Indefeasibility (2008) 32 Melb U L Rev 672; Kelvin F.K. Low, 'The Story of "Personal Equities" in Singapore: Thus Far and Beyond' [2009] SJLS 161; Kelvin F.K. Low, 'The Nature of Torrens Indefeasibility: Understanding the Limits of Personal Equities' (2009) 33 Melb U L Rev 205; Barry C. Crown, 'Whiter Torrens Title in Singapore?' (2010) 22 SAcLJ 9 at 29–35; Barry C. Crown, 'Back to Basics: Indefeasibility of Title Under the Torrens System' [2007] SJLS 117.
533. [1967] 1 AC 569 at 585.
534. [1980] 2 MLJ 159 at 165.

gave rise to a constructive trust over the land.[535] However, in *Bebe*, the Court of Appeal reminded that many of the in personam exceptions found in the older Australian cases have since been codified in the LTA.[536] Thus, as far as possible, one should turn to section 46(2) in search of an exception. The Court of Appeal said:

> As regards all other unspecified personal equities, we are of the view that having regard to the policy objectives of the LTA to reduce uncertainty and to give finality in land dealings, our courts should be slow to engraft onto the LTA personal equities that are not referable directly or indirectly to the exceptions in s 46(2) of the LTA. These exceptions are, as we have shown, capable of encompassing most of the in personam actions at common law or in equity that a court exercising in personam jurisdiction may grant.[537]

270. The hostility towards in personam exceptions was followed through in two subsequent cases. In *Malayan Banking Bhd v. Sivakolunthu Thirunavukarasu*, Kan J rejected an attempt to defeat a registered mortgage on the ground of undue influence because it does not fall within the statutory exceptions.[538] In *Sim Lian (Newton) Pte Ltd v. Gan Beng Cheng Raynes*, Paul Tan AR remarked that *Bebe* recognised the 'philosophical inconsistency' between section 46(2) and the in personam exceptions and that 'the court all but prospectively overruled its decision in *Betsy Lim*'.[539]

271. Several things could be said in response to the prevailing judicial hostility towards in personam exceptions. Firstly, Baalman (the drafter) did not claim to set out a closed list of exceptions. There is good reason to believe that he was merely attempting to list down as many exceptions recognised by the Australasian courts which he regarded as appropriate.[540] But that was in the early 1950s. Are we to disregard subsequent legal development? Worthy of particular mention is the area of proprietary remedies, which has since undergone important developments. Just to list a few examples: (a) the remedial constructive trust in response to a transfer based on mistake[541] or other cases involving unjust enrichment and fault;[542] (b) the

535. [2001] SGCA 62; [2001] 3 SLR(R) 220 at [47]–[53]. *See also United Overseas Bank v. Victor Sakayamary* [1996] SGHC 98; [1996] 2 SLR(R) 20 at [27]–[32]; *Teo Siew Peng v. Neo Hock Pheng* [1998] SGHC 312; [1998] 3 SLR(R) 472 at [19].
536. [2006] SGCA 30; [2006] 4 SLR(R) 884 at [78], citing John Baalman, *The Singapore Torrens system: being a commentary on the Land Titles Ordinance 1956 of the State of Singapore* (Singapore: Govt. Printer, 1961) at 84–85.
537. [2006] SGCA 30; [2006] 4 SLR(R) 884 at [91].
538. [2007] SGHC 161; [2008] 1 SLR(R) 149 at [43]–[44].
539. [2007] SGHC 84 at [48].
540. Kelvin F.K. Low, 'The Story of 'Personal Equities' in Singapore: Thus Far and Beyond' [2009] SJLS 161 at 171.
541. *Ching Mun Fong v. Liu Cho Chit* [2001] SGCA 36; [2001] 1 SLR(R) 856.
542. *Wee Chiaw Sek Anna v. Ng Li-Ann Genevieve* [2013] SGCA 36; [2013] 3 SLR 801.

imposition of a trust remedy in a case of proprietary estoppel;[543] and (c) an ambulatory constructive trust in the case of shared homes.[544] If the principle of indefeasibility is to be construed strictly, then many important cases must be regarded as wrongly decided in so far as they relate to registered land.

272. Secondly, the scope of the principle of indefeasibility may have been overestimated. As Low explained, the Torrens system aims to protect a proprietor only from an adverse claim based on a prior title.[545] Put simply, a person who previously owned the property could not recover it merely by claiming that it was his. The way the LTA deals with a beneficial interest under a trust provides an excellent illustration. Recall our discussion of *Betsy* under the trust exception.[546] Mdm Ho did not succeed in her claim against RHB simply by arguing that she had a beneficial interest in the property. This would constitute an adverse title-based claim which the Torrens system abhors. Mdm Ho succeeded because she could establish some unconscionability (fraud, according to *Bebe*) on RHB's part. The Torrens system does not insulate a proprietor from claims against his property due to his misconduct. The fraud exception is the best example. However, in *Bebe* the Court of Appeal said:

> [T]he inclusion of the exception of fraud to which the registered proprietor or his agent is a party would, by implication, also exclude from such exception all conduct which in law or equity has a lesser degree of moral turpitude than actual fraud.[547]

273. With respect, this cannot be right. For example, the contract exception was included although one would not regard a breach of contract to be as culpable as the commission of a fraud. If one accepts that the principle of indefeasibility only abhors a title-based claim, then in principle all other claims should be allowed. Obvious examples are proprietary remedies awarded in response to the proprietor's misconduct, e.g. for breach of fiduciary duty. Also possible are claims in unjust enrichment based on vitiated intention, e.g. mistake, duress and undue influence.[548] However, one shall refrain from relying simply on the broad notion of unconscionability, the vagueness of which has contributed to the hostility towards in personam exceptions. Finally, one needs to be mindful of claims that may be clad in the language of wrongdoing or unjust enrichment but are aimed at protecting a prior

---

543. *Low Heng Leon Andy v. Low Kian Beng Lawrence* [2013] SGHC 101; [2013] 3 SLR 710 at [27]: '[A] trust may be imposed over the property if it is required as the minimum right necessary to do justice between the parties'.
544. *Chan Yuen Lan v. See Fong Mun* [2014] SGCA 36; [2014] 3 SLR 1048 at [160].
545. Kelvin F.K. Low, 'The Nature of Torrens Indefeasibility: Understanding the Limits of Personal Equities' (2009) 33 Melb U L Rev 205.
546. *See* §5.IV. above.
547. [2006] SGCA 30; [2006] 4 SLR(R) 884 at [91].
548. Kelvin F.K. Low, 'The Nature of Torrens Indefeasibility: Understanding the Limits of Personal Equities' (2009) 33 Melb U L Rev 205 at 222–28. *Cf* Barry C. Crown, 'Whiter Torrens Title in Singapore?' (2010) 22 SAcLJ 9 at 33, who suggested that these vitiating factors could come within the fraud exception.

title, such as trespass and restitution on the ground of ignorance.[549] These are, in essence, title-based claims and should therefore be disallowed.

§7. The Assurance Fund

274. From the fees collected by the Registrar[550] a portion is to be set aside for the assurance fund.[551] The assurance fund serves mainly to compensate an aggrieved part identified in section 155(1). Two conditions must be satisfied. First, the person claiming compensation must have been deprived of land or sustained loss or damage through any omission, mistake or misfeasance of the Registrar, or any member of his staff, in the registration of any instrument. Second, the person must be barred from bringing any action for the recovery of land, proceeds of the sale of land, moneys secured by a registered mortgage or interests protected by a caveat. For example, an action for recovery of land shall lie only against a person who acquired title through fraud or a person who took the title from that proprietor otherwise than by purchaser.[552] Thus, a person who could bring an action for recovery of land on the ground of fraud could not claim compensation from the assurance fund.

275. In deciding the amount to be compensated, the court shall take into account any neglect, default or incaution on the claimant's part that may have contributed to the loss and may withhold or reduce the compensation accordingly.[553] It need only to be added that the assurance fund shall not be used to compensate for any loss caused by an incorrect description of the parcels, the boundaries or dimensions (including area) of any land[554] and any loss suffered as a result of the proprietor's breach of trust.[555]

276. To date, the only reported case where a claim for compensation from the assurance fund succeeded was *Bebe*.[556] In that case the registry staff was found to have registered the mortgage by mistake. Bebe could not bring an action for the recovery of the property as she failed to establish fraud on UOB's part. A claim for compensation from the assurance fund was thus possible.[557] Nothing turned on whether Bebe was at some fault for losing the original certificate of title.

549. *See* Kelvin F.K. Low, 'The Nature of Torrens Indefeasibility: Understanding the Limits of Personal Equities' (2009) 33 Melb U L Rev 205 at 216–17.
550. For an excellent examination of whether the insurance principle is sufficiently given effect to by the LTA, see Barry C. Crown, 'Whiter Torrens Title in Singapore?' (2010) 22 SAcLJ 9 at 14–25.
551. LTA, section 151(1).
552. *Ibid.*, section 154(1)(d) provides that an action for recovery of land shall lie only against a person who acquired title through fraud or a person who took title from that proprietor otherwise than by purchaser. A person bringing such a claim is barred from claiming compensation from the assurance fund.
553. *Ibid.*, section 154(2).
554. *Ibid.*, section 154(3).
555. *Ibid.*, section 151(5).
556. [2006] SGCA 30; [2006] 4 SLR(R) 884.
557. [2006] SGCA 30; [2006] 4 SLR(R) 884 at [98].

Chapter 5. Caveats

§1. Introduction

277. Under the Torrens system,[558] a registered proprietor takes his title free from any unregistered interest unless an indefeasibility exception could be established against him.[559] Importantly, the indefeasibility of his title is not undermined by the mere fact he had knowledge of the existence of an unregistered interest.[560] For the protection of unregistered interests, the system of caveats was introduced in place of the obsolete doctrine of notice.[561] The law governing private caveats, i.e. caveats lodged by individuals,[562] is set out in Part XII of the LTA.[563]

278. The main function of a caveat is to prohibit registration of dealings that are adverse to the interest claimed by the caveator.[564] A caveat may serve a temporary protective function. For example, a purchaser of land lodges a caveat merely to preserve status quo until he acquires registration of the title in his name. In the case of interests that are not registrable, e.g. equitable leases or mortgages, a caveat affords protection for as long as the interest subsists. When challenged, the caveator will be asked to prove his claim. If he succeeds in doing so, the court will allow the caveat to remain.

558. *See generally* Shannon Lindsay, *Caveats Against Dealings in Australia and New Zealand* (Federation Press, 1995); John Baalman, *The Singapore Torrens system: being a commentary on the Land Titles Ordinance 1956 of the State of Singapore* (Govt. Printer, 1961) at 193–210; Tang Hang Wu and Kelvin F.K. Low, *Tan Sook Yee's Principles of Singapore Land Law*, 3rd edn (LexisNexis 2009) Chapter 15.
559. *See* Land Titles Act (Cap. 157, 2004 Rev. Ed.) (LTA), section 46.
560. LTA, section 47.
561. John Baalman, *The Singapore Torrens system: being a commentary on the Land Titles Ordinance 1956 of the State of Singapore* (Govt. Printer, 1961) at 193; *Eng Mee Yong v. Letchumanan s/o Velayutham* [1980] AC 331 at 335; *Alrich Development Pte Ltd v. Rafiq Jumabhoy* [1993] SGCA 27; [1993] 1 SLR(R) 598 at [37]; *United Overseas Finance Ltd v. Mutu Jeras* [1989] SGHC 41; [1989] 1 SLR(R) 446 at [11].
562. The Controller of Residential Property may also lodge a private caveat: LTA, section 115A.
563. The other type of caveat not covered in this chapter is a Registrar's caveat, which is lodged by the Registrar 'for the prevention of fraud or improper dealing whenever he has reason to think that fraud or improper dealing may occur, or for the prevention of any dealing with any registered land which has been found to be erroneous'. *See* LTA, section 7(1)(b).
564. *Alrich Development Pte Ltd v. Rafiq Jumabhoy* [1993] SGCA 27; [1993] 1 SLR(R) 598 at [37]; *Cathay Theatres Pte Ltd v. LKM Investments Holdings* [1998] SGCA 4; [1998] 1 SLR(R) 234 at [32]. *See also Ho Seek Yueng Novel v. J & v. Development Pte Ltd* [2006] SGHC 63; [2006] 2 SLR(R) 742; *Ong Chay Tong & Sons (Pte) Ltd v. Ong Hoo Eng* [2008] SGCA 42; [2009] 1 SLR(R) 305.

§2. CAVEATABLE INTERESTS

I. Overview

279. Section 115(1) of the LTA states that any person who claims an interest in land may lodge a caveat with the Registrar. The reference to 'any person' includes the owner of a piece of land. A landowner who had been induced by fraud to sign a transfer form may lodge a caveat to prevent the transfer.[565] A landowner may also lodge a caveat to prevent the mortgagee's wrongful exercise of its power of sale.[566]

280. The LTA does not lay down any clear definition of what amounts to an 'interest in land' for the purposes of lodging a caveat. Section 4 merely states that 'interest', in relation to land, 'means any interest in land recognised as such by law, and includes an estate in land'.[567] Neither does the LTA set out a list of caveatable interests. Thus, the task of determining whether a certain interest should be admitted to the list of caveatable interests is left mainly to the courts.

281. At the time of lodgement the caveator is not required to prove that he in fact has a caveatable interest.[568] As section 117(5) of the LTA provides, when notifying a caveat in the land register the Registrar 'shall not be concerned to consider whether or not a caveator's claim is justified'. It is sufficient that the interest the caveator claims to have is a caveatable interest. It is only when the caveat is challenged that the caveator is required to prove his claim. If it turns out that the caveator does not in fact have a caveatable interest, the caveatee may apply to have the caveat removed[569] and claim compensation for loss if the caveat was lodged wrongfully, vexatiously or without reasonable cause.[570]

282. The following is a non-exhaustive list of recognised caveatable interests:[571]

(a) Lease not exceeding 7 years[572]

565. *Barry v. Heider* (1914) 19 CLR 197.
566. *Société Générale v. Good Property Land Development Pte Ltd* [1989] SGHC 5; [1989] 1 SLR(R) 27.
567. In *Tan Soo Leng David v. Wee, Satku & Kumar Pte Ltd* [1993] SGHC 199; [1993] 2 SLR(R) 741 at [20], Selvam JC clarified that the word 'law' also 'comprises the principles of equity'. *See also Alrich Development Pte Ltd v. Rafiq Jumabhoy* [1993] SGCA 27; [1993] 1 SLR(R) 598 at [41].
568. *Alrich Development Pte Ltd v. Rafiq Jumabhoy* [1993] SGCA 27; [1993] 1 SLR(R) 598 at [38]; *The Asiatic Enterprises (Pte) Ltd v. UOB Ltd* [1999] SGCA 85;[1999] 3 SLR(R) 976 at [27]; *Tan Soo Leng David Wee, Satku & Kumar Pte Ltd* [1993] SGHC 199; [1993] 2 SLR(R) 741 at [21]; *Ho Seek Yueng Novel v. J & v. Development Pte Ltd* [2006] SGHC 63; [2006] 2 SLR(R) 742 at [59].
569. *Ibid.*, section 127.
570. *Ibid.*, section 128.
571. In most of the cited cases below, the recognition is implied rather than explicit.
572. *Cathay Theatres Pte Ltd v. LKM Investment Holdings Pte Ltd* [1998] SGCA 4; [1998] 1 SLR(R) 234.

(b) Equitable mortgage[573]
(c) Easement[574]
(d) Restrictive covenant[575]
(e) Purchaser's interest under an unconditional contract of sale[576] or an exercised option to purchase[577]
(f) Right of pre-emption or first refusal[578]
(g) Mortgagor's equity of redemption[579]
(h) Beneficiary's interest in a trust property[580]
(i) Possessory interest[581]
(j) Vendor's lien[582]
(k) Purchaser's lien[583]
(l) Tenant's right to recover security deposit[584]

283. The question of what other interests come within the list must await judicial pronouncement when the issues come to be litigated. However, the decided cases do shed some light on the general principles relating to the identification of caveatable interests.

---

573. *United Overseas Finance Ltd v. Mutu Jeras* [1989] SGHC 41; [1989] 1 SLR(R) 446; *City Development Ltd v. Goh Yoke Hian* [1990] SGHC 9; [1990] 1 SLR(R) 120; *Power Knight Pte Ltd v. Natural Fuel Pte Ltd* [2010] SGHC 75; [2010] 3 SLR 82.
574. John Baalman, *The Singapore Torrens system: being a commentary on the Land Titles Ordinance 1956 of the State of Singapore* (Govt. Printer, 1961) at 196.
575. *Ibid.*, at 227.
576. *Virginia Developments Pte Ltd v. Behem Investment Pte Ltd* [1988] SGHC 31; [1988] 1 SLR(R) 302. *See also* LTA, section 115(1)(h). For discussion on whether a purchaser under a conditional contract has a caveatable interest, see Tang Hang Wu and Kelvin F.K. Low, *Tan Sook Yee's Principles of Singapore Land Law*, 3rd edn (LexisNexis, 2009) at 332–35. The authors suggest that, as a matter of policy, the purchaser should be allowed to lodge a caveat. *See also Ong Chay Tong & Sons (Pte) Ltd v. Ong Hoo Eng* [2008] SGCA 42; [2009] 1 SLR(R) 305 at [70].
577. *Alrich Development Pte Ltd v. Rafiq Jumabhoy* [1993] SGCA 27; [1993] 1 SLR(R) 598; *Eng Bee Properties v. Lee Foong Fatt* [1993] SGHC 202; [1993] 2 SLR(R) 778; *Tan Soo Leng David Wee, Satku & Kumar Pte Ltd* [1993] SGHC 199; [1993] 2 SLR(R) 741.
578. *Ong Chay Tong & Sons (Pte) Ltd v. Ong Hoo Eng* [2008] SGCA 42; [2009] 1 SLR(R) 305; *Ho Seek Yueng Novel v. J & v. Development Pte Ltd* [2006] SGHC 63; [2006] 2 SLR(R) 742.
579. *Société Générale v. Good Property Land Development Pte Ltd* [1989] SGHC 5; [1989] 1 SLR(R) 27.
580. *Lai Min Tet v. Lai Min Kin* [2004] SGHC 3; [2004] 1 SLR(R) 499; *Diaz v. Diaz* [1997] SGCA 55; [1997] 3 SLR(R) 759; *Shaan Taseer v. Aamna Taseer* [2012] SGCA 52; [2012] 4 SLR 1049; *Lim Kaling v. Hangchi Valerie* [2003] SGHC 99; [2003] 2 SLR(R) 377 at [13].
581. John Baalman, *The Singapore Torrens system: being a commentary on the Land Titles Ordinance 1956 of the State of Singapore* (Govt. Printer, 1961) at 196.
582. *Re Caveat No CV/21366D lodged by Lim Saw Hak* [1996] SGHC 11; [1996] 1 SLR(R) 70.
583. *Chip Thye Enterprises Pte Ltd v. Development Bank of Singapore Ltd* [1994] SGCA 59; [1994] 2 SLR(R) 68; *PACC Offshore Services Holdings Ltd v. Kensteel Engineering Pte Ltd* [2017] SGHC 175.
584. *United Malayan Banking Corp v. Goodhope Realty* [1989] SGHC 14; [1989] 1 SLR(R) 151.

II. Pre-existing Interest

284. Since a caveator need not actually have a caveatable interest to lodge a caveat, it must also be true that the lodgement of a caveat does not establish the existence of a caveatable interest. But would it be possible for the parties to specify the lodgement of caveat as the mechanism for creating a caveatable interest?

285. In *The Asiatic Enterprises (Pte) Ltd v. United Overseas Bank Ltd*, the Court of Appeal answered in the negative as such an arrangement falls foul of the requirement that a person must have a pre-existing caveatable interest when lodging the caveat.[585] In this case the loan agreement provided in clause 10 that in the event of the borrower's default 'the Bank shall … be entitled (as equitable chargee) to attach the [debt] to any property of [the borrower's] (whether real or personal) and to lodge a caveat against any real property that may now or hereafter be registered in [the borrower's] name whether singly or jointly'. When the borrower defaulted, the bank lodged caveats against the borrower's properties claiming interests as an equitable chargee. The Court of Appeal held that the bank had no caveatable interest.[586] According to the court's interpretation, clause 10 did not create a charge but merely entitled the bank to take a charge in any of the borrower's properties upon the latter's default. However, clause 10 did not specifically state how the bank could unilaterally obtain a charge over the borrower's property.[587] The lodgement of a caveat does not create an interest in land and in this case, it was not an appropriate mechanism for taking a charge. Even if it were, section 115(1) requires that the caveatable interest exists prior to the lodgement of the caveat.[588] It is 'impossible, in terms of chronology, for the lodgement of a caveat to be the act which also gives rise to the claim to an interest in land needed to support the same caveat'.[589]

III. Interest in Respect of Specific Property

286. The pre-existing interest must be an entitlement in respect of a specific property. In *Aamna Taseer v. Shaan Taseer*, the house was registered in the joint

585. [1999] SGCA 85; [1999] 3 SLR(R) 976 (Yong CJ, Thean and Chao JJA).

586. For a contrary view, see Barry C. Crown, 'Requirement of a Pre-Existing Interest to Support a Caveat Under the Land Titles Act' [2000] SJLS 341.

587. However, it might be argued that the agreement contemplated the creation of an equitable charge upon the bank pinpointing the property to which the debt was to be attached. *See Ho Soo Fong v. Standard Chartered Bank* [2004] SGHC 258; [2005] 1 SLR(R) 316 at [24]. For other contrary views, see Victor C.S. Yeo, 'No Security For the Unsecured Creditors' (2000) SAcLJ 218 at 226–28; Tan Cheng Han, 'Springing Security Interests and Registration' (2001) SAcLJ 451 at 452.

588. However, section 115(1) could also be interpreted as allowing the creation of an interest in land and the lodgement of the caveat to be simultaneous. *See* Barry C. Crown, 'Requirement of a Pre-Existing Interest to Support a Caveat Under the Land Titles Act' [2000] SJLS 341.

589. [1999] SGCA 85; [1999] 3 SLR(R) 976 at [29], applied in *Ho Soo Fong v. Standard Chartered Bank* [2004] SGHC 258; [2005] 1 SLR(R) 316; *Salbiah Bte Adnan v. Micro Credit Pte Ltd* [2014] SGHC 249; [2015] 1 SLR 601.

names of the deceased and his wife.[590] After the deceased's death, his wife procured the registration of the house in her sole name. It was accepted that the deceased's estate was to be distributed according to intestacy law. However, when the wife drew up a list of distributable assets, she excluded the house. The deceased's children lodged a caveat over the house claiming to be its beneficiaries. The wife sought an order for the removal of the caveat. In the High Court, Choo J held that the children had no caveatable interest in the house and granted the order sought. The learned judge explained:

> [O]nly persons who have a direct interest in the property will have a caveatable interest in that property. The [children] had only a share in the assets of an unadministered estate and their claim is not a claim in respect of any specific property of the estate. It is a claim for a portion of the value of the estate. That is a different proposition altogether.[591]

The Court of Appeal agreed with Choo J.[592] In contrast, where the beneficiary of the property is identified in the will, the beneficiary would have a caveatable interest.[593]

287. The decision in *Taseer* is helpful in solving the disagreement as to whether a power conferred on the family court to order distribution of matrimonial assets gives rise to a caveatable interest. Section 112(1) of the Women's Charter provides that the power could be exercised upon granting a judgment of divorce, judicial separation or nullity of marriage.[594] In *Chai Mei Leng v. William Cheng*, Lee JC held that the grant of a *decree nisi* gave rise to a caveatable interest in the matrimonial property.[595] However, in *Lim Kaling v. Hangchi Valerie*, Rajendran J disagreed:

> It is relevant to note that – until exercised – that power remains only a power. Whilst a spouse may hope that the court will order the division of certain properties, until the order for division is in fact made, that hope will remain merely a hope: an inchoate expectation. Even after a *decree nisi* is pronounced, the court may not order division under s 112(1) and, even if it does, that order may not extend to the particular property/properties in question.[596]

288. The learned judge held that such 'amorphous hope' that the division will be ordered does not give rise to a caveatable interest.[597] The issue was revisited in *Eu Yee Kai Alexander Junior v. Hanson Ingrid Christina* where the parties were

590. [2012] SGHC 32; [2012] 2 SLR 348.
591. [2012] SGHC 32; [2012] 2 SLR 348 at [6].
592. *Shaan Taseer v. Aamna Taseer* [2012] SGCA 52; [2012] 4 SLR 1049 (Chan CJ, Phang and Rajah JJA).
593. *See Diaz v. Diaz* [1997] SGCA 55; [1997] 3 SLR(R) 759
594. (Cap 353, Rev. Ed. 2009).
595. [1998] SGHC 381.
596. [2003] SGHC 99; [2003] 2 SLR(R) 377 at [12].
597. [2003] SGHC 99; [2003] 2 SLR(R) 377 at [14].

divorced by *decree nisi*.[598] Unlike the earlier cases, however, the hearing for the division of matrimonial assets had already taken place and the family court had made an interim order that the property shall not be sold pending its decision. Lai J allowed the caveat to remain mainly because of the interim order.[599] It was akin to an order for injunction, which gives rise to a caveatable interest.[600] This case is therefore distinguishable from the two earlier cases and is arguably neutral to the disagreement. However, in *Tan Huat Soon v. Lee Mee Leng*, Choo J preferred the approach in *Chai Mei Leng* due to practical considerations:

> [W]hen a decree nisi has been obtained, there will be two claimants to the same property and, while the party in whose name the property is registered has no need to lodge a caveat (because it is ostensibly his - or hers), legitimate claims may be made of what was once joint property. Each party to the marriage may attempt to deny the other a share in the matrimonial assets. The spouse who is not a registered co-owner will thus, by virtue of her entitlement to claim a share, have an equitable interest in the property. A purely injunctive relief may not sufficiently protect that spouse's interests because she might have no recourse against a bona fide purchaser without notice.[601]

289. Between the two opposing strands of authorities, it is clear that *Lim Kaling* is consistent with *Taseer*. In the absence of any entitlement to a specific property, one cannot claim to have a caveatable interest. The practical concerns identified in *Tan Huat Soon* could be addressed by requiring the person claiming to have an interest to first obtain an injunctive relief before lodging a caveat.

IV. More Than Merely a Personal Right

290. It is sometimes said that a mere personal or contractual right does not amount to an interest in land.[602] However, some of the recognised caveatable interests are not strictly speaking property rights but contractual rights. To be sure, section 115(1) refers to 'interest in land', not 'property right'. The question of when a personal right could amount to an interest in land has been considered in a few recent cases.

291. In *Ho Seek Yueng Novel v. J & v. Development Pte Ltd* (*Novel Ho*), the defendant, who was in financial difficulties, sold twelve properties to the plaintiffs.[603] In respect of the sale of each property, it was orally agreed that the plaintiffs need not pay the defendant the portion of purchase price which was not financed by

598. [2004] SGHC 214; [2004] 4 SLR(R) 586.
599. [2004] SGHC 214; [2004] 4 SLR(R) 586 at [27]–[28].
600. LTA, section 115(3)(b).
601. [2009] SGHC 199.
602. *See e.g. United Overseas Bank Ltd v. Chia Kin Tuck* [2006] SGHC 87; [2006] 3 SLR(R) 322 at [9]–[10].
603. [2006] SGHC 63; [2006] 2 SLR(R) 742.

a bank loan. This unpaid sum was to be treated as an interest-free loan to the plaintiffs. In return, the plaintiffs were to grant the defendant a right of pre-emption in respect of each property. If the plaintiffs decide to sell any of the properties, they were obliged to first offer it to the defendant. If the defendant purchases it, the debt owed by the plaintiffs would be set off against the sale price. But if the defendant does not and the property was sold to a third party, the plaintiffs would repay the debt from the sale proceeds. It was further agreed that if the defendant calls on any of the loans and the plaintiffs were unable to repay, the plaintiffs were obliged to resell the property to the defendant. The defendant planned the transactions in such a way so that he may regain his stable of property if his financial situation improves. The defendant later discovered that the plaintiffs agreed to sell one of the properties to a third party without first offering it to the defendant or notifying him. The defendant then lodged caveats against all twelve properties. The plaintiffs applied to have the caveat removed on the ground that the defendant had no caveatable interest. In the High Court, Phang J (as he then was) held that the defendant had two distinct caveatable interests, one based on the right of pre-emption and the other based on his interest in the sale proceeds.

292. The right of pre-emption was clearly the main focus of the judgment. The prevailing position under English law is that a contractual right of pre-emption crystallises into an interest in the land only when the owner of the property decides to sell it.[604] The learned judge was of the view that this approach did not go far enough in protecting the right holder and arguably 'inconsistent with the rationale and spirit underlying the lodging of a caveat under the LTA'.[605] The function of a caveat is to maintain status quo until the caveator is given an opportunity to make out his case. If the defendant were allowed to lodge a caveat only when the plaintiffs decide to sell the property, there is a real possibility that a stealthy and speedy sale could be completed before the defendant finds out about it. It would then be too late for the defendant to lodge a caveat. In fact, in the present case, it was only by chance that the defendant discovered that the plaintiffs attempted to sell one of the twelve properties. The learned judge was 'uncomfortable leaving the issue of protection (or otherwise) via a caveat under the LTA to the vagaries of circumstances'.[606] This practical concern weighed heavily in favour of admitting a right of pre-emption into the list of caveatable interests. Furthermore, in response to the argument that a right of pre-emption is a mere contractual right, the learned judge highlighted its similarities with the option to purchase, in particular the ability to attract the equitable remedies of injunction and possibly specific performance. Thus, like an option to purchase, the right of pre-emption is more than a mere contractual right.[607]

293. In *Ong Chay Tong & Sons (Pte) Ltd v. Ong Hoo Eng*, the Court of Appeal agreed with Phang J that a right of pre-emption is 'a right concerning land' mainly

604. *Pritchard v. Briggs* [1980] Ch 338.
605. [2006] SGHC 63; [2006] 2 SLR(R) 742 at [57].
606. [2006] SGHC 63; [2006] 2 SLR(R) 742 at [62].
607. [2006] SGHC 63; [2006] 2 SLR(R) 742 at [91]–[93].

because its breach could be restrained by way of an injunction.[608] The focus on the availability of injunctive relief as an important criterion for finding a caveatable interest was obviously influenced by the fact that a person who has obtained an injunction over a piece of land is deemed to have an interest in the land for the purposes of lodging a caveat.[609] The Court of Appeal was of the view since injunctive relief would invariably be granted it would be duplicative to require the right holder to first obtain an injunction before lodging a caveat.[610]

294. The other aspect of Phang J's decision in *Novel Ho* was more problematic.[611] The learned judge held that the defendant's interest in the sale proceeds amounted to a caveatable interest. The learned judge relied on section 115(3)(a), which states: '[A] reference to a person claiming an interest in land shall include ... any person who has an interest in the proceeds of sale of land'.[612] However, the learned judge did not explain why a mere contractual right to have a debt repaid from the sale proceeds constitutes interest in land. If the defendant's interest were purely monetary, there would be no room for injunctive relief since an award of damages would be adequate compensation.

295. More recently, in *Salbiah Bte Adnan v. Micro Credit Pte Ltd*, Leow JC preferred a more restrictive interpretation of section 115(3)(a).[613] In this case, a borrower and his wife signed a document authorising and consenting to the lodgement of caveat over their property, the purpose of which was 'to secure [the lender's] interest in the sale proceeds of the Property to fully repay all loans granted or to be granted by [the lender] to [the borrower] from time to time'. When the borrower defaulted, the lender lodged a caveat over the property, claiming that the pursuant to the said document the lender was granted an interest in the sale proceeds of the property. Referring to Baalman, the learned judge found that the classic example where section 115(3)(a) would apply is the case of a trust for sale of land, where the beneficiary's interest in the property is notionally converted into an interest in the future proceeds of sale by virtue of the equitable doctrine of conversion.[614] What section 115(3)(a) does is to reconvert the interest in the proceeds into an interest in the property to allow the beneficiary to protect the property by a caveat. Another possible example is where a foreign person inherits by will or by the law of intestate succession a residential property in Singapore.[615] The Residential Property Act (RPA)[616] prohibits the transfer of interest in the property to the foreign person but

608. [2008] SGCA 42; [2009] 1 SLR(R) 305 at [79]–[80] (Chan CJ, Chao and Phang JJA).
609. LTA, section 115(3)(b).
610. [2008] SGCA 42; [2009] 1 SLR(R) 305 at [79].
611. *See* W.J.M. Ricquier, *Land Law*, 5th edn (LexisNexis, 2017) at 154–55.
612. [2006] SGHC 63; [2006] 2 SLR(R) 742 at [38]–[39].
613. [2014] SGHC 249; [2015] 1 SLR 601.
614. John Baalman, *The Singapore Torrens system: being a commentary on the Land Titles Ordinance 1956 of the State of Singapore* (Govt. Printer, 1961) at 196.
615. Tang Hang Wu and Kelvin F.K. Low, *Tan Sook Yee's Principles of Singapore Land Law*, 3rd edn (LexisNexis 2009) at 328; W.J.M. Ricquier, *Land Law*, 5th edn (LexisNexis, 2012) at 155–56.
616. (Cap. 274, 2009 Rev. Ed.).

instead requires the personal representative of the deceased's estate to sell the property and distribute the proceeds to the foreign person.[617] Pending sale, the foreign person is allowed to lodge a caveat over the property by virtue of section 115(3)(a). The learned judge explained that in both examples 'the caveator has a definite entitlement to the proceeds of sale because the trustee or personal representative is charged with a *duty* of sale'.[618] In contrast, in *Novel Ho* and in the present case, there was no such entitlement. Any interest in the sale proceeds was wholly contingent on the owners deciding to sell. In the absence of such entitlement, the requirement that a caveatable interest be a proprietary one should be strictly applied.[619] The learned judge said:

> To hold that a person with a mere contractual right to be paid from the sale proceeds of a property can lodge a caveat on that property would effectively allow such agreements to function as a form of quasi-security, since the caveatee would be unable to register dealings in respect of the property until he pays up. This is not a purpose of the caveat mechanism; a caveat is meant to protect pre-existing interests in land, not operate in and of itself as a form of quasi-security for otherwise unsecured debts.[620]

296. For these reasons, the learned judge was of the view that section 115(3)(a) should have no application in the present case (and in *Novel Ho*). It may be added that in the two examples provided earlier, the caveator has a clear interest in how much the property is sold for. This was not the case in *Salbiah* where the debt was far less than what the property was worth. Neither was it the case in *Novel Ho*. Since the sale proceeds would be used to repay the debt owed to the defendant, it would be in the plaintiff's interest (not the defendant's) to sell the properties at the best possible prices.

§3. Form of the Caveat

297. The caveat must be in the approved form[621] specifying the following particulars:[622]

(a) the name of the caveator and the caveatee;
(b) an address in Singapore at which notices may be served on the caveator and the caveatee;
(c) nature of the interest claimed by the caveator;
(d) the grounds in support of the claim;
(e) the nature of the prohibition of the dealing in land;

617. RPA, section 3(4).
618. [2014] SGHC 249; [2015] 1 SLR 601 at [31].
619. [2014] SGHC 249; [2015] 1 SLR 601 at [41].
620. [2014] SGHC 249; [2015] 1 SLR 601 at [41].
621. Forms 49 and 50.
622. LTA, section 115(1).

(f) the lot affected by the caveat and, where that lot is comprised in a folio, the folio;
(g) where the caveat relates to only part of the land, such description of that part as will enable it to be identified to the satisfaction of the Registrar;
(h) if the caveator is a purchaser or sub-purchaser of the interest in the land, the amount of the purchase price and the date of the caveator's contract or the date on which he exercised the option to purchase the interest in the land, as the case may be; and
(i) the particulars required by section 19 of the Residential Property Act (Cap. 274).

298. In *Alrich Development Pte Ltd v. Rafiq Jumabhoy* the Court of Appeal expressed doubt that section 115(1) requires a caveator to provide elaborate details of his claim within the narrow confines of the caveat form.[623] The court explained:

> The contest in regard to the validity of the caveat should not be so much on the form of it as the underlying transaction giving rise or alleged to give rise to a caveatable interest. When a right to caveat is challenged, the full facts giving rise to the right or the alleged right must necessarily be gone into by the court. It is highly unlikely that such cases could ever be decided without reference to facts external to the four corners of the caveat form.[624]

299. Thus, it is sufficient that the caveat gives a fair indication of the interest the caveator claims to have and the grounds of his claim.[625] So long as the caveat is not positively misleading to the prejudice of the other party, a court should not be overly astute in striking out caveats for minor defects.[626]

300. In this case Jumabhoy granted to Ho an option to purchase a particular piece of land. The option could be exercised by Ho herself or by her nominee. Two days before the expiry of the option, Jumabhoy purportedly revoked the option. Ho refused to accept the revocation. The next day, Ho's nominee, Alrich, exercised the option using the agreed method and lodged a caveat over the property. The caveat reads:

> The caveator Alrich Development Pte Ltd claims interest as purchaser by virtue of an option dated 8 June 1990 given by the registered proprietor and duly exercised by the caveator on 6 August 1990 as to the estate or interest of the registered proprietor in the land above described, and hereby prohibits the registration of any instrument affecting the abovementioned land unless the caveator has consented in writing to such registration.

---

623. [1993] SGCA 27; [1993] 1 SLR(R) 598 at [42] (Lai, Khoo and Chua JJ).
624. [1993] SGCA 27; [1993] 1 SLR(R) 598 at [43]. Applied in *Cathay Theatres Pte Ltd v. LKM Investment Holdings Pte Ltd* [1998] SGCA 4; [1998] 1 SLR(R) 234 at [28]–[29]; *Ow Chor Seng v. Tjinta Pte Ltd* [1994] SGHC 259; [1994] 3 SLR(R) 536; *Sim Kwang Mui Ivy v. Goh Peng Khim* [1994] SGHC 169; [1994] 2 SLR(R) 814.
625. [1993] SGCA 27; [1993] 1 SLR(R) 598 at [44]
626. [1993] SGCA 27; [1993] 1 SLR(R) 598 at [45].

Jumabhoy applied to have the caveat removed complaining that three aspects of the caveat were incorrectly stated. First, on the nature and the extent of interest claimed, it is insufficient to simply state 'claims interest as purchaser'. Second, the caveat gave the impression that the option was granted to Alrich when in fact it was granted to Ho. Third, the option was exercised on 7 August 1990, not on 6 August 1990 as stated. The Court of Appeal held that none of these were serious enough to invalidate the caveat. It was obvious that Alrich had contracted to purchase the whole of the estate or interest Jumabhoy had in the property.[627] In this case it was an estate in fee simple in the property. As for the second complaint, Jumabhoy failed to demonstrate why it is important to specify the person whom the option was first given to.[628] Finally, the incorrect date did not mislead Jumabhoy since there was only one transaction between the parties. The court went as far as to say that the date of the exercise of the option could have been omitted without any harm.[629]

301. A good contrasting case is *Ong Chay Tong & Sons (Pte) Ltd v. Ong Hoo Eng* where a family company sold a property to one of the founder's sons.[630] The sale was subject to a special condition that the son shall not sell or otherwise dispose of the property except to the company for $100,000. The contract was later varied to allow sale or disposal of the property to the founder's own lineal descendants bearing the surname of 'Ong'. The company then lodged a caveat to protect its interest in the property. However, the caveat referred to the original special condition instead of the varied one. The Court of Appeal held that the defect was a serious one because there was substantial difference in the scope of the restriction imposed by the original and varied special conditions.[631]

§4. Extent of the Prohibition

302. Section 115(2) of the LTA states:

> A caveator may, according to the extent of his interest, prohibit the registration under this Act of any dealing affecting the land against which the caveat is directed, either –
>
> (a) unless the dealing is expressed to be subject to the interest claimed by the caveator; or
> (b) unless the caveator or some person nominated by him in the caveat has consented in writing to such registration.

303. The caveator must choose either (a) or (b) as an exception to the prohibition of dealing with the property. Exception (a) is useful in protecting the caveator's

627. [1993] SGCA 27; [1993] 1 SLR(R) 598 at [47]–[49].
628. [1993] SGCA 27; [1993] 1 SLR(R) 598 at [51].
629. [1993] SGCA 27; [1993] 1 SLR(R) 598 at [52].
630. [2008] SGCA 42; [2009] 1 SLR(R) 305.
631. [2008] SGCA 42; [2009] 1 SLR(R) 305 at [82].

interest while allowing the property to be dealt with in a manner that is not inconsistent with the caveator's interest. If the caveator does not wish the property to be dealt with at all, he should choose the narrower exception (b) and withhold consent. Even if the caveator gives his consent for the registration of a particular dealing, the caveat remains good in prohibiting the registration of other dealings.

304. The caveator must choose wisely between these two exceptions. The prohibition cannot be any wider than is justified by the extent of his interest. For example, the existence of an equitable lease does not usually impose any restriction on the landlord's freedom to deal with the reversion. In such a case the caveator ought to choose exception (a).[632] However, in a rare case where the lease agreement expressly provides that the landlord shall not dispose of or otherwise deal with the reversion without the tenant's consent, the caveator will be justified in choosing exception (b).

305. The way in which a title registered pursuant to exception (a) is subject to the caveator's interest was examined by the Court of Appeal in *Cathay Theatres Pte Ltd v. LKM Investment Holdings Pte Ltd.*[633] Cathay leased a property from the Housing Development Board (HDB) for a 99-year duration. Cathay then subleased a part of the property to McDonald. Because HDB only allowed a sublease for a maximum of two years, Cathay agreed to grant McDonald several consecutive two-year leases. McDonald lodged a caveat to protect its current and future subleases. The caveat prohibited registration of a transfer unless the transfer was expressly subject to the interest claimed in the caveat (i.e., exception (a)). Later, Cathay agreed to sell the property to LKM subject to McDonald's subleases. However, LKM refused to complete the sale unless the caveat lodged by McDonald was removed. LKM argued that the future subleases were not caveatable interests, and if the transfer was registered subject to McDonald's interests LKM would be taken to have admitted those interests and precluded from challenging their validity. The Court of Appeal disagreed that registration via exception (a) has the effect of rendering the unregistered interest unchallengeable. It merely precludes the registered proprietor from defeating the caveated interest on the ground of indefeasibility. Importantly, the registered proprietor is not precluded from challenging the validity of the interest on other grounds.

§5. Upon Successful Lodgment of a Caveat

I. Registrar to Notify the Caveatee

306. When a caveat is lodged and accepted, the Registrar shall notify the caveatee(s) of the caveat.[634] Section 4(1) defines a caveatee as 'the proprietor or other

632. John Baalman, *The Singapore Torrens System: Being A Commentary on the Land Titles Ordinance 1956 of the State of Singapore* (Govt. Printer, 1961) at 197.
633. [1998] SGCA 4; [1998] 1 SLR(R) 234 (Yong CJ, Karthigesu and Thean JJA).
634. LTA, section 117(1).

owner of land described in a caveat'. In *United Overseas Finance Ltd v. Mutu Jeras*, Chan J held that this includes an owner of an equitable interest in the property.[635] In this case an equitable mortgagee who had a caveat lodged against the property was not notified of a subsequent lodgement of caveat. The learned judge held that notwithstanding the Registrar's oversight the equitable mortgagee was not deprived of its status as a caveatee.[636] A caveatee may challenge the other caveat if he wishes to.[637]

II. Registration of a Dealing Prohibited by the Caveat

307. Section 119(4) provides that the Registrar shall not register any dealing which is prohibited by the caveat for so long as the caveat remains effective. However, pursuant to section 120(1), where a dealing prohibited by the caveat is lodged for registration, the Registrar shall serve on the caveator a notice of the Registrar's intention, at the expiration of 30 days from the date of service of the notice, to register the dealing unless:

(a) an order has been obtained from the court extending the operation of the caveat for such further period as may be specified in the order or for such further periods as may be specified in subsequent orders made by the court and the order or a duly certified copy thereof is served on the Registrar; or
(b) the dealing has been uplifted or withdrawn or otherwise becomes incapable of registration.

308. In other words, the status quo will be maintained for only 30 days. Within this period the caveator must satisfy a court why the caveat should remain. If he does not obtain the necessary court order, the Registrar shall proceed to register the dealing. The caveat will automatically lapse but only to the extent necessary to permit the registration.[638] For example, if the caveat seeks to protect two distinct unregistered interests and the registered dealing is only inconsistent with one of the unregistered interests, the caveat is still effective to prevent registration of a dealing inconsistent with the other unregistered interest.

§6. Duration

309. A caveat begins to take effect when it is in order for notification in the land register[639] and lasts for 5 years[640] unless it is earlier withdrawn,[641] removed[642] or

635. [1989] SGHC 41; [1989] 1 SLR(R) 446 at [7].
636. [1989] SGHC 41; [1989] 1 SLR(R) 446 at [7].
637. LTA, section 127.
638. *Ibid.*, section 121(1)(a) and (4).
639. *Ibid.*, section 119(1).
640. *Ibid.*, section 121(1)(b).
641. *Ibid.*, section 126.
642. *Ibid.*, section 127.

lapsed because the caveator failed to obtain a court order specified in section 120(1)(a).[643] A caveat which lapses ceases to affect the property.[644]

310. Where the caveator lodges for registration a dealing which gives the caveator the same interest he was seeking to protect with the caveat, the Registrar may register the dealing, upon which the caveat will lapse.[645] For example, *A* agrees to sell Greenacre to *B*. *B* lodges a caveat against the Greenacre to protect his interest as a purchaser. When *B* presents the instrument of transfer for registration, the Registrar shall register the transfer notwithstanding the caveat. If *B* had to first withdraw his caveat, his interest may become vulnerable if there are more than one caveats lodged against the property.[646]

311. At any time before a caveat lapses, the caveator may lodge an extension of the caveat claiming the same interest.[647] Where a caveat is extended, it will lapse at the expiration of 5 years from the date of the lodgement of the extension,[648] or where the caveat was extended more than once, at the expiration of 5 years from the date of lodgement of the last extension.[649]

§7. Lodgement of Fresh Caveat

312. Where a caveat lapses, the caveator may lodge a fresh caveat.[650] However, where the caveat lapses because the caveator failed to obtain a court order specified in section 120(1)(a),[651] a fresh caveat lodged to protect the same interest has no effect unless the caveator has obtained leave of the court to lodge that caveat.[652]

313. A fresh caveat is effective only from the date of its lodgement, not at the date of the lodgement of the original caveat. Thus, the lodgement of a fresh caveat is less advantageous compared to an extension of caveat in protecting the caveat's priority against other caveats.[653]

§8. Priorities

314. Section 49(1) provides that except in the case of fraud, the entry of a caveat protecting an unregistered interest shall give that interest priority over any other

643. *Ibid.*, section 121(1)(a). *See* §5.II. above.
644. *Ibid.*, section 121(1).
645. *Ibid.*, sections 121(2) and (3).
646. This is to prevent the difficulty encountered in *Re Tan Kiong Hwa* [1972] SGHC 3; [1971–1973] SLR(R) 330.
647. LTA, section 122(1).
648. *Ibid.*, section 122(1)(a).
649. *Ibid.*, section 122(1)(b).
650. *Ibid.*, section 121(6).
651. *Ibid.*, section 121(1)(a). *See* §5.II. above.
652. *Ibid.*, section 121(7).
653. On priority, see LTA, section 49. *See* §8 below.

unregistered interest not so protected at the time when the caveat was entered. In other words, the priority between unregistered interests protected by caveats is to be determined by the date of the entry of the caveats. Subsection (2) further states that knowledge of the existence of a prior unregistered interest which is not protected by a caveat shall not be imputed as fraud. As to what amounts to fraud, it is helpful to refer to the discussion on the fraud exception to indefeasibility in the previous chapter.[654]

§9. Voluntary Withdrawal of Caveat

315. A caveator may withdraw a caveat either wholly or partially.[655] A partial withdrawal reduces the area of the property which is subject to the prohibition of the caveat. This allows part of the property to be dealt with freely.

§10. Removal of Caveat

I. Application to Court

316. Section 127(1) provides that a caveatee may summon the caveator to attend before the court to show cause why the caveat should not be removed and the court may make such order as seems just.[656] In *Eng Mee Yong Letchumanan s/o Velayutham*, the Privy Council laid down the following test for determining whether a caveat should be allowed to remain:

> [The caveator] must first satisfy the court that on the evidence presented to it his claim to an interest in the property does raise a serious question to be tried; and, having done so, he must go on to show that on the balance of convenience it would be better to maintain the status quo until the trial of the action, by preventing the caveatee from disposing of his land to some third party.[657]

317. Where the caveator could show that there is a serious question to be tried, the balance of convenience would normally be in favour of allowing the caveat to remain.[658] The serious question to be tried could be one of facts or law. In *Ow Chor Seng v. Tjinta Pte Ltd*, for example, Singh JC held that the question of whether a

654. *See* Chapter 4 (Torrens System) §5.
655. LTA, section 126.
656. *Ibid.*, section 127(1).
657. [1980] AC 331 at 337, accepted as applicable to LTA, section 127 in *Société Générale v. Good Property Land Development Pte Ltd* [1989] SGHC 5; [1989] 1 SLR(R) 27; *Ow Chor Seng v. Tjinta Pte Ltd* [1994] SGHC 259; [1994] 3 SLR(R) 536; *Tan Cheow Gek v. Gimly Holdings Pte Ltd* [1992] SGHC 157; [1992] 2 SLR(R) 240; *Sim Kwang Mui Ivy v. Goh Peng Khim* [1994] SGHC 169; [1994] 2 SLR(R) 814; *Tan Yow Kon v. Tan Swat Ping* [2006] SGHC 123; [2006] 3 SLR(R) 881; *Jhaveri Darsan Jitendra v. Salgaocar Anil Vassudeva* [2018] SGHC 24.
658. [1980] AC 331 at 338.

mistaken transfer gives rise to a constructive trust was a serious issue to be determined at trial and thus allowed the caveat to remain.[659] The *Eng Mee Yong* test is also helpful in dealing with cases where, although the interest claimed is not within the list of recognised caveatable interests, it has the potential of being admitted to the list. In such cases the caveat should be allowed to remain pending determination of whether the interest claimed could amount to a caveatable interest.

318. Where a caveat is allowed to remain, the court may order that the caveator provide an undertaking or security to indemnify the caveatee for any possible loss resulting from the disposition of the property being delayed.[660] The court may also direct the caveator to take further proceedings on his caveat for determination of the validity of the interest claimed.[661]

319. Where the court orders a caveat to be removed, the court may additionally order that the caveatee provide security to meet any potential claim by the caveator.[662] In *Tan Yow Kon v. Tan Swat Ping*, Menon JC (as he then was) held that 'it is appropriate in weighing the balance of convenience to have regard to the financial means of each of the respective parties and in particular their ability to meet a claim for damages should it later transpire that the caveat ought not to have been extended or removed as the case may be'.[663]

320. Interestingly, section 127 does not specifically state the grounds for removal of caveat. However, recall that in *Alrich* the Court of Appeal said that any contest to the validity of the caveat must focus on substance rather than the form of the caveat.[664] In other words, it is for the caveatee to challenge the caveat on substantive grounds. There are three main substantive grounds for removal of caveat.

659. [1994] SGHC 259; [1994] 3 SLR(R) 536.
660. LTA, section 124(a).
661. *Ibid.*, section 124(c).
662. *Ibid.*, section 124(d), which allows the court to 'make any other order considered just'.
663. [2006] SGHC 123; [2006] 3 SLR(R) 881 at [90].
664. [1993] SGCA 27; [1993] 1 SLR(R) 598 at [43]. Of course, a caveat that is seriously defective in form can be ordered to be withdrawn: *Ong Chay Tong & Sons (Pte) Ltd v. Ong Hoo Eng* [2008] SGCA 42; [2009] 1 SLR(R) 305.

First, the interest claimed is not a caveatable interest.[665] Second, although the interest claimed is a caveatable interest, the caveator did not in fact have such an interest.[666] Third, the caveator had a caveatable interest but the interest had ceased to exist.[667]

II. Application to Registrar

321. A caveatee who opposes a caveat on the ground that it has been lodged, or is allowed to remain, vexatiously or frivolously or not in good faith, may lodge a complaint with the Registrar.[668] If the Registrar is satisfied with the complaint, he shall give notice to the caveator that he intends to remove the caveat, and he shall remove it unless within 30 days from the date of the service of the notice the caveator obtains a court order to the contrary.[669] In *Ho Soo Fong v. Standard Chartered Bank*, the Court of Appeal observed that this is a simpler method of removing a caveat than by court order.[670] However, the ground for removal is also stricter. As Baalman explained, the subsection 'is directed primarily against eccentric individuals whose claim to land is only imaginary' and therefore the Registrar 'should not take it on himself to cancel a caveat where there is even a semblance of good faith on the part of the caveator'.[671] He further clarified that the provision applies also to

665. *Shaan Taseer v. Aamna Taseer* [2012] SGCA 52; [2012] 4 SLR 1049 (beneficiaries do not have interest in specific assets of an unadministered estate); *Salbiah Bte Adnan v. Micro Credit Pte Ltd* [2014] SGHC 249; [2015] 1 SLR 601 (creditor had no interest in sale proceeds); *United Overseas Bank Ltd v. Chia Kin Tuck* [2006] SGHC 87; [2006] 3 SLR(R) 322 (judgment creditor had no interest in debtor's land); *Power Knight Pte Ltd v. Natural Fuel Pte Ltd* [2010] SGHC 75; [2010] 3 SLR 82 (unsecured creditors have no caveatable interest in the assets of an insolvent company).

666. *Tan Soo Leng David v. Wee, Satky & Kumar Pte Ltd* [1993] SGHC 199; [1993] 2 SLR(R) 741 (where the required consent for the sale was withheld by a joint tenant); *Tan Cheow Gek v. Gimly Holdings Pte Ltd* [1992] SGHC 157; [1992] 2 SLR(R) 240 (where the contract was null and void for illegality); *Eng Bee Properties Pte Ltd v. Lee Foong Fatt* [1993] SGHC 202; [1993] 2 SLR(R) 778 (the option to purchase had expired); *Sim Kwang Mui Ivy v. Goh Peng Khim* [1994] SGHC 169; [1994] 2 SLR(R) 814 (no contract of sale was concluded); *Mookka Pillai Rajagopal v. Khushvinder Singh Chopra* [1996] SGCA 58; [1996] 3 SLR(R) 210 (the option to purchase was not signed by all three joint tenants); *The Asiatic Enterprises (Pte) Ltd v. UOB Ltd* [1999] SGCA 85; [1999] 3 SLR(R) 976 (the loan agreement did not create an equitable mortgage or charge); *Ho Soo Fong v. Standard Chartered Bank* [2004] SGHC 258; [2005] 1 SLR(R) 316 (for the same reason in *Asiatic*).

667. *Virginia Developments Pte Ltd v. Behem Investment Pte Ltd* [1988] SGHC 31; [1988] 1 SLR(R) 302 (where the purchaser rescinded and repudiated the contract of sale); *Société Générale v. Good Property Land Development Pte Ltd* [1989] SGHC 5; [1989] 1 SLR(R) 27 (where the mortgagor's equity of redemption was extinguished by the mortgagee's power of sale); *Mookka Pillai Rajagopal v. Khushvinder Singh Chopra* [1996] SGCA 58; [1996] 3 SLR(R) 210 (the supplemental agreement of sale was rescinded for undue influence).

668. LTA, section 127(2).

669. *Ibid.*

670. [2007] SCGA 4; [2007] 2 SLR(R) 181 at [36] (Chan CJ, Phang JA and Lee J).

671. John Baalman, *The Singapore Torrens system: being a commentary on the Land Titles Ordinance 1956 of the State of Singapore* (Govt. Printer, 1961) at 208.

'caveats which, though having a genuine origin, have subsequently lose their propriety but are still *allowed to remain*, instead of being withdrawn'.[672] Citing Baalman, the Court of Appeal in *Ho Soo Fong* held that the word 'vexatiously' implies a lodgement of caveat that is 'utterly groundless and would clearly have no prospect of withstanding a challenge to cancel it'.[673]

§11. COMPENSATION

322. To prevent abuse of the caveat system, section 128(1) provides that any person who wrongfully, vexatiously or without reasonable cause lodges a caveat, refuses or fails to remove a caveat, or procures a lapsing of a caveat, shall be liable to any person who has sustained a pecuniary loss as a result of the aforementioned acts or omissions. Although the section could be invoked against both a caveator and a caveatee, a claim for compensation against the caveatee is rare since a caveator who fails to show a serious question to be tried is unlikely to succeed at trial in establishing his claim. A claim against the caveator may also be brought by a person other than a caveatee. For example, where the caveatee has agreed to sell the property to a third party and completion was delayed by a caveat that was wrongfully lodged, the third party may claim compensation from the caveator if he has suffered a pecuniary loss from the delay.

323. In *Ho Soo Fong v. Standard Chartered Bank*, the Court of Appeal laid down the definitions for the terms wrongfully, vexatiously and without reasonable cause.[674] The term 'wrongfully' suggests 'an improper motive or an extraneous purpose', e.g. 'where the caveator lodged the caveat deliberately in an attempt to infringe the rights of the caveatee'.[675] Similarly, the term 'vexatiously' suggests an 'objective of wishing to annoy or not intending to lead to a serious result', e.g. where the caveat was 'utterly groundless and would clearly have no prospect of withstanding a challenge to cancel it'.[676] Finally, the phrase 'without reasonable cause' means 'no honest belief based on reasonable grounds that he has a caveatable interest'.[677] This essentially means negligence. There is no need to prove improper motive.[678] Section 128(4) also states that if a caveator does not remove his caveat within 7 days after his interest in the property has been terminated, he shall be deemed to have allowed the caveat to remain without reasonable cause.

672. *Ibid.*
673. [2007] SCGA 4; [2007] 2 SLR(R) 181 at [36].
674. [2007] SCGA 4; [2007] 2 SLR(R) 181.
675. [2007] SCGA 4; [2007] 2 SLR(R) 181 at [34], rejecting the wide interpretation of the term 'wrongfully' in *Tan Soo Leng David v. Wee, Satku & Kumar Pte Ltd* [1993] SGHC 199; [1993] 2 SLR(R) 741*; Eng Bee Properties Pte Ltd v. Lee Foong Fatt* [1993] SGHC 202; [1993] 2 SLR(R) 778.
676. [2007] SCGA 4; [2007] 2 SLR(R) 181 at [36], following *Goh Koon Suan v. Heng Gek Kiau* [1990] SGHC 110; [1990] 2 SLR(R) 705. *See also* §10.II. above.
677. [2007] SCGA 4; [2007] 2 SLR(R) 181 at [35].
678. [2007] SCGA 4; [2007] 2 SLR(R) 181 at [35].

324. As it is clearly easier to prove the absence of reasonable cause, Baalman suggested that the words 'wrongfully' and 'vexatiously' are 'probably redundant'.[679] However, the presence or absence of improper motive may make a difference on the quantum of compensation. In *Ho Soo Fong*, the Court of Appeal alluded to the possibility that if a caveat was lodged with an improper motive, the usual reasonable foreseeability test might not apply to limit the losses that are compensable.[680] However, the court refrained from deciding on this issue as it was not argued.

325. The grounds for removal of a caveat do not align perfectly with the grounds for claiming compensation. While the absence of a caveatable interest is a straightforward ground for removal of a caveat, compensation does not necessarily follow since the caveat may not have been lodged without reasonable cause.[681] If there is reason to believe that the caveator's claim has some prospect of success, the caveat should be regarded as having been lodged with reasonable cause. Put differently, if the caveator could show that there is a serious question to be tried, he should not be liable to pay compensation if it is eventually decided that he has no caveatable interest.[682] It should be reminded that because the LTA does not specify clearly which interests are caveatable, the list of caveatable interests has been determined mainly through litigation. This process will be stultified if potential liability to pay compensation deters lodgement of caveats although there is some probability of success.

326. Section 128 is often understood as creating a new statutory tort.[683] Thus, the rules of causation, remoteness and mitigation apply.[684] In *Mookka Pillai Rajagopal v. Khushvinder Singh Chopra*, the owners of a property entered into a contract to sell the property but completion was prevented by the existence of a caveat lodged by another interested purchaser. The caveator was earlier granted an option to purchase but it was missing the signature of one co-owner. The Court of Appeal ordered that the caveat be removed on the ground that the caveator had no interest in the property and further ordered an inquiry into the compensation to be awarded under section 128.[685] Before the High Court, the owners claimed compensation for

679. John Baalman, *The Singapore Torrens system: being a commentary on the Land Titles Ordinance 1956 of the State of Singapore* (Govt. Printer, 1961) at 210.
680. [2007] SCGA 4; [2007] 2 SLR(R) 181 at [37].
681. [2007] SCGA 4; [2007] 2 SLR(R) 181 at [35].
682. Tang Hang Wu and Kelvin F.K. Low, *Tan Sook Yee's Principles of Singapore Land Law*, 3rd edn (LexisNexis, 2009) at 374.
683. John Baalman, *The Singapore Torrens system: being a commentary on the Land Titles Ordinance 1956 of the State of Singapore* (Govt. Printer, 1961) at 209; *Ho Soo Fong v. Standard Chartered Bank* [2007] SCGA 4; [2007] 2 SLR(R) 181 at [33]; *Mookka Pillai Rajagopal v. Khushvinder Singh Chopra* [1997] SGHC 205; [1997] 2 SLR(R) 689 at [21].
684. *Mookka Pillai Rajagopal v. Khushvinder Singh Chopra* [1997] SGHC 205; [1997] 2 SLR(R) 689, affirmed in *Khushvinder Singh Chopra v. Mookka Pillai Rajagopal* [1999] SGCA 7; [1999] 1 SLR(R) 130; *Ho Soo Fong v. Standard Chartered Bank* [2007] SCGA 4; [2007] 2 SLR(R) 181.
685. *Mookka Pillai Rajagopal v. Khushvinder Singh Chopra* [1996] SGCA 58; [1996] 3 SLR(R) 210. The basis for invoking section 128 was not stated. In a subsequent judgment, the Court of Appeal

three heads of loss. First, due to the delay in completion, the purchasers had commenced proceedings against the owners thus resulting in the latter having to pay late completion interest and associated litigation costs. Second, the owners had to continue paying interests on the mortgage loan. If the sale had been completed as scheduled, the owners could have used the purchase price to pay off the entire debt. The caveator knew about this outstanding debt. Third, the owners incurred interests on two judgment debts which were unrelated to the present dispute. Again, the owners could have used the purchase money to pay off the debts, thus avoiding the incurrence of interests. Chao J allowed the first two claims but not the third on the ground that the judgment debts were 'wholly unforeseen' and therefore the loss was 'too remote'.[686] The caveator appealed against Chao J's decision on the second head of loss. Reversing the decision of Chao J in part, the Court of Appeal disallowed the second claim, noting that the loan interest could have been avoided by redeeming the property and the inability to do so was due to the owners' impecuniosity rather than the presence of the caveat.[687]

327. In *Ho Soo Fong v. Standard Chartered Bank*, the borrowers obtained three loan facilities from SCB to assist refinancing of their existing loans. The loan agreement provided that the borrowers were to grant to SCB first legal mortgages over three of their properties. SCB proceeded to lodge caveats against the three identified properties. Subsequently, as a condition for disbursement of the loan was not satisfied, the borrowers cancelled the loan facilities. However, SCB refused to withdraw the caveats because the borrowers disputed that they were liable to pay cancellation fees. In the High Court, Ang J held that SCB had no caveatable interest.[688] It was obvious from the loan agreement that SCB negotiated for a first legal mortgage, not an immediately enforceable equitable mortgage. Thus, the caveats were lodged without reasonable cause.[689] The learned judge thus ordered an inquiry into the compensation to be awarded under section 128. Additional facts relevant to the issue of compensation are as follows: SCB knew that the borrowers needed to refinance their existing loans to reduce the interests payable and they could not do so unless the caveats were removed. SCB also knew that the borrowers were offered a new financing facility by another financial institution. Before the High Court, the borrowers claimed that SCB's caveats obstructed their attempt to refinance their loans, thus causing the following losses. First, the borrowers had to pay higher interest rates than what they would have had to if they had successfully refinanced their loans. Second, one of the borrowers' properties was sold by the mortgagee at a price

said that the caveats were lodged wrongfully or without any reasonable cause because the caveator had no interest in the property. *See* [1999] SGCA 7; [1999] 1 SLR(R) 130 at [10].

686. [1997] SGHC 205; [1997] 2 SLR(R) 689 at [9].
687. [1999] SGCA 7; [1999] 1 SLR(R) 130 (Karthigesu JA, Thean JA and Lai J).
688. [2004] SGHC 258; [2005] 1 SLR(R) 316.
689. [2004] SGHC 258; [2005] 1 SLR(R) 316 at [24]. Although this point was not argued on appeal, the Court of Appeal observed that SCB's motive for refusing to remove the caveats was to pressure the borrowers into paying the cancellation fees. Had the issue been argued, the Court of Appeal might well have found SCB to be wrongful and vexatious in its conduct ([2007] SCGA 4; [2007] 2 SLR(R) 181 at [38]).

allegedly $1.2m lower than what the property could have fetched in the open market. The borrowers could have prevented the forced sale had the refinancing been successful. In the High Court, Ang J awarded compensation for the first head of loss but not the second.[690] One reason the learned judge gave for why the second head of loss was not compensable was that it was caused by the borrowers' own impecuniosity. The learned judge found herself bound by the Court of Appeal's decision in *Mookka Pillai*.

328. On appeal, the Court of Appeal reversed the Ang J's decision in part and held that the second head of loss was compensable.[691] On the requirement of causation, the court was satisfied that SCB's failure to withdraw the caveats was the cause of the loss. The court clarified that test is not one of proximate cause but contributory cause. Importantly, the court also overruled its own decision in *Mookka Pillai*, thus excluding consideration of the borrower's impecuniosity. Indeed, even if the borrower's impecuniosity in some way caused the loss, it cannot be denied that SCB's refusal to remove the caveats was a contributory cause to the loss. On the issue of remoteness, the court was also satisfied that in the circumstances it was reasonably foreseeable that the obstruction of the borrower's attempt to refinance their loans would result in one or more of their properties being sold by the mortgagees. Finally, the court was satisfied that the borrowers discharged their duty to mitigate by offering to pay part of the cancellation fees. Although it could be argued that instead of engaging in prolonged negotiations with SCB the borrowers should have applied to have the caveat removed, the court decided not to pursue this issue as it was not argued.

690. [2006] SGHC 90; [2006] 3 SLR(R) 263.
691. [2007] SCGA 4; [2007] 2 SLR(R) 181.

Chapter 6. Leases

§1. Introduction

329. A lease (or tenancy)[692] is created when a landowner grants to another the exclusive possession of his land for a term certain in consideration of a lump sum payment or periodic payments.[693] Historically, a lease was the creation of contract and therefore gave rise only to personal obligations between the contracting landlord and tenant.[694] In time, however, it came to be accepted that a tenant, although not an owner of the freehold estate, had a possessory right in the land protectable from third-party interference by way of an action of ejectment. The tenant's right was thus elevated to the status of an estate in the land.[695] For the duration of the lease, the tenant is regarded as the owner of the land. The tenant may deal with the land as he wishes, subject of course to the terms of the lease. The lease is also inheritable. Despite this development, a lease retains the characteristics of a contract due to its origin. This hybrid nature of a lease has important practical implications, some of which will be addressed in this chapter.

330. Three important pieces of legislations that set out provisions relating to leases: the Land Titles Act (LTA),[696] the Conveyancing and Law of Property Act (CLPA)[697] and the Civil Law Act (CLA).[698] However, much of the law on leases remains heavily based on the common law.

§2. Types of Leases

I. Fixed-Term Lease

331. A fixed-term lease is one where the start and end dates of the lease have been determined at the outset, e.g. for 3 years beginning 1 January 2017. The lease will subsist for the entire duration unless the parties agree that the lease is terminable at an earlier time. For avoidance of doubt, merely because rent is payable periodically does not mean that the lease is a periodic one. In the example above, even if the rent is payable on a monthly basis, the lease is still for a fixed term of 3 years.

692. For comprehensive works on this topic, see Lye Lin Heng, *Landlord and Tenant* (Butterworths, 1990); Tang Hang Wu and Kelvin F.K. Low, *Tan Sook Yee's Principles of Singapore Land Law*, 3rd edn (LexisNexis, 2009) Chapter 17; Kevin Gray and Susan Francis Gray, *Elements of Land Law*, 5th edn (OUP, 2009) Part 4.
693. *Street v. Mountford* [1985] AC 809.
694. *Ibid., v.* at 814.
695. A leasehold estate is technically called a 'term of years absolute'. *See Bruton v. London & Quadrant Housing Trust* [2000] 1 AC 406 at 415.
696. (Cap. 157, 2004 Rev. Ed.).
697. (Cap. 61, 2004 Rev. Ed.), Part III (sections 10–18A) of the CLPA applies to registered land: LTA, section 86(2).
698. (Cap. 43, 1999 Rev. Ed.).

II. Periodic Lease

332. Unlike a fixed-term lease, a periodic lease continues from period to period (e.g., from year to year, month to month, etc). The lease does not expire at the end of each period and renew itself at the start of the following period.[699] Rather, it extends itself until it is determined by the appropriate advance notice to quit. The lease is to be viewed retrospectively as a single term.[700]

333. The phrases 'year to year' (yearly) or 'month to month' (monthly) merely indicate the advance notice required to determine the lease. In the case of a yearly lease, a six-month advance notice must be given. For a monthly lease, a one-month advance notice is required. There is no reason why the parties could not agree on a shorter or longer advance notice.[701]

334. A joint-tenanted periodic lease can be determined if just one joint tenant gives notice to quit.[702] Since the omission to give a notice to quit amounts to implied assent to the extension of the term for a further period (e.g., for another month or year), the notice serves to withhold the assent. The notice being merely to prevent the automatic extension of the lease, it does not amount to a dealing of the property by one joint tenant (which has no effect).[703]

335. While a periodic lease may be created by agreement, it usually arises in more informal situations. For example, if after the expiration of a fixed-term lease the tenant holds over and continues to pay, and the landlord accepts, a periodic rent, a periodic lease is created.[704] The periodic lease will inherit the terms of the earlier lease in so far as there is no inconsistency. A periodic lease may also arise in place of an invalid fixed-term lease. For example, in *Chiam Heng Luan v. Chiam Heng Hsien*, the lease purportedly created by the parties was void for uncertainty of duration.[705] However, because the tenant paid rent on either quarterly or monthly basis, a periodic lease was created.[706]

---

699. *Mellows v. Low* [1923] 1 KB 522.
700. *Hammersmith and Fulham LBC v. Monk* [1992] 1 AC 478.
701. Tang Hang Wu and Kelvin F.K. Low, *Tan Sook Yee's Principles of Singapore Land Law*, 3rd edn (LexisNexis, 2009) at 463.
702. *Hammersmith and Fulham LBC v. Monk* [1992] 1 AC 478; *Newton Housing Trust v. Alsulaimen* [1999] 1 AC 313; *Harrow LBC v. Johnstone* [1997] 1 WLR 459.
703. *See* Chapter 3 (Co-ownership).
704. This is provided that the earlier lease agreement did not explicitly set out a formal procedure for renewal of the lease. *See Kim Seng Orchid Pte Ltd v. Lim Kah Hin (trading as Yik Zhuan Orchid Garden)* [2017] SGHC 4; [2018] 3 SLR 34.
705. [2007] SGHC 132; [2007] 4 SLR(R) 305. *See also Prudential Assurance Co Ltd v. London Residuary Body* [1992] 2 AC 386.
706. [2007] SGHC 132; [2007] 4 SLR(R) 305 at [72], [74].

III. Tenancy At Will

336. Where the owner of a property lets another person into exclusive possession of his property on terms that either party may determine the tenancy at any time, a tenancy at will is created.[707] A classic situation of a tenancy at will arising is where the parties are still negotiating the terms of a formal lease but the owner allows the other party to enter into possession of the property as a gesture of goodwill.[708] As the tenancy is terminable at any time by the landlord and the tenant does not acquire any estate in the property, it is akin to a bare licence.

IV. Tenancy at Sufferance

337. Where a tenant remains in possession of the property after the lease has expired and the landlord has yet to decide whether to evict the tenant, the tenant is a tenant at sufferance. Instead of evicting the tenant, the landlord may charge him/her double rent.[709] Like a tenant at will, a tenant at sufferance does not acquire any estate in the property.

V. Reversionary Lease

338. A lease that commences only at a future date is known as a reversionary or future lease. The reversionary lease can either be a fixed-term lease or a periodic lease. Prior to the commencement of a reversionary lease, the tenant acquires a vested interest, an *interesse termini*, which gives him/her the right to take possession of the property when the lease commences.

339. Importantly, prior to taking possession, the tenant does not acquire any estate in land. In a sense, there is no lease yet. It is only when he enters into possession that his interest crystalises into an estate in the land. In *Pontiac Land Pte Ltd v. P-Zone Services Pte Ltd*, Rockingham granted to Pontiac 11 consecutive leases each separated by one day.[710] All leases were shorter than 7 years and therefore unregistrable. Later, Rockingham sold the property to ESH, who in turn sold it to PZS. PZS argued that it took the title free of Pontiac's leases. In the High Court, Lee J held that PZS's title was subject to any lease in force at the time of the transfer. The existing lease would be an overriding interest by virtue of section 46(1)(vi)

707. A tenancy at will was implicitly recognised in *Cheung Woh Metal (Pte) Ltd v. Chuan Eng Seng Trading (Pte) Ltd* [1998] SGHC 409; *Kassim Oil Mohamed v. Noordin* [1967] SGHC 8; [1965–1967] SLR(R) 597; *Midlink Development Pte Ltd v. The Stansfield Group Pte Ltd* [2004] SGHC 182; [2004] 4 SLR(R) 258 at [53] (although the example given is better understood as giving rise to a tenancy at sufferance).

708. *See Javad v. Mohammed Aqil* [1991] 1 WLR 1007.

709. CLA, section 28(4).

710. [2010] SGHC 171; [2010] 4 SLR 111.

of the LTA.[711] However, the learned judge opined that the future leases are not protected in the same way since they are not yet in force. In *Cathay Theatres Pte Ltd v. LKM Investments Holdings*, the Court of Appeal refrained from expressing its view on whether a reversionary lease is capable of supporting a caveat.[712] In principle, the tenant's *interesse termini*, being an interest relating to land, should amount to a caveatable interest.

VI. Tenancy by Estoppel

340. Where an occupier of land purports to grant a lease although he has no sufficient title to make such a grant, e.g. he has only a licence or a lease of shorter duration, a tenancy by estoppel may arise so as to preclude one or both parties from denying that a tenancy has arisen as between them.[713] The tenancy by estoppel runs with the land and binds the parties' successors in title.[714] But the tenant's interest is precarious for it is liable to be defeated by the true landowner and persons claiming under him.[715] If the landlord subsequently acquires the necessary title, however, the estoppel is fed with the title, and the tenant is regarded as having acquired a proper lease from the date of the initial grant.[716]

341. In *Methani v. Perianayagam*, the plaintiff, a licensee of a piece of land, purportedly granted the defendant a lease over the land.[717] The plaintiff later argued that because of his own lack of title the grant to the defendant could only be a licence, not a lease. The aim was to deprive the defendant of the protections afforded to a tenant by the Control of Rent Ordinance. In the High Court, Wee J held that the plaintiff was estopped from denying that a lease had arisen. Although in this case the defendant did not seek to deny the existence of the tenancy, the learned judge explained the doctrine in bilateral terms:

> The doctrine is that a tenant may not question his landlord's title and, conversely, that a landlord having by his offer of a tenancy induced a tenant to enter into (or remain in) occupation and to pay rent, cannot deny the validity of the tenancy by alleging his own want of title to create it.[718]

342. An example where the doctrine operated against a tenant is *Ritzland Investment Pte Ltd v. Grace Management & Consultancy Services Pte Ltd*.[719] In this case

711. LTA, section 46(1)(vi) refers to 'the rights of any person in occupation of the land under a tenancy when the proprietor became registered'.
712. [1998] SGCA 4; [1998] 1 SLR(R) 234 at [39] (Yong CJ, Karthigesu and Thean JJA).
713. Although the landlord's lack of title may render the lease unregistrable, section 45(3) of the LTA states that nothing prevents the unregistered instrument from operating as a contract.
714. *First National Bank Plc v. Thompson* [1996] Ch 231 at 239.
715. *Thode Gerd Walter v. Mintwell Industry Pte Ltd* [2009] SGHC 44 at [10].
716. *Universal Permanent Building Society v. Cooke* [1952] Ch 95.
717. [1961] 1 MLJ 5 (Singapore).
718. *Ibid.*
719. [2014] SGHC 62; [2014] 2 SLR 1342.

the Singapore Land Authority (SLA) granted the plaintiff a lease of a state land for 3 years with the option to renew the lease twice (the 'master lease'). In effect, the SLA was prepared to let the property to the plaintiff for 9 years in three terms. During the second term of the master lease, the plaintiff subleased parts of the land to the defendant. There were three agreements, each purporting to grant a sublease for a term of 3 years with an option to renew for a further 3 years but subject to the renewal of the master lease. The end dates of the subleases were all after the expiry of the second term of the master lease. However, the terms of the master lease were made known to the defendant and the defendant was allowed, for two of the subleases, to terminate them in the event that renewal of the master lease is refused by the SLA. The defendant duly entered into possession of the premises. However, after a year, the defendant stopped paying rent for one of the premises and later vacated the premises. The plaintiff claimed arrears in rent. The defendant resisted, claiming that the sublease was invalid. The defendant argued that the plaintiff lacked the necessary title from which the sublease could be carved since the master lease would expire during the currency of the sublease. In the High Court, Coomaraswamy J held that the plaintiff did not lack title in granting the sublease as it had every reason to expect the master lease to be renewed. However, even if the plaintiff's title was insufficient, the doctrine of tenancy by estoppel operated in the plaintiff's favour. The learned judge referred to section 118(1) of the Evidence Act,[720] which sets out part of the doctrine pertaining to estoppel of the tenant:

> No tenant of immovable property, or person claiming through such tenant, shall during the continuance of the tenancy be permitted to deny that the landlord of the tenant had at the beginning of the tenancy a title to the immovable property.

343. The obvious problem with section 118(1) is that it operates only during the continuance of the tenancy. In the present case, the sublease had ended when the dispute came to be adjudicated. Having observed a number of anomalies pertaining to section 118(1), the learned judge came to the conclusion that it does not preclude the operation of the full doctrine as recognised under the common law.[721] Thus, the defendant was estopped from denying that a contractual relationship of landlord and tenant had arisen between them.[722] The defendant was therefore liable to pay the arrears in rent.

344. The estoppel of the defendant in *Ritzland* is plainly justified. The defendant, having been informed about the terms of the master lease, had notice of the alleged lack of title.[723] Moreover, the defendant's possession of the premises was also undisturbed. As Martin B said in *Cuthbertson v. Irving*, 'so long as a lessee enjoys everything which his lease purports to grant, how does it concern him what

720. (Cap. 97, 1997 Rev. Ed.).
721. [2014] SGHC 62; [2014] 2 SLR 1342 at [88]–[91].
722. [2014] SGHC 62; [2014] 2 SLR 1342 at [71].
723. Lye Lin Heng, *Landlord and Tenant* (Butterworths, 1990) at 82: 'A tenant will only be so estopped if it is shown that at the time at which the rent was paid, he knew or had notice of, the true facts about the lessor's title'.

the title of the lessor[?]'.[724] However, what would be the position if the tenant has no notice of the landlord's lack of title? Surely it would be unfair to estop the tenant from rescinding the contract either on the ground of mistake or misrepresentation. In *Ritzland*, the learned judge acknowledged that the contract between the parties would be avoidable if the defendant could establish a vitiating factor.[725] What the learned judge did not consider, however, is whether such a claim would be inconsistent with section 118(1), which states the doctrine in unqualified terms.

345. What, then, is the nature of a tenancy by estoppel? In *Bruton v. London & Quadrant Housing Trust*, Lord Hoffmann explained that a tenancy (or lease) is the sheer product of contract and, in itself, does not necessarily imply any conferment of estate in land.[726] Whether the contract has the effect of granting a leasehold estate depends on whether the landlord has the necessary title to support such a grant. In a case where the tenancy is purely contractual, neither party can deny the existence of the landlord–tenant relationship on the ground that the landlord has no title. Thus, it is the not the estoppel which creates the tenancy, but the tenancy which creates the estoppel. As the learned judge in *Ritzland* observed, 'this view does away with a tenancy by estoppel altogether since there will on this view always be an actual tenancy arising from the contract between the parties whether or not the contract is capable of giving rise simultaneously to a proprietary interest'.[727] Having recognised the potential difficulties with this view, the learned judge preferred to express no opinion on whether it should form part of Singapore law.[728] This cautious attitude is plainly justified. While a lease has its origin in contract, it has, through centuries of evolution, acquired a significant proprietary dimension. Importantly, it is this proprietary dimension that distinguishes a lease from a licence.[729]

VII. Tenancy Coupled with an Equity

346. Suppose *L* grants *T* a monthly lease. During the subsistence of the lease, *L* represents to *T* that the latter may occupy the land for a longer period, e.g. as long as *T* wishes. In reliance of *L*'s representation, *T* expends considerable money for the improvement and maintenance of the land. If *L* tries to evict *T* by giving a notice to quit, it is likely that *T* would succeed in a claim for proprietary estoppel.[730] The court has a wide discretion as to what remedy to award. Although rare, a possible remedy is the imposition of a lease, thus allowing *T* to continue occupying the land.

724. (1859) 4 H & N 742 at 758.
725. [2014] SGHC 62; [2014] 2 SLR 1342 at [63]–[64].
726. [2000] 1 AC 406 at 415–16.
727. [2014] SGHC 62; [2014] 2 SLR 1342 at [70].
728. For criticisms of the view in *Bruton*, see e.g., Martin Dixon, 'The Non-Proprietary Lease: The Rise of the Feudal Phoenix' (2000) 59 CLJ 25; Susan Bright, Leases, Exclusive Possession and Estates' (2000) 116 LQR 7.
729. *See e.g., Street v. Mountford* [1985] AC 809 at 816.
730. *See generally* Tang Hang Wu and Kelvin F.K. Low, *Tan Sook Yee's Principles of Singapore Land Law*, 3rd edn (LexisNexis, 2009) Chapter 7.

This is sometimes referred to as a tenancy coupled with an equity.[731] The duration of the tenancy necessarily depends on the nature of the representation and the extent of *T*'s detriment. In *Chiam Heng Luan v. Chiam Heng Hsien* there was a clear intention that the tenant was entitled to occupy the property for as long as it carried on the hotel business.[732] In reliance of this expectation the tenant had been paying the property tax and maintaining the premises for the past 50 years. Prakash J held that this gave rise to an equity which 'operated to prevent the owners from demanding the return of the Property as long as the Hotel was operating'.[733] This was notwithstanding the separate finding of a periodic lease, which was terminable by a notice to quit. However, when the dispute was brought before the court, the tenant was no longer operating the hotel. Thus, the landlord was no longer estopped from recovering possession of the property.

§3. Hallmarks of a Lease

I. Certainty of Duration

347. Section 87(2)(b) of the LTA allows the Registrar to deny registration of a lease if its date of commencement and maximum duration are uncertain. This replicates the common law rule that a lease must be certain in its duration. In *Lace v. Chantler*, Lord Greene MR said: 'A term created by a leasehold tenancy agreement must be expressed either with certainty and specifically or by reference to something which can, at the time when the lease takes effect, be looked to as a certain ascertainment of what the term is meant to be'.[734] This was subsequently affirmed by the House of Lords in *Prudential Assurance Co Ltd v. London Residuary Body*.[735]

348. In Singapore, the certainty of duration rule has not been consistently applied. In *Tan Swee Eng v. Assoland Pte Ltd*, Thean J held that an agreement to let a property until such time the landlord required the property for redevelopment gave rise to a lease.[736] However, in *Chiam Heng Luan v. Chiam Heng Hsien*, Prakash J applied *Prudential* to hold that a lease purporting to last as long as the tenant carried on a hotel business on the property was invalid.[737]

731. *Lim Hock Kim v. Sim Seng Quee* [1980] SGHC 11; [1979–1980] SLR(R) 494; *Khew Ah Bah v. Hong Ah Mye* [1971] SGHC 8; [1971–1973] SLR(R) 107.
732. [2007] SGHC 132; [2007] 4 SLR(R) 305.
733. [2007] SGHC 132; [2007] 4 SLR(R) 305 at [89]. *Cf Khew Ah Bah v. Hong Ah Mye* [1971] SGHC 8; [1971–1973] SLR(R) 107, where Singh J decided to award compensation instead of imposing a tenancy coupled with an equity. In this case the tenant of a monthly lease had been occupying the land for 34 years, during which he had rebuilt the house he was staying in.
734. [1944] KB 368 at 370.
735. [1992] 2 AC 386 at 394.
736. [1987] SGHC 10; [1987] SLR(R) 204.
737. [2007] SGHC 132; [2007] 4 SLR(R) 305 at [72]–[74].

349. The status of *Prudential* in Singapore remains uncertain following the recent decision of the Court of Appeal in *Y.E.S. F&B Group Pte Ltd v. Soup Restaurant Singapore Pte Ltd.*[738] The plaintiff, who was granted a three-year lease in a shop unit, subleased part of it to the defendant. Clause 4 of the sublease agreement provided: 'This agreement shall survive as long as the [plaintiff's] lease with the Landlord is not terminated'. When the head lease ended, the plaintiff immediately entered into a new lease agreement with the landlord on materially different terms. The plaintiff then sought to recover possession of the premises on the ground that the sublease ended with the head lease. The defendant resisted, arguing that the effect of clause 4 was that the sublease would persist so long as the plaintiff had a lease in that shop unit. The Court of Appeal held in the defendant's favour but made no mention of the certainty of duration rule.

350. To be sure, the certainty of duration rule is not free from criticisms. In *Prudential*, Lord Browne-Wilkinson said: 'No one has produced any satisfactory rationale for the genesis of this rule. No one has been able to point to any useful purpose that it serves at the present day'.[739] In light of the existing uncertainty, the Court of Appeal is invited to clarify the status of the certainty of duration rule at the next available opportunity.

351. Assuming that the certainty of duration requirement is here to stay, a few things could be said about its application to fixed-term leases. First, it is not necessary to state the beginning and end of a lease by reference to calendar dates. If an event is bound to occur at a known date, reference to that event should be sufficient. For example, a lease that begins today and ends on the coming Christmas is sufficiently certain in duration.

352. Second, the parties may agree to include an early termination clause. Provided that the maximum duration of the lease is fixed, it matters not that the time at which the early termination clause could be exercised is not be precisely determined. For example, it is not uncommon for residential leases to contain a diplomatic clause allowing the tenant to terminate the lease if he is unable to remain in Singapore.[740] Similarly, the lease in *Chiam Heng Luan* could be saved by redrafting it to read: the lease is for 99 years, subject to the landlord's right to terminate the lease if the tenant ceases to conduct business on the property prior to the expiry of 99 years.[741]

353. On its face, a periodic lease appears to offend the certainty of duration requirement. A monthly tenancy, for example, may last indefinitely so long as neither party gives a notice to quit. However, recall that in *Prudential* the House of

738. [2015] SGCA 55; [2015] 5 SLR 1187 (Menon CJ, Chao and Phang JJA).
739. [1992] 2 AC 386 at 396.
740. *See e.g. Malayan Credits Properties (Pte) Ltd v. Betz Pte Ltd* [1986] SGHC 4; [1985–1986] SLR(R) 518; *Chen Con-Ling Tony v. Quay Properties Pte Ltd* [2004] SGHC 31; [2004] 2 SLR(R) 181.
741. *Prudential Assurance Co Ltd v. London Residuary Body* [1992] 2 AC 386 at 389–90, 395.

Lords held that the certainty of duration requirement equally applies to periodic leases. There Lord Templeman explained:

> A tenancy from year to year is saved from being uncertain because each party has power by notice to determine at the end of any year. The term continues until determined as if both parties made a new agreement at the end of each year for a new term for the ensuing year. A power for nobody to determine or for one party only to be able to determine is inconsistent with the concept of a term from year to year.[742]

354. However, it is possible to place restrictions on either party's right to terminate the lease so long as the restriction does not result in uncertainty. A yearly lease that neither party can terminate within the first 5 years is certain.[743] A monthly lease that neither party can terminate until the rental market improves is uncertain. To be sure, the restriction on termination may be imposed on one or both parties. In the latter case the restrictions need not be the same for both parties. It is sufficient that both restrictions do not result in uncertainty.

II. Exclusive Possession

355. Where a person is allowed to be in possession of a property, he may either be a tenant or a licensee. Whether a lease or a licence has been created necessarily depends on the intention of the parties. It is clear from the authorities that the courts place little weight on the parties' description of the grant, emphasising instead on inferring the true state of affairs from all the relevant circumstances.[744] The enjoyment of exclusive possession by the occupant is obviously an important consideration, for a lease necessarily entails the granting of exclusive possession. This is hinted in section 87(2)(c) of the LTA, which allows the Registrar to deny registration of a lease if it does not purport to grant the tenant exclusive possession. However, the inquiry is complicated by the fact the granting of exclusive possession does not necessarily create a lease. There may be circumstances which negative an intention to create a tenancy despite the granting of exclusive possession.[745] If the occupier pays rent, it is likely that a contractual licence has been created.[746] It is also

742. [1992] 2 AC 386 at 394.
743. [1992] 2 AC 386 at 395.
744. *Abdul Rahim v. British & Malayan Trustees Ltd* [1966] SGFC 8; [1965–1967] SLR(R) 390 at [7] (Wee CJ, Tan and Chua JJ); *Re Tan Tye* [1966] SGFC 4; [1965–1967] SLR(R) 226 at [14] (Tan FJ, Chua and Winslow JJ); *Goh Gin Chye v. Peck Teck Kian Realty Pte Ltd* [1987] SGCA 9; [1987] SLR(R) 195 at [14] (Kulasekaram J, Chua and Rajah J). The same approach is adopted when interpreting the terms of a lease: *Per Ah Seng Robin v. Housing and Development Board* [2014] SGHC 70; [2015] 2 SLR(R) 19 at [64]. For the leading English authority, see *Street v. Mountford* [1985] 1 AC 809.
745. *Goh Gin Chye v. Peck Teck Kian Realty Pte Ltd* [1987] SGCA 9; [1987] SLR(R) 195 at [15]; *Re Tan Tye* [1966] SGFC 4; [1965–1967] SLR(R) 226 at [13].
746. *See e.g. Daly v. Edwardes* (1900) 83 LT 548; *Clore v. Theatrical Properties Ltd and Westby & Co Ltd* [1936] 3 All ER 483. *See also Mehta v. Royal Bank of Scotland* [1999] L & TR 340.

possible for exclusive possession to be granted out of sympathy or generosity, in which case the reasonable inference is that the landowner had no intention to create a legal relationship.[747]

356. Where the landlord retains significant control over the property, the likely inference is that no lease is created. This is illustrated in several cases. In *Abdul Rahim v. British & Malayan Trustees Ltd*, the plaintiff granted to the defendant a 'monthly tenancy' in respect of a space in the common passageway of a building, described as 'second pillar on the right-hand side of the Arcade from the entrance from Raffles Place, six feet high, four feet wide and eight inches depth'. In the High Court, Winslow J held that the agreement did not create a tenancy because the plaintiff retained sufficient control of the passageway.[748] A watchman was employed to guard the place and the defendant was allowed to use the designated space only during the hours when the gates were kept. In these circumstances, it cannot be said that the defendant had been granted exclusive possession of the said space. The Federal Court agreed.[749]

357. In *Runme Shaw v. Habibulah*, the landlord sought to repossess the property on the ground that the tenant had sublet the property and received rent exceeding the amount permitted by the Control of Rent Ordinance.[750] The property consisted of a shop, a bedroom and a kitchen. The tenant allowed two tradesmen to use parts of the shop to conduct their businesses in return for payment of monthly fees. The tenant lived in the property and would allow the tradesmen into the shop only from 8 am to 8 pm on the first six days of the week and from 8 am to 1 pm on Sunday. At night the property was locked and the tradesmen had no access. Based on these facts Thorogood J held that the tenant did not intend to give exclusive possession of any part of the property to the tradesmen. The tenant merely granted them licences, which fell outside the purview of the Control of Rent Ordinance.

358. In *Ng Heng Keang v. Kim Poh Eng*, the defendant allowed the four plaintiffs to set up food stalls in his coffee shop in consideration of monthly payments.[751] The plaintiffs were not allowed to sleep in the premises and were not given the keys in the beginning. Instead, they would arrive before dawn and wake up the manager to open the door. It was only many years later that the assistant manager of the premises handed a duplicate key to one of the plaintiffs. This was a private arrangement between them because the assistant manager was unwell. In these circumstances, Chua J held that the landlord merely granted licenses to the plaintiffs.

359. Even if the landlord is not in physical control of the property, an agreement conferring on the landlord extensive rights to supervisory control would usually

747. *See e.g. Marcroft Wagons Ltd v. Smith* [1951] 2 KB 496.
748. [1966] SGHC 6; [1965–1967] SLR(R) 234.
749. [1966] SGFC 8; [1965–1967] SLR(R) 390.
750. [1950] MLJ 111 (Singapore).
751. [1976] SGHC 11; [1974–1976] SLR(R) 836.

point to the creation of a licence. In *Re Tan Tye* the trustee granted to one Mr Goh a licence over a trust property.[752] The beneficiaries, however, contended that the trustee had in fact granted a lease, which he had no power to. The property concerned was an amusement park. Pursuant to the agreement between the trustee (licensor) and Mr Goh (licensee), the latter was allowed to collect admission fees to the park and licence fees from the other occupiers of the park. However, the agreement also provided, *inter alia*, that the licensee shall (i) observe and conform to all the rules and regulations from time to time made by the licensor for the management of the amusement park; (ii) permanently reserve a table in the office of the amusement park for use by the licensor or his agents; and (iii) discharge any servant of the licensee who shall be guilty of any conduct considered by the licensor to be prejudicial to the proper management of the park. The Federal Court held that these major restrictions showed that control and supervision of the property remained with the trustee, which in turn meant that the third party was not intended to have exclusive possession. The agreement created not a lease, but a licence.

360. Where it is the occupier who exercises control of the property, it is more likely that a lease has been created. In *Goh Suat Neo v. W Roberts & Ors*, the tenant sublet rooms in the property to several persons.[753] Although the tenant reserved a room for himself, the occupants had exclusive control of their own rooms, which they secured using their own locks. They had unrestricted access to their rooms through the back door, passages and stairs. When the landlord sought to recover possession of the property, the occupants claimed to be subtenants protected under the Control of Rent Ordinance 1947. Evans J held that the occupants were subtenants and not mere lodgers because they had exclusive control over their rooms. The learned judge was of the view that if the arrangements were such that the tenant was to retain control of the property, he would have objected to the use of private locks by the occupants. The fact that he did not object was strong evidence that he had given up control of the property to the occupants.

361. In *Goh Gin Chye v. Peck Teck Kian Realty Pte Ltd*,[754] the landlord sought recovery of the property on the ground that the tenant had sublet the property at the monthly rental in excess of 110% of the reasonable rent of $26 per month, thus in breach of section 15(1)(g) of the Control of Rent Act.[755] The tenant argued that although there was initially a sublease it was soon converted into a licence, which falls outside the ambit of the statute. There were seven consecutive agreements between the tenant and the subtenant made in 1961, 1964, 1967, 1970, 1973, 1975 and 1977. Although the first two agreements were described as tenancy agreements, the subsequent agreements were explicitly referred to the grant of licences. The other terms of the agreements were substantially the same. Importantly, despite the change in the form of the agreements, the subtenant had all along enjoyed exclusive

752. [1966] SGFC 4; [1965–1967] SLR(R) 226.
753. [1950] MLJ 285 (Singapore).
754. [1987] SGCA 9; [1987] SLR(R) 195.
755. (Cap. 58, 1985 Rev. Ed.).

possession of the property and had carried on his food business as usual. The Court of Appeal held that all seven agreements created subleases, not licences.

362. Although the cases do not explicitly say so, they hint at an obvious reason why the courts were sceptical of the label used by the parties. A landlord may disguise a lease as a licence to avoid the application of the Control of Rent Act, which imposed restrictions on the rent chargeable and the right to repossess the premises. Although the Rent Control Act had been abolished,[756] the CLPA continues to protect tenants by imposing limitations on a landlord's right to forfeit a lease.[757] However, there is no evidence of these limitations being significant enough to cause a landlord to avoid describing a grant as a lease.[758]

363. Given this change in circumstances, it is submitted that the focus should be on whether a *right* of exclusive possession was granted, not whether exclusive possession was actually enjoyed. Where there is no hint of pretense or scam, the description of the grant should be conclusive of what it is. This approach promotes certainty since the relationship of the parties is determined once and for all at the very outset. For example, a landlord may have his reasons for wanting to grant only a licence. If this intention is made clear to the licensee, the mere fact that the landlord does not exercise physical or supervisory control over the property should not turn the licence into a lease. Likewise, if the parties clearly intended to create a lease, the mere fact that the landlord exercises some physical or supervisory control over the tenant's enjoyment of property should not turn it into a licence. Suppose a landlord demands to inspect the property more frequently than what was permitted under the lease agreement. The tenant may yield to the demand out of courtesy. This should not turn the lease into a licence. The tenant should not be deprived of his right to exclude the landlord if the latter's frequent visits becomes overly intrusive.

III. Rent

364. Because a lease has its origin in contract, the tenant must provide consideration in exchange for being given exclusive possession of the property. While this is usually in the form of periodic rent, it could also be in other forms. For a fixed long-term lease, the tenant may make a lump sump payment as though he is purchasing the property. Another example is in the case of a sale and leaseback agreement under which *S* agrees to sell his property to *P* subject to *P* agreeing to lease back the property to *S*. Instead of *S* paying rent periodically, it may be agreed that the purchase price would be reduced to take into account what *S* would have had to pay for rent.[759]

756. Control of Rent (Abolition) Act 2001 (No.14 of 2001).
757. CLPA, sections 18 and 18A. *See* §9.VI.C., D. & F. below.
758. Following the abolishment of the Control of Rent Act, there has been no reported cases where parties disagree on whether the grant created a lease or a licence.
759. *See e.g. Pontiac Land Pte Ltd v. P-Zone Services Pte Ltd* [2010] SGHC 171; [2010] 4 SLR 111, although the agreement also provided for the payment of peppercorn rent of $1 per annum.

§4. Creation of Leases

365. A contract for a lease arises upon the parties agreeing on the four basic ingredients: (i) the parties; (ii) the property; (iii) the date of commencement and duration; and (iv) the rent payable.[760]

366. Leases exceeding 7 years[761] must be in the prescribed form and registered.[762] In calculating the duration of the lease, an option to renew the lease shall be taken into consideration.[763] Thus, a lease of 5 years with an option to renew for a further 5 years is to be regarded as a lease for 10 years. Where the maximum duration of the lease exceeds 7 years, it is irrelevant that the lease is terminable at an earlier time.[764] Thus, a periodic lease is registrable if the maximum duration is specified to be more than 7 years. For example, a monthly lease that shall expire at the end of the 10th year if neither party gives a notice to quit is registrable. Registration confers on the tenant an indefeasible title that is reflected in the land register.[765]

367. It is possible to grant a lease over 7 years without using the mechanism provided by the LTA.[766] In *Golden Village Multiplex Pte Ltd v. Marina Centre Holdings Pte Ltd* the Court of Appeal answered in the affirmative.[767] In this case Marina Centre agreed to grant to Golden Village a lease over parts of a building for a term of 15 years. As Marina Centre was not prepared to obtain subdivision of the building, the lease was not in a form prescribed by the LTA and therefore unregistrable. The lease agreement contained a term precluding Golden Village from demanding a registrable lease. Aside from being unregistrable, the lease was also void at law. Being a lease over 7 years, it should have been made by deed but it wasn't.[768] However, the Court of Appeal held that Golden Village acquired an equitable lease by virtue of the doctrine of *Walsh v. Lonsdale*.[769] Under the doctrine, an equitable lease

760. *Ritzland Investment Pte Ltd v. Grace Management & Consultancy Services Pte Ltd* [2014] SGHC 62; [2014] 2 SLR 1342 at [28]; *Asirham Investment Pte Ltd v. JSI Shipping (S) Pte Ltd* [2007] SGHC 171; [2008] 1 SLR(R) 117 at [10]; *Maresse Collections Inc v. Trademart Singapore Pte Ltd* [1999] SGHC 123 at [20]; *Klerk-Elias Liza v. K T Chan Clinic Pte Ltd* [1993] SGCA 28; [1993] 1 SLR(R) 609.
761. The lease must purport to run continuously for more than 7 years. *See Pontiac Land Pte Ltd v. P-Zone Services Pte Ltd* [2010] SGHC 171; [2010] 4 SLR 111.
762. LTA, section 87; Form 38.
763. *Ibid.*, section 87(3)(a).
764. *Ibid.*, section 87(3)(b).
765. *See* Chapter 4 (Torrens System).
766. In *United Malayan Banking Corp v. Goodhope Realty* [1989] SGHC 14; [1989] 1 SLR(R) 151 at [1], Thean J expressed surprise that the lease was not in registrable form but proceeded on the assumption that it was valid.
767. [2002] SGCA 6; [2002] 1 SLR(R) 169 (Yong CJ, Thean and Chao JJA), noted in Tan Sook Yee, 'Equitable Leases, Subdivision and Section 4, Planning Act' (2002) 14 SAcLJ 133; Kelvin F.K. Low and Tan Sook Yee, 'Equity and Trust' (2002) 3 SAL Ann Rev 202 at 202–204. *See also* Tang Hang Wu and Kelvin F.K. Low, *Tan Sook Yee's Principles of Singapore Land Law*, 3rd edn (LexisNexis, 2009) at 474–76.
768. CLPA, section 53.
769. (1882) 21 Ch D 9. *See also Parker v. Taswell* (1858) 2 De G & J 560.

arises where the contract is specifically enforceable. The Court of Appeal extended the doctrine by holding that even if specific performance was not possible, the court could enforce the agreement by ordering an injunction. *Golden Village* was recently applied in *Power Knight Pte Ltd v. Natural Fuel Pte Ltd.*[770] However, where neither specific performance nor injunction could be ordered, e.g. because the claim was against the Government,[771] the doctrine of *Walsh v. Lonsdale* does not apply.[772]

368. Leases not exceeding 7 years (short leases) are created by agreement alone. An agreement to grant a lease, being a contract for the disposition of an interest in land, must be evidenced in writing to be enforceable.[773] However, even if the formality requirements are not complied with, the doctrine of part performance could apply to make it enforceable.[774]

369. Although short leases are not registered, it is incorrect to refer to them as equitable leases. Short leases are automatically binding as overriding interests.[775] The reason for excluding them from registration is to avoid clogging the land register.

§5. Dealings with Leases

I. Assignment

370. A tenant may assign (i.e., transfer) the lease to someone else.[776] For example, *L* grants to *T1* a five-year lease. If *T1* assigns the lease to *T2*, *T2* will step into the shoes of *T1*. There will be a relationship of landlord and tenant between *L* and *T2*. In the case of a registered lease, the approved form for transfer must be used and registered.[777] For unregistered leases, presumably the assignment must be by deed.[778]

371. The landlord's interest in recovering possession of the property at the expiry of the lease is known as the reversion. The landlord may assign the reversion

---

770. [2010] SGHC 75; [2010] 3 SLR 82. *See also Ong Beng Chong v. Jayaram Victoria* [2009] SGHC 66 (although this case was decided on the basis of proprietary estoppel).
771. Government Proceedings Act (Cap. 121, 1985 Rev. Ed.), section 27.
772. *Koh Ah Kow v. Public Prosecutor* [1995] SGCA 47; [1995] 2 SLR(R) 162 at [21].
773. CLA, section 6(d). *See SM Integrated Transware Pte Ltd v. Schenker Singapore (Pte) Ltd* [2005] SGHC 58; [2005] 2 SLR(R) 651; *Maresse Collections Inc v. Trademart Singapore Pte Ltd* [1999] SGHC 123 at [20]; *Tiananmen KTV (2013) Pte Ltd and others v. Furama Pte Ltd* [2015] SGHC 83; [2015] 3 SLR 433 at [32]–[38]. For more in-depth discussion, see Part III (Acquisition of Property Rights) Chapter 1 (Contract for the Sale of Land) §2.I.
774. *Midlink Development Pte Ltd v. The Stansfield Group Pte Ltd* [2004] SGHC 182; [2004] 4 SLR(R) 258 at [66]–[67]. *See also* Part III (Acquisition of Property Rights) Chapter 1 (Contract for the Sale of Land) §2.III.
775. LTA, section 46(1)(vi).
776. The formality requirements prescribed by section 6(d) of the CLA applies, subject to exceptions: *Hu Lee Impex Pte Ltd v. Lim Aik Seng* [2013] SGHC 142; [2013] 4 SLR 176.
777. LTA, section 63; Form 19.
778. CLPA, section 53.

to someone else.[779] Where he assigns his entire interest of reversion, this amounts to a transfer and the approved form must be used and registered.[780] Where the assignment is only for a limited duration (i.e., partial assignment), it is known as a lease of the reversion. During the continuance of the lease of the reversion, the grantee steps into the shoes of the landlord. For example, *L* grants *T* a 10-year lease. *L* also grants *R* a five-year lease of the reversion. Let us assume that both leases commence at the same time. During the first 5 years, *R* will be *T*'s landlord. When the lease of the reversion expires, *L* will regain his status as *T*'s landlord. As there appears to be no approved form for granting a lease of reversion under the LTA, presumably it must be made by deed.[781]

II. Sublease

372. A tenant may sublease (or sublet) the property to someone else. Unlike an assignment, a sublease does not amount to a transfer. Even during the duration of the sublease, the sublessor remains a tenant under the main lease. For example, *L* grants a five-year lease to *T*. *T* then sublets the property to *ST* for three years. The first lease is known as a head lease while the second lease is known as a sublease (or subtenancy). During the continuance of the sublease, *T* is the landlord of *ST*. At the same time, however, *T* is a tenant of *L* under the head lease. There is no relationship between *L* and *ST*. In the case of a sublease exceeding 7 years, the approved form must be used and registered.[782]

373. Because a sublease is essentially an estate carved out of another estate, the head lease must be of longer duration. Thus, from a head lease of 10 years one may carve out a sublease of 9 years and 11 months. However, where the tenant is given an option to renew the head lease, the maximum duration is to be taken into account provided that there is no reason to disbelief that the option could not be exercised.[783]

374. A periodic lease, on the other hand, raises some difficult issues. In theory, a periodic lease is capable of lasting indefinitely. Thus, it has been suggested that a tenant of a periodic lease may sublease for any fixed term or for a periodic lease of similar periods.[784] In *Teo Chwee Geok v. Ng Hui Lip & Co*, the Federal Court did not take issue with a monthly sublease granted by a tenant who had a monthly lease.[785] In practice, however, a tenant is unlikely to grant a sublease that could *potentially* outlast the head lease. If the landlord gives a notice to quit and proceeds

779. *See Raffles Hotel Ltd v. Malayan Banking Ltd (No 2)* [1965] MLJ 262 (Singapore).

780. LTA, section 63; Form 19.

781. CLPA, section 53.

782. LTA, section 87; Form 38.

783. *See Ritzland Investment Pte Ltd v. Grace Management & Consultancy Services Pte Ltd* [2014] SGHC 62; [2014] 2 SLR 1342 (see §2.VI. above).

784. Tang Hang Wu and Kelvin F.K. Low, *Tan Sook Yee's Principles of Singapore Land Law*, 3rd edn (LexisNexis, 2009) at 479.

785. [1967] SGFC 4; [1965–1967] SLR(R) 500.

to recover the property, the tenant will be in breach of contract towards the subtenant. A simple solution is to include a clause in the sublease allowing for early termination in the event that the landlord gives the tenant a notice to quit.

375. If a tenant purports to grant a sublease for a term equal to or exceeding the remaining duration of the head lease, the tenant is deemed to be assigning his lease.[786]

§6. Rights and Obligations of Landlords and Tenants

I. Express Terms

376. Most professionally drafted leases set out comprehensively the rights and obligations of the landlord and tenant. Some terms are meant to avoid unnecessary disputes. For example, responsibility for repair is usually apportioned between the landlord and the tenant based on the cost of the repair. Also common are terms for the convenience of one or both party. For example, the tenant may be allowed to terminate the lease early if certain conditions are satisfied or may be given an option to renew the lease upon its expiry.

377. Most formal leases will expressly include a term prohibiting the tenant from assigning, subletting or parting possession with the property. The prohibition is usually absolute in residential leases since the landlord must have taken into account the identity of the tenant before letting out the property. In the case of commercial leases, the prohibition is usually qualified; assignment, subletting or parting possession is allowed if the landlord gives his consent. In such a case it would be beneficial to the tenant to negotiate for the inclusion of a term that the landlord shall not unreasonably withhold such consent.[787] Where a tenant assigns or sublets the property in breach of the covenant, the assignment or sublease is nonetheless valid[788] but is subject to forfeiture by the landlord.[789] If the landlord, having knowledge of the breach, accepts rent from the assignee of the lease or the subtenant, he must be taken to have waived the right of forfeiture.[790] The waiver, however, applies only to the particular breach and does not amount to a general waiver for all future breaches.[791]

786. Kevin Gray and Susan Francis Gray, *Elements of Land Law*, 5th edn (OUP, 2009) at 371.
787. *See e.g. Raffles Hotel Ltd v. Rayner* [1965] MLJ 60 (Singapore); *Raffles Hotel Ltd v. Malayan Banking Ltd (No 2)* [1965] MLJ 262 (Singapore).
788. *Jubilee Electronics Pte Ltd v. Tai Wah Garments and Knitting Factory Pte Ltd* [1996] SGCA 8; [1996] 1 SLR(R) 352 at [32], [36]. *Cf Nagappan v. Chen Chi Ya* [1949] MLJ 271 (Singapore).
789. *Jubilee Electronics Pte Ltd v. Tai Wah Garments and Knitting Factory Pte Ltd* [1996] SGCA 8; [1996] 1 SLR(R) 352 at [36]. *Koh Lan Eng v. Tee Choon Yong* [1968–1970] SLR(R) 575.
790. *Hong Cheok Lam v. Ong Sing Mai* [1951] MLJ 34 (Singapore).
791. CLPA, section 15(1).

II. Implied Covenants

378. Where the parties agree on the most basic terms of a lease and nothing more, additional terms will be implied. The two most important covenants that the landlord impliedly undertakes are the covenants for quiet enjoyment and of non-derogation of grant. Both covenants aim to protect the tenant's enjoyment of the tenanted property against substantial interference by the landlord and persons claiming under him.[792]

379. The covenant for quiet enjoyment applies whether or not the tenanted property is let for a special purpose. In *Lim Kau Tee v. Lee Kay Li*, Lai J said:

> The covenant for quiet enjoyment operates to secure the lessee not merely in the possession, but also in the employment of the premises for all usual purposes; and where the ordinary and lawful enjoyment of the demised premises is substantially interfered with by the acts or omission of the lessor or those lawfully claiming under him, the covenant is broken.[793]

380. Whether the landlord's conduct is sufficiently intrusive to interfere with the tenant's quiet enjoyment is necessarily a question of fact. Minor conducts may collectively amount to substantial interference even if they do not by themselves have that effect.[794]

381. On the other hand, the covenant of no derogation from grant applies where the landlord knows that the property was to be used for a special purpose. In this case the landlord impliedly covenants to abstain from doing anything that will substantially interfere with the carrying out of that purpose.

382. The question of whether there is a substantial interference for the purposes of both covenants is necessarily a question of fact. However, it is helpful to bear a few points in mind.[795] First, the covenant of non-derogation from grant does not amount to an implied obligation on the landlord's part to underwrite the profitability of the tenant's business. Second, the landlord is not obliged to take extraordinary precautions to protect the tenant's use of the property unless specifically bargained for in the lease. Third, the landlord's interference could be physical or non-physical. Fourth, the tenant takes the property subject to the existing use of the adjoining or surrounding premises.

383. In *Cold Storage Singapore (1983) Pte Ltd v. Management Corporation of Chancery Court*, Cold Storage was a tenant in a housing estate known as Chancery Court. A dispute arose when in 1989 the management corporation of Chancery

792. *Overseas Union Enterprise Ltd v. Three Sixty Degree Pte Ltd* [2013] SGHC 71; [2013] 3 SLR 1 at [55]–[57] (Coomaraswamy J).
793. [2005] SGHC 162 at [48].
794. *See e.g. iHub Solutions Pte Ltd v. Freight Links Express Logisticentre Pte Ltd* [2017] SGHC 6.
795. *Overseas Union Enterprise Ltd v. Three Sixty Degree Pte Ltd* [2013] SGHC 71; [2013] 3 SLR 1 at [60]–[75].

Court introduced a parking scheme under which all non-resident motorists were to pay $1 at entry. The purpose of the scheme was to reduce the surface wear and tear of the roads in Chancery Court by deterring motorists who use them as a thoroughfare. Cold Storage protested, arguing that the premises were let to them for the purpose of operating a supermarket and thus the scheme, having adversely affected its business, amounted to derogation from the grant of the lease. In the High Court, Chan J phrased the question as whether Cold Storage, by virtue of being a tenant operating a supermarket, could claim that their customers were entitled to free entry into the Chancery Court.[796] The learned judge held that a term to this effect should not be implied because it was neither necessary nor reasonable in preserving the operation of the supermarket. The scheme only affected customers who wished to park their vehicles in Chancery Court. Even so they had unrestricted access to the supermarket. Although the interference caused the business to be less profitable, it did not amount to a derogation of a grant, especially considering the legitimate purpose of the parking scheme. The Court of Appeal agreed.[797]

384. In *Overseas Union Enterprise Ltd v. Three Sixty Degree Pte Ltd*, OUE leased to Three Sixty the 39th floor of the Orchard Wing of the Mandarin Orchard Singapore hotel.[798] Three Sixty intended to operate a bar on the 39th floor. However, as the public passenger lift stops at the 38th floor (of which OUE retained control), the public gains excess to the 39th floor via a staircase from the 38th floor. As the staircase is an open structure, air circulates freely between the two floors. The Singapore Civil Defence Force (SCDF) thus regarded the two floors as a single compartment for the purposes of fire safety. The SCDF granted Three Sixty a fire safety certificate but subject to a condition that the combined occupancy load for both floors shall not exceed 120 persons. This condition was difficult to comply since Three Sixty had no control over how many people OUE would let in on the 38th floor. OUE proposed, based on the floor area of both premises, that the occupancy load be apportioned 90–30 between the 38th and 39th floors. Three Sixty disagreed and sued OUE for breach of the covenants of quiet enjoyment and non-derogation of grant on many grounds. Coomaraswamy J held in OUE's favour. When Three Sixty requested for assistance, OUE rendered assistance to the best of its ability. Even if it was true, as Three Sixty alleged, that OUE failed to provide sufficient assistance, there was no evidence that this had caused the SCDF to grant a lower occupancy load. The proposed apportionment of occupancy load was also a fair one.

385. Where the property is let furnished for short-term dwelling, i.e. not sold as an estate,[799] the landlord also covenants to ensure that it is fit for human habitation.[800] There is no implied covenant on the landlord's part to keep the property in

796. [1989] SGHC 71; [1989] 2 SLR(R) 180.
797. [1991] SGCA 49; [1991] 2 SLR(R) 992 (Yong CJ, Sinnathuray and Thean JJ).
798. [2013] SGHC 71; [2013] 3 SLR 1.
799. Where the property is sold as an estate, all risks pass to the purchaser.
800. *Smith v. Marrable* (1843) 11 M & W 5; *Hart v. Windsor* (1843) 12 M & W 68. In both cases the premises were infested with insects.

repair.[801] However, where a building is let to different persons, it is fair to imply that the landlord covenants to keep the common access paths, including lifts and staircases, in a reasonable state of repair.[802]

386. The tenant, on the other hand, impliedly covenants to pay rent, to occupy the property in a tenant-like manner[803] and not to commit voluntary waste (i.e., damage or destroy the property).[804] The tenant must also allow the landlord, if the obligation to repair lies with him, to enter the premises and carry out repairs if necessary.[805] In the case of a registered lease,[806] section 93(1)(a)–(c) of the LTA implies in favour of the landlord the power to enter the premises for inspection and repair.[807] In so far as a state lease is concerned, certain covenants are implied by section 6 of the State Lands Act (SLA).[808]

§7. Enforceability of Covenants

I. Original Landlord and Tenant

387. The original landlord (*L*) and tenant (*T*) are parties to the lease agreement.[809] It follows that they are bound by all the terms set out in the lease agreement. Even after their respective interests are assigned to third parties, *L* and *T* continue to be bound by the lease agreement. Suppose *T* assigns the lease to *T2*. *T2* breaches a covenant set out in the lease agreement. *L* may sue *T*. If the covenant also binds *T2*, *T* and *T2* are jointly and severally liable.[810] Thus, if *L* suffers a loss as a result of *T2*'s breach, *L* may sue either *T* or *T2*, or both, for compensation subject to the prohibition against double recovery. To protect himself/herself, *T* could specifically state in the assignment agreement that *T2* takes the lease subject to the same terms in the lease agreement. Thus, if *T* becomes liable to pay *L* for a breach committed by *T2*, *T* could in turn sue *T2* for indemnification.

388. If *L* commits a breach of the lease agreement, *T* could sue *L* but only in respect of covenants specifically for the benefit of *T*. On the other hand, for a breach that affects the property, the proper claimant is *T2*. Although, in theory, *T* could sue *L* for the breach, it would be difficult for *T* to show that he has suffered a loss since he no longer has any interest in the property.

---

801. *See Sim Khoon Seng v. Thio Eeng Theng* [1965] SGHC 4; [1965–1967] SLR(R) 32.
802. *Liverpool City Council v. Irwin* [1977] AC 239.
803. *Warren v. Keen* [1954] 1 QB 15; *Nachiappin v. Lakshmi Ammal* [1966] 2 MLJ 95.
804. CLA, section 4(3) and (4).
805. *Mint v. Good* [1951] 1 KB 517.
806. LTA, section 93, refers to leases 'made under this Act', which means registered leases. Also, LTA, section 87(5) states that nothing in Part IX (sections 86–93) applies to leases not exceeding 7 years.
807. The operation of LTA, section 93(1)(a)–(c) may be excluded by agreement: LTA, section 93(2).
808. (Cap. 314, 1996 Rev. Ed.).
809. *See* Kevin Gray and Susan Francis Gray, *Elements of Land Law*, 5th edn (OUP, 2009) Chapter 4.5.
810. On whether the covenant binds *T2*, see §7.II.B. below.

II. Successors in Title

389. Suppose *L* assigns his reversion to *L2* and *T* assigns his lease to *T2*. Although *L2* and *T2* are not privy to the lease agreement, covenants which touch and concern the land will bind them. Having stepped into the shoes of *L* and *T*, *L2* and *T2* are now privy to the estate.

A. *Privity of Estate*

390. The distinction between an assignment and a sublease is an important one for the present purpose. While an assignee steps into the shoes of the assignor, a subtenant does not step into the shoes of his landlord. Suppose *L* grants a 10-year lease to *T*. *T* assigns the lease to *T2*, who in turn subleased the property to *ST*. Later, *L* assigns his reversion to *L2*. In this example, *L2* steps into the shoes of *L* while *T2* steps into the shoes of *T*. *L2* and *T2* are privy to the estate. Although the possession of the property is now with *ST*, *ST* does not step into the shoes of *T2* since his interest is acquired not by way of an assignment. There is no privity of estate between *L2* and *ST*.[811] The sublease constitutes a separate estate with *T2* as the landlord and *ST* as the tenant. Between *T2* and *ST* there is privity of estate. Any covenants which touch and concern land set out in the sublease will bind the assignees of *T2* and *ST*.

391. In the case of an equitable lease, the traditional view is that no estate is created and thus the doctrine of privity of estate does not apply. In light of the fusion of law and equity, the preferable view is that an equitable lease similarly gives rise to an estate as a legal lease does.[812]

B. *Covenants Touching and Concerning Land*

392. Covenants which touch and concern land run with the estate. As Gray and Gray observed, '[i]t is notoriously difficult to propose a definition of 'touching and concerning' which is now flawed by circularity'.[813] However, in *P&A Swift Investments v. Combined English Stores Group Plc*, Lord Oliver proposed a working test for identifying whether a covenant touches and concerns the land.[814] First, the covenant must benefit the covenantee only when he is still privy to the estate. Second, the covenant affects the nature, quality, mode of user or value of the land. Third, the covenant must not be expressed to be personal, i.e. not for the benefit of a specific landlord or tenant. From these criteria it is clear that a covenant which does not benefit the covenantee *qua* landlord or *qua* tenant does not run with the estate.

---

811. *Teo Chwee Geok v. Ng Hui Lip & Co* [1967] SGFC 4; [1965–1967] SLR(R) 500.
812. *See Boyer v. Warbey* [1953] 1 QB 234 at 246 (Denning LJ).
813. Kevin Gray and Susan Francis Gray, *Elements of Land Law*, 5th edn (OUP, 2009) at 537.
814. [1989] AC 632 at 642.

393. From the existing English cases, one may draw up a non-exhaustive list of covenants recognised as touching and concerning land.[815] On the tenant's part, the list includes obligations to pay rent, to repair the premises, to insure the premises, to use the premises for a particular purpose only, not to assign or sublet without landlord's consent, etc. On the landlord's part, the list includes obligations to renew the lease, to accept a surrender of the lease, to repair the premises, to insure the premises, to ensure quiet enjoyment, etc. It shall be observed that these are all covenants *in esse*, i.e. covenants having reference to things that are already on the land. A covenant requiring *T* to do something new, e.g. to construct a building on the land, is called a covenant *in posse*. A covenant *in posse* will run with the land to bind *T2* only if *T* expressly covenants for himself/herself and his/her assigns.[816]

394. In Singapore, this issue is very rarely litigated. To date there are only a small handful of relevant cases. In *Teo Chwee Geok v. Ng Hui Lip*, the Federal Court opined that if the defendants were assignees of the lease 'the principle established by *Goldstein v. Sanders* [1915] 1 Ch 549 might have applied so as to make [the covenant against assignment and subletting] run with the land'.[817] However, in this case the defendants were subtenants and therefore the covenant did not bind them.

395. In *United Malayan Banking Corp v. Goodhope Realty*, the tenant paid the landlord a deposit as security for the tenant's due performance and observance of the covenants of the lease.[818] This was pursuant to an express term in the lease agreement, which also provided that the landlord shall repay the deposit after the lease expires. During the continuance of the lease, the landlord mortgaged the property to a bank. Before the expiration of the lease, the landlord defaulted on the loan, causing the bank to appoint a receiver to collect the incomes of the property. Essentially, the bank became the landlord. The tenant lodged a caveat over the property, claiming to be entitled to repayment of the deposit from the bank. Following the Privy Council's decision in *Hua Chiao Commercial Bank Ltd v. Chiphua Industries Ltd*,[819] Thean J held that the term providing for repayment of the deposit did not amount to a covenant which touches and concerns the land.[820] The term gave rise to a personal obligation on the part of the original landlord only.

396. In the case of a state lease, all exceptions, reservations and covenants contained in the lease automatically bind the tenant's assignee.[821]

815. Kevin Gray and Susan Francis Gray, *Elements of Land Law*, 5th edn (OUP, 2009) at 538–39.
816. *Spencer's Case* (1583) 5 Co Rep 16.
817. [1967] SGFC 4; [1965–1967] SLR(R) 500 at [11].
818. [1989] SGHC 14; [1989] 1 SLR(R) 151.
819. [1987] AC 99 (on appeal from Hong Kong).
820. [1989] SGHC 14; [1989] 1 SLR(R) 151 at [16].
821. State Lands Act (Cap. 314, 1996 Rev. Ed.), section 8.

C. *Half of the Principle Codified*

397. It is interesting to note that one-half of the principle is codified in sections 10 and 11 of the CLPA.[822] The two sections provide that where the landlord assigns his reversion, all benefits (section 10) and burdens (section 11) having reference to the subject matter of the lease shall run with the reversion.[823] The phrases 'touching and concerning land' and 'reference to the subject matter of the lease' are merely different expressions of the same idea.[824] Put simply, the two sections allow *L2* and *T1* to sue each other for any breach of covenants which touch and concern land.[825] This essentially replicates the position under the common law.

398. There are two possible advantages in relying on the statutory scheme. First, sections 10 and 11 clearly apply regardless of whether the lease is legal or equitable.[826] However, as said earlier, there is no good reason why the common law should continue to deny the existence of an estate where an equitable lease is created. Second, the powers implied in favour of the landlord by section 93(1) of the LTA shall be treated as if they were stated in the registered lease for the purposes of section 10 of the CLPA.[827] In other words, these powers are exercisable by *L2* against *T*.

399. There is only one local case where the statutory scheme was applied. In *Syed Yassin v. Euvon Industries Pte Ltd*, the lease agreement contained an option to renew the lease for two more years.[828] The option clause also provides that the rent payable shall be the market rate prevailing at the time the tenant gives a notice to renew. Nearing the end of the lease, the tenant exercised the option to renew but the parties disagreed on the amount of rent payable. During the dispute, the landlord sold the land to a third party. The new landlord sought to enforce against the tenant the covenant to pay rent set out in the option clause. The tenant, however, resisted on the ground that the new landlord was not privy to the lease agreement. Thean J held that section 10 of the CLPA applied to annex the covenant to the reversion, thus allowing the new landlord to enforce the covenant.[829]

400. Finally, it is important to note that as sections 10 and 11 do not state that benefits or burdens run with the lease, they have no application in respect of the

822. Both sections apply to registered land by virtue of LTA, section 86(2).
823. LTA, section 93(4) provides that the powers of the landlord implied in s 93(1) shall be regarded as if contained in a registered lease for the purposes of section 10 of the CLPA.
824. *Hua Chiao Commercial Bank Ltd v. Chiphua Industries Ltd* [1987] AC 99 at 106–107.
825. *See* Kevin Gray and Susan Francis Gray, *Elements of Land Law*, 5th edn (OUP, 2009) at 544–48, referring the Law of Property Act 1925, sections 141(1) and 142(2), which is the English equivalents of the CLPA, sections 10 and 11.
826. CLPA, section 2 provides that a 'lease' includes 'an agreement for a lease where the lessee has become entitled to have his lease granted'.
827. LTA, section 93(4).
828. [1990] 2 SLR(R) 627.
829. It is interesting to note that, for unknown reason, Thean J did not apply section 11 of the CLPA in *United Malayan Banking Corp v. Goodhope Realty* [1989] SGHC 14; [1989] 1 SLR(R) 151.

enforceability of covenants touching and concerning land by or against *T2*. The position of *T2* continues to be governed by the common law.

D. Contracts (Rights of Third Parties) Act

401. By virtue of the CRTPA,[830] a stranger to the estate may enforce the terms of a lease agreement if the agreement explicitly states that he may or that the terms are for his benefit.[831] The stranger may be identified by name, as a member of a class or as answering a particular description.[832] Thus, it appears that a covenant could be expressed to be enforceable by or for the benefit of 'successors in title'.[833]

E. Restrictive Covenant

402. Where a lease contains a covenant that is restrictive in nature, the law on restrictive covenant applies. Suppose *T* covenants with *L* not to use the property for commercial purposes. If the covenant touches and concerns the land, and was expressed to be made on behalf of *T* and anyone deriving title from him,[834] then *ST* will be bound unless he had no notice of the covenant.[835] *L*'s reversionary interest is regarded as the equivalent of a dominant tenement.[836]

§8. Determination of Lease

403. There are several ways in which a lease could come to an end. Upon the determination of a lease, the landlord may apply to the Registrar to have a notification of the determination entered on the folio of the land.[837]

830. (Cap. 53B, 2002 Rev. Ed.) (CRTPA).
831. CRTPA, section 2(1).
832. *Ibid*., section 2(3).
833. Tang Hang Wu and Kelvin F.K. Low, *Tan Sook Yee's Principles of Singapore Land Law*, 3rd edn (LexisNexis, 2009) at 517–18.
834. There is a hint that automatic annexation is possible by virtue of section 57(2) of the CLPA: see *RSP Architects Planners & Engineers v. Ocean Front Pte Ltd* [1995] SGCA 79; [1995] 3 SLR(R) 653 at [22]. *See* Chapter 9 (Covenants Relating to Land).
835. *See* Lye Lin Heng, *Landlord and Tenant* (Butterworths, 1990) at 236–37; Barry C. Crown, 'Passing the Benefit and Burden of Restrictive Covenants Governing Land in Singapore' [1998] SJLS 98 at 105–106.
836. *Hall v. Ewin* (1887) 37 Ch D 74.
837. LTA, section 92.

I. Effluxion of Time

404. A fixed-term lease automatically comes to an end at the predetermined end date. If the agreement contains an option to renew, the tenant may extend the lease by giving the required advance notice.[838]

II. Notice to Quit

405. A periodic lease may be determined by the giving of notice to quit by either party. As explained earlier, the advance notice required depends on the period of the lease.[839] Take the example of a monthly lease commencing 15th January. If neither party gives a notice to quit, the lease extends itself on the fifteenth day of every subsequent months. Suppose that the tenant wishes to quit the lease sometime in June. For the month of June, the new period will commence on the 15 June. Thus, to prevent the lease from extending itself on 15 June, a notice to quit must be given by 14 May. A notice given on 14 May will expire on 14 June, thus constituting a one-month advance notice. It is also important to note that even if the notice to quit is given earlier, e.g. on 1 May, the lease will still come to an end only on 14 June.[840] This is because the notice does not affect the lease period commencing 15 April and ending 14 May.

III. Exercise of an Express Power

406. A lease agreement may also contain a term allowing one or both parties to terminate the lease early, usually upon the happening of a certain event. For example, a residential lease usually contains a diplomatic clause, allowing the tenant to determine the lease if he is no longer able to reside in Singapore.

838. On option to renew, see *AREIF (Singapore I) Pte Ltd v. NTUC Fairprice Co-operative* [2015] SGHC 28; [2015] 2 SLR 630; *iHub Solutions Pte Ltd v. Freight Links Express Logisticentre Pte Ltd* [2017] SGHC 6; *Ngee Ann Development Pte Ltd v. Takashimaya* [2017] SGCA 42; [2017] 2 SLR 627.

839. *See* §2.II. above.

840. *Ko Teck Kin v. Watkinson* [1961] 1 MLJ 73 (Singapore); *Cheung Woh Metal Works (Pte) Ltd v. Chuan Eng Seng Trading (Pte) Ltd* [1998] SGHC 409.

IV. Surrender and Merger

A. Surrender

407. Section 91(1) of the LTA provides that a lease may be surrendered by an instrument of surrender in the approved form or by operation of law. If an instrument of surrender is used,[841] the landlord and the tenant, as well as the mortgagee if the property is mortgaged, must execute it.[842]

408. Surrender by operation of law arises from an agreement accompanied by an act of surrender.[843] In *Fong Holdings Pte Ltd v. Computer Library (S) Pte Ltd*, the tenant, after obtaining the landlord's consent to the surrender, delivered to the latter the keys to the property.[844] Chan J held that the lease was surrendered by operation of law. In *Song Kim Puah v. Lim Hoe Chye*, the tenant, at the landlord's demand, agreed that he would leave the premises.[845] However, he continued to remain in it. Brown J held that the verbal agreement did not amount to a notional delivery up of possession and therefore there was no surrender.

409. The Registrar shall register a surrender by the entry of a memorial on the relevant folio of the land.[846] In the case of surrender by operation of law, the person who seeks to have the surrender registered may apply to the Registrar and support his application with evidence of the surrender.[847]

B. Merger

410. A merger occurs where the lease and the reversion become vested in the same person. It could arise where the tenant purchases the landlord's reversion or where a third-party purchases the landlord's reversion and the tenant's lease.[848] Section 67 of the LTA provides that where the interests of the landlord and the tenant vest in the same person, any intention to merge the interests shall be evidenced by a surrender of the lease. In other words, the procedure for surrender equally applies to merger.[849]

841. Form 39.
842. LTA, section 91(4).
843. *Tan Soo Leng David v. Lim Thian Chai Charles* [1998] SGHC 89; [1998] 1 SLR(R) 880 at [24].
844. [1991] SGHC 61; [1991] 1 SLR(R) 834.
845. [1953] 00 SLR 32.
846. LTA, section 91(2).
847. LTA, section 91(5).
848. *See e.g. Goodland v. Lim Ban Toon* [1966] SGHC 9; [1965–1967] SLR(R) 264 (although the court referred to surrender by operation of law).
849. *See* LTA, section 91(1).

C. Effect on Sublease

411. Section 91(3) of the LTA provides that registration of a surrender or merger does not extinguish a sublease. The Registrar shall enter a memorial of registration of the sublease on the folio of the land, and the landlord's estate shall, for the purpose of preserving the sublease and its covenants, be deemed to be the reversion expectant on the sublease. In other words, the landlord (*L*) steps into the shoes of the tenant (*T*) and becomes the landlord of the subtenant (*ST*) under the sublease.

V. Frustration

412. Where a person purchases a leasehold estate by making a lump sum payment, all risks pass to him. Thus, if the property is destroyed by fire, there is no basis for the purchaser to ask for a refund of the purchase money and to return the property to the seller. Their relationship is essentially one of seller and purchaser, not of landlord and tenant.[850]

413. However, in the case of a typical short(er) term landlord and tenant relationship, contract principles are applicable.[851] In *Singapore Woodcraft Manufacturing Co (Pte) Ltd v. Mok Ah Sai*, the premises were subleased for 10 years.[852] The subtenant used the premises for a retail business and paid a monthly rent. On the seventh year, the sublease was terminated by operation of law when the property was compulsorily acquired by the state. Singh J held that this amounted to a frustrating event[853] which attracted the application of the Frustrated Contracts Act.[854] The tenant was thus allowed to recover the deposit as well as rent paid after the notice of possession was served by the state.

414. The same was held in *Sheng Siong Supermarket Pte Ltd v. Carilla Pte Ltd* where the reversioner, the Housing and Development Board, refused to grant approval for the intended use.[855] As Ang J found that the lease agreement was conditional upon the tenant being allowed to use the premises to operate a supermarket, HDB's refusal amounted to a frustrating event.[856] Importantly, for frustration of purpose to be successfully argued, the purpose must be commonly held by both parties. This would naturally restrict the applicability of the doctrine to disputes between original the landlord and tenant.

850. However, where a contract of sale remains executory, i.e. prior to passing of title, the doctrine of frustration may apply: *Lim Kim Som v. Sheriffa Taibah bte Abdul Rahman* [1994] SGCA 15; [1994] 1 SLR(R) 233.
851. *See e.g. National Carriers Ltd v. Panalpina (Northern) Ltd* [1981] AC 675.
852. [1979] SGHC 37; [1979–1980] SLR(R) 159.
853. Applying *Davis Contractors Ltd v. Fareham Urban District Council* [1956] AC 696.
854. (Cap. 115, 2014 Rev. Ed.).
855. [2011] SGHC 204; [2011] 4 SLR 1094.
856. However, this decision can also be explained on the basis of the non-fulfilment of a condition precedent.

VI. Termination for Repudiatory Breach

415. In *Tan Soo Leng David v. Lim Thian Chai Charles*, Khoo J held that a distinction ought to be drawn between, on the one hand, a lease having the element of a purchase of an interest in land and, on the other hand, a lease giving rise to a typical landlord and tenant relationship.[857] A lease of the first kind is usually for a longer duration (e.g., 99 years) and the primary consideration from the tenant is a lump sum payment of the purchase price. Upon completion of the purchase, the landlord, for all practical purposes, drops out of the picture. There is no meaningful relationship between landlord and tenant. In contrast, a lease of the second kind is characterised by a continuing relationship under which the landlord and the tenant undertake to perform certain obligations throughout the duration of the lease. In particular, the tenant undertakes to pay rent on a regular basis. As the relationship is governed primarily by contract, ordinary contractual principles of repudiatory breach ought to apply.[858] Where either party has committed a repudiatory breach of the lease agreement, the innocent party may accept the repudiation and bring the lease to an end.

416. The tenant's abandonment of the lease is an obvious example of a repudiatory breach.[859] Other breaches of covenants are less straightforward. The tenant's obligations to pay rent when due being severable, it follows that failure to pay rent once is unlikely to amount to a repudiatory breach. In *Shevill v. Builders Licensing Board*, Gibbs CJ said:

> It is clear that a covenant to pay rent in advance at specified times would not, without more, be a fundamental or essential term having the effect that any failure, however slight, to make payment at the specified times would entitle the lessor to terminate the lease.[860]

417. A tenant's non-payment of rent must either be persistent or deliberate for it to amount to a repudiatory breach.[861] Although rarely, the parties may agree that payment of rent is not a condition, in which case non-payment of rent does not amount to a repudiatory breach.[862] The same principles apply in respect of other

857. [1998] SGHC 89; [1998] 1 SLR(R) 880 at [22], citing Lye Lin Heng, *Landlord and Tenant* (Butterworths, 1990) at 5.
858. [1998] SGHC 89; [1998] 1 SLR(R) 880 at [28], applied in *Lim Kau Tee v. Lee Kay Li* [2005] SGHC 162 (where it was the landlord who committed a repudiatory breach). *See also Progressive Mailing House Pty Ltd v. Tabali Pty Ltd* (1985) 157 CLR 17; *Shevill v. Builders Licensing Board* (1982) 149 CLR 620; *Reichman v. Beveridge* [2007] Bus LR 412.
859. *Klerk-Elias v. K T Chan Clinic Pte Ltd* [1993] SGCA 28; [1993] SLR(R) 609; *Tan Soo Leng David v. Lim Thian Chai Charles* [1998] SGHC 89; [1998] 1 SLR(R) 880.
860. (1982) 149 CLR 620 at 627.
861. *Progressive Mailing House Pty Ltd v. Tabali Pty Ltd* (1985) 157 CLR 17.
862. *See Syed Ahmad Jamal Alsagoff (administrator of the estates of Shaikah Fitom bte Ghalib bin Omar Al-Bakri and others) and others v. Harun bin Syed Hussain Aljunied and others and other suits* [2016] SGHC 252; [2017] 3 SLR 386. The 999-year lease commencing in 1877 required the tenant to pay just one Spanish Dollar per year.

continuing obligations, e.g. to pay utility bills or to maintain the premises in a reasonable state of repair. As for other covenants the breach is likely to be one-off, it is necessary to determine whether they have been cast as conditions.[863]

418. Instead of accepting the repudiation, the innocent party may choose to affirm the contract and continue to treat the lease as subsisting.[864] The right to affirm is particularly relevant where a tenant wishes to abandon the lease while the landlord insists on holding the tenant to the lease. In *Tan Soo Leng David v. Lim Thian Chai Charles*, the landlords, who owned a unit in Mount Elizabeth Medical Centre, agreed to lease it to the tenant for 3 years at a monthly rent of $5,000.[865] However, after a month, the tenant changed his mind about renting the unit and decided to purchase another unit in the same building. The tenant's abandonment of the lease clearly amounted to a repudiatory breach of the lease agreement. However, instead of accepting the repudiation, the landlords chose to hold the tenant to the lease and continued to demand for the payment of rent. A new tenant who was willing to pay the same rent was found only a year later. It was only when the landlords agreed to lease the unit to the new tenant that they the repudiation was accepted. As the loss was completely mitigated, the landlords were not entitled to any damages for loss of future rent. However, they were entitled to claim full rent for the duration the unit was left vacant.

419. What is unclear from the judgment, however, is whether a landlord would be entitled to insist on holding the tenant to the lease in all circumstances. While the learned judge did not directly address this point, he cited the Malaysian case of *Teh Wan Sang & Sons Sdn Bhd v. See Teow Chuan*,[866] where it was held that a duty to mitigate arose only upon the landlord's acceptance of the tenant's repudiation.[867] In other words, it is only when the landlord decides to accept the tenant's repudiation by reletting the premises that he is expected to mitigate his loss by accepting a reasonable offer. Curiously, however, the learned judge in *Tan Soo Leng* found it necessary to consider whether the landlords have made reasonable efforts to look for a new tenant. The landlords had advertised their unit for rent in four monthly issues of the Singapore Medical Association Newsletter. The learned judge found that these efforts were reasonable as the advertisements were directed at the right

863. *See generally* Andrew Phang et al., *The Law of Contract in Singapore* (Academy Publishing, 2012) Chapter 17.

864. Affirmation could either be express or implied. In *Leivest International Pte Ltd v. Top Ten Entertainment Pte Ltd* [2006] SGHC 1; [2006] 1 SLR(R) 888, for example, affirmation was implied from the landlord's continued acceptance of rent payment from the tenant. Where the innocent party chooses to affirm the contract, he waives his right to accept the repudiation. However, if the repudiatory breach is a continuing one, the innocent party may subsequently choose to accept the repudiation and bring the lease to an end.

865. [1998] SGHC 89; [1998] 1 SLR(R) 880, noted in Aedit Abdullah, 'Repudiation of Leases' [1998] SJLS 438.

866. [1984] 1 MLJ 130. *See Tan Soo Leng David v. Lim Thian Chai Charles* [1998] SGHC 89; [1998] 1 SLR(R) 880 at [25]–[26].

867. The High Court applied the House of Lords' decision in *White and Carter (Councils) Ltd v. McGregor* [1962] AC 413.

audiences. The obvious difficulty is in reconciling, on the one hand, the landlords' right to hold the tenant onto the lease and, on the other hand, a duty to make reasonable efforts to look for a new tenant.

420. It is interesting to note that English law similarly adopts a landlord-friendly approach. In *Reichman v. Beveridge*, the Court of Appeal explained that a landlord has a legitimate interest in keeping the lease as subsisting despite the tenant's abandonment.[868] The court cited an old authority which stood for the proposition that a landlord who accepts the tenant's repudiation is precluded from claiming damages for prospective loss of rent.[869] Thus, it is not unreasonable for the landlord to hold the tenant to the lease until he could find an offer equalling or exceeding the terms of the lease.[870] Even where the rental market is healthy, the onus is on the tenant to find a new tenant. If an offer of reasonable terms is found and presented to the landlord, he is expected to mitigate the loss by accepting the offer.

421. Under Singapore law, however, a landlord who elects to terminate the lease may also claim damages for prospective loss of rent.[871] If the landlord subsequently relets the premises at a lower rent, the tenant will only be liable for the shortfall. From the tenant's perspective, this would be less harsh than being held to the lease and having to pay full rent. Importantly, it makes little or no difference to the landlord, whose loss would be made good in either case.

422. Clearly, a law that encourages a landlord to hold the tenant to the lease although the latter has every intention to abandon it is not only economically wasteful but also inconsistent with the policy of maximising space, which is especially important in land-scarce Singapore. Moreover, the burden of having to search for a new tenant is also not overly onerous and, in any case, the cost of doing so could be claimed from the tenant. Thus, it is suggested that if the landlord is presented with a reasonable offer, he should be expected to accept it. If he decides to reject it, the onus should be on him/her to explain any legitimate reason that he might have for the rejection.

VII. Forfeiture

423. Where a landlord forfeits a lease, the lease comes to an end. More shall be said below about a landlord's right to forfeit a lease.[872]

868. [2007] Bus LR 412. This was in response to the Lord Reid's 'legitimate interest' exception laid down in *White and Carter (Councils) Ltd v. McGregor* [1962] AC 413 at 431.
869. *Walls v. Atcheson* (1826) 11 Moo CP & Ex 379.
870. The decision in *Reichman* has been doubted for its failure to consider cases where the landlord was allowed to claim damages for future rent: *Marshall v. Macintosh* (1898) 78 LT 750; *Gray v. Owen* [1910] 1 KB 622; *Williams v. Lewis* [1915] 3 KB 493. *See* Mark Pawlowski, 'Tenant abandonment – damages for loss of future rent' (2010) 126 LQR 361.
871. *Klerk-Elias v. K T Chan Clinic Pte Ltd* [1993] SGCA 28; [1993] SLR(R) 609. *See* §9(iii) below.
872. *See* §9.VI. below.

§9. REMEDIES

I. Double Rent or Value

424. Where a tenant remains on the premises after the determination of the lease, he is said to be holding over.[873] In such a case, section 28(4) of the CLA allows the landlord to charge the tenant 'double the amount of his rent until possession is given up by him or with double the value during the period of detention of the land'. The difference between double rent and double value, as well as the advantages and disadvantages of claiming under each head, have been helpfully explained by Lee J in *UDL Marine (Singapore) Pte Ltd v. Jurong Town Corporation*:

> … it would be more logical for the first option to refer to the rent last paid and the second option to refer to the market rent during the holding over period. This would give the landlord the option to charge double the last rent paid if the market value of the land had fallen in the holding over period, or if it has risen, to charge double the market rent. Further, if the landlord opts for double market value, he has the burden of proving the market value which may be a difficult task. He can simply opt for double rent which relieves him of this evidential burden.[874]

425. The fact that the tenant has remained on the premises after determination of the lease does not necessarily amount to holding over. *In Lee Wah Bank Ltd v. Afro-Asia Shipping Co (Pte) Ltd*, the lease agreement contained a covenant requiring the tenants to restore the premises to its original state prior to handing it over to the landlord when the lease expires.[875] When the lease expired, the tenants vacated the premises and handed over its keys to the landlords. However, the tenants continued to perform the required restoration work on the premises. For about a month and a half after the expiry of the lease, the tenants would obtain the keys from the landlords' maintenance supervisor and hand them back at the end of the day. The landlords claimed that the tenants had held over and were therefore liable to pay double rent. The Court of Appeal rejected the claim. According to the court:

> To establish that there was a holding over of the demised premises, the [landlords] must show that even after the expiration of their tenancy, the [tenants] continued to exercise a degree of possession and control over the demised premises which precluded the [landlords] from excluding them from the demised premises at their (the [landlords']) will.[876]

426. The court further said the expression 'holding over' in section 28(4) requires 'an intention on the part of the tenant to refuse to deliver up the premises

873. Walter Woon, 'Mesne Profits, Double Rent and Double Value in Singapore' [1985] MLJ lxiv.
874. [2013] SGHC 236 at [92].
875. [1992] SGCA 23; [1992] 1 SLR(R) 740 (Yong CJ, Chan and Goh JJ), applied in *Kiat Lee Machinery Pte Ltd v. Comfortdelgro Engineering Pte Ltd and Thong Huat Brothers* [2012] SGDC 458.
876. [1992] SGCA 23; [1992] 1 SLR(R) 740 at [15].

with knowledge that he has no right to remain in possession'.[877] None of these were satisfied in the present case. The possession of the premises was returned to the landlords when the leases expired.

II. Recovery of Rent and Distress

427. Where a tenant fails to pay rent when it becomes due, the landlord is entitled to bring an action for an agreed sum. Alternatively, if the tenant has valuable goods in the premises, the landlord may apply for a writ of distress for the appointment of a sheriff to seize the goods and sell them to satisfy the debt. The rules and procedures for distress are set out in the Distress Act (DA).[878] A landlord may apply for a writ of distress only if the arrears in rent do not exceed 12 months.[879] This remedy is available even after the determination of the lease, provided that either the tenant is still in occupation or where his goods are still on the premises.[880] However, the landlord must not have ceased to be a landlord before the determination of the lease. In *Falcon Properties Pte Ltd v. Ng Sun Kok Mould Making Co*, the Court of Appeal held that a landlord who sold his reversion ceased to be a landlord for the purposes of the DA.[881]

428. Section 8 of the DA sets out a list of property exempted from seizure:

(a) things in actual use in the hands of a person at the time of the seizure;
(b) tools and implements not in use where there is other movable property in or upon the house or premises sufficient to cover such amount and costs;[882]
(c) the tenant's necessary wearing apparel and necessary bedding for himself and his family;
(d) goods in the possession of the tenant for the purpose of being carried, wrought, worked up or otherwise dealt with in the course of his ordinary trade or business;[883]
(e) goods belonging to guests at an inn; and
(f) goods in the custody of the law.

---

877. [1992] SGCA 23; [1992] 1 SLR(R) 740 at [17]. However, it has also been said that the holding over need not be wilful: *Teo Gracie v. Tay Leng Hong* [1987] SGHC 19; [1987] SLR(R) 315 at [21]; *Mount Elizabeth Health Centre Pte Ltd v. Mount Elizabeth Hospital Ltd* [1992] SGHC 265; [1992] 3 SLR(R) 155.
878. (Cap. 84, 2013 Rev. Ed.).
879. DA, section 5(1).
880. *Ibid.*, section 5(3).
881. [1985] SGCA 3; [1985–1986] SLR(R) 57 (Wee CJ, Thean and Chua JJ).
882. Referring to tools and implements of trade.
883. In *Cupid Jewels Pte Ltd v. Orchard Central Pte Ltd* [2014] SGCA 2; [2014] 2 SLR 156, the Court of Appeal (Menon CJ, Phang and Rajah JJA) interpreted the phrase 'otherwise dealt with' to mean the management of the goods belonging to a principal. An example is where the tenant sells goods for the principal in return for commissions. In this case there was no agency relationship since the tenant was entitled to sell the goods at whatever price it likes and was only liable to pay the owner of the goods the cost price.

429. Subject to section 8, the sheriff may seize any goods found on the premises, including goods belonging to a subtenant, a lodger or any other person not having any beneficial interest in the premises. Pursuant to section 10, a subtenant may apply to the court to have the goods released.[884] However, no order for release will be made unless he pays to the landlord an amount equal to the arrears of rent and also undertake to pay to the landlord future rent, if any, due from the tenant.[885] Where the subtenant is paying at least 75% of the full monthly letting value of the premises, he shall not be liable to pay to the landlord a sum greater than the rent which he owes to the tenant.[886] For the purposes of recovery of any sums payable by the subtenant under the above-mentioned undertaking, the subtenant shall be deemed to be the immediate tenant of the landlord and the sums payable shall be deemed to be rent.[887] Where the subtenant makes such payment to the landlord, he may deduct an equivalent sum from any rent due or which may become due to the tenant.[888]

430. Importantly, section 12 provides that section 10 shall not apply to:

(a) goods belonging to the husband or wife of the tenant whose rent is in arrear, or to goods comprised in any bill of sale, hire purchase agreement, or settlement made by such tenant, or to goods in the possession, order or disposition of such tenant by the consent and permission of the true owner under such circumstances that such tenant is the reputed owner thereof;[889]
(b) goods of a partner of the immediate tenant;
(c) goods (not being goods of a lodger) upon premises where any trade or business is carried on in which both the immediate tenant and the undertenant have an interest;
(d) goods (not being goods of a lodger) on premises used as offices or warehouses where the owner of the goods neglects for one calendar month after notice (which shall be given in like manner as a notice to quit) to remove the goods and vacate the premises; or
(e) goods belonging to and in the offices of any company or corporation on premises the immediate tenant whereof is a director or an officer, or is in the employment of such company or corporation.

884. DA, section 10(1).
885. *Ibid.*, section 10(2).
886. *Ibid.*, section 10(3).
887. *Ibid.*, section 11(1).
888. *Ibid.*, section 11(2).
889. It is for the true owner to disprove that the tenant is a reputed owner of the goods. In *Plaza Singapura (Pte) Ltd v. Cosdel (S) Pte Ltd* [1990] SGCA 9; [1990] 2 SLR(R) 22 at [22], the Court of Appeal (Thean J, Wee CJ and Sinnathuray J) laid down the test to be 'whether in all the circumstances, a reasonable man would necessarily infer that the tenant was the owner of the articles in question'. In *Cupid Jewels Pte Ltd v. Orchard Central Pte Ltd* [2014] SGCA 2; [2014] 2 SLR 156 at [81], the Court of Appeal clarified that the reasonable person refers to the landlord. *See also Jurong Town Corp v. Shutters 31 Pte Ltd* [2002] SGHC 175; [2002] 2 SLR(R) 673.

431. A tenant who disputes the landlord's claim may apply to the court for the discharge or suspension of the execution of the writ, or for the release of some or all the goods that were seized.[890] Where the landlord has no reasonable cause in applying for the writ of distress, any person who is aggrieved by the writ of distress may sue the landlord for malicious prosecution.[891] The aggrieved person may also bring a claim in negligence if the execution of the writ is not properly carried out.[892]

432. In the case of a state lease, the collector of Land Revenue may sell the land by public auction and use the proceeds to satisfy the arrears of rent.[893]

III. Compensatory Damages

433. The aim of awarding compensatory damages is to place the innocent party, in so far as money can do it, in the position which he would have been if the contract had been performed.[894] If a tenant has been wrongfully evicted, he may be awarded relocation costs and any increase in rent which he has to pay for a similar place.[895] Where a party responsible for repair of the premises fails to do so, the cost of repair may be awarded to the other party. In all cases the principles of remoteness and mitigation apply.[896]

434. Where the tenant has abandoned the lease, the landlord may refuse to accept the repudiation and continue to request for the payments of rent as they become due.[897] If the tenant refuses to pay, the landlord may bring an action for an agreed sum.[898] Because this is essentially an action to recover a debt, principles of remoteness and mitigation do not apply.

435. However, where the landlord accepts the tenant's repudiation and terminates the lease, he may claim damages for prospective loss of rental income. In *Klerk-Elias v. K T Chan Clinic Pte Ltd*, the parties entered into an agreement for the grant of a three-year lease for a monthly rent of $9180.[899] Following a dispute between the parties, the tenant vacated the premises. The landlord accepted the repudiation and claimed damages for loss of future rent. In assessing the damages

890. DA, section 16.
891. *Comfort Management Pte Ltd v. Afco East Pte Ltd* [2012] SGHC 137; [2012] 4 SLR 66; *Ginsin Holdings Pte Ltd v. Tan Mui Khoon* [1996] SGHC 245; [1996] 3 SLR(R) 500; *Chop Chye Hin Chong v. Ng Yeok Seng* [1934] 1 MLJ 265 (Singapore).
892. *Heng Chyu Kee v. Far East Square Pte Ltd* [2001] SGHC 348; [2001] 3 SLR(R) 651.
893. Land Revenue Collection Act (Cap. 155, 1985 Rev. Ed.), Part II.
894. *Alvin Nicholas Nathan v. Raffles Assets (Singapore) Pte Ltd* [2016] SGCA 18; [2016] 2 SLR 1056 at [23]–[29].
895. *Alvin Nicholas Nathan v. Raffles Assets (Singapore) Pte Ltd* [2016] SGCA 18; [2016] 2 SLR 1056.
896. *Alvin Nicholas Nathan v. Raffles Assets (Singapore) Pte Ltd* [2016] SGCA 18; [2016] 2 SLR 1056; *Klerk-Elias v. K T Chan Clinic Pte Ltd* [1993] SGCA 28; [1993] 1 SLR(R) 609.
897. *Tan Soo Leng David v. Lim Thian Chai Charles* [1998] SGHC 89; [1998] 1 SLR(R) 880.
898. *See* §9.II. above.
899. [1993] SGCA 28; [1993] 1 SLR(R) 609 (Thean, Khoo and Karthigesu JJ).

claimable by the landlord, the Court of Appeal took into account the efforts of the landlord in looking for a new tenant. At first the landlord (who was a doctor) advertised the premises for rent in the Singapore Medical Association Newsletter. But there was no taker. The landlord then engaged a property agent, who managed to find a new tenant who was willing to pay $6300 per month. Between the termination of the lease and the reletting, 9 months had elapsed. The Court of Appeal held that the landlord had not done enough to find a new tenant sooner especially considering the falling rental market. The landlord should have advertised in a publication that is more accessible to the public or engaged a property agent sooner.[900] If the landlord had done any of these, it would be reasonable to expect that a new tenant could be found within three months. Thus, by virtue of the principle of mitigation, the tenant is liable for the full rent only for the first three months after the breach ($9180 x 3). For the remaining 31 months, the measure of damages was represented by the rent reserved by the terminated lease ($9180 x 31) less the rent receivable under the new lease ($6300 x 31).[901] This was assuming that $6300 per month was a fair rental rate. Indeed, there was no evidence that the premises were relet at undervalue. Additionally, the landlord was allowed to claim the advertising costs and agent's fee.

IV. Equitable Set-Off

436. In *Batshita International (Pte) Ltd v. Lim Eng Hock Peter*, the Court of Appeal held that a tenant is entitled to withhold rent to set-off a claim against the landlord for breach of a covenant to repair the premises.[902] In *Overseas Union Enterprise Ltd v. Three Sixty Degree Pte Ltd*, Coomaraswamy J explained that the equitable set-off is a self-help remedy, allowing a tenant lawfully to withhold a payment of rent which is contractually due.[903] A right to equitable set-off is available 'if the tenant's cross-claim against the landlord is so closely connected to the landlord's claim for rent as to go to the root of that claim'.[904]

437. A right to set-off may be excluded by a term of the lease. In *Three Sixty*, the learned judge held that the expression 'without any deduction or set off whatsoever' accompanying the tenant's covenant to pay rent was sufficient to exclude the tenant's right to set-off. However, the simpler expression 'without any deduction' is insufficient.[905]

900. Unlike in *Tan Soo Leng*, where the unit was within a medical centre, here the premises was in a shopping mall.
901. Where the premises were relet at the same rent, no damages is claimable thereafter since the landlord has suffered no loss. *See e.g. Tan Soo Leng David v. Lim Thian Chai Charles* [1998] SGHC 89; [1998] 1 SLR(R) 880.
902. [1996] SGCA 68; [1996] 3 SLR(R) 563 at [12] (Karthigesu JA, Thean JA and Yong CJ).
903. [2013] SGHC 71; [2013] 3 SLR 1 at [35].
904. [2013] SGHC 71; [2013] 3 SLR 1 at [36].
905. *Batshita International (Pte) Ltd v. Lim Eng Hock Peter* [1996] SGCA 68;[1996] 3 SLR(R) 563 at [12].

438. Traditionally, unless otherwise stated, the obligations of each party to the lease are independent. Thus, one party's non-performance of his obligation does not excuse the other party from performing his obligations. For example, a landlord who withholds performance of his covenant to repair in response to the tenant's failure to pay rent commits a breach of the contract. However, a tenant's withholding of rent in exercise of an equitable right to set-off is an exception. In *Three Sixty*, the learned judge said: 'The [landlord] cannot rely on the [tenant's] withholding of payment to trigger extra-judicial rights and remedies for breach including a right to terminate the contract.'[906]

V. Specific Performance and Injunction

439. It is trite law that a remedy of specific performance will not be awarded where damages is adequate. Thus, if one party breaches his covenant to repair, this is easily remedied by awarding the other party damages for the cost of repair, which the latter could use to employ someone else to perform the repair. A court will also not order specific performance or an injunction having the effect of compelling performance even if damages are inadequate. The case of *Parkway Properties Pte Ltd v. Page One – The Book Shop Pte Ltd* is a good example.[907] There the landlords leased shop lots in a shopping mall to several persons. The lease agreements contained a term requiring the tenants to keep their respective units open for business from 10 am to 10 pm daily. Dispute arose when several tenants closed their shops for one day for the purpose of pressuring the landlord to reduce their rents in light of the poor economic climate. When a concession could not be reached, the tenants threatened to again close their shops. The landlord sought an interim injunction claiming that the reputation and letting value of the shopping mall would be adversely affected by the tenants' conduct. Ghows J dismissed the landlord's application on the ground that they had no real prospect of succeeding at trial. A court would not order specific performance of an obligation to carry on a business. Likewise, an injunction having the effect of compelling the tenants to carry on their businesses will also not be ordered. The learned judge was obviously concerned that granting an injunction would force the tenants to conduct their business at a loss, which might eventually result in bankruptcy.[908]

440. A prohibitive injunction is more readily awarded where the covenant is a negative one, e.g. the landlord's covenant to ensure quiet enjoyment and the tenant's covenant not to commit waste.

906. [2013] 3 SLR 1 at [35].
907. [1985] SGHC 17; [1985–1986] SLR(R) 204.
908. *See also Co-operative Insurance Society Ltd v. Argyll Stores (Holdings) Ltd* [1997] 2 WLR 898.

VI. Forfeiture

A. Grounds for Forfeiture

441. Perhaps the most powerful remedy a landlord may exercise against a tenant is forfeiture of the lease. A right to forfeiture may arise in several situations.[909] First, where the landlord may expressly reserve in the agreement a right to forfeiture in respect of specific breaches. Second, where the tenant commits a repudiatory breach. The landlord's right to terminate the lease necessarily entails a right to forfeit the lease.[910] Third, in the case of a registered lease,[911] a right to forfeiture is implied where: (i) rent is in arrears for 30 days; (ii) the tenant has defaulted in the fulfilment of any covenant, whether expressed or implied, for a period of 30 days; or (iii) the tenant has failed to comply with a notice to repair the premises within the time specified in the notice.[912]

B. Waiver

442. A right to forfeiture is lost if a landlord waives the tenant's breach. Whether the landlord has waived the breach is necessarily a question of fact. Normally a waiver may be inferred where the landlord, having knowledge of the tenant's breach, continues to accept rent.[913] However, the mere receipt of rent does not necessarily constitute waiver. In *Protaz Co-operative Society Ltd v. Toh Teng Seng*, the landlord wrote to the tenant requesting payment of outstanding rent.[914] The letters stated that unless the tenant pays within a stipulated date, the landlord would exercise its right of re-entry. When the tenant failed to pay within the grace period, the landlord applied for a writ of possession. However, before the writ of possession was served on the tenant, the tenant directly paid a portion of the rent into the landlord's account by bank transfer. Chan JC held that there was no waiver in this case.

C. Exercising the Right of Forfeiture

443. A right of forfeiture may be exercised either by physical re-entry of the premises or by way of formal proceedings, i.e. by applying for a writ of possession.[915]

909. For a State lease, see section 7(1)(e) of the SLA. For a Housing and Development Board (HDB) flat, see section 55 of the Housing and Development Act (Cap. 129, 2004 Rev. Ed.).
910. *See Ritzland Investment Pte Ltd v. Grace Management & Consultancy Services Pte Ltd* [2014] SGHC 62; [2014] 2 SLR 1342 at [97]–[100]; *Oriental Investments (SH) Pte Ltd v. Catalla Investments Pte Ltd* [2012] SGHC 245; [2013] 1 SLR 1182.
911. LTA, section 87(5) provides that nothing in Part IX (sections 86–93) applies to leases not exceeding 7 years.
912. LTA, section 93(1)(d).
913. *Leivest International Pte Ltd v. Top Ten Entertainment Pte Ltd* [2006] SGHC 1; [2006] 1 SLR(R) 888; *Hong Cheok Lam v. Ong Sing Mai* [1951] MLJ 34 (Singapore).
914. [2001] SGHC 84.
915. Rules of Court (2014 Rev. Ed.) Order 45, rule 3; Order 81.

In *Oriental Investments (SH) Pte Ltd v. Catalla Investments Pte Ltd*, where the landlord who re-entered the premises was found to have wrongfully repudiated the lease, Pillai J warned:

> A prudent landlord having an independent common law self-help right of forfeiture would need to weigh the advantages of exercising this self-help right of forfeiture against … the availability of court processes to mitigate the risk of unlawful repossession and termination which may subsequently expose it, as here, to liability for wrongful termination of the lease.[916]

444. Where a tenant assigns the lease in breach of a covenant prohibiting assignment, the assignment is nonetheless valid.[917] However, the lease is liable to be forfeited. The notice of forfeiture shall be addressed to the assignee, i.e. the existing tenant.[918] Where a tenant subleases the premises in breach of a covenant prohibiting subletting, presumably the notice of forfeiture must be addressed to both the tenant and the subtenant. Where the head lease is forfeited, the sublease, which was carved out of the head lease, equally ceases.[919]

D. General Limitations, Relief Against Forfeiture and Protection of Subtenants

445. Section 18(1) of the CLPA states:

> A right of re-entry or forfeiture under any provision or stipulation in a lease, for a breach of any covenant or condition in a lease, shall not be enforceable, by action or otherwise, unless the lessor serves on the lessee a notice specifying the particular breach complained of and, if the breach is capable of remedy, requiring the lessee to remedy the breach, and, in any case, requiring the lessee to make compensation in money for the breach, and the lessee fails, within a reasonable time thereafter, to remedy the breach, if it is capable of remedy, and to make reasonable compensation in money, to the satisfaction of the lessor, for the breach.[920]

446. At first glance, the reference to a right to forfeit 'under any provision or stipulation in a lease' suggests that section 18(1) applies only to an express forfeiture clause. However, there is a strong case for extending its application to a right of forfeiture implied into a registered lease by section 93(1)(d) of the LTA. Section 93(3) specifically states that the rights implied under section 93(1) shall be read subject to 'any written law imposing restrictions or conditions on re-entry or forfeiture or on ejectment of tenants'. However, it may be that section 18(1) does not apply to

916. [2012] SGHC 245; [2013] 1 SLR 1182.
917. *Jubilee Electronics Pte Ltd v. Tai Wah Garments and Knitting Factory Pte Ltd* [1996] SGCA 8; [1996] 1 SLR(R) 352 at [32]–[35]. *Cf Nagappan v. Chen Chi Ya* [1949] MLJ 271 (Singapore).
918. *Old Grovebury Manor Farm Ltd v. Seymour (W) Plant Sales & Hire Ltd (No. 2)* [1979] 1 WLR 1397.
919. *Great Western Railway Co v. Smith* (1876) 2 Ch D 235 at 253.
920. For the purposes of this section, 'lease' includes 'underlease' (i.e., sublease): CLPA, section 18(7).

a right of forfeiture arising from the tenant's repudiatory breach.[921] In such a case, the right of forfeiture arises not from any provision or stipulation in the lease but by operation of law. It is also clear that section 18(1) does not apply where the tenant's breach relates to a covenant to pay rent[922] or a covenant against the assigning, subletting or with the possession of the premises.[923]

447. A common dispute pertaining to section 18(1) is whether the complained breach is remediable.[924] If it is, the landlord must give a notice requiring the tenant to remedy the breach within a reasonable time.[925] If it is not, then no such notice needs to be given. The prevailing view is that a breach is remediable if the harm caused could be effectively remedied within a reasonable time.[926] Cases where the harm is incapable of being remedied within a reasonable time are rare. One example is where very serious damage is inflicted on the premises. Another example is where the breach causes a long-term stigma on the property. In *Rugby School (Governors) v. Tannahill*, the tenant, in breach of a covenant not to use the premises for illegal or immoral purposes, allowed it to be used as a brothel.[927] The English Court of Appeal held that the breach was irremediable and therefore the landlord need not give a notice to remedy.

448. The purpose of section 18(1) is to provide the tenant with an opportunity to pre-empt the landlord's right of forfeiture by remedying the breach. In *Lee Tat Realty Pte Ltd v. Limco Products Manufacturing Pte Ltd*, Chao J held that 'for a notice to be valid it must contain sufficient particulars of the alleged breaches'.[928] In this case the notice was invalid because its particulars were so vague that the tenant could not know what precisely it was supposed to do to avoid forfeiture.

449. A tenant may also pre-empt the landlord's right of forfeiture by applying to a court for relief.[929] The court may grant or refuse relief, having regard to the conduct of the parties and to other relevant factors,[930] e.g. whether granting the relief would cause substantial prejudice or damage to the landlord.[931] It is submitted that

---

921. *See Apriaden Pty Ltd v. Seacrest Pty Ltd* (2005) 12 VR 319; *Marshall v. Snowy River Shire Council* (1994) 7 BPR 14, 447. *Cf Ritzland Investment Pte Ltd v. Grace Management & Consultancy Services Pte Ltd* [2014] SGHC 62; [2014] 2 SLR 1342 at [99]; *Abidogun v. Frolan Health Care Ltd* [2001] EWCA Civ 1821; [2002] L&TR 16.
922. CLPA, section 18(9).
923. *Ibid.*, section 18(8).
924. *See* Kevin Gray and Susan Francis Gray, *Elements of Land Law*, 5th edn (OUP, 2009) at 487–92.
925. *Ng Poh Guan v. Chan Ai Leng* [2001] SGHC 353; [2001] 3 SLR(R) 671.
926. *Expert Clothing Service & Sales Ltd v. Hillgate House Ltd* [1986] Ch 340. The English equivalent of section 118(1) is to be found in the Law of Property Act 1925, section 146(1).
927. [1935] 1 KB 87.
928. [1998] SGHC 150; [1998] 2 SLR(R) 258 at [13].
929. CLPA, section 18(2).
930. *Ibid.*, section 18(3).
931. *Lee Tat Realty Pte Ltd v. Limco Products Manufacturing Pte Ltd* [1998] SGHC 150; [1998] 2 SLR(R) 258 at [49].

a relief against forfeiture should be denied where the tenant has committed a repudiatory breach. Otherwise, the principle of repudiatory breach would be rendered redundant.

450. A relief against forfeiture may be granted with conditions attached, e.g. to pay compensation, to remedy the breach or to refrain from future breaches.[932] In *Lee Tat Realty*, the tenant, in breach of a term of the lease, fixed to the premises two signboards without the landlord's consent.[933] When the landlord complained about the breach, the tenants removed the signboards. Chao J held that the breach was purely technical as the purpose of the term was to give the landlord a measure of control over the kind of signboard that is allowed and where it should be put. In granting relief against forfeiture, the learned judge also ordered the tenant to either restore the wall to its original condition or to pay the landlord $5000 as compensation.

451. Where a lease is forfeited, the court may, on the application of a subtenant, make an order vesting the lease in him, upon such conditions the court deems fit. [934] However, the subtenant shall not be given a term that is longer than what he had in his sublease.

E. Non-payment of Rent and Relief Against Forfeiture

452. Where the right of forfeiture arises from the tenant's non-payment of rent, section 18A of the CLPA gives the tenant two opportunities to avoid forfeiture.[935] Unlike the relief against forfeiture in section 18, the relief in section 18A is not discretionary but automatic. The tenant may, within the time given for acknowledging service of the writ, pay into court all the rent in arrears and the costs of the action. If he makes such payment, there shall be no forfeiture of the lease.[936] If he does not, the court shall make an order that possession of the premises be given to the landlord upon the expiration of 4 weeks or for any longer period. Within this period the tenant may pay into court the arrears in rent and costs of the action. If he does so, the order of possession will cease to be effective.[937] But if he does not, the order of possession shall be enforced and the tenant shall be barred from all relief.[938]

932. CLPA, section 18(4).
933. [1998] SGHC 150; [1998] 2 SLR(R) 258.
934. CLPA, section 18(6).
935. *Ibid.*, section 18A(6) states that section 18A shall not apply if in the same action the landlord seeks to enforce his right of forfeiture by relying also on other grounds.
936. *Ibid.*, section 18A (2).
937. *Ibid.*, section 18A(3)–(5).
938. *Ibid.*, section 18A(7).

F. *Equitable Relief Against Forfeiture*

453. For cases where sections 18 and 18A have no application, it is arguable that a court may exercise its general equitable jurisdiction to grant relief where appropriate.[939] Recall that section 18 of the CLPA does not apply in a case where the tenant has breached a covenant prohibiting assignment, subletting or parting possession with, the premises. If the tenant could somehow regain possession of the premises at his own cost, it would seem unfair to allow forfeiture of the lease. Another example is where a subtenant wishes to pay the rent owed by the tenant to avoid forfeiture.[940] Unlike section 18, the right to obtain relief against forfeiture in section 18A is available only to a tenant. Neither does section 18A allow a subtenant to take the place of the tenant in the event of forfeiture.

454. The factors to be taken into account in deciding whether to grant a relief are broadly those stated in sections 18 and 18A. In *Shiloh Spinners v. Harding*, Lord Wilberforce said that the word 'appropriate' involves 'consideration of the conduct of the applicant for relief, in particular whether his default was wilful, of the gravity of the breaches, and of the disparity between the value of the property of which forfeiture is claimed as compared with the damage caused by breach'.[941]

939. CLA, section 3.

940. Tang Hang Wu and Kelvin F.K. Low, *Tan Sook Yee's Principles of Singapore Land Law*, 3rd edn (LexisNexis, 2009) at 508.

941. [1973] AC 691 at 723–24.

Chapter 7. Licences

§1. Introduction

455. A landowner (*A*) may permit someone else (*B*) to enter his land or to use the land in a particular manner.[942] Where *B*'s permitted use of the land does not significantly conflict with *A*'s right to possession, the permission is likely to take the form of a licence. Although, in principle, *A* may grant *B* exclusive possession by way of a licence, the more likely inference in such a case is that a lease has been created.[943] A licence also has the tendency to be less formal in its description[944] and less certain in its duration.[945]

456. The nature and strength of a licence necessarily depend on the type of licence one is dealing with. In this chapter, four types of licences will be examined: (i) bare licence; (ii) contractual licence; (iii) licence coupled with a grant of an interest; and (iv) licence coupled with an equity.[946] From a licensee's perspective, a bare licence is clearly the weakest while a contractual licence is arguably the strongest.

457. In recent years the situations in which it is necessary to distinguish a lease from a licence have been gradually reduced. Tenants no longer receive special protection since the abolition of the Control of Rent Act.[947] The courts are also increasingly willing to protect a licensee's interest. Where a licensee is in possession with effective control of the land, or has a right to possession of the land, he may sue third-party intruders for trespass and bring proceedings to recover possession of the land.[948] More significantly, a licensee who has been granted a *right* to exclusive possession[949] of the land is entitled to specific and injunctive relief against the licensor's interference.[950] In light of these, Gray and Gray made an interesting observation:

> If the proprietary quality of a right is measured in terms of the protection afforded to it (particularly against comers), many contractual licences can justifiably be claimed to have some proprietary dimension. Proprietary character

942. Kevin Gray and Susan Francis Gray, *Elements of Land Law*, 5th edn (OUP, 2009) Chapters 10.2–10.5; Tang Hang Wu and Kelvin F.K. Low, *Tan Sook Yee's Principles of Singapore Land Law*, 3rd edn (LexisNexis, 2009) Chapter 19.
943. *See* Chapter 6 (Leases) §3.II.
944. *See e.g. Abdul Rahim v. British & Malayan Trustees Ltd* [1966] SGFC 8; [1965–1967] SLR(R) 390.
945. *See e.g. Ng Heng Keang v. Kim Poh Eng* [1976] SGHC 11; [1974–1976] SLR(R) 836.
946. *Chiam Heng Luan v. Chiam Heng Hsien* [2007] SGHC 132; [2007] 4 SLR(R) 305 at [53].
947. (Cap 58, 1985 Rev. Ed.); abolished by the Control of Rent (Abolition) Act 2001 (No. 14 of 2001). *See* Chapter 6 (Leases) §3.II.
948. *Manchester Airport Plc v. Dutton* [2000] 1 QB 133; *Countryside Residential (North Thames) Ltd v. T* (2001) 81 P & CR 2.
949. This excludes a bare licence and a licence coupled with a grant of an interest, neither of which entails the granting of exclusive possession of the land.
950. *See* §2.II. below. *See also Jal Mehta v. Royal Bank of Scotland Plc* [1999] L&TR 340, where the evicted licensee successfully sued the licensor for trespass.

is not the cause, but rather the consequence, of curial relief in support of a right. Equity's increasing willingness to protect contractual licences by specific performance and injunction has inevitably enhanced the proprietary content of the licensee's entitlement.[951]

458. While it is true that a contractual licence increasingly resembles a lease in many respects, there remain important differences between the two. Unlike a lease, a licence is not an estate in land.[952] This has a number of implications. First, a licence is not inheritable.[953] It automatically determines if the licensee dies. Second, a licence does not generally bind the licensor's successor in title.[954] Thus, a licence is less desirable where the letting is for a long term.

§2. Types of Licences

I. Bare Licence

459. A bare licence is a licence that is granted gratuitously. An invitation to one's place for dinner is a classic example. A bare licence may also be implied. For example, if the pathway leading to the entrance of a house is unobstructed and there is no notice prohibiting visitors, the law implies a licence in favour of any members of the public to approach the entrance for the purpose of lawful communication with the owner of the house.[955] A bare licence gives no right to occupy the land.[956] It is a mere privilege with the function of preventing the licensee from being regarded as a trespasser.[957] It follows that the licensee has nothing to assign and nothing out of which he could grant a sublicence.[958]

460. A bare licence may be revoked by notice at any time without reasonable cause,[959] although the licensee does not immediately become a trespasser upon the notice being conveyed to him.[960] He is to be allowed a reasonable time to leave the house. Thereafter he no longer has a privilege to enter the house. The case of *Wee Kang Whye v. Lee Woon Tong* appears to be the only local authority on point.[961]

951. Kevin Gray and Susan Francis Gray, *Elements of Land Law*, 5th edn (OUP, 2009) at 1327–28.
952. *Chiam Heng Luan v. Chiam Heng Hsien* [2007] SGHC 132; [2007] 4 SLR(R) 305 at [53]; *Neo Hock Pheng v. Teo Siew Peng* [1999] SGCA 97; [1999] 1 SLR(R) 592 at [19]; *Tan Hin Leong v. Lee Teck Im* [2001] SGCA 7; [2001] 1 SLR(R) 167 at [18], [25]–[27]; *Street v. Mountford* [1985] AC 809 at 814.
953. *Tan Hin Leong v. Lee Teck Im* [2000] SGHC 70; [2000] 1 SLR(R) 891 at [32] (Selvam J).
954. *See* §3 below.
955. *Halliday v. Nevill* (1984) 155 CLR 1.
956. *Thomas v. Sorrell* (1673) Vaugh 330 at 351; *Goldsack v. Shore* [1950] 1 KB 708 at 714.
957. *Thomas v. Sorrell* (1673) Vaugh 330 at 351, cited with approval in *Tan Hin Leong v. Lee Teck Im* [2000] SGHC 70; [2000] 1 SLR(R) 891 at [16] (Selvam J).
958. Kevin Gray and Susan Francis Gray, *Elements of Land Law*, 5th edn (OUP, 2009) at 1290.
959. *Winter Gardens Theatre (London) Ltd v. Millennium Productions Ltd* [1948] AC 173 at 188.
960. *Winter Gardens Theatre (London) Ltd v. Millennium Productions Ltd* [1948] AC 173 at 188–89.
961. [1971–1973] SLR(R) 826 at [13].

II. Contractual Licence

461. Where a licence is conferred by way of a contract, its scope and revocability is necessarily determined by the terms of the contract.[962] A licence can be granted for a fixed term. It may also be granted on a periodic basis, e.g. from month to month, in which case the necessary advance notice must be given to terminate the licence. Where the contract is silent on these matters, the intention of the parties is to be inferred from the circumstances of the case. Much depends on the purpose for which the licence was granted. A classic example would be a person who has purchased a ticket to watch a movie. In this case it is fair to imply that he has a right to be on the premises when the movie is being shown and to be allowed a reasonable time to leave the premises after the movie ends.[963] This is a straightforward case because the licence is given for a purpose which is more or less definite in duration.

462. Where the contract does not specify when the licence can be revoked, the courts are usually reluctant to find that the licence is to last perpetually. In *Winter Garden Theatre (London) Ltd v. Millennium Productions Ltd*, the plaintiffs, who were owners of a theatre, granted the defendants a licence to use the theatre for the purpose of producing stage plays, concerts or ballets in return for a weekly payment.[964] A dispute arose when the plaintiffs sought to terminate the agreement by giving the defendants a month's notice. The House of Lords held that it was unlikely that the parties intended to create a perpetual licence, i.e. an irrevocable licence. On the issue of revocability, Lord MacDermott observed that the use of the theatre necessarily involved considerable expenditure and a host of contractual relationships with those who provide and those who seek the entertainment offered. Taking these into account, it was unlikely that the parties intended for the licence to be withdrawn instantly, regardless of the defendants' commitments. In such circumstances, while it is fair to imply that the plaintiffs may give a notice to revoke the licence at any time, the defendants must be given sufficient time to settle their affairs and to vacate the premises. However, as the defendants have failed to show that one month was insufficient to settle their affairs, the notice was held to be valid. Similarly, in *Ng Heng Keang v. Kim Poh Eng*, Chua J held that one month's advance notice is sufficient for the licensees to vacate their stalls from the coffee shop.[965]

463. The reluctance to find a perpetual licence is also illustrated in two local cases. In *Neo Hock Pheng v. Teo Siew Peng*, the boundary fences of the defendants' properties encroached into an adjacent land due to a mistake by the property developer.[966] The adjacent land belonged to the same developer. Upon discovering the mistake, the developer entered into a contract with the defendants' predecessors,

962. *Tan Hin Leong v. Lee Teck Im* [2001] SGCA 7; [2001] 1 SLR(R) 167; *Victoria Hotel v. Ho See Teck* [1965] SGHC 5; [1965–1967] SLR(R) 42. *See also Winter Gardens Theatre (London) Ltd v. Millennium Productions Ltd* [1948] AC 173.
963. *Winter Gardens Theatre (London) Ltd v. Millennium Productions Ltd* [1948] AC 173 at 189.
964. [1948] AC 173.
965. [1976] SGHC 11; [1974–1976] SLR(R) 836.
966. [1999] SGCA 97; [1999] 1 SLR(R) 592 (Yong CJ, Karthigesu and Thean JJA).

agreeing not to sell the encroached portion of the land and to grant to the latter a licence to use the said land. The agreement stated that the licence was 'granted in perpetuity'. Subsequently, the developer sold the land to the plaintiffs. Upon discovering that their land was being encroached upon, the plaintiffs sued the defendants for trespass and sought to recover the encroached portion of their land. The defendants resisted the claim and joined the developer as a third party to the proceedings. The Court of Appeal held that the licence, being one for an indefinite period, was revocable at will.[967] In this case the licence was revoked when the developer sold the land to the plaintiffs without excluding the encroached portion.[968]

464. In *Tan Hin Leong v. Lee Teck Im*, a stepson agreed to let his stepmother have possession of his house.[969] In return, she agreed to pay an annual rent of $12 and undertook certain obligations in relation to the maintenance of the house. The agreement expressly stated that the licence was personal to the stepmother and shall automatically lapse upon her death. The agreement also stated that the licence could be immediately revoked if she breaches any of the obligations that she undertook. The Court of Appeal affirmed its own decision in *Neo Hock Pheng*, but held that contractual licence in the present case was limited to the lifetime of the stepmother and not for an indefinite period.[970] The licence could be revoked during her lifetime only if she commits a breach of contract.

465. In the earlier case of *Victoria Hotel v. Ho See Teck*, the proprietor of a hotel granted the defendant a licence to run a restaurant on the ground floor for as long as the hotel continued to exist and the defendant being personally ready and willing to run the restaurant. [971] In return, the defendant made an upfront payment of $6,000 and undertook to pay the plaintiff 10% commission on his gross monthly takings. A dispute arose when the plaintiff sought to revoke the licence by giving three days' notice. Winslow J, applying *Winter Garden*, said that the revocability of the licence depended on the terms of the contract. The learned judge came to the conclusion that an irrevocable licence had been granted. At first sight, this decision appears to be inconsistent with *Neo Hock Pheng*. The licence was clearly for an indefinite period. However, following *Tan Hin Leong*, it is obvious that what the courts truly abhor is a perpetual licence, not an indefinite licence. In *Victoria Hotel*, the licence would last only as long as the defendant was *personally* ready and willing to run the restaurant. Put differently, the licence will not outlast the defendant's lifetime. It was not intended to be a perpetual licence.

466. The extent to which a contractual licensee who is entitled to remain on the land may resist repossession by the landlord is a more difficult question. Can the landlord revoke the licence notwithstanding his contractual obligation not to do so?

---

967. [1999] SGCA 97; [1999] 1 SLR(R) 592 at [22].
968. [1999] SGCA 97; [1999] 1 SLR(R) 592 at [23].
969. [2001] SGCA 7; [2001] 1 SLR(R) 167 (Yong CJ, Thean and Chao JJA).
970. [2001] SGCA 7; [2001] 1 SLR(R) 167 at [17].
971. [1965] SGHC 5; [1965–1967] SLR(R) 42.

Is the licensee confined to a claim for damages for breach of contract? In *Thompson v. Park*, where an injunction was granted in favour of the landlord, Goddard LJ said: 'That licence has been withdrawn. Whether it has been rightly withdrawn or wrongly withdrawn matters nothing for this purpose'.[972] This decision has been criticised in subsequent cases. In *Hounslow LBC v. Twickenham Garden Developments Ltd*, Megarry J suggested that a court ought not to grant an injunction in the landlord's favour unless the contract has been validly terminated.[973] This view found favour with the English Court of Appeal in *Verrall v. Great Yarmouth Borough Council* where specific performance was ordered against the landlord who wrongfully repudiated the contract to grant a licence.[974] Lord Denning MR explained:

> Since the *Winter Garden* case, it is clear that once a man has entered under his contract of licence, he cannot be turned out. An injunction can be obtained against the licensor to prevent his being turned out. On principle it is the same if it happens before he enters. If he has a contractual right to enter, and the licensor refuses to let him come in, then he can come to the court and in a proper case get an order for specific performance to allow him to come in.[975]

467. In Singapore, *Thompson v. Park* was considered in *Victoria Hotel*, where the learned judge said: 'All that this case decided was that once such a licence has been revoked by the exercise of a lawful power any reentry by the licensee would amount to a trespass'.[976] While this interpretation of *Thompson v. Park* is arguably doubtful, the learned judge clearly took the view that revocation of a licence could only be done lawfully. The issue was put beyond doubt in *Tan Hin Leong* where the Court of Appeal said: 'In addition to damages, equitable remedies such as specific performance or injunction are available to ensure that a licence will not be wrongfully revoked against the terms of the bargain'.[977]

468. While a contractual licence is assignable, there are disadvantages in doing so. The basic rule of assignment is that only benefits of the licence are assignable. The licensee's assignee, while entitled to enjoy the benefits of the licence, is under no legal obligation to perform the duties under the licence. Without the benefit of the doctrine of estate, covenants which touch and concern the land do not bind the assignee. Thus, the licensee will be constantly at risk of being sued by the licensor for the assignee's breach. A licensee may also grant a sublicence.[978] However, where the contract explicitly states that the licence is personal to the licensee, the licensee shall not assign or sublicence.[979] While an assignment or sublicensing in breach of

972. [1944] KB 408 at 410.
973. [1971] 1 Ch 233.
974. [1981] 1 QB 202, cited with approval in *Tan Hin Leong v. Lee Teck Im* [2000] SGHC 70; [2000] 1 SLR(R) 891 at [22]–[24] (Selvam J).
975. [1981] 1 QB 202 at 216.
976. [1965] SGHC 5; [1965–1967] SLR(R) 42 at [19].
977. [2001] SGCA 7; [2001] 1 SLR(R) 167 at [23].
978. *Winter Gardens Theatre (London) Ltd v. Millennium Productions Ltd* [1948] AC 173 at 202.
979. *Tan Hin Leong v. Lee Teck Im* [2000] SGHC 70; [2000] 1 SLR(R) 891 at [32] (Selvam J).

the contract is likely to be valid, the licensee has arguably committed a repudiatory breach entitling the licensor to terminate the contract and revoke the licence.

III. Licence Coupled with a Grant of an Interest

469. Where a landowner enters into a contract to sell something on his land on terms that the purchaser is responsible for removing that thing, the purchaser is granted a licence coupled with a grant of interest, which entitles him/her to enter the land and remove the thing.[980] Such a licence gives the licensee a right, not a mere privilege. It is irrevocable until the purpose for which the licence is granted ceases.[981] During the subsistence of the licence, it is assignable[982] unless assignment is restricted by a contrary term.[983]

470. Although the word 'interest' was once given an expansive meaning,[984] in *Hounslow*, Megarry J strongly argued for a more restrictive approach:

> ... I feel great doubt whether the word 'interest' means anything more than an interest in property, though it matters not whether that property is real or personal, or legal or equitable. Today, with contractual licences recognised as being capable of being made irrevocable in their own right, there is no need to torture the word 'interest' into embracing miscellaneous collections of rights.[985]

Indeed, many of the older cases purportedly dealing with a licence coupled with a grant of interest are better understood as concerning contractual licences.[986]

IV. Licence Coupled with Equity

471. A licence coupled with an equity, or an equitable licence, is 'a licence arising from the conduct or representation of the parties operating as an estoppel'.[987] A classic situation is where *A*, a landowner, allows *B* to occupy the land and makes certain representation to the effect that *B* would have some interest in the land. In

980. *See e.g. James Jones & Sons v. Earl of Tankerville* [1909] 2 Ch 441 (where the licensee was allowed to enter the land and to cut and remove timbers); *Muskett v. Hill* (1839) 5 Bing 694 (where the licensee was allowed to enter the land, mine minerals and carry the minerals away).
981. *James Jones & Sons v. Earl of Tankerville* [1909] 2 Ch 441; *Hounslow LBC v. Twickenham Garden Developments Ltd* [1971] 1 Ch 233.
982. *Muskett v. Hill* (1839) 5 Bing 694 at 710.
983. *Woods v. Donnelly* [1982] NI 257.
984. *See e.g. Vaughan v. Hampson* (1875) 33 LT 15; *Hurst v. Picture Theatres Ltd* [1915] 1 KB 1.
985. [1971] 1 Ch 233 at 254.
986. *See e.g. Winter Gardens Theatre (London) Ltd v. Millennium Productions Ltd* [1948] AC 173 at 189, reinterpreting *Hurst v. Picture Theatres Ltd* [1915] 1 KB 1 as concerning a contractual licence.
987. *Tan Hin Leong v. Lee Teck Im* [2001] SGCA 7; [2001] 1 SLR(R) 167 at [23]. *See also National Provincial Bank Ltd v. Hastings Car Mart Ltd* [1964] Ch 665 at 686–87.

reliance of *A*'s representation, *B* expends money for the benefit of the land. If *A* tries to evict *B*, *B* is likely to succeed in a claim for proprietary estoppel.[988] The court has a wide discretion as to what remedy to award.[989] Although rare, a possible remedy is an order for an equitable licence to be created, thus allowing *B* to continue staying on the land.[990] The duration of the licence necessarily depends on the nature of the representation and the extent of *B*'s detriment.

§3. Licences and Third Party

472. A bare licence does not bind a third party.[991] The licensor's act of transferring or selling his title in the land automatically revokes the licence.[992] As for a licence coupled with a grant of interest, there is no clear authority that it is binding on a third party.[993]

473. A licence coupled with an equity is binding on a third party.[994] The licensee ought to protect it by lodging a caveat. It is important to note, however, that prior to a declaration by the court, all that the claimant has is an inchoate equity, which may or may not crystallise into an equitable licence.[995] Where the land is transferred to a third party before the licensee could seek a declaration, the court is unlikely to award an equitable licence unless the conscience of the third party is materially affected in some way (see below).

474. A contractual licence is traditionally regarded as strictly personal and therefore does not bind the licensor's successor in title.[996] This view is most strongly held in respect of short-term contractual licences. As Lathan CJ said in *Cowell v. Rosehill Racecourse Co Ltd*, '[f]ifty thousand people who pay to see a football match do

988. *See generally* W.J.M. Ricquier and Soon Choo Hock, 'The "Licence Coupled with Equity" in Singapore and Malaysia' (1981) 23 Malaya LR 123; W.J.M. Ricquier, *Land Law*, 5th edn (LexisNexis, 2017) at 245–47; Tang Hang Wu and Kelvin F.K. Low, *Tan Sook Yee's Principles of Singapore Land Law*, 3rd edn (LexisNexis, 2009) at Chapter 7.
989. The court may award compensation instead of imposing an equitable licence: see e.g. *Lee Suat Hong v. Teo Lye* [1987] SGCA 4; [1987] SLR(R) 70. Although the headnote of the judgment referred to a claim for a tenancy coupled with an equity, this is arguably inaccurate since the occupier did not pay any rent. A better view is that the occupier was claiming a licence coupled with an equity.
990. Impliedly recognised in *Wee Kang Whye v. Lee Woon Tong* [1971–1973] SLR(R) 826.
991. For the present purposes, the term 'third party' refers to the licensor's successor in title, e.g. a purchaser or a gratuitous transferee.
992. An analogy could be drawn with the case of *Neo Hock Pheng v. Teo Siew Peng* [1999] SGCA 97; [1999] 1 SLR(R) 592 (see §2.II. above).
993. Unless the licence amounts to an easement. *See* Chapter 8 (Easements).
994. *National Provincial Bank Ltd v. Car Mart Ltd* [1964] Ch 665 at 686.
995. Tang Hang Wu and Kelvin F.K. Low, *Tan Sook Yee's Principles of Singapore Land Law*, 3rd edn (LexisNexis, 2009) at 170–76, 612–13.
996. *King v. David Allen and Sons, Billposting, Ltd* [1916] AC 54; *Clore v. Theatrical Properties Ltd* [1936] 3 All ER 483.

not obtain fifty thousand interests in the football ground'.[997] In the case of long-term contractual licences, the courts have been more willing to protect the licensees' interests. However, there is much disagreement about the situations in which protection should be afforded to the licensee.

475. In *Binions v. Evans*, the landowners entered into an agreement with the widow of a former employee under which the latter was allowed to occupy a house on the Estate's land rent-free for the remainder of her life.[998] In return, the widow undertook obligations to maintain the house and its garden. The landowners subsequently sold the land but sought to protect the widow's interest by inserting a special clause in the contract of sale. The special clause provided that the land was sold subject to the widow's interest and the purchaser shall not raise any objection regarding this matter. By reason of this special clause the purchaser paid a reduced price for the land. Six months after the sale, the purchaser sought to evict the widow. The Court of Appeal found in the widow's favour but their reasoning differed. Megaw and Stephenson LJJ held that the agreement created a tenancy for life under the Settled Land Act 1925. On the other hand, Lord Denning MR held that the agreement created a contractual licence and went on to lay down two broad propositions on its effect on third parties. First, a licensee in actual occupation has an equitable interest in the land.[999] This is binding on the licensor's successor in title except a purchaser for value without notice.[1000] Second, where a purchaser agrees to purchase land subject to an existing licence and pays a reduced price, a constructive trust will be imposed to protect the licensee's interest on the simple reason that it would be inequitable for the purchaser to resile on his promise.[1001]

476. In *Ashburn Anstalt v. Arnold*, the Court of Appeal approved the second proposition but not the first.[1002] Fox LJ, who delivered the judgment of the court, was of the view that the first proposition was contrary to the orthodox view that a contractual licence does not give rise to any estate or interest in land.[1003] The second proposition was also further refined and clarified.[1004] A constructive trust will only be imposed where the conscience of the licensor's successor in title is affected.[1005] Mere notice of the contractual licence is insufficient. It must be a case where the successor in title has undertaken to give effect to the licence. *Binions v.*

997. (1937) 56 CLR 605 at 616.
998. [1972] Ch 359.
999. [1972] Ch 359 at 367–68.
1000. Lord Denning MR expressed the same view in a few other cases: *National Provincial Bank Ltd v. Hastings Car Mart Ltd* [1964] Ch 665 at 686–88; *Errington v. Errington and Woods* [1952] 1 KB 290 at 299; *DHN Food Distributors Ltd v. Tower Hamlets Borough Council* [1976] 1 WLR 852 at 859.
1001. [1972] Ch 359 at 368.
1002. [1989] Ch 1.
1003. [1989] Ch 1 at 22, 24. *See also Chiam Heng Luan v. Chiam Heng Hsien* [2007] SGHC 132; [2007] 4 SLR(R) 305 at [53]; *Neo Hock Pheng v. Teo Siew Peng* [1999] SGCA 97; [1999] 1 SLR(R) 592 at [19]; *Tan Hin Leong v. Lee Teck Im* [2001] SGCA 7; [2001] 1 SLR(R) 167 at [18], [25]–[27].
1004. [1989] Ch 1 at 25–26.
1005. Cited with approval in *Guy Neale and others v. Ku De Ta SG Pte Ltd* [2015] SGCA 28; [2015] 4 SLR 283 at [80]; *UJT v. UJR* [2018] SGHC 44 at [72]–[73].

Evans was clearly such a case. The fact that the purchaser had paid a discounted purchase price was also an important consideration.

477. It is important to ask how all these fit within the Torrens system. The third-party purchaser acquires an indefeasible title by virtue of section 46 of the Land Titles Act.[1006] To defeat the purchaser's title, the licensee must be able to invoke a statutory exception to indefeasibility.[1007] While section 46 sets out a trust exception, the Court of Appeal in *United Overseas Bank Ltd v. Bebe bte Mohammad* expressed reservation about whether a constructive trust could come within this exception.[1008] However, it might be possible to understand *Binions v. Evans* as a case coming within the fraud exception[1009] in light of the Court of Appeal's reinterpretation[1010] of its previous holding in *Ho Kon Kim v. Lim Gek Kim Betsy*.[1011]

478. The focus on the principle of indefeasibility, however, assumes that the contractual licence amounts to a prior proprietary interest. This appears to be placing the cart before the horse since the question of whether a contractual licence amounts to a property right, and thus binding on a third party, has yet to receive a firm answer. Section 95(2) of the LTA appears to shed some hint. The section states that no licence shall be notified in the land register but 'where a licence relating to the use or enjoyment of land is by law binding on assigns of the licensor, the licensee thereunder shall be deemed to have an interest in the land for the purposes of section 115'. According to Baalman, the insertion of this section was 'necessitated by the fact that English Courts have recently given birth to a new interest in land, a licence to occupy land which is binding on assigns of the licensor'.[1012] He cited *Errington v. Errington*.[1013] However, in *Ashburn Anstalt v. Arnold*, the Court of Appeal held that the result of that case was explicable on other grounds and disapproved Denning LJ's reasoning that a contractual licence gave rise to an equitable interest.[1014] Thus, the continued relevance of section 95(2) is now in doubt.

479. Perhaps the protection of the licensee can be achieved by other means without having to argue that contractual licences constitute property rights. In an interesting article, Bright suggested that the third-party purchaser may incur tortious or contractual liability towards the licensee in three situations.[1015] First, where the property is acquired solely for the purpose of defeating the licensee's interest. Second, where the third party knew that the transfer would violate a term of the licence agreement. Third, where the third party has contractually assumed a responsibility

1006. (Cap. 157, 2004 Rev. Ed.).
1007. LTA, section 46(2)(a)–(e).
1008. [2006] SGCA 30; [2006] 4 SLR(R) 884 at [10].
1009. LTA, section 46(2)(a).
1010. *United Overseas Bank Ltd v. Bebe bte Mohammad* [2006] SGCA 30; [2006] 4 SLR(R) 884 at [73], [76].
1011. [2001] SGCA 62; [2001] 3 SLR(R) 220. *See* Chapter 4 (Torrens System), §5.II.
1012. John Baalman, *The Singapore Torrens system: being a commentary on the Land Titles Ordinance 1956 of the State of Singapore* (Govt. Printer, 1961) at 162.
1013. [1952] 1 KB 290.
1014. [1989] Ch 1 at 16–17.
1015. Susan Bright, 'The Third Party's Conscience in Land Law' [2000] Conv 398.

to respect the licensee's interest. *Binion v. Evans* is a good example of the third situation. Although there is no privity of contract between the licensee and the third party, a liberal interpretation of the Contracts (Rights of Third Parties) Act would allow the licensee to enforce the obligation against the third party.[1016] If there is any issue of indefeasibility, the contract exception may be invoked.[1017]

1016. (Cap 53B, 2002 Rev. Ed.).
1017. LTA, s 46(2)(b).

Chapter 8. Easements[1018]

§1. Definition and Characteristics

480. An easement, broadly stated, is a right to derive some limited benefit from another person's land.[1019] As an easement constitutes a property right, its categories are deliberately limited. Under the common law, a right must satisfy the following conditions to qualify as an easement.[1020]

481. First, there must be a servient land over which the right is enjoyed and a dominant land which benefits from the right.[1021] There can be no easement in gross, i.e. one that does not benefit any land.[1022] It follows that the right must also benefit the dominant owner as an occupier of the dominant land and not in a purely personal capacity. Furthermore, as a general rule, the servient and dominant lands must be owned by separate persons. No person may create for himself/herself an easement over his own land.[1023] However, in the case of tenanted property, it suffices that the reversion and the lease are in separate ownerships.[1024]

482. Second, the right must be sufficiently definite to be capable of grant. There cannot be an easement for general purposes (e.g., for pleasure) or for an unclear duration. It is possible, however, to grant a perpetual easement.[1025]

483. Third, the right must not impose a positive burden on the servient owner, e.g. to keep a road in repair or to supply utilities.[1026] The duty on the servient owner

---

1018. *See* Kevin Gray and Susan Francis Gray, *Elements of Land Law*, 5th edn (OUP, 2009) Chapters 5.1–5.3; Tang Hang Wu and Kelvin F.K. Low, *Tan Sook Yee's Principles of Singapore Land Law*, 3rd edn (LexisNexis, 2009) Chapter 20.
1019. Kevin Gray and Susan Francis Gray, *Elements of Land Law*, 5th edn (OUP, 2009) at para. 5.1.4.
1020. *Muthukumaran s/o Varthan v. Kwong Kai Chung* [2015] SGCA 69; [2016] 1 SLR 1273 at [39]–[41] (Menon CJ, Phang JA and Chong J); *Wee Siew Bock v. Chan Yuen Yee Alexia Eve* [2012] SGCA 33; [2012] 3 SLR 1053 at [58]–[61] (Chao, Phang and Rajah JJA); *Fragrance Realty Pte Ltd v. Rangoon Investment Pte Ltd* [2013] SGHC 70; [2013] 2 SLR 1007 at [30]. For English authorities, see *Re Ellenborough Park* [1956] Ch 13; *Moncrieff v. Jamieson* [2007] UKHL 42; [2007] 1 WLR 2620.
1021. *See* Land Titles Act (Cap 157, 2004 Rev. Ed.) (LTA), section 94(1): '... 'dominant tenement' and 'servient tenement' mean, respectively, the land to which the benefit of an easement has been made appurtenant, and the land which is subject to the burden of an easement'.
1022. LTA, section 95(1)(b).
1023. *Seah Sye Kim v. Chua Mui Ying* [1988] SGHC 15; [1988] 1 SLR(R) 116 at [33]: 'A man cannot have an easement over his own land, because all acts which he does upon his own land are acts done in respect of his rights as owner of the land, and the law does not allow the coexistence of an easement over land with the possession of the land itself.' Subsequently affirmed in *Management Corporation Strata Title Plan No 549 v. Chew Eu Hock Construction Co Pte Ltd* [1998] SGCA 41; [1998] 2 SLR(R) 934 at [37].
1024. *Ohna Mohamed Abubakar v. Tho Yan Poh* [1915] 13 SSLR 39.
1025. *Lian Kok Hong v. Lee Choi Kheong* [2010] SGCA 19; [2010] 3 SLR 378 at [24]; *Frontfield Investment Holding (Pte) Ltd v. Management Corporation Strata Title Plan No 938* [2001] SGHC 161; [2001] 2 SLR(R) 410 at [31].
1026. *Regis Property co Ltd v. Redman* [1956] 2 QB 612.

should be wholly negative, i.e. to refrain from interfering with the dominant owner's right or from doing something that is expressly prohibited under the grant.

484. Fourth, since an easement is, by definition, a right to derive some limited benefit from the servient land, it must not deprive the servient owner of all beneficial proprietorship of the servient land.[1027] In *Fragrance Realty Pte Ltd v. Rangoon Investment Pte Ltd*, the defendants erected a retaining wall across the plaintiff's land, thus creating a compound within which the defendants parked their cars and stored their goods.[1028] Ang J held that the right claimed by the defendants could not amount to an easement as the retaining wall prevented the plaintiff from exercising beneficial use and control of the encroached portion of its land.[1029] The result would have been different had the servient owner retained control and possession of the area serving the alleged easement such that he could use it for other purposes that do not interfere with the easement.[1030]

485. Easements can be positive or negative. Most recognised easements are positive. They concern rights to use servient lands for clearly defined purposes, e.g. as an access way[1031], to store goods[1032] or to park vehicles.[1033] Negative easements, which impose prohibitions on the use of the servient land, are viewed with caution due to their potential to unduly restrict the servient owner's enjoyment of his land and hamper legitimate development.[1034] The few negative easements that are presently recognised include a right to receive sufficient light through a defined aperture (e.g., a window of a building)[1035] and a right to non-interference of existing electricity or water supply to the dominant land.[1036]

486. The nature and characteristics of an easement recognised under the common law are mostly preserved under the LTA.[1037] Thus, section 95(1)(a) provides:

> The Registrar shall not register as an easement any instrument purporting to create an interest –
>
> (a) of a kind which has not been recognised by law as an easement; or

---

1027. *Fragrance Realty Pte Ltd v. Rangoon Investment Pte Ltd* [2013] SGHC 70; [2013] 2 SLR 1007 at [32]–[35].
1028. [2013] SGHC 70; [2013] 2 SLR 1007.
1029. [2013] SGHC 70; [2013] 2 SLR 1007 at [35]. The same conclusion was arrived at in *Lim Hong Seng v. East Coast Medicare Centre Pte Ltd* [1994] SGHC 270; [1994] 3 SLR(R) 680, although the issue of ouster was not clearly addressed.
1030. *See Moncrieff v. Jamieson* [2007] UKHL 42; [2007] 1 WLR 2620.
1031. *Lim Hong Seng v. East Coast Medicare Centre Pte Ltd* [1994] SGHC 270; [1994] 3 SLR(R) 680.
1032. *Yim Yip Kae v. Kwong Hock Cheng Sawmill & Co Ltd* [1954] MLJ 21 (Singapore).
1033. *Fragrance Realty Pte Ltd v. Rangoon Investment Pte Ltd* [2013] SGHC 70; [2013] 2 SLR 1007 at [35].
1034. *Phipps v. Pears* [1965] 1 QB 76 at 82–84.
1035. *Colls v. Home and Colonial Stores Ltd* [1904] AC 179.
1036. *Rance v. Elvin* (1985) 50 P & CR 9; *Duffy v. Lamb* (1997) 75 P & CR 364.
1037. *Muthukumaran s/o Varthan v. Kwong Kai Chung* [2015] SGCA 69; [2016] 1 SLR 1273 at [41] (Menon CJ, Phang JA and Chong J).

(b) which is not expressed to be appurtenant to land (whether registered land or otherwise) of a person other than the proprietor or owner of the site of the easement.

487. However, the LTA introduced limited exceptions to the prohibition against exclusive possession by the dominant owner. For example, section 96 provides:

> [T]he fact that a right to lay or maintain pipes or other installations through the land of a proprietor confers on the person or authority entitled to that right the exclusive possession or occupation of the soil, or of the space occupied by the pipes or other installations, shall not of itself prevent the right of passage of matter or energy through the pipes or other installations being registrable as an easement.

488. Similarly, section 104 permits the granting of an easement for the construction of a party wall along the common boundaries of the servient and dominant lands. This is notwithstanding the fact that the wall, being a permanent structure, necessarily entails exclusive occupation of the soil on which it is erected.

489. The proprietary nature of easements is partly reflected in section 101, which provides that where the dominant land is transferred or leased, the easement shall pass to the transferee or leasee without the need for express mention in the transfer or lease.[1038] Although the LTA does not say the same with regards to the burden of an easement, it is generally assumed that upon a transfer of the servient land the burden automatically passes to the transferee.[1039]

§2. Easement Distinguished from Other Rights

I. Natural Rights

490. Natural rights are ordinary incidents of ownership in land. Common examples include right to lateral support for lands and buildings,[1040] right to waterway serving the land,[1041] right to drain naturally collected water through and over a lower adjacent land,[1042] and etc.[1043] Although natural rights are sometimes

1038. LTA, section 101(1).
1039. *See e.g. Lian Kok Hong v. Lee Choi Kheong* [2010] SGCA 19; [2010] 3 SLR 378.
1040. State Lands Act (Cap 157, 2004 Rev. Ed.) section 3C. *See also Xpress Print Pte Ltd v. Monocrafts Pte Ltd* [2000] SGCA 37; [2000] 2 SLR(R) 614 (Yong CJ, Thean and Chao JJA), noted in Tang Hang Wu, 'The Right of Lateral Support of Buildings from the Adjoining Land' (2002) Conv 237; Teo Keng Sood, 'Right of Support for Buildings Revisited' (2004) 78 ALJ 20; Prakash Pillai, 'The Primacy of the Principle of Reciprocity in the Singapore Land Regime' (2001) SAcLJ 198.
1041. *Yim Yip Kae v. Kwong Hock Cheong Sawmill & Co Ltd* [1954] MLJ 21.
1042. *Medway Investments Pte Ltd v. Trustees of the Estate of Cheong Eak Chong, deceased* [1997] SGCA 18; [1997] 1 SLR(R) 934 (Yong CJ, Karthigesu and Thean JJA).

referred to as easements, they are different in that natural rights come into existence automatically without the need for acquisition by grant.[1044]

II. Profit-à-*Prendre*

491. A profit-à-*prendre* is a right granted by a landowner allowing the grantee to sever and take natural resources capable of ownership from the land.[1045] Like an easement, a profit-à-*prendre* constitutes a property interest in the grantor's land.[1046] However, unlike an easement, a profit-à-*prendre* may exist in gross, i.e. it need not appertain to any dominant tenement.[1047] Today, profits-à-*prendre* have little role to play due to the high level of urbanisation in Singapore. When the LTA was revised in 1993, the provision providing for the grant and registration of profits-à-*prendre* was omitted.[1048]

III. Restrictive Covenants

492. Restrictive covenants[1049] are sometimes referred to as negative easements. However, while an easement is normally created by way of grant, a restrictive covenant normally arises from a contract between landowners. It follows that an easement can be acquired by prescription, i.e. implied grant from long continuous user, but a restrictive covenant cannot. Another difference is that the restriction that may be imposed on the servient land is less circumscribed if imposed by way of a covenant. In recognition of the fact that easements and restrictive covenants are distinct creatures, the LTA deals with them in separate provisions.

IV. Licence

493. Depending on the manner in which it is created, a licence may either constitute a privilege or a right to use the grantor's land.[1050] Even where the licence constitutes a right, it is merely a personal right, binding only between the grantor and grantee.[1051] Unlike an easement, a licence may exist in gross and may entail the granting of exclusive possession of the premises to the licensee.

1043. *See* LTA, section 4(1): ' … the proprietorship of land includes natural rights to air, light, water and support and the right of access to any highway on which the land abuts'. *See also* LTA, section 94(2).
1044. *Bettison v. Langton* [2000] Ch 54 at 61.
1045. *Duke of Sutherland v. Heathcote* [1892] 1 Ch 475 at 484–85.
1046. *R v. Toohey, Ex parte Meneling Station Pty Ltd* [1982] HCA 69; (1982) 158 CLR 327 at 352.
1047. *Bettison v. Langton* [2001] UKHL 24; [2002] 1 AC 27.
1048. *See* Land Title Ordinance (No. 21 of 1956) section 84.
1049. *See* Chapter 9 (Covenants Relating to Land).
1050. *See* Chapter 7 (Licences).
1051. Only in exceptional cases would a licence bind a third party

§3. CREATION

494. The manner of acquiring an easement over registered land are clearly set out in Part XIV of the LTA[1052] Importantly, section 97(1) provides that an easement 'shall not be acquired over registered land by long-continued user adverse to a proprietor, nor by prescription, nor by any presumption of a lost grant, nor by any implication of law except as may be provided in this Act'.[1053] Where a parcel of land has been brought within the registration system, any acquisition of easement thereafter must be through the methods prescribed by the LTA.

495. However, section 46(1)(ii) provides that any easement in existence when the servient land becomes registered land shall continue to bind the title of the servient land as overriding interests. Therefore, in the case of an easement allegedly created before the servient land became registered land, the old common law methods of acquiring easements continue to be relevant.[1054]

I. Registered Land

A. *Express Grant*

496. A landowner may grant an easement by executing an instrument of grant in the approved form or by an appropriate description in an instrument of transfer.[1055] The instrument shall indicate clearly:[1056] (a) the dominant and servient lands;[1057] (b) the nature of the easement and its extent over the servient land;[1058] and (c) any condition, limitation or restriction intended to affect the enjoyment of the easement.[1059] The easement shall be registered by entry of a memorial on the folio of the servient land.[1060] A notification shall also be entered on the folio of the dominant land unless the dominant owner agrees to dispense with any notification.[1061] Where the servient

1052. *See* John Baalman, *The Singapore Torrens system: being a commentary on the Land Titles Ordinance 1956 of the State of Singapore* (Govt. Printer, 1961) at 222–34.
1053. In *Management Corporation Strata Title Plan No 549 v. Chew Eu Hock Construction Co Pte Ltd* [1998] SGCA 4; [1998] 2 SLR(R) 934 at [41], the Court of Appeal held that the rule in *Wheeldon v. Burrows* (1879–80) 12 Ch D 31 (see §2.II.A.(ii). below), although not expressly excluded by section 97(1), does not apply after a land has become registered land.
1054. *Lian Kok Hong v. Lee Choi Kheong* [2010] SGCA 1; [2010] 3 SLR 378 at [14].
1055. LTA, section 97(1).
1056. *Ibid.*, section 97(3) & (4).
1057. According to Baalman, the actual site of the easement must be clearly delineated: John Baalman, *The Singapore Torrens system: being a commentary on the Land Titles Ordinance 1956 of the State of Singapore* (Govt. Printer, 1961) at 167.
1058. This avoids vague descriptions, which are likely to give rise to disputes. For example, in *Lim Hong Seng v. East Coast Medicare Centre Pte Ltd* [1994] SGHC 270; [1994] 3 SLR(R) 680, the grant referred to 'all rights of way' without more. While the plaintiff argued that the right of way allowed motorised vehicles to pass the servient land, the defendant contended that the right of way only allowed access by foot, pushcarts and bicycles.
1059. For example, the duration of the easement may be specified.
1060. LTA, section 97(5).
1061. *Ibid.*, section 97(6).

land is subsequently transferred or leased, the easement shall pass to the transferee or leasee without the need for any express mention in the document of conveyance.[1062]

B. Express Reservation

497. Reservation is the converse of grant. Suppose *A* owns Blackacre and Whiteacre, two adjoining parcels of land. *A* then transfers or leases Blackacre to *B*. If *A* wishes to reserve an easement over Blackacre for the benefit of Whiteacre, he may do so by including a reservation clause in the instrument of transfer or lease.[1063] The instrument, upon registration, shall be effective as a regrant of an easement to *A* without the need for execution by *B*.[1064]

C. Implied by Law

498. Where a parcel of land is subdivided into two or more lots, section 98 implies, in favour of each subdivided lot, easements for the passage of water, electricity, gas, sewerage and drainage. Section 99 further provides that where the competent authority has approved the development and subdivision of any land, there shall be implied easements of way and easements for the construction of party walls in respect of each subdivided lot.[1065]

499. In three important decisions, the Court of Appeal provided clarifications on the scope of section 99. First, the easements will be implied upon subdivision of the land, regardless of whether a development plan has been obtained.[1066] Second, the easements must be indicated in the subdivision plan.[1067] Where the subdivision plan merely hints at such easements without indicating their precise locations, other relevant documents containing the required information may be referred to.[1068] Third, as the easements are implied for the reasonable enjoyment of the subdivided lots and of any building 'at any time thereon', the scope of the easements may vary from

1062. *Ibid.*, section 100(1).
1063. *Ibid.*, section 97(2).
1064. *Ibid.*, section 97(2).
1065. In *Andrew John Hanam v. Lam Vui* [2013] SGHC 159; [2013] 4 SLR 554, Ang J held that section 99 does not imply in favour of the dominant owner a right to access the servient land for the purposes of inspecting or repairing a party wall.
1066. *Cheng-Wong Mei Ling Theresa v. Oei Hong Leong* [2006] SGCA 12; [2006] 2 SLR(R) 637 at [47] (Yong CJ, Chao JA and Kan J).). *See also Muthukumaran s/o Varthan v. Kwong Kai Chung* [2015] SGCA 69; [2016] 1 SLR 1273 at [57] (Menon CJ, Phang JA and Chong J); *Management Corporation Strata Title Plan No 549 v. Chew Eu Hock Construction* [1998] SGCA 41; [1998] 2 SLR(R) 934 at [31]–[32] (Yong CJ, Karthigesu and Thean JJA).
1067. *Muthukumaran s/o Varthan v. Kwong Kai Chung* [2015] SGCA 69; [2016] 1 SLR 1273 at [60]–[62].
1068. *Cheng-Wong Mei Ling Theresa v. Oei Hong Leong* [2006] 2 SLR(R) 637 at [37]–[45]; *Muthukumaran s/o Varthan v. Kwong Kai Chung* [2015] SGCA 69; [2016] 1 SLR 1273 at [63]–[69].

time to time. The easements arise prior to the subdivided lots being developed[1069] and may later extend to serve future developments on the lands.[1070]

500. The Land Titles (Strata) Act[1071] further implies, in respect of each lot in a strata title development, easements of subjacent and lateral support,[1072] of shelter,[1073] of light,[1074] for the passage of water, sewerage, drainage and other services.[1075] Ancillary rights reasonably necessary to make these easements effective are also implied.[1076]

501. These statutorily implied easements are enforceable without the need for notification on the land register.[1077] The invisibility of these easements in the land register is unlikely to be an issue given that they are clearly spelled out in the LTA and the LTSA, and they benefit the owners of the subdivided lots equally.

D. *By Court Order*

502. Section 97A of the LTA allows a court, on application by an interested person, to order the creation of an easement if it is reasonably necessary for the effective use or development of the dominant land. The court will only make such an order if it is satisfied with the following conditions.[1078] First, the land to be benefitted by the easement will not be used in a manner that is inconsistent with public interest. Second, the owner of the land to be burdened by the easement can be adequately compensated for any loss or disadvantage. Third, the applicant has made all reasonable attempts to procure a grant of the easement.

503. Where the court decides to order the creation of an easement, it shall specify in the order the nature and terms of the easement as well as the particulars required under section 97(3).[1079] The easement becomes binding only when it is registered in accordance with section 97.[1080]

1069. *Muthukumaran s/o Varthan v. Kwong Kai Chung* [2015] SGCA 69; [2016] 1 SLR 1273 at [51].
1070. *Management Corporation Strata Title Plan No 549 v. Chew Eu Hock Construction* [1998] SGCA 41; [1998] 2 SLR(R) 934 at [54].
1071. (Cap. 158, 2009 Rev. Ed.) (LTSA).
1072. LTSA, section 16.
1073. *Ibid.*, section 17.
1074. *Ibid.*, section 19.
1075. *Ibid.*, section 18.
1076. *Ibid.*, section 20.
1077. LTA, sections 98(7) and 99(5); LTSA, section 21.
1078. LTA, section 97A(2).
1079. *Ibid.*, section 97A(3).
1080. *Ibid.*, section 97A(5).

II. Unregistered Land

A. *Grant*

1. Express

504. An easement may be expressly granted, either independently or in a conveyance of the dominant tenement. In either case, the grant of the easement must be made by deed in the English language.[1081]. However, if an informal grant (i.e., otherwise than by deed) is relied upon by the grantee to his detriment, the court may declare that the grantee acquires an equity by way of proprietary estoppel[1082] and direct the grantor to satisfy the equity by making a formal grant.[1083]

2. Implied

505. Suppose *A* owns Blackacre and Whiteacre, two adjoining parcels of land. Subsequently, *A* transfers or leases Blackacre to *B*. In certain situations, an easement over Whiteacre may be implied in *B*'s favour to give effect to the parties' common intention.[1084] A simple example is where it is within the contemplation of *A* and *B* that Blackacre will be used for some definite and particular purpose and that purpose cannot be carried out without an easement over Whiteacre. The implication of the easement is based on the principle of non-derogation from grant: 'a grantor having given a thing with one hand is not to take away the means of enjoying it with another'.[1085]

506. In *Wong v. Beaumont Property Trust Ltd*, the owners of a building granted a twenty-one-year lease over three underground cellars for the purpose of operating a restaurant business.[1086] However, the cellars were so badly ventilated that the public health inspector found it absolutely necessary for a new ventilation system to be installed. This required an air duct to be fixed to the back of the building, which belonged to the landlords. As the landlords objected, the tenant argued that he had an easement for this purpose. The Court of Appeal held that an easement was to be implied on the ground of necessity.

507. While necessity is often listed as a separate ground for the implication of an easement, it is now clear that its underlying rationale is to give effect to the parties' common intention.[1087] In *Nickerson v. Barraclough*, Brightman LJ explained

1081. CLPA, section 53.
1082. *ER Ives Investment Ltd v. High* [1967] 2 QB 379.
1083. *Crabb v. Arun DC* [1976] Ch 179.
1084. *Pwllbach Colliery Co Ltd v. Woodman* [1995] AC 634 at 646–47.
1085. *Birmingham, Dudley and District Banking Co v. Ross* (1888) 38 Ch D 295 at 313.
1086. [1965] 1 QB 173.
1087. In *Wong v. Beaumont Property Trust Ltd* [1965] 1 QB 173 at 180, Lord Denning MR, after referring to Lord Parker's dicta in *Pwllbach Colliery Co Ltd v. Woodman* [1995] AC 634, said: 'That is the principle which underlies all easements of necessity'.

that 'the doctrine of way of necessity is not founded upon public policy at all but upon an implication from the circumstances'.[1088] It follows that 'a way of necessity is never found to exist except in association with a grant of land'.[1089]

508. Even if the parties did not contemplate any definite or particular purpose for which Blackacre was to be used, an easement of necessity may still be implied if the absence of an easement would prevent the ordinary use of the land. A straightforward example is where Blackacre is landlocked.[1090] This issue arose for consideration in *Kian Seng & Co v. Ban Hin Lee Bank Ltd.*[1091] There the owner of a building divided it into three parts (front, middle and rear) and let all three parts to different persons. The plaintiff was the tenant of the middle part, which had a side entrance accessible from a path along the side of the building. The land on which the said path was situated belonged to the City Council. Two years later, the City Council closed off the path, thus completely depriving the plaintiff of access to the middle part. The plaintiff claimed to have a right of way through the front part. Tan FJ, although accepting that an easement of necessity could arise in this situation, was reluctant to imply one because it would significantly affect the tenant of the front part. Instead, the learned judge held that the tenancy was subject to an implied term that it would last as long as the middle part was accessible by the said path. When the path was closed off, the tenancy came to an end. While the decision is plainly right, the suggestion that there was an issue of necessity for the purposes of implying an easement is open to question. The middle part was not landlocked when the tenancy was granted. As the Court of Appeal said in *Seah Sye Kim v. Chua Mui Ying*: 'The surrounding circumstances must, of course, be those prevailing at the time when the land was conveyed. If there was no common intention then, it could not have arisen thereafter'.[1092]

509. An easement may also be implied by virtue of the rule in *Wheeldon v. Burrows.*[1093] Thesiger LJ said:

> [O]n the grant by the owner of a tenement of part of that tenement as it is then used and enjoyed, there will pass to the grantee all those continuous and apparent easements (by which, of course, I mean quasi-easements), or, in other words, all those easements which are necessary to the reasonable enjoyment of

1088. [1981] 1 Ch 426 at 440.
1089. *Ibid.*
1090. It is insufficient that the absence of an easement will greatly inconvenience *B*. In *Seah Sye Kim v. Chua Mui Ying* [1988] SGHC 15; [1988] 1 SLR(R) 116, the plaintiff argued that if an easement of way was not implied, she would have had to leave her house by reversing her car down a long and narrow driveway to reach the public road. Grimberg JC held that the absence of an easement did not render the plaintiff's land completely inaccessible and therefore no easement will be implied on the ground of necessity.
1091. [1964] 1 MLJ 207 (Singapore).
1092. [1991] SGCA 30; [1991] 2 SLR(R) 457 at [35].
1093. (1879–80) 12 Ch D 31 at 49.

the property granted, and which have been and are at the time of the grant used by the owners of the entirety for the benefit of the part granted.[1094]

510. It is clear that the rule contemplates a very specific situation. Suppose *A* has been using a driveway running through Whiteacre to access his house on Blackacre. As both parcels of land are in common ownership, *A* cannot be said to have an easement of way over Whiteacre. However, *A* can be said to enjoy a quasi-easement. If *A* subsequently transfers or leases Blackacre to *B*, the same easement of way will be implied in *B*'s favour unless there is an agreement to the contrary. The rule converts the quasi-easement into an easement in favour of *B* by implying a grant. The rule also applies where *A* simultaneously transfers or leases Blackacre and Whiteacre to different persons, e.g. Blackacre to *B* and Whiteacre to *C*.[1095] The right of way will be implied over *C*'s land in favour of *B*.

511. There are three conditions that must be satisfied for the rule to apply. First, the quasi-easement enjoyed by *A* must be necessary for the reasonable enjoyment of Whiteacre. Common examples include rights of way, support, light and drainage. Second, *A*'s enjoyment of the quasi-easement must be continuous up to the time of the transfer, sale or lease to *B*. Third, *A*'s enjoyment of the quasi-easement must be apparent, i.e. discoverable on careful inspection.

3. Section 6 of the CLPA

512. Section 6 of the CLPA[1096] provides that a conveyance[1097] of an unregistered land shall be deemed to include all 'easement, rights and advantages whatsoever, appertaining or reputed to appertain to the land, or any part thereof, or at the time of conveyance demised, occupied or enjoyed with or reputed or known as part or parcel of or appurtenant to the land'.[1098] By implying these general words into a conveyance, the section operates to transfer subsisting easements or rights.[1099]

513. Curiously, this section became best known for its capability to transmute lesser rights or mere advantages into easements. Suppose *A*, who owns Blackacre

1094. (1879–80) 12 Ch D 31 at 49.
1095. *Swansborough v. Coventry* (1832) 9 Bing 305.
1096. The English equivalent is section 6 of the Conveyancing Act 1881, which has since been replaced by section 62 of the Law of Property Act 1925.
1097. A conveyance includes a transfer or a lease made by deed: CLPA, section 2.
1098. CLPA, section 6(1) and (2).
1099. *Lim Hong Seng v. East Coast Medi Care Centre Pte Ltd* [1994] SGHC 270; [1994] 3 SLR(R) 680 at [68]–[72]. *See also* W.J.M. Ricquier, *Land Law*, 5th edn (LexisNexis, 2017) at 255–57. *Cf* Tang Hang Wu and Kelvin F.K. Low, *Tan Sook Yee's Principles of Singapore Land Law*, 3rd edn (LexisNexis, 2009) at 640: 'Section 6 has no effect on existing easements or profits appurtenant to the land conveyed, as these pass with it automatically and without express mention' (citing *Godwin v. Schweppes Ltd* [1902] 1 Ch 926).

and Whiteacre, transfers or leases Blackacre to *B*. If *B* had been in apparent and continuous enjoyment of a right or an advantage over Whiteacre prior to the conveyance,[1100] and the right or advantage is capable of being an easement,[1101] section 6 operates to transform the right or advantage into a full easement that benefits Blackacre.[1102] This transformative effect of section 6 is widely regarded as having originated from the decision of Farwell J in *International Tea Stores Co v. Hobbs*.[1103] There the defendant, who owned two houses separated by a yard, let one to the plaintiff company to be used as a shop. The defendant retained possession and control of the yard but the plaintiff was given permission to use it as a passageway during business hours. The plaintiff eventually bought the reversion of the shop from the defendant. However, for unknown reasons, the permission to use the yard was revoked. Farwell J held that the plaintiff, having enjoyed access through the yard, had acquired a right of way, which passed with the conveyance by virtue of section 6 of the Conveyancing Act 1881. In *Lewis v. Meredith*, Neville J regarded *International Tea Stores* as having laid down the proposition that a mere permission 'may become a legal right upon the grant by force of the general words in s. 6 of the Conveyancing Act, 1881'.[1104] This was cited with approval by the Court of Appeal in *Wright v. Macadam*,[1105] which was in turn followed by the same court in several other cases.[1106]

514. Section 6 also operates to pass to *B* any quasi-easement continuously and apparently enjoyed by *A* over Whiteacre,[1107] thus overlapping with the rule in *Wheeldon v. Burrows*.[1108] Although section 6 is easier to satisfy given the absence of any statutory requirement that the quasi-easement be reasonably necessary for the enjoyment of Whiteacre, it does not apply where there is no formal conveyance of Blackacre to B, e.g. the lease of Blackacre to *B* is by mere agreement, not by deed. In this case, only the rule in *Wheeldon v. Burrows* will apply.

B. Prescription and the Lost Modern Grant

515. Where *B* manages to prove that he had continuous use of *A*'s land as of right for a period of 20 years, the law presumes that *A* had granted *B* an easement

1100. *Payne v. Inwood* (1997) 74 P & CR 42; *Broomfield v. Williams* [1897] 1 Ch 602.
1101. *Burrows v. Lang* [1901] 2 Ch 502 at 512; *Lewis v. Meredith* [1913] 1 Ch 571 at 579; *Wright v. Macadam* [1949] 2 KB 744 at 750, 752; *Regis Property Co Ltd v. Redman* [1956] 2 QB 612 at 627–28, 632.
1102. *See* Simon Douglas, 'How to reform section 62 of the Law of Property Act 1925' [2015] Conv 13.
1103. [1903] 2 Ch 165.
1104. [1913] 1 Ch 571.
1105. [1949] 2 KB 744.
1106. *Goldberg v. Edwards* [1950] Ch 247; *Graham v. Philcox* [1984] QB 747; *P & S Platt Ltd v. Crouch* [2004] P & CR 18.
1107. *P & S Platt Ltd v. Crouch* [2004] P & CR 18.
1108. *See* §2.II.A.(ii). above.

by deed but the deed been misplaced and lost.[1109] The easement is acquired by prescription, specifically based on the doctrine of lost modern grant.[1110] The presumption of lost grant is a recognised fiction and thus it matters not that in fact no grant was ever made.[1111] However, the presumption can be rebutted by any evidence inconsistent with a grant, e.g. the servient owner was incompetent to make such a grant due to incapacity or illegality.[1112]

516. In Singapore, the doctrine of lost modern grant was applied in four instances[1113] and recognised in several other decisions.[1114] Where the land has been registered, it is for the alleged dominant owner to prove 20 years' continuous user prior to the servient land becoming registered land.[1115]

517. The user must be continuous but need not be frequent. The degree of continuity required is dependent on the nature of the easement claimed. The user must also be sufficiently certain and uniform.[1116] Where there is great variation in the user, e.g. in terms of intensity, the prescriptive claim will fail.

518. The user must also be as of right, i.e. exercised without force (*nec vi*), without secrecy (*nec clam*) and without permission (*nec percario*).[1117] All three elements relate to an important ingredient of a prescriptive claim: acquiescence of the user by the servient owner.[1118] If the user is forced or is exercised secretly, the servient owner cannot be said to have acquiesced to the user. The last element requires

---

1109. The seminal case in England is *Dalton v. Angus* (1881) 6 App Cas 740.
1110. The easement is presumed to have been granted at some date after 1189, hence modern. Before the doctrine of lost modern grant was introduced, an easement can be acquired by prescription only upon proof of immemorial user, i.e. since 1189. This method of prescription was held not to apply in Singapore as the history of Singapore began only in 1819 (*Angullia v. Ong Boon Tat* (1910) 15 SSLR 190).
1111. *Lim Hong Seng v. East Coast Medicare Centre Pte Ltd* [1994] SGHC 270; [1994] 3 SLR(R) 680 at [61]; *Fragrance Realty Pte Ltd v. Rangoon Investment Pte Ltd* [2013] SGHC 70; [2013] 2 SLR 1007 at [29].
1112. *Neaverson v. Peterborough Rural District Council* [1902] 1 Ch 557; *Tehidy Minerals Ltd v. Norman* [1971] 1 QB 528 at 552.
1113. *Ohna Mohamed Abubakar v. Tho Yan Poh* [1915] 13 SSLR 39; *Yim Yip Kae v. Kwong Hock Cheng Sawmill & Co Ltd* [1954] MLJ 21 (Singapore); *Lim Hong Seng v. East Coast Medicare Centre Pte Ltd* [1994] SGHC 270; [1994] 3 SLR(R) 680; *Fragrance Realty Pte Ltd v. Rangoon Investment Pte Ltd* [2013] SGHC 70; [2013] 2 SLR 1007.
1114. *MCST Plan No 549 v. Chew Eu Hock Construction Co Pte Ltd* [1998] SGCA 41; [1998] 2 SLR(R) 934 at [39]; *Xpress Print Pte Ltd v. Monocrafts Pte Ltd* [2000] SGCA 37; [2000] 2 SLR(R) 614 at [36]; *Trustees of the Estate of Cheong Eak Chong, deceased v. Medway Investments Pte Ltd* [1996] SGHC 154; [1996] 2 SLR(R) 607 at [26]; *Lee Quee Siew v. Lim Hock Siew* [1895–6] 3 SSLR 80.
1115. *Lim Hong Seng v. East Coast Medicare Centre Pte Ltd* [1994] SGHC 270; [1994] 3 SLR(R) 680 at [51]–[52]; *Fragrance Realty Pte Ltd v. Rangoon Investment Pte Ltd* [2013] SGHC 70; [2013] 2 SLR 1007 at [29]; *Management Corporation Strata Title Plan No 549 v. Chew Eu Hock Construction Co Pte Ltd* [1998] SGCA 41; [1998] 2 SLR(R) 934 at [38].
1116. *Hulley v. Silversprings Bleaching and Dyeing Co Ltd* [1922] 2 Ch 268.
1117. *Gardner v. Hodgson's Kingston Brewery co Ltd* [1903] AC 229 at 239.
1118. *Sturges v. Bridgman* (1879) 11 Ch D 852 at 863; *Mills v. Silver* [1991] Ch 271, applied in *Fragrance Realty Pte Ltd v. Rangoon Investment Pte Ltd* [2013] SGHC 70; [2013] 2 SLR 1007 at [36]–[37].

a distinction to be drawn between tolerated and permitted user. It is only in the case of tolerated user can the servient owner be said to have acquiesced.

519. Finally, it should be noted that whether a prescriptive claim may be brought against an occupier of a leasehold land is unclear. In *Ohna Mohamed Abubakar v. Tho Yan Poh*, Bucknill CJ held that an easement of support could be acquired over a 999-year leasehold estate.[1119] However, in *Angullia v. Ong Boon Tat*, Sproule J preferred the contrary view,[1120] which has the support of English authorities.[1121] The reason is that the doctrine presumes a grant of an easement in perpetuity, which can only be supported by a fee simple estate.[1122] However, there is no logical reason why the presumption cannot be modified such that the servient owner is presumed to have granted an easement for a term of years, rather than in perpetuity. In subsequent local cases in which the doctrine was applied or considered, no attention was paid to whether the servient owner had a fee simple estate or a leasehold estate.

C. *Reservation*

1. Express

520. Reservation of an easement over unregistered land can be achieved only through indirect means. First, *A* may include the reservation in the conveyance and require *B* to execute it. This would essentially be grant by *B*.[1123] Second, *A* may employ the device of a use as provided in section 60 of the CLPA.

2. Implied

521. In *Wheeldon v. Burrows*, Thesiger LJ remarked that 'if the grantor intends to reserve any right over the tenement granted, it is his duty to reserve it expressly in the grant.[1124] This is notwithstanding that *A* was enjoying a quasi-easement over Blackacre before transferring or leasing it to *B*. The principle of non-derogation of grant does not apply here.

522. A reservation may be implied on the ground of necessity or to give effect to the parties' common intention. However, it is very difficult to succeed based on

---

1119. [1915] 13 SSLR 39.
1120. [1910] 15 SSLR 190.
1121. *Simmons v. Dobson* [1991] 1 WLR 720; *Davis v. Whitby* [1973] 1 WLR 629; *Pugh v. Savage* [1970] 2 QB 373; *Bright v. Walker* (1834) 1 CM & R 211.
1122. Kevin Gray and Susan Francis Gray, *Elements of Land Law*, 5th edn (OUP, 2009) at 5.2.58.
1123. *Durham & Sunderland Railway v. Walker* (1842) 2 QB 940 at 967.
1124. (1879–80) 12 Ch D 31 at 49.

the latter ground.[1125] The existing cases show that no easement of support will be implied even if *B* knew that *A* intended to build on Whiteacre.[1126]

§4. Right to Enjoyment of the Easement

523. An easement is infringed if its enjoyment is substantially interfered, whether by the servient owner, another dominant owner or a third party. As the following cases will illustrate, whether the interference is substantial is necessarily a question of fact. The scope of the grant is obviously of great relevance. The principle of non-derogation from grant requires the implication of such ancillary rights as are reasonable necessary to the enjoyment of the easement, but not rights which merely improve the enjoyment of the easement.[1127] Thus, an ordinary easement of way was held not to include a right to park or a right to generous turning space.[1128]

524. Substantial interference with an easement is actionable by the tort of nuisance and the aggrieved dominant owner may personally abate the interference with reasonable force (e.g., breaking open a locked gate) or apply to the court for an injunction and/or damages.

525. Where the dispute is between a dominant owner and a servient owner, a balance must be struck between their respective rights.[1129] While the focus is often on the dominant owner's rights, the servient owner, having ownership and possession of the servient land, also has the right to use it as he pleases provided that the dominant owner's enjoyment of the easement is not substantially interfered with.[1130] In *Wee Siew Bock v. Chan Yuen Yee Alexia Eve*, the servient owner granted to the dominant owner an easement over a paved driveway, which provided both the dominant and servient lands with the only means of accessing a public road.[1131] A dispute arose when the servient owner installed an automatic remote-controlled gate at the entrance the driveway. The servient owner offered the dominant owner equal access by means of a remote control and a set of keys for the gate. However, the dominant owner insisted that the gate must be kept open at all times. The Court of Appeal held that that the gate did not substantially interfere with the dominant owner's enjoyment of the easement.[1132] The court remarked: '[T]he dominant owner

1125. *Seah Sye Kim v. Chua Mui Ying* [1991] SGCA 30; [1991] 2 SLR(R) 457.
1126. *Lee Quee Siew v. Lim Hock Siew* [1895–6] 3 SSLR 80; *Tan Mee Neo v. Tan Tug* [1894] 2 SSLR 29.
1127. *Jones v. Pritchard* [1908] 1 Ch 630 at 638.
1128. *Wee Siew Bock v. Chan Yuen Yee Alexia Eve* [2012] SGCA 33; [2012] 3 SLR 1053 at [72], [79], [90]–[92]; *Lim Hong Seng v. East Coast Medicare Centre Pte Ltd* [1994] SGHC 270; [1994] 3 SLR(R) 680 at [44]. *See also* LTA, The Schedule, Parts I and II on the meaning of 'right of carriage way' and 'right of footway'.
1129. *Wee Siew Bock v. Chan Yuen Yee Alexia Eve* [2012] SGCA 33; [2012] 3 SLR 1053 at [66].
1130. *Wee Siew Bock v. Chan Yuen Yee Alexia Eve* [2012] SGCA 33; [2012] 3 SLR 1053 at [58]–[63].
1131. [2012] SGCA 33; [2012] 3 SLR 1053 at [63] (Chao, Phang and Rajah JJA).
1132. *See also Lian Kok Hong v. Lee Choi Kheong* [2010] SGCA 19; [2010] 3 SLR 378, where the dispute similarly arose from the servient owner's construction of a gate. The Court of Appeal affirmed

has no right to insist on maintenance of the status quo if changes to or on the easement land do not substantially interfere with his reasonable enjoyment of the easement'.[1133]

526. The same issue, albeit involving a more significant alteration to the servient land, arose in *Yickvi Realty Pte Ltd v. Pacific Rover Pte Ltd.*[1134] The dominant and servient owners were real estate developers and both were granted permissions to erect residential apartments on their respective lands. The servient owner wished to realign the route of the easement of way so as to allow better development of the servient land. The dominant owner, who refused to give permission for the realignment, applied for an injunction. The Court of Appeal refused to grant an injunction because the realignment would cause no inconvenience to the dominant owner. The new road would still allow the dominant owner to access the public road. In fact, the dominant owner stood to benefit from the realignment, for the new road would better serve the needs of its new development. The court was also influenced by two policy considerations. First, 'because of the scarcity of land in Singapore, land should be allowed to be developed to its optimal potential as permitted by planning law'.[1135] Second, allowing the realignment would avoid potential disputes regarding the dominant owner's right to enjoy the easement.[1136] When the easement was granted to the predecessor of the dominant owner, it was only to provide for basic access for one residential house on the dominant land. With the completion of the new development on the dominant land, at least ten households will be enjoying the easement. This could amount to excessive use not contemplated by the grant.[1137]

527. Section 105A of the LTA now allows the courts to balance the interests of the parties in a more direct manner.[1138] A court may, on application by any person interested in the servient land, make an order varying an easement if it is satisfied that: (a) due to change in circumstances, the continued existence of the easement, unless varied, will impede the development of the servient land without securing practical benefits to the dominant owner; or (b) the proposed variation will not substantially injure the dominant owner. Where the court orders that the easement be varied, it may direct the servient owner to pay compensation to the dominant owner.

528. The Grange Heights saga, which consisted of four sets of court proceedings spanning over 30 years, raised interesting issues on excessive use by a dominant owner. The disputes concerned an easement of way over a long and narrow strip of land known as Lot 111-31 (the servient land). This easement, which leads

the High Court's decision that there will be no substantial interference with the dominant owner's enjoyment of the easement of way if he was allowed to pass freely.

1133. [2012] SGCA 33; [2012] 3 SLR 1053 at [63].

1134. [2009] SGCA 44; [2009] 4 SLR(R) 951 (Chan CJ, Phang and Rajah JJA).

1135. [2009] SGCA 44; [2009] 4 SLR(R) 951 at [15].

1136. [2009] SGCA 44; [2009] 4 SLR(R) 951 at [16].

1137. On excessive use, see *Lee Tat Development Pte Ltd v. Management Corporation Strata Title Plan No 301* [2008] SGCA 47; [2009] 1 SLR(R) 875.

1138. The new section was inserted in response to the suggestion made by Chong J in *Botanica Pte Ltd v. Management Corporation Strata Title Plan No 2040* [2012] SGHC 98; [2012] 3 SLR 476.

to a public road, served Lots 111-32 and 111-33 belonging to Lee Tat Development Pte Ltd (formerly Collin Development (Pte) Ltd) as well as Lot 111-34 belonging to Hong Leong Holdings Ltd. Lot 111-34 was amalgamated with Lot 561 to form a larger piece of land, on which the Grange Heights development was constructed. Lot 111-34 was located between Lot 111-31 and Lot 561.

529. When the first dispute arose, the three blocks of apartment under the Grange Heights development were still under construction on Lot 561. In *Grange Heights (No 1)*, Collin Development (Pte) Ltd applied for a *quia timet* injunction to restrain Hong Leong Holdings Ltd from inviting purchasers of the apartment units to use the servient land to access the apartment blocks. In the High Court, Chua J refused to grant an injunction.[1139] As the future residents of Grange Heights would have alternative access to their flats, it was unlikely that vehicular traffic over the servient land would be so heavy as to substantially interfere with the enjoyment of the easement by Collin Development (Pte) Ltd. The Court of Appeal upheld Chua J's decision.[1140]

530. The dispute in *Grange Heights (No 2)* arose when Lee Tat Development Pte Ltd installed an iron gate and fencing on the servient land, thus depriving the residents of Grange Heights of access to and from the public road. Lee Tat Development Pte Ltd argued that the amalgamation of Lot 111-34 and Lot 561 had caused the easement to be extinguished. In response, the Management Corporation of Grange Heights applied for an injunction to restrain Lee Tat Development Pte Ltd from obstructing the right of way. In the High Court, Coomaraswamy J held that the amalgamation did not extinguish the easement and proceeded to grant an injunction.[1141] The Court of Appeal, in upholding the High Court's decision, added that as the residents of Grange Heights had been using the servient land only as a footpath, there was no excessive user so as to substantially interfere with the defendant's enjoyment of the easement.[1142]

531. Grange Heights (No 4) concerned a separate proceeding in which Lee Tat Development Pte Ltd sought to argue that the use of the easement by the residents of Grange Heights was in breach of the principle in *Harris v. Flower*, which states: 'If a right of way be granted for the enjoyment of close A, the grantee, because he owns or acquires close B, cannot use the way in substance for passing over close A to close B'.[1143] The majority in the Court of Appeal held that Lee Tat Development Pte Ltd was estopped from raising this issue as it had already been decided in the

1139. [1976] SGHC 3; [1974-1976] SLR(R) 618.

1140. *Collin Development (Pte) Ltd v. Hong Leong Holdings Ltd* [1976] SGHC 3; [1974–1976] SLR(R) 618 (Wee CJ, Kulasekaram and Singh JJ).

1141. [1990] SGHC 103; [1990] 2 SLR(R) 634.

1142. *Lee Tat Development Pte Ltd v. Management Corporation Strata Title Plan No 301* [1992] SGCA 61; [1992] 3 SLR(R) 1 at [23]–[24] (Yong CJ, Thean and Goh JJ).

1143. (1904) 91 LT 816 at 819.

previous decision.[1144] In holding that the easement in Lot 111-31 survived the amalgamation of Lots 111-34 and 561 and continued to serve Lot 111-34, the principle in *Harris v. Flower* was not followed.[1145]

532. In *Grange Heights (No 3)*, the Management Corporation of Grange Heights sought a declaration that it was entitled to carry out certain repair and maintenance work on the servient land. Lee Tat Development Pte Ltd continued to resist the right of the Management Corporation to use the servient land. In an unexpected turn of event, the Court of Appeal held that the majority of the Court of Appeal in *Grange Heights (No 4)* had gotten the estoppel issue wrong.[1146] In the first two proceedings, Lee Tat Development Pte Ltd was suing as the dominant owner of Lots 111-32 and 111-33. However, Lee Tat Development Pte Ltd subsequently purchased the servient land. Thus, in *Grange Heights (No 4)*, Lee Tat Development Pte Ltd was suing as the owner of the servient land.[1147] It was only in this latter proceeding that Lee Tat Development Pte Ltd had the *locus standi* to invoke the principle in *Harris v. Flower*.[1148] Applying the said principle, the Court of Appeal held that the residents of Grange Heights have no right to use the servient land to access Lot 561, a non-dominant land.[1149] Such use was deemed to be excessive.

§5. Extinguishment

533. In the case of an easement over registered land, the dominant owner may expressly release an easement by executing an instrument of release in the approved form.[1150] Where part of the dominant land is transferred subject an express agreement that the easement shall not pass to the transferee, registration of the transfer shall operate to release the easement to the extent to which it had been appurtenant to the part transferred.[1151] In the case of an easement over unregistered land, the release must be made by deed.[1152]

534. Extinguishment of a notified easement over registered land other than by way of express release is governed in part by section 106 of the LTA. Subsection

1144. *Lee Tat Development Pte Ltd v. Management Corporation Strata Title Plan No 301* [2005] SGCA 22; [2005] 3 SLR(R) 157.
1145. *Ibid., v.* at [25] (Yong CJ and Ang J) (Chao JA dissenting).
1146. [2008] SGCA 47; [2009] 1 SLR(R) 875 (Chan CJ, Phang and Rajah JJA).
1147. [2008] SGCA 47; [2009] 1 SLR(R) 875 at [69].
1148. [2008] SGCA 47; [2009] 1 SLR(R) 875 at [32]. *C.f.* Tang Hang Wu and Kelvin F.K. Low, *Tan Sook Yee's Principles of Singapore Land Law*, 3rd edn (LexisNexis, 2009) at 656–57, where the authors argued that the principle in *Harris v. Flower* was relevant in *Grange Heights (No 2)*. In attempting to remove the obstructions installed by Lee Tat Development Pte Ltd, the Management Corporation had to first establish title to their easement, specifically the right to access Lot 561 using the servient land. Applying the principle in *Harris v. Flower*, it was clear that there was no such right.
1149. [2008] SGCA 47; [2009] 1 SLR(R) 875 at [85].
1150. LTA, section 105(1).
1151. *Ibid.*, section 101(2).
1152. *Lee Tat Development Pte Ltd v. Management Corporation Strata Title Plan No 301* [2008] SGCA 47; [2009] 1 SLR(R) 875 at [94].

(1) provides that the Registrar shall cancel the notification of the easement if he is satisfied that: (a) any period of time for which the easement was intended to subsist has expired; (b) any event upon which the easement was intended to determine has occurred; or (c) the easement has been abandoned. Subsection (2) further provides for a situation of presumed abandonment:

535. Where an application is made to the Registrar in the approved form and evidence is furnished to the Registrar of non-user of an easement for a period exceeding 12 years, he may, without further evidence of abandonment, give notice to the proprietor of the dominant tenement and, in the absence of objection by that proprietor within one month from the service of the notice, treat the easement as abandoned.

536. The common law doctrine of abandonment continues to apply to easements generally, whether notified or not.[1153] Abandonment of an easement will not be lightly inferred, especially where the easement was granted in perpetuity.[1154] In *Wee Siew Bock v. Chan Yuen Yee Alexia Eve*, the Court of Appeal explained that save in exceptional cases, mere non-user of an easement is not by itself sufficient to establish abandonment.[1155] The Court of Appeal further said:

> [W]here the servient owner is able to show a long period of non-user of an easement by the dominant owner, the evidential burden shifts to the dominant owner to explain and show that he nonetheless consistently intended to preserve his rights under the easement.[1156]

537. This suggests that prolonged non-user is an exceptional case where a presumption of abandonment may arise. The Court of Appeal added that in light of section 106(2) of the LTA, 'it will be difficult for any claimant to establish abandonment at common law unless a lapse in the use of the easement for more than 12 years is likewise established'.[1157]

538. The non-user must be examined in light of the surrounding circumstances. For example, where the servient owner has introduced alteration(s) to the servient land so as to affect the enjoyment of the easement, absence of protest from the dominant owner coupled with prolonged non-user is likely to amount to acquiescence. Acquiescence of the infringement amounts to an abandonment. The nature of the

1153. *Wee Siew Bock v. Chan Yuen Yee Alexia Eve* [2012] SGCA 33; [2012] 3 SLR 1053 at [33].
1154. *Lian Kok Hong v. Lee Choi Kheong* [2010] SGCA 19; [2010] 3 SLR 378 at [24]; *Frontfield Investment Holding (Pte) Ltd v. Management Corporation Strata Title Plan No 938* [2001] SGHC 161; [2001] 2 SLR(R) 410 at [31].
1155. [2012] SGCA 33; [2012] 3 SLR 1053 at [39]–[42]. *See also Lian Kok Hong v. Lee Choi Kheong* [2010] SGCA 19; [2010] 3 SLR 378 at [24].
1156. [2012] SGCA 33; [2012] 3 SLR 1053 at [30].
1157. [2012] SGCA 33; [2012] 3 SLR 1053 at [35].

alteration will obviously be relevant.[1158] The more significant the alteration is, the more the dominant owner is expected to protest if he still intends to retain the easement.

539. The case of *Lian Kok Hong v. Lee Choi Kheong* provides an excellent illustration.[1159] A landowner subdivided his land into two parts and sold one part. The landowner reserved an easement of way over the part sold (Land A) and granted an easement of way over the part retained (Land B). Both easements of way ran in parallel and allowed access to the main public road. Prior to the dispute, both parcels of land have changed ownerships several times. At some point in time, the owner of Land A constructed a chain-linked fence along the common boundary of both parcels of land, effectively preventing the owner of Land B from enjoying the easement of way running along Land A. Disputes arose when the present owner of Land B (Owner B) decided to construct a gate on the road serving the easement of way over Land B. The present owner of Land A (Owner A) sought an injunction, claiming that the gate would interfere with his enjoyment of the easement over Land B. Owner B in turn counterclaimed that the fencing of Land A amounted to an infringement of the easement on Land A. The Court of Appeal held that the easement over Land A had been abandoned by the previous owners of Land B. When Land B was conveyed to Owner B, Land A had been fenced off for more than 20 years. None of the previous owners of Land B protested. Even after Owner B took possession of Land B, the situation subsisted for another 13 years until this issue was raised in the present dispute. The Court of Appeal held that the easement over Land A had been abandoned due to acquiescence of the predecessors of Owner B.

540. Similarly, in *Wee Siew Bock v. Chan Yuen Yee Alexia Eve*, the servient owner planted trees on the side of the driveway serving the easement.[1160] The trees were allowed to grow for more than 20 years without protest from the dominant owner. The Court of Appeal held that the dominant owner had partially abandoned the easement.

541. Certain alterations to the dominant land may also give rise to an inference of abandonment. In *Frontfield Investment Holding (Pte) Ltd v. Management Corporation Strata Title Plan No 938*, the manner in which the condominium on the dominant land was constructed strongly indicated that the easement was no longer needed.[1161] First, a more convenient access way was constructed. Second, the condominium was fenced in a way that its residents could not access the pathway on the servient land. Third, the location swimming pool and other facilities rendered vehicular access between the dominant and servient lands was impossible. Prakash J held that these factors, taken together with prolonged non-user, pointed to the abandonment of the easement by the dominant owner.

1158. *Wee Siew Bock v. Chan Yuen Yee Alexia Eve* [2012] SGCA 33; [2012] 3 SLR 1053 at [38].
1159. [2010] SGCA 19; [2010] 3 SLR 378.
1160. *Wee Siew Bock v. Chan Yuen Yee Alexia Eve* [2012] SGCA 33; [2012] 3 SLR 1053 at [33].
1161. [2001] SGHC 161; [2001] 2 SLR(R) 410.

542. If two easements over two different parcels of land were created with the intention that they shall mutually coexist, one cannot be abandoned without the abandonment of the other.[1162] For example, where *A* and *B* agree to create mutual easements benefiting their respective parcels of land, *A* cannot, without abandoning the easement granted to him, claim that the easement granted to *B* has been abandoned. An intention to create mutual easements must be clearly expressed and will not be lightly inferred. Where one easement can be abandoned without affecting enjoyment of the other easement, the reasonable inference is that they are not intended to mutually coexist. For example, in *Lian Kok Hong v. Lee Choi Kheong*, the easement over Land A could be abandoned without affecting enjoyment of the easement over Land B, which was itself wide enough to provide for vehicular access.[1163] Thus, the Court of Appeal refused to infer an intention that both easements shall mutually coexist.[1164]

543. Finally, an easement may also be extinguished by operation of law. One straightforward situation is provided in section 100(1) of the LTA. Where both the dominant and servient lands become vested in the same person,[1165] the Registrar shall, upon request of the common owner, cancel the notification of the easement.[1166] However, there are two exceptions. First, where either of the two parcels of land is subject to a registered mortgage, charge or lease, both parcels of land shall not be deemed to be in common ownership for the purposes of section 100(1).[1167] Second, easements implied under sections 98 and 99 are merely suspended until the cessation of the unity of possession.[1168]

544. Another situation is where the servient and dominant lands have amalgamated into a single parcel of land, in which case the Registrar shall, as soon as he becomes aware of that amalgamation, cancel the notification of the easement.[1169]

545. A third situation is where the easement is no longer capable of serving the dominant land in the manner intended by the grant due to radical alteration of the dominant land. The Grange Heights saga provides a good illustration.[1170] When the easement was granted, only one bungalow stood on the dominant land, Lot 111-34. Lot 111-34 was subsequently amalgamated with Lot 561 for the Grange Heights development. Three apartment blocks were built on Lot 561 while the recreational facilities for the residents were built on Lot 111-34. As a result of this development, the easement was required to serve 120 households. This significant increase in the

---

1162. *Lian Kok Hong v. Lee Choi Kheong* [2009] SGHC 18.
1163. [2010] SGCA 19; [2010] 3 SLR 378 (Chan CJ, Phang and Rajah JJA) (see above for facts).
1164. [2010] SGCA 19; [2010] 3 SLR 378 at [12]–[13].
1165. *See also Lee Tat Development Pte Ltd v. Management Corporation Strata Title Plan No 301* [2008] SGCA 47; [2009] 1 SLR(R) 875 at [95].
1166. LTA, section 100(1) and (2).
1167. *Ibid.*, section 100(3).
1168. *Ibid.*, sections 98(6), 99(6) and 100(1).
1169. *Ibid.*, section 100(2).
1170. [2008] SGCA 47; [2009] 1 SLR(R) 875 at [95]–[109].

quantum of use could not have been within the contemplation of the grantor. Moreover, Lot 111-34 can no longer be used as a stand-alone lot, but only as an ancillary to Lot 561. As the alteration of Lot 111-34 was permanent and irreversible, the Court of Appeal declared that the easement was extinguished by operation of law.

546. The power of the court to make such an order extinguishing an easement over registered land is now provided in section 105A of the LTA. A court may, on application by any person interested in the servient land, make an order extinguishing the easement if it is satisfied that: (a) due to change in circumstances, the continued existence of the easement will impede the development of the servient land without securing practical benefits to the dominant owner; or (b) the proposed extinguishment will not substantially injure the dominant owner. Where the court orders that the easement be extinguished, it may direct the servient owner to pay compensation to the dominant owner.

Chapter 9. Covenants Relating to Land

§1. INTRODUCTION

547. A covenant relating to land refers to a contractual undertaking by a landowner to do, or to refrain from doing, something on his land. The covenantor's land is known as the servient land while the covenantee's land is known as the dominant land. Between the covenantor and the covenantee, the bindingness of the covenant derives from the contract between them. What remains unclear is in what circumstances would the covenant also bind their successors in title. The law on this topic is highly complex due to the different rules that apply for the passing of benefit to the covenantee's successor and the passing of burden to the covenantor's successor. Fortunately, in the case of a restrictive covenant over registered land, the legal position has been greatly simplified by the provisions of the Land Titles Act (LTA).[1171] However, for all other covenants relating to land, the complex rules under common law and equity continue to apply. In light of a dearth of local authority on this topic, which may be reflective of the unpopularity of covenants relating to land in Singapore, this chapter intends to do no more than providing a brief overview of the subject.[1172]

§2. RESTRICTIVE COVENANTS

I. Creation

548. Part XIV of the LTA[1173] applies to restrictive covenants created by agreements between landowners.[1174] A restrictive covenant may be created using an instrument in the approved form and the restriction shall be notified by the Registrar in the folio of the servient land.[1175] Unless so notified, the restriction will not bind the assignees of the covenantor and covenantee.[1176] A restrictive covenant that is not notified remains valid, but is only binding between the covenantor and covenantee.

1171. (Cap. 157, 2004 Rev. Ed.).

1172. For more comprehensive works on this topic, see Barry C. Crown, 'Passing the Benefit and Burden of Restrictive Covenants Governing Land in Singapore' [1998] SJLS 98; Tang Hang Wu and Kelvin F.K. Low, *Tan Sook Yee's Principles of Singapore Land Law*, 3rd edn (LexisNexis, 2009) Chapter 21; W.J.M. Ricquier, *Land Law*, 5th edn (LexisNexis, 2010) Chapter 13.

1173. *See* John Baalman, *The Singapore Torrens system: being a commentary on the Land Titles Ordinance 1956 of the State of Singapore* (Govt. Printer, 1961) at 222–34.

1174. To be sure, the provisions in Part XIV apply to restrictive covenants affecting all kinds of estate, not only those affecting freehold estates. *See* John Baalman, *The Singapore Torrens system: being a commentary on the Land Titles Ordinance 1956 of the State of Singapore* (Govt. Printer, 1961) at 223–34. However, restrictive covenants contained in a mortgage (affecting mortgagor and mortgagee) or a lease (affecting landlord and tenant) fall outside the ambit of Part XIV (LTA, section 138).

1175. LTA, section 139(1).

1176. *Ibid.*, section 139(2). *Cf.* LTA, section 45(1), which merely states that no instrument until registered is effective to pass any interest or estate under the provisions of the LTA.

549. The covenant must be restrictive[1177] and relate to the user of the servient land.[1178] Whether a covenant is restrictive or positive is a matter of substance, not form. Importantly, a covenant purporting to restrict the right of the owner of the servient land to alienate or otherwise dispose of his land is not eligible for notification on the land register.[1179]

550. The instrument must clearly indicate the dominant and servient land.[1180] Dominant land is defined as 'the land to which the benefit of a restriction is annexed' while servient land is defined as 'the land subject to the burden of a restriction'.[1181] Traditionally, annexation of the covenant's benefit to the dominant land and annexation of the covenant's burden to the servient land are effected by the use of appropriate annexation formulae.[1182] For registered land, however, annexation is automatically effected by section 62(1) of the LTA, which states:

551. In instruments registered under the provisions of this Act, unless a contrary intention is expressed, covenants relating to land shall be deemed to be made by the covenantor and his successors in title with the covenantee and his successors in title and shall have effect as if such successors were expressly referred to therein.[1183]

552. The notification of the restriction does not give the restrictive covenant any greater effect than it would have without the notification.[1184] Under the common law, the benefit and burden of the covenant will pass only if the covenant touches and concerns the dominant land.[1185] If it is apparent that the restrictive covenant is only for the personal benefit of the covenantee, subsequent owners of the affected land may apply to the court for a declaration that the restrictive covenant has no binding effect on third parties.[1186] If the court so declares, the Registrar shall cancel the notification.[1187]

1177. LTA, section 139(3)(a) & (4).
1178. *Ibid.*, section 138.
1179. *Ibid.*, section 139(5).
1180. *Ibid.*, section 139(3)(b).
1181. *Ibid.*, section 138.
1182. *See* §3.I.B.(ii). below.
1183. *See* Barry C. Crown, 'Passing the Benefit and Burden of Restrictive Covenants Governing Land in Singapore' [1998] SJLS 98 at 119; Tang Hang Wu and Kelvin F.K. Low, *Tan Sook Yee's Principles of Singapore Land Law*, 3rd edn (LexisNexis, 2009) at 694. *Cf* W.J.M. Ricquier, *Land Law*, 5th edn (LexisNexis, 2017) at 275–76.
1184. LTA, section 139(6).
1185. *Rogers v. Hosegood* [1900] 2 Ch 388.
1186. John Baalman, *The Singapore Torrens system: being a commentary on the Land Titles Ordinance 1956 of the State of Singapore* (Govt. Printer, 1961) at 226, 229–30.
1187. LTA, section 139(8).

II. Discharge

A. By Agreement Between the Parties

553. The current owners of the affected lands may agree on the variation or release of a restrictive covenant. For this purpose, an instrument in the approved form executed by the owner of the dominant land is required.[1188] Upon application by the owner of the servient land, the Registrar will notify the variation or release on the folio of the servient land.[1189]

B. By Court Order

554. Where the granting of a planning permission has altered the permitted use of the servient land and the continued existence of a restriction will impede the development of the said land, the court may, upon an application by the owner of the servient land, order that the restriction be varied or extinguished (either wholly or in part).[1190] The court may also order the same if it is satisfied that the proposed extinguishment or variation will not materially injure the owner of the dominant land.[1191] If the order extinguishing or varying the restriction will cause a loss or disadvantage to the owner of the dominant land, the court may order the owner of the servient land to make the necessary compensation.[1192] The restriction will be extinguished or varied when the Registrar makes the necessary notification on the land register.[1193]

C. By Efflux ion of Time

555. A restrictive covenant will cease to be enforceable against the assigns of the covenantor and covenantee on the expiry of 20 years from the date the restriction is notified on the land register,[1194] following which the Registrar will cancel the notification of the restriction.[1195] Before a restrictive covenant becomes unenforceable, it can, from time to time, be extended by an instrument in the approved form executed by any person having an interest in the dominant land.[1196] Upon notification of the extension, the duration of the restriction will be prolonged for a period

1188. *Ibid.*, section 140(1).
1189. *Ibid.*, section 140(2).
1190. *Ibid.*, section 140(5)(a).
1191. *Ibid.*, section 140(5)(b).
1192. *Ibid.*, section 140(6)(a).
1193. *Ibid.*, section 140(11).
1194. *Ibid.*, section 141(1). Where the restrictive covenant was created before the servient land had become registered land, the restriction ceases to be enforceable against the owner or his assigns on the latest among the following dates: (a) 20 years from the date of creation of the restriction; (b) 5 years from the date of entry of a notification; or (c) 24 months from 20th August 2001. LTA, section 141(2).
1195. *Ibid.*, section 141(3).
1196. *Ibid.*, section 141(4).

of 10 years.[1197] However, where the restriction is stated to be for a specific period, an instrument of extension will not be effective in prolonging the duration of the restriction beyond the stated period.[1198]

§3. Other Covenants Relating to Land

556. All other covenants relating to land continue to be governed by the rules developed under the common law and equity. As these covenants are not notified on the land register, they are best protected by way of a caveat.

I. Passing of Benefit

A. By Express Assignment

557. The benefits of a covenant may be expressly assigned. Section 4(8) of the Civil Law Act provides that assignment must be in writing, and express notice must be given to the covenantor.[1199] Upon assignment, the assignee of the covenantee may enforce the covenant against the covenantor.

B. By Annexation

1. At Common Law

558. At common law, the benefit of a covenant will be annexed to the dominant land if three conditions are satisfied. First, the covenant must touch and concern the dominant land. In short, it must be for the benefit of whoever may be the owner of the land, not merely for the personal benefit of the covenantee. Second, the covenantee must have a legal estate in the dominant land. Third, the covenantee's successor in title must have the same legal estate as the covenantee. Thus, where the covenantee owns an estate in fee simple, benefit of the covenant will only pass to a transferee of the estate in fee simple.

2. In Equity

559. Where the covenantee's assign has only an equitable interest in the land (e.g., he is a beneficiary), he must satisfy the more stringent equitable rules on the passing of the covenant's benefit.

1197. *Ibid.*, section 141(5).
1198. *Ibid.*, section 141(6).
1199. (Cap. 43, 1999 Rev. Ed.).

560. For the covenant's benefit to pass in equity, two conditions must be satisfied. First, the covenant must touch and concern the dominant land. Second, the covenant must be annexed to dominant land. Annexation can be effected by using the appropriate annexation formulae to show that the benefit of the covenant is intended to run with the dominant land. For example, the covenant may be stated to be for the benefit of the covenantee and his assigns.

561. Whether annexation can be effected by statute is a more difficult question. A potentially relevant statutory provision is section 57 of the Conveyancing and Law of Property Act (CLPA), which states:[1200]

> (1) A covenant relating to freehold land shall be deemed to be made with the covenantee, his heirs and assigns, and shall have effect as if heirs and assigns were expressed.
> (2) A covenant relating to leasehold land shall be deemed to be made with the covenantee, his executors, administrators and assigns, and shall have effect as if executors, administrators and assigns were expressed.

562. In *J Sainsbury plc v. Enfield LBC*, Morritt J preferred a conservative interpretation of the English equivalent of section 57[1201] and held that the section did not effect statutory annexation.[1202] However, in an excellent article, Crown convincingly argued that *Sainsbury* should not be followed in Singapore and section 57 should be regarded as effecting statutory annexation.[1203]

563. The scope of section 57 was further curtailed in *RSP Architects Planners & Engineers v. Ocean Front Pte Ltd*, where the Court of Appeal held that subsection (2) is only concerned with 'the passing of the benefit of any covenant or undertaking in a lease to the assigns or successors in title of the lessee where such covenant or undertaking has been made between the lessor and lessee'.[1204] This will mean that subsection (2) does not apply to a covenant entered into between two owners of leasehold lands. With all due respect, this is an overly restrictive reading of subsection (2). Moreover, it is not immediately clear how the same reading could be applied to the similarly worded subsection (1).

C. Contracts (Rights of Third Parties) Act

564. Where the covenant is expressed to be for the benefit of the covenantee's assigns, the covenantee's successor in title may enforce the covenant by virtue of

1200. (Cap. 61, 2004 Rev. Ed.).
1201. Conveyancing and Law of Property Act 1881 (UK), section 58.
1202. [1989] 2 All ER 817.
1203. Barry C. Crown, 'Passing the Benefit and Burden of Restrictive Covenants Governing Land in Singapore' [1998] SJLS 98 at 112–17.
1204. [1995] SGCA 79; [1995] 3 SLR(R) 653 at [22] (Karthigesu JA, Thean JA and Goh J).

the CRTPA.[1205] Importantly, he may do so regardless of whether the covenant touches and concerns the land. However, as the CRTPA does not provide for the passing of burden, the covenant can only be enforced against the covenantor. Whether the burden of the covenant has passed to the covenantor's successor in title has to be separately established.

II. Passing of Burden

A. Chains of Covenants

565. While the burden of a covenant cannot be assigned, it can be indirectly passed on by way of a chain of covenants. For example, when *A*, the owner of the servient land, sells the land to *B*, *A* may protect himself/herself by insisting on a term that *B* would uphold the covenant. *B* may do the same when he sells the land to *C*. Thus, *C*'s failure to uphold the covenant causes the owner of the dominant land to sue *A*, *A* can sue *B*, who can in turn sue *C*. The downside of relying on a chain of covenants is obvious. If *C* fails to include the aforesaid term in a sale of the servient land to *D*, *D* and his assigns will be entirely free from the burden of the covenant.

B. Doctrine of Mutual Benefit and Burden

566. The doctrine gives expression to the principle that he who takes the benefit must bear the burden.[1206] A classic example is where the owner of Blackacre (*A*) grants the owner of Whiteacre (*B*) a right to use a road on Blackacre. In return, *B* covenants to contribute to the maintenance of the road. If *B* sells Whiteacre to *C*, who continues to enjoy the benefit of the road on Blackacre, *A* may enforce the covenant against *C*. To prevent the doctrine from being extended too widely, two preconditions must be fulfilled before the doctrine can be invoked.[1207] First, the benefit must be directly related to the obligation to discharge the covenanted burden. Second, *B*'s successor must have a choice of accepting or rejecting the benefit.

567. The statutory equivalent of the doctrine can be found in section 102(1) of the LTA, which reads:

> Where an instrument creating an easement contains a covenant binding either party to contribute to the cost of construction, maintenance or repair of any way, wall, drain or any other matter (the subject of the easement), then, unless a contrary intention is expressed in the instrument, so long as the easement subsists the covenant shall bind any successor in title to that party as if the successor had been a party to the original covenant.

1205. (Cap. 53B, 2002 Rev. Ed.) (CRTPA).
1206. *See Halsall v. Brizell* [1957] Ch 169; *Tito v. Waddell* (No.2) [1977] Ch 106.
1207. *Thamesmead Town Ltd v. Allotey* (2000) 79 P & CR 557; *Rhone v. Stephens* [1994] 2 AC 310.

C. Implied Easements and Implied Covenants

568. In the case of easements implied by the provisions of the LTA, the same provisions also imply, as against every person enjoying the benefit of the easements, a covenant to contribute towards the construction, maintenance or repair of the subject of the easement.[1208]

1208. LTA, sections 98(1) & (4), 99(1) & (3).

Chapter 10. Mortgages

§1. Introduction

569. Land is arguably the most valuable and accepted form of security owing to its immovability, durability and endless demand. Even if a person does not already own land, he could purchase land by way of a bank loan and simultaneously grant a mortgage over the land to secure the debt. In fact, this is the usual method of financing the purchase of land. In the context of land, the most common form of security interest granted is a mortgage. In this chapter, we will examine the different types of mortgage, the rights and duties of the mortgagor and mortgagee, as well as the remedies available to a mortgagee in the event of the mortgagor's default.

§2. Types of Mortgage over Registered Land

I. Registered Mortgage

570. A classic legal mortgage entails a transfer of the land to the lender-mortgagee, who becomes the legal owner of the property. The borrower-mortgagor retains a beneficial interest in the land known as an equity of redemption, which entitles him/her to obtain a retransfer of the land when the debt is fully repaid. A mortgage is commonly distinguished from a charge, which does not entail any transfer of the land to the lender-chargee. The lender-chargee simply obtains a security interest in the land while the borrower-chargor remains its legal owner. From a lender's perspective, a mortgage is a more advantageous form of security interest as it gives him/her more control over the land.

571. For a mortgage over registered land, to which section 68 of the Land Titles Act (LTA)[1209] applies, the traditional distinction between a mortgage and a charge has been significantly diluted.[1210] Subsection (3) states that a registered mortgage 'shall not operate as a transfer of the land mortgaged, but shall have effect as a security only'. Instead of operating by way of a transfer of the land to the mortgagee, the land merely becomes encumbered by the mortgage, which is reflected in the land register. The mortgagor remains the registered owner of the land.

572. This characteristic of a registered mortgage was emphasised by the Court of Appeal in *Rimmon Watch Pte Ltd v. Great Pacific Finance Ltd.*[1211] However, there remain two important distinctions between a registered mortgage and a registered charge. First, while the function of a mortgage is to secure repayment of debt,[1212] the function of a charge is to secure payment of 'a rentcharge, annuity or

1209. (Cap. 157, 2004 Rev. Ed.).
1210. *See* John Baalman, *The Singapore Torrens system: being a commentary on the Land Titles Ordinance 1956 of the State of Singapore* (Govt. Printer, 1961) at 127–133.
1211. [1989] SGCA 2; [1989] 1 SLR(R) 66 at [18] (Wee CJ, Sinnathuray and Thean JJ).
1212. LTA, section 68(1).

other periodical sum, or of any money other than a debt'.[1213] Due to this delineation of functions, a mortgage is the more commonly encountered security interest. Second, the available remedies appear to differ. The self-help remedies of sale, possession and appointment of receiver are not available to a chargee.[1214] Neither is the remedy of foreclosure.[1215]

573. The creation of a mortgage under the LTA must be by way of an instrument in the approved form.[1216] The mortgage is validly created only when the instrument is registered.[1217] Upon registration, the mortgagee becomes indefeasible, subject to exceptions.[1218] Where the property is encumbered by several registered mortgages, the priority of the mortgages is to be determined by their dates of registration.[1219]

574. Besides setting out a number of important provisions relating to registered mortgage, the LTA also states that certain provisions in the Conveyancing and Law of Property Act (CLPA)[1220] shall be applicable, with necessary modifications, to registered mortgages.[1221] In the event of inconsistency between the statutes, the LTA shall prevail.[1222]

II. Equitable Mortgage

575. As explained in an earlier chapter, the Torrens system accommodates unregistered interests.[1223] In the case of mortgages, it has been accepted that an owner of a registered land may grant an equitable mortgage, i.e. a mortgage that is not registered.[1224] Like a registered mortgage, an equitable mortgage operates as an encumbrance on the mortgagor's land.

576. An agreement (usually by way of deed) expressing the necessary intention is sufficient to create an equitable mortgage.[1225] Since this amounts to a disposition

1213. *Ibid.*, section 68(2).
1214. *Power Knight Pte Ltd v. Natural Fuel Pte Ltd (in compulsory liquidation)* [2010] SGHC 75; [2010] 3 SLR 82 at [22]–[25].
1215. LTA, section 76.
1216. *Ibid.*, section 68(1); Form 29 (Mortgage)
1217. LTA, section 45.
1218. *Ibid.*, section 46.
1219. *Ibid.*, section 48.
1220. (Cap. 61, 1994 Rev. Ed.), sections 19–30 (Part IV), 31(2).
1221. LTA, section 69(1) & (2).
1222. *Ibid.*, section 69(4).
1223. *See* Chapter 4 (Torrens System).
1224. *See Société Générale v. Good Property Land Development Pte Ltd* [1989] SGHC 8; [1989] 1 SLR(R) 76; *United Overseas Finance Ltd v. Mutu Jeras* [1989] SGHC 41; [1989] 1 SLR(R) 446; *Power Knight Pte Ltd v. Natural Fuel Pte Ltd (in compulsory liquidation)* [2010] SGHC 75; [2010] 3 SLR 82.
1225. *Cheetham v. 805 Archer Road Pty Ltd* (in liq) [2015] VSC 96; *Pelenoy Pty Ltd v. Donovan Oates Hannaford Mortgage Corp* [2004] NSWSC 4; *Express Business Finance Pty Limited v. Monaco*

of an interest in land, it needs to be evidenced in writing and signed by the mortgagor for it to be enforceable.[1226] In many cases, the agreement is also accompanied by the depositing of the duplicate certificate of title with the mortgagee.[1227]

577. On the applicable law, Chan J said in *Société Générale v. Good Property Land Development Pte Ltd*: 'Since the LTA has nothing to say in relation to unregistrable mortgages of registered land except that it provides a means of protecting such interests by caveats, the question of whether such mortgagees have the statutory powers of mortgagees of non-registered land is left to the general law to determine'.[1228] The general law in this case would be the relevant provisions in the CLPA.[1229] On the facts of this case, the mortgage was only provisionally registered and therefore it was to be regarded as an equitable mortgage. Whether the equitable mortgagee was entitled to exercise a statutory power of sale under the CLPA depended on whether the relevant requirements are satisfied, such as the use of deed in the creation of the mortgage.[1230]

578. In deciding whether to accept an equitable mortgage to secure a loan, it is important for the lender to understand the advantages and disadvantages of the interest offered. Unlike a registered mortgage, an equitable mortgage does not have the benefit of registration: indefeasibility and its validating effect. Instead, the equitable mortgage is protected by the lodgment of a caveat. Unlike registration, the lodgement of a caveat does not have a validating effect. If an equitable mortgage is tainted by forgery, for example, it is simply invalid under the common law notwithstanding the lodgment of the caveat. Assuming, on the other hand, that the equitable mortgage has been validly created, the caveat will prevent the registration of any subsequent dealing that is inconsistent with the mortgagee's interest before he is given an opportunity to invoke the assistance of the court to give effect to his interest. Between unregistered interests (e.g., two equitable mortgages), the one protected by an earlier caveat has priority, except in the case of fraud.[1231]

579. Where no caveat is lodged, the equitable mortgage is not binding on a subsequently registered proprietor unless any of the exceptions to indefeasibility can be established.[1232] Where both unregistered interests (e.g., both equitable mortgages)

& anor [2010] NSWSC 206; *Perpetual Trustee Company Ltd (original plaintiff), Performance Capital Mortgage Pty Ltd v. Motive Finance & Leasing Pty Ltd* [2010] NSWSC 429.

1226. Civil Law Act (Cap. 43, 1999 Rev. Ed.), section 6(d).

1227. *Ng Wei Teck Michael v. Oversea-Chinese Banking Corp Ltd* [1998] SGCA 21; [1998] 1 SLR(R) 778; *J&H Just (Holdings) Pty Ltd v. Bank of New South Wales* (1971) 125 CLR 456.

1228. [1989] SGHC 8; [1989] 1 SLR(R) 76 at [6].

1229. [1989] SGHC 8; [1989] 1 SLR(R) 76 at [3]

1230. *See* CLPA, section 24(1).

1231. LTA, section 49.

1232. *Ibid.*, section 46. *See* Chapter 4 (Torrens system).

are not protected by the lodgment of caveats, the priority rules at general law presumably apply. The question would be whether the prior interest holder is at fault, i.e. contributed in some way to the creation of the subsequent unregistered interest.[1233]

§3. Rights of the Mortgagor

I. Equity of Redemption

A. *Mortgagor's Right to Discharge the Mortgage*

580. A mortgagor who has fully repaid the debt is entitled to redeem the property. In the case of a classic legal mortgage, the mortgagee would be under a duty to retransfer the property to the mortgagor. However, since registered and equitable mortgages operate only as encumbrances on land, it is more accurate to speak of the mortgagor as having a power to discharge the mortgage. Having said this, the language of redemption is still used in the LTA,[1234] perhaps due to its popular use and also to avoid perceived inconsistency with the relevant provisions imported from the CLPA, which employ the same language.[1235]

581. The mortgagor's power to discharge the mortgage is usually provided for in the mortgage agreement. The date on which the power could be exercised is also usually specified. Even if the mortgage agreement is silent, the power is implied by statute. Section 77 of the LTA provides that the mortgagor, upon fulfilling his obligations under the mortgage agreement, may obtain from the mortgagee a registrable discharge. Section 31(2)(b) of the CLPA further provides that the following proviso to the mortgagee's right to repayment shall be deemed to be included in every mortgage created by way of deed:

> [I]f the mortgagor, on the stated day, pays to the mortgagee the stated mortgage money, and has duly paid the interest thereon in the meantime at the stated rate, the mortgagee shall at any time thereafter, at the request and cost of the mortgagor, reconvey the mortgaged property to the mortgagor, or as he shall direct.

582. If the mortgagor misses the contractually stipulated date for discharging the mortgage, he may nevertheless revive the power to discharge using the methods provided in section 22 of the CLPA. The mortgagor could give a three months' written notice of his intention to discharge the mortgage. Alternatively, if he is in a hurry, he could pay 3 months' interest in lieu of such notice. However, even if the power to discharge is revived, it is, of course, not exercisable until the mortgagor

---

1233. *See Rice v. Rice* (1853) 2 Drew 73; *Northern Counties of England Fire Insurance Co v. Whipp* (1884) 26 Ch D 482; *Butler v. Fairclough* (1917) 23 CLR 78 at 91.
1234. *See e.g.* LTA, sections 76, 77 and 78.
1235. *See* CLPA, sections 19, 20, 21 and 30.

repays the debt. During the period of continuing default by the mortgagor, the mortgagee is entitled to pursue the available remedies, including the exercise of the power to sell the property.[1236]

583. Even if the debt is not fully repaid, the mortgage may be discharged with the consent of both parties.[1237] Where a debt is secured by mortgages over more than one property, both parties may also agree to a partial discharge, e.g. removal of one or more of the properties as security for the debt.[1238]

584. A discharge shall be in the prescribed form duly executed by the mortgagee and registered.[1239] Upon registration, the property shall be 'freed from the mortgage and from all rights and powers of the mortgagee, either absolutely or to any lesser extent as expressed in the discharge'.[1240]

B. Clogs

585. As a mortgage arises from a contract, the parties may mutually agree on their respective rights and obligations. However, the law abhors terms that impede the mortgagor's ability to redeem the property or to obtain a discharge of the mortgage. These are known as clogs to the mortgagor's equity of redemption. Clog can take different forms. They may directly concern the security, e.g. one that specifies the mode of repayment or the timing of redemption or discharge. Or they may appear to be independent of the security but indirectly affects the mortgagor's ability to redeem or discharge, e.g. an option to purchase the mortgaged property granted to the mortgagee. Such a term, being beneficial to the mortgagee, is also known as a collateral advantage.

586. Identifying whether a particular term amounts to a clog is largely a fact-specific exercise. The process, however, is made difficult by the many inconsistent and irreconcilable authorities. It has been said that 'the law in this area oscillate between two competing policies: (a) the paternalistic impulse of the law to protect [the mortgagor]; and (b) freedom of contract'.[1241] As shall be observed, however, the more recent authorities tend to uphold the mortgage agreement so long as both parties have negotiated at arm's length and no unconscionability or oppression is involved.

587. Two of the most common situations in which the courts have identified a clog are where the contractual date of redemption is postponed for an unreasonably

1236. *Shaik Sahied bin Abdullah Bajarai v. Tan Boon Guan* [1936] 1 MLJ 107.
1237. LTA, section 78(1).
1238. *Ibid.*, section 78(1).
1239. *Ibid.*, section 78(2); Form 31 (Total Discharge); Form 32 (Partial discharge)
1240. LTA, section 78(2)
1241. Tang Hang Wu and Kelvin F.K. Low, *Tan Sook Yee's Principles of Singapore Land Law*, 3rd edn (LexisNexis, 2009) at 527–28.

long period[1242] and where the interest rate is exorbitant.[1243] However, the older authorities concerning these two situations are arguably of less relevance today. Most modern mortgage agreements allow early redemption subject to payment of a fee. So long as the amount chargeable is not so disproportionate to the mortgagee's loss so as to offend the law against penalties, the courts are unlikely to interfere. A relevant consideration is the amount that the mortgagee would have earned had the loan run its full course.[1244] Similarly, given that moneylending is a heavily regulated business, disputes about interest rates are unlikely to arise.[1245]

588. On the other hand, collateral benefits continue to attract judicial attention. The interesting question of whether an option to purchase the mortgaged property granted to the mortgagee amounts to a clog was indirectly addressed in *Citicorp Investment Bank (Singapore) Ltd v. Wee Ah Kee*.[1246] In this case, Wee borrowed money from Citicorp to purchase shares and agreed that the shares shall be charged to Citicorp as security for the loan. Wee also granted Citicorp an option to purchase 30% of the said shares. The Court of Appeal held that the option to purchase was not a clog because the parties clearly intended something more than a simple loan and security agreement. The agreement incorporated elements of investment and profit-sharing.[1247] As the court observed:

> The [borrower] was a businessman who required funds to buy the shares of a company; the [lender] was an investment bank looking for potentially profitable joint ventures, while at the same time being in the business of lending money'.[1248]

589. The Court of Appeal also mentioned two other points in support of its reluctance to intervene. First, there was nothing to indicate that Wee was a victim of oppression. He was an experienced businessman who was well advised by competent lawyers.[1249] Second, there is no compelling reason to restrict commercial parties from pursuing legitimate expectations through the employment of flexible and innovative financing schemes.[1250]

1242. *See Fairclough v. Swan Brewery* [1912] AC 565; *cf Knightsbridge Estates Trust v. Byrne* [1939] 1 Ch 441.
1243. *Cityland and Property (Holdings) Ltd v. Dabrah* [1968] Ch 166
1244. *Fiscal Consultants Pte Ltd v. Asia Commercial Finance Ltd* [1981] SGHC 13; [1981-1982] SLR(R) 149.
1245. *See e.g.*, Moneylenders Act (Cap 188, Rev Ed 2010).
1246. [1997] SGCA 64; [1997] 2 SLR(R) 1 (Yong CJ, Karthigesu and Thean JJA), noted in Lee Eng Beng, 'Not Quite Unclogged' [1997] SJLS 597.
1247. [1997] SGCA 64; [1997] 2 SLR(R) 1 at [35], [36]. *See also G & C Kreglingerv v. New Patatonia Meat and Cold Storage Co Ltd* [1914] AC 25.
1248. [1997] SGCA 64; [1997] 2 SLR(R) 1 at [35].
1249. [1997] SGCA 64; [1997] 2 SLR(R) 1 at [41].
1250. [1997] SGCA 64; [1997] 2 SLR(R) 1 at [42].

590. The decision would most likely be different if the case concerned a simple housing loan and an anxious borrower who has little choice but borrow on the lender's terms. In such a case, it is difficult to perceive what meaningful role does an option to purchase play except to defeat the borrower's equity of redemption.

591. Another interesting case that warrants attention is *Esso Petroleum Ltd v. Harper's Garage (Stourport) Ltd*, where the agreement provided that the mortgaged property was irredeemable for 21 years and during its continuance the mortgagor must purchase fuel only from the mortgagee.[1251] The House of Lords, having considered the amount loaned and the duration of the restraint, held that the agreement imposed an unreasonable restraint of trade. Importantly, because the tie was so closely linked to the term postponing redemption, that term was also unenforceable.

592. Although the cases appear to address clogs as though they are governed by an independent doctrine, one cannot help but wonder if the courts were merely applying established vitiating factors in contract law, particularly unconscionability. If the possibility of this linkage has yet to be noticed, then it is submitted that much could be gained by amalgamating the two supposedly distinct areas of the law.

II. Rights as the Registered Owner

A. *Possession of the Mortgaged Property*

593. Since the mortgagor remains the registered owner of the property, he is prima facie entitled to possession of the property, unless otherwise agreed. The mortgagor may stay in the property without having to pay rent to the mortgagee and is not accountable to the mortgagee for any profits derived from the property.

B. *Transfer of the Mortgaged Property*

594. The mortgagor may sell or transfer the mortgaged property to a third party. The transferee takes the property subject to the mortgage and becomes the mortgagor. Where the property is encumbered by a registered mortgage, section 64 of the LTA implies into the transfer a covenant by the transferee to observe all obligations secured by the mortgage, such as the repayment of the debt. On the other hand, in the case of an equitable mortgage, such obligations remain with the original mortgagor. If it is intended that the transferee should assume such obligations, the intention should be clearly stipulated and it would be prudent for the original mortgagor to insure itself against the transferee's default by including an indemnity clause in the agreement.

1251. [1966] 2 QB 514.

C. Lease of the Mortgaged Property

595. For a traditional legal mortgage, where title in the property passes to the mortgagee, the default rules regarding the leasing of the property are set out in section 23 of the CLPA. Unless otherwise agreed, section 23 of the CLPA limits any leasing of the mortgaged property by the mortgagor to 3 years and requires the mortgagor to lease at the best rent that can reasonably be obtained. This section does not apply to a registered or equitable mortgage. Since title in the property remains with the mortgagor, he is entitled to lease the property as he wishes, subject to the terms of the mortgage agreement.

596. However, unless the lease is expressly or impliedly authorised by the mortgage agreement or by law, or granted with the mortgagee's consent, the lease will not be binding on the mortgagee.[1252] The case of *Singapore Finance Ltd v. Matterhorn (Pte) Ltd*, although decided prior to the addition of section 89, remains helpful in shedding light on the requirement of consent.[1253] In that case, the mortgagor leased the mortgaged property to various parties without obtaining the mortgagee's prior consent, as required by the mortgage agreement. Although the mortgagee knew that the mortgagor was letting the property, it did not know to whom exactly the tenants were. Thean J held that such knowledge alone did not constitute consent. There must be positive acts from which one can reasonably infer consent or acquiescence to the leases.

D. Granting of Subsequent Mortgages

597. A property may be offered as security for more than one debt. For example, a property worth $750,000 is mortgaged to secure a debt of $100,000. There is nothing to prevent the mortgagor from offering the same property as security to obtain further loans. The only limitation is a practical one. As the total debt amount secured by the property approaches its value, lenders will be unwilling to accept the property as security for fear that in the case of default the proceeds of sale may be insufficient to satisfy the debt after deducting the necessary expenses and paying the prior mortgagees.

598. Where the granting of a subsequent mortgage is not prohibited by the terms of the first mortgage, the mortgagor may request that the first mortgagee, who is entitled to the custody of the documents of title, to produce those documents at the Land Titles Registry to allow the registration of the subsequent mortgage.[1254] On the other hand, where the mortgagor grants a subsequent mortgage in breach of the terms of the first mortgage agreement, the first mortgagee is entitled to withhold

1252. LTA, section 89.

1253. [1989] SGHC 64; [1989] 2 SLR(R) 105. *See also Win Supreme Investment (S) Pte Ltd v. Joharah bte Abdul Wahab (Sjarikat Bekerjasama Perumahan Kebangsaan Singapura, third party)* [1996] SGHC 255; [1996] 3 SLR(R) 583.

1254. LTA, section 72.

delivery of the documents of title. However, the subsequently granted mortgage may still be valid although only as an equitable mortgage.

§4. Rights and Duties of the Mortgagee

I. Rights Independent of the Mortgagor's Default

A. Repayment

599. The right of the mortgagee to repayment of the debt is usually stipulated in the loan and mortgage agreement. Even if the agreement is silent, this duty will be implied either in fact or by statute.[1255]

B. Transfer of the Mortgage

600. The mortgagee may transfer the mortgage to a third party by an instrument of transfer in the approved form and by having it registered.[1256] Upon registration, the transferee shall become entitled, by virtue of section 63(2) of the LTA, to all the rights, powers and remedies of the mortgagee expressed or implied in the mortgage, including the right to repayment.

C. Submortgage

601. A mortgage, being an interest in land, could itself be offered as a security. Section 71 of the LTA provides that a mortgage may be mortgaged, thereby creating a submortgage.[1257] The same section also mentions the need to register a submortgage, although no specific form has been prescribed for this purpose. According to Baalman, the standard mortgage form[1258] could be adapted for this purpose simply by stating the subject matter of the mortgage as another mortgage instead of an estate.[1259]

602. Upon registration of the submortgage, the powers and rights of the mortgagee (i.e., the head mortgagee) become exercisable by the submortgagee, and the mortgagee shall not exercise such rights and powers during the currency of the submortgage.[1260] It is not entirely clear how a submortgage is different from a transfer of a mortgage. One possibility is that a submortgage operates only as an assignment

1255. CLPA, section 31(2)(a).
1256. LTA, section 63(1); Form 28 (Transfer of Mortgage).
1257. LTA, section 71(1).
1258. Form 29 (Mortgage).
1259. John Baalman, *The Singapore Torrens system: being a commentary on the Land Titles Ordinance 1956 of the State of Singapore* (Govt. Printer, 1961) at 135.
1260. LTA, section 71(2).

of rights and powers exercisable upon the mortgagor's default. Other rights independent of default, e.g. the right to repayment, remains with the mortgagee. In any case, a submortgage shall not affect the rights of a mortgagor who has not been given notice of the submortgage.[1261]

D. Possession of the Mortgaged Property

603. Unlike the mortgagee in the case of a classic legal mortgage, a registered mortgagee and an equitable mortgagee have no immediate right to possession of the mortgaged property. However, they may be given possession either by a term of the mortgage agreement or by the consent of the mortgagor. Unless otherwise agreed, a mortgagee in possession is liable to account to the mortgagor for the rents and profits received, or which ought to have been generated. In *Lee Nyet Khiong v. Lee Nyet Yun Janet*, the mortgagee, without the mortgagor's consent, took possession of the mortgaged property and allowed his family members to move in.[1262] The Court of Appeal held that the mortgagee was liable to pay to the mortgagor rent at the market rate.

E. Leasing of the Mortgaged Property

604. Where the mortgage agreement does not prohibit a mortgagee in possession from letting the mortgaged property, he may grant an agricultural or occupational lease for a term not exceeding 21 years or a building lease for a term not exceeding 99 years.[1263]

F. Tacking

605. Where the property is encumbered by more than one mortgage, the prior mortgagee may make further advances to the mortgagor and have that additional debt secured by the prior mortgage if: (i) the prior mortgage agreement expressly allows the further advances; or (ii) if the subsequent mortgagee(s) agrees to the further advances.[1264] Thus, where a lender is offered a second mortgage, it is important that he checks the term of the prior mortgage agreement to see if further advances by the first mortgagee are allowed.

1261. *Ibid.*, section 71(3).
1262. [1997] SGCA 25; [1997] 2 SLR(R) 173 (Yong CJ, Karthigesu and Thean JJA).
1263. CLPA, section 23(2).
1264. LTA, section 80.

II. Remedies of the Mortgagee in the Event of the Mortgagor's Default

606. Where the mortgagor has defaulted in repayment of his debt, a range of remedies becomes available to the mortgagee. As the law stands, the mortgagee is under no duty to have regard to the mortgagor's interest when choosing his remedy.[1265] For example, the mortgagee is not obliged to sell the property at the most opportune moment. He is not even obliged to sell it in the first place even though that may be the most beneficial course of action for both parties. It is only when the mortgagee has chosen his remedy that he must exercise it with reasonable care. More shall be said below about the mortgagee's duties when exercising the various available remedies.

A. Entry into Possession

607. The right of a registered mortgagee to enter into possession of the mortgaged property in the event of the mortgagor's default in repayment is provided for under section 75 of the LTA. The mortgagee is required to give one month's prior notice before entering into possession. Alternatively, the mortgagee may apply to the court for an order for possession. In *Hong Leong Finance Ltd v. Tan Gin Huay*, the Court of Appeal held that where the mortgagor is clearly in default the court has no power to decline to make an order for possession.[1266] However, the court may 'adjourn a summons for possession to afford to the mortgagor a chance of paying off the mortgagee in full or otherwise satisfying him, but not if there is no reasonable prospect of this occurring'.[1267]

608. As section 75 does not apply to equitable mortgages, and there is no equivalent provision in the CLPA, an equitable mortgagee may enter into possession only if the right to do so has been expressly reserved in the mortgage agreement.

609. In most cases, entry into possession is a preliminary step to the exercise of the mortgagee's statutory power of sale.[1268] Having possession of the property will facilitate the sale, especially when the mortgagee intends to sell the property by way of private contract instead of a public auction. Once in possession, the mortgagee is also entitled to receive rents and profits of the mortgaged property by giving notice to persons liable to account for them.[1269]

1265. *China and South Sea Bank Ltd v. Tan Soon Gin* [1990] 1 AC 536; *Roberto Building Material Pte Ltd v. Oversea-Chinese Banking Corp* [2003] SGCA 30; [2003] 3 SLR(R) 217.
1266. [1999] SGCA 18; [1999] 1 SLR(R) 755 (Yong CJ, Karthigesu and Thean JJA).
1267. [1999] SGCA 18; [1999] 1 SLR(R) 755 at [12]. *See also The Bank of East Asia v. Tan Chin Mong Holdings (S) Pte Ltd* [2000] SGHC 250; [2000] 3 SLR(R) 769 at [34].
1268. *Lee Nyet Khiong v. Lee Nyet Yun Janet* [1997] SGCA 25; [1997] 2 SLR(R) 173.
1269. LTA, section 75(4).

610. If the mortgaged property is tenanted, the mortgagee is entitled to evict the tenant and acquire vacant possession only if the lease is not binding on the mortgagee. Where the lease predates the mortgage, the mortgagee is allowed to enter into possession only after the expiry of the lease.[1270] During the continuance of the lease, however, the mortgagee may repossess the property if the tenant has delayed in paying rent for 30 days,[1271] subject to the tenant's right to obtain relief against forfeiture.[1272] Where, on the other hand, the lease postdates the mortgage, the focus is on whether the lease was granted with the mortgagee's consent.[1273] In *Singapore Finance Ltd v. Matterhorn (Pte) Ltd*, the mortgagee was allowed to evict the tenants because the mortgagor did not obtain the mortgagee's consent in letting the property.[1274] In contrast, in *Rimmon Watch Pte Ltd v. Great Pacific Finance Ltd*, since the mortgagee had consented to the mortgagor's granting of a three-year lease, during the continuance of the lease the mortgagee was only entitled to the collection of rent.[1275]

611. Where a mortgagee exercises his statutory right to enter into possession of the mortgaged property, he does not become the owner of the reversion.[1276] In *Rimmon Watch*, the tenants sought to argue that the mortgagee stepped into the shoes of the landlord-mortgagor and was thus automatically bound by the option to renew the lease granted to the tenant. The Court of Appeal disagreed, clarifying that the mortgagee, in entering into possession, does not acquire any title to the property:

> In exercising his statutory power of entering into possession, a mortgagee under the Land Titles Act remains aloof from the legal estate. His right derives its force entirely from [section 75] and is of a wholly different character from the legal mortgagee's right under common law title. The section makes no attempt to equate the position enjoyed by a mortgagee of Torrens title land with that of a mortgagee of land under common law title.[1277]

612. As explained earlier, a mortgagee in possession owes a duty to the mortgagor to put the property to beneficial use. Even where the purpose for entering into possession of the mortgaged property was to sell it, the mortgagee is under a duty not to leave it vacant for an unreasonable period of time. In *Lee Nyet Khiong v. Lee Nyet Yun Janet*, the Court of Appeal said:

> … if the sale does not take place within a reasonable period, the mortgagee will be accountable to the mortgagor for any loss occurring between the date

1270. *United Overseas Bank Ltd v. Loh Boon Hua* [2015] SGHCR 9.
1271. LTA, sections 75(3) and 93(1)(d).
1272. *Ibid.*, section 18A.
1273. *See ibid.*, section 89.
1274. [1989] SGHC 64; [1989] 2 SLR(R) 105 at [26], [27].
1275. [1989] SGCA 2; [1989] 1 SLR(R) 66.
1276. The landlord's interest in recovering possession of the property at the expiry of the lease is known as the reversion.
1277. [1989] SGCA 2; [1989] 1 SLR(R) 66 at [19] (Wee CJ, Sinnathuray and Thean JJ).

of taking possession and the date of sale. The position in law is that during the time he is in possession, he must exercise due diligence to put the property to beneficial use.[1278]

613. This principle is best illustrated in *Indian Overseas Bank v. Motorcycle Industries (1973) Pte Ltd.*[1279] There the mortgaged property was sold at a public auction but the purchaser decided not to complete the purchase. Instead of accepting the purchaser's repudiation and reselling the property, the mortgagee instituted legal proceedings against the purchaser. The property was eventually resold 10 years after the mortgagee took possession of it. During that entire period, the property was left vacant despite the mortgagor's complaint. The mortgagor brought a claim for account of rent that should have been generated. The Court of Appeal held that the mortgagee was in breach of duty for not putting the property to profitable use. Even if the mortgagee decided to pursue a claim of specific performance against the defaulting purchaser, it should have predicted that litigation would be protracted and could have taken steps to let out the property on short terms. The same decision was arrived at in *Overseas Union Bank Ltd v. Chua Kok Kay* where the mortgaged property was left unlet for 13 ½ months.[1280]

614. In *The Bank of East Asia v. Tan Chin Mong Holdings (S) Pte Ltd*, Selvam J warned against seeking possession of the mortgaged property 'with a hidden agenda, in disregard of the harm that it might cause to someone with a vested interest in it.[1281] Although the court did not explicitly say so, this is most likely in reference to a mortgagee's general duty of good faith.

B. *Power of Sale*

1. General

615. In the event of the mortgagor's default, the mortgagee may exercise the power of sale to liquidate the mortgaged property and apply the proceeds towards repayment of debt. In most cases, this is the fastest and surest way of recovering a debt. From the mortgagor's perspective, however, the mortgagee's exercise of a power of sale has serious implications. First, the mortgagor will lose possession of his property. Second, the amount for which the property is sold directly affects the extent to which the debt would be repaid and the amount of surplus (if any) from the proceeds that the mortgagor is entitled to have. Thus, many of the disputes on this topic arise from the mortgagor's allegation that the mortgagee did not sell the mortgaged property at the best possible time and price.

1278. [1997] SGCA 25; [1997] 2 SLR(R) 173 at [20] (Yong CJ, Karthigesu and Thean JJA).
1279. [1993] SGCA 16; [1993] 1 SLR(R) 364 (Thean, Rajendran and Karthigesu JJ).
1280. [1992] SGHC 239; [1992] 2 SLR(R) 811.
1281. [2000] SGHC 250; [2000] 3 SLR(R) 769 at [31].

2. Exercising the Power of Sale

616. In most cases, a power of sale is expressly provided as a term of the mortgage agreement. The manner in which the power of sale may be exercised is usually also governed by the agreement.[1282]

617. Where the agreement is silent, the relevant provisions in the CLPA apply. Section 24(1)(a) implies a power of sale, which arises upon the mortgagor's default in repayment. Section 25 further states that a power of sale is not exercisable unless: (a) a notice requiring repayment of the mortgage money has been served on the mortgagor and default has been made in payment of the mortgage money or part thereof for three months after the service; (b) some interest is in arrears and unpaid for one month; or (c) there has been a breach of some other provision contained in the mortgage agreement. The grounds most commonly invoked are (a) and (b). A mortgagee who wishes to avoid delay in selling the property is better off relying on (b) due to the absence of a notice requirement.[1283] A power of sale could only be defeated by the mortgagor's payment of whatever amount that was due and owing.

618. The sale of the mortgaged property may be by public auction or by private contract.[1284] Upon a successful sale, and upon registration of the transfer to the purchaser, the interest of the mortgagor passes to the purchaser and the purchaser takes the property free of the mortgage and any prior encumbrances binding on the mortgage.[1285] In a case where the property is subject to a first registered mortgage and a subsequent equitable mortgage protected by a caveat, and it is the first mortgagee who wishes to exercise a power of sale, the caveat does not prohibit registration of the transfer pursuant to the sale.[1286]

619. The manner in which the proceeds of sale shall be applied is prescribed by section 74(1).[1287] After discharging any prior encumbrances (e.g., a prior mortgage), the remainder of the proceeds shall be held by the mortgagee 'on trust' to be applied: (a) first, in payment of all costs and expenses properly incurred as incidental to the sale or any attempted sale; (b) second, in discharge of money liability secured by the mortgage belonging to the mortgagee who exercised the power of sale; and (c) third, in payment of subsequent mortgages and charges (if any) in the order of their priority; and (d) any residue shall be paid to the person who appears from the land register to be entitled to the mortgaged property.

620. In *Good Property Land Development Pte Ltd (in liquidation) v. Société-Générale*, the Court of Appeal sought to clarify the reference to 'trust' in section 74:

1282. *See* CLPA, section 24(2) and (3).
1283. *Tye Ong Choon v. Mohamed Ismail* [1948] MLJ 39.
1284. CLPA, section 24(1)(a).
1285. LTA, section 73.
1286. *Ibid.*, section 129(1A)(c).
1287. *See also* the equivalent provision in CLPA, section 26(3), which applies to equitable mortgages.

> ... it is clear that a mortgagee is a trustee of the proceeds of sale. But for whom? From a reading of the section, it would appear that he could be a trustee for all the subsequent encumbrancers coming after him ... or perhaps a trustee for the mortgagor, subject to his duties to apply the surplus funds in a certain way in accordance with priority ... We think that whether the surplus funds were held for the mortgagor or all subsequent encumbrancers, one position is undoubted and it is this: the proceeds of sale were held on trust but the right of the mortgagor to any residue will only crystallise or, to phrase it in another way, the beneficial interest will only become clear and ascertained after all prior encumbrancers are paid.[1288]

621. In *Chip Thye Enterprises Pte Ltd v. Development Bank of Singapore Ltd*, the Court of Appeal explained that the person referred to in category (d) need not be a registered proprietor.[1289] In this case, the mortgagor entered into an agreement to sell the property to a third party. The third party lodged a caveat to protect its interest as a purchaser. As the agreement was specifically enforceable, the purchaser acquired an equitable interest in the property. However, before the property could be transferred to the purchaser, the mortgagor defaulted in repayment of its debt and the mortgagee sold the property at a public auction in exercise of its power of sale. Although the purchaser was never a registered owner of the property, the Court of Appeal held that it was entitled to the surplus of the sale proceeds. The lodgment of the caveat, which was notified in the land register, was sufficient to bring the purchaser within category (d).

3. Mortgagee's Duties in Respect of the Power of Sale

622. As alluded to earlier, the exercise of a power of sale has serious implications on the mortgagor's interest. Thus, although the power of sale is clearly for the mortgagee's benefit, it is only fair that the interest of the mortgagor should not be ignored entirely. The issue of how the interests of the mortgagor and the mortgagee should be balanced has been a much-debated topic.[1290] As the law stands, the mortgagor owes only a general duty of good faith and also a duty of care in exercising the power of sale. Such duties are owed to the mortgagor as well as other parties who will be affected by the manner in which the power of sale is exercised, e.g. subsequent encumbrancers[1291] and sureties.[1292]

1288. [1996] SGCA 25; [1996] 1 SLR(R) 884 at [18] (Yong CJ, Lai and Goh JJ).
1289. [1994] SGCA 59; [1994] 2 SLR(R) 68 (Yong CJ, Karthigesu and Thean JJA).
1290. *See* Wee Meng Seng, 'Duties of a Mortgagee and a Receiver: Where Singapore Should and Should Not Follow English Law' (2008) 20 SAcLJ 559; Kelry Loi, 'Mortgagees Exercising Power of Sale: Nonfeasance, Privilege, Trusteeship & Duty of Care' [2010] JBL 576.
1291. *Downsview Nominees v. First City Corp Ltd* [1993] 3 All ER 626.
1292. *The Bank of East Asia v. Tan Chin Mong Holdings (S) Pte Ltd* [2000] SGHC 250; [2000] 3 SLR(R) 769.

623. In *Roberto Building Material Pte Ltd v. Oversea-Chinese Banking Corp*, the Court of Appeal acknowledged that a mortgagee must act in good faith.[1293] A duty of good faith is breached only if the mortgagee acted dishonestly or for an improper motive.[1294] While acting recklessly may amount to bad faith,[1295] negligence alone is insufficient.[1296] In practice, it is difficult to find that a mortgagee has breached a duty of good faith if all that he intended to do is to protect his own interest by realising the security.[1297]

624. The courts have persistently maintained that the mortgagee owes no general duty of care to the mortgagor. The mortgagee is entirely free to decide whether or not to sell the mortgaged property, and if so, when.[1298] In *How Seen Ghee v. Development Bank of Singapore Ltd*, the Court of Appeal said: 'A mortgagee is not a trustee of his power of sale *vis-a`-vis* the mortgagor. Thus, he is not required to wait for the most propitious market conditions to sell or to delay a sale in the hope of obtaining a better price.[1299]

625. There is also no duty to sell even in a falling market. In *Teo Siew Har v. Oversea-Chinese Banking Corp Ltd*, the mortgagor complained that the mortgagee should have acceded to the former's request to sell the property early to avoid an expected decline in the property market.[1300] The Court of Appeal held that even though the power of sale had arisen, the mortgagee was under no obligation to sell the property.

626. In *The Bank of East Asia v. Tan Chin Mong Holdings (S) Pte Ltd*, Selvam J explained the policy underlying the existing law:

> The basis of the principle is this: it is the duty of the borrower and the guarantor to activate themselves and discharge their obligations. If they don't then they bear the risk of a falling market. It is not desirable to turn the right of a mortgagee into a duty. To do so would be baneful to the business of property financing. The lender is entitled to sit tight and wait until he feels that he has to act in his interest.[1301]

627. However, the mortgagee does owe a duty of care in the exercise of a power of sale. In the English case of *Cuckmere Brick Co Ltd v. Mutual Finance Ltd*, the

---

1293. [2003] SGCA 30; [2003] 3 SLR(R) 217 at [51] (Chao JA, Prakash and Tan JJ).
1294. [2003] SGCA 30; [2003] 3 SLR(R) 217 at [24].
1295. [2003] SGCA 30; [2003] 3 SLR(R) 217 at [28].
1296. [2003] SGCA 30; [2003] 3 SLR(R) 217 at [24].
1297. *Kennedy v. De Trafford* [1897] AC 180.
1298. *Roberto Building Material Pte Ltd v. Oversea-Chinese Banking Corp* [2003] SGCA 30; [2003] 3 SLR(R) 217 at [51].
1299. [1993] SGCA 88; [1993] 3 SLR(R) 610 at [23] (Karthigesu JA, Thean JA and Khoo J). *See also Good Property Land Development Pte Ltd v. Société Générale* [1989] SGHC 10; [1989] 1 SLR(R) 97 at [5]; *Ng Muimui v. Indian Overseas Bank* [1985] SGCA 10; [1985–1986] SLR(R) 262 at [38].
1300. [1999] SGCA 43; [1999] 2 SLR(R) 619 (Karthigesu JA, Thean JA and Tan J).
1301. [2000] SGHC 250; [2000] 3 SLR(R) 769 at [28].

Court of Appeal held that the mortgagee owed to the mortgagor a duty 'to take reasonable care to obtain the true market value of the mortgaged property at the date on which he decides to sell it'.[1302] The court preferred to avoid the terms 'proper price', which is 'a little nebulous', and 'best price', which 'may suggest an exceptionally high price'.[1303] In several Singapore cases, reference was made to the best price reasonably obtainable at the time of the sale or in the circumstances of the case.[1304] Although the language used may appear to be different, it is unlikely that the Singapore courts intended to set the standard any higher than to sell the property at its true market value.

628. Since the test of liability is not whether the mortgagee has obtained the best price, the courts have demonstrated reluctance in finding liability on the mortgagee's part merely because there is evidence that the property could have been sold for more.[1305] Instead, the courts have focused primarily on whether the mortgagee has done all that is reasonable in conducting the sale. Before examining four cases that helpfully illustrate how a mortgagee's duty of care may be breached, one important point must be noted. If the mortgaged property is not sold, the duty of care does not arise at all.[1306] In such a case it is irrelevant that the failure to sell the property was due to the mortgagee's negligence.

629. In *Kian Choon Investments (Pte) Ltd v. Société Générale*, the mortgagee took possession of the mortgaged building following the mortgagor's default and sold the property by way of a private sale.[1307] The purchase price was agreed based on professional valuations. Importantly, the agreement of sale contained two peculiar terms requiring the purchaser to grant to the mortgagee: (a) a lease over four floors of the building for a period of 5 years; and (b) on option to purchase exercisable within 6 months. The mortgagor challenged the sale. In the High Court, Thean J observed that there was a conflict between the mortgagee's interest to derive benefits for itself and its duty to sell the building at the best price available. In such a case, the burden was on the mortgagee to show that it had taken reasonable precautions to obtain the best price reasonably obtainable in the circumstances. On the facts, the mortgagee failed to discharge this burden. It had made no effort to obtain the best possible price either by advertising the building for sale, by inviting tenders, or by selling the building by individual floors given that strata subdivision of individual floors had been obtained.[1308] On the whole, the mortgagee's conduct reflected a 'calculated indifference to the position of the mortgagor' and amounted

1302. [1971] Ch D 949.
1303. *Ibid.*, at 966.
1304. *Lee Nyet Khiong v. Lee Nyet Yun Janet* [1997] SGCA 25; [1997] 2 SLR(R) 173; *Good Property Land Development Pte Ltd v. Société Générale* [1989] SGHC 10; [1989] 1 SLR(R) 97; *Ng Muimui v. Indian Overseas Bank* [1985] SGCA 10; [1985–1986] SLR(R) 262.
1305. *See e.g. Ng Muimui v. Indian Overseas Bank* [1985] SGCA 10; [1985-1986] SLR(R) 262; *Good Property Land Development Pte Ltd v. Société Générale* [1989] SGHC 10; [1989] 1 SLR(R) 97.
1306. *Roberto Building Material v. OCBC* [2003] SGCA 30; [2003] 3 SLR(R) 217 at [57].
1307. [1990] SGHC 2; [1990] 1 SLR(R) 7.
1308. [1990] SGHC 2; [1990] 1 SLR(R) 7 at [25].

to 'recklessness'.[1309] The mortgagor succeeded in obtaining an injunction to retrain the mortgagee and the purchaser from completing the sale.

630. In *How Seen Ghee v. Development Bank of Singapore Ltd*, the defaulting mortgagor managed to solicit a firm and serious offer to purchase the property for \$725,000.[1310] As the debt owed was \$1.1 million, the mortgagee refused to approve sale unless the mortgagor suggested a proposal for repayment of the shortfall. As the mortgagor was unable to propose a solution, the mortgagee proceeded to sell the property by public auction. Based on a valuation it obtained, the mortgagee set the reserve price at \$650,000. The property was eventually sold for \$670,000. The Court of Appeal held that the mortgagee, in selling the property for such a low price, had sacrificed the mortgagor's interest without any discernable gain to itself and was therefore in breach of a duty of care. The court commented:

> An auction is not always the best way of securing a good price, as shown in the instant case. It is often possible for the mortgagor himself/herself, who has every reason to try to do so, to secure a good price by a private treaty sale. There is seldom any harm in allowing the mortgagor a reasonable opportunity to do so. While the mortgagor is engaged in such efforts, the mortgagee should refrain from doing anything which is liable adversely to affect the mortgagor's efforts.[1311]

The court assessed the damages payable by the mortgagee at \$55,000, being the difference between \$725,000 and \$670,000.

631. In *Lee Nyet Khiong v. Lee Nyet Yun Janet*, the mortgagee obtained a valuation which showed that the property was worth \$7m if sold in open market and \$5.95 on forced sale.[1312] The mortgagee placed an advertisement in newspaper for the sale of the property by tender. At the close of the tender only one tender of \$6.85m accompanied by a \$150,000 deposit was received. Soon after, the mortgagor informed the mortgagee that the former had received a genuine offer of \$7.1m. However, the offeror refused to tender for the purchase on the mortgagee's terms. Instead, he demanded to proceed by way of an option to purchase with an option period of one month. He offered an option fee of \$100,000. Despite reminders by the mortgagor that the property should not be sold for less than \$7.1m, the mortgagee proceeded to accept the tender of \$6.85m. The mortgagor claimed that the mortgagee had breached a duty of care in exercising his power of sale. The Court of Appeal found for the mortgagor. The court rejected the mortgagee's argument that the sale price of \$6.85m was reasonable because it was very close to the valuation obtained. Instead, the court focused on whether the mortgagee 'had taken

1309. [1990] SGHC 2; [1990] 1 SLR(R) 7 at [39].
1310. [1993] SGCA 88; [1993] 3 SLR(R) 610.
1311. [1993] SGCA 88; [1993] 3 SLR(R) 610 at [24] (Karthigesu JA, Thean JA and Khoo J).
1312. [1997] SGCA 25; [1997] 2 SLR(R) 173 (Yong CJ, Karthigesu and Thean JJA).

reasonable efforts to obtain the best price that was available in the circumstances'.[1313] The court found that he had not on several grounds. First, the advertisement contained insufficient information about the property. It merely stated the property's location, its land area and the nature of the tenure. It failed to state the condition of the property, especially the fact that it was a recently renovated luxurious bungalow. Second, the mortgagee placed only one advertisement inviting tenders. Third, invitation for tenders was open only for only a short period of two weeks. Fourth, the mortgagee sold the property too hastily. Even though the subsequent offer of $7.1m was to proceed by way of an option to purchase, it should have been given serious consideration given that it was significantly higher than the tender of $6.85m. The mortgagee should also have tried to negotiate with both offerors for better terms. As the property market was healthy at that time, there was no risk of loss to the mortgagee in taking some time to do so. All these factors led the court to the conclusion that the mortgagee was solely concerned about his own interest and sacrificed the mortgagor's interest. The mortgagee was in breach of a duty of care and was liable to pay the shortfall of $250,000.

632. In *Sri Jaya (Sendirian) Bhd v. RHB Bank Bhd*, the mortgagee decided not to advertise the mortgaged property for sale to avoid objections from the tenants.[1314] Instead, the mortgagee informed its branches in Singapore to spread the words around. Several offers to purchase were received, although many of the offerors came to know about the sale from their own channels. There were two offers of $6.5m, which were the highest received. The mortgagee sold the property for that amount to the offeror whom it considered to be more reliable. Within three months, the purchaser resold the property for $14m. Rajendran J held that the mortgagee had failed to sell the property at its true market value. Several reasons were given. First, although the mortgagee was not obliged to publicly advertise the property the sale,[1315] it could have done more to attract a wider pool of potential purchasers, e.g. by entrusting the sale to a reputable property firm.[1316] Second, the mortgagee did not try to obtain a better offer by making the two offerors of $6.5m compete against each other. Third, the mortgagee failed to pay due consideration to the phenomenal rise in the amounts offered for the property, which was an indication of a healthy demand for the property. In awarding damages, the learned judge relied on the valuation provided by the expert called by the mortgagee. The property was valued at $15.54m if sold unencumbered. The learned judge accepted the true market value of the property to be $9.69m after deducting $5.85m as the estimated compensation to the tenants to obtain vacant possession. Damages were assessed at $3.19m, being the difference between $9.69m and $6.5m.

1313. [1997] SGCA 25; [1997] 2 SLR(R) 173 at [36].
1314. [2000] SGHC 206; [2000] 3 SLR(R) 365.
1315. [2000] SGHC 206; [2000] 3 SLR(R) 365 at [31], [49]; citing *Ng Muimui v. Indian Overseas Bank* [1985] SGCA 10; [1985-1986] SLR(R) 262.
1316. [2000] SGHC 206; [2000] 3 SLR(R) 365 at [51].

633. Finally, it shall be observed that the disputes often involve competing valuations of the mortgaged property. In *The Bank of East Asia v. Tan Chin Mong Holdings (S) Pte Ltd*, Selvam J said: '[W]hen a competent firm of estate agents and property valuers market a property and conclude a sale, the price obtained by them is conclusive of the correct market price'.[1317]

634. However, in other cases, the courts have expressed reservation about the reliability of property valuations in shedding light on the true market value of the property.[1318] It should come as no surprise that property valuations are often biased towards the party who adduces them. More importantly, it must be recognised that property valuation is not an exact science. In *Cuckmere Brick Co v. Mutual Finance Ltd*, the English Court of Appeal said:

635. The valuation of a plot of land depends upon the knowledge, experience, expertise and ability of the valuer. Valuation is not an exact science. Equally careful and competent valuers may differ within fairly wide limits about the value of any piece of land.[1319]

C. Appointment of Receiver

636. A mortgage agreement may expressly allow the mortgagee to appoint a receiver in the event of the mortgagor's default. The function of the receiver may also be expressly stated, e.g. to enter into possession of the mortgaged property for the purposes of receiving income from the property, managing any business operating on the property, selling the property.

637. Even where the mortgage agreement is silent, section 24(1)(c) of the CLPA confers on the mortgagee a power to appoint a receiver. However, the appointment can only be made when the power of sale arises.[1320] Under such appointment, the receiver's function is limited to receiving the income of the property and applying it to discharge the debt owed to the mortgagee.

638. Unless the mortgage agreement otherwise provides, the receiver shall be deemed to be the mortgagor's agent.[1321] The receiver owes a duty of care to the mortgagor in the performance of those functions.[1322] Where the receiver is tasked with exercising a power of sale, the receiver is subject to the same duty of care that is imposed on a mortgagee exercising the same.[1323]

1317. [2000] SGHC 250; [2000] 3 SLR(R) 769 at [42].
1318. *See Ng Muimui v. Indian Overseas Bank* [1985] SGCA 10; [1985-1986] SLR(R) 262 at [25].
1319. [1971] Ch 949 at 959; cited with approval in *The Bank of East Asia v. Tan Chin Mong Holdings (S) Pte Ltd* [2000] SGHC 250; [2000] 3 SLR(R) 769 at [41].
1320. CLPA, section 29(1).
1321. *Ibid.*, section 29(2).
1322. *Medforth v. Blake* [2000] Ch 86.
1323. *Roberto Building Material Pte Ltd v. Oversea-Chinese Banking Corp* [2003] SGCA 30; [2003] 3 SLR(R) 217 at [51]; *Downsview Nominees v. First City Corp Ltd* [1993] 3 All ER 626 at 634.

639. Income received by the receiver shall be applied based on the following priority: (a) in discharge of the property's outgoings, e.g. rents and taxes; (b) to satisfy repayment obligation under any mortgage that ranks in priority to the mortgage under which he is appointed; (c) to pay his commission, insurance premiums for the property and repair cost; and (d) to pay interest accruing under the mortgage under which he is appointed.[1324]

D. *Foreclosure*

640. An action of foreclosure is traditionally brought by a mortgagee to forfeit the mortgaged property by extinguishing the mortgagor's equity of redemption. For a registered mortgage, section 76 of the LTA preserves the right of a mortgagee to apply to the court for an order of foreclosure. Upon obtaining a court order for foreclosure, the mortgagee may have it registered, which has the effect of vesting the property in him/her free of the mortgagor's equity of redemption. The mortgagee may further apply for an order for delivery of the possession of the property to him.[1325]

641. Section 76 is silent on when an order for foreclosure may be granted. That is left to the general law. However, besides a handful of cases making references to successful foreclosure, none of them shed any light on when a court would grant an order for foreclosure.[1326] It is submitted that a court should only make an order for foreclosure if the value of the property roughly equals the debt still owing to the mortgagee. To order foreclosure where the value of the property exceeds the debt still owing would give the mortgagee a windfall. This would go beyond the function of a mortgage as a mere security device. Where the court decides against ordering foreclosure, it may instead order a sale.[1327]

§5. Judicial Sale

642. Section 30(2) of the CLPA states:

> In any action, whether for foreclosure, or for redemption, or for sale, or for the raising and payment in any manner of mortgage money, the court, on the request of the mortgagee, or of any person interested either in the mortgage money or in the right of redemption, and notwithstanding the dissent of any

---

1324. CLPA, section 29(8).
1325. Rules of Court (2014 Rev. Ed.) Order 83 Rule 5.
1326. *See e.g. Hong Leong Singapore Finance Ltd v. United Overseas Bank Ltd* [2006] SGHC 205; [2007] 1 SLR(R) 292; *Ho Soo Fong v. Standard Chartered Bank* [2006] SGHC 90; [2006] 3 SLR(R) 263; [2004] SGHC 258; [2005] 1 SLR(R) 316; *Ng Soo Khim v. Heng Teo Bong* [1992] SGHC 235; [1992] 2 SLR(R) 729.
1327. CLPA, section 32(2).

other person, … and without allowing any time for redemption or for payment of any mortgage money, may, if it thinks fit, direct a sale of the mortgaged property, on such terms as it thinks fit ...

643. In the English case of *Palk v. Mortgage Services Funding Plc*, the mortgagors owed the mortgagee £358,587 and could not keep up with repayment.[1328] The mortgagors wished to sell the property to reduce the debt. Although the property could only fetch £283,000 in the depressed market, the proceeds would at least stop interest accruing on most of the debts. The mortgagee, however, refused to consent to a sale. The mortgagee obtained an order for possession, wishing to let the property on a short term and sell it when the market improves. However, the projected income from letting the property was insufficient to cover the accruing interests. The debt would continue to grow by £30,000 each year. There was also no indication that the market will improve anytime soon. The Court of Appeal, relying on a statutory provision identical to section 30(2) of the CLPA, ordered the property to be sold. The court found this to be an exceptional case where it would be manifestly unfair to the mortgagors if the property was not sold: 'If a sale is refused, then [the mortgagors] are in a situation of financial haemorrhage for an indefinite period while the [mortgagee] continues to speculate at their expense on an increase in the value of the property'.[1329]

644. It is important to note that the court in *Palk* did not go as far as to say that the mortgagee would be in breach of a duty of care by preferring not to sell the property. Thus, in *Teo Siew Har v. Oversea-Chinese Banking Corp Ltd*, the Court of Appeal opined that *Palk* does not support the mortgagor's claim that the mortgagee had breached a duty of care by not selling the property earlier.[1330] Section 30(2) does not erode the mortgagee's freedom to choose what to do in the case of the mortgagor's default. Instead, it gives the court the power to override that freedom. If the mortgagor is of the view that a sale is more beneficial but the mortgagee decides to wait, he should simply apply to the court and ask for a judicial sale.

1328. [1993] 1 Ch 330.
1329. [1993] 1 Ch 330 at 344–45.
1330. [1999] SGCA 43; [1999] 2 SLR(R) 619 at [23] (Karthigesu JA, Thean JA and Tan J).

Chapter 11. Planning Law

§1. Introduction

645. Traditionally, a landowner is often regarded as having the freedom to use his land as he pleases. As population density increases, much of this freedom is now curtailed to reduce conflicts between neighbours.[1331] Aside from specific aspects of criminal, tort and statutory laws, which prohibit certain conducts even if performed on one's own land, perhaps the most influential regulation by the state operating at the background is through planning law. More than merely prohibiting certain conducts or activities, planning law goes further to promote broader policy goals, such as the maximisation of space, ensuring sustainable development, nature and heritage conservation, etc.

§2. Town Planning

I. The Urban Redevelopment Authority

646. The most important statutory body in charge of land planning[1332] in Singapore is the Urban Redevelopment Authority (URA) established in 1973.[1333] The broad functions and duties of the URA are listed in section 6 of the URAA. Among the more important ones are 'to undertake land planning and to manage and control the development of land in Singapore', 'to manage such lands, buildings or other property as the Authority may think fit', 'to sell, lease or grant licences to use or occupy such land belonging to the Authority for the purposes of the development and redevelopment of the land as the Authority may think fit' and to prepare and/or execute proposals, plans and projects for the above-mentioned purposes.

647. For the furtherance of its functions, the URA may make regulations,[1334] carry on such activities that it regards to be 'advantageous, necessary or convenient'[1335] and exercise one or more powers specified in the Second Schedule. Moreover, the URA may, from time to time, with the approval of the Minister, declare an area to be an urban redevelopment area, the result being that the land may be acquired by the state within three years.[1336]

1331. *See also* Chapter 12 (Neighbourhood and Urban Problems).
1332. *See* Tang Hang Wu and Kelvin F.K. Low, *Tan Sook Yee's Principles of Singapore Land Law*, 3rd edn (LexisNexis, 2009) Chapter 23; W.J.M. Ricquier, *Land Law*, 5th edn (LexisNexis, 2017) Chapter 15.
1333. Urban Redevelopment Authority Act (Cap. 340, Rev Ed 1990) (URAA).
1334. *Ibid.*, section 17.
1335. *Ibid.*, section 7.
1336. *Ibid.*, section 8.

II. Planning Act and the Master Plan

648. In making its land development decisions, the URA works within the ambit of the Planning Act.[1337] The Master Plan, first submitted to the Governor in Council in 1958,[1338] and revised every 5 years,[1339] forms the backbone of land planning.[1340] The most recent Master Plan, published in 2014, 'features a comprehensive and integrated planning approach that ensures our social and economic needs are met, while maintaining a liveable and sustainable environment'.[1341]

649. The Master Plan sets out, inter alia, the following matters: (a) zoning; (b) plot ratios; (c) height restrictions; (d) designation of conservation areas; and etc. In this way, the Master Plan restricts how land may be used or developed. For example, a parcel of land designated for residential use cannot be used for farming or other non-residential purposes.

650. Any development of land can only be carried out with a planning permission.[1342] Section 3(1) of the PA defines 'development' to mean 'the carrying out of any building, engineering, mining, earthworks or other operations in, on, over or under land, or the making of any material change in the use of any building or land'. While each case is necessarily fact specific, the PA provides a list of operations which shall not be deemed to involve development,[1343] and a separate list of operations which amount to developments.[1344]

651. In deciding whether to grant a planning permission, the URA will refer to the Master Plan and also take into account other relevant policy considerations, such as safety and security concerns. The URA may also impose conditions on the grant, such as conditions relating to height, design, appearance and siting of any building.[1345] Where planning permission has been obtained, the developer is required to pay to the URA a development charge.[1346]

§3. Buildings: Use and Occupation

652. As explained earlier, a landowner is not free to build whatever he wants on his land, or use his building in whichever way he prefers. Under the Master Plan, every parcel of land is zoned for a specific type of use, such as for 'Residential',

1337. (Cap. 232, Rev Ed 1998) Part III (PA).
1338. Singapore Improvement Ordinance (Cap. 259, Ed 1955).
1339. PA, section 8.
1340. The most recent Master Plan was published in 2014.
1341. URA, 'About Master Plan 2014': https://www.ura.gov.sg/uol/master-plan/view-master-plan/master-plan-2014/master-plan/Introduction
1342. PA, section 12(1).
1343. *Ibid.*, section 3(2).
1344. *Ibid.*, section 3(3).
1345. *Ibid.*, sections 14 and 15.
1346. *Ibid.*, section 35.

'Commercial', 'Business', 'Road', etc. Thus, a land that is zoned for residential use cannot be used for commercial purposes.

653. Even if the proposed use is consistent with the zoning of the land, any material change to an existing land use requires a planning permission.[1347] Examples of material change include the use of a single house as separate houses and the use of any building for any purpose other than that for which it was originally constructed, such as using a dwelling house for non-dwelling purposes, and vice versa.[1348]

654. An interesting recent development in Singapore is the URA's regulation of short-term lettings of private homes through online portals such as Airbnb. Under the Planning Act, using a dwelling house to provide dormitory accommodation, or for lettings for a period of less than three consecutive months, amounts to a development which requires a planning permission from the URA.[1349] The policy of the URA is to reject any application for planning permission to preserve the residential character of the buildings in question. The legal position in relation to HDB flats is similar. The minimum rental period prescribed by HDB is 6 months.

§4. Agricultural Land

655. Being a small city state, the agriculture industry has been rapidly shrinking and now forms a very small part of Singapore's economy. Today, clusters of land specifically designated for agricultural use, also known as Agrotechnology Parks, comprise about 1,465 hectares, which translate to less than 1% of Singapore's total land area.[1350] This is in stark contrast to the situation in 1961, where there were 14,000 hectares of agriculture land, translating to 21% of the total land area.[1351] With the reduction in available farmland, more than 90% of Singapore's food supply is imported.

656. As explained earlier, only certain parcels of land are specifically designated in the Master Plan to be for agricultural use. In other words, one could not simply acquire any parcel of land and use it for agricultural purposes. Most agricultural lands are owned by the Singapore Land Authority (SLA) and regulated by the Agri-Food & Veterinary Authority of Singapore (AVA). In the past, parcels of agricultural land are usually let to private farmers on 10-year leases. Recently, however, the standard lease duration has been increased to 20 years. This is to encourage farmers to invest in high tech agriculture methods to maximise the very limited agriculture space. Towards this end, agriculture land tenders will emphasise on the

1347. *Ibid.*, section 12(1).
1348. *Ibid.*, section 3(3).
1349. *Ibid.*, section 3(3)(ca).
1350. AVA, 'Farming in Singapore': https://www.ava.gov.sg/explore-by-sections/farms/land-farms/farming-in-singapore.
1351. Data from World Bank's website: https://data.worldbank.org/indicator/AG.LND.AGRI.ZS?locations=SG

quality of proposals received, with a focus on the following factors: (i) production capacity; (ii) production track record; (iii) relevant experience and qualification of the farmer; and (iv) innovation and sustainability.

657. To start an animal farm, farm layout plans and building plans have to be submitted to both the AVA and the Building and Construction Authority (BCA) for approvals. After the required approvals are obtained, the farmer will have to apply for a farm licence.

Chapter 12. Neighbourhood and Urban Problems

§1. Introduction

658. Population and building densities are major contributors to conflicts between neighbours in Singapore. The law of torts, through which most of these disputes are resolved, has undergone interesting developments by taking these factors into consideration.[1352] In this chapter, we will consider three common types of neighbourhood disputes: (1) physical intrusion of airspace, (2) interference with a neighbour's enjoyment of land and (3) withdrawal of lateral support. We will then consider the manner in which some of these disputes are managed and resolved in strata developments.

§2. Intrusion of Airspace

659. A typical dispute involving landed properties is the intrusion of airspace. This is generally resolved by reference to the torts of trespass and nuisance.[1353] In *Nasrat Lucas Muzayyin v. Shi Ka Yee*, the branches of a huge rain tree growing on the defendant's land overhung the plaintiffs' land and dead branches from the tree were found on the plaintiff's land.[1354] There was a real possibility of the plaintiff's house being damaged by falling branches. In light of such evidence, Chiah DJ held that the intrusion amounted to a nuisance given its substantial interference with the plaintiff's enjoyment of his land. Interestingly, the case was not argued on the basis of trespass. Unlike nuisance, trespass is a strict liability tort. The mere fact of intrusion gives rise to a liability without requiring the proof of substantial interference.[1355] However, the advantage of adducing such proof is that it may increase the quantum of damages that the plaintiffs were entitled to claim.

660. There is no fixed height at which a landowner may claim exclusive enjoyment. However, a complaint in respect of overflying aircrafts is unlikely to succeed as it is now recognised that airspace beyond a certain height is a public pathway.[1356] In the English case of *Bernstein of Leigh (Baron) v. Skyviews & General Ltd*, where the defendant's employee flew a plane several hundred meters above the plaintiff's land to photograph the plaintiff's farm, it was held that no trespass was committed.[1357] Griffith J explained that between the landowner's right and the public's right of passage an appropriate balance is struck by 'by restricting the rights of an owner in the airspace above his land to such height as is necessary for the ordinary use and

1352. *See* Goh Yihan, 'Tort Law in the Face of Land Scarcity in Singapore' (2009) 26 Arizona J Int'l & Comp L 335.
1353. *See generally* Gary Chan, *The Law of Torts in Singapore*, 2nd edn (Academy Publishing, 2015) Chapter 10.
1354. [2016] SGMC 26, affirmed by the High Court in *Shi Ka Yee v. Nasrat Lucas Muzayyin* [2016] SGHC 138.
1355. *Cf Lemmon v. Webb* [1894] 3 Ch 1.
1356. *See United States v. Causby* (1946) 328 US 256.
1357. [1978] 1 QB 479.

enjoyment of his land and the structures upon it, and declaring that above that height he has no greater rights in the airspace than any other member of the public'.[1358] This principle was approved by the Singapore High Court in *Kim Beng Lee Construction Ltd v. Kosion Enterprise (S) Pte Ltd*.[1359] While the cases did not expressly say so, the height of existing structures on the land is obviously a relevant consideration in determining the extent of the landowner's right to the airspace above. For example, flying an aircraft a kilometre above ground is normally unobjectionable. However, flying an aircraft at the same height over a skyscraper could potentially amount to trespass or nuisance.

661. It is also pertinent to note that the height at which an aircraft may fly is regulated by statute. While there is a minimum height below which aircrafts shall not fly, this prohibition is exempted in the case of take-off and landing.[1360] Thus, a person who owns land near an air base is unlikely to have any legal recourse against low-flying aircrafts that are taking off from or landing at the air base. This does not necessarily mean that the landowner does not own that column or airspace through which the aircrafts fly. Rather, any infringement is permitted by legislation. In reality, the dispute in *Bernstein* is unlikely to occur in Singapore given the stringent regulation of air traffic. However, the recent rise in popularity of small remote-controlled aircrafts might give rise to disputes that can test the limits of a landowner's right to the airspace above.[1361]

§3. Interference with Enjoyment of Land

662. A dispute between neighbours may also arise in the absence of direct intrusion. It may instead arise from an act or omission that has substantially interfered with another person's enjoyment or use of land. Common examples, usually arising in multistorey buildings, include damage caused by water leakage from one unit to another[1362] and fire spread from one unit to another.[1363] In such cases, the basis of the claim is usually private nuisance or negligence. Where the damage is caused by the escape of a dangerous thing which the defendant had brought onto his land, liability may also arise on the basis of the rule in *Rylands v. Fletcher*, which may be regarded as a specific form of nuisance.[1364]

1358. [1978] 1 QB 479 at 488.
1359. [1993] SGHC 312; [1993] 3 SLR(R) 909.
1360. Air Navigation Order (O. 2, 1990 Rev. Ed.), Eleventh Schedule, rule 3.1.2.
1361. For regulation of unmanned aircrafts, see Air Navigation Order, Part XA.
1362. *Goh Sin Huat Electrical Pte Ltd v. Ho See Jui (trading as Xuanhua Art Gallery)* [2012] SGCA 32; [2012] 3 SLR 1038; *PC Connect Pte Ltd v. HSBC Institutional Trust Services (Singapore) Ltd (trustee of CapitaMall Trust)* [2010] SGHC 154; *Hygeian Medical Supplies Pte Ltd v. Tri-Star Rotary Screen Engraving Works Pte Ltd* [1993] SGHC 158; [1993] 2 SLR(R) 411.
1363. *Epolar System Enterprise Pte Ltd v. Lee Hock Chuan* [2003] SGCA 10; [2003] 2 SLR(R) 198.
1364. *Rylands v. Fletcher* (1868) LR 3 HL 330; applied in *Tesa Tape Asia Pacific Pte Ltd v. Wing Seng Logistics Pte Ltd* [2006] SGHC 73; [2006] 3 SLR(R) 116.

663. In *Epolar System Enterprise Pte Ltd v. Lee Hock Chuan*, the Court of Appeal provided guidance to the question of who may bring a claim for private nuisance:

> Generally, only a person with a proprietary interest, whether by virtue of his freehold or leasehold interest, can bring proceedings. Thus, a tenant can sue. Where an owner has leased out his property, in order to be able to sue, he must prove that the nuisance has damaged or is likely to be adverse to his reversionary interest.[1365]

However, the court also recognised that a nuisance claim may be brought by a plaintiff who has a right to exclusive possession of the land, even if the right is a purely contractual one (i.e., a contractual licence).[1366] While the court did not explicitly say so, it is likely that the same principles apply to a claim in negligence.

§4. Withdrawal of Lateral Support

664. Another type of dispute between neighbours, although less common, arises from the withdrawal of lateral support which causes damage to a neighbouring land. The classic case is where one landowner excavates his land in preparation for the construction of a building, and a defective retaining wall causes soil in the adjacent land to subside. The law on this area has seen interesting developments eventually leading to a solution that is unique to Singapore.

665. Where a piece of land remains in its natural state, it enjoys a natural right of support from adjoining lands.[1367] Such a right is not in the nature of an easement; it is an ordinary incident of land ownership. But this principle is of limited significance in the modern world, especially in Singapore, where lands are rarely left in their natural state. More important is the question of whether an owner of a building (or other man-made structures) could claim a right of support in respect of the building that is exigible against owners of adjoining parcels of land. Although common sense would dictate an affirmative answer, the law, unfortunately, started off on a less than unsatisfactory footing.

666. In the Straits Settlement case of *Lee Quee Siew v. Lim Hock Siew*, the defendant excavated soil from his land, thus removing necessary lateral support for a wall on the plaintiff's adjoining land.[1368] The wall bulged and cracked to such

1365. *Epolar System Enterprise Pte Ltd v. Lee Hock Chuan* [2003] SGCA 10; [2003] 2 SLR(R) 198 at [10] (Yong CJ, Chao JA and Prakash J).

1366. *Epolar System Enterprise Pte Ltd v. Lee Hock Chuan* [2003] SGCA 10; [2003] 2 SLR(R) 198 at [11]–[17], citing with approval *Hunter v. Canary Wharf Ltd* [1997] AC 655 at 692.

1367. *Xpress Print Pte Ltd v. Monocrafts Pte Ltd & Anor* [1999] SGHC 320; *Trustees of the Estate of Cheong Eak Chong, deceased v. Medway Investments Pte Ltd* [1996] SGHC 154; [1996] 2 SLR(R) 607.

1368. [1895–6] 3 SSLR 80.

extent that the plaintiff was ordered by the Municipality to demolish the wall. However, the Court of Appeal held that the plaintiff had no right of support from the defendant's land in respect of the wall.

667. In arriving at this conclusion, the court relied on the seminal English case of *Dalton v. Angus*.[1369] There the defendants demolished a house on his land and excavated the land to a depth of several feet. This resulted in the collapse of the plaintiff's factory, which relied on lateral support from the defendant's land. The five-member bench of the House of Lords, taking advice from seven other judges, held by way of majority decision that an easement of support could be acquired only through 20 years of uninterrupted enjoyment of such support. Such an easement is acquired by way prescription, specifically by a fiction of lost (modern) grant, i.e. a presumption that an easement had been granted but was later lost. In this case, the factory was built more than 20 years before the occurrence of the ill-fated event. Thus, an easement by prescription was found in the plaintiff's favour.[1370]

668. Curiously, the judgment of *Lee Quee Siew v. Lim Hock Siew* did not address the question of when exactly the plaintiff's wall erected. The holding against the plaintiff appeared to be based on an assumption that the wall was built within 20 years prior to the dispute. Similarly curious is the case of *Trustees of the Estate of Cheong Eak Chong, deceased v. Medway Investments Pte Ltd*, where the High Court held that the plaintiff's building enjoyed an easement of lateral support by prescription even though, as a matter of fact, the building was completed less than 10 years prior to the commencement of legal proceedings.[1371]

669. The glaring problem with a strict application of *Dalton v. Angus*, as Lord Penzance (dissenting) observed, is that 'at any time within 20 years after the house is built the owner of the adjacent soil may with perfect legality dig that soil away and allow his neighbour's house, if supported by it, to fall in ruins to the ground'.[1372] The matter was revisited by the Singapore Court of Appeal in *Xpress Print Pte Ltd v. Monocrafts Pte Ltd*.[1373] The plaintiff and the defendant were adjoining landowners. On the plaintiff's land stood an eight-storey building that was completed in 1996. In 1997, the defendant engaged a contractor to construct a building on its land. The contractor erected a retaining wall between the two plots of land

1369. (1881) 6 App Cas 740.

1370. *Dalton v. Angus* (1881) 6 App Cas 740 was applied by the Federal Malay States Supreme Court in *Yong Joo Lin & Ors v. Fung Poi Fong* [1941] MLJ 63 to find an easement of support.

1371. [1996] SGHC 154; [1996] 2 SLR(R) 607. The building was completed in 1986 whilst legal proceedings commenced in 1994.

1372. (1881) 6 App Cas 740 at 804. *See also Xpress Print Pte Ltd v. Monocrafts Pte Ltd* [2000] SGCA 37; [2000] 2 SLR(R) 614 at [34].

1373. [2000] SGCA 37; [2000] 2 SLR(R) 614 (Yong CJ, Thean and Chao JJA), noted in HW Tang, 'The Right of Lateral Support of Buildings from the Adjoining Land' (2002) Conv 237; KS Teo, 'Right of Support for Buildings Revisited' (2004) 78 ALJ 20; P Pillai, 'The Primacy of the Principle of Reciprocity in the Singapore Land Regime' (2001) SAcLJ 198.

and commenced excavation work on the defendant's land. Unfortunately, the retaining wall provided inadequate lateral support for the plaintiff's land, resulting in subsidence of soil leading to cracks in the driveway. In a landmark judgment, the Court of Appeal held that the defendant owed to the plaintiff a strict duty to provide lateral support to the latter's building from the time it was erected.[1374] The content of the duty, simply stated, is to refrain from damaging another's land by interfering with its support.[1375] The duty is non-delegable such that the landowner cannot shift the liability to an independent contractor who performs the actual excavation work.[1376] Where the duty is breached, the measure of damages is based on the general tort measure, i.e. to compensate for all foreseeable loss.[1377]

670. This change in the law was motivated by the court's displeasure with the insensitivity of the prior law to realities of modern Singapore. In favouring the imposition of a strict duty of support, the court said:

> We believe that the true legal justification for the right of support is the legal principle encapsulated in the Latin maxim *sic utere tuo ut alienum non loedas*, which translates in English to: use your own property in such a manner as not to injure that of another. The importance of that principle is compounded in Singapore in view of our land-use pattern, whereby all land available for commercial, industrial or residential purposes is used to a high intensity. The damage that might be caused if landowners were lackadaisical in their excavation works could be astronomical, not to mention the cost in human lives or injury to property.[1378]

671. The recent amendment to the State Lands Act codifies the solution introduced in *Xpress Print*. Section 3C(1) provides that each parcel of land enjoys an implied easement for subjacent support by any other parcel of land capable of affording such support. Subsection (5) further provides that such easement is enforceable without the need for registration or notification. However, to the extent that the precise details of the easement are left unstated, the decision in *Xpress Print* continues to be relevant in interpreting the section.

672. Interestingly, the State Lands Act also provides, in section 3C(2), that the implied easement of support entitles the owner of a dominant tenement to have, upon giving reasonable notice, such access to the servient tenement as is reasonably required for erecting or installing any structure necessary to support the dominant tenement, or for maintaining, replacing, renewing or restoring any such structure. Such a right was not mentioned in *Xpress Print* but was hinted in the earlier case of

1374. [2000] SGCA 37; [2000] 2 SLR(R) 614 at [50]. *Xpress Print* was later applied in *Afro-Asia Shipping Company (Pte) Ltd v. Da Zhong Investment Pte Ltd and others* [2003] SGHC 286; [2004] 2 SLR(R) 117.
1375. [2000] SGCA 37; [2000] 2 SLR(R) 614 at [51].
1376. [2000] SGCA 37; [2000] 2 SLR(R) 614 at [53].
1377. [2000] SGCA 37; [2000] 2 SLR(R) 614 at [52].
1378. [2000] SGCA 37; [2000] 2 SLR(R) 614 at [48].

Trustees of the Estate of Cheong Eak Chong, deceased v. Medway Investments Pte Ltd.[1379] There, the High Court said, in relation to a retaining wall that was damaged by accumulation of rainwater:

> [T]he plaintiffs are entitled to demand of the defendants that they permit the remedial measures to repair the retaining wall, put right the landslide and construct adequate drainage for rain water that falls on the shed and the area between the mansion and the defendants' property.[1380]

673. Section 3C(3) qualifies this right in two respects. First, the right must not be exercised in a way that unreasonably prevents another person's enjoyment of his land. Second, in exercising the right, reasonable steps must be taken to minimise damage to the land or other property of other persons.

674. It is only necessary to add that, in *Xpress Print*, the Court of Appeal acknowledged the availability of an alternative claim in negligence.[1381] However, the duty is not strict, but rather one of reasonable care.[1382] Thus, the defendant could defend against the plaintiff's claim by showing that reasonable care has been taken. Despite this, a negligence claim will continue to be useful against persons other than the landowner, e.g. the contractor, who is not subject to the strict duty to provide support.

§5. Overloading of Neighbouring Land

675. In *Eng Yuen Yee v. Grandfort Builders Pte Ltd*, the defendants' newly erected building tilted toward the plaintiff's building.[1383] The lateral load that was exerted on the plaintiff's building caused damage to its structural frame. The plaintiff sought summary judgment by arguing that this involved a straightforward application of *Xpress Print*. The High Court, however, was unconvinced that the principle laid down in that case is applicable beyond cases involving *removal* of lateral support. Instead, this situation should be governed by the law of negligence, which would require the plaintiff to establish its basic elements. The refusal to extend the principle in *Xpress Print* is arguably consistent with the narrow ambit of the doctrine of non-delegable duty as recognised in recent Court of Appeal decisions.[1384]

1379. [1996] SGHC 154; [1996] 2 SLR(R) 607.
1380. [1996] SGHC 154; [1996] 2 SLR(R) 607 at [21].
1381. [2000] SGCA 37; [2000] 2 SLR(R) 614 at [53].
1382. [2000] SGCA 37; [2000] 2 SLR(R) 614 at [42].
1383. [2018] SGHCR 01.
1384. *See Ng Huat Seng v. Munib Mohammad Madni* [2017] SGCA 58 [2017] 2 SLR 1074; *MCST Plan No 3322 v. Tiong Aik Construction Pte Ltd* [2016] SGCA 40; [2016] 4 SLR 521.

§6. Strata Developments

676. For strata developments, where occupation densities are typically very high, the rights of subsidiary proprietors to use their own units and common properties are regulated by the by-laws set out in the Second Schedule of the Building Maintenance (Strata Management) Regulations 2005.[1385] These by-laws prohibit, among other things, the making of excessive noise, unauthorised parking of vehicles, unauthorised depositing of rubbish on common property and any obstruction of, alteration or damage to, common property.

677. For the purposes of maintaining common property and regulating use of the building generally, the Land Titles (Strata) Act provides for the constitution of a management corporation.[1386] The duties and powers of the management corporation are set out in the BMSMA.[1387] Importantly, the management corporation is empowered to make additional by-laws so long as they are not inconsistent with the statutorily prescribed by-laws.[1388]

678. Both types of by-laws are binding on the management corporation, the subsidiary proprietors and occupiers as though they had been signed and sealed by all the parties.[1389] In *Choo Kok Lin v. MCST Plan No 2405*, Prakash J (as she then was) described such by-laws as 'statutorily constituted contracts between the management corporation and the subsidiary proprietors and between the subsidiary proprietors *inter se*'.[1390]

679. The BMSMA also provides for the establishment of one or more Strata Titles Board to adjudicate disputes, either between individual subsidiary proprietors or between the management corporation and individual subsidiary proprietors, by way of mediation–arbitration.[1391] Proceedings of a Board are deemed to be judicial proceedings.[1392] An appeal against a Board's order may lie to the High Court only if it concerns a point of law.[1393]

1385. *See also* Chapter 2 (General Classifications) §2.II.A.(ii).
1386. LTSA, section 10A.
1387. (Cap. 30C, 2008 Rev. Ed.) (BMSMA).
1388. BMSMA, sections 32 and 33.
1389. BMSMA, section 32(6).
1390. [2005] SGHC 144; [2005] 4 SLR(R) 175 at [23].
1391. BMSMA, section 89.
1392. BMSMA, section 92.
1393. BMSMA, section 98. The term 'point of law' has been interpreted broadly: *Ng Eng Ghee v. Mamata Kapildev Dave and others (Horizon Partners Pte Ltd, intervener)* [2009] SGCA 30; [2009] 4 SLR(R) 155 (Chan CJ, Phang and Rajah JJA).

Chapter 13. Comparative Property Law

§1. Introduction

680. Four Civilian property concepts, *usufruct*, *emphyteusis*, *superficies* and apartment rights, are briefly considered in this chapter for the purposes of comparative study. Sensitive to the fact that these concepts may vary across the different civil law jurisdictions, to avoid confusion, this chapter adopts the most basic definitions set out in Dutch law.[1394]

§2. Usufruct

681. The term *usufruct*, which is derived from the words *usus* (use) and *fructus* (fruit), refers to a right to use and derive benefits (e.g., rent) of another person's property.[1395] Once such a right is created, it operates as a burden on the landowner's ownership in favour of the grantee, also known as the *usufructuary*. The landowner, who retains only a bare ownership, can no longer exercise a right to use and enjoy the land. It is only upon expiry of the right of *usufruct* that he regains absolute ownership. The right of *usufruct* is usually created for the duration of the *usufructuary*'s life (hence, it is sometimes called a 'liferent'), but it can also be for a fixed term. Importantly, it cannot operate beyond the lifetime of the *usufructuary*.[1396] In this sense, the right of *usufruct* is often regarded as a form of personal servitude.[1397] However, its true nature is that of a property right. During its subsistence, it is enforceable not only against the landowner but also against the world, and it can be assigned to a [1398]

682. Perhaps the closest equivalent of a *usufruct* in a common law system is the life estate.[1399] The analogy is not obvious possibly because of the different conceptions of ownership between the two systems. As the Civilian model subscribes to a unitary notion of ownership, i.e. there can only be one owner at any given time, the *usufruct* has to be classified as a limited property right.[1400] In contrast, the common law doctrine of estates recognises concurrent ownerships. Where a life estate is carved out of a fee simple estate, both the grantor and the grantee are owners, although only one (in this case the life tenant) is entitled to exclusive possession and

1394. *See generally* Sjef van Erp and Bram Akkermans (eds), *Cases, Materials and Text on National, Supranational and International Property Law* (Oxford: Hart Publishing, 2012) Chapter 3.
1395. The right of use, while narrower in scope, is similar in nature.
1396. This is unlike a lease, which is inheritable if its duration outlasts the tenant's life.
1397. *Cf* WW Buckland, 'The Conception of Usufruct in Classical Law' (1927) 43 LQR 326.
1398. The right enjoyed by the assignee ceases upon the *usufructuary*'s death.
1399. A.J. McClean, 'The Common Law Life Estate and the Civil Law Usufruct: A Comparative Study' (1963) 12 ICLQ 649; Alain-Laurent Verbeke, Bart Verdickt and Dirk-Jan Maasland, 'The Many Faces of Usufruct' in Cornelius van der Merwe and Alain-Laurent Verbeke (eds), *Time-Limited Interests in Land* (Cambridge: CUP, 2012) Chapter 4, at 38. For a brief description of the life estate, see Chapter 2 (General Classifications) §4.I.
1400. Giovanni Pugliese 'On Roman Usufruct' (1966) 40 Tulane L Rev 523 at 528.

enjoyment of the land. However, despite their conceptual differences, both the *usufruct* and the life estate may be employed to achieve the very same outcome.

§3. Emphyteusis

683. A right of *emphyteusis* is essentially a long-term lease.[1401] In so far as it entitles the right holder to use and enjoy the land, it is very similar to the right of *usufruct*. Classified as a property right, the right of *emphyteusis* is enforceable against the world and can be assigned to a third party. However, unlike a right of *usufruct*, the right of *emphyteusis* is not a form of personal servitude. In other words, it is connected to the land rather than to the grantee. This being the case, the right of *emphyteusis* survives the grantee's death (hence, it is sometimes called a 'hereditary land lease'). The right of *emphyteusis* is therefore employed to achieve longer grants. A common example is a right of *emphyteusis* for a term of 99 years, which is inheritable when the grantee dies.

684. In civil law, a right of *emphyteusis* is distinguished from a lease, which is merely a personal right. Not being a property right, a lease is binding only between the landlord and the tenant. However, as we have seen, the common law lease was historically a chattel real but was subsequently elevated to the status of an estate in land.[1402] A lease is to be distinguished from a contractual licence, which is generally binding only between the licensor and the licensee.[1403] Thus, at the broadest level, one may equate the right of *emphyteusis* with a common law lease, and the civil law lease with a common law licence.

685. There is, however, one aspect of the right of *emphyteusis* that is difficult to explain from a common law perspective. In some civil law jurisdictions, the right can be created for perpetuity. Under the common law, this amounts to an outright transfer of ownership. Perhaps the closest analogy is with the estate in perpetuity, which is created by statute, and granted over state land by the state.[1404]

§4. Superficies

686. The status of things found on land, such as buildings and plants, is generally determined by the maxim *quicquid plantatur solo, solo cedit*, which translates to mean whatever is affixed to the soil belongs to the soil.[1405] In civil law, however, ownership of the land can be separated from ownership of the building if the landowner grants the building owner a right of *superficies*. Being a property right, the

1401. *See* William R Johnston, 'Emphyteusis: A Roman "Perpetual" Tenure' (1940) 3 U Toronto LJ 323.
1402. *See* Chapter 6 (Leases).
1403. *See* Chapter 7 (Licences).
1404. For a brief description of the life estate, see Chapter 2 (General Classifications) §4.III.
1405. *See* Chapter 2 (General Classifications) §5.

right of *superficies* burdens the ownership of the land by preventing the landowner from evicting the building owner. The duration of the right of superficies is to be agreed upon between the parties.

687. While the right of *superficies* is alien to the common law, a long-term lease may be employed to achieve the same outcome. Before constructing a building, the developer should acquire a lease, e.g. for 99 years. Being an estate in land, the lease grants the developer exclusive possession of the land for 99 years, which in turn grants him/her ownership of the building. If the principle of accession is strictly applied, however, upon the lapsing of the lease the building will belong to the reversioner/landlord. A simple solution would be for the developer to purchase a fee simple estate (which is perpetual in duration)[1406] or an even longer lease such that this issue becomes practically irrelevant.

§5. Apartment Rights

688. A building may be divided into several parts for individual ownerships. In civil law, this is achieved by the granting of apartment rights in respect of defined areas to individual owners. In Singapore, the same outcome is achieved through the system of strata titles, under which the owner of each subdivided lot acquires a distinct subsidiary strata certificate of title [1407]

1406. *See* Chapter 2 (General Classifications) §4.I.
1407. *See* Chapter 2 (General Classifications) §3.II.A.

Part II. Personal Property

Chapter 1. General Classifications

689. Personal property, which is understood to mean any asset other than land, can be very broadly divided into two categories: (1) tangible and (2) intangible. Given that the two types of personal property are very different in nature, the manner in which they may be dealt with and how they are protected in law, are also very different. In this regard, unlike land law, there is no single coherent set of law applying to personal property.[1408]

§1. Tangible (Choses in Possession)

690. As its name suggests, this category covers all things that can be physically held. Everyday examples include fiat money, book, car and mobile phone. Such properties are also known as chattels or choses in possession, which hints at the crucial role of the concept of possession in determining who has title in them.[1409] Ownership in personal property is protected by the law of tort, specifically trespass and the overlapping torts of conversion and detinue.[1410]

§2. Intangible (Choses in Action)

691. All assets that cannot be physically held fall within this category. Such assets are in the form of rights which are enforceable in court, and hence they are also called choses in action. A simple example is money in a bank account, which is essentially a debt owed by the bank to the customer. Based on the contract between the bank and its customer, the bank is not required to keep the money segregated and safeguard it. The bank is free to mix the money with money from other

1408. For a comprehensive account of personal property law in Singapore, see Tan Yock Lin, *Personal Property Law* (Academy Publishing, 2014). *See also* Michael Bridge, *Personal Property Law*, 4th edn (OUP, 2015); Michael Bridge, Louise Gullifer, Kelvin Low and Gerard McMeel, *The Law of Personal Property*, 2nd edn (Sweet & Maxwell, 2017); David Fox, *Property Rights in Money* (OUP, 2008); Duncan Sheehan, *The Principles of Personal Property Law*, 2nd edn (Hart Publishing, 2017).
1409. *See* Chapter 3 (Possession and Appropriation) §1.
1410. *See* Pey-Woan Lee, 'Interference with Goods' in Gary Chan, *The Law of Torts in Singapore*, 2nd edn (Academy Publishing, 2015) Chapter 11.

sources and apply them for its own purpose such as the generation of profits. In other words, title in the money passes to the bank. In return, the customer is owed a contractual debt, the value of which is reflected in his account balance. If the bank refuses to fulfil this debt (e.g., by dispensing cash) upon the customer's request, the customer may sue the bank for breach of contract. Where bank money is appropriated by a third party, e.g. through hacking of the customer's account, the customer may sue the third party in the law of unjust enrichment.

692. Given the very broad ambit of this category, it is not easy to determine where precisely the line between property and non-property should be drawn. While bank money and shares are commonly accepted forms of property, less clear is cryptocurrencies,[1411] carbon credits[1412] or even contractual rights generally.[1413] Even for the recognised categories of intangible property, the concepts of property and ownership have to be understood in the broadest sense, differing from the traditional conceptions applying to tangible assets. Lee thus explained, with specific reference to contracts:

> [C]ontrary to common perception, contracts and property are better seen as different shades of a similar phenomenon. In particular, property does not exist as a reified 'thing' with stable features and structure; it is a relative rather than an absolute concept. At its core, property may be understood as a state endorsed power relation that regulates access to valuable resources. To qualify for such protection, a resource must minimally be capable of being excluded from the rest of the world. The question whether intangibles are amenable to such exclusivity has to be determined by evaluating the relevant practical, legal and moral considerations.[1414]

693. Finally, a subcategory of intangible property that is often dealt with separately is intellectual property, such as copyrights, trademarks and patents. Most intellectual properties are recognised, regulated and protected by specific legislations.[1415] Given the very specific rules applying to intellectual property, they will not be dealt with in this book.[1416]

1411. *See* Kelvin FK Low and Ernie GS Teo, 'Bitcoins and other cryptocurrencies as property?' (2017) Law, Innovation and Technology 235
1412. *See* Kelvin FK Low and Jolene Lin, 'Carbon Credits as EU Like It: Property, Immunity, TragiCO2medy?' (2015) 27 J Environmental L 377.
1413. *See* Pey-Woan Lee, 'Inducing Breach of Contract, Conversion and Contract as Property' (2009) 29 OJLS 511.
1414. Pey-Woan Lee, 'Inducing Breach of Contract, Conversion and Contract as Property' (2009) 29 OJLS 511 at 513.
1415. *See*, e.g., Copyright Act (Cap. 63, 2006 Rev. Ed.); Trade Marks Act (Cap. 332, 2005 Rev. Ed.); Patents Act (Cap. 221, 2005 Rev. Ed.).
1416. For intellectual property law, see Ng-Loy Wee Loon, *Law of Intellectual Property of Singapore*, 2nd edn (Sweet & Maxwell, 2014).

Chapter 2. Security Interests

§1. Introduction

694. In earlier chapters,[1417] we have seen that land is immovable and permanent and are subject to many formality requirements in its dealings. In comparison, personal property is often more volatile and is more easily transacted. In light of these differences, the law has provided for a wider range of security interests that may be created over personal property.[1418] This chapter focuses only on two very common types of personal property: (1) chattels and (2) shares. For how security interests are created over other choses in action, e.g. book debts and intellectual property rights, reference should be made to specialist texts.

695. Security interests may be broadly divided into two types, (1) possessory and (2) non-possessory, depending on whether possession of the property by the lender is necessary for the creation of the security interest. Pledges and liens are examples of possessory security interests while mortgages and charges are non-possessory security interests.[1419] Precisely which type of security interest to use will depend on the needs of the parties concerned. Non-possessory security interests are useful where it is important that the borrower has possession of, and right to deal with, the property. For example, if money is lent to a manufacturer for the purpose of purchasing machinery, it only makes sense that the manufacturer is allowed to have possession of the machinery and use it. In the case of stock-in-trade, which changes from time to time, a more specific type of non-possessory security interest known as the floating charge will be more appropriate.

696. This topic is also complicated by the fact that there is no single governing statute. While charges and mortgages granted by a company are regulated by the Companies Act (CA),[1420] charges and mortgages granted by an individual or an unincorporated association over chattels (but not choses in action) are governed by the Bills of Sale Act (BSA).[1421] The Conveyancing and Law of Property Act (CLPA)[1422] also sets out default rules relating to the remedies of a mortgagee or chargee in situations where the BSA does not apply. This chapter is structured in such a way that the applications of these different statutes are carefully reflected.

1417. *See generally* Duncan Sheehan, *The Principles of Personal Property Law*, 2nd edn (Hart, 2017) Chapters 11–14; Loo Wee Ling, *Law of Credit and Security* (LexisNexis, 2012) Chapters 10–11; Tan Yock Lin, *Personal Property Law* (Academy Publishing, 2014) Chapters 21–24.
1418. Quasi-security devices, such as hire purchase and the *Quistclose* trust, will not be dealt with in this chapter. For retention of title clauses, see Part III (Acquisition of Property Rights) Chapter 2 (Contract for the Sale of Goods) §3.
1419. The parties to an agreement creating a charge or mortgage are of course free to decide who shall have possession of the property.
1420. (Cap. 50, 2006 Rev. Ed.).
1421. (Cap. 24, 2011 Rev. Ed.).
1422. (Cap. 61, 1994 Rev. Ed.).

§2. Mortgages

697. The main characteristic of a mortgage is the transfer of title to the lender subject to an equity or redemption in favour of the borrower, which allows the latter to recover the property upon full repayment of the debt.[1423]

I. Individuals or Unincorporated Associations

A. Chattels

698. A chattel mortgage, if created in writing, amounts to a bill of sale and is valid only if the requirements set out in the BSA are complied with. First, it must be in the prescribed form set out in the First Schedule of the BSA,[1424] which provides for the transfer of title in the chattel to the grantee and the right of the grantee to seize or take possession of the chattel in the event of the grantor's default.[1425] Second, it must be accompanied by a schedule listing all chattels to which it applies.[1426] As the bill of sale is void in respect of any chattel not included in the schedule, it is not a suitable form of security in the case of goods that may be replaced from time to time. Third, it must be duly attested and registered within three clear days of its execution.[1427] Aside from validity, registration of a bill of sale gives it priority over other bill(s) of sale in the event that they relate to the same chattel.[1428] A bill of sale has to be renewed every 12 calendar months, failing which it becomes void.[1429]

699. The situations in which the grantee may seize the chattel is provided for in section 8 of the BSA, which include: (a) where the grantor defaults in repayment; (b) where the grantor becomes a bankrupt;[1430] (c) where the chattel becomes available for distrain for rent, property tax or otherwise; (d) where the grantor fraudulently removes the chattel from his premises; and (e) where execution has been levied against the goods of the grantor under process of any court. After seizure, the chattel may be sold only by public auction.[1431] Although the statute is silent, it is obvious that any balance from the proceeds after repayment of the debt to the grantee must be handed over to the grantor.

1423. *See generally* Part I (Land) Chapter 10 (Mortgages).
1424. BSA, section 6.
1425. *See also* the definitions of a bill of sale in BSA, sections 2 & 3. For the only one local case to have considered the meaning of a bill of sale, see *Tan Tien Choy v. Kiaw Aik Hang Co Ltd* [1965] SGFC 2; [1965-1967] SLR(R) 16.
1426. BSA, section 5.
1427. BSA, section 4.
1428. BSA, section 11.
1429. BSA, section 13.
1430. *See also* Bankruptcy Act (Cap. 20, 2009 Rev. Ed.) section 78(2)(d).
1431. BSA, section 9.

B. Shares

700. A legal mortgage of shares is created by the transfer of title in the shares to the lender subject to the borrower's equity of redemption. The BSA does not apply as shares are not personal chattels.[1432] In most cases the rights and duties of the parties will be clearly set out in the agreement. Where the mortgage is created by deed, certain default remedies and how they may be exercised are provided for in the CLPA[1433] to the extent that they are not inconsistent with the terms of the mortgage agreement.

701. An equitable mortgage is usually created by agreement and is usually accompanied by the deposit of the share certificates and the necessary transfer form with the lender. Where the shares are subject to an earlier mortgage, in which case the share certificates will be in the possession of the first mortgagee, an agreement evincing the necessary intention suffices. The subject matter of the equitable mortgage will be the mortgagor's equity of redemption under the first mortgage. For this reason, an equitable mortgage is often a second mortgage. The disadvantage is that it is prone to be defeated by a bona fide purchaser for value without notice of it. As the equitable mortgagor does not acquire legal title in the shares, an equitable mortgage is essentially and practically a charge, hence the not infrequent broad reference to 'equitable mortgage or charge'.[1434]

II. Companies

702. The BSA does not apply to mortgages granted by a company.[1435] Such mortgages are instead governed by the CA, under which a mortgage is included within the definition of a charge.[1436] Moreover, the CA does not distinguish between a charge over chattels and a charge over choses in action. The requirements for creating a charge or mortgage and the priority rules under the CA will be discussed below.[1437]

§3. Charges

703. Unlike a mortgage, the creation of a charge does not require a transfer of title from the chargor to the chargee. The charge operates as an encumbrance on the title of the chargor. While charges and mortgages are functionally very similar, the flexibility of the former makes it the preferred security device outside the realm of land transactions.

1432. BSA, section 3(1).
1433. CLPA, sections 24–30. *See* Part I (Land) Chapter 10 (Mortgages) §4.II.B.
1434. *See e.g. Chase Manhattan Bank NA v. Wong Tui Sun* [1992] SGCA 82; [1992] 3 SLR(R) 436.
1435. BSA, section 2(1).
1436. CA, section 4.
1437. *See* §3.III. below.

I. Fixed and Floating Charges

704. There are two kinds of charges: (1) fixed charge and (2) floating charge.[1438] A fixed charge operates against identified assets much like a conventional mortgage. In contrast, a floating charge is usually granted over a class of assets which may include both existing and after-acquired assets. In determining whether a fixed or floating charge has been created, emphasis is placed on the substance of the transaction and not on what the parties call it. A floating charge is most likely found if the assets charged changes from time to time and, until some steps are taken by the lender to enforce the charge, the borrower is at liberty to deal with the assets.[1439]

705. While a fixed charge immediately attaches to identified assets, a floating charge attaches to identified assets within the specified class only upon the happening of a predetermined event. This is known as crystallisation, the effect of which is to convert the floating charge into a fixed charge. In *Dresdner Bank AG v. Ho Mun-Tuke Don*, where the floating charges were created over shares, the Court of Appeal found that crystallisation had occurred when the banks demanded delivery up of the shares and, upon the borrower's default, instituted legal proceedings for possession of the shares.[1440]

II. Individuals or Unincorporated Associations

706. A fixed charge over chattels, like a chattels mortgage, is governed by the BSA.[1441] As the BSA does not allow for a security to be given over future assets, it is not possible to create floating charge over stock-in-trade generally. The creation of a floating charge over shares, however, is not regulated by the BSA and does not appear to be subject to any formality requirements.

III. Companies

707. No distinction is made in the CA between the different kinds of property over which a charge can be granted by a company. Section 131(3) sets out a list of security transactions that require registration:

(a) a charge to secure any issue of debentures;
(b) a charge on uncalled share capital of a company;
(c) a charge on shares of a subsidiary of a company which are owned by the company;

1438. *Illingworth v. Houldsworth* [1904] AC 355.
1439. *Dresdner Bank AG v. Ho Mun-Tuke Don* [1992] SGCA 75; [1992] 3 SLR(R) 307 at [39]; *Re Lin Securities (Pte) Ltd; Chi Man Kwong Peter and others v. Asia Commercial Bank and others* [1998] SGHC 24; [1998] 1 SLR(R) 220.
1440. [1992] SGCA 75; [1992] 3 SLR(R) 307 at [54] (Yong CJ, Thean and Khoo JJ).
1441. *See* §2.I.A. above.

(d) a charge created or evidenced by an instrument which, if executed by an individual, would require registration as a bill of sale;
(e) a charge on land wherever situate or any interest herein but not including any charge for any rent or other periodical sum issuing out of land;
(f) a charge on book debts of the company;
(g) a floating charge on the undertaking or property of a company;
(h) a charge on calls made but not paid;
(i) a charge on a ship or aircraft or any share in a ship or aircraft; and
(j) a charge on goodwill, on a patent or a licence under a patent, on a trademark or a licence to use a trademark, or on a copyright or a licence under a copyright or on a registered design or a licence to use a registered design.

The purpose of registration is to give notice to outsiders about the financial status of the company, specifically how much its assets are encumbered.

708. A charge must be registered within 30 days of the creation of a charge, failing which it is 'void against the liquidator and any creditor of the company'.[1442] An unregistered charge is void against a liquidator only where the company has become insolvent and a liquidator has been appointed during the subsistence of the charge. Thus, where a liquidator is appointed only after a registered charge has been realised, section 131(1) does not operate retrospectively to render the charge void.[1443]

709. Less straightforward is the meaning of 'creditor' for the purposes of section 131(1). While the company is a going concern, an unregistered charge is not void against unsecured creditors.[1444] They have no *locus standi* to prevent the company from paying off the debt secured by the unregistered charge. Less clear is the position of other secured creditors. In *Re City Securities Pte*, Chao JC (as he then was) held that an unregistered charge is void only against 'a creditor who has acquired a proprietary right to or an interest in the subject matter of the unregistered charge'.[1445] The remark being a passing one, no distinction was not made between a competing charge that is registered and one that is not. Certainly, an unregistered charge would be void against a registered charge. Between two competing charges that are unregistered, presumably priority is to be determined by the basic rules (explained below) given that neither is void against unsecured creditors.

710. Where, on the other hand, the company has become insolvent and a winding-up order has been made, an unregistered charge is void even against unsecured creditors.[1446] The chargee becomes an unsecured creditor.[1447]

1442. *Duncan, Cameron Lindsay v. Diablo Fortune Inc* [2017] SGHC 172 at [74].
1443. *Ng Wei Teck Michael v. Oversea-Chinese Banking Corp Ltd* [1998] SGCA 21; [1998] 1 SLR(R) 778 at [19] (Karthigesu and Thean JJA, Chao J).
1444. *Ng Wei Teck Michael v. Oversea-Chinese Banking Corp Ltd* [1998] SGCA 21; [1998] 1 SLR(R) 778 at [31].
1445. [1990]; SGHC 31; [1990] 1 SLR(R) 413 at [76].
1446. *Media Development Authority of Singapore v. Sculptor Finance (MD) Ireland Ltd* [2013] SGCA 58; [2014] 1 SLR 733 at [43]–[50] (Menon CJ; Rajah JA and Prakash J); *Power Knight Pte Ltd v. Natural Fuel Pte Ltd* [2010] SGHC 75; [2010] 3 SLR 82. *See also* Lee Eng Beng, 'Unsecured

711. In the case of competing charges that are duly registered, the priority rules to be applied depend on the type of charges in question. Between fixed charges, priority is determined by the order of creation. Between competing fixed and floating charges, generally the fixed charge has priority. There are, however, two exceptions. First, where the floating charge has crystallised before the creation of the fixed charge. Second, where the floating charge contains a term restricting the creation of a subsequent charge over the same asset and the subsequent fixed chargee has notice of the term.[1448]

712. Unlike the BSA, the CA does not specify the remedies of the chargee (and their limits) in the event of the chargor's default. However, where the charge is created by deed, certain default remedies and how they may be exercised are provided for in the CLPA[1449] to the extent that they are not inconsistent with the terms of the charge agreement.

§4. Pledges

I. General Principles

713. A pledge is essentially a contractual bailment, under which possession of the property is handed over to the lender (also known as the pledgee or bailee) subject to the right of the borrower (also known as the pledgor or bailor) to redeem the property upon full repayment of the debt. Since title in the property remains with the borrower, a pledge and a charge may appear similar. The key difference, however, is that while a charge is valid even if possession of the property is with the borrower, the validity of a pledge depends on the continued possession of the property by the lender. As the Court of Appeal said in *Chase Manhattan Bank NA v. Wong Tui Sun*, '[f]or there to be a pledge, the property or the thing must be actually or constructively delivered to the pledgee'.[1450] However, where possession of the property is with the lender, the transaction can either be a pledge or a charge. Emphasis is of course placed on the substance of the transaction. One important factor is whether the property offered as security is fixed. Where the borrower is allowed to swap from time to time the subject matter of the security, most likely a floating charge, has been created.[1451]

714. Delivery can be actual or constructive. As Lord Wright explained in *Official Assignee of Madras v. Mercantile Bank of India Ltd*:

Creditor Versus Unregistered Charge' (1998) 10 SAcLJ 241; Wee Meng Seng, 'The Avoidance of Unregistered Charge and Extension of Time to Register' (2014) 26 SAcLJ 750.

1447. *Chase Manhattan Bank NA v. Wong Tui Sun* [1992] SGCA 82; [1992] 3 SLR(R) 436.
1448. *Kay Hian & Co (Pte) v. Phua Ooi Yong Jon* [1988] SGHC 90; [1988] 2 SLR(R) 439.
1449. CLPA, sections 24–30. *See* Part I (Land) Chapter 10 (Mortgages) §4.II.B.
1450. [1992] SGCA 82; [1992] 3 SLR(R) 436 at [24]. *See also United Malayan Banking Corp Bhd v. Lim Kang Seng* [1994] SGHC 70; [1994] 1 SLR(R) 802 at [26]–[29].
1451. *Chase Manhattan Bank NA v. Wong Tui Sun* [1992] SGCA 82; [1992] 3 SLR(R) 436 at [24]; *Re EG Tan & Co (Pte)* [1990] SGHC 82; [1990] 2 SLR(R) 386.

> If the pledgor had the actual goods in his physical possession, he could effect the pledge by actual delivery; in other cases he could give possession by some symbolic act, such as handing over the key of the store in which they were. If, however, the goods were in the custody of a third person, who held for the bailor so that in law his possession was that of the bailor, the pledge could be effected by a change of the possession of the third party, that is by an order to him from the pledgor to hold for the pledgee, the change being perfected by the third party attorning to the pledgee, that is acknowledging that he thereupon held for him; there was thus a change of possession and a constructive delivery: the goods in the hands of the third party became by this process in the possession constructively of the pledgee. But where goods were represented by documents the transfer of the documents did not change the possession of the goods, save for one exception, unless the custodier (carrier, warehouseman or such) was notified of the transfer and agreed to hold in future as bailee for the pledgee. The one exception was the case of bills of lading, the transfer of which by the law merchant operated as a transfer of the possession of, as well as the property in, the goods.[1452]

715. While this suggests that a pledge can only be created over chattels, in Singapore the question of whether documentary intangibles such as shares can be pledged remains an open one. In *Re Lin Securities (Pte) Ltd; Chi Man Kwong Peter v. Asia Commercial Bank*, Chao JC (as he then was) expressed doubt that a pledge can be created over shares.[1453] When the question arose for consideration in *Chase Manhattan*, the Court of Appeal did not find it necessary to express an opinion; the agreement was found to have given rise to an equitable mortgage or charge.[1454] While the possibility of creating a pledge over shares has not been categorically dismissed, courts are generally inclined to find an equitable charge or mortgage where share certificates are deposited with the lender.[1455] The prevailing trend may be explicable by the fact that share certificates are not documents of title and hence depositing them with the lender does not amount to delivery of the property.[1456]

716. While the chattel is in the lender's possession, he is not allowed to use the chattel as his own and profit from them, unless the borrower allows him/her to do so.[1457] The lender's power to sell the property arises upon the borrower's

1452. [1935] AC 53 (Privy Council) at 58–59. For an example of delivery of a documentary intangible, see *Malayan Banking Bhd v. Hwang Rose* [1997] SGCA 10; [1997] 1 SLR(R) 353 (bearer bonds). For an example of the bill of lading exception, see *The 'Jag Shakti'* [1985] SGPC 8; [1985–86] SLR(R) 448.
1453. [1998] SGHC 24; [1998] 1 SLR(R) 220 at [36].
1454. [1992] SGCA 82; [1992] 3 SLR(R) 436 at [23]–[27].
1455. *See also Pacrim Investments Pte Ltd v. Tan Mui Keow Claire* [2008] SGCA 16; [2008] 2 SLR(R) 898; *Re Lin Securities (Pte) Ltd; Chi Man Kwong Peter v. Asia Commercial Bank* [1998] SGHC 24; [1998] 1 SLR(R) 220; *Chase Manhattan Bank NA v. Wong Tui Sun* [1992] SGCA 82; [1992] 3 SLR(R) 436; *Re EG Tan & Co (Pte)* [1990] SGHC 82; [1990] 2 SLR(R) 386.
1456. *Cf Public Prosecutor v. Koh Beng Oon* [2000] SGHC 262; [2000] 3 SLR(R) 857, where it was held that the depositing of vehicle log cards created a pledge. However, the judgment was unclear on whether the pledge was created over the log cards or over the corresponding vehicles.
1457. *The Odessa* [1916] 1 AC 145 at 159.

default.[1458] However, the borrower may redeem the property by repaying the lender at any time before the power of sale is exercised. Where the lender exercises his power of sale, he 'must take care that the sale is a provident sale, and if the goods are in bulk he must not sell more than is reasonably sufficient to pay off the debt'.[1459] The lender will apply the sale proceeds towards discharging the debt owed to him/her and he must account to the borrower for any surplus.[1460]

717. As explained earlier, the lender does not have a better title than the borrower. However, when the lender exercises his power of sale, the purchaser acquires a good title to the property. This is because the power of sale 'is exercisable by virtue of an implied authority from the [lender]'.[1461] In other words, it is as though the lender acts as the borrower's agent in exercising the power of sale.

II. Pawnbroking

718. Where a property is pledged to a pawnbroker, i.e. a person who carries on the business of taking goods in pawn, act of pledging is also known as pawning and is regulated by the Pawnbrokers Act (P).[1462] To extend the protection conferred by the statute to small borrowers, section 3(1) provides that a person is deemed to be a pawnbroker if he:[1463]

(a) receives or takes of or from any person whomsoever any goods or chattels by way of security for the repayment of any sum or sums of money, not exceeding $1,000 advanced thereon; or
(b) purchases or receives or takes in goods or chattels and pays or advances or lends thereon any sum or sums of money, not exceeding $1,000, with or under an agreement or understanding express or implied or to be from the nature and character of the dealing reasonably inferred that those goods or chattels may be afterwards redeemed or repurchased on any terms.

However, section 3(1) does not apply where the rate of interest does not exceed 10% per annum.[1464]

719. The PA imposes various duties on a pawnbroker, which include the duties to obtain an annual licence,[1465] to keep proper records of articles pawned[1466] and to provide a pawn ticket.[1467] The pawnbroker is also prohibited from making a profit

1458. *Malayan Banking Bhd v. Hwang Rose* [1997] SGCA 10; [1997] 1 SLR(R) 353 at [62]–[65].
1459. *The Odessa* [1916] 1 AC 145 at 159.
1460. *The Odessa* [1916] 1 AC 145 at 159.
1461. *The Odessa* [1916] 1 AC 145 at 159.
1462. (Cap. 222, 1994 Rev. Ed.).
1463. PA, section 3(1).
1464. PA, section 3(2).
1465. PA, sections 8
1466. PA, section 14
1467. PA, section 15.

in excess of what is allowed under the Second Schedule.[1468] Moreover, the pawnbroker bears the risk of damage to or destruction of the pawned chattel.[1469]

720. The PA sets out different rules relating to redemption and sale depending on the amount of money advanced. If the amount advanced does not exceed $50, the period of redemption is statutorily fixed at 6 months from the day of pawning.[1470] Where the property is not redeemed within this period, it becomes the property of the pawnbroker.[1471] As for an advance exceeding $50, the period of redemption can be specifically agreed between the parties.[1472] Even after the expiry of the redemption date, the property continues to be redeemable until it is sold by the pawnbroker.[1473] The sale has to be by public auction and conducted by a licensed auctioneer.[1474] Any surplus from the sale proceeds must be paid to the pledgor if a demand is made within four months after the sale.[1475] If no demand is made, the surplus shall be paid to the Accountant-General.[1476]

§5. Liens

721. A lien is essentially a right to withhold delivery of chattel. A lien can arise in a variety of situations, each explicable on its own terms. To illustrate how a lien differs from other security interests discussed earlier, it would be helpful to confine our discussion to three common types of lien: (1) the unpaid vendor's lien, (2) the mechanic's lien and (3) the carrier's lien.

722. Under the Sale of Goods Act (SGA),[1477] a seller of goods who has not been paid may exercise a lien by retaining possession of the goods.[1478] If the seller has parted with possession of the goods, he may stop them in transit if the purchaser becomes insolvent.[1479] In either situation, the seller may rescind the contract and resell the goods.[1480] These self-help remedies are available to the unpaid seller even if the title in the goods had passed to the purchaser.

723. Similarly, the mechanic who repaired or improved goods, and a carrier who received goods for delivery, acquire a lien over the goods if they are not paid when payment is due. Unlike the earlier situation, where title in the goods could either be

1468. PA, section 16.
1469. PA, sections 28–29.
1470. PA, section 17
1471. PA, section 18.
1472. PA, section 17
1473. PA, section 19.
1474. PA, section 20.
1475. PA, sections 23–24.
1476. PA, section 24.
1477. (Cap. 393, 1999 Rev. Ed.).
1478. SGA, sections 41–42. For comparison, see also Part III (Acquisition) Chapter 1 (Contract for the Sale of Land) §6.I.
1479. SGA, sections 44–46.
1480. SGA, section 48.

with the seller or the purchaser, here the mechanic or carrier holds the goods on a bailment, under which title remains with the owner of the goods. In this regard the mechanic's lien and the carrier's lien may appear similar to a pledge or a charge.

724. From the brief descriptions of the lien, however, important differences with a pledge or a charge can be readily discerned. While a pledge or a charge is created by agreement, the lien arises by operation of law to confer on the unpaid vendor a self-help remedy. The goods are not delivered by their owners specifically to be held as security but for some other purposes. In the case of the unpaid vendor's lien, possession or control of the goods has always been with the seller. Moreover, except in the case of the unpaid vendor's lien, a lien does not give rise to a power to sell the goods. This is unlike a pledge or a charge where the power to sell is an important characteristic. Presumably, a sale under a lien is possible by resort to a writ of seizure and sale or where the owner of the goods can be regarded as having abandoned them.

Part III. Acquisition of Property Rights

Chapter 1. Contract for the Sale of Land[1481]

§1. CONTRACT FORMATION

I. Option to Purchase

A. Introduction

725. An agreement for the sale and purchase of land often begins with an option to purchase (OTP).[1482] Upon agreeing on the purchase price, the seller will usually grant the purchaser an OTP in return for an option fee (typically 1% of the purchase price). Besides particulars of the parties, the property and the purchase price, the OTP will also set out an option period (e.g., 14 working days) and the manner in which it could be exercised (usually by signing on the option and payment of a deposit). During the option period, the seller is bound to keep the property for the purchaser. If the purchaser decides to proceed with the purchase, he will exercise the OTP by the prescribed method within the option period, upon which the seller is obliged to complete the transaction. The option fee will either be returned to the purchaser or count towards the purchase price.

726. Clearly, the OTP is mainly for the purchaser's benefit. At a small cost, it gives the purchaser an opportunity to reconsider his decision to purchase the property and sufficient time to source for financing if he decides to proceed with the purchase. The seller, on the other hand, does not lose out because he is entitled to forfeit the option fee if the purchaser does not exercise the OTP within the option period. In this case the OTP lapses and the seller is free to sell the property to someone else.

B. Ways of Obtaining an Option to Purchase

727. Where a purchaser is convinced that a property that is put up for sale satisfies his expectation in every way, he may wish to proceed to purchase it without

1481. *See* Kelvin F.K. Low, 'Sale of Land' in Michael Hwang and Yeo Tiong Min (eds.), *Law Relating to Specific Contracts in Singapore* (Sweet & Maxwell Asia, 2008) Chapter 12.
1482. *See generally* Andrew Phang Boon Leong *et. al.*, *The Law of Contract in Singapore* (Academy Publishing, 2012) Chapters 3–5.

further negotiation with the seller. Usually, the purchaser will send to the seller a letter of intent requesting for an OTP. In basic contract terms, this amounts to an invitation to treat. The seller is free to ignore this request. Or he may grant an OTP, which may amount to an offer. Up to this point no contractual relationship arises. This explains why the seller is free to stipulate the terms of the OTP, even to the extent of setting out terms which do not meet the purchaser's expectation. If the purchaser is satisfied with the terms of the OTP, he may accept it, usually by paying the option fee. At this point a contractual relationship arises.

728. An interested purchaser may also take a more proactive step to procure an OTP. In *Woo Kah Wai v. Chew Ai Hua Sandra*, the purchaser sent to the sellers an offer to purchase an OTP containing certain terms (compliant OTP) and enclosed a cheque to pay for the option fee.[1483] The sellers accepted the offer by signing in acknowledgment of receiving the cheque, banking in the cheque and instructing their agent to prepare a draft OTP. According to the Court of Appeal, this gave rise to a contract for the purchase of a compliant OTP (or 'Pre-Option Contract'), thus obliging the seller to grant an OTP on terms indicated in the offer.[1484] In this case the seller breached the contract by granting an OTP that ended earlier than what was indicated in the offer.

729. Another possible situation is where the seller and purchaser have come to an agreement by negotiations and decided to proceed by way of an OTP. In such a case, the grant of the OTP is pursuant to a concluded contract of sale. It does not constitute a separate contract. A good example is *Alrich Development Pte Ltd v. Rafiq Jumabhoy*, where the parties came to an agreement for the sale and purchase of a property.[1485] Pursuant to this contract, the seller granted an OTP to the purchaser, but subsequently sought to revoke it. The Court of Appeal held that the seller's conduct amounted to a breach of the contract of sale.

C. The Nature of an Option to Purchase

730. In *Alrich Development*, the Court of Appeal drew an analogy between an OTP and a 'unilateral contract along the lines of *Carlill v. Carbolic Smoke Ball Company*'.[1486] In the classic case, the contract was formed between the smoke ball company and a smoke ball user when the latter had performed the terms of the offer,

1483. [2014] SGCA 41; [2014] 4 SLR 166 (Menon CJ, Phang and Chao JJA), noted in Alvin W.L. *See*, 'Contract for the Grant of a Compliant Option to Purchase' [2015] SJLS 241.

1484. *See also Joseph Mathew v. Singh Chiranjeev* [2009] SGCA 51; [2010] 1 SLR 338 and *Ong Kok Ming (alias Ong Henardi) v. Happy Valley Holdings Pte Ltd* [2011] SGHC 199, where the pre-OTP contract was inferred from the facts. Both cases were relied on in *Woo Kah Wai v. Chew Ai Hua Sandra* [2014] SGCA 41; [2014] 4 SLR 166.

1485. [1995] SGCA 53; [1995] 2 SLR(R) 340 (Thean JA, Goh and Rajendran JJ).

1486. [1995] SGCA 53; [1995] 2 SLR(R) 340 at [41]. The analogy was suggested by Lord Diplock in *United Dominions v. Eagle Aircraft Services* [1968] 1 All ER 104 at 109; cited in *Lee Hooi Lian v. Kuay Guan Kai* [1990] 2 MLJ 345; *Lo Geok Kwee v. Suriyakumari d/o Kandasamy Gopal* [1991] SGHC 199. *See also Teo Siew Peng v. Guok Sing Ong* [1982] SGCA 20; [1981–1982] SLR(R) 699 at [14].

i.e. by using the smoke ball three times a day for three weeks.[1487] However, the company's obligation to pay the promised £100 only arose upon the smoke ball user contracting influenza. The term 'unilateral contract' describes the fact that only the company was under an obligation to do something. The purchaser was never under any obligation to use the smoke ball, let alone by the recommended method.

731. Similarly, in the case of an OTP, the purchaser is not under any obligation to exercise it. However, the term 'unilateral contract' only tells half the story. It fails to emphasise the point that the seller's obligation only arises upon the occurrence of a certain event brought about by the purchaser. Moreover, it is incapable of explaining cases where the occurrence of the said event also brings about obligation(s) on the purchaser's part. For instance, after exercising the OTP, the purchaser will be under an obligation to pay the purchase price. Thus, the term 'conditional contract' may be more appropriate. In *Alrich*, the contract of sale was made conditional upon the purchaser's exercise of the OTP.

732. As *Alrich* was a case where the contract of sale preceded the grant of the OTP, it does not provide direct support for the proposition that the grant of an OTP would by itself give rise to a contract of sale. In *Laybutt v. Amoco Australia Pty Ltd*, however, Gibbs J of the High Court of Australia preferred the view that an OTP 'is a contract to sell the land upon condition that the grantee gives the notice and does the other things stipulated in the option'.[1488]

733. Similarly, in *Griffith v. Pelton*, the Court of Appeal said:

734. An option in gross for the purchase of land is a conditional contract for such purchase by the grantee of the option from the grantor, which the grantee is entitled to convert into a concluded contract of purchase, and to have carried to completion by the grantor, upon giving the prescribed notice and otherwise complying with the conditions upon which the option is made exercisable in any particular case.[1489]

735. In *Woo Kah Wai*, however, the Court of Appeal held (*obiter*) that a contract of sale would only arise upon the purchaser exercising the OTP.[1490] This suggests that the grant of an OTP does not give rise to a conditional contract, thus requiring an alternative explanation. One possibility is that the OTP is an irrevocable offer, i.e. an offer to sell the property coupled with a contract preventing its revocation. Thus, in *Helby v. Matthews*, the House of Lords said:

1487. *Carlill v. Carbolic Smoke Ball Company* [1893] 1 QB 256.
1488. (1974) 4 ALR 482 at 498.
1489. [1958] Ch 205 at 225. *See also Weeding v. Weeding* (1861) 70 ER 812 at 815.
1490. [2014] SGCA 41; [2014] 4 SLR 166 at [51].

> From a legal point of view the [seller] was in exactly the same position as if he had made an offer to sell on certain terms, and had undertaken to keep it open for a definite period. Until acceptance by the person to whom the offer is made, there can be no contract to buy.[1491]

736. Based on this analysis, the Pre-Option Contract in *Woo Kah Wai* functioned to procure an offer to sell from the seller and to prevent the seller from revoking this offer. The irrevocable offer analysis also finds support in some local cases. The case of *Seah Kiat Seng v. Amtel Exports Pte Ltd* was unusual in that the OTP explicitly referred to an offer to sell the property.[1492] This led Rubin J to find that the OTP amounted to an irrevocable offer. However, the irrevocable offer analysis has also found favour with the courts even where the term 'offer' was not used. In *Lim Hwee Meng v. Citadel Investment Pte Ltd*, the Court of Appeal referred to 'the offer contained in the option' and focused its attention on whether the purchaser had accepted the offer.[1493] In *Lo Geok Kwee v. Suriyakumari d/o Kandasamy Gopal*, one of the terms of the OTP stated: 'This Option shall be treated a legally binding contract upon the same being exercised … and no further contract is necessary.' [1494] Chan J, preferring an irrevocable offer explanation of the OTP, held that no contract of sale arises until the exercise of the OTP.

737. There is one situation where the granting of an OTP will not give rise to a contract of sale. This is where the OTP requires the parties to enter into a formal contract of sale. In *Tai Tong Realty Co (Pte) Ltd v. Galstaun*, the OTP provided that 'the sale is subject to contract' and that a contract of sale must be executed within six weeks from the date of exercise of the OTP.[1495] The purchaser exercised the OTP and paid a deposit. However, the seller refused to proceed with the sale. The Court of Appeal held that there was no binding contract.[1496] Arguably, this case does not shed any light on the debate about the nature of an OTP. By imposing a further condition for a contract of sale to arise, especially one where the fulfilment of which could be prevented by the seller, the OTP is rendered illusory in so far as the purchaser is concerned.

738. In light of the uncertainty, one might prefer the view that an OTP is really *sui generis*, having the characteristics of both an irrevocable offer and a conditional

1491. [1895] AC 471 at 480.
1492. [1996] SGHC 156; [1996] 2 SLR(R) 636.
1493. [1998] SGCA 46; [1998] 3 SLR(R) 101 at [35] (Karthigesu JA, Thean JA and Lai J).
1494. [1991] SGHC 199.
1495. [1973] SGCA 5; [1971–1973] SLR(R) 810 (Wee CJ, Chua and Tan JJ). *See also JT Chanrai (S) Pte Ltd v. Consolidated Hotels Ltd* [1985] SGHC 32; [1985–1986] SLR(R) 390; *Koh Peng Moh v. Yahiya* [1965] MLJ 320 (Singapore); *Koh Peng Moh v. Tan Chwee Boon* [1962] MLJ 353 (Singapore); *Huang Han Chao v. Tan Hong Moh Milton* [1994] SGCA 144; [1994] 3 SLR(R) 1080; *Yap Eng Thong v. Faber Union Ltd* [1973] SGHC 7; [1971–1973] SLR(R) 690.
1496. But the court did make a reference to 'a mere conditional contract of sale' ([1973] SGCA 5; [1971–1973] SLR(R) 810 at [1]).

contract.[1497] However, in refusing to commit to one explanation, two practical matters are rendered uncertain. First, is stamp duty payable for an OTP?[1498] Second, must an OTP satisfy the formalities requirement of section 6(d) of the Civil Law Act (CLA) for it to be enforceable?[1499] If an OTP gives rise to a conditional contract of sale, then both questions can be readily answered in the affirmative.

739. Perhaps there is no fixed explanation of an OTP. Where the parties have already arrived at an agreement to sell and purchase the property but decided to proceed by way of an OTP, then it might be that the grant of an OTP gives rise to a contract of sale, if it has not already arisen.[1500] If there is any explicit or implicit postponement of the contract of sale until a certain condition is satisfied, then an irrevocable offer explanation would seem appropriate. In a simple grant of an OTP without more, however, either analysis is possible. If it is right that the nature of a particular OTP depends on the manner in which it is procured, then the questions of whether stamp duty and formalities requirement apply to OTPs cannot be answered in abstract but require examination of the specific facts of each case.

740. One might ask whether the two views differ in the protection of the purchaser's interest. Where the seller wilfully revokes the OTP, the purchaser's case appears stronger if the seller's conduct is regarded as a breach of a contract of sale. However, it has also been compellingly argued that an offeror's attempts to revoke his offer 'can be nothing more than a repudiation of the contracted duty to keep the offer open' and the offeree may 'ignore the repudiation and accept the offer'.[1501] This view finds implicit support in the case of *Woo Kah Wai*, where Yee JC refused to order specific performance only because the property had been sold to a third party and the purchaser had unduly delayed in seeking the remedy.[1502]

II. Contract of Sale

741. For a contract for the sale of land to arise, the parties must have agreed on the three P's: (1) the parties, (2) the property and (3) the purchase price.[1503] Where

1497. *Spiro v. Glencrown Properties Ltd* [1991] Ch 537 at 544.
1498. *See* Stamp Duties Act (Cap. 312, 2006 Rev. Ed.), First Schedule.
1499. (Cap. 43, 1999 Rev. Ed.). *See* discussion below.
1500. *See Joseph Mathew v. Singh Chiranjeev* [2009] SGCA 51; [2010] 1 SLR 338 and *Ong Kok Ming (alias Ong Henardi) v. Happy Valley Holdings Pte Ltd* [2011] SGHC 199. Although these cases were said to be analogous to *Woo Kah Wai v. Chew Ai Hua Sandra* [2014] SGCA 41; [2014] 4 SLR 166, they are perhaps closer in nature to the *Alrich Development Pte Ltd v. Rafiq Jumabhoy* [1995] SGCA 53; [1995] 2 SLR(R) 340.
1501. D.O. McGovney, 'Irrevocable Offers' (1914) 27 Harv L Rev 644.
1502. *Chew Ai Hua Sandra v. Woo Kah Wai* [2013] SGHC 120; [2013] 3 SLR 1088.
1503. *Woo Kah Wai v. Chew Ai Hua Sandra* [2014] SGCA 41; [2014] 4 SLR 166 at [139]; *Lee Christina v. Lee Eunice* [1993] SGCA 56; [1993] 2 SLR(R) 644 at [30].

the completion date is not specified, there would be an implied term that completion is to take place within a reasonable time.[1504] This is known as an 'open contract'.[1505]

742. The usual rules of contract formation govern the finding of a contract for the sale of land. As hinted earlier, where the parties have agreed to proceed by way of an OTP, it is not always clear when exactly a contract of sale arises. The inquiry is even more difficult where no OTP was granted. In such a case it is necessary to carefully examine the parties' correspondence, which could be lengthy and take various forms, to determine whether there is any meeting of minds. Other important factors that might shed light on the matter include whether the negotiation led to the drafting of a formal document,[1506] whether the document was signed by the parties and whether the seller accepted a deposit from the purchaser.[1507]

743. Where the parties' written correspondences are marked 'subject to contract', they are not bound until the signing of a formal contract of sale. Even if the document is not marked 'subject to contract', an intention to that effect may nonetheless be inferred from the wording of the documents.[1508] The effect of an OTP made subject to contract has been discussed earlier. In *Tai Tong Realty Co (Pte) Ltd v. Galstaun*, the Court of Appeal appeared to suggest that there could be exceptional cases where a contract of sale could nonetheless arise even if the relevant documents were marked 'subject to contract'. [1509] However, the court did not elaborate on what would constitute such a case. It is also important to note that even if the phrase is subsequently omitted, it is not conclusive that a contract of sale has arisen. In *Ong Chong Soo v. Tan Eng Tai*, the first letter from the purchaser was marked 'subject to contract' but the phrase was omitted in subsequent exchange letters.[1510] Having examined the subsequent letter exchanges between the parties, Sinnathuray J concluded that there was no change in the parties' intention to create a binding legal relation by way of a formal contract.

1504. *Lee Christina v. Lee Eunice* [1993] SGCA 56; [1993] 2 SLR(R) 644 at [30]; *Lim Hoe Heng v. Poh Choon Kia* [2012] SGCA 58; [2013] 1 SLR 152 at [28]–[30]; *Singh Chiranjeev v. Joseph Mathew* [2008] SGHC 222; [2009] 2 SLR(R) 73 at [37].
1505. *Mt Elizabeth Hospital Ltd v. Allan Ng Clinic for Women* [1994] SGCA 47; [1994] 1 SLR(R) 821.
1506. *Choo Si Sen v. Lee Boon Sai* [1986] 1 MLJ 466.
1507. *Koh Kia Hiong v. Guo Enterprises Pte Ltd* [1989] SGHC 106; [1989] 2 SLR(R) 673; *Loh Chin Kok v. Lee Teck Seng Paul* [1996] SGHC 168; [1996] 2 SLR(R) 767; *SM Integrated Transware Pte Ltd v. Schenker Singapore (Pte) Ltd* [2005] SGHC 58; [2005] 2 SLR(R) 651; *Yeo Long Seng v. Lucky Park (Pte) Ltd* [1970] SGHC 20; [1968–1970] SLR(R) 859.
1508. *See Quek Choon Huat v. Seow R M* [1980] SGCA 14; [1979–1980] SLR(R) 828.
1509. [1973] SGCA 5; [1971–1973] SLR(R) 810.
1510. [1982] SGHC 8; [1981–1982] SLR(R) 361.

§2. FORMALITIES

I. Formality Requirements

744. For centuries,[1511] dealings in land have been subjected to formality requirements.[1512] The intention was originally to prevent fraud and therefore the formality requirements served mainly as an evidentiary function. In light of recent improvements to the law of evidence, this function now takes a back seat. Today, the formality requirements serve mainly a cautionary function, preventing parties from being bound inadvertently or prematurely. The parties are required to satisfy the formality requirements to sufficiently demonstrate their seriousness about entering into the transaction.

745. In Singapore the relevant provision is section 6 of the Civil Law Act (CLA), which states:[1513]

> No action shall be brought against –
>
> ...
>
> (d) any person upon any contract for the sale or other disposition of immovable property, or any interest in such property;
>
> ...
>
> unless the promise or agreement upon which such action is brought, or some memorandum or note thereof, is in writing and signed by the party to be charged therewith or some other person lawfully authorised by him.

746. Where the parties have entered into a formal contract, the requirements of section 6(d) are usually satisfied. But section 6(d) does not require that the contract itself be in writing. Where the contract is an oral one, it is sufficient if it is evidenced by some note or memorandum.[1514] Such note or memorandum must contain all the material terms of the contract. In the case of a simple contract of sale, only the 3 P's must be recorded. In *Lee Christina v. Lee Eunice*, for example, the Court of Appeal held that the following note that the seller signed and sent to her lawyer constituted sufficient memorandum of the contract of sale:[1515]

> Dear Sir
> I shall be glad if you will act for me in the sale of my house No 21 Fifth Avenue, Bukit Timah Rd subject to existing tenancy to Mrs Christina Loke for the sum of $250,000 of which I have received a deposit of $25,000.

1511. *See* UK Law Commission, 'Transfer of Land: Formalities for Contracts for Sale Etc. of Land' (Law Com. No.164, 1987).
1512. *See e.g.* the Statute of Frauds 1677, section 4.
1513. (Cap. 43, 1999 Rev. Ed.).
1514. *Cheong Kok Leong v. Cheong Woon Weng* [2017] SGCA 47 at [7].
1515. [1993] SGCA 56; [1993] 2 SLR(R) 644 (Yong CJ, Goh and Karthigesu JJ).

Yours faithfully
[Seller's signature]

747. If the parties have agreed on any other terms, e.g. the date of completion, such terms must also be recorded in the note or memorandum.[1516]

748. The note or memorandum must be in writing. In *SM Integrated Transware Pte Ltd v. Schenker Singapore (Pte) Ltd*, Prakash J held that the writing requirement could also be satisfied by a memorandum or note that is in electronic form.[1517] It is interesting to note while the Electronic Transactions Act (ETA)[1518] provides that an electronic record can satisfy the writing requirement,[1519] the statute explicitly excluded itself from applying to transactions relating to land.[1520] However, this merely means that the ETA could not be relied upon in interpreting section 6(d) of the CLA. Prakash J justified her decision by relying instead on the broad definition of 'writing' in section 2 of the Interpretation Act[1521] as well as the policy need to serve modern business practices.[1522] Prakash J's decision was later affirmed by the Court of Appeal in *Joseph Mathew v. Singh Chiranjeev*.[1523]

749. The memorandum or note must be signed by 'the party to be charged', i.e. the party against whom the contract is sought to be enforced. For example, if an aggrieved purchaser wishes to sue a defaulting seller, it is important that the memorandum or note contains the seller's signature. As to what constitutes signature, the common law takes a pragmatic approach and adopts a loose interpretation. It need not be in the popular sense of putting pen to paper. In *Schenker Singapore*, however, Prakash J went as far as to hold that the automatic insertion of the sender's name and e-mail address in the e-mail (From: 'Tan Tian Tye' <tiantye.tan@schenker.com>) constituted signature for the purposes of section 6(d).[1524] As this sufficiently identified the sender, it performed the authenticating function of a signature.[1525]

750. The Court of Appeal in *Joseph Mathew* agreed, although in this case the signature requirement was satisfied by the seller typing out his name at the end of his e-mail message.[1526] In both cases the courts were clearly conscious about to need to interpret section 6(d) in a way that keeps up with modern times, especially in light of the rise of e-commerce. However, the relaxation of the signature requirement in

---

1516. *Tay Joo Sing v. Ku Yu Sang* [1994] SGCA 45; [1994] 1 SLR(R) 765.
1517. [2005] SGHC 58; [2005] 2 SLR(R) 651.
1518. (Cap. 88, 2011 Rev. Ed.).
1519. ETA, section 7.
1520. ETA, section 4(1); First Schedule.
1521. (Cap. 1, 2002 Rev. Ed.) section 2: '"writing" and expressions referring to writing include printing, lithography, typewriting, photography and other modes of representing or reproducing words or figures in visible form'.
1522. [2005] SGHC 58; [2005] 2 SLR(R) 651 at [85].
1523. [2009] SGCA 51]; [2010] 1 SLR 338.
1524. [2005] SGHC 58; [2005] 2 SLR(R) 651 at [92].
1525. [2005] SGHC 58; [2005] 2 SLR(R) 651 at [87], [92].
1526. [2009] SGCA 51]; [2010] 1 SLR 338 at [7], [45].

Schenker Singapore may be criticised for having gone too far. As explained earlier, the requirements of section 6(d) serve mainly as a cautionary function. Thus, a signature should, at the very least, be something that is consciously appended to the message by its sender.[1527]

751. Section 6(d) does not specify the time at which the note or memorandum must be created. Thus, in *Ong Kok Ming (alias Ong Henardi) v. Happy Valley Holdings Pte Ltd*, the Prakash J explained that even a note or memorandum that is created after the conclusion of the oral contract of sale is sufficient, so long as they exist before the commencement of the proceedings.[1528]

752. A contract that does not comply with the requirements of section 6(d) is merely unenforceable, not invalid. An orally concluded contract of sale is as valid as a written one. Thus, in the case of a completed contract, where there is no issue of enforceability, neither party can demand the return of considerations that have passed hands on the ground that there was no valid contract.

753. As alluded to earlier, it is generally assumed that an OTP must comply with section 6(d) despite the fact that the grant of an OTP does not necessarily amount to a contract of sale. The usual explanation is that a valid OTP confers on the purchaser an interest in the property, sufficient at least to support the lodgment of a caveat in the land register, so as to amount to a disposition of an interest in land.[1529] But the nature and effect of such an interest are often left unexplained.[1530] In fact, the Court of Appeal in *E C Investment Holding Pte Ltd v. Ridout Residence Pte Ltd* held that the grant of an OTP does not, by itself, give the purchaser any substantial interest in the property.[1531] There, although the purchaser had properly exercised the OTP, the court refused to award specific performance, which is essential for attracting the application of the doctrine in *Lysaght v. Edwards*.[1532] Thus, the assumption that every OTP must comply with section 6(d) requires rethinking. As a matter of good practice, however, the parties should make an effort to ensure that an OTP complies with section 6(d) for it would then serve as a memorandum of the contract of sale that arises later.

1527. *J Pereira Fernandes SA v. Mehta* [2006] EWHC 813 (Ch); [2006] 1 WLR 1543. *See also* Kelvin F.K. Low, 'Informal Dealings with Land: Retaining the Knotty Apron Strings' (2010) 22 Sing Ac LJ 704 at 712.

1528. [2011] SGHC 199. *See also Lee Christina v. Lee Eunice* [1993] SGCA 56; [1993] 2 SLR(R) 644.

1529. *Mountford v. Scott* [1975] Ch 258 at 265; *Ong Chay Tong & Sons (Pte) Ltd v. Ong Hoo Eng* [2008] SGCA 42; [2009] 1 SLR(R) 305 at [75]; *Eng Bee Properties Pte Ltd v. Lee Foong Fatt* [1993] SGHC 202; [1993] 2 SLR(R) 778 at [26]; *Ho Seek Yueng Novel v. J & v. Development Pte Ltd* [2006] SGHC 63; [2006] 2 SLR(R) 742 at [52]; *Joseph Mathew v. Singh Chiranjeev* [2009] SGCA 51; [2010] 1 SLR 338 at [22], [23]; *Ong Kok Ming (alias Ong Henardi) v. Happy Valley Holdings Pte Ltd* [2011] SGHC 199 at [41].

1530. But see *Pritchard v. Briggs* [1980] Ch 338 at 418, where Templeman LJ explained the interest as such: '[T]he grant of the option creates a contingent equitable interest which, if registered as an estate contract, is binding on successors in title of the grantor and takes priority from the date of its registration.'

1531. [2011] SGCA 50; [2012] 1 SLR 32.

1532. (1876) 2 Ch D 499.

754. In the case of HDB flats[1533] and properties offered for sale by a developer,[1534] the parties are obliged to use the prescribed OTP and contract of sale.

II. Joinder of Documents

755. Where the parties have manifested sufficient intention to be bound by a contract of sale, the courts are generally unwilling to allow a party to escape from the contract on the ground that the formality requirements have not been complied with. This has led the courts to adopt a less stringent approach to the formality requirements. Where there is no single document that forms the required memorandum, the court may invoke the doctrine of joinder, allowing two or more documents to be joined and read together. However, the doctrine of joinder does not apply to documents that are marked 'subject to contract'. In *Schenker Singapore*, Prakash J held that because the letter of intent was marked 'subject to contract', 'there is no way that, even if it had been signed, it could have served as a memorandum of agreement for the purpose of s 6 of the CLA'.[1535]

756. The rules on joinder are not entirely clear but it appears to be accepted that documents can be joined in at least two situations. The first situation is where a document that is signed by the defendant expressly or impliedly refers to another document, or to a transaction which is recorded in another document.[1536] The second document can then be joined to the first. Although the second document usually predates the first document, it need not be the case if both documents were created 'more or less contemporaneously'[1537] or if the first document envisaged the creation of the second document.[1538]

757. This rule of joinder is conveniently illustrated by the English case of *Long v. Millar.*[1539] There, the parties agreed to the sale and purchase of three plots of land at Hammersmith. When the seller reneged on his promise to sell, the purchaser sued. The purchaser had signed a document stating that he agreed to purchase the said properties for £310 and to pay a deposit of £31. However, this document could not by itself constitute sufficient memorandum because it did not contain the seller's signature. The purchaser thus sought to join a receipt issued and signed by the seller acknowledging receipt of £31 as a deposit for the purchase of the said properties. The Court of Appeal allowed the joinder because the receipt referred to the purchase, which was in turn recorded in the first document.[1540]

1533. Housing and Development (Agreement for Sale and Purchase) Rules (R.11, 2004 Rev. Ed.).
1534. Housing Developers Rules (R.1, Rev. Ed. 2008), rules 10 and 12; Sale of Commercial Properties Rules (R.1, 1999 Rev. Ed.) rules 5 and 7.
1535. [2005] SGHC 58; [2005] 2 SLR(R) 651 at [73].
1536. *Timmins v. Moreland Street Property Co Ltd* [1958] Ch 110 at 130.
1537. *Timmins v. Moreland Street Property Co Ltd* [1958] Ch 110 at 123, 133.
1538. *Alrich Development Pte Ltd v. Rafiq Jumabhoy* [1995] SGCA 53; [1995] 2 SLR(R) 340 at [51].

1539. (1879) 4 CPD 450. *See also Burgess v. Cos* [1951] Ch 383.
1540. *See also Burgess v. Cos* [1951] Ch 383.

758. The second situation in which joinder is possible is where the documents, when placed side by side, manifestly refer to the same transaction.[1541] The more recent English cases, however, appear to adopt a cautious attitude when invited to apply this second rule of joinder. In *Timmins v. Moreland Street Property Co Ltd*, the purchaser, having agreed to purchase a property, handed to the seller a signed cheque for £3900.[1542] The seller issued a signed receipt acknowledging receipt of £3900 as a deposit for the sale of the property for a sum of £39,000. When the purchaser reneged on this promise to sell, the seller sought to join the receipt to the cheque.

759. The Court of Appeal held that there could be no joinder because the cheque did not refer to any other document or transaction other than the order to pay the seller. Although the two documents, when placed side by side, would appear to be connected, the court did not apply the second rule of joinder, preferring to limit its application. Jenkins LJ said:

760. The laying of documents side by side may no doubt lead to the conclusion as a matter of res ipsa loquitur that the two are connected. But before a document signed by the party to be charged can be laid alongside another document to see if between them they constitute a sufficient memorandum, there must, I conceive, be found in the document signed by the party to be charged some reference to some other document or transaction.[1543]

761. Similarly, in *Stokes v. Wicher*, the High Court preferred to apply the first rule of joinder even though the two documents were clearly duplicates: one was the original while the other was the carbon copy.[1544]

762. In contrast, the second rule of joinder appears to find favour with the Singapore courts.[1545] A good example is *Ong Kok Ming*, where the aggrieved purchaser sought to join the following documents: (i) a draft OTP containing all the essential terms of the contract and specifying an option fee of $145,000; and (ii) the photocopy of two cheques for the sums of $139,000 and $6000 respectively, signed at the back by the seller's agent. [1546] Although the two cheques did not on their faces refer to the transaction, Prakash J nonetheless allowed them to be joined to the draft OTP on the ground that they are so obviously connected. The joinder supplied the memorandum with the seller's signature, which was originally lacking.

1541. *Sheers* v *Thimbleby* (1897) 13 TLR 451.
1542. [1958] Ch 110.
1543. [1958] Ch 110 at 130.
1544. [1920] 1 Ch 411.
1545. In an old case, *Wee Alice v. Yeo Gek Lang* [1978] SGHC 2; [1977-78] SLR(R) 254, the judgment of Jenkins LJ in *Timmins* was cited with approval. However, the High Court applied the rule of joinder without considering whether the defendant had signed any of the documents. This issue was not challenged on appeal: *Yeo Gek Lang v. Wee Alice* [1979] SGCA 2; [1979-1980] SLR(R) 12.
1546. *Ong Kok Ming (alias Ong Henardi) v. Happy Valley Holdings Pte Ltd* [2011] SGHC 199 at [47]–[48].

763. A liberal approach to the joinder of documents is also demonstrated by the case of *Joseph Mathew*, again concerning a seller who reneged on his promise to sell.[1547] The following documents were adduced before the courts:

(i) A cheque for the sum of $5060 issued and signed by the purchaser. The property agent wrote the following on the back of the cheque: '1% Deposit Sale of 26 Upper Serangoon View #04-32 RIO VISTA (S) 534206';
(ii) E-mail from the property agent to the seller, informing that the purchaser offered to buy the property for $506,000 and that a 1% deposit, which will serve as the option fee, was collected;
(iii) E-mail from the property agent to the seller, informing that the cheque for $5060 will be sent to the latter together with the draft option to purchase; and
(iv) E-mail from seller to property agent, agreeing to proceed with the sale of the property at $506,000 and instructing the property agent to bank the cheque into the seller's bank account.

In the High Court, Ang J held that the three e-mails 'clearly form a chain of correspondence and must thus be read together'.[1548] However, as the e-mails only mentioned 'Rio Vista' instead of the full address of the property, Ang J also allowed the cheque, which was referred to in the e-mails, to be joined.[1549] This was notwithstanding that it was not the seller who wrote at the back of the cheque.[1550] On appeal to the Court of Appeal, this liberal approach to joinder was affirmed.[1551]

764. While this approach is obviously helpful where a large number of documents are adduced before a court, it is submitted that the courts ought to exercise some caution when joining documents that are created outside the negotiation process and without the knowledge of the party to be charged. Take the example of an oral contract where the purchaser, after paying the deposit by way of a cheque, decides not to proceed with the purchase. The seller, intending to enforce the contract, subsequently records the particulars of the contract on a piece of paper and requests that this paper be joined to the cheque containing the purchaser's signature. If joinder were allowed in this case, section 6(d) would be rendered otiose for its requirements would be overly easy to satisfy.

III. Doctrine of Part Performance

765. Where a contract has been partially performed by one party, the other party cannot deny its enforceability by claiming that the formality requirements have not been complied with. Although the CLA does not explicitly preserve the doctrine of

1547. [2009] SGCA 51; [2010] 1 SLR 338 (CA); [2008] SGHC 222; [2009] 2 SLR(R) 73 (HC).
1548. [2008] SGHC 222; [2009] 2 SLR(R) 73 at [33].
1549. [2008] SGHC 222; [2009] 2 SLR(R) 73 at [35].
1550. [2008] SGHC 222; [2009] 2 SLR(R) 73 at [32], [35].
1551. [2009] SGCA 51; [2010] 1 SLR 338 at [42]–[43] (Chan CJ, Phang and Rajah JJA).

part performance, in *Joseph Mathew*, the Court of Appeal held that the doctrine continues to be a recognised exception to the section 6(d) formality requirements.[1552] Unlike the doctrine of joinder, the doctrine of part performance is a true exception in that it operates to completely exempt the formality requirements. The rationale is to disallow a defaulting party from using the statute as an instrument of fraud.[1553]

766. In *Joseph Mathew*, Ang J held that even if the cheque containing the address of the property could not be joined to the e-mails, the contract was nonetheless enforceable because it had been partially performed. Curiously, however, Ang J referred to the defaulting sellers' act of accepting the purchasers' cheque as constituting part performance.[1554] This appears to be contrary to the traditional focus on the part performance of the party seeking to enforce the contract, the purchasers in this case. However, the authors of a leading textbook commented:

> [T]he reference to the defendant vendors' actions ought not to be regarded as a reference to the act of part performance itself. Rather, it should regarded as evidence that the act of part performance was known by the vendors who had acquiesced in the act so as to indicate the requisite fraud upon which the doctrine is based.[1555]

The Court of Appeal, in referring to the payment of money by way of a cheque as constituting part performance, appeared to have focused instead on the purchasers' conduct, thus confirming the traditional approach.[1556]

767. In *Hu Lee Impex Pte Ltd v. Lim Aik Seng*, Ang J held that the act relied upon as constituting part performance must unequivocally point to the existence of a contract fitting the description of the alleged oral contract.[1557] This stringent test would make it more difficult to establish part performance, especially where no part of the contract is evidenced in writing and where there is more than one contract that could have induced the act. However, this is unlikely to be a problem for most contracts for the sale of land. In *Joseph Mathew*, for example, there was no doubt that the cheque was delivered as payment of the option fee.

1552. [2009] SGCA 51; [2010] 1 SLR 338 at [47]–[62]. *See also Cheong Kok Leong v. Cheong Woon Weng* [2017] SGCA 47 at [8].
1553. [2009] SGCA 51; [2010] 1 SLR 338 at [48], [52]. *See also Steadman v. Steadman* [1976] AC 536; *Broughton v. Snook* [1938] Ch 505.
1554. [2008] SGHC 222; [2009] 2 SLR(R) 73 at [29], [48].
1555. Tang Hang Wu and Kelvin F.K. Low, *Tan Sook Yee's Principles of Singapore Land Law*, 3rd edn (LexisNexis, 2009) at 398.
1556. [2009] SGCA 51; [2010] 1 SLR 338 at [64].
1557. [2013] SGHC 142; [2013] 4 SLR 176, following *Elizabeth Maddison v. John Alderson* (1883) 8 App Cas 467. *Cf Steadman v. Steadman* [1976] AC 536, where the House of Lords held that part performance could be established only if it is more probable than not that the act was performed in reliance of the oral contract.

§3. OBLIGATIONS OF THE PARTIES

I. Disclosure of Latent Defect in Title

768. For the sale of a registered land,[1558] the seller is no longer required to undertake the laborious task of proving good root title.[1559] The seller is also under no duty to actively disclose anything other than a latent defect in title. The onus is on the purchaser to do a land search to verify whether the seller has what he had promised to sell. Anything that could be revealed by a land search is not regarded as a latent defect in title. In *Indian Overseas Bank v. Cheng Lai Geok*, where the purchaser sought to terminate the contract of sale on the ground that the seller had failed to disclose the existence of four caveats lodged over the property, Goh JC said:

> The caveats had been notified on the Land Register and they were there for the whole world to see. The general rule in contracts for the sale of land is still undoubtedly *caveat emptor* and a vendor's duty to disclose only applies to latent defects of title.[1560]

769. An example of an encumbrance that a land search will not reveal, and thus constituting a latent defect of the title, is a short-term lease, i.e. for the duration of 7 years or less.

II. Completion of the Contract

770. After a contract of sale is concluded, and upon the satisfaction of any condition precedent, the next step is for the parties to complete the sale and purchase. The purchaser is obliged to pay the purchase price. The seller is obliged to convey good title, i.e. one that the seller promised to give (usually free of encumbrances) and to deliver vacant possession of the property (unless otherwise agreed). The timing of performance is usually stipulated in the contract. It is customary to require the purchaser to first pay the purchase price in exchange for vacant possession of the property. Registration of the property in the purchaser's name will follow thereafter.

771. An obligation to perform may be made subject to a condition precedent, e.g. subject to approval by the relevant authority for the proposed use of the property.[1561] Where the condition is exclusive for the benefit of one party, that party may

1558. *See e.g.* the Law Society of Singapore's Conditions of Sale 2012, which parties may in corporate into their contracts by reference.

1559. On good root title, see the Conveyancing and Law of Property Act (Cap. 61, 1994 Rev. Ed.) (CLPA), section 3(4).

1560. [1991] SGHC 141; [1991] 2 SLR(R) 574 at [46].

1561. *See* Tang Hang Wu and Kelvin F.K. Low, *Tan Sook Yee's Principles of Singapore Land Law*, 3rd edn (LexisNexis, 2009) at 400–403.

waive the condition.[1562] The other party's obligation to perform will then arise. To avoid dispute, it is advisable for the parties to stipulate a deadline by which the condition must be fulfilled.

772. Prior to the completion date, the purchaser cannot complain that the seller does not have good title to give. In *Siti v. Lee Kay Li*, where two caveats have been lodged over the property by a third party, the Court of Appeal held that the seller was under no obligation to remove the caveats before the completion date.[1563]

773. The court explained:

774. In so far as the withdrawals of the two caveats are concerned, the vendor's obligation was to procure and deliver to the purchasers at the time of completion properly signed withdrawals. There was no obligation on his part to submit copies of completed and properly executed withdrawals before completion. In our judgment, the failure on the part of the vendor's solicitor to produce a copy of a properly executed withdrawal of the caveat did not relieve the purchasers' solicitor from proceeding with the completion. He should proceed to complete as scheduled, and if on completion such withdrawal was not handed over he could refuse to complete and would be entitled so to do.[1564]

775. The Court of Appeal's decision was later applied in *Teo Beng Ngoh v. Quek Kheng Leong Nicky*, where the purchaser refused to pay the purchase price on the ground that the seller had no good title due to a caveat lodged over the property.[1565] Lai J held that the purchaser's objection was premature as it was before the completion date.

776. Despite the *obiter* in *Siti*, a different approach was adopted in two other High Court decisions. Curiously, *Siti* was not cited in both cases. In *Coastland Properties Pte Ltd v. Ho San Kong Hoey*, the purchasers claimed that the sellers were unable to deliver a good title at the completion date due to the existence of a caveat lodged over the property.[1566] The sellers failed to show that the caveator's claim to the property was unsubstantiated. Thus, had the purchasers gone on to complete the purchase, it is likely that they would become embroiled in a prolonged and costly litigation with the caveator. For this reason, Lau JC held that the purchasers were entitled to refuse completion of the purchase. The learned judge explained:

Where the title of the vendor is subject to potential or actual adverse claims, as for example by the existence of a caveat, it is the duty of the vendor to clear his title so long as the claims are not fanciful or theoretical. The fact that the vendor's title

---

1562. *Chip Thye Enterprises Pte Ltd v. Development Bank of Singapore* [1994] SGCA 59; [1994] 2 SLR(R) 68; *Cheng-Wong Mei Ling Theresa v. Oei Hong Leong* [2006] SGCA 12; [2006] 2 SLR(R) 637.

1563. [1996] SGCA 51; [1996] 2 SLR(R) 934 (Karthigesu JA, Thean JA and Lai J).

1564. [1996] SGCA 51; [1996] 2 SLR(R) 934 at [31], citing *See Bee Hoon v. Quah Poe Hoe* [1989] SGHC 54; [1989] 1 SLR(R) 623.

1565. [2008] SGHC 228 at [41].

1566. [1998] SGHC 129; [1998] 2 SLR(R) 95.

which is subject to such an adverse claim is subsequently proved not to be bad but essentially good does not alter the fact that it is sufficiently doubtful not to be forced upon the purchaser.[1567]

777. In *Indian Overseas Bank v. Cheng Lai Geok*, the seller was a mortgagee bank exercising a power of sale.[1568] The purchaser was the successful bidder for the mortgaged property at a public auction. However, the purchaser refused to complete the contract when he discovered that there were caveats lodged over the property. The caveators were third parties who had earlier entered into an agreement to purchase the property from the mortgagor. The caveats were lodged following the mortgagor's failure to complete the sale. Goh JC held that despite the existence of these caveats the purchaser would have acquired good title upon registration.[1569] Although the learned judge did not elaborate, this was most likely because the caveats were obviously unsustainable. As the mortgage was created earlier in time and duly registered, the bank's interest had priority over the caveators' interest. Proceedings to remove the caveats would have been straightforward. As a matter of substance, the bank had a good title to give to the purchaser.[1570]

778. It is submitted that the approach adopted in the latter cases is to be preferred. The entry of a caveat says nothing about the substance of the caveator's claim.[1571] It is merely a procedural tool.[1572] Thus, the mere existence of a caveat should not, by itself, be regarded as an encumbrance on, or a defect in, the seller's title.[1573] The substance of the caveator's claim must be examined, at least on a *prima facie* basis. If a purchaser is truly concerned about potential inconvenience resulting from a non-removal of caveat, he should negotiate for the inclusion of a term requiring the seller to prove, at a specific point in time prior to completion, that the title is 'free from encumbrances and caveats'.

779. Where a purchaser, having knowledge of a prior interest protected by a caveat, agreed to purchase the property subject to that interest, the purchaser has no right to insist on the removal of the caveat. In *Cathay Theatres Pte Ltd v. LKM Investment Holdings Pte Ltd*, the property in question was subject to existing and future leases.[1574] The tenant lodged a caveat, prohibiting registration of any dealing with the property unless it is expressed to be subject to these leases. Later the landlord entered into an agreement to sell the property subject to the leases. However, the purchaser refused to complete the purchase unless the seller first removes the

1567. [1998] SGHC 129; [1998] 2 SLR(R) 95 at [4].
1568. [1991] SGHC 141; [1991] 2 SLR(R) 574.
1569. [1991] SGHC 141; [1991] 2 SLR(R) 574 at [36].
1570. *See also* LTA, section 73; CLPA, section 26.
1571. *See* LTA, sections 49(4) and 117(5).
1572. *See* Part I (Land) Chapter 5 (Caveats).
1573. *See Forster v. Finance Corporation of Australia Ltd* [1980] VR 63. *See also Godfrey Constructions Pty Ltd v. Kanangra Park Pty Ltd* (1972) 128 CLR 529; *Leros Ptv Ltd v. Terara Pty Ltd* (1991) 174 CLR 407.
1574. [1998] SGCA 4; [1998] 1 SLR(R) 234 (Yong CJ, Karthigesu and Thean JJA).

caveat. The Court of Appeal held that the purchaser was not entitled to insist on the removal of the caveat because it had agreed to take the property subject to the leases.[1575]

§4. Protection of the Purchaser Pending Registration of Transfer

780. As alluded to earlier, it is inevitable that a gap in time exists between the conclusion of the contract of sale and registration of the transfer. During this period, there is a risk that the seller might, in breach of contract, sell the property to someone else. To address this problem, it was held in *Lysaght v. Edwards* that when parties enter into a valid contract of sale, a constructive trust arises in the purchaser's favour.[1576]

781. For the purposes of the doctrine in *Lysaght v. Edwards*, a valid contract arises if three things are satisfied.[1577] First, the contract must be sufficient in substance. There must be no ground for the seller to set the contract aside. Second, the contract must be sufficient in form. A contract that is unenforceable for failure to comply with the formality requirements does not attract the application of the doctrine. Third, the seller must possess good title. In other words, he must be in a position to give what he had promised to give.

782. Additionally, the purchaser must be able to show that he is entitled to compel a transfer of the property into his name by way of specific performance.[1578] This is because the basis for imposing a constructive trust is the purchaser's entitlement to a remedy of specific performance. Since the availability of specific performance would ensure the eventual transfer of the property into the purchaser's name, equity simply accelerates his interest.[1579]

783. In Lim Kim Som v. Sheriffa Taibah bte Abdul Rahman, the Court of Appeal said:

1575. [1998] SGCA 4; [1998] 1 SLR(R) 234 at [27].
1576. (1876) 2 Ch D 499. *See also Chen Con-Ling Tony v. Quay Properties Pte Ltd* [2004] SGHC 31; [2004] 2 SLR(R) 181 at [20]–[22].
1577. *Lysaght v. Edwards* (1876) 2 Ch D 499 at 507.
1578. *British & Malayan Trustees Ltd v. Sindo Realty Pte Ltd (in liquidation)* [1999] SGCA 2; [1999] 1 SLR(R) 61 at [66]; *Lim Kim Som v. Sheriffa Taibah bte Abdul Rahman* [1994] SGCA 15; [1994] 1 SLR(R) 233 at [40].
1579. Tang Hang Wu and Kelvin F.K. Low, *Tan Sook Yee's Principles of Singapore Land Law*, 3rd edn (LexisNexis, 2009) at 416.

> The passing of the beneficial ownership to a purchaser of land is premised on the availability of specific performance, as equity looks upon as done what has been agreed to be done and the purchaser is deemed the owner in equity as of the date of contract.[1580]

784. This aspect of the doctrine is now uncertain following the Court of Appeal's decision in *E C Investment Holding Pte Ltd v. Ridout Residence Pte Ltd.*[1581] There the court held that the remedy of specific performance is no longer available as of right to a purchaser of land.[1582] Instead, all the circumstances of the case must be considered in determining whether specific performance is an appropriate remedy. It is not yet clear how this would affect the doctrine in *Lysaght v. Edwards*.[1583] It could be that the parties must now litigate and await the availability of specific performance to be judicially determined. If the court orders specific performance, it would simply declare retrospectively that a constructive trust arose from the time the contract was concluded.

785. In *Lee Christina v. Lee Eunice*, although there was an enforceable contract of sale, no constructive trust arose.[1584] As the property was encumbered by a mortgage at the completion date, the seller could not give that which she had promised to give. While the purchaser could have opted to accept the defective title, she did not.[1585] Had she done so, a constructive trust would have arisen. Instead, she elected to accept the seller's repudiation of the contract, which also had the effect of barring her from claiming specific performance.

786. Where the sale is subject to a certain condition, e.g. subject to approval by the relevant authority, no equitable interest will pass to the purchaser until that condition is satisfied.[1586] It would be different, however, if the condition is exclusively for the purchaser's benefit. In *Cheng-Wong Mei Ling Theresa v. Oei Hong Leong*, the contract of sale was subject to the seller obtaining a court declaration that the property enjoyed a statutorily implied easement.[1587] The Court of Appeal held that

---

1580. [1994] SGCA 15; [1994] 1 SLR(R) 233 at [39] (Karthigesu JA, Thean JA and Khoo J). *See also Cheng-Wong Mei Ling Theresa v. Oei Hong Leong* [2006] SGCA 12; [2006] 2 SLR(R) 637; *British & Malayan Trustees Ltd v. Sindo Realty Pte Ltd (in liquidation)* [1999] SGCA 2; [1999] 1 SLR(R) 61 at [35]; *Chen Con-Ling Tony v. Quay Properties Pte Ltd* [2004] SGHC 31; [2004] 2 SLR(R) 181 at [20]. *See also Howard v. Miller* [1915] AC 318 at 326; *Oughtred v. Inland Revenue Commissioners* [1960] AC 206 at 240.
1581. [2011] SGCA 50; [2012] 1 SLR 32 (Chao, Phang and Rajah JJA).
1582. [2011] SGCA 50; [2012] 1 SLR 32.
1583. *See* Robert Chambers, 'The Importance of Specific Performance' in Simone Degeling and James Edelman (eds.), *Equity in Commercial Law* (Law Book, 2005) at 431.
1584. [1993] SGCA 56; [1993] 2 SLR(R) 644 at [48].
1585. *Lysaght v. Edwards* (1876) 2 Ch D 499 at 507: '… for however bad the title may be the purchaser has a right to accept it, and the moment he has accepted the title, the contract is fully binding upon the vendor'.
1586. *Chi Liung Holdings Sdn Bhd v. Attorney-General* [1994] SGCA 68; [1994] 2 SLR(R) 314; *British & Malayan Trustees Ltd v. Sindo Realty Pte Ltd (in liquidation)* [1999] SGCA 2; [1999] 1 SLR(R) 61; *Lim Kim Som v. Sheriffa Taibah bte Abdul Rahman* [1994] SGCA 15; [1994] 1 SLR(R) 233.
1587. [2006] SGCA 12; [2006] 2 SLR(R) 637 (Yong CJ, Chao JA and Kan J).

as the condition was exclusively for the purchaser's benefit, she was entitled to waive it. Importantly, the court held that it did not matter whether she had actually waived the condition:

> On the facts, it is unlikely that there would be a waiver by the [purchaser], but that is not the issue. The question is whether specific performance is available to her, and the answer is it is if she wants it. When the agreement was signed, specific performance was available to the [purchaser], and she had thereby acquired the equitable interest ...[1588]

787. The effect of the constructive trust was thoroughly examined by Rajah JC (as he then was) in *Chen Con-Ling Tony v. Quay Properties Pte Ltd.*[1589] The seller, who is a trustee of the property, must hold it for the purchaser pending completion. He must also be reasonably prudent in preserving the property and any rights that run with the property (e.g., a profitable lease). However, the risk of any deterioration or destruction that is not due to the fault of the seller lies with the purchaser. The purchaser, who is the equitable owner of the property, is entitled to lodge a caveat to protect his interest. However, he cannot insist on taking possession of the property before the purchase price is paid. Pending such payment, the seller is entitled to retain possession of the property by virtue of a lien over it.

§5. Remedies

I. Purchaser's Remedies

A. *Specific Performance*

788. In light of the ever-increasing property prices, a purchaser is likely to prefer the remedy of specific performance.[1590] If the property is bought for residential use, the courts are usually willing to order specific performance, subject of course to the usual bars. Where the contract of sale is to proceed by way of an OTP and the seller refuses to grant one, the court may order the seller to grant the OTP, failing which the Registrar of the Supreme Court shall have the power to grant and sign the OTP on the seller's behalf.[1591]

B. *Abatement*

789. Where the seller delivers to the purchaser a property which differs substantially from that which the purchaser had contracted to buy, the latter may accept or

1588. [2006] SGCA 12; [2006] 2 SLR(R) 637 at [23].
1589. [2004] SGHC 31; [2004] 2 SLR(R) 181.
1590. *See generally* Andrew Phang Boon Leong *et. al.*, *The Law of Contract in Singapore* (Academy Publishing, 2012) Chapters 20–21.
1591. *Singh Chiranjeev v. Joseph Mathew* [2008] SGHC 222; [2009] 2 SLR(R) 73 at [42].

reject it. Where the purchaser decides to accept it, he is entitled to abatement, i.e. reduction of the contracted purchase price provided that the property delivered could be shown to be less valuable.[1592] A claim for abatement is usually successful where the floor area of the property is less than what was described in the contract, which obviously renders the property less valuable.[1593]

C. Damages

790. The primary purpose of damages is to compensate a plaintiff for any expectation loss suffered. If the purchaser is buying the property for his own use, damages are assessed by the difference between the purchase price and the market price of a similar property at the completion date.[1594] If, on the other hand, the property is bought for investment purposes, e.g. to be rented out or to be resold for a profit, those losses must be proven, subject to the usual rules on remoteness of loss.

791. Where the vendor wrongfully revokes an OTP, the court has to consider whether the purchaser would have been able to exercise it in time and whether he would be able to complete the purchase. In *Woo Kah Wai*, the Court of Appeal was satisfied with the purchaser's ability to do both and awarded her damages based on her expectation loss, assessed by the difference between the contract price and the value of the property at the putative date of completion.[1595]

II. Seller's Remedies

A. Forfeiture of Deposit

792. Where the purchaser refuses to complete the purchase, the seller is entitled to forfeit any deposit paid. However, the seller is not entitled to forfeit a part payment of the purchase price, unless otherwise agreed. The amount of deposit to be paid is usually described in the contract. Any other payment must thus be taken to be a part payment. Where the amount which the seller seeks to forfeit is excessive, the purchaser is likely to challenge the forfeiture on the ground that the term allowing forfeiture amounts to a penalty clause.[1596] While a deposit could be forfeited even if the seller has suffered no loss, a liquidated damages clause is enforceable only if the sum to be forfeited is a genuine estimate of the seller's loss.

1592. *Kassim Syed Ali v. Grace Development Pte Ltd* [1998] SGCA 38; [1998] 2 SLR(R) 558.

1593. *See e.g. Chin Tien Sung v. Yat Yuen Hong Co Pte Ltd* [1993] SGHC 103; [1993] 1 SLR(R) 784 (shortfall of 3.82%); *Hew Tze Yin v. Ming Teck Co Pte Ltd* [1990] SGHC 74; [1990] 2 SLR(R) 301 (shortfall of 4.8%); *Chong Ah Kwee v. Viva Realty Pte Ltd* [1990] SGHC 20; [1990] 1 SLR(R) 244 (shortfall of 16.47%); *Yeo Brothers C (Pte) Ltd v. Atlas Properties (Pte) Ltd* [1987] SGHC 38; [1987] SLR(R) 490 (10.77%).

1594. *Lie Kie Siang v. Han Ngum Juan Marcus* [1991] SGHC 130; [1991] 2 SLR(R) 511.

1595. [2014] SGCA 41; [2014] 4 SLR 166.

1596. *See e.g. Indian Overseas Bank v. Cheng Lai Geok* [1993] SGCA 4; [1993] 1 SLR(R) 32; *Allgreen Properties Ltd v. Lim Lay Bee* [1998] SGHC 73; [1998] 1 SLR(R) 703.

B. Damages

793. The seller is also entitled to damages, to be assessed by the difference between the contracted purchase price and the amount the seller has, or could have, sold the property for. The usual rules on mitigation apply.

§6. VENDOR'S AND PURCHASER'S LIEN

I. Vendor's Lien

794. Where the purchaser has yet to pay the purchase price, the seller is entitled to a lien over the property to secure the debt. Where the property is still with the seller, the lien entitles him/her to retain possession of the property.[1597] On the other hand, where the property has already been transferred to the purchaser, the lien entitles the seller to apply to the court for either a retransfer of the property or for the property to be sold so that the debt could be satisfied using the sale proceeds.[1598]

II. Purchaser's Lien

795. Where the seller refuses to complete the sale, the purchaser is entitled to a lien over the property to secure the return of any deposit or part payment.[1599] Even where it was the purchaser who refused to complete the purchase, a lien may arise to secure the purchaser's claim for the return of a part payment (if it is not forfeitable) but not for the return of a deposit (which is forfeitable).[1600]

1597. *Lysaght v. Edwards* (1876) 2 Ch D 499 at 506; *Phillips v. Silvester* (1872) 8 Ch App 173.
1598. *Re Caveat No CV/21366D lodged by Lim Saw Hak* [1996] SGHC 11; [1996] 1 SLR(R) 70 at [15].

1599. *Chip Thye Enterprises Pte Ltd v. Development Bank of Singapore Ltd* [1994] SGCA 59; [1994] 2 SLR(R) 68; *PACC Offshore Services Holdings Ltd v. Kensteel Engineering Pte Ltd* [2017] SGHC 175.
1600. *Bestland Development Pte Ltd v. Manit Udomkunnatum and another* [1997] SGCA 4; [1997] 1 SLR(R) 177.

Chapter 2. Contract for the Sale of Goods

§1. Introduction

796. Unlike a contract for the sale of land, the creation of a contract for the sale of goods need not satisfy any formality requirements for it to be valid and enforceable. Basic principles of contract formation apply. However, this area of the law is unique in that it is governed by the Sale of Goods Act (SGA).[1601] However, while the detailed provisions set out in the SGA address almost the entire range of issues relating to contracts for the sale of goods, this chapter will focus less on the purely contractual aspects of such contracts and more on the rules relating to the passing of title in goods as well as the specific enforceability of such contracts.[1602]

§2. Transfer of Title by Seller

I. Passing of Title Based on Intention

797. Once the contract is concluded, the seller is under a duty to deliver the goods to be purchaser. The transfer of title in the goods, however, is independent from the physical delivery of the goods. Section 17 of the SGA provides that title will be transferred to the purchaser 'at such time as the parties to the contract intend it to be transferred' and that the parties' intention shall be ascertained by having regard to 'the terms of the contract, the conduct of the parties and the circumstances of the case'.[1603] In other words, the contract, on its very own, is sufficient to effect a transfer of title.[1604]

II. Default Rules on Passing of Title

798. Section 18 of the SGA further sets out five default rules for determining when title in the goods passes. Rule 1 provides that, where there is an unconditional

1601. (Cap. 393, 1999 Rev. Ed.). Section 61(1) defines 'goods' to mean 'all personal chattels other than things in action and money', and 'includes emblements, industrial growing crops, and things attached to or forming part of the land which are agreed to be severed before sale or under the contract of sale and includes an undivided share in goods'.

1602. *See* Tan Yock Lin, *Personal Property Law* (Academy Publishing, 2014) Chapter 11; Howard Hunter, *The Law of Sales in Singapore* (Academy Publishing, 2017) Chapter 11. For other comprehensive accounts of the subject, see also Michael Bridge, *The Sale of Goods*, 3rd edn (OUP, 2014); Michael Bridge (ed.), *Benjamin's Sale of Goods*, 10th edn (Sweet & Maxwell, 2017); Christian Twigg-Flesner, Rick Canavan and Hector MacQueen, *Atiyah and Adam's Sale of Goods*, 13th edn (Pearson, 2016).

1603. *See BP Refinery Singapore Pte Ltd v. Amazon Group Ltd* [1998] SGHC 256; [1998] 3 SLR(R) 4.

1604. This was first recognised in *Cochrane v. Moore* (1890) 25 QBD 57 at 71. The legal position for contracts for the sale of land is very different. Recall that, after a contract of sale is entered into, the vendor must complete the sale by effecting a registrable transfer of the title in the purchaser's favour. *See* Chapter 1 (Contract for the Sale of Land) §3.II.

contract for the sale of specific goods in a deliverable state, title passes to the purchaser at the time of contract, notwithstanding that the time of payment and time of delivery might have been postponed to a later time.[1605]

799. However, where the goods are specific (i.e., identified) but are not in a deliverable state, Rule 2 provides that title passes only when they have been put into a deliverable state and the purchaser has notice of this.[1606]

800. As for specific goods in a deliverable state which require measurement or testing for the purpose of ascertaining their price, Rule 3 provides that title passes only when the measurement or testing has been performed and the purchaser has notice of it.[1607]

801. Rule 4 provides that if the goods are delivered to the purchaser on approval or on a sale or return (i.e., the purchaser has the right to reject or return the goods), title in the goods passes to the purchaser when he signifies his approval.[1608] Where he does not signify his approval but retains the goods, the title will pass upon the expiration of a stipulated deadline or, in the absence of such deadline, upon the expiration of a reasonable time.[1609]

802. Finally, Rule 5 lays down the default rules for the sale of unascertained or future goods by description. When goods fitting the agreed description is unconditionally appropriated to the contract, either by the seller with the assent of the purchaser or by the purchaser with the assent of the seller, title in the goods passes to the purchaser.[1610] There are two situations in which the goods are to be regarded as having been unconditionally appropriated to the contract. First, where the seller, pursuant to its contractual obligation and without reserving a right of disposal,[1611] delivers the goods to the purchaser or to a carrier, bailee or custodier for the purpose of transmission to the purchaser.[1612] The mere preparation of the goods for shipment, however, does not constitute unconditional appropriation.[1613] Second, where a specified quantity of the unascertained goods are to be appropriated from an identified bulk, and the bulk is reduced to (or to less than) that quantity, title in the remaining goods will pass to the purchaser if he is the only person whose goods are due out of the bulk.[1614] Where there is more than one purchaser whose goods

1605. SGA, section 18, Rule 1.
1606. SGA, section 18, Rule 2. *See Siang Hoa Goldsmith Pte Ltd v. The Wing On Fire and Marine Insurance Co Ltd* [1998] SGCA 31; [1998] 2 SLR(R) 408.
1607. SGA, section 18, Rule 3.
1608. SGA, section 18, Rule 4(a). *See Wang Wang Pawnshop Pte Ltd v. K J Tiffany* [2004] SGHC 50; [2004] 2 SLR(R) 222.
1609. SGA, section 18, Rule 4(b).
1610. SGA, section 18, Rule 5(1).
1611. For a seller's reservation of the right of disposal, see SGA, section 19. *See also Hua Seng Sawmill Co Bhd v. QBE Insurance (Malaysia) Bhd* [2003] SGHC 233; [2003] 4 SLR(R) 449.
1612. SGA, section 18, Rule 5(2).
1613. *Yap Chin Hock v. Cheng Wang Loong* [1964] MLJ 276 (Singapore).
1614. SGA, section 18, Rule 5(3) & 4.

are due out of an identified bulk, and the purchase price has been paid, then the purchasers will become owners in common of the bulk.[1615]

III. The Importance of Locating Title

803. Determining who has title to the goods is important for several reasons. There are implications that matter to both the seller or the purchaser. First, unless otherwise agreed, risk passes with the title.[1616] Thus, if the title has passed to the purchaser, and the goods perished while in the seller's possession, the loss is to be borne by the purchaser unless otherwise agreed. Second, where the goods are damaged or destroyed due to the negligence of a third party, e.g. a carrier, only the person having title to the goods could sue.[1617] Third, where the party having possession of the goods becomes insolvent, the goods will not be included within the pool of assets for *pari passu* distribution if title belongs to the other party.

804. From the purchaser's perspective, having title to the goods is important for a few reasons. First, where the seller fails to deliver the goods, the purchaser's title may strengthen his claim for specific performance, and avail him/her of alternative actions in conversion and detinue.[1618] However, this is subject to the self-help remedies available to an unpaid seller, such as the right to enforce a lien or to retain the goods, to stop goods in transit, and to rescind and resell.[1619] Second, where the seller disposes of the goods to a third party, the purchaser has a claim against the third party in conversion or detinue[1620] unless the third party is a bona fide purchaser for value[1621] or where one of the statutory exceptions apply.[1622]

§3. Retention of Title by Seller

805. The contract of sale may provide that, even upon delivery of the goods to the purchaser, title in the goods shall remain with the seller until the price is paid. Often employed as a quasi-security measure, a contractual term to this effect is known as a retention of title clause or a *Romalpa* clause,[1623] and may be understood as a reservation of the right of disposal allowed under section 19 of the SGA.[1624] The relevant provision reads:

1615. SGA, section 20A.
1616. SGA, section 20.
1617. *The 'ASL Power'* [2002] SGHC 164; [2003] 1 SLR(R) 545.
1618. *See* §3 below.
1619. SGA, sections 38–48.
1620. *Langton v. Higgins* (1859) 4 H&N 402; *Denny v. Skelton* (1916) 115 LT 305.
1621. *See* Chapter 4 (Possession and Appropriation).
1622. *See* §5 below.
1623. After the eponymous case, *Aluminium Industrie Vaassen BV v. Romalpa Aluminium Ltd* [1976] 1 WLR 676.
1624. *Clough Mill Ltd v. Martin* [1985] 1 WLR 111.

> Where there is a contract for the sale of specific goods or where goods are subsequently appropriated to the contract, the seller may, by the terms of the contract or appropriation, reserve the right of disposal of the goods until certain conditions are fulfilled; and in such a case, notwithstanding the delivery of the goods to the buyer … the property in the goods does not pass to the buyer until the conditions imposed by the seller are fulfilled.

806. Difficult issues arise from the many variants of the *Romalpa* clause. For example, an attempt to claim not just the goods but also any sale proceeds will succeed only if the seller can establish a trust or fiduciary relationship which would allow tracing.[1625] Similarly difficult is where the passing of title is conditioned not only upon payment of the price but also upon the purchaser discharging all liabilities arising between the purchaser and seller, e.g. an earlier unsecured indebtedness, or even future indebtedness.[1626] Either of these situations can potentially be construed as creating a charge, which is void if not registered.[1627] These complex issues are beyond the scope of this chapter.[1628]

807. Another interesting question is whether a *Romalpa* clause is effective in retaining the title in goods that are incorporated into manufactures or affixed to land or buildings. The simple answer is that it loses effect when the goods have lost their identity[1629] or have become fixtures.[1630] As this requires consideration of the principles of accession and specification, it will be addressed in a separate chapter.[1631]

§4. Specific Performance

808. Where the seller fails to deliver specific or ascertained goods, the court may, if it thinks fit, orders specific performance in the purchaser's favour.[1632] As a discretionary remedy, the court will order specific performance only if the goods are 'of peculiar and practically unique value' to the purchaser.[1633]

1625. *Aluminium Industrie Vaassen BV v. Romalpa Aluminium Ltd* [1976] 1 WLR 676; *Precious Shipping Co Ltd v. OW Bunker Far East (Singapore) Pte Ltd* [2015] SGHC 187; [2015] 4 SLR 1229 at [35]–[38].
1626. *See Thyssen v. Armour Edelstahlwerke AG* [1991] 2 AC 339.
1627. *Cf Thyssen v. Armour Edelstahlwerke AG* [1991] 2 AC 339.
1628. *See* Louise Gullifer, '"Sales" on retention of title terms: is the English law analysis broken?' (2017) 133 LQR 244; Gerard McCormack, 'Reservation of title – past, present and future' [1994] Conv 129; Kelry CF Loi, '*Quistclose* Trusts and *Romalpa* Clauses: Substance and *Nemo Dat* in Corporate Insolvency' (2012) 128 LQR 412; Kelry CF Loi, 'Tracing and the Future of *Romalpa* Clauses' [2008] RLR 76.
1629. *Borden (UK) Ltd v. Scottish Timber Products Ltd* [1981] 1 Ch 25.
1630. *Gebrueder Buehler AG v. Chi Man Kwong Peter* [1986] SGHC 28; [1985-1986] SLR(R) 845.
1631. *See* Chapter 5 (Accession and Specification).
1632. SGA, section 52.
1633. *Behnke v. Bede Shipping Co Ltd* [1927] 1 KB 649 at 661. *See also Phillips v. Lamdin* [1949] 2 KB 33; *Dougan v. Ley* [1946] HCA 3; (1946) 71 CLR 142.

809. The remedy is available whether or not title in the goods has passed to the purchaser. Where a title has passed, the purchaser may also bring an alternative claim in detinue for delivery up of the goods. However, for consistency, delivery up will be ordered only in the very same circumstances where an order for specific performance will be made.[1634] While this might suggest that the passing of title is immaterial, the courts seem to be more inclined to order specific performance where the purchaser claims as an owner.[1635]

810. Where a title has not passed to the purchaser, e.g. because the contract provides that title is to pass only upon delivery, an interesting issue arises as to whether, in the appropriate circumstances, the purchaser may become the equitable owner of the goods under a vendor-purchaser constructive trust. Recall that, in the context of sale of land, the availability of specific performance will lead to the imposition of a constructive trust in the purchaser's favour.[1636] Although there is no reported example, the same principle ought to also apply to sale of goods. Thus, *in Holroyd v. Marshall*, Westbury LC said:

> A contract for valuable consideration, by which it is agreed to make a present transfer of property, passes at once the beneficial interest, provided the contract is one of which a Court of Equity will decree specific performance. In the language of Lord Hardwicke, the vendor becomes a trustee for the vendee; subject, of course, to the contract being one to be specifically performed. And this is true, not only of contracts relating to real estate, but also of contracts relating to personal property, provided that the latter are such as a Court of Equity would direct to be specifically performed.[1637]

811. Where the seller disposes of the goods to a third party, the purchaser, who is an owner in equity, may recover the goods by bringing an equitable ownership claim, except where the third party is a bona fide purchaser for value.

§5. Transfer of Title by Non-owner

812. Where a person having possession of goods belonging to someone else gives it away to a third party without the latter's consent,[1638] the general rule is that the third party acquires no better title than the seller.[1639] This is the effect of the nemo dat rule. However, where the transfer is by way of sale, several statutory exceptions to the nemo dat rule exist to give the third party a good title.

1634. *Whiteley Ltd v. Hilt* [1918] 2 KB 808; *Cohen v. Roche* [1927] 1 KB 169.
1635. Christian Twigg-Flesner, Rick Canavan and Hector MacQueen, *Atiyah and Adam's Sale of Goods*, 13th edn (Pearson, 2016) at 466.
1636. *Lysaght v. Edwards* (1876) 2 Ch D 499; *Lim Kim Som v. Sheriffa Taibah bte Abdul Rahman* [1994] SGCA 15; [1994] 1 SLR(R) 233. *See* Chapter 1 (Contract for the Sale of Land) §4.
1637. (1862) HLC 191 at 209.
1638. *See* Tan Yock Lin, *Personal Property Law* (Academy Publishing, 2014) Chapter 11; Howard Hunter, *The Law of Sales in Singapore* (Academy Publishing, 2017) Chapter 12.
1639. *See* Chapter 4 (Possession and Appropriation).

I. Voidable Title

813. Where a seller of goods who has only voidable title to them sells them to a third party before the original owner avoids the earlier transaction, the third-party purchaser acquires good title to the goods provided that he buys them in good faith and without notice of the seller's defect of title.[1640] This is the effect of section 23 of the SGA. In most of the cases on this topic, the earlier transaction between the original owner and the seller is a contract of sale tainted by a vitiating factor. Here the distinction between a void and voidable contract is crucial. If the contract is void, e.g. because there was an operative mistake, no title passes to the seller and section 23 does not apply. Section 23 specifically refers to a voidable contract, e.g. a contract induced by misrepresentation or duress. Unlike the four other exceptions to the nemo dat rule discussed below, section 23 may be understood as setting out a weak exception, for the seller does have title to the goods, albeit a voidable one.

II. Estoppel Arising from the Owner's Conduct

814. Where a person who is in possession of another person's goods sells them to a third party, section 21(1) of the SGA provides that the third party acquires no better title than the seller unless the owner is 'by his conduct precluded from denying the seller's authority to sell'. For the proviso to apply, the owner's conduct must give the third-party purchaser the impression that the seller had authority to sell the goods, such as by arming the former with the indicia of title, and the third party must also be a bona fide purchaser for value.[1641]

III. Mercantile Agent

815. Section 2(1) of the Factors Act[1642] provides that, where an owner of goods places them (or documents of title)[1643] in the hands of a mercantile agent, any sale made by the latter in the ordinary course of business of a mercantile agent[1644] shall be valid as though he was expressly authorised by the owner, provided that the purchaser has acted in good faith and had no notice of the seller's lack of authority.

1640. For a famous example of the earlier transaction being rescinded in time, see *Car & Universal Finance Co Ltd v. Caldwell* [1965] 1 QB 525.
1641. *Commercial & Savings Bank of Somalia v. Joo Seng Co* [1988] SGHC 62; [1988] 2 SLR(R) 57.
1642. (Cap. 386, 1994 Rev. Ed.).
1643. *See Tan Siah Poh v. Orient Consumer Credit Pte Ltd (Fullhouten Credit Pte Ltd and another, third parties)* [1999] SGHC 130; [1999] 2 SLR(R) 430 (where it was held that the registration book of a car is not a document of title).
1644. *See Commercial & Savings Bank of Somalia v. Joo Seng Co* [1988] SGHC 62; [1988] 2 SLR(R) 57 (where the charterers were held not to be mercantile agents).

IV. Seller in Possession

816. A seller in possession is one who, having sold certain goods, continues to be in possession of those goods (or the documents of title to those goods). Section 24 of the SGA provides that, where such a seller sells and delivers the goods to a third party, and the third party receives the goods in good faith and has no notice of the earlier sale, the sale is effective as though it were expressly authorised by the earlier purchaser.[1645] As the section refers to the earlier purchaser as 'the owner of the goods', it is clear that the title to the goods must have passed under the earlier sale. By giving the third-party purchaser a better title, the section creates an exception to the nemo dat rule.

V. Buyer in Possession

817. A buyer in possession is one who obtains, with the seller's consent, possession of the goods or the documents of title to the goods. Section 25 of the SGA provides that, where such a buyer sells and delivers the goods to a third party, and the third party receives the goods in good faith and has no notice of the right of the seller, the sale is effective as though the purchaser were a mercantile agent in possession of the goods (or documents of title) with the seller's consent.[1646] In other words, the sale is effective to give the third-party purchaser good title.[1647] As the section also refers to the seller as 'the owner', it is clear that title in the goods did not pass to the buyer under the earlier sale.[1648] By giving the third-party purchaser a better title, the section creates another exception to the nemo dat rule.

1645. *See also* Factors Act, section 8.
1646. *See also* Factors Act, section 9.
1647. *See* §5.II. above.
1648. *Cf* Tan Yock Lin, *Personal Property Law* (Academy Publishing, 2014) at 650–51.

Chapter 3. Transfer upon Death

§1. Testamentary Disposition by Will

818. A testamentary disposition may be made by will. For a will to be valid, the formality requirements prescribed by the Wills Act[1649] (WA) must be complied with. The will must be executed in writing, signed by the testator and attested by at least two witnesses.[1650] Any gift under the will to an attesting witness or his (or her) spouse is void, except where the attestation of that witness is not necessary for the execution of the will (e.g., where there are two other attesting witnesses).[1651]

819. The person responsible for administering the will is called an executor (or personal representative). The executor holds the assets on a trust for the beneficiary. Prior to the completion of administration, the beneficiary has 'a direct and real interest', specifically a vested (albeit contingent) right to obtain the trust asset at some future time.[1652] This is a chose in action which the beneficiary is free to dispose of to a third party, either by assignment or by declaration of trust.[1653] Where the asset in question consists of land, the chose in action is a caveatable interest.[1654]

820. Where a will fails to carry out the testator's intention due to a clerical error or a failure to understand the testator's instructions, a court has a statutory power to order that the will be rectified so as to carry out the testator's intention.[1655] The identical statutory provision in the UK has been broadly interpreted in *Marley v. Rawlings*[1656] such that the phrase 'clerical error' is not confined to a mistake in the copying or writing of the will but includes also any 'mistake arising out of office work of a relatively routine nature, such as preparing, filing, sending, organising the execution of, the [will]'.[1657]

821. Aside from the existence of vitiating factors invalidating the will,[1658] revocation of the will can occur in four situations.[1659] First, where the testator marries after the execution of the will.[1660] Second, where the testator executes another

1649. (Cap. 352, 1996 Rev. Ed.).
1650. WA, section 6.
1651. WA, section 10.
1652. *Sheares Betty Hang Kiu v. Chow Kwok Chi* [2006] SGHC 34; [2006] 2 SLR(R) 285 at [34]–[38].
1653. *Sheares Betty Hang Kiu v. Chow Kwok Chi* [2006] SGHC 34; [2006] 2 SLR(R) 285; *BOK v. BOL* [2017] SGHC 316 at [138].
1654. *See Diaz v. Diaz* [1997] SGCA 55; [1997] 3 SLR(R) 759.
1655. WA, section 28. On the interpretation of wills, see Goh Yihan and Yip Man, '*Marley v. Rawlings*: Reflections from Singapore' [2014] SJLS 218.
1656. [2014] UKSC 2; [2014] 2 WLR 213.
1657. [2014] UKSC 2; [2014] 2 WLR 213 at [75]. For comment on this decision, see Barry C. Crown, 'Where There's a Will, There's a Way' (2015) 27 SAcLJ 222.
1658. *See e.g. Chee Mu Lin Muriel v. Chee Ka Lin Caroline* [2010] SGCA 27; [2010] 4 SLR 373 (testamentary incapacity); *BOK v. BOL* [2017] SGHC 316 (misrepresentation, mistake, undue influence and unconscionability).
1659. WA, section 15.
1660. WA, section 13.

will.[1661] Third, where the testator revokes the will by a duly executed written declaration.[1662] Fourth, where the testator destroys the will with the intention of revoking it.[1663]

§2. Intestate Succession

822. Where a person passes away intestate (i.e., without leaving a will), his assets shall be distributed in accordance to the rules set out in section 7 of the Intestate Succession Act[1664] (ISA). Given the clear and fixed rules on distribution, there are far fewer reported disputes among family members over the assets of an intestate. Under the ISA, there are generally four categories of persons with a prospect of inheriting from the deceased's estate: spouse, issues, parents and siblings.

823. *Rule 1*: If the deceased leaves only a spouse, the spouse shall be entitled to the whole of the estate.

824. *Rule 2*: If the deceased leaves only a spouse and a child, the spouse shall be entitled to one-half of the estate while the remaining half belongs to the child.

825. *Rule 3*: As an extension of the situation in *Rule 2*, if the deceased has more than one child, the remaining half shall be distributed equally among the children or, if any of them has passed away, to his or her descendant(s).

826. *Rule 4*: If the deceased leaves only a spouse and a parent, the spouse shall be entitled to one-half of the estate and the parent to the other half. If there is more than one parent, the other half of the estate shall be distributed equally among them.

827. *Rule 5*: If the deceased leaves only a parent, the parent shall take the entire estate. If there is more than one parent, the estate shall be distributed equally among them.

828. *Rule 6*: If there are no surviving spouse, issue or parent, any sibling shall be entitled to the entire estate. If there is more than one sibling, the estate shall be distributed equally among them. If a sibling has passed away, his or her share shall be distributed to his or her issue(s).

829. *Rule 7*: If the deceased leaves only a grandparent, the grandparent shall take the whole of the estate. If there are more than one surviving grandparents, they shall take the estate in equal shares.

1661. WA, section 15(b).
1662. WA, section 15(c).
1663. WA, section 15(d).
1664. (Cap. 146, 2013 Rev. Ed.).

830. *Rule 8*: If there are no surviving spouse, descendant, parent, sibling (or his/her descendant) but uncles and aunts, the uncles and aunts shall take the whole of the estate in equal portions.

831. *Rule 9*: In default of distribution under *Rules 1* to *8*, the Government shall be entitled to the whole of the estate.

832. The estate will be administered by an appointed administrator, who holds the property on trust for the beneficiaries in accordance to the statutory distribution rules. However, prior to administration, the beneficiaries do not have an equitable or beneficial interest in any particular asset comprised in the estate. Thus, where a parcel of land is comprised in the estate, no beneficiary has a specific interest in it to support the lodgment of a caveat.[1665] This, however, does not deprive the beneficiaries of the *locus standi* to sue the administrator or a third party for the preservation of the trust assets.[1666]

§3. Rule of Survivorship

833. In the case of a joint-tenanted property, the death of one joint tenant will result in the entire interest vesting in the surviving joint tenant(s). In contrast, where a tenant in common dies, his interest passes either to a beneficiary under a will or, in the absence of a will, to his statutory next of kin based on the distribution rules under the ISA.

834. The distinction between a joint tenancy and a tenancy in common is of utmost importance in the context of co-ownership of land.[1667] Given that the purchase of land will require significant financial commitment, it is reasonable to assume that most co-purchasers of land would have made a conscious and informed decision in choosing between the two forms of co-ownership. However, this assumption is now undermined by equity's dislike of a joint tenancy. The presumption of resulting trust (or of advancement), if established, operates to override the mode of holding reflected in the land register.[1668]

835. The distinction between the two modes of co-ownership also frequently arises in the context of bank accounts in joint names.[1669] Where the banking agreement does not specify the mode of co-ownership, the courts are inclined to find that

1665. *Shaan Taseer v. Aamna Taseer* [2012] SGCA 52; [2012] 4 SLR 1049.

1666. *Wong Moy (administratrix of the estate of Theng Chee Khim, deceased) v. Soo Ah Choy* [1996] SGCA 52; [1996] 3 SLR(R) 27; *Ching Chew Weng Paul v. Ching Pui Sim* [2009] SGHC 277; [2010] 2 SLR 76; *Omar Ali bin Mohd v. Syed Jafaralsadeg bin Abdulkadir Alhadad* [1995] SGHC 137; [1995] 2 SLR(R) 407.

1667. *See* Part I (Land), Chapter 3 (Co-ownership) §2.

1668. *See* Part I (Land), Chapter 3 (Co-ownership) §6.II.C.

1669. *See Tsu Soo Sin v. Oei Tjiong Bin* [2008] SGCA 46; [2009] 1 SLR(R) 529; *Sabnani Kan v. Lachmandas Ramesh* [1994] SGCA 72; [1994] 2 SLR(R) 474; *One Investment and Consultancy Ltd v.*

the account is held on a joint tenancy. In *Tsu Soo Sin v. Oei Tjiong Bin* the Court of Appeal held that 'an account named 'Tony Oei/Oei Boon Wan', without any provision for how the two persons named should share the account, indicate a joint tenancy rather than a tenancy in common'.[1670] Where there is clear evidence of the respective contribution of each account holder, a presumption of resulting trust will likely be found, thus creating a tenancy in common in equity.

Cham Poh Meng (DBS Bank Ltd, garnishee) [2016] SGHC 208; [2016] 5 SLR 923; *Soo Yen Sun v. Oversea-Chinese Banking Corp Ltd* [2009] SGHC 243.

1670. [2008] SGCA 46; [2009] 1 SLR(R) 529 at [65] (Chao, Phang and Rajah JJA).

Chapter 4. Possession and Appropriation

§1. Introduction

836. In the realm of property law,[1671] there is an old saying that possession is nine tenths of the law. In other words, it is easier for a person who has possession of an asset to establish and enforce ownership in it. While the saying is not without truth, one can say with some confidence that it has lost much of its significance in modern property law.

§2. Possession of Land

837. In Singapore, the erosion of the importance of possession is most clearly seen in land law. The doctrine of adverse possession was abolished in 1994. In an attempt to reinforce the principle of indefeasibility, section 50 of the Land Titles Act now states that no title adverse to that of a registered proprietor can be acquired by any length of possession.[1672] Moreover, even if an occupier of land has a right to exclusive possession (e.g., he was granted a lease), his interest is in a precarious state unless it is a lease not exceeding 7 years (in which case it is an overriding interest) or if it is registered or protected by a caveat.[1673] This is to be contrasted with the position under English law where an interest of a person in actual occupation constitutes an overriding interest.[1674] From this comparison, one can say that Singapore's land registration system prioritises the mirror principle at the expense of the concept of possession.

§3. Possession of Chattels

I. Delivery of Possession

838. The concept of possession plays a far more important role in so far as chattels are concerned.[1675] Outside the context of sale of goods, title in chattels would pass only if the donor has manifested an intention to make a gift (donative intent) and has handed over the chattel to the donee (delivery). In other words, the donee does not acquire title in the chattel until he takes possession of it from the donor.

1671. *See* Eric Descheemaeker (ed.), *The Consequences of Possession* (Edinburg University Press, 2014).
1672. (Cap. 157, 2004 Rev. Ed.).
1673. *See* Part I (Land), Chapter 4 (Torrens System).
1674. Land Registration Act 2002 (Cap. 9) section 29(2)(a)(ii); Schedule 3, para. 2.
1675. *See* Robin Hickey, *Property and the Law of Finders* (Hart Publishing, 2010); David Fox, 'Relativity of Title in Law and at Equity' [2006] CLJ 330.

II. Possessory Title by Appropriation

839. A person can also acquire title in chattels by appropriation, i.e. the taking of possession without the original owner's consent. The *locus classicus* for this proposition is the old case of *Armory v. Delamirie*.[1676] The plaintiff, a chimney sweeper, found a ring while cleaning a chimney and brought it to the defendant goldsmith for appraisal. The defendant's apprentice, who under the pretense of weighing it, removed the stones attached to the ring and refused to return them. The court held that, although the plaintiff did not acquire absolute title in the ring, he nevertheless acquired such title that is enforceable against all but the rightful owner(s). The plaintiff was thus able to maintain an action of trover against the defendant.

840. The principle in *Armory* was briefly considered in *Wong Seng Kwan v. Public Prosecutor*.[1677] The accused found a lost wallet at a casino washroom and kept the money for himself. He was convicted of dishonest misappropriation under section 403 of the Penal Code.[1678] While the main issue was squarely within the remit of criminal law, the court emphasised that because a finder acquires possessory title, the act of taking possession does not by itself give rise to any civil or criminal liability. This is consistent with Explanation 2 to the section, which states that liability for dishonest misappropriation arises only if the finder appropriates the chattel to his own use 'when he knows or has the means of discovering the owner, or before he has used reasonable means to discover and give notice to the owner, and has kept the property a reasonable time to enable the owner to claim it'.

841. From the judgment, one could imply that had the accused made a reasonable attempt to return the wallet, he would be entitled to keep it if the true owner could not be found. Indeed, this was the conclusion arrived at in the English case of *Parker v. British Airways Board*.[1679] Mr Parker found a gold bracelet in the executive lounge of British Airways. He handed it to an employee at the lounge and requested that the bracelet be returned to him if the owner could not be found. The bracelet remained unclaimed and British Airways sold it for £850. Mr Parker sued for the value of the bracelet. The Court of Appeal found in Mr Parker's favour as he had discharged his obligation as a finder. Although the bracelet was found within the premises of British Airways, the fact that they did not manifest any intention to take control of the bracelet meant that they did not acquire a possessory title before Mr Parker did.

842. What would the legal position be had Mr Parker kept the bracelet without attempting to find its true owner? Unlike in *Wong Seng Kwan*, where the owner of the wallet was eventually identified, the bracelet remained unclaimed by its true

1676. (1721) 1 Stra 505.
1677. [2012] SGHC 81; [2012] 3 SLR 12.
1678. (Cap. 224, 2008 Rev. Ed.).
1679. [1982] 1 QB 1004.

owner. Does the British Airways Board acquire a better possessory title? The judgment is not entirely on this point. The Court of Appeal made a passing reference to the case of a trespassing finder:

843. Some qualification has also to be made in the case of the trespassing finder. The person vis a vis whom he is a trespasser has a better title. The fundamental basis of this is clearly public policy. Wrongdoers should not benefit from their wrongdoing. This requirement would be met if the trespassing finder acquired no rights. That would, however, produce the free-for-all situation to which I have already referred, in that anyone could take the article from the trespassing finder. Accordingly, the common law has been obliged to give rights to someone else, the owner ex hypothesi being unknown. The obvious candidate is the occupier of the property upon which the finder was trespassing.[1680]

844. However, Mr Parker was clearly not a trespasser. He entered the lounge as a flight passenger with the permission of the British Airways Board. The better view is that he does acquire a possessory title,[1681] but this should not absolve him of any criminal liability.[1682]

III. Relativity of Title

845. The doctrine of relativity of title is a simple means of resolving title disputes. From the judgment in *Armory*, it can be implied that the defendant also acquired a possessory title to the stones. However, as the plaintiff had acquired a possessory title before the defendant did, the plaintiff's title was stronger. The first in time prevails. Certainly, had the true owner of the ring appeared before the court, his title would trump the titles of the plaintiff and defendant. In short, while each possessor along the chain acquires a possessory title, the doctrine of relativity of title operates to determine who among them has the best (or a better) title. As a general rule, the possessory titles become weaker down the chain.

846. For avoidance of doubt, it is not always the case that all titles within the chain are possessory titles. A possessory title can be trumped by an earlier non-possessory title. Suppose *A* agrees to sell a rare book to *B*. Under the Sale of Goods Act,[1683] title in the book may pass from *A* to *B* even prior to delivery if they intended it to pass or if one of the statutory default rules apply.[1684] Before delivery, the book was stolen by *C*. In such a case, *B*'s non-possessory title would trump *C*'s possessory title. The decision in *Aero-Gate Pte Ltd v. Engen Marine Engineering Pte Ltd* is explicable in the same way.[1685]

1680. [1982] 1 QB 1004 at 1009.
1681. *See*, e.g., *Kowal v. Ellis* (1977) 76 DLR (3d) 546 (Manitoba Court of Appeal).
1682. *Wong Seng Kwan v. Public Prosecutor* [2012] SGHC 81; [2012] 3 SLR 12.
1683. (Cap. 393, 1999 Rev. Ed.).
1684. *See* Chapter 2 (Contract for the Sale of Goods) §2.
1685. [2013] SGHC 148; [2013] 4 SLR 409. *See also* Chapter 5 (Accession and Specification) §2.

IV. The Nemo Dat Rule and the Money Exception

847. Suppose *A*'s car is stolen by *X*, who in turn sold it to *B*. As *A*'s title prevails over *X*'s, and *B* cannot acquire a better title than *X*, it follows that *A*'s title prevails over *B*'s. The *nemo dat* rule is premised on the idea that the transfer from *X* to *B* is derivative in nature, i.e. *B*'s title is derived from *X*'s. There is, however, an important exception to the *nemo dat* rule. This is where money is received by a bona fide purchaser for value.[1686] Thus, if X steals $10 from *A* and uses it to buy something from *B*, *B* acquires a fresh (i.e., non-derivative) and absolute title to the money. This is to facilitate the wider goal of efficient circulation of money.

1686. *See* David Fox, *Property Rights in Money* (OUP, 2008) Chs 2 and 8; David Fox, 'The Transfer of Legal Title to Money' [1996] RLR 60.

Chapter 5. Accession and Specification

§1. INTRODUCTION

848. Besides first possession,[1687] accession and specification are two other original modes of acquiring property rights.[1688] Original acquisition entails the creation of a new property right. This is to be contrasted with derivative acquisition such as receipt via transfer of an existing property right previously owned by someone else. The principles of accession and specification are often employed to determine ownership of goods sold on hire purchase or subject to a retention of title clause that were subsequently attached to land or other chattels.

§2. ACCESSION

849. In an earlier chapter,[1689] we have seen that, in the context of land, the principle of accession finds expression in the maxim *quicquid plantatur solo, solo cedit*, which translates to mean whatever is affixed to the soil belongs to the soil.[1690] Buildings and vegetation become part of the land, and chattels that are affixed to buildings become part of the building if the fixtures test is satisfied. The basic idea being that a minor object becomes an integral part of a principal object to which it is attached, the doctrine of fixtures presupposes that land and buildings are always the principal objects.

850. The principal–minor distinction is often more difficult to draw in the case of chattels unless one is very obviously larger (or more valuable) than the other.[1691] In *The 'Safe Neptunia'*, the court had to consider whether a crawler crane became part of a work barge.[1692] This presupposes, logically, that the work barge was the principal object while the crawler crane was the minor object. On the facts, however, Thean J found that accession did not occur notwithstanding that the crawler crane was included with the vessel in the charterparty and that it enhanced the capabilities and performance of the barge. More crucial were the facts that the crane was mobile and removable, and was not purpose-built for the barge or for marine work.

1687. The taking of possession of a thing that is not previously owned.

1688. *See generally* Gerard McCormack, 'Mixture of Goods' (1990) 10 LS 293; Earl C Arnold, 'Law of Accession of Personal Property' (1922) 22 Columbia L Rev 103.

1689. *See* AG Guest, 'Accession and Confusion in the Law of Hire-Purchases' (1964) 27 MLR 505; Thomas W Merill, 'Accession and Original Ownership' (2009) 1 J Legal Analysis 459.

1690. *See* Part I (Land), Chapter 2 (General Classifications) §5.

1691. A comparison in terms of value, however, is not always conclusive. In *McKeown v. Cavalier Yachts Pty Ltd and another* (1988) 13 NSWLR 303, for example, the yacht hull was regarded as the principal object although the components that were added to it cost some twelve times as much.

1692. [1988] SGHC 33; [1988] 1 SLR(R) 314.

851. The decision in *Aero-Gate Pte Ltd v. Engen Marine Engineering Pte Ltd* is less easy to explain.[1693] The plaintiff entered into two contracts to purchase 10 containerised diesel generators from the defendant. Under these contracts, the defendant was required to procure a specific model of generators, modify them and fit them into containers. When the defendant received delivery of six generators, it executed a written transfer of title in those generators to the plaintiff in return for a part payment.[1694] Eventually, only two completed units were delivered to the plaintiff. The plaintiff sued for breach of contract and also delivery up of the remaining generators. The issue of accession arose in respect of two of the generators, which were fitted with additional components belonging to the defendant, such as exhaust silencers and electrical equipment on the unit control panel. Coomaraswamy J held, applying the principle of accession, that the components, being the minor objects, became part of the generators, which were the principal objects. However, even assuming that the principal–minor distinction was correctly made, the learned judge did not appear to place sufficient emphasis on the ease or difficulty in removing the components from the generators, which is often regarded as a crucial factor.

852. In the Australian case of *Rendell v. Associated Finance Pty Ltd*, one Pell bought a truck from the defendants and an engine from the plaintiff, both on hire purchase terms. Unknown to both sellers, Pell installed the engine to the truck.[1695] The truck was later repossessed by the defendants when Pell defaulted on his payments. In finding that the engine did not accede to the truck, O'Bryan J said:

> In our opinion, [the plaintiff] is entitled to rely on the presumption that he continued to remain the owner, so that in the absence of evidence to the contrary the engine continued to belong to him, which, in this case, would require evidence from the defendants that as a matter of practicability it had been so attached to the truck that it could not be detached therefrom.[1696]

853. Similarly, in the New Zealand case of *Thomas v. Robinson,* the plaintiff bought a car and made considerable improvements to it, the most significant of which was the fitting of a new engine and carburettor.[1697] It transpired that the seller from whom the plaintiff bought the car defaulted on payments to the defendant hire purchase company. When the defendant repossessed the car, the question arose as to whether the components which the plaintiff added to the car acceded to it. Applying *Rendell*, Speight J held that they did not, as they can be detached from the car.[1698]

1693. [2013] SGHC 148; [2013] 4 SLR 409.
1694. Although the court did not say so, the transfer of title was effective only by virtue of section 17 of the Sale of Goods Act (Cap. 393, 1999 Rev. Ed.). *See* Chapter 2 (Contract for the Sale of Goods) §2.I.
1695. [1957] VR 604.
1696. [1957] VR 604 at 610.
1697. [1977] 1 NZLR 385
1698. [1977] 1 NZLR 385 at 292

854. Interestingly, *Rendell* was cited with approval by Thean J in *The 'Safe Neptunia'*,[1699] which was in turn acknowledged by Coomaraswamy J to have laid down the correct principle.[1700] However, the learned judge preferred instead to adopt a flexible, fact-specific test:

> [T]he broad idea is [to] keep the test flexible so as to do practical justice based on the particular circumstances of each individual case. The characteristics of the owners of the respective chattels will probably be very relevant: for instance, what they know, and whether either of them can be said to be a 'wrongdoer' (and it may matter whether the wrongdoer was 'innocently' or wilfully so). The owner of the principal chattel might have had it wrongfully appropriated from him by another, or he might have wrongfully appropriated the minor chattels. The owner of the minor chattels might be a contractor attaching those minor chattels to a principal chattel which he knows full well belongs to another, or he might be a consumer who attaches minor chattels to a principal chattel which he believes to be his but to which a third party (of whom he has no knowledge) has better title ... [W]hile it may in some instances be right to favour one owner, there will be other instances in which it is right to favour the other. Everything in reality depends on the facts of each case.[1701]

855. Applying this test to the facts, Coomaraswamy J held that the principle of accession applied because the defendant was fully aware that the generators belonged to the plaintiff.[1702] This is indeed consistent with *Thomas v. Robinson* where Speight J placed considerable emphasis on the fact that the plaintiff improved the car in the bona fide belief that it belonged to him.[1703] However, Coomaraswamy J went on to observe that 'to remove the installed components would be to destroy what would, with more work, become working Completed Generators'.[1704] With respect, this observation was not supported by detailed factual findings and, for this reason, appears to be inconsistent with the decision in *Rendell.*

856. Finally, it need only be added that while the principle of accession operates to extinguish title in the minor object, it is not a precondition that the minor object shall lose its original character before it can be regarded as having become part of the major object. In *Gebrueder Buehler AG v. Chi Man Kwong Peter*, Thean J held that the doctrine of fixtures applied even though the machinery attaching to a building retained its original character.[1705] This is consistent with the broader principle of accession, which may apply outside the situation of one object attaching to another. For example, wild animals belong to the owner of the *locus in quo*,[1706] and

1699. [1988] SGHC 33; [1988] 1 SLR(R) 314 at [16].
1700. [2013] SGHC 148; [2013] 4 SLR 409 at [151].
1701. [2013] SGHC 148; [2013] 4 SLR 409 at [153].
1702. [2013] SGHC 148; [2013] 4 SLR 409 at [156].
1703. [1977] 1 NZLR 385 at 291.
1704. [2013] SGHC 148; [2013] 4 SLR 409 at [156].
1705. [1986] SGHC 28; [1985-1986] SLR(R) 845.
1706. *Blades v. Higgs* (1862) 11 HLC 521.

offspring of a female animal belong to the person who owns that animal (the rule of natural increase).[1707] In the latter example, the offspring are regarded as integral to their mother on the basis of biological rather than physical connection.

§3. SPECIFICATION

857. The inquiry into whether the machinery has lost its identity in *Gebrueder Buehler* is more relevant to the issue of specification.[1708] In short, where a chattel is used in the manufacture of a new product and thereafter loses its original character, title in that chattel is extinguished and title in the new product is ascribed to the manufacturer.

858. The English case of *Borden (UK) Ltd v. Scottish Timber Products Ltd*,[1709] which was cited with approval in *Gebrueder Buehler*, is instructive on when the principle of specification applies. The plaintiff supplied the defendant with resin for the manufacture of chipboards, subject to a retention of title clause for unpaid goods. The resin was mixed with hardener and wax emulsion to form a glue mix. The glue mix was then blended with wood chippings and pressed together to form chipboards. This process is irreversible in the sense that none of the raw materials could be recovered in their original states. When the defendant became insolvent, the plaintiff sought to trace its title in the resin into the chipboards by invoking the retention of title clause. Since the tracing claim was premised on the plaintiff having title in the resin, the claim failed following the court's finding that title in the resin had been extinguished. As Bridge LJ explained, the process involved 'a mixture of heterogeneous goods in a manufacturing process wherein the original goods lose their character and what emerges is a wholly new product'.[1710] This is to be distinguished from a mixture of homogeneous goods where the character of the original goods remains unaltered. By the principle of specification, title in the new product is ascribed to its creator, in this case the defendant.

859. Whether a chattel has lost its identity through a manufacturing process is a question of fact. Attention must necessarily be paid to the degree to which it has become integrated with other raw materials. The facts of *Borden* are usefully contrasted with those of *Hendy Lennox (Industrial Engines) Ltd v. Grahame Puttick Ltd*.[1711] The plaintiff supplied a number of diesel engines to the defendant. The sale was on credit and was subject to a retention of title clause. Upon receipt, the defendant incorporated each engine into a diesel generating set. While this entailed attachment by bolts and by various other connections, the engines themselves were not physically changed. They remained identifiable by unique serial numbers and

1707. *Case of Swans* (1592) 7 Co Rep 15b. *See also* William Blackstone, *Commentaries on the Laws of England*, Book 2 (Clarendon Press, 1765) at 390.
1708. Ernest G Lorenzen, 'Specification in the Civil Law' (1925) 35 Yale LJ 29.
1709. [1981] 1 Ch 25.
1710. [1981] 1 Ch 25 at 41. *See also Re Bond Worth* [1980] Ch 228 (yarn made into carpet); *Re Peachdart* [1984] Ch 131 (leather made into handbags).
1711. [1984] 1 WLR 485.

could be disconnected from the generating sets in a matter of hours. The court thus held that the plaintiff's titles to the engines were not extinguished by specification. In the end, the plaintiff's claim failed only because the retention of title clause ceased to be effective when titles in the engines have passed to sub-buyers of the generating sets.

Chapter 6. Expropriation

§1. Introduction

860. Expropriation refers to a lawful act which results in the extinguishment of an existing property right owned by one person and the simultaneous creation of a new property right in favour of another person.[1712] This chapter offers a broad overview of four kinds of expropriation of property. The first two methods are initiated by the state whereas the latter two are initiated by private individuals.

§2. Compulsory Acquisition of Private Land by the State

861. With a population of 5.6 million living in an area of 720 km^2, Singapore is the densest country in the world.[1713] One direct solution is land reclamation, which has increased the land area of Singapore by more than 20% since its independence in 1965. The President may declare any reclaimed land to be state land.[1714] The other solution is compulsory acquisition of private land. The power of the state to do so is provided for in the Land Acquisition Act (LAA).[1715] The objective is not only to create more land area but also to ensure that enough space is used for development of public infrastructure. The purposes for which private land may be compulsorily acquired are set out in section 5 of the LAA:

> (1) Whenever any particular land is needed –
> (a) for any public purpose;
> (b) by any person, corporation or statutory board, for any work or an undertaking which, in the opinion of the Minister, is of public benefit or of public utility or in the public interest; or
> (c) for any residential, commercial or industrial purposes,
>
> the President may, by notification published in the *Gazette*, declare the land to be required for the purpose specified in the notification

862. In the 1960s, the development of public infrastructure to meet public needs was a matter of great urgency. To facilitate this goal, the protection of the right to

1712. To be sure, this chapter is not concerned with misappropriation of property even if the priority rules operate to extinguish the title of the previous owner and to grant a new title to the recipient. On misappropriation, see Chapter 4 (Possession and Appropriation) §3.IV.

1713. Bryan Chew, Vincent Hoong, Tay Lee Koon and Manimegalai d/o Vellasamy, 'Compulsory Acquisition of Land in Singapore' (2010) 22 SAcLJ 166; WJM Ricquier, 'Compulsory Purchase in Singapore' in Tsuyoshi Kataka and David L Callies (eds), *Taking Land* (University of Hawaii Press, 2002) Chapter 8; N Khublall, *Compulsory Land Acquisition—Singapore and Malaysia*, 2nd edn (Butterworths, 1994); Lim Chin Joo, 'Compulsory Land Acquisition in Singapore' (1968) 10 Malaya L Rev 1; TTB Koh, 'The Law of Compulsory Land Acquisition in Singapore' (1967) 2 Malayan LJ ix.

1714. Foreshores Act (Cap. 113, 1985 Rev. Ed.) section 5.

1715. (Cap. 152, 1985 Rev. Ed.). *See also* Rapid Transit System Act (Cap. 263, 2004 Rev. Ed.) sections 5–7A; Urban Redevelopment Authority Act (Cap. 340, 1990 Rev. Ed.) section 8.

property found in the Federal Constitution of Malaysia[1716] was dropped from Singapore Constitution following its separation from the federation in 1965.[1717] The concern was that, given the many large-scale projects that were planned, the constitutional right to 'adequate compensation' would place too much financial burden on the new developing country.[1718] To address this problem, the compensation provisions were drafted with one broad principle in mind: no landowner should benefit from development which has taken place at public expense. Thus, any appreciation in land value which resulted mainly from good land planning and infrastructure development by the state is to be excluded in the computation of compensation. The compensation framework is now set out in sections 33 to 35 of the LAA.

863. Prior to 2007, compensation for acquired land was based on its value at the date of gazette or at the fixed statutory date, whichever was lower. The various statutory dates adopted in the past were: 30 November 1973, 1 January 1986, 1 January 1992 and 1 January 1995. As property prices were generally on an upward trajectory over the long term, most owners whose land were compulsorily acquired were paid less than market price. For example, the owner of a property compulsorily acquired in 1980 will be paid the market value of the property in 1973, which is almost always lower than the market rate in 1980. However, in response to the perceived unfairness and to alleviate potential hardships, *ex gratia* payments were sometimes made, on a case-by-case basis, to owner-occupiers of residential property to top up the shortfall. However, with effect from 12 February 2007, the compensation system based on a statutory date was abolished. Compensation will thereafter be based on the current market rate. The change in pattern of land ownership was an important reason for the shift in compensation policy. As Chew *et al* explained:

> The cost of acquisition in the early years of nation building could have been a major concern. Land ownership then was mainly in the hands of a few individual owners. Clearly the compensation regime in the early years was structured in favour of the tax-paying public, who had to bear the cost of public development rather than a small group of individual landowners. Although this was obviously unfair from the landowners' point of view, it was nevertheless

---

1716. Federal Constitution (Malaysia), Art. 13:

> (1) No person shall be deprived of property save in accordance with law.
> (2) No law shall provide for the compulsory acquisition or use of property without adequate compensation.

1717. *Cf* Constitution of the State of Singapore (1963); Constitution of the Republic of Singapore (1965).

1718. *See* the *Report of Constitutional Commission* (1966); elaborated upon by the then Minister for Law and National Development, EW Barker, in *Singapore Parliamentary Debates, Official Report* Vol. 25 at col. 1424 (17 March 1967).

reasonable from the State's perspective. Where the acquisition affected the wider population however, the State was prepared to be more accommodating.[1719]

864. Unsatisfied landowners may appeal to a quasi-judicial tribunal known as the Appeals Board (Land Acquisition).[1720] Besides the quantum of compensation, another source of dispute is where the compulsorily acquired land is not eventually used for the proposed purpose.[1721] However, a claim to have the acquisition quashed on the ground of bad faith is unlikely to succeed as a change of purpose over time is not in itself evidence of bad faith.[1722] As the then Minister of Law, Prof S Jayakumar explained, 'sometimes due to new factors which arise after the acquisition, it is no longer optimal to put the land to the original planned use'.[1723]

§3. Compulsory Repossession of Public Flat

865. We have seen in an earlier chapter that the ownership and use of HDB flats are subject to conditions imposed by the Housing and Development Board.[1724] Where a flat owner breaches a condition, the Board may compulsorily acquire his flat. Some of the more specific grounds for compulsory acquisition are listed in section 56 of the Housing and Development Board Act,[1725] and these include: where the owner and his spouse have ceased to occupy the flat; where the owner, his spouse or any authorised occupier has acquired an interest in another property; where the flat has been used for a non-approved purpose; where the owner allowed a person who is not an authorised occupier to reside in the flat; and where the flat has been sublet without the prior approval of the Board.

§4. Collective Sale of Strata Title Development

866. To facilitate urban renewal,[1726] Part VA of the Land Titles (Strata) Act (LTSA)[1727] was introduced in 1999 to allow a process known as collective sales (or *en bloc* sales), under which buildings under the strata title scheme may be sold (usually to a developer) if the majority of subsidiary proprietors agree and approval has been obtained from the Strata Titles Board or the High Court. For buildings below

1719. Bryan Chew, Vincent Hoong, Tay Lee Koon and Manimegalai d/o Vellasamy, 'Compulsory Acquisition of Land in Singapore' (2010) 22 SAcLJ 166 at 172.
1720. LAA, section 23.
1721. *Teng Fuh Holdings Pte Ltd v. Collector of Land Revenue* [2007] SGCA 14; [2007] 2 SLR(R) 568.
1722. *Teng Fuh Holdings Pte Ltd v. Collector of Land Revenue* [2006] SGHC 93; [2006] 3 SLR 507 at [41] (Phang J).
1723. *Singapore Parliamentary Debates, Official Report* Vol.83 at col. 376 (Prof S. Jayakumar, Minister for law) (11 April 2007).
1724. *See* Part I (Land) Chapter 2 (General Classifications) §3.I.
1725. (Cap. 129, 2004 Rev. Ed.).
1726. Ter Kah Leng, '*En Bloc* Sales in Singapore: Critical Developments in the Law' (2009) 21 SAcLJ 485.
1727. (Cap 158, 2009 Rev. Ed.).

10 years of age, the approval votes of subsidiary proprietors owning no less than 90% of the share values and no less than 90% of the total area of all the lots are required. For buildings older than 10 years, the required percentage is reduced to 80%.

867. The main incentive for selling a building *en bloc* is the premium to be gained compared to individual sales. For owners who are unwilling to sell, however, the process is essentially expropriation of their property rights. On one view, this is justified because of the lesser property right acquired by a subsidiary proprietor. When the idea was introduced, the then Minister of Law, Professor S Jayakumar drew a comparison with the ownership of landed property:

> [I]n the case of landed property a person owns both the land and the premises which are identifiable and is free to dispose of it without consultation or agreement with any other party. Whereas in the case of strata titles, to put it in layman's term, he does not own an identifiable part of the land as being his but he owns it in common with the other subsidiary proprietors as far as the land is concerned.[1728]

868. This is, of course, open to debate. While the land on which the building sits is owned in common, a subsidiary proprietor may be understood as having absolute ownership in the delineated airspace that defines his lot. Therefore, to force a sale would not only deprive him/her of a co-owned interest in the land but also his individual property right in the defined airspace. If this is right, then the justification for *en bloc* sales is best found in public policy, specifically the need to facilitate urban renewal.

869. The detailed procedures for commencing and carrying out a collective sale are set out in section 84A and the Third Schedule of the LTSA. To introduce a certain level of safeguard, the LTSA provides that the High Court or a Board shall not approve the collective sale if it is satisfied that the transaction is not in good faith after taking into account the following factors: (a) the sale price for the lots and the common property; (b) the manner of distributing the proceeds of sale; and (c) the relationship of the purchaser to any of the subsidiary proprietors.[1729]

870. In *Ng Eng Ghee v. Mamata Kapildev Dave and others (Horizon Partners Pte Ltd, intervener)*, the Court of Appeal held that the specific reference to 'sale price' does not confine the inquiry to whether the amount is fair or not.[1730] The manner in which the sale price is arrived at is obviously relevant. The court said:

1728. *Report of the Select Committee on the Land Titles (Strata) Amendments Bill* (1999) at [144].

1729. LTSA, section 84A(9)(a)(i).

1730. [2009] SGCA 14; [2009] 3 SLR(R) 109 at [131] (Chan CJ, Phang and Rajah JJA). *See also N K Rajarh and others v. Tan Eng Chuan and others* [2014] 1 SLR 694; [2014] 1 SLR 694; *Ngui Gek Lian Philomene v. Chan Kiat and others (HSR International Realtors Pte Ltd, intervener)* [2013] SGHC 166; [2013] 4 SLR 694; *Lim Choo Suan Elizabeth v. Goh Kok Hwa Richard* [2009] SGHC 114; [2009] 4 SLR(R) 193.

> In our view, the term 'good faith' under s 84A(9)(a)(i) must be read in the light of the [sale committee's] role as fiduciary agent (at general law and, now, under s 84A(1A)), and whose power of sale is analogous to that of a trustee of a power of sale. Thus, in our view, the duty of good faith under s 84A(9)(a)(i) requires the [sale committee] to discharge its statutory, contractual and equitable functions and duties faithfully and conscientiously, and to hold an even hand between the consenting and the objecting owners in selling their properties collectively. In particular, [a sale committee] must act as a prudent owner to obtain the best price reasonably obtainable for the entire development.[1731]

§5. ORDER FOR PARTITION OR SALE OF CO-OWNED PROPERTY

871. In the case of co-owned land, any of the co-owners may apply to the court for an order to have the property partitioned, or to be sold in the open market and for the proceeds to be distributed among the co-owners. Suppose *A* and *B* co-own Greenacre. Regardless of the form of co-ownership, each of them has (co)ownership over the whole of Greenacre. If the court orders that Greenacre be partitioned into two equal halves, and that *A* and *B* will each own one-half, the extent of ownership for each of them is obviously reduced by half. From the perspective of an unwilling co-owner, the effect of the order would be to expropriate his ownership in the other half of Greenacre. The expropriatory effect of an order for sale is, of course, self-explanatory. The power of the court to make either order is found in paragraph 2 of the First Schedule of the Supreme Court of Judicature Act.[1732] In deciding whether to make either order, the court will consider a range of factors such as whether there is any difficulty in achieving a fair partition of the property and whether the unwilling co-owner will suffer undue hardship if the property is sold.[1733]

872. Interestingly, there is no equivalent statutory provision for co-owned personal property. However, in a dispute between a separated couple over the possession of their co-owned dog, the High Court gave sole possession of the dog to the female owner who had been taking care of it and who shared a strong bond with it.[1734] Curiously, the expropriation order was not accompanied by an order that the male owner be compensated by the female owner.

1731. [2009] SGCA 14; [2009] 3 SLR(R) 109 at [133].
1732. (Cap. 322, 2007 Rev. Ed.).
1733. *See* Part I (Land) Chapter 3 (Co-ownership) §7.
1734. *Tan Huey Kuan (alias Chen Huijuan) v. Tan Kok Chye and another* [2011] SGHC 86; [2011] 3 SLR 960.

Chapter 7. Insolvency

873. Where a bankruptcy order is made against a person, the assets of the bankrupt will vest in the Official Assignee.[1735] Similarly, when an insolvent company is wound up, the liquidator may apply to the court for the vesting of the company's assets in him.[1736] Both the Official Assignee and the liquidator are given the power to sell the assets of the insolvent debtor and apply the proceeds in satisfaction of his/its debts.[1737] The exercise of such power has the effect of expropriating the insolvent debtor's property rights.

874. Basic property law also plays an important role in the insolvency regime. In the first place, only assets belonging to the insolvent debtor may be realised to meet his liabilities. What precisely the insolvent debtor owns is necessarily a question of property law and the relevant rules have been examined in some of the earlier chapters. The fact that the insolvent debtor has possession of the asset is not conclusive of ownership.[1738] In sale of goods context, the passing of title, which is independent of delivery of possession, depended on the parties' intention or, where no such intention was expressed, on the statutory default rules.[1739]

875. But even if the insolvent debtor is found to hold the legal title in an asset, he might be holding it on trust for someone else, in which case it is not truly his. While trust law is examined only in the later parts of this book, one specific example that we have examined earlier, the vendor-purchaser constructive trust, serves as a good illustration. Where there is a specifically enforceable contract for the sale of land, the vendor holds the land under a constructive trust for the purchaser pending registration of the transfer.[1740] Since the land belongs beneficially to the purchaser, the vendor's insolvency will not prevent completion of the sale in the purchaser's favour.

876. Instead of leaving it to chance, a creditor may decide to take active steps to pre-empt the negative consequence of the defaulting debtor's insolvency. We have seen how the purchase or land is usually financed by a bank loan secured by a mortgage over the land,[1741] and how various forms of security interests such as mortgage, charge and pledge may be created over personal property to secure a debt.[1742] The power of an Official Assignee or liquidator to realise the insolvent debtor's assets and distribute the proceeds among creditors does not affect the right of a

1735. Bankruptcy Act (Cap. 20, 2009 Rev. Ed.) (BA) section 76.
1736. Companies Act (Cap. 50, 2006 Rev. Ed.) (CA) section 269.
1737. BA, sections 111(a) and 117–121A; CA, sections 272(2)(c) and 300.
1738. Chapter 4 (Possession and Appropriation).
1739. Chapter 2 (Contract for the Sale of Goods).
1740. Chapter 1 (Contract for the Sale of Land).
1741. Part II (Personal Property) Chapter 2 (Security Interests).
1742. Part I (Land) Chapter 10 (Mortgages).

secured creditor to realise his security.[1743] The asset used as security is removed from the common pool from which *pari passu* distribution to the unsecured creditors is made.[1744]

877. Thus, an unsecured creditor who stands to lose has obvious incentive to argue that the insolvent debtor is both the legal and beneficial owner of certain assets, or to challenge the validity of a security interest, in the attempt to enlarge the pool of assets available for distribution to the unsecured creditors. For this reason, many insolvency disputes are essentially property disputes.

1743. BA, section 76(3); CA, section 327(2) and 328(1).
1744. A floating charge, however, ranks below preferential creditors: CA, section 328.

Part IV. Trusts

Chapter 1. Introduction to Trusts

§1. Definition of a Trust

878. The trust has had a long history dating back to the 13th century.[1745] It was then known as the 'use' and was a conveyancing device for the holding of land for financial and inheritance reasons.[1746] The person who transferred the land was known as the trustor, for he transferred his land in someone he trusted, known as a trustee. The trustee held the land for a third party known as a beneficiary, since that person benefited from the use of land.

879. It is in that light that the trust has come to be defined in terms of the relationship between trustor (or settlor), trustee and beneficiary. Maitland has suggested what Virgo has termed 'one of the most helpful definitions':[1747]

> When a person has rights which he is bound to exercise upon behalf of another or for the accomplishment of some particular purpose he is said to have those rights in trust for that other or for that purpose and he is called a trustee.[1748]

880. Virgo suggests that this definition should be supplemented by referring to the property being held by the trustee.[1749] In this regard, property would encompass both tangible assets and intangibles, such as personal rights. From this supplication, it can be seen that the trust has two fundamental features, *viz*, that a person holds property rights (tangible or intangible) for a person or purpose; and that person is obliged under the rules of equity to exercise those rights for that person or purpose.

881. In Singapore, as with elsewhere where the concept has been recognised, the trust has been put to both commercial and social uses. For example, the trust enables

1745. *See* John McGhee (ed.), *Snell's Equity*, 33rd edn (Sweet & Maxwell, 2015) Chapter 21; Lynton Tucker, Nicholas Le Poidevin and James Brightwell, *Lewin on Trusts*, 19th edn (Sweet & Maxwell, 2015) Chapter 1
1746. S.F.C. Milsom, *Historical Foundations of the Common Law*, 2nd edn (OUP, 1981) Chapter 9.
1747. Graham Virgo, *The Principles of Equity and Trusts*, 2nd edn (OUP, 2016) at 46.
1748. F.W. Maitland, *Equity: A Course of Lectures* (John Brunyate, 2nd rev edn) (CUP, 1936) at 44. *See also* Walter G. Hart, 'What is a Trust?' (1899) 15 LQR 294; Peter Jaffey, 'Explaining the Trust' (2015) 131 LQR 377.
1749. Graham Virgo, *The Principles of Equity and Trusts*, 2nd edn (OUP, 2016) at 46–47.

assets to be segregated from those of the settlor, which helps protects them from the settlor's insolvency or tax liability. It also enables assets to be managed by people with expertise in managing particular types of assets, for the benefit of beneficiaries who may not have such expertise or may simply be too young. The multiple uses of the trust, especially as it extends beyond the family home to the commercial world, means that the nature and variety of trusts, as well as the rules of equity that govern them, will continue to evolve and become more complex.

§2. Fundamentals of the Trust

882. In the House of Lords decision of *Westdeutsche Landesbank v. Islington LBC*, Lord Browne-Wilkinson identified four fundamentals of the trust, namely that: (a) equity operates on the conscience of the owner of the legal interest; (b) a person can only be a trustee of the property if he is aware that he is intended to hold the property for the benefit of others; (c) there must be identifiable trust property; and (d) the beneficiary will have in equity a proprietary interest in the trust property once the trust is established and this interest will be enforceable against any subsequent holder of the property other than a purchaser for value of the legal interest without notice.[1750]

I. Settlors, Trustees and Beneficiaries

883. Lord Browne-Wilkinson's identification of the fundamentals of a trust point to three parties essential in a trust. As mentioned earlier, these are the settlor, the trustee and the beneficiary. Before a trust is created, a party who is to become the settlor has full ownership in the property concerned. He will also have the beneficial interest to the property, since he is entitled to its benefit. As Lord Browne-Wilkinson said in *Westdeutsche Landesbank v. Islington LBC*:

> A person solely entitled to the full beneficial ownership of money or property, both at law and in equity, does not enjoy an equitable interest in that property. The legal title carries with it all rights. Unless and until there is a separation of the legal and equitable estates, there is no separate equitable title.[1751]

At this stage, there is therefore no trust yet, and there is no separation of the legal and equitable interests in the property concerned.

884. In the case of the creation of trust by transferring property to a trustee, it is only when the settlor conveys the property to the trustee that there is a separation of the legal and equitable interests in the property. In this case, the settlor will lose both the legal interest in the property and the beneficial interest in it. The trustee will now have legal interest to the property. However, since the trustee holds the property on

---

1750. [1996] AC 669 at 705.
1751. [1996] AC 669 at 706.

trust for a beneficiary, he does not have the beneficial interest; the benefits of legal interest vests in the beneficiary. This beneficial interest may entitle the beneficiary to certain benefits, such as income or a right of possession, but that is dependent on the nature of the trust. In the case of the creation of trust by self-declaration as trustee, the act of declaration by the settlor will separate the legal ownership from the beneficial ownership, the latter is then held by the beneficiary.

885. If the trustee transfers the legal interest to the beneficiary, the beneficiary will have full ownership in the property and the equitable interest will be extinguished. This was the case in *Saunders v. Vautier*, which laid down the rule that the adult beneficiary of a trust, in whom the whole beneficial interest is vested, can direct the trustees to transfer the trust property to him/her, in which case the trust would be terminated because both the legal and beneficial titles are vested in the beneficiary.[1752] However, if the trust was not properly constituted at the outset, legal interest would still have passed to the trustees, but an equitable proprietary interest will be created in the settlor's favour by operation of the rules of equity, i.e., a resulting trust.[1753]

II. Separation of Legal and Equitable Interests

886. The most important consequence upon the creation of a trust is the separation of legal and equitable interests to the property concerned. In some cases, the trustees' actions can 'overreach' the beneficiary's equitable interest. For example, where the trustees are authorised to sell the property under the terms of the trust, such a sale will overreach the beneficiary's equitable interest.[1754] Upon the transfer of the legal interest of the trust property to a purchaser, the beneficiary's equitable interest in that property is extinguished and substituted by the creation of an equivalent interest in the asset obtained in exchange. This principle is important for the functioning of trusts, for it enables a third-party purchaser to acquire the property free of the beneficiary's equitable interest; in other words, he does not hold it on trust for the beneficiary.

887. However, if the trustee deals with trust property without authorisation, the outcome will be quite different. The equitable interest will only be extinguished if the third-party purchaser was a bona fide purchaser for value of the property (equity's darling). In that case, the third party purchaser takes the property from the trustees free of any equitable interest in the beneficiary. The beneficiary will then only be able to sue the trustees for breach of trust.

1752. (1841) 4 Beav 115.
1753. *See* Chapter 5 (Resulting Trusts).
1754. *See* Charles Harpum, 'Overreaching, Trustees' Powers and the Reform of the 1925 Legislation' (1990) 49 CLJ 277.

III. Nature of Beneficiary's Equitable Interest

888. By traditional analysis, the beneficiary's equitable interest is conceived as a proprietary right against a particular asset enforceable against the world at large.[1755] This is known as a right *in rem*. However, an equitable interest is somewhat unique. For one, it can be defeated by a bona fide third party purchaser for value. This means that it is weaker than a legal proprietary right, which can be so defeated only in exceptional situations.[1756] Also, if the property is negligently damaged, the beneficiary generally has no recourse against the tortfeasor because only a person with the legal proprietary interest or possessory interest may sue. In the usual course of things, the beneficiary has no possessory right to the property. Traditional analysis therefore requires the law to recognise two systems of proprietary rights.

889. McFarlane and Stevens challenge the traditional view and argues instead that the beneficiary's equitable interest is a right against rights, namely the beneficiary's right against the trustee's rights of ownership.[1757] Under their analysis, the trustee holds his right of ownership of the property (or even a personal right) on trust for the beneficiary, who has a right against that right of ownership. This analysis overcomes the shortcomings of the traditional ways of characterising the beneficiary's equitable interest by explaining simultaneously why the beneficiary has a right against a third party purchaser without value and a right against the trustee for breach of trust. Because the third party in this case acquires the property subject to the trustee's right of ownership held on trust for the beneficiary, the third party is now subject to the beneficiary's right against his right of ownership. Thus, the beneficiary will now have a right against the third party's right of ownership, except where the third party is a bona fide purchaser for value. This analysis also explains why a beneficiary is not able to sue a third party who has stolen or damaged trust property. In that case, the third party's right to the property does not derive from the trustee's right since the third party's right is an original possessory right. The beneficiary therefore has no claim against the third party. Finally, where the trustee is in breach of trust, the beneficiary is able to assert his right against the trustee's right of ownership, thereby explaining the beneficiary's right against the trustee personally.

890. However, notwithstanding its explanatory usefulness, it has been suggested that the 'right against a right' analysis should not be adopted because it 'involves an artificial and unnecessarily complex analysis'.[1758] Moreover, the language of a right against a right is foreign to equity and has not been used by the courts, which have conventionally analysed the beneficiary's equitable interest in more traditional language of property rights. Virgo suggests characterising a beneficiary's equitable

1755. *See* John McGhee (ed.), *Snell's Equity*, 33rd edn (Sweet & Maxwell, 2015) Chapter 2.

1756. *See* Part III (Acquisition of Property Rights) Chapter 4 (Possession and Appropriation) §3.IV. and Chapter 2 (Contract for the Sale of Goods) §5.I.

1757. Ben McFarlane and Robert Stevens, 'The Nature of Equitable Property' (2010) 4 J Eq 1. *See also* Ben McFarlane, *The Structure of Property Law* (Hart Publishing, 2008).

1758. Graham Virgo, *The Principles of Equity and Trusts*, 2nd edn (OUP, 2016) at 58–62.

interest may well be to recognise that it is *sui generis* and cannot be explained adequately by looking at it as either *in rem* or *in personam* rights.[1759] Instead, this equitable interest should be looked upon as a modified proprietary right that, unlike a legal proprietary right, is not enforceable against the world at large, specifically, not against a bona fide third-party purchaser for value. On another view, the equitable interest can be understood as having both characteristics. As Nolan explains: 'A beneficial interest under a trust is a package of constituent elements, some of which can consistently be viewed as matters of property, others of which can consistently be viewed as matters of obligation.'[1760]

891. The proprietary nature of the beneficiary's equitable interest is demonstrated in the old case of *Saunders v. Vautier*.[1761] In that case, shares were held on trust for Vautier until he reached the age of 25, upon which the shares and dividends were to be transferred to him. When Vautier reached 21, he argued that he was entitled to have the shares and dividends transferred to him since he was an adult and had now an indefeasible interest in the trust. Lord Chancellor Cottenham held that a proper construction of the trust showed that the vesting of the beneficial interest was not contingent on Vautier reaching 25, but that his enjoyment of it was. Thus, the beneficial interest vested in Vautier upon reaching the age of 21 and he could direct the trustees to transfer the shares and dividends to him, thereby terminating the trust. This result therefore acknowledges that the property held on trust for the beneficiary is regarded in equity as his property, who can decide what they wish to do with it. This also thereby recognises the proprietary nature of the beneficiary's equitable interest.

892. The English Court of Appeal's decision in *Shell UK Ltd v. Total UK Ltd* is a good illustration of why the beneficiary's equitable interest might be characterised as a modified proprietary right.[1762] In that case, the defendant negligently damaged tanks and pipelines that had been held on trust for the plaintiff. Since the plaintiff only had an equitable interest in the tanks and pipelines, the question was whether it could sue for the damage and also for consequential economic loss. While the court did not use the language of a modified equitable proprietary right, its analysis was consistent with such an understanding of the beneficiary's interest. The court held that the plaintiff did not have a direct claim against the defendant for consequential economic loss because it was not the legal owner of the tanks and pipelines and also not in possession of them. This is consistent with a modified proprietary right analysis of equitable interest as proposed by Virgo – it helps explains why this right, despite being a proprietary right, is not the same as the legal proprietary or possessory right that is necessary to establish the claim. It was only through joining the trustee in the action – with whom the legal proprietary right resided – that the plaintiff would be able to claim against the defendant. Ultimately, the plaintiff succeeded in claiming compensation for the economic loss it suffered because the court

1759. Graham Virgo, *The Principles of Equity and Trusts*, 2nd edn (OUP, 2016) at 58–62.
1760. R.C. Nolan, 'Equitable Property' (2006) 122 LQR 232 at 254.
1761. (1841) 4 Beav 115.
1762. [2011] QB 86.

held that a duty of care in tort could be owed to the beneficiary of a trust and a legal owner of the property; this does not, however, change the fact that the court's reasoning is at least consistent with the modified equitable proprietary right understanding of the beneficiary's equitable interest.

§3. Distinguishing a Trust from Other Legal Relationships

893. A trust is distinguishable from other legal relationships. However, as we have seen earlier, with the increasing assimilation between common law and equity, such distinctions may become increasingly unclear.

I. Contract

894. Whereas a contract is based on agreement between two parties, a trust involves a settlor transferring property to a trustee for the benefit of a beneficiary. And unlike a contract, where promises must be supported by consideration, the beneficiary usually supplies no consideration to the settlor or trustee and is thus a volunteer. Finally, whereas a contract is only enforceable between the contracting parties – with the notable exception of the Contract (Rights of Third Parties) Act[1763] – the beneficiary, who is not a party to any bargain, is able to assert a beneficiary interest against the trustee. Notwithstanding these differences, there are some overlaps; for instance, contracts can modify the application of the rules of trust and exclude them.

II. Debt

895. In a debt, the debtor is personally liable to the creditor. However, in a trust, the beneficiary has an equitable proprietary right in the trust property. The consequence of this difference is that, if the debtor becomes insolvent, the creditor does not gain a priority over other creditors, but if the trustee becomes insolvent, the beneficiary can claim the trust property over the trustee's creditors. In the trust scenario, the trust property is not considered as part of the insolvent trustee's pool of assets.

896. A debt can, however, sometimes give rise to a trust – known as a *Quistclose* trust.[1764] The characterisation of this trust is a matter of controversy. We will consider this issue in greater detail in Chapter 5.

1763. (Cap. 53B, 2002 Rev. Ed.).
1764. *Barclays Bank Ltd v. Quistclose Investments Ltd* [1968] 3 WLR 1097; *Twinsectra Ltd v. Yardley* [2002] UKHL 12; [2002] 2 AC 164.

III. Agency

897. Both trust and agency are traditional fiduciary relationships. As such, both the trustee and agent are subject to fiduciary duties. However, a trust relationship necessarily involves property but an agency relationship is not so restricted. An agent is usually appointed to help bring the principal into a contractual relationship with third parties.

IV. Bailment

898. In a trust, the full ownership is separated into legal interest and beneficial interest held by different persons. In a relationship of bailment, the bailor (the equivalent of the settlor) retains full ownership, and only possessory title is transferred to the bailee. For this reason, bailment can only arise in respect of chattels. This difference affects whether the beneficiary/bailor has the right to sue a third party, to whom the trustee/bailee illegally sold the property, for the tort of conversion. Moreover, a relationship of bailment arises in common law, whereas a trust relationship arises in equity.

§4. Classification of Trusts

899. As we will see in the course of this book, trusts are divided traditionally by reference to the context in which the trust arises. Under the traditional context-based way of classifying trusts, the main form of trust is the express trust, which is created intentionally by the settlor or the testator. Under express trusts, there can be subdivision based on the purpose of the trust. Thus, trusts created for public purposes are known as public or charitable trusts, whereas trusts created for individuals or purposes (exceptionally recognised) are known as private purpose trusts.

900. Express trusts can also be classified based on when it is intended to take effect. A trust that is intended to take effect as soon as it is declared, which invariably means when the settlor is alive, is called an *inter vivos* trust. A testamentary trust, on the hand, takes effect upon the death of the testator. This is achieved by executing a will.

901. Not all trusts are created by declaration by the settlor. Some trusts arise by operation of law (that is, not by the settlor's intention): the constructive and resulting trusts. These trusts will be considered in Chapters 5 and 6

Chapter 2. Express Trusts

§1. TYPES OF EXPRESS TRUSTS

902. Express trusts are established pursuant to the express intention of the settlor or testator who creates the trust.[1765] There are different types of express trusts. A fixed trust provides for fixed beneficiaries and fixed proportions in which they will share the trust property. The trustee have no discretion in either choosing the beneficiaries or deciding their respective shares. A fixed trust can be subject to a condition precedent or subsequent, such that the trust property is not distributed until and unless the condition is satisfied. In contrast, a discretionary trust confers a discretion on the trustee to decide who the beneficiaries are, and/or their respective shares in the trust property.

903. As a general rule, private express trusts are valid only if they are created in favour of human beneficiaries. This is known as the beneficiary principle. Only exceptionally are express purpose trusts recognised to be valid. The most prominent example of these is the charitable purpose trust (a trust for public purposes), which is an express trust for a charitable purpose that falls within the four recognised categories laid down by Lord Macnaghten in *Commissioner for Special Purposes of Income Tax v. Pemsel.*[1766] There are also exceptional cases in which trusts in favour of private purposes are held to be valid and enforceable, but these circumstances are very limited.[1767]

§2. CERTAINTY OF THE TRUST

904. Although the settlor is given great discretion in formulating the express trust, his or her intention alone does not always lead to the successful creation of a trust. Other than certainty of intention, to create a valid trust, certainty of subject matter as well as certainty of objects are required.[1768] The rationale for requiring the three certainties for the substantive validity of the trust has been explained in *Zhao Hui Fang v. Commissioner of Stamp Duties:*

> The requirement for the three certainties is connected to the ownership of legal and equitable rights under a trust, and serves broadly the purpose of enabling the trustee, or the court in default, to execute the trustee's duties (*Snell's Equity* at paragraph 22-012).[1769]

1765. *See generally* Jamie Glister and James Lee (eds), *Hanbury & Martin: Modern Equity*, 20th edn (Sweet & Maxwell, 2015) Chapter 5; Graham Virgo, *The Principles of Equity and Trusts*, 2nd edn (OUP, 2016) Chapter 5.
1766. [1891] AC 531 at 583.
1767. *See* §4 below.
1768. *Knight v. Knight* (1840) 3 Beav 148 at 173; *Guy Neale v. Nine Squares Pty Ltd* [2015] SGCA 64; [2015] 1 SLR 1097 at [51].
1769. [2017] SGHC 105; [2017] 4 SLR 945 at [57].

905. However, this need for certainty is not carried to extremes, and is moderated by the principle that judges will try to uphold a trust if they can, on the basis that the settlor's intention should not be frustrated too easily. Thus, Lord Wilberforce acknowledged in *McPhail v. Doulton* that a trust should be upheld so long as there is 'sufficient practical certainty in its definition for it to be carried out' and 'if necessary with the administrative assistance of the court'.[1770] Thus, what is required is not absolute certainty, but practical certainty sufficient to give effect to the trust. Likewise, in *Re Gulbenkian's Settlement Trusts*, Lord Upjohn said that it is the court's duty:

> by the exercise of its judicial knowledge and experience in the relevant matter, innate common sense and desire to make sense of the settlor's … expressed intentions, however obscure and ambiguous the language that may have been used, to give a reasonable meaning to that language if it can do so without doing violence to it.[1771]

In *Ong v. Ping*,[1772] the English Court of Appeal was able to find that a settlor had intended to subject her house to the trusts of the settlement, even though she left the 'settled property' field in the trust deed blank when she executed it. The court was satisfied, based on the correspondence between settlor and her solicitor, that she evinced an intention to subject the house to the trusts.

906. The interaction between the need for certainty in a trust on the one hand and the courts' desire to uphold a trust as best as they can on the other creates complication in the relevant law as the definition of what is 'certain' can be stretched and distinguished across different cases. This is unsurprising given that the practical certainty of any trust sufficient for its working is highly dependent on the particular facts of the case, but this also means that the cases are at times difficult to reconcile with one another. Ultimately, there will come a point at which the courts' desire to uphold trusts run out, and a trust is held to be invalid because it is just impossible to tell what the trustees are required to do under the trust, such that the court is similarly unable to execute the trust.

§3. The Three Certainties

I. Introduction

907. Be that as it may, it is uncontroversial that there are three relevant certainties that need to be established for the creation of an express trust, namely, certainty of intention to create a trust, certainty of subject matter and certainty of objects.[1773]

1770. [1971] AC 424.
1771. [1970] AC 508 at 522.
1772. [2017] EWCA Civ 2069.
1773. *Guy Neale v. Nine Squares Pty Ltd* [2014] SGCA 64; [2015] 1 SLR 1097 [51]; *Chiang Sing Jeong v. Treasure Resort Pte Ltd* [2013] SGHC 126 at [53].

The creator must intend first and foremost to establish a trust (certainty of intention), which vests identifiable property in a trustee (certainty of subject matter), who is bound to hold it for the benefit of another (certainty of object) or for the accomplishment of some purpose.[1774]

908. Before discussing the three certainties, it is important to note that the settlor must have the capacity to create a trust in addition to having the requisite intention. A child[1775] or mentally incapacitated person[1776] lacks the capacity to create a trust even if they subjectively 'intended' to do so.

II. Certainty of Intention

A. General Principles

909. The key test in ascertaining whether there is certainty of intention to create a trust is to ask whether the creator of the trust 'wanted somebody to hold the property for the benefit of another person so that he or she is under a duty to do so'.[1777] Given that equity looks to substance rather form, a trust will be formed on that basis even if the creator did not understand that this was the legal outcome of his actions.[1778]

910. The explicit use of the word 'trust' is not necessary for the creation of a trust, so long as the substance of the arrangement amounts to a trust.[1779] This has been endorsed by the Singapore courts.[1780] In *Chiang Sing Jeong v. Treasure Resort Pte Ltd*, the High Court explained:

> While the intention to create a trust must be certain, there is no requirement that certain words or that words referring to 'trust', 'in trust' or 'upon trust' must be employed. Where the creator of the trust is to be the trustee, any expression will suffice if it is clear that the person using them considers himself a trustee and adopts that character. The intention is collected first from the words used including the context, and second from the surrounding circumstances at the time the purported trust was created.[1781]

1774. F.W. Maitland, *Equity: A Course of Lectures*, 2nd edn (CUP, 1936) at 44.
1775. *Edwards v. Carter* [1893] AC 360.
1776. *See* Mental Capacity Act (Cap. 177A, 2010 Rev. Ed.), section 4.
1777. Graham Virgo, *The Principles of Equity and Trusts*, 2nd edn (OUP, 2016) at 87.
1778. *Paul v. Constance* [1977] 1 WLR 527.
1779. *Guy Neale v. Nine Squares Pty Ltd* [2015] SGCA 64; [2015] 1 SLR 1097 at [52].
1780. *Guy Neale v. Nine Squares Pty Ltd* [2014] SGCA 64; [2015] 1 SLR 1097 at [52]–[53].
1781. [2013] SGHC 126 at [57]; citing *Halsbury's Laws of Singapore* (Singapore: LexisNexis, 2012), vol. 9(3), at [110.488].

1. Where the Term 'Trust' Is Not Used

911. In *Hinckley Singapore Trading Pte Ltd v. Sogo Department Stores (S) Pte Ltd (under judicial management)*, the Singapore Court of Appeal explained that where the word 'trust' is not used, the court must look for indicators of the intention to create a trust.[1782] In this connection, 'the maintenance of a separate account by the agent is crucial to constituting the money as trust money'.[1783] However, while the segregation of the beneficiary's monies from the trustee's own funds is a strong indicator of an intention to create a trust, it is not by itself conclusive. In the words of the Court of Appeal in *Vintage Bullion DMCC v. Chay Fook Yuen*, segregation is a 'necessary' but not a 'sufficient' condition.[1784] If on the facts of the case, there is no requirement of segregation of funds, then the court must look for other indicators of an intention to create a trust.[1785]

912. Where the alleged trust was to arise in a commercial context, the court would also consider whether a trust relationship would be compatible with the particular business model in the process of determining if there is certainty of intention.[1786]

2. Precatory Words

913. Indeed, even if the word 'trust' is used, the courts will still look to the substance of the arrangement, for the word 'trust' may, in the given context, not refer to the equitable concept of a trust. In the past, the courts treated 'precatory' words as sufficient to indicate an intention to create a trust. The modern judicial attitude is that these words are not conclusive. This is because a trust relationship mandates the trustee to hold the property for the benefit of the beneficiary, whereas precatory words merely convey a desire that this be the case.

914. In *Re Adams and the Kensington Vestry*, the testator provided in his will that:

1782. [2001] SGCA 59; [2001] 3 SLR(R) 119 at [22].
1783. [2001] SGCA 59; [2001] 3 SLR(R) 119 at [22].
1784. *Vintage Bullion DMCC (in its own capacity as representative of the customers of MF Global Singapore Pte Ltd (in creditors' voluntary liquidation)) v. Chay Fook Yuen (in his capacity as joint and several liquidator of MF Global Singapore Pte Ltd (in creditors' voluntary liquidation)* [2016] SGCA 49; [2016] 4 SLR 1248 at [61].
1785. *Hinckley Singapore Trading Pte Ltd v. Sogo Department Stores (S) Pte Ltd (under judicial management)* [2001] SGCA 59; [2001] 3 SLR(R) 119 at [29].
1786. *Hinckley Singapore Trading Pte Ltd v. Sogo Department Stores (S) Pte Ltd (under judicial management)* [2001] SGCA 59; [2001] 3 SLR(R) 119 at [40].

> I give, devise, and bequeath all my real and personal estate and effects ... unto and to the absolute use of my dear wife ... in full confidence that she will do what is right as to the disposal thereof between my children, either in her lifetime or by will after her decease.[1787]

The question in this case was whether the testator intended to create a trust by which the wife was to hold the property for the children. It was held that there was no intention to create a trust. Instead, the testator was found to have intended the wife to continue his position as head of the family and carry out the moral obligation to provide properly for the family.[1788]

915. A similar result was also reached in *Re Hamilton*, where a testatrix by her will bequeathed to her nieces a sum of £2,000 each and 'wish[ed] them to bequeath the same equally between the families of ... Oliver and ... Pakenham in such mode as they shall consider right'.[1789] The question was whether this will created a trust for the families of Oliver and Pakenham. The English Court of Appeal held that it did not. The court instead found that the will showed that the testatrix intended to give the sums of £2,000 absolutely, trusting to the nieces' affection and honour to follow her wish for the sum to be bequeathed to the families of Oliver and Pakenham. There was no intention to fetter what the nieces could or should do with the sums of money. In the event, there was no intention to create a trust in favour of the families of Oliver and Pakenham.

916. A contrasting case where the requisite intention to create a trust was found upon an examination of all the relevant circumstances is *Comiskey v. Bowring-Hanbury*.[1790] In that case, the testator left his estate to his wife on the following terms:

> in full confidence that she will make such use of it as I should have made myself and that at her death she will devise it to such one or more of my nieces as she may think fit and in default of any disposition by her thereof by her will ... I hereby direct that all my estate and property acquired by her under this will shall at her death be equally divided among the surviving said nieces.

The House of Lords, by a 4-1 majority, found that the testator's bequest to his wife was subject to a trust for the nieces upon her death, although she had a discretion as to how the gift was to be shared among the nieces. However, if she did not exercise this discretion, then the estate was to be distributed equally. The Lord Chancellor's judgment neatly sums up how the majority came to the conclusion. First, he found that the testator instructed for his estate to remain in the same character at his wife's death as it did at his. This was evident from the sentence 'in full confidence that she will make such use of *it* as I should have made myself and that at her death

1787. (1884) 27 Ch D 394.
1788. (1884) 27 Ch D 394 at 409.
1789. [1895] 2 Ch 370.
1790. [1905] AC 84.

she will devise *it*'. The use of the word 'it' to refer to the estate at the time of the wife's death showed an intention that it should be unchanged as at the time of the testator's death.[1791] Second, the Lord Chancellor pointed out that the testator left directions as to what should happen to his estate if the wife did not leave a will. This showed that the testator did not intend for the wife to be the absolute owner of the estate and do what she pleased with it.[1792]

3. Other Considerations

917. The circumstances in which words are used are also relevant. Thus, if certain phrasing had been considered by a court to be sufficient to create a trust before, then a document prepared by a lawyer containing those same words would likely be found to be have created a trust .[1793] In *Chiang Sing Jeong v. Treasure Resort Pte Ltd*, the Singapore High Court also considered that documents created *after* the creation of the express trust may be relevant for proving an intention to create the trust,[1794] citing the English case of *Grant v. Grant*.[1795] In that case, Sir John Romilly MR had said:

> Any words that shew that the donor means, at the time he speaks, to divest himself of all beneficial interest in the property are, in my opinion, sufficient for the purpose of creating the trust. I think it is also sufficient for the purpose of shewing that the trust has been created, if he afterwards states that he has so created the trust, though there was no witness except the donee present at the time the trust was created.[1796]

Interestingly, this is different from the impermissibility of using documents created after the creation of a contract to infer the intention to create the contract. The rationale there is that such documents being created after the contract was formed, cannot accurately shed light on the circumstances in which the contract was formed in the first place. If that rationale is correct, then it is difficult to see why a different rule should apply for inferring the intention to create a trust.

918. Ultimately, whether there is certainty of intention to create a trust will be determined by a consideration of all the facts of the case, such as the parties' conduct and the objective meaning of relevant documents. It is therefore possible to analyse the cases according to the circumstances in which they have arisen.

1791. [1905] AC 84 at 87–88.
1792. [1905] AC 84 at 88.
1793. *Re Steele's Will Trust* [1948] Ch 603.
1794. [2013] SGHC 126 at [60].
1795. (1865) 34 Beav 623.
1796. (1865) 34 Beav 623 at 625.

B. Self-Declaration of Trusts

1. Domestic Context

919. The second category of cases in which the question of certainty of intention arises concerns the self-declaration of trusts. In certain cases, a person or company may behave in such a way as to give rise to the possibility that he/she is holding his/her property ion trust for another. But because there is no express declaration as such, whether there is the necessary intention to create a trust will need to be inferred from the circumstances of the case.

920. The difficulty is especially pronounced in the domestic context given the general informality of dealings in such a setting. However, the relevant principles are the same and the ultimate question is whether that person had the intention of creating a trust. But because persons acting in a domestic context are generally not legally advised and may not have acted with legal consequences in mind, the more relevant proxy to the requisite intentions will be found in the words of the purported creator of the trust. Indeed, Scarman LJ in *Paul v. Constance* said that the courts should be aware that, in such situations, they are 'dealing with simple people, unaware of the subtleties of equity, but understanding very well indeed their own domestic situation'.[1797]

921. Thus, in *Paul v. Constance*, the deceased had separated from the defendant in 1965.[1798] In 1967, he began to live with the plaintiff although they were never married when the deceased died in 1974. Because of the circumstances, the deceased did not have a joint bank account with the plaintiff but had an account in his sole name. However, he had a special arrangement with the bank that allowed the plaintiff to draw on the account with a special note from the deceased authorising her to do so. He used the account both for himself and for the plaintiff. For example, when he received compensation for a work-related injury, the money was deposited into this account. When he and the plaintiff both won money from bingo, the winnings were credited into this account. He also drew on this account to pay for their holiday. The deceased had said on various occasions that the money in the account was 'as much [the plaintiff's] as [his]'. When he died intestate, the defendant as his widow took out letters of administration of the estate. The plaintiff sought a declaration that the deceased held that money in this account on trust for her so that the said money would not pass to the defendant according to the rules of intestacy.

922. The English Court of Appeal upheld the lower court's decision that there had been a trust created for the deceased and the plaintiff. The court found that, as a starting point, the settlor's words and conduct must show a clear intention to dispose of property so that someone else would acquire a beneficial interest. In this

1797. [1977] 1 WLR 527 at 530. *See also Jones v. Lock* (1865–66) LR 1 Ch App 25.
1798. [1977] 1 WLR 527.

case, there had indeed been a trust because the deceased had said on multiple occasions that the money as the plaintiff's as much as it was his own. Indeed, this conclusion was strengthened when the other circumstances, such as the special arrangement in relation to the bank account and the deposit of their winnings from bingo, were examined. They all supported the conclusion that the deceased had intended to create a trust when he said that the money was the plaintiff's as much as it was his own. What is not clear is when did the trust arise, an issue that was not germane to the resolution of the dispute in the case. However, the timing at which the trust arose might be crucial in other cases where for example, there are allegations of breach of trust or tax liability.

2. Commercial Context

923. We now turn to consider the commercial context where special considerations arise. In the first place, there is a general judicial reluctance to find a trust arising from a commercial relationship.[1799] This is because, as was said in *Henry v. Hammond*, trusts can introduce unnecessary 'intricacies and doctrines' into commercial transactions and complicate them.[1800] However, where it is clear that there existed an intention to create a trust, a trust will nonetheless be found. In contrast to the domestic context, commercial actors are more likely to be legally advised and will be taken to know of the legal consequences of their actions.[1801] An obligation to segregate property hints strongly, but not decisively, that there is an intention to create a trust.

924. For example, in *Re Kayford*, a company carried out a mail order business, where customers either paid the full price or a deposit in advance of delivery.[1802] When the company's suppliers got into financial difficulties and the company could not fulfil its orders, it was advised by its accountants to open a separate bank account to deposit money it had received from its customers whose goods could not yet be delivered. By this arrangement, the company would only withdraw the money upon the goods being delivered to the customers. The company took the advice but did not open a new account. It instead paid the money into a dormant deposit account in the company's name. It only changed the name of the account to 'customers' trust deposit account' in the same month it went into voluntary liquidation. The liquidator took out a summons to determine whether the money formed part of the company's general assets or were held on trust for the customers in the proportion of the amounts they had paid.

1799. *Vintage Bullion DMCC (in its own capacity as representative of the customers of MF Global Singapore Pte Ltd (in creditors' voluntary liquidation)) v. Chay Fook Yuen (in his capacity as joint and several liquidator of MF Global Singapore Pte Ltd (in creditors' voluntary liquidation)* [2016] SGCA 49; [2016] 4 SLR 1248 at [63].

1800. [1913] 2 KB 515 at 521, citing *New Zealand and Australian Land Co v. Watson* (1881) 7 QBD 374 at 397.

1801. *See* further Man Yip, 'The Commercial Context in Trust Law' [2016] Conv 347.

1802. [1975] 1 WLR 279.

925. The English High Court held that there was a trust in favour of the customers. Megarry J found that, despite some 'loose ends' in the form of the company depositing the money into its own dormant account, there was an intention to create a trust.[1803] The learned judge placed particular emphasis on the fact that the company had accepted the advice to establish a trust account at the bank from the outset, with the purpose being to ensure that the money remained in the beneficial ownership of those who sent them. Thus, although the money was not paid into a dedicated and separate bank account,[1804] that by itself did not negate the intention to create a trust when, taking the circumstances on the whole, the company did have such an intention.

926. Similarly, in *Re Lewis's of Leicester Ltd*, a company allowed traders to trade on its store premises as 'concessionaires'.[1805] When the company went into financial difficulties, arrangements were made at the end of 1993 to segregate money received by the company from some of its traders. There were three different types of traders. The first type sold their goods but put their takings into tills controlled by the company. Some traders had their takings paid into a separate account and some, through error, did not. The company would then pay the traders at the end of the month with money, less its commission. The second type of traders withdrew from the proceedings. The third type of traders provided for their takings, less the company's commission, to be held on trust. Some traders within the third category also had their takings made into a separate bank account. When the company entered into administration, the question was whether the money in the separate account was held on trust for the traders.

927. The English High Court held that the money was held on trust. Robert Walker J accepted that the mere opening of a new account was not sufficient to create a trust, but he found further evidence of such an intention on the facts. In particular, the company had decided to segregate the money in order to protect the traders from the consequences of administration. The company's directors were concerned that money belonging to third parties such as the traders should be protected. Indeed, one director said that that money should be held on 'trust' for them, which resulted in the opening of a separate account. All these facts pointed to a clear intention that the money was to be held ion trust for the traders.

928. While the existence of a separate account is important, it is often said to be inconclusive as to the intention to create a trust. Nonetheless, it should not be missed that the segregation of property is a key indication of the intention to create a trust in cases where the words 'trust' or 'in trust' are not explicitly used. For example, in the Singapore Court of Appeal decision of *Hinckley Singapore Trading*

1803. [1975] 1 WLR 279 at 281.
1804. It may be said that the deposit of money into the dormant account (with £47.80 to its credit) amounted to segregation.
1805. [1995] 1 BCLC 428.

Pte Ltd v. Sogo Department Stores (S) Pte Ltd, Sogo granted Hinckley a concessionaire agreement to sell its products in Sogo's store.[1806] Under the agreement, the products belonged to Hinckley and the proceeds received from their sale were collected by Sogo's cashiers. The proceeds were then banked into Sogo's general account together with the sale proceeds of all other goods in the store. The parties would then settle payment monthly. Importantly, the agreement did not stipulate that the payment for Hinckley's products could only be made at a dedicated cashier or that the proceeds were to be paid into a separate account. When Sogo went under judicial management, Hinckley argued that Sogo held the proceeds from the sale of its product on trust for it.

929. The Singapore Court of Appeal held that since there was no express term creating a trust, the maintenance of a separate account was crucial, though not conclusive, in determining whether there had been a trust. On the facts, there was no separate account and also no other indicators of a trust.[1807] In fact, the commercial context, that this was a business arrangement involving a large number of items, would have made it wholly unrealistic that the parties expected a trust to arise in relation to the sale proceeds for each item. There were also other concessionaries operating in Sogo's store and this explained why all the sale proceeds were paid into a general account.[1808] The court therefore found that the parties had not intended for the creation of a trust over the proceeds.

930. In *Vintage Bullion*, on the other hand, certainty of intention was not established even though there was segregation of property in practice. The case concerned leveraged foreign exchange and leveraged commodity transactions. The commodity broker, in the ordinary course of business, segregated from its own funds a sum of money that represented the aggregate value of the different types of profits that could arise from the transactions. In particular, one type of profits (referred to as 'Unrealised Profits') related to notional assessment of what would be the gain to the customer for that day but as the relevant customer's position remained open, such profits would fluctuate from day to day as they were subject to market rates. Notably, for the same reason, certainty of subject matter was also not established on the facts. This demonstrates that there is a link between certainty of intention and certainty of subject matter. In other words, the commodity broker (alleged trustee) could not have intended to create a trust over property that was not certain.

931. In international commercial transactions, parties might have been negotiating their agreement with reference to a certain legal system. If the court found on the facts that the parties had carried out their negotiations with reference to a legal system that does not recognise the concept of trust, the court would not find that the

1806. [2001] SGCA 59; [2001] 3 SLR(R) 119.
1807. [2001] SGCA 59; [2001] 3 SLR(R) 119 at [38]–[39].
1808. [2001] SGCA 59; [2001] 3 SLR(R) 119 at [40].

settlor (one of the contracting parties) had the intention to create a trust, even if 'the documents did have elements that resemble a trust or terms that resemble 'trust-like' obligations'.[1809]

C. *Consequence of Absence of Certainty of Intention*

932. If certainty of intention is not established on the facts of a case, no trust has been created. If the creator of the purported trust has transferred property to another person, what the legal outcome of that transfer is would depend on the circumstances. It may amount to an outright gift to the transferee;[1810] the creation of charge; or the creation of a simple debt.

D. *Identification of Trust Property and Certainty of Intention*

933. The requirement of identifiable property overlaps with the determination of certainty of intention, even though the certainty of subject matter is a distinct concept and an independent requirement from certainty of intention.[1811] As Bridge points out:

> It is well known that, in order to declare a trust, it is not necessary to use explicit trust language. Commercial imperatives may persuade a court to infer a trust from language that does not obviously bespeak trust ... in extreme financial circumstances, a court will be prepared to conjure a trust out of thin air and prompts the following question: does the arrogation to a trustee of an extreme freedom to deal beneficially with trust assets tend towards negativing any intention to create a trust, or is it so inconsistent with a trust that a trust cannot be constituted whatever the intention of the parties may be? Are assets really identified to a trust as trust property if the so-called trustee is given such a wide-ranging personal freedom ... .[1812]

934. As discussed above, the segregation of property (which relates to the identification of trust property) is also relevant to the determination of an intention to create a trust. Here, one must distinguish between the obligation of segregation (e.g., based on parties' agreement) and the practice of segregation that is not based

---

1809. *The State-Owned Company Yogoimport SDPR (also known as Jogoimport-SDPR) v. Westacre Investments Inc* [2016] SGCA 51; [2016] 5 SLR 372 at [59].

1810. *Lassence v. Tierney* (1849) 1 Mac & G 551 at 561.

1811. *See Hinckley Singapore Trading Pte Ltd v. Sogo Department Stores (S) Pte Ltd (under judicial management)* [2001] SGCA 59; [2001] 3 SLR(R) 119; *Vintage Bullion DMCC (in its own capacity as representative of the customers of MF Global Singapore Pte Ltd (in creditors' voluntary liquidation)) v. Chay Fook Yuen (in his capacity as joint and several liquidator of MF Global Singapore Pte Ltd (in creditors' voluntary liquidation)* [2016] SGCA 49; [2016] 4 SLR 1248.

1812. Michael Bridge, 'Certainty, Identification and Intention in Personal Property Law' in Paul S. Davies and James Penner (eds), *Equity, Trusts and Commerce* (Hart Publishing, 2017) Chapter 4 at 102–103.

on an obligation.[1813] Where parties' agreement stipulates the obligation of segregation of property, the fact that this has not been performed in practice is not fatal to the finding of certainty of intention – the party who failed to perform this obligation would be in breach of trust (other than breach of contract). Conversely, the practice of segregation that is not being based on an obligation does not always support the finding of certainty of intention.[1814] In the commercial context, a party may have done so for good business/accounting practice as a matter of internal administration.

III. Certainty of Subject Matter

A. *General Principles*

935. As discussed previously, trusts can be declared over all types of property, whether tangible or intangible. However, in order for the trust to be valid, there must be certainty of subject matter. There are two aspects of this certainty, the first being certainty as to the description of the subject matter. A proper description enables the subject matter to be capable of conceptual definition. Whether this requirement is satisfied will depend on the description being considered, as well as all relevant circumstances, which may include background knowledge that a reasonable person is taken to have. For example, in *Re Golay's Will Trusts*, the expression 'reasonable income' was deemed to be sufficiently certain because it provided an effective determinant (that courts are familiar with) by which effect could be given to the testator's intention.[1815] It was held that this referred to the court's objective assessment of what is reasonable, and so the expression was not uncertain. In contrast, in *Palmer v. Simmonds*, the phrase 'the bulk of my said residuary estate' was held to be uncertain because the word 'bulk' did not express a definite part of her estate.[1816]

936. In particular, the court will not be overly technical in the determination of certainty of subject matter. In *BOK v. BOL*, it was alleged that the provision ' … all assets, both personal and immoveable, owned by me, whether legally or beneficially … ' was uncertain because the phrase 'owned by me' could be interpreted to include ownership of future property which cannot be the subject of a trust.[1817] The High Court rejected the argument, taking into account that on actual evidence, the relevant parties had never understood the phrase to include reference to future property.[1818]

937. The second aspect concerns the identity of the subject matter. Even if it is possible to conceptually define the subject matter, the *actual* property that is the

1813. *Ong Han Ling v. American International Assurance Co Ltd* [2017] SGHC 327 at [254].
1814. *Cf Re Kayford* [1975] 1 WLR 279.
1815. [1965] 1 WLR 969.
1816. (1854) 2 Drew 221.
1817. [2017] SGHC 316.
1818. [2017] SGHC 316, [136].

subject of the trust must be capable of identification. One way in which uncertainty as to the identity of the subject matter could arise is where there is uncertainty as to which beneficiary is entitled to what property that is held on trust. In *Boyce v. Boyce*, one beneficiary was given the right to select the property that she would be entitled to, and the trustees were to give the other property to the other beneficiary.[1819] Ordinarily, this would not result in uncertainty in subject matter but on the facts of the case, the beneficiary with the right to choose died before the selection was made.

938. More usually, uncertainty in relation to the identity of subject matter arises in respect of cases concerning trusts purportedly declared over unidentified part of a bulk, such as five out of ten bottles of wine. It needs to be ascertained which five of the ten bottles the description refers to. It is to this second aspect of certainty of subject matter that this section will now turn.

B. Identity of Subject Matter: Unidentified Part of a Bulk

1. Where Trust Property Has Not Been Segregated

939. Where the trust property has not been segregated, the determination of whether there is certainty of subject matter will usually turn on whether the assets concerned are tangible or intangible in nature. This is because intangible assets usually, but not always, are identical in their qualities. For example, shares of a defined class in a company are usually identical in their qualities such that it makes no difference to its functioning whichever share is being referred to. Thus, it makes no difference which 50 of the shares are being referred to when a trust refers to '50 of 100' shares. It is immaterial that each share may bear a different number, because this difference does not affect the *quality* of the share.[1820] This is of course not always the case for there may be different classes of shares in one company, in which case it would certainly matter which 50 of the 100 shares the trust is referring to. Thus, it has been said in *Re Harvard Securities Ltd* that the courts adopt a more benevolent approach to certainty of the identity of the subject matter insofar as intangible properties are concerned.[1821]

940. In contrast, tangible properties, or chattels, are usually not identical notwithstanding their generally identical outward appearances. For example, a trust may refer to five of ten cars. Even supposing that the ten cars are of the same model and manufactured on the same day, there will still be differences in, for example, the mechanical performance of each car or the grooves on the tyres due to the inherent randomness of the manufacturing process. In this case, it would make a difference which five out of the ten cars the trust is referring to. And if it is not possible to determine the exact five cars that are to be held on trust, the trust will fail.

1819. (1849) 16 Sim 476.
1820. Graham Virgo, *The Principles of Equity and Trusts*, 2nd edn (OUP, 2016) at 99.
1821. [1997] 2 BCLC 369 at 383.

941. The rule for determining certainty of subject matter for intangible property was established in the landmark decision by the English Court of Appeal in *Hunter v. Moss*.[1822] *Hunter v. Moss* was subsequently endorsed and explained by Neuberger J in *Re Harvard Securities Ltd*.[1823] Neuberger J saw that a satisfactory way of distinguishing *Hunter v. Moss* from other cases is that *Hunter v. Moss* was concerned with shares, whereas other cases were concerned with chattels.[1824] In *Hunter v. Moss*, the defendant owned 950 out of 1,000 shares in a company. He declared that he held five per cent of the issued share capital, which was interpreted as meaning 50 shares on trust for the plaintiff. The question was whether the identity of the subject matter had been sufficiently certain, since it might be unclear which 50 of his shares this referred to. In holding that there was a valid trust, the court paid particular attention to the fact that the shares were of a single class in a single company. Because each share was identical in quality as the next, it did not matter that the trust did not clearly identify exactly which 50 of the 950 shares was the subject matter.

942. A different rule applies for determining the certainty of subject matter for chattels. In *Re London Wine Co (Shippers) Ltd*,[1825] a company acquired a stock of wine that was deposited in various warehouses. Various quantities of wine were sold to customers, but none were actually delivered and remained as part of the general stock in the warehouses. Each customer was instead issued with a document of title confirming the purchaser to be the sole and beneficial owner of the wine purchased. The contract for sale of the wine provided that the wine would belong to the customer and would be stored for him by the company. When the company went into receivership, the issue was whether the wine was held on trust for the various customers. The English High Court held that there was no trust because the customers' respective quantities had not been segregated from the bulk. While there was certainty of intention to create a trust as evident from the documents, there was no certainty of subject matter as it was not certain which part of the stock any supposed trust was referring to.

943. While the distinction between tangible and intangible properties may help explain the respective results reached in *Hunter v. Moss* and *Re London Wine Co (Shippers) Ltd*, it does not explain all the cases. For example, in *MacJordan Construction Ltd v. Brookmount Erostin Ltd*, Brookmount engaged MacJordan as subcontractors for a building project.[1826] Brookmount retained three percent of the money due to MacJordan as retention money that was contractually stated to be held on trust for MacJordan. However, the retention money was not set aside in a separate fund. Eventually, a receiver was appointed by Brookmount's bank and the question was whether MacJordan was entitled to the retention money in priority over the receiver on the basis of a trust. The English Court of Appeal held that there was no

1822. [1994] 1 WLR 452.
1823. [1997] 2 BCLC 369.
1824. [1997] 2 BCLC 369 at 383.
1825. [1986] PCC 121.
1826. (1991) 56 BLR 1.

trust and hence no equitable interest created in the retention money in favour of MacJordan. Since there was certainty of intention to create a trust as gleaned from the contract concerned, the court's holding must have been premised on there being no certainty in the subject matter. However, despite the property concerned being intangible, the result reached is the opposite of that reached in *Hunter v. Moss*. While *MacJordan Construction Ltd v. Brookmount Erostin Ltd* was referred to by Dillon LJ in *Hunter v. Moss*, it was not satisfactorily distinguished.[1827]

944. The distinction between tangible and intangible properties also leads to some difficulties in practice. While it may not matter at the creation of the trust which specific part of a bulk is being referred to, this may matter subsequently if part of the trust property is sold. For example, while it is immaterial that a trust refers to 50 of 950 shares so far as the certainty of the identity of subject matter is concerned, it will be material when 50 of the 950 shares are subsequently sold. In this case, the question arises as to whose 50 shares are sold. It has been suggested that this question could be resolved by tracing rules.[1828] However, the tracing rules solution is circular. This is because in principle tracing rules can only be invoked after determining that an express trust has been created; tracing rules should not be brought into play to justify the creation of an express trust.

945. There is an alternative and less difficult analysis based on the concept of co-ownership that may explain some of the cases involving intangible property. This analysis posits that where a settlor declares himself/herself trustee of 5 percent of the shares for a beneficiary, he/she does not mean that the beneficiary has a beneficiary interest in any 50 shares, but rather intends that the beneficiary should have a beneficial interest in 50/950 (or 1/19) of the shares, such that they will be tenants in common of the whole. The beneficiary will become a co-owner of a single legally indivisible asset. This analysis can only work, however, if the part of property that is intended to be held on trust is denoted as a proportional share.

946. The English High Court in *Pearson v. Lehman Brothers Finance SA* accepted the tenancy-in-common analysis.[1829] In that case, it was held that it was sufficient so long as the mass from which the subject matter is to be apportioned is sufficiently defined and the beneficiary's proportionate share of the mass is not uncertain. It was also held that 'such a trust works by creating a beneficial co-ownership share in the identified fund, rather than in the conceptually much more difficult notion of seeking a particular part of that fund which the beneficiary owns outright'.[1830]

1827. *See* insightful analysis on distinguishing between the two cases in Sarah Worthington, 'Sorting Out Ownership Interests in a Bulk: Gifts, Sales and Trusts' [1999] JBL 1.
1828. Sarah Worthington, 'Sorting Out Ownership Interests in a Bulk: Gifts, Sales and Trusts' [1999] JBL 1 at 18–20.
1829. [2010] EWHC 2914 (Ch) at [224].
1830. [2010] EWHC 2914 (Ch) at [232].

2. Where Trust Property Has Been Segregated

947. There will usually be certainty in subject matter if the property has been segregated. In such a case, it is clear which part of the bulk that the trust is referring to. It would not make a difference whether the property is tangible or not, although by the nature of the property concerned, it is more natural to speak of tangible properties being segregated.

948. Thus, in *Re Goldcorp Exchange Ltd*, customers paid a company for gold bullion but the company became insolvent before it was delivered to them.[1831] While most of the customers failed in their argument that there had been a trust, the few customers that succeeded did so because their gold bullion had been segregated from the bulk. For these few customers, legal title had passed to the customers because a trust could be found from the fact that their gold bullion were specifically segregated from the rest of the bullion.

949. Where a sale is concerned, as in *Re Goldcorp Exchange Ltd*, such a situation is now governed by section 20A of the Sale of Goods Act,[1832] which provides relevantly as follows:

> **Undivided shares in goods forming part of bulk**
>
> (1) This section applies to a contract for the sale of a specified quantity of unascertained goods if the following conditions are met:
> (a) the goods or some of them form part of a bulk which is identified either in the contract or by subsequent agreement between the parties; and
> (b) the buyer has paid the price for some or all of the goods which are the subject of the contract and which form part of the bulk.
>
> (2) Where this section applies, then (unless the parties agree otherwise), as soon as the conditions specified in paragraphs (*a*) and (*b*) of subsection (1) are met or at such later time as the parties may agree –
> (a) property in an undivided share in the bulk is transferred to the buyer; and
> (b) the buyer becomes an owner in common of the bulk.

The effect of section 20A is, if the conditions in section 20A(1)(*a*) and (*b*) are met, and the parties have not agreed to the contrary, then the purchaser of an unascertained part of an identified bulk of goods acquires property rights as tenants in common in that bulk.

1831. [1995] 1 AC 74.
1832. (Cap. 393, 1999 Rev. Ed.).

3. Future Property

950. It is trite law that a settlor cannot create a trust over future property, that is, property which the settlor does not presently own.[1833] Future royalties, the mere expectancy of receiving an interest under the will of a living relative and compensation that one hopes to receive in future court proceedings are examples of future property.

951. However, it is important to examine if the settlor has an immediate proprietary interest to convey or not. In *Sheares Betty Hang Kiu v. Chow Kwok Chi*, it was contended that the subject matter of a trust could not include assets inherited by the settlor pursuant to a testator's will because the testator's estate had not been administered when the trust was declared.[1834] As such, it was argued that the settlor had no valid interest that could be conveyed in the trust. By this argument, the settlor only had a future interest in the property. The Singapore High Court rejected this argument because the settlor's interest in the testator's estate amounted to more than a bare expectancy.

952. The settlor was a named beneficiary and had a direct and real interest in his assets. Future property does not include existing vested or contingent right to obtain property at some future time.[1835] While the legatee may not have an equitable interest in any particular property during the period of administration, he does have a right to ensure that the assets are properly safeguarded, and this right may be disposed of by will or *inter vivos*.[1836]

C. Consequence of Absence of Certainty of Subject Matter

953. -If the certainty of subject matter cannot be established in a case, the intended trust does not arise. As such, in a situation where the purported settlor declared himself/herself to be the trustee, he would remain the owner of the property. In a situation where the entire property has been transferred to a third party who is to become the trustee of part of the property for a third party, and it is unclear as to which part of the property is to be held on trust, the third party will take the entire property absolutely. There will not be a resulting trust in favour of the purported settlor for the same reason why a trust has not been created: it is not possible to tell which part of the property should be the subject matter of a resulting trust.

1833. *Re Ellenborough* [1903] 1 Ch 697.
1834. [2006] SGHC 34; [2006] 2 SLR(R) 285.
1835. [2006] SGHC 34; [2006] 2 SLR(R) 285 at [34].
1836. [2006] SGHC 34; [2006] 2 SLR(R) 285 at [36]–[37].

IV. Certainty of Objects

A. General Principles

954. It is trite law that a private trust must be created for ascertainable beneficiaries.[1837] The underlying rationale is simple: the beneficiaries are the enforcers of the trust. As Lord Eldon explained in *Morice v. Bishop of Durham*:

> As it is a maxim, that the execution of a trust shall be under the control of the court, it must be of such a nature, that it can be under that control; so that the administration of it can be reviewed by the court; or, if the trustee dies, the court itself can execute the trust; a trust therefore, which, in case of maladministration could be reformed; and a due administration directed; and then, unless the subject and the objects can be ascertained, upon principles, familiar in other cases, it must be decided, that the court can neither reform maladministration, nor direct a due administration.[1838]

955. Different textbooks may have slightly different ways of explaining the relevant test. For example, Virgo notes that six different aspects of certainty need to be considered each for different types of trust and power, namely, (a) the essential test of certainty; (b) conceptual certainty; (c) evidential certainty; (d) locational certainty; (e) size of the class; and (f) capriciousness.[1839] While this is certainly a possible way of understanding the relevant test, it might be clearer to simply say that each type of trust is governed by its own test to ascertain whether there is certainty of objects. Each test has conceptual and/or evidential aspects that may (or may not) need to be satisfied in order the trust is validly created. Conceptual certainty refers to the possibility of defining the class of objects. Evidential certainty refers to the ease of proving that someone is an object. Evidential certainty must be distinguished from ascertainability. As Lord Wilberforce made clear *McPhail v. Doulton*, ascertainability refers to the ease of 'ascertaining the existence or whereabouts of members of the class'.[1840] The trust does not fail for issues of ascertainability.

956. Apart from the relevant test (which encompasses both conceptual and evidential aspects), there are two other distinct considerations, namely administrative workability and capriciousness. As we shall see below, in some cases where the size of the class is too large, the courts may find the trust to be administratively unworkability *even if* the relevant certainty of objects is satisfied. Similarly, if the trust is declared for a nonsensical purpose, the courts may invalidate the trust for capriciousness, *even if*, again, the relevant certainty of objects test is satisfied.

1837. *Re Vandervell's Trusts (No 2)* [1974] Ch 269 at 319.
1838. (1805) 10 Ves Jr 522 at 539–40.
1839. Graham Virgo, *The Principles of Equity and Trusts*, 2nd edn (OUP, 2016) at 102.
1840. [1971] AC 424 at 457. *See* further C.T. Emery, 'The Most Hallowed Principle—Certainty of Beneficiaries of Trusts and Powers of Appointment' (1982) 98 LQR 551.

B. Fixed Trusts

1. Conceptual Certainty

957. The relevant test to determine certainty of objects for fixed trusts is the 'complete list' test. In *IRC v. Broadway Cottages*, it was explained that this test requires the complete identification of all the beneficiaries from the moment the trust comes into operation.[1841] In that case, the settlor purported to create a trust of a sum of money in favour of all or any of a class of beneficiaries specified in a schedule. In particular, the trustees held the capital sum for the beneficiaries in equal shares and had discretion to distribute the income from the capital sum amongst the beneficiaries in proportions as they shall decide. The English Court of Appeal held that this trust was invalid for uncertainty as it was not possible to ascertain the whole range of objects eligible for selection. Insofar as the capital sum was concerned, the court held that this was uncertain because 'there can be no division in equal shares amongst a class of persons unless all the members of the class are known'.[1842] As for the income, the court rejected an argument that the trust could be enforced because it was possible to ascertain whether any particular person was a member of the class of beneficiaries and that the trustees could distribute amongst those beneficiaries. The court held instead that the trust obliged the trustees to exercise their discretion on a defined class, and if that class were unascertainable or incapable of being ascertained, then the trust would be invalid for uncertainty.[1843]

958. If the underlying rationale for certainty of objects, *viz.*, to enable the trustee to execute the trust, is considered, it is easy to understand why the test is framed as such. In a fixed trust, the trustee has no discretion as to who are the beneficiaries of the trust. The trustee also has no say as to each beneficiary's share in the trust property. These factors are fixed at the outset. Thus, if the trust does not by its terms tell the trustee how to determine the complete list of beneficiaries, the trust cannot be executed because the trustee does not have discretion to decide who those beneficiaries might be. However, this complete list only needs to be drawn up at the time the trust property is to be distributed so that a trust will not be invalidated simply because a complete list cannot be drawn up at the time of the trust's creation.

959. The conceptual certainty aspect of the complete list test requires the object to be clearly defined so that the trustee can execute the trust. For example, a fixed trust declared for the settlor's 'friends' will be conceptually uncertain in objects because there are many shades of friendship such that the trustee, who has no discretion in deciding who the beneficiaries should be, is unable to execute the trust by reference to a clearly defined class. The evidential certainty aspect requires that there be a method of proving who the persons on the conceptually certain list are. As discussed above, a fixed trust in favour of members of a particular university's science club in a certain year may be conceptually certain because it is possible to

1841. [1955] Ch 20.
1842. [1955] Ch 20 at 29.
1843. [1955] Ch 20 at 35–36.

define what that means. However, if the science club does not keep records of its previous members, then the trust may fail for evidential uncertainty of objects, because there is no *method* of determining who is a member of the science club in the relevant year.

2. Administrative Unworkability

960. According to Virgo, there is no evidence that the size of the class is a relevant consideration when determining the validity of a fixed trust.[1844] This is supposedly because 'all the necessary work is being done by the complete list test' – if it is possible to list the objects completely, then there should not be a problem in administering the trust.[1845] However, it may be possible to draw a distinction between *defining* a class and *administering* the trust. Thus, even if it is possible to list all the objects, if the size of the class is too large, it might still be difficult to administer the trust. Indeed, it appears that the real reason why administrative unworkability is never considered for fixed trusts is because they tend to be small by their very nature.[1846]

3. Capriciousness

961. There is no case law suggestion that the courts have had regard to the capriciousness of the objects in a fixed trust. It follows that the settlor is free to choose the objects as he pleases, so long as the relevant test is satisfied.[1847]

C. Discretionary Trusts

1. Conceptual Certainty

962. Unlike a fixed trust, a discretionary trust gives the trustee a discretion to decide who the beneficiaries are and/or their proportionate shares of the trust property. The relevant test to determine certainty of objects for discretionary trusts is the 'any given postulant' test, as established in *McPhail v. Doulton.*[1848] This test requires that it can be said with certainty whether a given person is or is not a member of the relevant class, although it is not necessary to identify everybody in the class. This test is therefore different from the 'complete list' test.

1844. Graham Virgo, *The Principles of Equity and Trusts*, 2nd edn (OUP, 2016) at 103.
1845. Graham Virgo, *The Principles of Equity and Trusts*, 2nd edn (OUP, 2016) at 103. *See* further I.M. Hardcastle, 'Administrative Unworkability – A Reassessment of an Abiding Problem' [1990] Conv 24.
1846. Graham Virgo, *The Principles of Equity and Trusts*, 2nd edn (OUP, 2016) at 103.
1847. Graham Virgo, *The Principles of Equity and Trusts*, 2nd edn (OUP, 2016) at 103.
1848. [1971] AC 424.

963. It used to be the case that the complete list test applied for both fixed and discretionary trusts.[1849] Indeed, it might be thought, having regard to the rationale for the certainty of objects, that it would not be wrong to say that the complete list test also enables the trustee to execute a discretionary trust: if the trustee cannot define the complete class to begin with, then he may not be able to exercise the discretion to choose from that class. The complete list test would also enable the court to distribute the property equally among all the beneficiaries if the trustee failed to exercise his/her discretion to select from the relevant class.

964. However, the application of the complete list test to discretionary trusts was difficult in practice. Unlike fixed trusts, discretionary trusts usually involve a large number of objects, and both the size, as well as the composition, of the relevant class made it very difficult to satisfy the complete list test. Furthermore, it was not always in line with the settlor's intention that the trust property be distributed equally among all members in the class if the trustee failed to make a selection from the class.[1850] Significantly, as Lord Wilberforce expressly acknowledged in *McPhail v. Doulton*, it would be difficult in practice to distinguish a discretionary trust from a fiduciary power, notwithstanding conceptual distinctions.[1851] The given postulant test applies to determine certainty of objects in respect of a fiduciary power. For this reason, Lord Wilberforce did not consider a need to differentiate a discretionary trust from a fiduciary power where the issue of validity is concerned.[1852]

965. Moreover, while the trustees of a discretionary trust have a duty to distribute, they have no duty to make a distribution to each and every object of the class. Their discretion in respect of distribution renders a complete list unnecessary and onerous. As Lord Wilberforce explained in *McPhail v. Doulton*:

> [A] trustee with a duty to distribute, particularly among a potentially very large class, would surely never require the preparation of a complete list of names, which anyhow would tell him little that he needs to know. He would examine the field, by class and category; might indeed make diligent and careful inquiries, depending on how much money he had to give away and the means at his disposal, as to the composition and needs of particular categories and of individuals within them; decide upon certain priorities or proportions, and then select individuals according to their needs or qualifications. If he acts in this manner, can it really be said that he is not carrying out the trust?[1853]

1849. *IRC v. Broadway Cottages* [1955] Ch 20.
1850. However, if the settlor's intention was indeed such, then the complete list test would need to be satisfied: see Graham Virgo, *The Principles of Equity and Trusts*, 2nd edn (OUP, 2016) at 108, citing *Burrogh v. Philcox* (1840) 5 Myl & Cr 72.
1851. [1971] AC 424 at 448–49.
1852. [1971] AC 424 at 448–49.
1853. [1971] AC 424 at 449.

966. In *McPhail v. Doulton*, the settlor established a fund for the benefit of the employees and ex-employees of the company, as well as their relatives and dependents. The House had to consider first whether this was a trust or power, since different tests of validity applied at the time. This was held to be a discretionary trust, but it was unclear whether 'relatives and dependents' were sufficiently certain objects, which required the House to consider what the proper test of validity ought to be. They decided that the given postulant test should apply.

967. The case was remitted to the English High Court to decide whether the trust satisfied the given postulant test. On appeal to the English Court of Appeal as *Re Baden's Deed Trusts (No. 2)*, the court upheld the High Court's decision that the trust was valid according to the given postulant test.[1854] However, each member of the court interpreted the test differently.

968. Insofar as conceptual certainty is concerned, the starting point is that it must be possible to define the class with sufficient clarity. However, this leaves unanswered just how clear the definition must be for each case. Indeed, most definitions have penumbral meanings that cannot be completely eradicated. Depending on the precise level of clarity required, the size of the potential class may be affected. Thus, in *Re Baden (No. 2)*, both Sachs and Megaw LJJ defined 'relatives' as descendants from a common ancestor,[1855] while Stamp LJ defined 'relatives' as the next of kin or nearest blood relations.[1856] While both definitions are conceptually certain, Stamp LJ's definition is clearly narrower than the definition put forward by Sachs and Megaw LJJ. This illustrates how the ambit of the class may change depending on what definition is taken to be of sufficient clarity in a given case. Nonetheless, all the judges agreed that 'dependents' could be defined as those who are wholly or partly dependent on somebody else.

969. The three judges in *Re Baden (No. 2)* understood the evidential certainty aspect of the given postulant test differently. Sachs LJ said that evidential certainty is not required in the given postulant test for the determination of certainty of objects. According to Sachs LJ, only conceptual certainty is required – once the class is defined with sufficient clarity, the trust would be validly created.[1857] If a particular person cannot show evidence that he comes within the class, then he is considered to fall outside of the class and cannot take benefit under the trust.

970. Megaw LJ understood the evidential aspect differently. According to him, it is necessary to show that a substantial number of objects fall within the class. If not, the trust would not be valid. What constitutes a 'substantial number' would depend on the facts of each case and is ultimately a matter of common sense.[1858]

1854. [1973] Ch 9.
1855. [1973] Ch 9 at 22.
1856. [1973] Ch 9 at 29.
1857. [1973] Ch 9 at 20.
1858. [1973] Ch 9 at 24.

971. Finally, Stamp LJ was of the view that the given postulant test requires both conceptual certainty and evidential certainty. In other words, it must be shown whether any given person *is or is not* within the class. However, there is no need to identify the complete list of objects.[1859] If it cannot be said of a potential member of the class whether he is a member of the class or not, the trust would fail.

972. While Stamp LJ's interpretation appears to best accord with Lord Wilberforce's speech in *McPhail v. Doulton*, the test may be unduly strict as it could lead to the invalidation of many discretionary trusts. As such, Sach LJ's interpretation is to be preferred.

2. Ascertainability

973. The inability to locate a particular object of a discretionary trust or establish that object's existence will not invalidate the trust.[1860]

3. Administrative Unworkability

974. Even if the relevant test is satisfied such that it is possible to conceptually define a class and for someone to prove that he is or is not a member of the class, the size of the class is another consideration that may invalidate the class. In *McPhail v. Doulton*, Lord Wilberforce suggested that if the class of objects is so wide that it cannot be considered to be anything like a class, the trust could be invalidated for administrative unworkability.[1861] There have been several explanations for this concept. For example, it has been suggested that the trustee would not be able to perform his duty to ascertain the range of objects if the size of the class is too large. It has also been suggested that should the trustee fail to exercise their discretion, the courts will be unable to execute a trust with a very wide class of objects.[1862] Finally, Hardcastle suggests that administrative workability should be considered as 'a logical extension of evidential certainty' and it may be exceptionally invoked to invalidate a trust where 'performance becomes an exercise in futility' by reason of both the width of the class and 'a total lack of provable definitional criteria'.[1863] However, Virgo suggests that none of these explanations is satisfactory. For example, the fact the size of the class is too large does not mean that the trustee is unable to exercise his discretion since he needs only to know the width of the field and adapt his method of ascertaining objects.[1864] He therefore proposes that the concept of administrative unworkability be abolished.[1865]

1859. [1973] Ch 9 at 28.
1860. *McPhail v. Doulton* [1971] AC 424 at 457 (Lord Wilberforce).
1861. [1971] AC 424 at 457.
1862. *Re Manisty's Settlement* [1974] Ch 17 at 29.
1863. I. M. Hardcastle, 'Administrative Unworkability – A Reassessment of an Abiding Problem' [1990] Conv 24 at 31.
1864. Graham Virgo, *The Principles of Equity and Trusts*, 2nd edn (OUP, 2016) at 112.
1865. *Ibid.*, at 113.

975. Be that as it may, the first case in which administrative unworkability was used to invalidate a trust is the case of *Ex p. West Yorkshire Metropolitan.*[1866] In that case, a discretionary trust was purportedly declared for the benefit of any, some, or all of the inhabitants of the county of West Yorkshire, which amounted to some 2.5 million persons. While the court accepted that the class of objects was conceptually certain, the size was so large as to make it administratively unworkable. In *Re Hay's Settlement Trust*, Sir Robert Meggary V-C said in obiter that he would be prepared to hold a discretionary trust in favour of anyone in the world other than a few specified people to be administratively unworkable.[1867]

4. Capriciousness

976. If the settlor had no sensible intent in establishing the trust, it may be void for capriciousness. In *Re Manisty's Settlement*, Templeman J suggested that a power given to trustees to benefit the 'residents of Greater London' by a settlor who had no connection to Greater London would be capricious because it does not show any sensible intention by the settlor to benefit the beneficiaries.[1868] However, that was said in respect of a power, although the principle could just as easily be applied to void a discretionary trust, although this has never been done.[1869] Crucially, it is not readily apparent what is the precise objection against a settlor establishing a trust for persons with whom he/she has no discernible connection. After all, a property owner should have the freedom to decide how he/she may like to deal with his/her property. 'Capriciousness' appears too arbitrary and vague a ground to invalidate a trust. If there is a specific policy objection against the creation or performance of a trust, that policy objection should be clearly articulated and the validity of the trust be decided on that basis.

D. Powers

1. The Relevant Test

977. Fiduciary powers are powers conferred upon a fiduciary. The donee of a fiduciary power is not under a duty to distribute but they must consider from time to time whether to exercise the power. In *McPhail v. Doulton*, Lord Wilbeforce described this duty incumbent upon the donee of a fiduciary power in the following terms:

1866. [1986] 26 RVR 24.
1867. [1982] 1 WLR 202 at 212.
1868. [1974] Ch 17.
1869. Graham Virgo, *The Principles of Equity and Trusts*, 2nd edn (OUP, 2016) at 114.

> Any trustee would surely make it his duty to know what is the permissible area of selection and then consider responsibly, in individual cases, whether a contemplated beneficiary was within the power and whether, in relation to other possible claimants, a particular grant was appropriate.[1870]

978. The relevant test of certainty of objects for fiduciary powers was set out in *Re Gulbenkian's Settlement Trusts*.[1871] The test is that it must be determinable whether an individual is or is not a member of the class. The settlement in that case contained a power to appoint in favour of Gulbenkian, his wife, children, remoter issue or anybody who employed him or with whom he resided. The House of Lords held that this power was not void for uncertainty because it could be said of any individual whether he was or was not a member of the class.

979. The conceptual certainty aspect of the test is illustrated by *Re Gulbenkian's Settlement Trusts*, in which it was held that the term 'residing' was not conceptually uncertain because the court could determine if a person matched that description. What counts as sufficiently certain will of course depend on the facts of the case. As for the evidential certainty aspect, it has been suggested that it would apply as it does to discretionary trusts.[1872]

2. Ascertainability

980. Since there is no obligation for the trustee to exercise the fiduciary power, it would not matter if a particular person who is an object of the trust cannot be located or ascertained.

3. Administrative Unworkability

981. Although Buckley LJ suggested in *Blausten v. IRC*[1873] that a power might be invalid for administrative unworkability, this has not been definitively settled. In *Re Hay's Settlement Trust*, Megarry V-C did not consider a power to trustees to appoint to anyone in the world save for a few specified individuals to be administratively unworkable. [1874] This is a defensible approach since donees of fiduciary powers lare not obliged to make any distribution.

1870. [1971] AC 424 at 449. Lord Wilberforce also commented that the duty of survey incumbent upon the trustee of a discretionary trust, in light of his/her duty to distribute, is more onerous – he/she is required to make 'a wider and more systematic survey'.
1871. *Re Gulbenkian's Settlement Trusts* [1970] AC 508.
1872. Graham Virgo, *The Principles of Equity and Trusts*, 2nd edn (OUP, 2016) at 115.
1873. [1972] Ch 256 at 272.
1874. [1982] 1 WLR 202 at 212. Megarry V-C appeared to suggest that the doctrine of administrative unworkability is directed at discretionary trusts.

4. Capriciousness

982. In *Re Manisty's Settlement*, Templeman J suggested that a fiduciary power may be invalidated on the basis of capriciousness if there is no discernible sensible link between the class of objects and the settlor.[1875] He gave the example of a power to benefit 'residents of Greater London' where 'the terms of the power negative any sensible intenion on the part of the settlor'.

E. Gifts Subject to a Condition Precedent

1. Conceptual Certainty

983. There are cases where the trustees are to distribute trust property upon the satisfaction of a stipulated condition. In that case, that condition must be certain. If the condition is a condition precedent, then the relevant test for certainty is whether it can be said of just one person that he satisfies the condition. In *Re Barlow's Will Trusts*, the testatrix left some pictures in her will for sale, but only after any of her family and friends were allowed by the trustee to buy them at a lower price first.[1876] The question was whether this condition precedent, specifically the word 'friends', was sufficiently certain. The court answered it in the affirmative. This is because the gift was regarded not as a gift for a class of persons, but as conferring 'on friends of the testatrix a series of options to purchase'.[1877]

984. While a word such as 'friends' may be uncertain for discretionary trusts or fiduciary powers due to the varying degrees of friendship, it was sufficient in the context of a condition precedent that just one person satisfied the condition. And because there would be some people who satisfied even the most stringent definition of 'friends', the condition precedent could be met and was not uncertain. The reason for the distinction is because, unlike discretionary trusts and fiduciary powers, a condition precedent does not actually create a class of objects but is merely a threshold requirement for someone to establish an entitlement to the property. The label 'friend' describes the option holder – all that is required is that 'the executors should be able to say of that individual whether he has proved that he is a friend'.[1878]

2. Ascertainability

985. There is no need to ascertain the location and existence of each object since it is the object who bears the burden of showing that he/she comes within the class. Thus, unascertainability of objects will not invalidate the condition precedent.

1875. [1974] Ch 17 at 27.
1876. [1979] 1 WLR 278.
1877. [1979] 1 WLR 278 at 282.
1878. [1979] 1 WLR 278 at 282.

3. Administrative Unworkability

986. Again, because the object bears the burden of showing that he/she comes within the condition precedent, there is no issue of administrative unworkability from the trustee's (or court's) point of view. Importantly, as explained above, the size of the class is irrelevant as the condition precedent operates as a threshold requirement, as opposed to creating a class of objects.

4. Capriciousness

987. There is no authority on this point although it has been suggested that if the condition can be characterised as capricious in the sense that the settlor or testator had no sensible intention for imposing the condition, then it should be invalidated.[1879] However, the concept itself appears too paternalistic and goes against the policy of upholding a trust where possible. After all, a property owner should have general liberty to decide what he wishes to do with his property, save where the proposed course of conduct is illegal. Hardcastle suggests that the doctrine of capriciousness is based on the policy that 'the court will not aid the settlor in all his eccentricities'.[1880] If this is to be accepted, it is suggested that the law should only intervene in the most extreme of cases.[1881]

F. Resolving Uncertainty

988. In some cases, the trust itself may give the trustee a power to resolve uncertainties in relation to the identity of objects. Or it may be that a third party has been appointed by the settlor to decide matters of evidential uncertainty. In *Re Tuck's Settlement Trusts*, any doubt or dispute as to 'approved wife' of 'Jewish blood' and 'Jewish faith' could, as authorised by the settlement, be resolved by referring the matter to a Chief Rabbi.[1882] Lord Denning affirmed that conceptual uncertainty could be resolved by the trustees or a third party if the settlor wished for this to be so.[1883] In any event, Lord Denning, agreeing with Lord Russell, also took the view that there was no conceptual uncertainty with the clause.[1884] Both Lord Russell and Eveleigh LJ said that 'Jewish blood' in the context meant 'some Jewish blood'.[1885] Lord Russell did not wish to defeat the settlement on the basis that 'adherence to the Jewish faith is an unintelligible concept'.[1886] Eveleigh LJ, on the other hand,

1879. Graham Virgo, *The Principles of Equity and Trusts*, 2nd edn (OUP, 2016) at 107.
1880. I. M. Hardcastle, 'Administrative Unworkability – A Reassessment of an Abiding Problem' [1990] Conv 24 at 32–33.
1881. The lack of case law evidence of the successful invocation of the doctrine indicates that the courts will not liberally apply the doctrine to invalidate trusts.
1882. [1978] Ch 49.
1883. [1978] Ch 49 at 61–62.
1884. [1978] Ch 49 at 62.
1885. [1978] Ch 49 at 64 (Lord Russell) and 65 (Eveleigh LJ).
1886. [1978] Ch 49 at 65.

offered the alternative analysis that the clause may be interpreted as meaning that the settlor had incorporated the Chief Rabbi's views as to 'Jewish faith' as his own definition.[1887] As such, the clause was not regarded by Eveleigh LJ as appointing the Chief Rabbi as the third party to resolve the uncertainty in the phrasing.

G. Consequence of Absence of Certainty of Objects

989. If the objects of a trust are not certain, the trust will fail. The third party trustee will not be allowed to keep the trust property since it is clear that the settlor or testator never intended for him/her to benefit from the property. The consequence is that the property will be held by the trustee on a resulting trust in favour of the settlor or testator. If the settlor is the intended trustee, he/she remains the owner of the property.

§4. The Beneficiary Principle

990. Even if the three certainties are satisfied, the law requires that the property must be held on trust for identified beneficiaries or objects in order that the trust is valid. This is known as the beneficiary principle. While this principle overlaps with the certainty of objects, they are independent requirements for the creation of an express trust. A trust may be manifestly created for persons but still fail for uncertainty of objects because of imprecise descriptions. Whereas certainty of objects is concerned with the trustee's ability to execute the trust, the beneficiary principle is concerned with whether there are beneficiaries who can enforce the trust. If there are no such beneficiaries, the trust is invalid because an express trust for persons must have identifiable persons in whose favour the court can order performance. Thus, it was said in *Morice v. Bishop of Durham* that '[e]very … trust must have a definite object. There must be somebody, in whose favour the court can decree specific performance'.[1888]

991. One obvious consequence of the beneficiary principle is that an express trust must be a trust for persons, and not for purposes. Thus, in *Morice v. Bishop of Durham*, a trust for 'such objects of benevolence and liberality as the Bishop of Durham in his own discretion shall most approve of' was held to be void.[1889] Whether an express trust is created for persons or for a private purpose is a matter of construction. Even if an express trust is clearly created for a private purpose, the beneficiary principle may be satisfied if it is possible to identify persons who will indirectly benefit from the trust. In *Re Denley's Trust Deed*, the trust deed provided that: 'The said land shall be maintained and used as and for the purpose of a recreation or sports ground primarily for the benefit of the employees of the company

1887. [1978] Ch 49 at 66.
1888. (1804) 9 Ves 399.
1889. (1805) 10 Ves Jr 522.

and secondarily for the benefit of such other person or persons (if any) as the trustees may allow to use the same'.[1890] Goff J held that the trust was valid by reinterpreting the beneficiary principle: 'Where, then, the trust, though expressed as a purpose, is directly or indirectly for the benefit of an individual or individuals, it seems to me that it is in general outside the mischief of the beneficiary principle'.[1891]

992. A notable exception whereby an express trust for purposes is valid is that of a charitable trust. In fact, the beneficiary principle is still fulfilled because the Attorney-General is able to enforce charitable trusts. Thus, it was said in *Leahy v. AG for New South Wales* that: '[A] trust may be created for the benefit of persons as *cestui que* trust but not as a purpose or object unless the purpose or object be charitable. For a purpose or object cannot sue, but if it be charitable the Attorney-General can sue to enforce it'.[1892]

993. There are also some very exceptional cases where express trusts for a private purpose have been recognised as valid: for example, trusts for the building of tombs and other memorials, trusts for the maintenance of animals and trusts for saying masses.[1893] However, these have been described in *Re Endacott* as 'troublesome, anomalous, and aberrant'.[1894] Where such private purpose trusts are recognised, the purpose must be sufficiently certain.

1890. [1969] 1 Ch 373.
1891. [1969] 1 Ch 373 at 383–84.
1892. [1959] AC 457.
1893. In Singapore, *see Bermuda Trust (Singapore) Ltd v. Wee Richard* [1998] SGHC 390; [1998] 3 SLR(R) 938 (a private purpose trust for the observance and performance of Sinchew rites).
1894. [1960] Ch 232 at 251. The lack of an enforcer issue is resolved, in some jurisdictions, by the introduction of an enforcer. However, Low argues that this does not resolve the enforcement problem and to the contrary, the office of an enforcer replicates the problem. *See* Kelvin FK Low, 'Non-Charitable Purpose Trusts: The Missing Right to Forgo Enforcement' in Richard Nolan, Kelvin FK Low and Tang Hang Wu (eds), *Trusts and Modern Wealth Management* (Hart Publishing, 2018, forthcoming). *Cf* David Hayton, 'Developing the Obligation Characteristic of the Trust' (2011) 117 LQR 96; Patrick Parkinson, 'Reconceptualising the Express Trust' (2002) 61 CLJ 657.

Chapter 3. Formalities

§1. Introduction

994. In this chapter,[1895] we examine the formality requirements for the creation of trusts of land and for the disposition of equitable interests. Similar to the formalities required for a contract for the sale of land, the formality requirements discussed in this chapter fulfil both cautionary and evidentiary functions.[1896]

§2. Inter Vivos Trust over Land or Interests in Land

I. Evidenced by Signed Writing

995. In most cases, a settlor can declare an inter vivos express trust without having to satisfy any formality requirements.[1897] One important exception is where the trust is declared over land or interests in land (e.g., a lease or a mortgage). Section 7(1) of the Civil Law Act[1898] (CLA) provides:

> A declaration of trust respecting any immovable property or any interest in such property must be manifested and proved by some writing signed by some person who is able to declare such trust or by his will.

996. From the wording of the section, it is clear that the signed writing has to be performed by the settlor.[1899] However, it has been argued that, where the trust involves a separate trustee, signed writing by that trustee would be sufficient. As Youdan explains:

> The trustee is of course the person against whom the trust would be enforced and, since it seems to be established that he may carry out the trust even in the absence of the required writing, it seems appropriate that he should be able to effect the formality that makes the trust enforceable against him.[1900]

While this might be difficult to square with the wording of the statute, 'it may be the most appropriate solution', bearing in mind that merely because the evidence is

---

1895. *See generally* Jamie Glister and James Lee, *Hanbury & Martin: Modern Equity*, 20th edn (Sweet & Maxwell, 2015) Chapter 6; Graham Virgo, *The Principles of Equity and Trusts*, 2nd edn (OUP, 2016) Chapter 5; Alistair Hudson, *Equity and Trusts*, 8th edn (Routledge, 2015) Chapter 5.

1896. *See* Part III (Acquisition of Property Right), Chapter 1 (Contract for the Sale of Land) §2.

1897. *See* T.G. Youdan, 'Formalities for Trusts of Land and the Doctrine in *Rochefoucauld v. Boustead*' (1984) 43 CLJ 306.

1898. (Cap. 43, 1999 Rev. Ed.).

1899. *Tay Jui Chuan v. Koh Joo Ann (alias Koh Choon Teck)* [2010] SGCA 29; [2010] 4 SLR 1069 at [28].

1900. T.G. Youdan, 'Formalities for Trusts of Land and the Doctrine in *Rochefoucauld v. Boustead*' (1984) 43 CLJ 306 at 317.

admissible does not necessarily mean that the trust exists.[1901] The existence of the trust has to be proven on a balance of probabilities.

997. As the trust is not required to be in writing, but merely to be evidenced by signed writing, failure to comply with section 7(1) merely renders the trust unenforceable, not void.[1902] Thus, the trustees can fulfil their obligations if they wish to, though they cannot be compelled to do so. Also, if the trust property has already been distributed to the beneficiary, in which case there would be no issue of enforceability, the settlor cannot recover the property on the basis that the formality requirements have not been complied with.

998. Since section 7(1) does not affect the validity of the trust but merely its enforceability, the formality requirements need not be complied with at the very outset. In *Rochefoucauld v. Boustead*, Lindley LJ said: 'it is not necessary that the trust should have been declared by such a writing in the first instance; it is sufficient if the trust can be proved by some writing signed by the defendant, and the date of the writing is immaterial'.[1903]

II. Instrument of Fraud Principle

999. A strict application of the formality requirements may sometimes lead to injustice. This may happen, for example, where a trustee seeks to retain the land by arguing that the trust is unenforceable for failing to satisfy the formality requirements. In such a case, equity will intervene and allow the trust to be enforced on the ground that the statute shall not be used as an instrument of fraud. Perhaps, the most quoted statement of the principle is that of Lindley LJ in the landmark decision of *Rochefoucauld v. Boustead*:

> [T]he Statute of Frauds does not prevent the proof of a fraud; and that it is a fraud on the part of a person to whom land is conveyed as a trustee, and who knows it was so conveyed, to deny the trust and claim the land himself. Consequently, notwithstanding the statute, it is competent for a person claiming land conveyed to another to prove by parol evidence that it was so conveyed upon trust for the claimant, and that the grantee, knowing the facts, is denying the trust and relying upon the form of conveyance and the statute, in order to keep the land himself.[1904]

1901. Jamie Glister and James Lee, *Hanbury & Martin: Modern Equity*, 20th edn (Sweet & Maxwell, 2015) at 133.
1902. *Gardner v. Rowe* (1828) 5 Russ 258.
1903. [1897] 1 Ch 196 at 206.
1904. [1897] 1 Ch 196 at 206. *See* Ying Kai Liew, '*Rochefoucauld v. Boustead* (1897)' in Charles Mitchell and Paul Mitchell (eds), *Landmark Cases in Equity* (Hart Publishing, 2012) Chapter 14; William Swadling, 'The Nature of the Trust in *Rochefoucauld v. Boustead*' in Charles Mitchell (ed.), *Constructive and Resulting Trusts* (Hart Publishing, 2010) Chapter 3.

1000. In *Rochefoucauld*, the plaintiff owned certain estates which were mortgaged. Unable to repay the mortgage debt, the plaintiff entered into an arrangement with the defendant, under which the defendant agreed to purchase the estates from the mortgagee and to hold them on trust for the plaintiff, subject to the plaintiff repaying the defendant the purchase price and expenses. Without the plaintiff's knowledge, defendant sold the estates at a profit. The defendant later became bankrupt and the plaintiff sought an account of the surplus from the sale on the basis that the estates were held on trust for her. The Court of Appeal allowed her claim notwithstanding that the agreement between the parties were not evidenced by signed writing. Had the defendant been allowed to invoke the formality requirements to deny the existence of the fraud, it would amount to using the statute as an instrument of fraud.

1001. In Singapore, the instrument of fraud principle has been applied in *Leong Sze Hian v. Teo Ai Choo.*[1905] The plaintiff had difficulties repaying his mortgage debt. The defendant, with whom he was in a close relationship, helped discharge the mortgage by obtaining a separate loan. This required the defendant to transfer the property to the defendant to be used as security for the new loan. The plaintiff continued living in the property with his family and made monthly payments of $500 to the defendant. When their relationship soured, the plaintiff filed a caveat over the property, claiming that it was held on a trust for him. The defendant, on the other hand, argued that it was an outright sale and in any event the trust was not enforceable for non-compliance with the necessary formalities. In the High Court, Rajah J held that the trust was enforceable by relying on the principle laid down in *Rochefoucauld.*[1906]

III. Implied Trusts Exempted

1002. Another way of circumventing section 7(1) is to find an implied trust. This is because, according to section 7(3), the formality requirements do not apply to 'resulting, implied or constructive trusts'. This method has the same effect as applying the instrument of fraud principle but with the added benefit of not being in conflict with the statute's wording.

1003. In *Bannister v. Bannister*, the defendant sold two cottages to the plaintiff at below market price, subject to the oral agreement that the latter will be allowed to live in one of the cottages rent-free.[1907] The plaintiff later sought to evict the defendant from the cottage. The Court of Appeal held that a constructive trust arose in the defendant's favour on the basis of the plaintiff's fraud:

1905. [1984] SGHC 5; [1983–1984] SLR(R) 324. *See also Yeo Kia Yong v. Yeo Kia Hock* [1998] SGHC 203; [1998] 2 SLR(R) 602 at [39].
1906. [1984] SGHC 5; [1983-1984] SLR(R) 324 at [21]–[22].
1907. [1948] 2 All ER 133.

> The fraud which brings the principle into play arises as soon as the absolute character of the conveyance is set up for the purpose of defeating the beneficial interest, and that is the fraud to cover which [the formality requirements] cannot be called in aid in cases in which no written evidence of the real bargain is available.[1908]

Interestingly, while the court referred to *Rochefoucauld*, the court characterised the trust as a constructive trust instead of an express trust.[1909] In Singapore, this approach finds indirect support from the case of *Koh Kim Eng v. Lim Geok Yian*, which is discussed below.[1910]

1004. Similarly, in *Hodgson v. Marks*, the plaintiff, intending to stop her nephew from turning a lodger out of the house, transferred legal title of the house to the latter.[1911] It was agreed, orally, that beneficial ownership was to remain with the plaintiff. The lodger later sold the house to the first defendant, who then executed a charge in favour of the second defendant. The question was whether the house was subject to a valid and enforceable trust for the plaintiff. The English Court of Appeal held that the trust was valid and enforceable on two alternative bases. First, the lodger could not rely on the Statute of Frauds to exclude evidence of the intention to create a trust on the basis of the instrument of fraud principle. Second, a resulting trust arose in favour of the plaintiff, either because the plaintiff did not intend to make a gift to the lodger or because the express trust failed. On this alternative basis, the formality requirements are exempted by the English equivalent of section 7(3) of the CLA.

IV. Enforcement by a Third-Party Beneficiary?

1005. The instrument of fraud principle has been applied mostly in two-party situations: where *A* transfers property to *B* to be held on trust for *A*. Suppose *A* transfers property to *B* to be held on trust for *C*. Should *C* be allowed to enforce the trust? On one view, an affirmative answer would go beyond preventing *B*'s fraud.[1912] It would be sufficient, for the purpose of preventing *B*'s fraud, to find that the property is held on a resulting trust for *A*. The problem is particularly acute where the competition is between *A* who had changed his mind and *C* who is merely a volunteer.

1006. On the other hand, Youdan suggested that *C* should be allowed to enforce the trust for three reasons:

1908. [1948] 2 All ER 133 at 136.
1909. *See also* Part I (Land), Chapter 7 (Licences) §3.
1910. [2001] SGHC 230; [2001] 2 SLR(R) 812.
1911. [1971] 1 Ch 892.
1912. *See* J.D. Feltham, 'Informal Trusts and Third Parties' [1987] Conv 246; Austin Wakeman Scott, 'Conveyances Upon Trusts Not Property Declared' (1924) 37 Harv L Rev 653; James Barr Ames, 'Constructive Trusts Based Upon the Breach of an Express Oral Trust of Land' (1907) 20 Harv L Rev 549.

> [T]he third party beneficiary should be entitled to enforce the trust … [I]t seems to be established that an oral trust of land is valid despite non-compliance with section 7; it is merely unenforceable. Consequently, where A conveys land to B on an oral trust for C, A has ordinarily no right to restitution since B is holding the property on a valid trust for C, and he may carry out that trust if he chooses to do so. The problem arises where B refuses to carry out the trust; the question then is whether A or C can claim the benefit of the *Rochefoucauld* doctrine. The claim of C is, I suggest, stronger for three main, related, reasons. First, it seems inappropriate that B, the trustee, should have the power to determine whether C or A should get the benefit of the property. Secondly, A has effectively divested himself of the property … Thirdly, the allowance of C's claim is not contrary to the purpose of the formality requirement.[1913]

1007. In English law, the debate is now settled in favour of allowing *C* to enforce the trust. In *Staden v. Jones*, Arden LJ held that placing a restriction on the instrument of fraud principle 'would not be consistent with the principle itself, which is to give effect to the arrangement informally made'.[1914]

1008. There is one Singapore case that provides indirect support for this view. The dispute in *Koh Kim Eng v. Lim Geok Yian* concerned a house which was purchased by a family business owned by two brothers.[1915] The house was registered in the name of the younger brother's wife on the understanding that she would later transfer a half-share in the property to the elder brother's wife. Tan J held that this gave rise to a constructive trust which, by virtue of section 7(3) of the CLA, was valid notwithstanding the absence of signed writing. The learned judge thus ordered that the younger brother's wife transfer a half-share in the property to the elder brother's wife. Interestingly, neither *Rochefoucauld*, *Bannister* nor *Hodgson* were cited. Neither did the learned judge explain on what basis the constructive trust arose. But the decision might be explained on an alternative basis. The younger brother's wife, being a mere donee, held a half-share in the house on a purchase money resulting trust for the two brothers.[1916] The arrangement between the parties amounted to an attempt by the two brothers to dispose of a beneficial half-share in the house to the elder brother's wife. While this would prima facie be ineffective for failing to comply with section 7(1), the younger brother's wife, by her conduct, was prevented from denying the enforceability of the disposition on the basis of the instrument of fraud principle.

1913. T.G. Youdan, 'Formalities for Trusts of Land and the Doctrine in *Rochefoucauld v. Boustead*' (1984) 43 CLJ 306 at 335–36. *See also* T.G. Youdan, 'Informal Trusts and Third Parties: A Response' [1988] Conv 267.
1914. [2008] EWCA Civ 936; [2008] 2 FLR 1931 at [32]; referring specifically to *Bannister v. Bannister* [1948] 2 All ER 133.
1915. [2001] SGHC 230; [2001] 2 SLR(R) 812.
1916. *See* Chapter 6 (Resulting Trusts).

§3. Inter Vivos Disposition of Equitable Interests

I. In Signed Writing

1009. Where a person who owns a beneficial interest in something wishes to dispose of that beneficial interest to another person,[1917] he must comply with the formality requirements provided for under section 7(2) of the CLA:

> A disposition of an equitable interest or trust subsisting at the time of the disposition must be in writing signed by the person disposing of the same or by his agent lawfully authorised in writing or by will.

The purpose of this section is to 'prevent equitable interests from being the subject of hidden oral transactions and to enable trustees to ascertain the beneficiaries'.[1918]

1010. Failure to comply with the formality requirements under section 7(2) renders the disposition void. However, if the intention to dispose of the beneficial interest is continuing, the disposition will be effective when the required signed writing has been supplied.[1919]

1011. Unlike section 7(1), which arises in fairly straightforward situations, section 7(2) arises in a wider variety of contexts. This prompted Lord Wilberforce to observe in *Vandervell v. IRC* that the section 'is certainly not easy to apply to the various transactions in equitable interests which now occur'.[1920] As the cases discussed later will illustrate, it is particularly difficult to identify with certainty what amounts to a disposition within the meaning of the section.

1012. A classic illustration is the English case of *Grey v. IRC.*[1921] The settlor transferred shares to a trustee to be held on trust for himself. Later, he orally directed his trustee to hold the shares on trust for his grandchildren. The UK House of Lords held that the oral directions were attempts by the settlor to dispose of his beneficial interests in the shares and were void for non-compliance with the English equivalent of section 7(2). However, the dispositions were effective when the settlor and trustee later executed the necessary written declarations. Since the dispositions were

---

1917. *See* Graham Battersby, 'Formalities for the Disposition of Equitable Interests Under Trust' [1979] Conv 17; B Brian Green, '*Grey, Oughtred and Vandervell* - A Contextual Reappraisal' (1984) 47 MLR 385.

1918. *Ong Siew Lay v. Ong Boon Chuan* [2009] SGHC 99 at [63]; *Ching Chew Weng Paul v. Ching Pui Sim* [2009] SGHC 277; [2010] 2 SLR 76 at [51]; *Vandervell v. Inland Revenue Commissioners* [1967] 2 AC 291 at 311.

1919. *See Grey v. IRC* [1960] AC 1.

1920. [1967] 2 AC 291 at 329.

1921. [1960] AC 1; noted in P V Baker, 'Case note on *Grey v. Inland Revenue Commissioners*' (1958) 74 LQR 180; J.W.A. Thornely, 'Trusts of Personalty–Disposition of Interests–Formality' (1960) 18 CLJ 31; Gareth Jones, 'Section 53(1)(c) and (2) of the Law of Property Act 1925 - Recent Developments' [1966] CLJ 19.

effected by the written declarations (and not the oral directions), they were chargeable with stamp duty. The principle laid down in *Grey* has been applied in Singapore on several occasions.[1922]

II. Disposition

1013. The distinction between a disposition and a (fresh) grant is not always easy to draw. This is best illustrated in by the *Vandervell* saga, which involved prolonged litigation and complex facts. For our present purposes, the simplified facts suffice. Mr Vandervell wanted to make a donation to the Royal College of Surgeons. He instructed his bank, who held certain shares on trust for him, to transfer those shares to the college. The bank executed a transfer deed in blank and delivered it to Mr Vandervell's lawyer along with the share certificates. The shares were eventually transferred to the college subject to an option to purchase, which was granted to Vandervell Trustee Ltd (VT). Dividends were subsequently declared and paid to the college. The legal dispute can be broadly divided into two parts.

1014. In the first part, the Inland Revenue argued that Mr Vandervell was liable to pay surtax on the dividends paid to the college. One argument was that Mr Vandervell remained the beneficial owner of the shares because his attempt to dispose of his beneficial interest in the shares was ineffective for non-compliance with the English equivalent of section 7(2). The House of Lords rejected this argument, finding that the section did not apply in this situation.[1923] Lord Upjohn said:

> [W]hen the beneficial owner owns the whole beneficial estate and is in a position to give directions to his bare trustee with regard to the legal as well as the equitable estate there can be no possible ground for invoking the section where the beneficial owner wants to deal with the legal estate as well as the equitable estate.[1924]

Similarly, Lord Wilberforce said:

> The case should then be regarded as one in which [Mr Vandervell] himself has, with the intention to make a gift, put the college in a position to become the legal owner of the shares, which the college in fact became. If [Vandervell] had died before the college had obtained registration, it is clear on the principle of

1922. *Ong Siew Lay v. Ong Boon Chuan* [2009] SGHC 99; *Ching Chew Weng Paul v. Ching Pui Sim* [2009] SGHC 277; [2010] 2 SLR 76; *Re Estate of Tan Kow Quee* [2017] SGHC 19; [2007] 2 SLR(R) 417.

1923. *Vandervell v. Inland Revenue Commissioners* [1967] 2 AC 291. For alternative explanations, see S.M. Spencer, 'Beneficiaries and Transferring Trustees' [1967] Conv 175; Nicholas Strauss, 'Imperfect Gifts and the Law of Property Act 1925, s. 53(1)(c)' (1967) 30 MLR 461; J.W. Harris, 'The Case of the Slippery Equity' (1975) 38 MLR 557; Graham Battersby, 'Formalities for the Disposition of Equitable Interests Under Trust' [1979] Conv 17; R.C. Nolan, '*Vandervell v. I.R.C.*: A Case of Overreaching' (2002) 61 CLJ 169.

1924. *Vandervell v. Inland Revenue Commissioners* [1967] 2 AC 291 at 311.

> *In re Rose* that the gift would have been complete, on the basis that he had done everything in his power to transfer the legal interest, with an intention to give, to the college. No separate transfer, therefore, of the equitable interest ever came to or needed to be made and there is no room for the operation of the subsection.[1925]

1015. The House of Lords, however, found that as the beneficiary of the option to purchase was not clearly specified, the benefit of the option was held on a resulting trust for Mr Vandervell. The Inland Revenue's claim that Mr Vandervell was liable for surtax succeeded on this ground. This was the prelude to the second part of the litigation. Concerned about liability for surtax in respect of future dividends, VT repurchased the shares by paying the college a cheque drawn from a settlement for Mr Vandervell's children. The evinced intention of both Mr Vandervell and VT was that the shares were to be held on trust for the children's settlement. Mr Vandervell soon passed away, after which the Inland Revenue assessed his estate for surtax in respect of dividends declared on the basis that he did not divest the beneficial interest in the shares. Specifically, the Inland Revenue argued that as the shares were held on a resulting trust for Mr Vandervell, his instruction to VT that the shares be held for the children's settlement amounted to a disposition of beneficial interest, which was ineffective for non-compliance with the English equivalent of section 7(2). The Court of Appeal disagreed. As Lawton LJ explained:

> Neither the extinction of the resulting trust of the option resulting from its exercise nor the creation of a beneficial interest in the shares by the declaration of trust amounted to a disposition of an equitable interest or trust within the meaning of sections 53(1)(c).[1926]

The learned judge was referring to the declaration of trust by VT. In other words, the beneficial interest of the children's settlement arose from a declaration of trust by VT as opposed to a disposition of an existing beneficial interest by Mr Vandervell. Thus, it has been cautioned that despite the fine distinction 'it is necessary to distinguish between activities that are properly seen as authorised acts of trustees and those that are properly seen as dispositions by beneficiaries'.[1927]

1016. The difficulty in distinguishing between a disposition and a grant also arises in the context of sub-trusts. If *A* holds an asset on trust for *B*, and *B* declares himself/herself a trustee for *C*, does this sub-trust fall within the meaning of disposition under section 7(2)? On one view, if *B* does not retain any active role as a

---

1925. *Vandervell v. Inland Revenue Commissioners* [1967] 2 AC 291 at 330.

1926. *Re Vandervell's Trusts (No. 2)* [1974] 1 Ch 269 at 326. *Cf* Graham Battersby, 'Formalities for the Disposition of Equitable Interests Under Trust' [1979] Conv 17.

1927. Jamie Glister and James Lee, *Hanbury & Martin: Modern Equity*, 20th edn (Sweet & Maxwell, 2015) at 141; R.C. Nolan, '*Vandervell v. I.R.C.*: A Case of Overreaching' (2002) 61 CLJ 169 at 186–87.

trustee, the sub-trust amounts to a disposition of beneficial interest.[1928] However, in *Nelson v. Greening & Sykes (Builders) Ltd*, Lawrence Collins LJ opined that one should not conflate the practical effect of a sub-trust with the legal position:

> [Saying that] the practical effect would seem to amount to or be capable of amounting to the 'getting rid' of the trust of the equitable interest then subsisting, is not the same as saying that as a matter of law it does get rid of the intermediate trust … [I]n the case of a trust and sub-trust of personal property the trustees may decide that as a matter of practicality it is more convenient to deal directly with the beneficiary of the sub-trust.[1929]

1017. In an excellent article, Tham explains that the authorities commonly cited in support of the first view have been misinterpreted.[1930] More importantly, the trustee of the main trust, *B*, could not possibly drop out because the subject matter of the primary trust is different from that of the sub-trust. As Tham explains:

> Even with a bare sub-trust, it is wrong to speak of the bare sub-trustee substantively dropping out because for there to be a sub-trust, there has to be subject-matter for that sub-trust to bite on. And when the subject matter of the sub-trust is the sub-trustee's chose against the primary trustee, it is conceptually impossible for the sub-trustee to be substituted by her sub-beneficiary.[1931]

III. Instrument of Fraud Principle

1018. Even assuming that a particular transaction amounts to a disposition, section 7(2) is not always strictly enforced. In *Ong Siew Lay v. Ong Boon Chuan*, the plaintiff's father was the beneficial owner of certain shares registered in the name of the plaintiff's mother.[1932] Before the father passed away, he instructed the mother to hold the shares on trust for the plaintiff. With the consent of the plaintiff, the mother sold the shares to the defendant, who is plaintiff's brother. When the plaintiff claimed the sale proceeds, the defendant denied the existence of a trust in the plaintiff's favour. Woo J found that the oral instruction by the father, which was similar to the settlor's instruction in *Grey*, amounted to a disposition of his beneficial interest in the shares to the plaintiff. Although the disposition was not made in signed writing, the defendant had known and acknowledged that the shares were beneficially the plaintiff's, and therefore he could not rely on the want of signed writing to defeat the plaintiff's claim.[1933]

1928. The authorities commonly cited for this view are: *Grainge v. Wilberforce* (1889) 5 TLR 436; *Re Lashmar* [1891] 1 Ch 258; *Onslow v. Wallis* (1849) 1 Mac & G 506; *Head v. Lord Teynham* (1783) 1 Cox 57.
1929. [2007] EWCA Civ 1358; [2007] All ER (D) 270 at [57].
1930. C.H. Tham, 'Exploding the Myth that Bare Sub-trustees "Drop Out"' (2017) 31 TLI 76.
1931. C.H. Tham, 'Exploding the Myth that Bare Sub-trustees "Drop Out"' (2017) 31 TLI 76 at 90.
1932. [2009] SGHC 99.
1933. [2009] SGHC 99 at [63]–[67].

1019. Similarly, in *Ching Chew Weng Paul v. Ching Pui Sim*, a father, who was the beneficiary of certain shares, orally instructed his trustees to hold them on trust for his son.[1934] After the father passed away, a dispute arose as to whether those shares should be held for the son or for the father's estate. The son conceded that the oral instructions by his father constituted attempts to dispose of the beneficial interests in those shares and were therefore prima facie ineffective for want of signed writing. However, he argued that the formality requirements should be relaxed based on the instrument of fraud principle, specifically the doctrine of part performance. This doctrine was invoked specifically against one of the trustees, who executed a trust deed acknowledging that she held some of the shares for the plaintiff. It was argued that since the trustee had taken steps which are referable to the trust and have acknowledged the existence of the trust, it would therefore be unconscionable for the trustee to rely on the non-compliance with formality requirements to deny its existence. While Chong J accepted that the doctrine of part performance could apply to mitigate the harshness of the formality requirements, he decided not to invoke it on the specific facts. As the plaintiff was the sole beneficiary of his father's estate, he would be similarly entitled to the shares even if the disposition were to be found to be ineffective. Thus, the learned judge invoked that principle that 'while equity will intervene to prevent unscrupulous claims, it is also trite that equity will not act in vain'.[1935]

1020. These cases suggest that the doctrine of part performance is merely one specific version of the wider instrument of fraud principle.[1936] In *Ong Siew Lay*, Woo J stressed that part performance is 'not an essential ingredient to prevent the abuse of the relevant statute'.[1937] The learned judge cited *Rochefoucald* as authority for the wider principle.[1938] Assuming this to be right, it is difficult to see when, if ever, will it be more advantages to rely on the doctrine of part performance instead of the wider instrument of fraud principle.

IV. Implied Trusts Exempted

1021. Section 7(3) of the CLA exempts implied trust from having to satisfy the formality requirements imposed by section 7(2). This is aptly illustrated in the case of *Oughtred v. IRC*.[1939] Mrs Oughtred was beneficially entitled to the life interest in a settled fund consisting of shares in a limited company. The same trustee held the absolute reversion of the very same shares for her son. By an oral agreement, the son agreed to give up his beneficial reversionary interest in those shares in exchange

1934. [2009] SGHC 277; [2010] 2 SLR 76.
1935. [2009] SGHC 277; [2010] 2 SLR 76 at [48], [51]–[53].
1936. *See also Cheong Kok Leong v. Cheong Woon Weng* [2017] SGCA 47 at [13]; *Tan Kim Heng v. Tan Kim Li* [2017] SGHC 177 at [39]–[44].
Re Estate of Tan Kow Quee [2017] SGHC 19; [2007] 2 SLR(R) 417 at [15].
1937. [2009] SGHC 99 at [65].
1938. [2009] SGHC 99 at [67].
1939. [1960] AC 206. *See* P.G. Turner, 'The High Court of Australia on Contracts to Assign Equitable Rights' [2006] Conv 390.

for other shares which the mother owned absolutely. Soon after, documents were executed to give effect to this agreement. The issue of tax liability ultimately turned on the interpretation of the Stamp Act 1891. However, the effect of the oral agreement was briefly considered by two Law Lords, Lord Radcliffe and Lord Cohen, according to whom a vendor-purchaser constructive trust arose to vest in the mother the beneficial interest to the shares.[1940] By virtue of section 7(3), such an implied trust is valid notwithstanding the absence of signed writing.

1022. In *Cheong Kok Leong v. Cheong Woon Weng*, the Court of Appeal relied on section 7(3) to hold that a common intention constructive trust is exempted from the formality requirements.[1941] While the result of the case is undoubtedly right, this is arguably not a situation that falls within section 7(2) for it concerns the creation of a trust as opposed to the disposition of a beneficial interest under a previously existing trust.

§4. Testamentary Disposition

1023. A testator may declare a testamentary trust by way of will. In doing so, the formality requirements prescribed by section 6 of the Wills Act[1942] must be complied with.[1943] In brief, a will is valid only if it is executed in writing, signed by the testator and attested by at least two witnesses. Importantly, this applies to all wills even if they do not involve land or disposition of beneficial interest. As the formality requirements under the Wills Act are more stringent than those imposed by section 7 of the CLA, compliance with the former automatically results in compliance with the latter.

1940. [1960] AC 206 at 227–28 (Lord Radcliffe); 231–32 (Lord Cohen). *See also Neville v. Wilson* [1997] Ch 144 at 157 (Nourse LJ).
1941. [2017] SGCA 47 at [12].
1942. (Cap. 352, 1996 Rev. Ed.).
1943. *See* Part III (Acquisition of Property Rights) Chapter 3 (Transfer Upon Death) §1.

Chapter 4. Constitution

§1. Introduction

1024. With the exception of a case where a settlor declares himself/herself a trustee, a trust will be constituted only when the subject matter is transferred to the appointed trustee.[1944] Similarly, in the case of an outright gift, the gift is complete only when the subject matter is delivered into the hands of the donee. Thus, in *Milroy v. Lord*, Turner LJ said:

> [In] order to render a voluntary settlement valid and effectual, the settler must have done everything which, according to the nature of the property comprised in the settlement, was necessary to be done in order to transfer the property and render the settlement binding upon him. He may of course do this by actually transferring the property to the persons for whom he intends to provide, and the provision will then be effectual, and it will be equally effectual if he transfers the property to a trustee for the purposes of the settlement, or declares that he himself holds it in trust for those purposes … [I]n order to render the settlement binding, one or other of these modes must, as I understand the law of this court, be resorted to, for there is no equity in this court to perfect an imperfect gift.[1945]

1025. Where a person has chosen one of these modes to dispose of an asset but fails to do what is necessary, e.g. a transfer, the courts will generally not perfect the imperfect gift by implying that a different mode of disposition was intended. This was again alluded to by Turner LJ in *Milroy v. Lord*:

> The cases I think go further to this extent, that if the settlement is intended to be effectuated by one of the modes to which I have referred, the Court will not give effect to it by applying another of those modes. If it is intended to take effect by transfer, the Court will not hold the intended transfer to operate as a declaration of trust, for then every imperfect instrument would be made effectual by being converted into a perfect trust.[1946]

1026. The constitution of the trust need not be done at the same time as its declaration. A settlor can declare a trust first and then transfer the legal title to the property to the trustee at a later point in time. Once the trust is constituted, the settlor will not be able to reclaim the property.

1027. If the settlor declares himself/herlsef as the trustee, no transfer of legal interest is necessary.

1944. *See generally* Jamie Glister and James Lee, *Hanbury & Martin: Modern Equity*, 20th edn (Sweet & Maxwell, 2015) Chapter 5; Graham Virgo, *The Principles of Equity and Trusts*, 2nd edn (OUP, 2016) Chapter 5; Alistair Hudson, *Equity and Trusts*, 8th edn (Routledge, 2015) Chapter 5.
1945. (1882) 4 De GF & J 264 at 274.
1946. (1882) 4 De GF & J 264 at 274.

§2. OUTRIGHT TRANSFER

1028. The most straightforward way for a person to dispose of his/her property is to make an outright transfer to a third party. Whether any formalities are required for the transfer will depend on the nature of the property in question.

1029. Special formality requirements apply to the transfer of an interest in land that is governed by the Land Titles Act.[1947] In particular, section 45(1) and 45(2) of the Act provides that any instrument transferring interest in land shall be ineffective until registered under the Act:

> **Instruments ineffectual until registered**
>
> 45. – (1) No instrument until registered as in this Act provided is effectual to pass any estate or interest in land under the provisions of this Act.
>
> (2) Upon registration of an instrument the estate or interest therein specified shall pass, or the land shall become liable as security for the payment of money (as the case may be), subject to such covenants and conditions as are set forth in the instrument and are capable of taking effect, and subject to such covenants and conditions as are by law declared to be implied in instruments of a like nature.

Other provisions of the Act provide for the registration requirements of certain interests in land. For example, section 87 provides for the form and registration of leases. Until these formality requirements under the Act are met, the transfer of interest in land that is governed by the Land Titles Act will not be effective.[1948]

1030. The assignment of debts and choses of action is also governed by special formality requirements found in the Civil Law Act.[1949] In this regard, section 4(8) of that Act provides as follows:

> **Assignment of debts and choses in action effectual to pass right and remedy**
>
> Any absolute assignment by writing under the hand of the assignor, not purporting to be by way of charge only, of any debt or other legal chose in action of which express notice in writing has been given to the debtor, trustee or other person from whom the assignor would have been entitled to receive or claim such debt or chose in action, shall be and be deemed to have been effectual in law, subject to all equities which would have been entitled to priority over the right of the assignee under the law as it existed before 23rd July 1909, to pass and transfer the legal right to such debt or chose in action, from the date of such notice, and all legal and other remedies for the same, and the power to give a good discharge for the same, without the concurrence of the assignor.

1947. (Cap. 157, 2004 Rev. Ed.).
1948. *See generally* Part I (Land) Chapter 4 (The Torrens System).
1949. (Cap. 43, 1999 Rev. Ed.). *See Tsu Soo Sin v. Oei Tjiong Bin* [2008] SGCA 46; [2009] 1 SLR(R) 529.

§3. Declaration of Self as Trustee

1031. The settlor may declare himself/herself as trustee of property for the benefit of a third party. If done effectively, this will constitute the trust. In this case, the settlor will retain the legal title to the property but he/she will no longer have a beneficial interest in it. Instead, the beneficiary will acquire the beneficiary interest. If the settlor declares that he/she holds the property on trust for himself/herself and another, then he/she would retain a beneficial interest to his/her share of property, in addition to the legal title. The other beneficiary will also acquire a beneficial interest to his/her share of the property.

I. The Requisite Intention

1032. The key question in a case involving a settlor declaring himself/herself as the trustee is whether he/she has the requisite intention of doing so. This question is one of fact and is to be answered by a holistic consideration of the circumstances of the case. In *Jones v. Lock*, a father put a cheque in the hand of his nine-month-old son and said: 'I give this to baby for himself.'[1950] He then took the cheque back and kept it. When the father died shortly after, the question was whether had given the cheque to the son or held it on trust for him. Lord Cranworth LC held that there was neither a gift nor a valid declaration of trust. He said that it was dangerous if 'loose conversations' of this sort should have the effect of establishing a trust and that the father would no doubt be very much surprised if he had been told that he could not deal with the money under the cheque.

1033. A case in which a settlor was found to have intended to hold the property in trust is *Paul v. Constance*.[1951] In that case, the deceased had separated from the defendant in 1965. In 1967, he began to live with the plaintiff although they were never married when the deceased died in 1974. Because of the circumstances, the deceased did not have a joint bank account with the plaintiff but had an account in his sole name. However, he had a special arrangement with the bank that allowed the plaintiff to draw on the account with a special note from the deceased authorising her to do so. He used the account both for himself and for the plaintiff. For example, when he received compensation for a work-related injury, the money was deposited into this account. When he and the plaintiff both won money from bingo, the winnings were credited into this account. He also drew on this account to pay for their holiday. On multiple occasions, the deceased had said that the money in the account was 'as much [the plaintiff's] as [his]'. When he died intestate, the defendant as his widow took out letters of administration of the estate. The plaintiff sought a declaration that the deceased held that money in this account on trust for her so that it would not pass to the defendant according to the rules of intestacy.

1950. (1865) LR 1 Ch App 25.
1951. [1977] 1 WLR 527.

1034. The English Court of Appeal upheld the lower court's decision that there had been a trust created for the deceased and the plaintiff. In this case, the deceased had said on multiple occasions that the money was the plaintiff's as much as it was his own. Indeed, this conclusion was strengthened when the other circumstances, such as the special arrangement in relation to the bank account, the deposit of their winnings from bingo and using the moneys in the account for their joint expenditure, were examined. They all supported the conclusion that the deceased had intended to create a trust when he said that the money was the plaintiff's as much as it was his own.

1035. Many cases turn on whether there had been an intention to make a gift or to declare a trust. If there had been an intention to make a gift, and the gift is not completely constituted, equity will not treat the failed outright gift as an instance of a trust (by declaration of self as trustee). This is because an intention to make a gift and an intention to declare a trust are very different: a donor intends to divest himself/herself of all responsibility for the property, whereas a trustee assumes onerous obligations as one. In *Richards v. Delbridge*, Delbridge purported to make a gift of his business interests to his grandson, Richards, by the following memorandum indorsed on the lease concerned: 'This deed and all thereto belonging I give to [Richards] from this time forth, with all the stock-in-trade'.[1952] The legal issue that arose after Delbridge died was whether there had been a valid declaration of trust in favour of Richards. Sir Jessel MR held that the legal owner of a property may transfer his/her property gratuitously either via a conveyance or a valid declaration of trust. Insofar as the latter is concerned, there is no need for the legal owner to use any particular words but his/her actions must be consistent with an intention to declare himself/herself trustee over the property concerned. On the facts, the words used by Delbridge were found not to be sufficient to constitute an expression of intention to make himself a trustee. Crucially, Sir Jessel MR affirmed the principled that equity would not recast a failed gift as an effectual declaration of trust.

1036. Although a court will not generally hold an imperfectly constituted gift to operate as a declaration of trust, that will not, as Arden LJ held in *Pennington v. Waine*, prevent the court from construing it as a trust if that is permissible from a holistic or benevolent interpretation of the facts and circumstances.[1953] This would be the case if the intention were never to make a gift but to declare a trust in the first place.

1037. An application of these principles can be seen in *Shah v. Shah*, in which the appellant signed a letter disposing shares in favour of his brother.[1954] More specifically, the letter provided as follows: 'This letter is to confirm that out of my shareholding of current 12,500.00 in the above company I am as from today holding 4,000 shares in the above company for you subject to you being responsible for all tax consequences and liabilities [arising] from this declaration and letter.' The

1952. (1874) LR 18 Eq 11.
1953. [2002] EWCA Civ 227; [2002] 1 WLR 2075 at [60].
1954. [2010] EWCA Civ 1408. *Cf Zeital v. Kaye* [2010] EWCA Civ 159.

letter was delivered with a signed stock transfer form but without the share certificates. This was ineffective to make a gift of the shares since the stock transfer form was incomplete. The question was whether there was nonetheless an intention to create a trust in favour of the brother.

1038. The English Court of Appeal, upholding the finding of the lower court, held that there was. Placing an objective interpretation on the letter, Arden LJ held that the appellant intended that the letter should take effect immediately, as shown by the words 'as from today'. To give effect to those words, there has to be a disposition only of a beneficial interest since legal title did not pass until the shares were registered. Arden LJ held that the parties clearly intended registration to take place later on because the appellant delivered the incomplete stock transfer form with the letter. Moreover, the appellant had used the words 'I am … holding' and the conception of him 'holding' the shares pending registration for his brother could only be given effect to by the imposition of a trust. In this case, the fact that the gift failed did not prevent the court from finding that there was an intention to declare a trust, because that was the only intention to begin with.

II. More Than One Trustee

1039. Where the settlor declares himself/herself and others as trustees, it is not necessary for title to the property to be transferred to those other trustees in order for the trust to be constituted. In *Choithram (T) International SA v. Pagarani*, the settlor executed a deed to establish a charitable foundation by way of a trust. He made himself and some others trustees.[1955] However, he died before legal title could be transferred to the other trustees. The Privy Council that the trust was properly constituted. It saw no distinction between a case where the settlor declares himself to be the sole trustee and one where the settlor declares himself to be one of the trustees. In both cases, the settlor's conscience is affected and it would be unconscionable and contrary to the principles of equity to allow the settlor to resile from his declaration that he was giving (and had given) property to the trust. The general principle laid down in the case is that, 'in the absence of special factors where one out of a larger body of trustees has the trust properly vested in him he is bound by the trust and must give effect to it by transferring the trust property into the name of all the trustees'.[1956]

§4. Transfer to Third Party as Trustee

1040. Finally, the settlor may vest titles to the property in a third party as trustee. The formality requirements for doing so will depend on the nature of the property

1955. [2001] 1 WLR 1.
1956. [2001] 1 WLR 1 at 12.

concerned. Thus, as discussed above, special formality requirements may apply to the transfer of interests in land (pursuant to the Land Titles Act) or choses in action (pursuant to the Civil Law Act).

1041. Once title to the property has been validly vested in the trustees, the trust will be constituted. Thus, in *Re Ralli's Will Trusts*, a testator left his estate on trust for his wife and two children, Helen and Irene.[1957] The testator died in 1899. By a marriage settlement dated January 1924, Helen covenanted to settle any property acquired subsequently for Irene's children. Helen's husband was appointed one of the trustees of this settlement. In 1946, the husband was also appointed a trustee under the testator's will. Helen died in 1956 and the testator's widow died in 1961, leaving the husband the sole surviving trustee of both the will and settlement. One of the questions that arose was whether the husband held Helen's share of the testator's estate on trust for Helen's estate or on trust for her settlement. Buckley J in the English High Court held that the husband held Helen's share on trust for her settlement. This was because the property had vested in him as trustee for the settlement, with the result that the trust for the settlement was constituted once the property had come to him. Thus, the circumstances in which a trustee became a legal owner of the property are irrelevant and it is the fact of legal title vesting that constitutes the trust.

§5. Incomplete Constitution: Enforcement

1042. An incompletely constituted trust is a failed trust. As a result of the principle that 'equity will not assist a volunteer', the beneficiary, who having provided no consideration is regarded as a volunteer, will have no right to enforce the trust.

1043. This principle can be seen in *Milroy v. Lord*.[1958] In that case, the settlor purportedly transferred shares to Lord by deed to be held on trust for the plaintiff. Although the settlor gave Lord the share certificates, this did not vest legal title in him since other formality requirements for effective transfer were not met. Lord also did not exercise his power of attorney as the settlor's agent to transfer the shares to him. The result was that the shares remained registered in the name of the settlor. When the plaintiffs sued to enforce the purported trust, the English Court of Appeal held that the trust had not been properly constituted. Since the settlor had not done everything required to transfer title to the shares, the title remained with him and the trust was not constituted. Although Lord had a power of attorney which would have enabled him to transfer the shares to himself, the court was unwilling to compel him to do so as the settlor's agent, when it could not make the settlor do so himself.

1957. [1964] Ch 288.
1958. (1882) 4 De GF & J 264.

I. The *Re Rose* Principle

A. *Whether the Settlor Has Done Everything Necessary to Transfer Title*

1044. Notwithstanding the principle that equity will not assist a volunteer, there are other ways by which equity can use to save a failed gift. One principle is that 'equity treats as done that which ought to be done'. By the application of this principle, where the settlor has done everything necessary in his/her power to transfer title to the trustee, but this has not happened for reasons outside of the settlor's control, equity will assume that title has passed to the trustee. This is despite the fact that the law still views the settlor as possessing the legal title to the property. The consequence of this is that there is a separation of title in that the settlor retains the legal title and the trustee has the equitable title. This gives rise to a trust by operation of law and is properly regarded as a constructive trust. The trustee can then seek the transfer of the legal title to the property to him/her. Once this is done, the trustee then holds the property on trust for the beneficiary.

1045. The principle was applied in *Re Rose.*[1959] In that case, the deceased had on 30 March 1943 transferred 10,000 shares in a company by way of gift. He also transferred another 10,000 shares to other transferees to hold on trust. The transfers were made in the form required by the company, which entitled the directors to decline to register any transfer. The transfers were also accompanied by the relevant share certificates. The transfers were stamped on 12 April 1943 and registered in the company's books on 30 June 1943. The question that arose in this case was whether the shares were transferred before 10 April 1943; if they were not, estate duty on the shares would be due.

1046. The English Court of Appeal, upholding the decision of the lower court, held that no estate duty was due because the shares were transferred on 30 March 1943. This was because the deceased had done everything in his power by executing the transfers to transfer his legal and beneficial interests in the shares to the transferees. The transferees therefore became beneficial owners of the shares on 30 March 1943, with the deceased as constructive trustee of the legal title in the shares, until the shares were properly registered on 30 June 1943. The court therefore distinguished *Milroy v. Lord*, holding that in that case, the transferor had not done everything within his power to make a transfer of the legal title in the shares as the wrong form had been used.

1047. A similar result would arise in the making of failed gift. In an earlier case also known as *Re Rose,*[1960] the testator gave a number of his shares to Hook but the gift was subject to the qualification that the shares had not been transferred to Hook before the testator's death. The question arose as to whether such a transfer had taken place because the testator had executed a transfer in the relevant form and

1959. [1952] Ch 499.
1960. [1949] Ch 78.

handed the transfer and certificate to Hook, although the transfer had not been registered before the testator died. It was held that the transfer had taken place effectively before the testator died because the testator had done all that he needed to do to vest legal title in the shares in Hook.

1048. Although these cases are said to have turned on the fact that the settlor (or donor) had done everything necessary to transfer title to the trustee (or donee), they do raise the question of just when exactly this has occurred. Indeed, it might be possible to say that the settlor and donor in the *Re Rose* cases had not done everything necessary, since consent of the directors was required and the directors could have requested for more information before allowing the transfer. However, this would be going too far since it is always possible for the settlor (or donor) to have done more, particularly when the transfer is dependent on a third party.[1961] The better view is that it should be sufficient so long as the settlor (or donor) has done everything within his/her power to effect the transfer of legal title.

B. *Re Rose* Principle Applied to Transfers Involving Property Other Than Shares

1049. The *Re Rose* principle has also been applied in situations not involving the transfer of shares. It therefore lays down a principle of general application to all types of property. For example, in *Mascall v. Mascall*, the question was whether a father had made an effective gift of his house to a son.[1962] The father had handed the land certificate to the son and executed the transfer document. But before the son could submit the transfer for stamping and to the Land Registry for registration, the father fell out with him and sought to revoke the gift. The English Court of Appeal held that there had been a valid transfer since the father had done all that was necessary on his part to transfer the house to his son. It rejected the argument that the father could have done more in the case by seeking registration of the transfer himself because in the ordinary way, it was for the transferee to register himself/herself as the proprietor of the property.

C. *Re Rose* Principle Applied on the Basis of Unconscionability

1050. The *Re Rose* principle was further extended in the English Court of Appeal decision of *Pennington v. Waine*, in which the strict requirement (in *Re Rose*) of delivery of the share transfers was dispensed with.[1963] In *Pennington v Waine*, the court held that where a transferor had done enough (though not everything in his/her power) such that a stage is reached when it would be unconscionable for him/her to recall the gift, equity would treat a gift as completely constituted such that the transferor would not be permitted to change his/her mind.

1961. Graham Virgo, *The Principles of Equity and Trusts*, 2nd edn (OUP, 2016) at 155.
1962. (1984) 50 P & CR 119.
1963. [2002] EWCA Civ 227; [2002] 1 WLR 2075. *See* an alternative analysis based on contract in Chee Ho Tham, 'Careless Share Giving' (2006) 70 Conv 411.

1051. In *Pennington v. Waine*, the donor intended to give her nephew 400 shares in a company and for him to become a director of that company. She communicated her intentions to the company auditor. Before the donor's death, the auditor had written to the nephew, enclosing a prescribed form of consent to act as a company director for the nephew's completion and informing the nephew that he had been appointed on 1 September 1998 and of the gift of shares intended by the donor. The auditor also assured the nephew that the transfer would not require any action on the nephew's part. The relevant share transfer form was accordingly signed by the nephew and countersigned by the donor and then delivered to the auditor. The auditor placed it 'on the company's file' and took no further action on the matter prior to the donor's death. The shares were thus not registered in the nephew's name. The question was whether the shares formed part of the donor's residuary estate or whether they had been validly transferred to the nephew. In this case, the donor had not done everything necessary to effect the transfer since the share transfer (in this case the share transfer form) had not been delivered to the company. In principle, therefore, the *Re Rose* exception would be inapplicable to save the failed gift.

1052. The English Court of Appeal nonetheless held that the nephew had an equitable interest in the shares. Arden LJ reasoned that since the nephew had been told of the gift of the shares, and had been made a director, it would have been unconscionable for the donor to revoke the gift before her death. The court articulated two relevant policy reasons for upholding the gift, namely that, first, this gave effect to the donor's intention and secondly, that it prevented the donor from acting unconscionably by revoking the gift. On the facts of the case, it was held that the donor's conduct had reached a stage where it would be unconscionable for her to revoke the gift: the donor had intended to make an immediate gift to the nephew; the the auditor had assured the nephew that no action on his part was necessary to finalise the transfer of the shares; and that the nephew was made a director, an office which required that he held shares in the company. Alternatively, Arden LJ said that the auditor was to be treated as an agent for the nephew for the purpose of delivering the share transfer to the company, since the auditor gave the assurance that the transfer would require no action on the nephew's part.

1053. There is some uncertainty as to the nature of the trust by which the donor holds the property for the donee. Although Clarke LJ characterised this as an express trust, this may not be correct since the donor had clearly intended to make an immediate gift to the nephew and equity will not rescue an invalid gift by treating it as a trust.[1964] The better view is therefore that of Arden LJ, who treated the trust as a constructive trust. Since a constructive trust arises by operation of law, it is immaterial that the donor did not intend to create an express trust in favour of her nephew. The problem with Arden LJ's analysis, however, is that it generates uncertainty as to what circumstances would amount to unconscionability such that equity would intervene to save an apparently incompletely constituted gift. As Arden LJ conceded in *Pennington v Waine*, 'unconscionability' cannot be determined by a

1964. Graham Virgo, *The Principles of Equity and Trusts*, 2nd edn (OUP, 2016) at 157–58.

comprehensive list of factors and must be assessed by an evaluation of all the relevant facts. In other words, the court is to engage in a discretionary exercise.

1054. Virgo characterises the unconscionability as flowing from the fact that the donor had made a representation to the nephew that had been relied upon, although not to his detriment. Thus, he thinks that the 'key test of unconscionability is a form of estoppel without needing to prove detriment'.[1965] However, in the later case of *Curtis v. Pulbrook*, Briggs J considered that detrimental reliance was necessary.[1966] He said that this requirement was satisfied in *Pennington v. Waine* because the nephew had detrimentally relied on the intended gift by becoming a director of the company, although it is difficult to characterise the taking on of corporate directorship as a form of detriment.

II. Covenants to Settle Property upon Trust

1055. Quite apart from the *Re Rose* principle, a beneficiary may enforce a term in a contract/deed if the settlor has contracted with the beneficiary to create a trust or if the settlor has covenanted by deed to settle property on trust for the beneficiary and the beneficiary is a party to the deed. However, a beneficiary may only sue on the basis of the Contracts (Rights of Third Parties) Act,[1967] if the settlor has contracted with the trustee for the creation of a trust to benefit the beneficiary or covenanted by deed to settle property on trust for the beneficiary to which only the trustee is a party. Before the commencement of the Act, the beneficiary could not sue due to the doctrine of privity. If the trustee had sued instead, he/she might be directed to not take proceedings to enforce the covenant or recover nominal damages if he/she proceeded to do so.[1968]

1056. However, if it can be shown that the trustees held the benefit of the covenant on trust for the beneficiaries, then the beneficiaries might be able to sue as the beneficiaries under a constituted trust of the covenant. To succeed on this line of analysis, it must be shown that the settlor has intended that it is the covenant (or promise), and not the property, that is to be held on trust. This is generally difficult to show on the facts of a case. While this solution was accepted in *Don King v. Warren*,[1969] this arguably escapes the problem of privity by way of a semantic re-understanding, and hence might still be substantively avoided in other cases. This solution is less frequently resorted to now that the Contracts (Rights of Third Parties) Act has come into effect, as many cases may now be brought under the Act.

1965. Graham Virgo, *The Principles of Equity and Trusts*, 2nd edn (OUP, 2016) at 157–58.
1966. [2011] EWHC 167 (Ch).
1967. (Cap. 53B, 2002 Rev. Ed.).
1968. *Re Cook's Settlement Trusts* [1965] Ch 902.
1969. [1998] 2 All ER 608.

III. Exceptions to the Rule That Equity Does Not Assist a Volunteer

1057. One problem that volunteers face is that equity does not insist on the constitution of a trust in so far as they are concerned. One exception to this is the so-called rule in *Strong v. Bird*.[1970] According to this rule, equity will perfect an imperfect gift if the donee is appointed as the donor's executor or is his administrator on intestacy. The rationale for the rule was explained by Jessel MR as follows:

> It appears to me that there being a continuing intention to give, and there being a legal act which transferred the ownership or released the obligation - for it is the same thing - the transaction is perfected, and he does not want the aid of the court of equity to carry it out, or to make it complete, because it is complete already, and there is no equity against him to take the property away from him.[1971]

1058. Another exception is the doctrine of *donatio mortis causa*, which operates where the donor intended to gift his property to the donee but only effective if he dies. In this case, even if the donor fails to effectively transfer the property to the done when he was alive, equity will insist that his executors or administrators perfect the gift. In *Koh Cheong Heng v. Ho Yee Fong*, Judith Prakash J explained the requirements for the application of the doctrine as follows:

(a) First, a gift must have been made in contemplation of impending death.
(b) Second, the gift must have been made upon the condition that it is to be absolute and complete only on the donor's death. The condition need not be express, and will normally be implied from the fact that the gift was made when the donor was ill.
(c) Third, there must have been delivery of the subject matter of the gift, or of something representing it, which the donee accepts. When the donor delivers the property, he must intend to part with dominion over it, rather than with mere physical possession.[1972]

In*Koh Cheong Heng*, a husband applied to court for the reconveyance of his flat, which was in the joint names of his wife and himself, to his sole name. He had earlier conveyed the flat to his wife and himself as joint owners when he was very ill, to ensure that she would be provided for if he should predecease her. Unfortunately, post-conveyance, his wife had lost testamentary capacity by reason of severe head injuries. He thus became concerned that if he should predecease his wife, she would become solely entitled to the property and on her death, the flat would pass to her relatives in accordance with intestacy rules, instead of his relatives as he had intended. He sought to revoke the gift on the basis that the gift was a *donatio mortis causa* and not an immediate inter vivos gift. The High Court allowed the husband's application. It ruled that delivery of

---

1970. [1874] LR 18 Eq 315. *See also Re James* [1935] Ch 449.
1971. [1874] LR 18 Eq 315 at 318.
1972. [2011] SGHC 48; [2011] 3 SLR 125 at [13].

the subject matter of the gift (the flat) was fulfilled on the facts of the case through the conveyance of the legal interest into the joint names of the wife and the husband. On revocation of the gift by the husband, the court said that a remedial constructive trust arose over the property such that the wife (the donee) held the property on trust for the husband (the donor).

Chapter 5. Resulting Trusts

§1. General Principles and Consideration

I. Categories of Resulting Trusts

1059. A resulting trust is labelled 'resulting' because the beneficial interest in the property returns or 'springs back'[1973] to the transferor under certain triggering circumstances, such that the property is held on trust by the transferee for the transferor.[1974]

1060. Singapore law[1975] presently adopts the traditional view that resulting trusts arise only in two sets of circumstances. These two categories of resulting trusts have been explained by Lord Browne-Wilkinson in *Westdeutsche Landesbank Girozentrale v. Islington London Borough Council*:

> Under existing law a resulting trust arises in two sets of circumstances: (A) where A makes a voluntary payment to B or pays (wholly or in part) for the purchase of property which is vested either in B alone or in the joint names of A and B, there is a presumption that A did not intend to make a gift to B: the money or property is held on trust for A (if he is the sole provider of the money) or in the case of a joint purchase by A and B in shares proportionate to their contributions. It is important to stress that this is only a *presumption*, which presumption is easily rebutted either by the counter-presumption of advancement or by direct evidence of A's intention to make an outright transfer … (B) Where A transfers property to B *on express trusts*, but the trusts declared do not exhaust the whole beneficial interest … Both types of resulting trust are traditionally regarded as examples of trusts giving effect to the common intention of the parties. A resulting trust is not imposed by law against the intentions of the trustee (as is a constructive trust) but gives effect to his presumed intention.[1976]

The first category is commonly referred to as the presumed resulting trusts; the second category is commonly referred to as the automatic resulting trusts.[1977]

1973. There is a view that the resulting trust operates by virtue of the beneficial interest in the property being *retained* by the transferor. *See Vandervell v. IRC* [1967] 2 AC 291 at 313.
1974. William Swadling, 'Explaining Resulting Trusts' (2008) 124 LQR 72.
1975. *Lau Siew Kim v. Yeo Guan Chye Terence* [2007] SGCA 54; [2008] 2 SLR(R) 108 at [34]; *Chan Yuen Lan v. See Fong Mun* [2014] SGCA 36; [2014] 3 SLR 1048 at [43].
1976. [1996] AC 669 at 708.
1977. *Re Vandervell's Trusts (No 2)* [1973] 3 WLR 744 at 763 (Megarry J). This category of resulting trusts is also sometimes referred to as the failed trust resulting trusts.

II. Jurisprudential Nature

1061. Resulting trusts are, like constructive trusts, trusts that arise by operation of law. However, resulting trusts are conceptually distinct from constructive trusts. It is said that constructive trusts arise by reason of unconscionability and are imposed regardless of the parties' intention, though, as we shall see in Chapter 6, this view has not gained universal acceptance. As for resulting trusts, it is equally contentious as to why they arise. It is difficult to rationalise the two categories of resulting trusts by a common account.

1062. The debate on the jurisprudential nature of resulting trusts is primarily centred on two competing accounts: (a) the intention-based account,[1978] which is often attributed to Lord Browne-Wilkinson's judgment in *Westdeutsche*;[1979] and (b) Robert Chambers' 'absence of intention' thesis.[1980] Neither account is, however, free from problems.

1063. The intention-based account explains resulting trusts as arising in response to the transferor's positive intention. There are two main contentions arising from this account. The first contention, and the less difficult of the two, relates to the content of the presumption, where the presumption of resulting trust applies. Swadling argues that the presumed resulting trust involves an evidential presumption of express declaration by the settlor/transferor of trust in favour of himself or herself.[1981] Mee, on the other hand, contends that what is being presumed is an intention to create a trust for the settlor or the provider of the purchase money.[1982] The second and greater contention relates to how one can explain automatic resulting trusts by reference to intention. Automatic resulting trusts are resulting trusts that arise on the failure of the declaration of express trust in favour of the settlor/transferor. Swadling has convincingly argued that this category of resulting trusts,

1978. There are different versions of the intention-based account. *See*, for example, William Swadling, 'A New Role for Resulting Trusts?' (1996) 16 LS 110 (Swadling later departed from this initial view); John Mee, 'Presumed resulting trusts, intention and declaration' (2014) 73 CLJ 86.

1979. It is incorrect to say that resulting trusts, even in respect of presumed resulting trusts, arise in response to the parties' *common intention*, as the requirement of a common intention is more closely associated with a common intention constructive trust. In *Jones v. Kernott* [2011] UKSC 53; [2012] 1 AC 776 at [8], Lord Walker and Lady Hale explained that the resulting trust 'depends upon the law's presumption as to the intention of the party who makes a financial contribution to the purchase'.

1980. Robert Chambers, *Resulting Trusts* (OUP, 1997). *See also* earlier works by Birks which laid the foundation for Chambers' thesis: Peter Birks, *An Introduction to the Law of Restitution,* revised ed (Oxford, 1989) at 54–73; Peter Birks, 'Restitution and Resulting Trusts' in Stephen R. Goldstein (ed.), *Equity and Contemporary Legal Developments* (Humaccabi Press, 1992) 335.
The 'absence of intention' account has been endorsed by Lord Millett in *Air Jamaica v. Charlton* [1999] 1 WLR 1399 at 1412. *Cf* Lord Goff's lack of enthusiasm for widening the scope of resulting trusts in *Westdeutsche Landesbank Girozentrale v. Islington LBC* [1996] AC 669 at 689.

1981. William Swadling, 'Explaining Resulting Trusts' (2008) 124 LQR 72. His earlier view, as expressed in William Swadling, 'A New Role for Resulting Trusts' (1996) 16 LS 110, was that the presumed resulting trust involves a presumption of an intention to create a trust.

1982. John Mee, 'Presumed resulting trusts, intention and declaration' (2014) 73 CLJ 86.

unlike presumed resulting trusts, does not involve the operation of any presumption.[1983] As he points out, in all likelihood, the settlor/transferor has not addressed his/her mind to what should happen to the property if the trust fails. To allocate beneficial ownership based on an imputed intention that a settlor, given self-interestedness, would want the property back in the event of failure of the trust is to operate on the basis of imputed intention,[1984] instead of presumed intention. Swadling in fact considers automatic resulting trusts as incapable of rationalisation.[1985]

1064. Mee disagrees with Swadling. He explains that a distinction needs to be drawn between two legal acts: (i) the creation of *a trust* by transferring property to a trustee to hold on trust; and (ii) the declaration of *a particular kind of trust* under which the trustee is to hold property.[1986] As he explains, the specific failure of certainty of objects (but other elements for the creation of the intended trust are present) in the context of automatic resulting trusts only means the intended express trust has failed. The failure of certainty of objects does not mean that the transferee trustee is to take the property beneficially. The only 'reasonable conclusion' and the preferable option to other alternatives, in view of the existence of a trust, is that the property should be held on trust for the transferor/settlor.[1987] Accordingly, on Mee's analysis, the intention to create a trust underlines both presumed resulting trusts and automatic resulting trusts. In respect of presumed resulting trusts, the intention is presumed. Mee thus offers a forceful intention-based account that unifies both categories of resulting trusts.

1065. We now turn our attention to the other competing school of thought based on the idea of an absence of intention to benefit the transferee. Chambers considers that all resulting trusts are restitutionary and arise in response to the transferor's absence of intention to benefit the transferee. On his thesis, where presumed resulting trusts apply, what is being presumed is that the transferor did not intend the transfer to be an outright gift to the transferee.[1988] In automatic resulting trusts cases, on the other hand, it is proved – by the fact that the transferor intends the transferee to take property as a trustee – that the transfer was made with an absence of intention to benefit the transferee. Chambers' 'absence of intention' account, if accepted, would mean that resulting trusts operate as a vehicle for proprietary restitution and can arise in many more situations beyond the presently recognised categories. For example, a resulting trust would arise where the property has been transferred by the claimant to the defendant by mistake or where the basis of the transfer has subsequently failed totally (total failure of consideration).

1983. William Swadling, 'Explaining Resulting Trusts' (2008) 124 LQR 72 at 94–99. *See also Vandervell v. IRC* [1967] 2 AC 291 at 329 (Lord Browne-Wilkinson).
1984. In other words, the intention is fictitious.
1985. William Swadling, 'Explaining Resulting Trusts' (2008) 124 LQR 72 at 102.
1986. John Mee, 'Automatic Resulting Trusts: Retention, Restitution, or Reposing Trust?' in Charles Mitchell (ed.), *Constructive and Resulting Trusts* (Hart Publishing, 2009) Chapter 7 at 232.
1987. John Mee, 'Automatic Resulting Trusts: Retention, Restitution, or Reposing Trust?' in Charles Mitchell (ed.), *Constructive and Resulting Trusts* (Hart Publishing, 2009) Chapter 7 at 233–35.
1988. Robert Chambers, *Resulting Trusts* (Clarendon Press, 1997) at 21. *Cf* William Swadling, 'Explaining Resulting Trusts' (2008) 124 LQR 72 at 86.

1066. The Singapore Court of Appeal has recently considered the debate concerning the jurisprudential nature of the resulting trust in *Chan Yuen Lan v. See Fong Mun.*[1989] The court was of the view that the 'lack of intention' analysis propounded by Chambers is the 'more sensible basis for the principled yet pragmatic development of this equitable doctrine'.[1990] The Court of Appeal nevertheless noted that accepting this account of resulting trust could potentially blur the distinctions between unjust enrichment claims and claims based on resulting trust, and that this 'might have unsettling effects on' third parties' rights and the security of commercial transactions.[1991] As such, the better reading of *Chan Yuen Lan* is a rejection of Chambers' wider thesis that the resulting trust operates as a vehicle of proprietary restitution to reverse unjust enrichment.[1992] The 'lack of intention' account has been affirmed in subsequent Court of Appeal decisions.[1993]

§2. Presumed Resulting Trusts

1067. There are two kinds of presumed resulting trusts: a voluntary conveyance resulting trust and a purchase money resulting trust.[1994] A voluntary conveyance resulting trust arises where a transferor voluntarily transfers a property to a transferee for no consideration. A purchase money resulting trust arises where a property is purchased in the name of a person who did not provide the purchase money or who only provided part of the purchase money. In both situations, equity presumes that the transferor (in a case of voluntary conveyance resulting trust) or the provider of purchase money (in a case of purchase money resulting trust) does not intend to make a gift. Accordingly, in the case of a voluntary conveyance resulting trust, the transferee will be presumed to hold the property on trust for the transferor; and in the case of a purchase money resulting trust, the property will be presumed to be held on a resulting trust for the provider of purchase money.[1995]

1989. [2014] SGCA 36; [2014] 3 SLR 1048. The two competing accounts of resulting trusts were first considered by the Court of Appeal in *Lau Siew Kim v. Terence Yeo Guan Chye* [2007] SGCA 54; [2008] 2 SLR 108 but the Court did not come to any resolution on that occasion. *See* Kelvin FK Low, 'Apparent gifts: re-examining the equitable presumption' (2008) 124 LQR 369.
1990. [2014] SGCA 36; [2014] 3 SLR 1048 at [44].
1991. [2014] SGCA 36; [2014] 3 SLR 1048 at [48].
1992. *See* further Rachel Leow and Timothy Liau, 'Resulting trusts: a victory for unjust enrichment' (2014) 73 CLJ 500.
1993. *Tan Yok Koon v. Tan Choo Suan* [2017] SGCA 13, [2017] 1 SLR 654 at [195]; *Chia Kok Weng v. Chia Kwok Yeo* [2017] SGCA 54; [2017] 2 SLR 964 at [47].
1994. William Swadling, 'Explaining Resulting Trusts' (2008) 124 LQR at 72–73.
1995. In a case where parties have contributed unequally to the purchase of the property, a presumed resulting trust arises such that the parties hold beneficial interests in proportions that are equivalent to their respective direct contributions.

I. The Presumption of Resulting Trust

1068. The Singapore Court of Appeal has recently affirmed the continued relevance of the presumptions of resulting trust and advancement in modern society,[1996] although the role of the twin presumptions is likely to be increasingly more limited than before.[1997] In *Lau Siew Kim*, the Court of Appeal clarified that the strength of the presumptions varies with changes in societal conditions and attitudes.[1998] In *Chan Yuen Lan*, the Court of Appeal further made clear that 'there can generally be no justification to resort to presumptions, however much they may reflect the norms, customs and mores of society, if the court is faced with the *actual* intentions and desires of the transferor'.[1999] However, the court also stressed that in determining if the presumption of resulting trust is brought to play, the question in each case is 'whether there is any direct *evidence that may adequately reveal the intention of the transferor*'.[2000]

1069. In relation to ownership of registered land, the Court of Appeal in *Lau Siew Kim* pointed out that section 53(1) of the Land Titles Act – which incorporates a statutory presumption of joint tenancy at law if parties have failed to specify the manner of holding in cases where the property is purchased in joint names – envisages that there are situations where parties have omitted to make a conscious and informed choice.[2001] The court explained that there is room for equitable intervention, through the presumed resulting trust, in such situations, with the result that parties hold as tenants in common. Of course, cogent evidence may be presented to show that the parties made an informed and voluntary choice to hold as joint tenants and accordingly, the presumption of resulting trust would be displaced.[2002] Such evidence could take the form of sworn testimony from the lawyer attesting to the completion of the transfer form or from one of the co-owners.[2003] Moreover, the court said that the strength of the presumption of resulting trust is 'much weaker' in cases where the spouses jointly contribute (whether equally or not) to the purchase of a property, especially if the property is their matrimonial home.[2004] The Court of Appeal's comments in *Lau Siew Kim* must be reappraised against the analytical framework laid down in *Chan Yuen Lan*:[2005]

> In view of our discussion above, a property dispute involving parties who have contributed unequal amounts towards the purchase price of a property and who

---

1996. *Chan Yuen Lan v. See Fong Mun* [2014] SGCA 36; [2014] 3 SLR 1048 at [152].
1997. *See also* Man Yip, 'The Presumptions of Resulting Trust and Advancement Under Singapore Law: Localisation, Nationalism and Beyond' in Andrew Robertson and Michael Tilbury (eds), *Divergences in Private Law* (Hart Publishing, 2016) Chapter 13 at 263–65.
1998. [2007] SGCA 54; [2008] 2 SLR(R) 108 at [52]–[61] and [67].
1999. [2014] SGCA 36; [2014] 3 SLR 1048 at [51].
2000. [2014] SGCA 36; [2014] 3 SLR 1048 at [52].
2001. [2007] SGCA 54; [2008] 2 SLR(R) 108 at [93].
2002. [2007] SGCA 54; [2008] 2 SLR(R) 108 at [95].
2003. [2007] SGCA 54; [2008] 2 SLR(R) 108 at [95].
2004. [2007] SGCA 54; [2008] 2 SLR(R) 108 at [101].
2005. [2014] SGCA 36; [2014] 3 SLR 1048 at [160] (emphasis added).

have not executed a declaration of trust as to how the beneficial interest in the property is to be apportioned can be *broadly* analysed using the following steps in relation to the available evidence:

(a) Is there sufficient evidence of the parties' respective financial contributions to the purchase price of the property? If the answer is 'yes', it will be presumed that the parties hold the beneficial interest in the property in proportion to their respective contributions to the purchase price (*ie*, the presumption of resulting trust arises). If the answer is 'no', it will be presumed that the parties hold the beneficial interest in the same manner as that in which the legal interest is held.
(b) Regardless of whether the answer to (a) is 'yes' or 'no', is there sufficient evidence of an express or an inferred common intention that the parties should hold the beneficial interest in the property in a proportion which is different from that set out in (a)? If the answer is 'yes', the parties will hold the beneficial interest in accordance with that common intention instead, and not in the manner set out in (a). In this regard, the court may not impute a common intention to the parties where one did not in fact exist.
(c) If the answer to both (a) and (b) is 'no', the parties will hold the beneficial interest in the property in the same manner as the manner in which they hold the legal interest.
(d) If the answer to (a) is 'yes' but the answer to (b) is 'no', is there nevertheless sufficient evidence that the party who paid a larger part of the purchase price of the property (X) intended to benefit the other party (Y) with the entire amount which he or she paid? If the answer is 'yes', then X would be considered to have made a gift to Y of that larger sum and Y will be entitled to the entire beneficial interest in the property.
(e) If the answer to (d) is 'no', does the presumption of advancement nevertheless operate to rebut the presumption of resulting trust in (a)? If the answer is 'yes', then: (i) there will be no resulting trust on the facts where the property is registered in Y's sole name (*ie*, Y will be entitled to the property absolutely); and (ii) the parties will hold the beneficial interest in the property jointly where the property is registered in their joint names. If the answer is 'no', the parties will hold the beneficial interest in the property in proportion to their respective contributions to the purchase price.
(f) Notwithstanding the situation at the time the property was acquired, is there sufficient and compelling evidence of a subsequent express or inferred common intention that the parties should hold the beneficial interest in a proportion which is different from that in which the beneficial interest was held at the time of acquisition of the property? If the answer is 'yes', the parties will hold the beneficial interest in accordance with the subsequent altered proportion. If the answer is 'no', the parties will hold the beneficial interest in one of the modes set out at (b)–(e) above, depending on which is applicable.

1070. Thus, if the parties have made an express declaration of trust regarding their beneficial interests in the property, according to *Chan Yuen Lan*, the declaration would preclude a reassessment based on the equitable doctrines of resulting trust and common intention constructive trust. This is consistent with the position under English law[2006] which made clear that a declaration of trust is conclusive of parties' beneficial interests in the property, unless a case has been established for it to be set aside.[2007] As for the point on cogent evidence of parties' intentions discussed by the Court of Appeal in *Lau Siew Kim*, it could be analysed under step (b).

1071. A resulting trust crystallises at the point of acquisition of property.[2008] As such, only 'direct' contributions to the purchase price of the property would be relevant to the presumed resulting trust analysis.[2009] Contribution to down payment and taking on mortgage liability are examples of 'direct' contributions.[2010] The Court of Appeal in *Lau Siew Kim* further affirmed that contribution to the costs of redevelopment of the property where the redevelopment takes place closely after purchase and increases the value of property would be considered a relevant contribution to the purchase price.[2011] As for contributions to the repayment of a mortgage, the court clarified that a distinction is to be drawn between contributions on the basis of an agreement made at the time the mortgage was executed and subsequent repayments of the mortgage liability that are not referable to any prior agreement.[2012] The court said that the former kind of contributions would be relevant, but not the latter.[2013] In the subsequent case of *Chan Yuen Lan*, the Court of Appeal commented that such a restrictive rule on mortgage repayments may need to be reviewed to take into account of 'the realities of mortgage repayment',[2014] highlighting the possibility of invoking equitable accounting[2015] as an adjustment mechanism.[2016]

1072. The principles of equitable accounting were more fully canvassed in *Su Emmanuel v. Emmanuel Priya Ethel Anne*[2017] and *Chia Kok Weng and Chia Kwok Yeo*.[2018] In *Su Emmanuel*, the Court of Appeal described equitable accounting as an accounting process 'where the court endeavours to do "broad justice or equity as

---

2006. *Pettitt v. Pettitt* [1970] AC 777 at 813 (Lord Upjohn); *Goodman v. Gallant* [1986] 1 FLR 513 at 517; *Pankhania v. Chandegra* [2012] EWCA Civ 1438; [2013] 1 P & CR 16 at [13].
2007. A declaration of trust can be set aside for fraud, mistake or undue influence: see *Pankhania v. Chandegra* [2012] EWCA Civ 1438; [2013] 1 P & CR 16 at [17] . Under Singapore law, the Singapore High Court has also held that a voluntary disposition may be set aside on the basis of the doctrine of unconscionability: see *BOK v. BOL* [2017] SGHC 316.
2008. [2007] SGCA 54; [2008] 2 SLR(R) 108 at [112].
2009. [2007] SGCA 54; [2008] 2 SLR(R) 108 at [113].
2010. [2007] SGCA 54; [2008] 2 SLR(R) 108 at [115].
2011. [2007] SGCA 54; [2008] 2 SLR(R) 108 at [126].
2012. [2007] SGCA 54; [2008] 2 SLR(R) 108 at [116].
2013. [2007] SGCA 54; [2008] 2 SLR(R) 108 at [116].
2014. [2014] SGCA 36; [2014] 3 SLR 1048 at [55].
2015. Applied in *Tan Chui Lian v. Neo Liew Eng* [2007] 1 SLR(R) 265 (renovation costs).
2016. [2014] SGCA 36; [2014] 3 SLR 1048 at [56].
2017. [2016] SGCA 30; [2016] 3 SLR 1222.
2018. [2017] SGCA 54; [2017] 2 SLR 964.

between co-owners'".[2019] As for the scope of application, the court noted that equitable accounting could be invoked to take into account matters such as 'mortgage repayments, improvements and repairs to the property and rents and profits derived'.[2020] Equitable accounting does not adjust the co-owners' financial burdens and benefits of land by adjusting their respective beneficial interests; instead, it 'operates as a remedy arising from the right of contribution which is an incident of one discharging another's obligation'.[2021] To clearly illustrate the operation of equitable accounting, the court quoted[2022] from Bagnall J's judgment in *Cowcher v. Cowcher*:

> Suppose land be conveyed to A for £24,000 B providing in cash £8,000 and A raising on mortgage of the property the remaining £16,000; suppose A has paid off £5,000 of the mortgage and B (though under no obligation) has paid off a further £2,000 leaving £9,000 outstanding: finally, suppose the property to be sold for £60,000. The shares under the resulting trust are one-third to B and two-thirds to A; but A must account for the outstanding mortgage of £9,000 and B is entitled to be reimbursed the £2,000 paid by him in part discharge of the mortgage. Thus out of £60,000 realised £9,000 goes to the mortgagee, B takes £22,000, his one-third share of £20,000 together with £2,000 paid off the mortgage, and A takes £29,000, that is his two-thirds share of £40,000 less £9,000 outstanding on the mortgage and £2,000 repayable to B.[2023]

1073. In *Chia Kok Weng*, the Court of Appeal, citing *Tan Chui Lian v. Neo Liew Eng*,[2024] endorsed the principle that 'the remedy of equitable accounting rests on equity and the court has a discretion as to how it may be given effect to'.[2025] It is ultimately a fact-sensitive exercise.[2026] In *Chia Weng Kok*, the ownership dispute arose out of a series of transfers of the family property between family members to keep the property safe from creditors' claims. In particular, relevant to the claim for equitable accounting, two registered co-owners of the property had contributed to the costs for the rebuilding of the property. The court said that relevant considerations would include: '(a) when the renovation works were done; (b) whether these were in the nature of works done to enhance the capital value or merely to attend to necessary repairs; (c) whether in fact there has been an enhancement in the resale value of the property as a result of the expenditure; and (d) whether these have already been enjoyed by a party in occupation so as to warrant no further remedy or to limit it'.[2027]

2019. [2016] SGCA 30; [2016] 3 SLR 1222 at [95], citing *Byford v. Butler* [2003] EWHC (Ch) 1267 at [40].
2020. [2016] SGCA 30; [2016] 3 SLR 1222 at [97].
2021. [2016] SGCA 30; [2016] 3 SLR 1222 at [100].
2022. [2016] SGCA 30; [2016] 3 SLR 1222 at [98].
2023. [1972] 1 WLR 425 at 432–33.
2024. [2006] SGHC 203; [2007] 1 SLR(R) 265 at [32]–[33].
2025. [2017] SGCA 54; [2017] 2 SLR 964 at [76].
2026. [2017] SGCA 54; [2017] 2 SLR 964 at [76].
2027. [2017] SGCA 54; [2017] 2 SLR 964 at [76].

1074. In *Chia Kok Weng*, the Court of Appeal clarified that to rebut the presumption of resulting trust, it needs to be proved that 'the transferor intended to benefit or to make a gift to the transferee'.[2028] The burden of proof lies with the transferee.[2029] It is not enough to show that the transferor did not have an intention to retain a beneficial interest. The court acknowledged that the distinction is immaterial in most cases because a transferor who did not intend to retain a beneficial interest would usually have intended a gift and vice versa. However, the case before the Court of Appeal was an exception: it was found that the transferor had not directed his mind to whether he intended to retain a beneficial interest in making the relevant transfer. He was found to be '*singularly* occupied' with carrying out the 'family compact' to keep the family home safe.[2030] It follows that the presumption of resulting trust which arose in the case was not rebutted.[2031]

1075. More generally, the presumption of resulting trust may be rebutted by direct evidence of an intention to execute a transaction that is contrary to retaining the beneficial interest,[2032] a common intention constructive trust or the countervailing presumption of advancement.[2033]

II. The Presumption of Advancement

1076. The presumption of advancement is a countervailing presumption that arises to mitigate the harshness of the operation of the presumption of resulting trust. It presumes that an absolute gift is intended in certain relationships. In *Lau Siew Kim*, the Singapore Court of Appeal, while affirming its contemporary relevance, said that the equitable presumption is confined to a 'last resort' device in cases where there is no direct evidence of the parties' intentions.[2034] In the subsequent case of *Chan Yuen Lan*, the Court of Appeal's prescribed framework of analysis underscores the 'last resort device' view of the presumption of advancement.[2035]

1077. Moreover, although the presumption of advancement continues to be relevant to the modern society, the Court of Appeal said in *Lau Siew Kim* that the strength of presumption would vary with the facts of the case. Two factors are crucial to measuring the strength of the presumption of advancement: (a) the nature of the relationship; and (b) the state of the relationship.[2036] 'Nature of the relationship'

2028. [2017] SGCA 54; [2017] 2 SLR 964 at [48].
2029. [2017] SGCA 54; [2017] 2 SLR 964 at [49].
2030. [2017] SGCA 54; [2017] 2 SLR 964 at [48] (emphasis as original).
2031. [2017] SGCA 54; [2017] 2 SLR 964 at [68].
2032. This may take the form of a gift but may also be other forms of transactions, such as a loan or the declaration of trust for a third party appointing the transferee as a trustee.
2033. *See* analytical framework laid down by the Singapore Court of Appeal in *Chan Yuen Lan v. See Fong Mun* [2014] SGCA 36; [2014] 3 SLR 1048 at [160].
2034. [2007] SGCA 54; [2008] 2 SLR(R) 108 at [59].
2035. [2014] SGCA 36; [2014] 3 SLR 1048 at [160]. The presumption of advancement inquiry is the fifth step in the six-step framework, after considering direct evidence of parties' intention and common intention between the parties.
2036. [2007] SGCA 54; [2008] 2 SLR(R) 108 at [77]–[78].

is concerned with the legal or moral obligation on one party to support the other or the dependency between the parties. 'State of the relationship' relates to how close and caring the relationships is. The point has been made above that the *Chan Yuen Lan* analytical framework affirms that the presumption of advancement can only be invoked as a last resort, as a means to plug evidential gaps. If so, it is not clear if the recommendation in *Lau Siew Kim* to assess the strength of the presumption by reference to the two aforesaid factors could be realistically applied in most cases, given that the equitable presumption is only brought into play in cases where there is scant evidence on parties' true intentions.[2037]

1078. The traditional rationale for presumption of advancement is based upon the transferor's legal or moral duty to support. The Court of Appeal in *Lau Siew Kim* was of the view that the legal/moral duty to support is not the sole basis for a presumption of advancement to arise – dependency is thus not the only consideration. The court, persuaded by Abella J's views in *Pecore v. Pecore*,[2038] said that a presumption of advancement could also arise from 'love and affection'.[2039] For this reason, a presumption of advancement could apply in respect of transfers from a parent to an adult child, although the strength of the presumption would depend on the circumstances of the case.

1079. Lau Siew Kim made clear that the categories of relationships to which the presumption of advancement applies are not closed. It is well established that the presumption applies to transfers from husband to wife, from father to child and from any one standing *loco parentis* to child. It expressed willingness to apply the presumption of advancement to transfers from mother to child,[2040] parent to adult child,[2041] and did not appear to object to extend the presumption to cover transfers from fiancé to his fiancée.[2042] However, the court did not think that the time had come to extend the presumption of advancement to cohabiting couples, owing to the lack of recognition of this kind of relationship legislatively and socially.[2043] In the subsequent case of *Ng So Hang v. Wong Sang Woo*, the High Court was similarly doubtful that the presumption of advancement should be extended to cohabiting couples who are not legally married.[2044] It indicated preference for an approach that is focused on the actual intentions of the parties. It also commented that the categories of relationships in which the presumption of advancement arises should not be 'unduly expanded', as '[t]here are limited categories of relationships in which it is more probable than not that a gift was intended simple by virtue of the nature of the relationship between the parties'.[2045]

2037. Evidence for assessing the state and nature of relationship would be relevant as circumstantial evidence for determining the intention to make a gift on a balance of probabilities.
2038. (2007) 279 DLR (4th) 513.
2039. [2007] SGCA 54; [2008] 2 SLR(R) 108 at [68].
2040. [2007] SGCA 54; [2008] 2 SLR(R) 108 at [62]–[67].
2041. [2007] SGCA 54; [2008] 2 SLR(R) 108 at [68].
2042. [2007] SGCA 54; [2008] 2 SLR(R) 108 at [69]–[72].
2043. [2007] SGCA 54; [2008] 2 SLR(R) 108 at [74].
2044. [2018] SGHC 162 at [114]–[115].
2045. [2018] SGHC 162 at [114].

III. Rebutting the Presumptions: The Rule in *Shephard v. Cartwright*

1080. The rule in *Shephard v. Cartwright*[2046] established the kind of evidence that can be relied upon to rebut the presumptions of resulting trust and advancement:

> The acts and declarations of the parties before or at the time of the purchase, or so immediately after it as to constitute a part of the transaction, are admissible in evidence either for or against the party who did the act or made the declaration; subsequent acts and declarations are only admissible as evidence against the party who made them, and not in his favour.[2047]

The rule addresses the concern of self-serving acts or declarations by rendering such evidence inadmissible.[2048]

1081. The *Shephard v. Cartwright* rule was abolished in Canadian law by the Supreme Court of Canada in *Pecore v. Pecore*.[2049] Canadian law considers post-transaction declarations/acts to be admissible evidence but addresses the risk of producing self-serving evidence by assessing the weight of the evidence. The position of the rule in English law is less clear. It was thought to have lost its force in *Lavelle v. Lavelle*[2050] but it was endorsed by the Privy Council subsequently in *Antoni v. Antoni*.[2051]

1082. In Singapore, the High Court recently considered the continued relevance of the *Shephard v. Cartwright* rule in *Chin Kim Yon v. Chin Kheng Hai*.[2052] It noted that it is possible to apply a 'looser' version of the rule by dealing with self-serving evidence as a matter of the probative weight of the evidence, as opposed to a matter of admissibility of evidence.[2053] As Coomaraswamy J said in *Tan Chin Hoon v. Tan Choo Suan (in her personal capacity and as executrix of the estate of Tan Kiam Toen (deceased))*, the 'looser' version is still consistent with the underpinning rationale of the stricter, traditional version: the courts ought to exercise caution in dealing with self-serving evidence because of the risk that a party may make unilateral post-transaction declarations/acts with a view of strengthening their case.[2054] The High Court did not conclusively resolve the issue as to which version applied under Singapore law because the application of the two versions to dispute would lead to the same outcome.

2046. [1955] AC 431.
2047. *Shephard v. Cartwright* [1955] AC 431 at 445 (Viscount Simonds), citing from a passage in *Snell's Equity* (24th edn) at 153.
2048. *See Teo Siew Har v. Lee Kuan Yew* [1999] SGCA 70; [1999] 3 SLR(R) 410 at [34].
2049. (2007) 279 DLR (4th) 513.
2050. [2004] 2 FCR 418 at [19] (Lord Phillips of Matravers MR). *See also* Eugene Fung, 'The scope of the rule in *Shephard v. Cartwright*' (2006) 122 LQR 651.
2051. [2007] WTLR 1335 at [20]–[21] (Lord Scott of Foscote).
2052. [2016] SGHC 2.
2053. [2016] SGHC 2 at [74]–[76].
2054. [2015] SGHC 306; [2016] 1 SLR 1150 at [195].

1083. In the subsequent case of *Tan Yok Kon*, the Court of Appeal held that there are strong policy reasons in support of relaxation of the rule in *Shephard v. Cartwright.*[2055] First, the court considered it to be an 'anachronistic application of the rule against hearsay in old common law' which has since been legislatively modified.[2056] Second, it observed that English law and Canadian law have moved away from such a strict approach. Third, the court pointed out that departing from this strict rule would 'allow the court to consider the parties' intentions more holistically and achieve a fairer result especially in complex cases where parties' intentions are not readily apparent'.[2057] The court thus refused to follow the strict *Shephard v. Cartwright* rule and instead would admit all evidence and weigh them accordingly. The dispute in *Tan Yok Koon* was indeed a complex case concerning the breakdown of sibling relations and the court noted there was 'a dearth of clear and objective evidence', as a consequence of the informal way in which the family business was conducted and the length of time during which the relevant events occurred.[2058] *Tan Yok Koon* thus provided the perfect factual pattern for the Court of Appeal to clearly observe the inadequacy of a strict rule.

IV. The Equitable Presumptions and Illegality

1084. A key context in which the operation of the twin equitable presumptions – more precisely, which presumption arises – used to matter is the enforcement of equitable interests in illegal transactions. Traditionally, the technical 'reliance' principle, attributable to the majority judgment in *Tinsley v. Milligan,*[2059] would apply. In essence, the party who relies on the illegality would not be able to assert his/her proprietary interest. Accordingly, a party who is able to invoke the presumption of resulting trust against a party who does not enjoy the benefit of a presumption of advancement would not need to rely on the underlying illegality. Likewise, a party who is able to invoke the presumption of advancement to displace the presumption of resulting trust would not need to rely on the underlying illegality to enforce his/her proprietary interest. The effect of the reliance principle is that the presumptions, as opposed to the merits of the case, are determinative of whether property could be recovered in cases of illegality.[2060] The *Tinsley v. Milligan* rule has thus been criticised as arbitrary and productive of inconsistent results in essentially like cases.[2061] In *Stone and Rolls Ltd v. Moore Stephens*, Lord Phillips doubted the utility of a rigid application of the reliance principle:

2055. [2017] SGCA 13; [2017] 1 SLR 654 at [110]. *See* further Alvin W-L See, 'Transferor's Intention, Trustee's Undertaking and the Scope of Fiduciary Liability' (2018) 32 TLI 50.
2056. [2017] SGCA 13; [2017] 1 SLR 654 at [110].
2057. [2017] SGCA 13; [2017] 1 SLR 654 at [110].
2058. [2017] SGCA 13; [2017] 1 SLR 654 at [2].
2059. [1994] 1 AC 340.
2060. *See Chettiar v. Chettiar* [1962] AC 294. *See generally* R.A. Buckley, *Illegality and Public Policy*, 3rd edn (Sweet & Maxwell, 2013) at [16-06]–[16-20].
2061. *See*, for example, H. Stowe, 'The 'Unruly Horse' has bolted' (1994) 57 MLR 441 at 446.

> I do not believe ... that it is right to proceed on the basis that the reliance test can automatically be applied as a rule of thumb. It is necessary to give consideration to the policy underlying *ex turpi causa* in order to decide whether the defence is bound to defeat [the claimant's] claim.[2062]

1085. Of course, the reliance principle is subject to the application of various defences. For example, where parties are not *in pari delicto* (not equally blameworthy)[2063] or where the *locus poenitentiae* principle[2064] applies.

1086. Since the House of Lords' decision in *Stack v. Dowden*,[2065] however, there was some uncertainty as to the continued applicability of the *Tinsley v. Milligan* reliance principle under English law, as domestic consumer cases are no longer subject to the resulting trust analysis. Buckley thus commented that 'it seems not unlikely that the [*Stack*] approach will render the avoidance of illegality issues by the 'proprietary interest' technique favoured in *Tinsley v. Milligan* more problematic and less readily applicable'.[2066] The *Tinsley v. Milligan* principle was also expected to further diminish in significance under English law when section 199 of the Equality Act 2010 is finally brought into force.[2067]

1087. But the demise of the reliance principle came sooner under English law and was brought about by judicial abolition. The unsatisfactory state of the general illegality doctrine under English law (which encompasses the reliance principle) came under intense scrutiny before the UK Supreme Court recently.[2068] *Patel v. Mirza*[2069] was the latest judgment handed down by the Supreme Court in its recent series of decisions that considered the doctrine of illegality. By a majority of six to three, a more flexible approach to the operation of the illegality defence was endorsed. Relevantly, the majority rejected the application of the reliance principle.[2070]

2062. [2009] UKHL 39; [2009] 1 AC 1391 at [25].
2063. *Mohamed v. Alaga and Co* [2000] 1 WLR 1815. *Cf Awwad v. Geraght and Co* [2001] QB 570.
2064. *Tribe v. Tribe* [1996] Ch 107. Neither genuine repentance nor voluntary change of mind is not required under English law. The defence is applicable even if the withdrawal from the illegal transaction was caused by the frustration of the transaction: see *Patel v. Mirza* [2014] EWCA Civ 1047; [2015] Ch 271 at [20] (Rimer LJ) and [102] (Vos LJ).
2065. [2007] UKHL 17; [2007] 2 AC 432.
2066. *See* R.A. Buckley, *Illegality and Public Policy*, 3rd edn (Sweet & Maxwell, 2013) at [16-19].
2067. *See* section 199(2) of the Equality Act 2010.
2068. *See Hounga v. Allen* [2014] UKSC 47; [2014] ICR 847; *Les Laboratoires Service v. Apotex Inc* [2014] UKSC 55; [2015] AC 430; *Jetivia SA v. Bilta (UK) Ltd* [2015] UKSC 23; [2016] AC 1.
2069. [2016] UKSC 42; [2016] 3 WLR 399, noted Graham Virgo, '*Patel v. Mirza*: one step forward and two steps back' (2016) 22 T&T 1090; Andrew Burrows, 'Illegality after Patel v Mirza' (2017) 70 CLP 55; James Goudkamp, 'The end of an era? Illegality in private law in the Supreme Court' (2017) 133 LQR 14. *See also* Man Yip, 'The Restitutionary Aftermath of Contractual Illegality' [2015] RLR 106.
2070. [2016] UKSC 42; [2016] 3 WLR 399 at [110] (Lord Toulson); and [136] (Lord Clarke).

1088. Lord Toulson, delivering the leading judgment in *Patel v. Mirza*,[2071] said that '[t]he essential rationale of the illegality doctrine is that it would be contrary to the public interest to enforce a claim if to do so would be harmful to the integrity of the legal system'.[2072] He identified three considerations in assessing whether the public interest would be harmed:

> (a) to consider the underlying purpose of the prohibition which has been transgressed and whether that purpose will be enhanced by denial of the claim, (b) to consider any other relevant public policy on which the denial of the claim may have an impact and (c) to consider whether denial of the claim would be a proportionate response to the illegality, bearing in mind that punishment is a matter for the criminal courts.[2073]

1089. Lord Toulson further emphasised that the assessment to be undertaken in each case must be 'principled and transparent'.[2074] In particular, he identified relevant factors to be considered under the proportionality consideration, though qualifying that he is not prescribing a closed list.[2075] The factors include seriousness of the conduct; the centrality of the conduct to the contract; whether the conduct was intention; and whether there was a marked disparity in the parties' respective culpability.

1090. After *Patel v. Mirza*, the fate of the *locus poenitentiae* defence is uncertain. It would appear to be subsumed into the three-consideration framework set out by Lord Toulson, as opposed to being of independent existence as a separate defence.[2076] Lord Sumption (who disagreed with the majority approach) and Lord Neuberger, on the other hand, considered the defence to be still relevant and of independent existence. But Lord Sumption, in particular, reinterpreted the defence to be grounded on total failure of basis (illegality caused the failure) for which restitution would be available.[2077]

1091. We now turn to consider the position under Singapore law. The *Tinsley v. Milligan* reliance principle has been endorsed by the Singapore Court of Appeal in the case of *Shi Fang v. Koh Pee Huat*,[2078] although the *dicta* endorsement of the

2071. With whom Lady Hale, Lord Kerr, Lord Wilson and Lord Hodge agreed. Lord Neuberger, whilst preferred a different approach, ultimately expressed some support for Lord Toulson's approach (see [2016] UKSC 42; [2016] 3 WLR 399 at [174]–[175]).

2072. [2016] UKSC 42; [2016] 3 WLR 399 at [120].

2073. [2016] UKSC 42; [2016] 3 WLR 399 at [120].

2074. [2016] UKSC 42; [2016] 3 WLR 399 at [120].

2075. [2016] UKSC 42; [2016] 3 WLR 399 at [107].

2076. Graham Virgo, '*Patel v. Mirza*: one step forward and two steps back' (2016) 22 T&T 1090 at 1097.

2077. [2016] UKSC 42; [2016] 3 WLR 399 at [249].

2078. [1996] SGCA 28; [1996] 1 SLR(R) 906.

majority view in *Tinsley v. Milligan* was given without the consideration of an earlier Singapore Court of Appeal decision in *Suntoso Jacob v. Kong Miao Ming*.[2079] Notably, the decision in *Suntoso Jacob* was consistent with the minority view in *Tinsley v. Milligan*:[2080] a property is not recoverable if it is transferred under an illegal transaction.

1092. Nevertheless, as a result of recent in-depth judicial review on the principles relating to contractual illegality, the retention of the equitable presumptions under Singapore law does not further entrench the *Tinsley v. Milligan* principle (and its problems) within local jurisprudence. In *Ting Siew May v. Boon Lay Choo*, a case on contractual illegality, the Singapore Court of Appeal clarified that the 'reliance principle'[2081] is a 'legal principle necessarily embodying normative elements'.[2082] It stressed that the question is therefore not whether the illegality had to be specifically pleaded by one party (a procedural issue), but whether the party is seeking to enforce an illegal contract (a substantive issue).[2083] The court explained that the law of illegality and public policy is underpinned by considerations of wider public interest.[2084]

1093. In *Ochroid Trading Ltd v. Chua Siok Lui*,[2085] the Court of Appeal had the opportunity to consider if Singapore law would follow the majority approach *in Patel v. Mirza*. *Ochroid* concerned contractual illegality. There were two issues: whether the contractual claim failed because the moneylending contracts were illegal and unenforceable under the Moneylenders Act;[2086] and whether the claim in unjust enrichment to recover the benefits conferred under the said contracts could succeed. Notably, the Court of Appeal had previously laid down a two-stage approach for dealing with contractual illegality and restitutionary consequences in *Ting Siew May*.[2087] The Court of Appeal declined to follow the majority approach in *Patel v. Mirza*. The court said that the majority approach engenders uncertainty and draws an unprincipled distinction between statutory illegality and common law illegality.[2088] The court went on to explain that it is unnecessary for Singapore law

2079. [1984] SGHC 12; [1983–1984] SLR(R) 458. The reliance principle in *Tinsley v. Milligan* had been later applied in *Chee Jok Heng Stephanie v. Chang Yue Shoon* [2010] SGHC 153; [2010] 3 SLR 1131; *Guillaume Levy-Lambert v. Goh See Yuen Pierre* [2010] SGDC 482; *Lim Leong Huat v. Chip Hup Hup Kee Construction Pte Ltd* [2010] SGHC 170; [2011] 1 SLR 657. None of these cases discussed the implications of the ruling in *Suntoso Jacob v. Koh Miao Ming* [1984] SGHC 12; [1983–1984] SLR(R) 458.

2080. *See* Lord Goff's judgment in *Tinsley v. Milligan* [1994] 1 AC 340 at 361, which has been concurred in by Lord Keith.

2081. The rule is generally associated with the decision of the English Court of Appeal in *Bowmakers v. Barnet Instruments* [1945] KB 65.

2082. [2014] SGCA 28; [2014] 3 SLR 609 at [127].

2083. [2014] SGCA 28; [2014] 3 SLR 609 at [127].

2084. *Ting Siew May v. Boon Lay Choo* [2014] SGCA 28; [2014] 3 SLR 609 at [128].

2085. [2018] SGCA 5.

2086. (Cap. 188, 2010 Rev. Ed.).

2087. *See* a summary of the approach in *Ochroid* [2018] SGCA 5 at [63]–[66].

2088. [2018] SGCA 5 at [114]–[125].

to follow *Patel v. Mirza*, in light of the *Ting Siew May* approach that has already been laid down under local jurisprudence.[2089]

1094. Importantly, in *Ochroid*, the Court of Appeal firmly rejected a procedural and formal application of 'reliance' as characterised by the application in *Tinsley v. Milligan*.[2090] The court endorsed the application of a normative or substantive principle of reliance – one that is '***only engaged when a plaintiff seeks to directly enforce and profit from the illegal contract***'.[2091] If an independent cause of action is brought to claim restitution of benefits transferred pursuant to a contract, the claim will be allowed as there is substantive reliance on the underlying illegality.[2092]

1095. Finally, the court said in obiter that the *locus poenitentiae doctrine* is 'best rationalised as falling within a narrow category of unjust enrichment where restitution is allowed based on the policy of discouraging unlawful conduct', and it is only engaged if there is genuine and voluntary withdrawal from the illegal transaction.[2093] The court recognised that this would mean a disagreement with the decision in *Tribe v. Tribe*, but it preferred not to render a conclusive view in the matter until a suitable opportunity arises in future where the issue is germane to a dispute that comes before the court.[2094]

§3. Failure of Express Trusts: 'Automatic' Resulting Trusts

1096. The second category of resulting trusts, also commonly referred to as the 'automatic' resulting trusts, arise on the failure of an express trust. In *Re Vandervell's Trusts (No 2)*, Megarry J said:

> [A] transfer to B is made on trusts which leave some or all of the beneficial interest undisposed of. B automatically holds on a resulting trust for A to the extent that the beneficial interest has not been carried to him or others.[2095]

1097. The express trust may have failed for various reasons, including initial failure of the trust,[2096] invalidity of the trust,[2097] incomplete exhaustion of the

2089. [2018] SGCA 5 at [125].
2090. [2018] SGCA 5 at [125].
2091. [2018] SGCA 5 at [137] (emphasis in original).
2092. [2018] SGCA 5 at [137].
2093. [2018] SGCA 5 at [174].
2094. [2018] SGCA 5 at [175].
2095. [1974] Ch 269 at 294; endorsed in *Goh Swee Fang v. Tiah Juah Kim* [1994] SGCA 118; [1994] 3 SLR(R) 556.
2096. *Morice v. Bishop of Durham* (1804) 9 Ves 399; *Essery v. Cowlard* (1884) 26 Ch D 191; *Re Ames' Settlement* [1946] Ch 217.
2097. *Vandervell v. IRC* [1967] 2 AC 291 (invalid by reason of non-compliance with formality).

beneficial interest (surplus),[2098] etc. In respect of cases of incomplete exhaustion of the beneficial interest, it should be noted that the resulting trust is not the only response or an appropriate response to some of these situations. For instance, in *Re Osoba*,[2099] the court found that the testator's intention was for the provision of *an absolute gift* to the beneficiary and the stated purposes of how the gift was to be applied were simply expression of the motive. In that case, the intention to make an absolute gift was construed from the fact that the testator had given the entire residuary estate to be applied for the benefit of the beneficiaries. In the case of a charitable purpose trust, the surplus funds will be applied cyprès.

§4. *QUISTCLOSE* TRUST

1098. The *Quistclose* trust doctrine has been accepted as part of Singapore law.[2100] In *Pacific Rim Palm Oil Ltd v. PT Asiatic Persada*, Ang J described the doctrine as follows:

> [W]here money is advanced by A to B, with the mutual intention that it should be used exclusively for a specific purpose, there will be implied (in the absence of any contrary intention) a stipulation that if the purpose fails the money will be repaid, and the arrangement will give rise to a relationship of a fiduciary character, or trust.[2101]

1099. The dominant judicial account of a *Quistclose* trust under English law is that it is a resulting trust, following Lord Millett's analysis in *Twinsectra v. Yardley*.[2102] Lord Wilberforce's dual-trusts analysis in *Barclays Bank Ltd v. Quistclose Investments Ltd*[2103] – the case from which the doctrine derived its name – has generally been rejected.[2104] Indeed, Lord Wilberforce's account would not have been able to fully explain the result in *Twinsectra* itself, where the loan was extended to perform the abstract purpose of acquiring properties, without also taking the major

2098. *Re the Trusts of the Abbott Fund* [1900] 2 Ch 326 (surplus of a private purpose express trust that was valid). In the case of a charitable purpose trust, the surplus will be applied cyprès.
2099. [1979] 1 WLR 247.
2100. *See generally* Alvin W-L See, 'The *Quistclose* Trust in Singapore' (2014) 20 T&T 362.
2101. *Pacific Rim Palm Oil Ltd v. PT Asiatic Persada* [2003] SGHC 243; [2003] 4 SLR(R) 731 at [16]. Although a number of Singapore cases endorsed the requirement of a 'mutual intention' for a *Quistclose* trust to arise, it remains a matter of debate whether this requirement is justified as a matter of principle. *See* Jamie Glister, 'Mutual Intention and *Quistclose* Trusts' (2012) 6 J Eq 221 at 231. *Cf* Man Yip, 'The commercial context in trust law' [2016] Conv 347 at 354–55.
2102. *Twinsectra v. Yardley* [2002] UKHL 12; [2002] 2 AC 164 at [92]. The resulting trust analysis has been affirmed by lower courts, for example, *Templeton Insurance Ltd v. Pennington Solicitors* [2006] EWHC 685 (Ch) at [18], *Cooper v. PRG Power Ltd* [2008] EWHC 498 (Ch) at [14].
2103. [1970] AC 567.
2104. William Swadling, 'Orthodoxy' in William Swadling (ed.), *The Quistclose Trust: Critical Essays* (Hart Publishing, 2004) Chapter 2. *Cf* A defence on a more limited premise: Barrie Lawrence Nathan, 'In Defence of The Primary Trust: *Quistclose* Revisited' (2012) 18 T&T 123.

step of abrogating the beneficiary principle.[2105] In contrast, according to the resulting trust account of *Quistclose* trust, the trust arises in response to the *absence* of the transferor's intention to benefit the recipient.[2106] The beneficiary is the transferor, and the trust arises from the outset. Its merit lies in being able to explain the outcome without offending the beneficiary principle.

1100. Yet, Lord Millett's analysis has attracted trenchant criticisms.[2107] Smolyansky has forcefully argued that the 'absence of intention to benefit' account is highly unsatisfactory because 'it cannot be rationally assumed that [parties] did not turn their minds' to an issue as fundamental as in whom the beneficial interest is intended to lie,[2108] given that it was a commercial transaction. Millett's analysis creates, somewhat bizarrely, an 'intermediate state' between a positive intention to transfer beneficial interest to the transferee and a positive intention to retain the beneficial interest, thereby lowering the standard that is required for the acquisition of a proprietary interest.[2109] Smolyansky further pointed out that the absence of intention was not a term in the contract; it was merely deduced from the finding that funds were not at the borrower's 'free disposal'.[2110] That the funds were not at the borrower's free disposal could, however and perhaps more conventionally, be interpreted as that the moneys were subject to contractual restriction of use.[2111] In his view, by allowing the lender to acquire a proprietary right that was not explicitly provided for in the contract, Lord Millett's analysis is inconsistent with contract law as well as subversive of insolvency principles. In response, Millett defended his decision in *Twinsectra*, disclaiming any suggestion that the trust analysis is the *only* interpretation in a commercial case; but insisting that in appropriate cases, the trust is consistent with the commercial reality of a transaction.[2112]

2105. *Re Endacott* [1960] Ch 232.

2106. *Twinsectra v. Yardley* [2002] UKHL 12, [2002] 2 AC 164 at [91] (Lord Millett). Lord Millett adopted Chambers' account of the resulting trust as the explanation for the *Quistclose* trust (see Robert Chambers, *Resulting Trusts* (OUP, 2004)), although Chambers himself did not characterise the *Quistclose* trust as such. Notably, his thesis for resulting trust was rejected by the House of Lords in *Westdeutsche Landesbank Girozentrale v. Islington LBC* [1996] AC 669.

2107. *See*, for example, Michael Smolyansky, 'Reining in the *Quistclose* Trust: a Response to *Twinsectra v. Yardley*' (2010) 16 T&T 558; James Penner, 'Lord Millett's Analysis' in William Swadling (ed.), *The Quistclose Trust: Critical Essays* (Hart Publishing, 2004) Chapter 3.

2108. Michael Smolyansky, 'Reining in the *Quistclose* Trust: a Response to *Twinsectra v. Yardley*' (2010) 16 T&T 558 at 561.

2109. Michael Smolyansky, 'Reining in the *Quistclose* Trust: a Response to *Twinsectra v. Yardley*' (2010) 16 T&T 558 at 561.

2110. Michael Smolyansky, 'Reining in the *Quistclose* Trust: a Response to *Twinsectra v. Yardley*' (2010) 16 T&T 558 at 565.

2111. *See* Robert Chambers, 'Restrictions on the Use of Money' in William Swadling (ed.), *The Quistclose Trust: Critical Essays* (Hart Publishing, 2004) Chapter 5 at 86–94, cited by Michael Smolyansky, 'Reining in the *Quistclose* Trust: a Response to *Twinsectra v. Yardley*' (2010) 16 T&T 558 at 563.

2112. Lord Millett, 'The *Quistclose* trust — a reply' (2011) 17 T&T 7.

1101. However, an express trust account of the *Quistclose* trust has been endorsed under Australian law.[2113] Notably, an express trust appointing the transferor as the beneficiary coupled with a power conferred upon the transferee trustee to apply the moneys for a specific purpose achieves the same legal effects as the resulting trust analysis. In this connection, Rhodes has forcefully pointed out that the classification of the *Quistclose* trust has profound implications because it determines the requisite evidence to establish the *Quistclose* trust and therefore the frequency with which a *Quistclose* trust is found.[2114] The subtle operation of a resulting trust type of *Quistclose* trust – through inference and the requirement of an absence of intention – is, in Rhodes' words, 'the antithesis of a sound commercial arrangement'.[2115]

1102. Singapore law has traditionally endorsed a resulting trust account of the *Quistclose* trust.[2116] More recently, the Singapore courts expressed approval of an express trust account of the *Quistclose* trust alongside the resulting trust account. In *Attorney-General v. Aljunied-Hougang-Punggol East Town Council,* the Singapore High Court endorsed both resulting trust-type *Quistclose* trust as well as express trust-type *Quistclose* trust.[2117] Loh J explained the differences between the two kinds *of Quistclose* trusts:[2118]

> For an express *Quistclose* trust, the settlor-donor must intend to constitute the recipient as a trustee, and confer a power or duty on the recipient-trustee to apply the money exclusively in accordance with the stated purpose.
>
> For a resulting *Quistclose* trust to arise, the donor must have a lack of intention to part with the entire beneficial interest in the transferred money. The recipient must not have free disposal of the money ... and must be under a power or duty to apply the money exclusively in accordance with the stated purpose ...

1103. On appeal, the Court of Appeal took the view that it would not be appropriate to 'add such private law overlays to the statutory relationship between the

2113. Australia: see *Lord v. Australian Elizabethan Theatre Trust* [1991] FCA 344, *Compass Resources Ltd v. Sherman* (2010) 42 WAR 1. *See also* Jamie Glister and James Lee (eds), *Hanbury & Martin: Modern Equity*, 20th edn (Sweet & Maxwell, 2015) at [11-002].

2114. A.L. Rhodes, 'The *Quistclose* Trust's Detrimental Effect on Commercial Transactions' (2013) 27 TLI 179 at 179–80.

2115. A.L. Rhodes, 'The *Quistclose* Trust's Detrimental Effect on Commercial Transactions' (2013) 27 TLI 179 at 181.

2116. *Pacific Rim Palm Oil Ltd v. PT Asiatic Persada* [2003] SGHC 243; [2003] 4 SLR(R) 731 at [16] and [19]; *Singapore Tourism Board v. Children's Media Ltd* [2008] SGHC 77; [2008] 3 SLR(R) 981 at [157]; *Sitt Tatt Bhd v. Goh Tai Hock* [2008] SGHC 220; [2009] 2 SLR(R) 44 at [58]; *Tee Yok Kiat v. Pang Min Seng* [2012] SGHC 85 at [28]; *Verona Capital Pty ltd v. Ramba Energy West Jambi Ltd* [2016] SGHC 55 at [88]. *Cf Aero-Gate Pte Ltd v. Engen Marine Engineering Pte Ltd* [2013] SGHC 148; [2013] 4 SLR 409 at [58]. The High Court noted that the classification of the resulting trust 'not free from controversy' but did not come to any conclusive view on the matter.

2117. [2015] SGHC 137; [2015] 4 SLR 474 at [112].

2118. *Attorney-General v. Aljunied-Hougang-Punggol East Town Council* [2015] SGHC 137; [2015] 4 SLR 474 at [112]. Neither type of *Quistclose* trust was established on the facts of the case.

Minister and the Town Councils' and this objection thus foreclosed the consideration of the *Quistclose* trust claim on the facts of the case.[2119] It did not, however, comment on whether an express trust type of *Quistclose* trust should or should not be recognised under Singapore law. In the later High Court case of *CCM Industrial Pte Ltd (in liquidation) v. Chan Pui Yee*, Chua JC, citing the High Court judgment in *Attorney-General v. Aljunied-Hougang-Punggol East Town Council*, approved both types of *Quistclose* trust. It remains to be seen whether the Singapore Court of Appeal would endorse an express trust type of *Quistclose* trust.

2119. *Attorney-General v. Aljunied-Hougang-Punggol East Town Council* [2015] SGCA 60; [2016] 1 SLR 915 at [123].

Chapter 6. Constructive Trusts

§1. General Principles

1104. A constructive trust is a real trust[2120] that arises by operation of law. Unlike an express trust, it is not created based on the settlor's intention.[2121] Constructive trusts also differ from resulting trusts, the latter of which arise in two fixed sets of circumstances[2122] and are said to respond to the lack of intention on the part of the transferor of property to benefit the transferee.[2123] By contrast, constructive trusts arise in a wide range of circumstances and the categories are not closed.[2124]

I. Jurisprudential Basis

1105. The question as to why constructive trusts arise is one of ceaseless debate. The main challenge with rationalising constructive trusts lies in the wide-ranging circumstances in which the constructive trust is imposed,[2125] making it particularly difficult to formulate a single unifying theory to explain all categories of constructive trusts. There are a number of accounts put forward by scholars,[2126] though none is free from problems.[2127] Courts generally endorse the view that a constructive trust is imposed in response to unconscionable conduct on the part of the defendant owner of a property.[2128] The 'unconscionability' account has been endorsed by the Singapore courts.[2129] Nevertheless, the Singapore Court of Appeal has also warned

2120. *Cf* the unorthodox view advanced by Swadling that constructive trusts are not real trusts but are one of two kinds of court orders that (a) the defendant pay a sum of money to the plaintiff and (b) that the defendant convey a certain right to the plaintiff. *See* William Swadling, 'The Fiction of the Constructive Trust' (2011) 64 CLP 1.

2121. *Air Jamaica Ltd v. Charlton* [1999] 1 WLR 1399 at 1412 (Lord Millett).

2122. *Lau Siew Kim v. Yeo Guan Chye Terence* [2007] SGCA 54; [2008] 2 SLR(R) 108 at [34], affirmed in *Chan Yuen Lan v. See Fong Mun* [2014] SCGA 36; [2014] 3 SLR 1048 at [43].

2123. *Chan Yuen Lan v. See Fong Mun* [2014] SCGA 36; [2014] 3 SLR 1048 at [44].

2124. *Carl-Zeiss Stiftung v. Herbert Smith & Co (No 2)* [1969] 2 Ch 276 at 300 (Edmund Davies LJ).

2125. Sir Terence Etherton, 'Constructive Trusts: A New Model for Equity and Unjust Enrichment' (2008) 67 CLJ 265.

2126. *See*, e.g., D.W.M. Waters, *The Constructive Trust* (Athlone Press, 1964) (constructive trust is a vehicle for effecting restitution of unjust enrichment); Gbolahan Elias, *Explaining Constructive Trusts* (Clarendon Press, 1990) (constructive trusts arise to fulfill one or more of three aims: (1) perfection; (2) restitution; and (3) reparation); A.J. Oakley, *Constructive Trusts* (Sweet & Maxwell, 1997) (constructive trusts cannot be rationalised).

2127. *See generally* Tang Hang Wu., 'The Constructive Trust in Singapore: Five Persistent Puzzles' (2010) 22 SAcLJ 136 at 152–61.

2128. *Westdeutsche Landesbank Girozentrale v. Islington London Borough Council* [1996] AC 669 at 705 (Lord Browne-Wilkinson); *Paragon Finance plc v. D B Thakerar & Co* [1999] 1 All ER 400 at 409 (Millett LJ); *De Bruyne v. De Bruyne* [2010] EWCA Civ 519; [2010] 2 FLR 1249 at [49] (Patten LJ).

2129. In *Guy Neale v. Nine Squares Pty Ltd* [2014] SGCA 64; [2015] 1 SLR 1097 at [124], the Court of Appeal said that an institutional constructive trust 'is imposed whenever the defendant knows that the property in question has been dealt with in an unconscionable manner'. In *Wee Chiaw Sek Anna v. Ng Li-Ann Genevieve (sole executrix of the estate of Ng Hock Seng, deceased)* [2013]

that the terms 'unconscionability' and 'in conscience' are 'capable of different shades of meaning and are too uncertain to be applied as a doctrine or test'.[2130] The court nevertheless approved of 'unconscionability' being used as a rationale to underpin a particular equitable doctrine or test, though it can only be utilised as such after the doctrine/test has been applied and not before.[2131] What this means is that notwithstanding Singapore law's acceptance of 'unconscionability' as the rationale for constructive trusts, such an account only has *explanatory* force but not *normative* force. That is, 'unconscionability' – on the Court of Appeal's preferred usage – cannot be directly employed to justify the recognition of a new category of constructive trust.[2132]

1106. The Singapore Court of Appeal's approach coheres with the UK Supreme Court's approach as recently expressed in *Bailey v. Angove's Pty Ltd.*[2133] In that case, Lord Sumption (delivering the judgment of the Supreme Court) stressed that '[p]roperty rights are fixed and ascertainable rights' that are based upon 'settled principles'.[2134] His Lordship said that while it is correct as a general proposition to say that 'a recipient of money may be liable to account as a constructive trustee if he cannot in good conscience assert his own beneficial interest in the money as against some other person whose rights he is aware', that is 'not a sufficient statement of the test'.[2135] Even under English law, therefore, there must be properly established basis, as opposed to mere reference to unconscionable conduct, upon which a constructive trust is imposed.

II. Terminology

A. *Institutional Constructive Trust and Remedial Constructive Trust*

1107. The institutional and remedial dichotomy[2136] in the law of constructive trusts has generated much controversy.[2137] In the main, there are two interrelated

SGCA 36; [2013] 3 SLR 801 at [171]–[185], the Court of Appeal affirmed that the remedial constructive trust arises in response to unconscionable conduct on the part of the defendant, although it clarified that the kind of unconscionability required is not in the general and loose sense of unfairness and injustice.

2130. *Wee Chiaw Sek Anna v. Ng Li-Ann Genevieve (sole executrix of the estate of Ng Hock Seng, deceased)* [2013] SGCA 36; [2013] 3 SLR 801 at [100]. *See also Royal Air Brunei Airlines v. Philip Tan Kok Ming* [1995] 2 AC 378 at 392.

2131. *Wee Chiaw Sek Anna v. Ng Li-Ann Genevieve (sole executrix of the estate of Ng Hock Seng, deceased)* [2013] SGCA 36; [2013] 3 SLR 801 at [101].

2132. *See also Aero-Gate Pte Ltd v. Engen Marine Engineering Pte Ltd* [2013] SGHC 148; [2013] 4 SLR 409 at [60].

2133. [2016] UKSC 47; [2016] 1 WLR 3179.

2134. [2016] UKSC 47; [2016] 1 WLR 3179 at [28].

2135. [2016] UKSC 47; [2016] 1 WLR 3179 at [28].

2136. The dichotomy can be traced to Roscoe Pound, 'The Progress of the Law – Equity' (1920) 33 Harvard L Rev 420 at 420–21.

2137. *See* Michael Bryan, 'Constructive Trusts: Understanding Remedialism' in Jamie Glister and Pauline Ridge (eds), *Fault Lines in Equity* (Hart Publishing, 2012) Chapter 10 at 217–18; Tang

issues: whether a remedial constructive trust should be recognised and how is it to be distinguished from an institutional constructive trust.

1108. The dichotomy is clearly relevant for Singapore law. Unlike English law which firmly rejects the concept of a remedial constructive trust,[2138] Singapore law has always been receptive to the remedial constructive trust.[2139] In *Guy Neale v. Nine Squares Pty Ltd*, the High Court, following Lord Browne-Wilkinson's definitions in *Westdeutsche Landesbank Girozentrale v. Islington London Borough Council*,[2140] explained that an institutional constructive trust refers to a trust that 'arises by operation of law as from the date of the circumstances which give rise to it: the function of the court is merely to declare that such trust has arisen in the past'.[2141] A remedial constructive trust, on the other hand, is 'a judicial remedy giving rise to an enforceable equitable obligation: the extent to which it operates retrospectively to the prejudice of third parties lies in the discretion of the court'.[2142] On appeal, the Court of Appeal affirmed that an institutional constructive trust arises by operation of law upon the occurrence of the requisite facts for its creation.[2143] Hence, under Singapore law, some constructive trusts are considered institutional and some constructive trusts are considered remedial.[2144]

1109. Although the institutional and remedial dichotomy is relevant under Singapore law, it is not clear how that line is to be precisely drawn in practice, given that the Singapore model of remedial constructive trust has yet to be fully developed. Moreover, whether the line needs to be redrawn with respect to some established categories of constructive trusts once the remedial constructive trust is fully developed under Singapore law is another question that the local courts will have to grapple with in due course. Finally, it remains unclear whether Singapore law will recognise new categories of constructive trust solely through the remedial constructive structure framework.[2145] Thus far, there is no indication from the Singapore courts that they will not recognise new categories of institutional constructive trust.

Hang Wu., 'The Constructive Trust in Singapore: Five Persistent Puzzles' (2010) 22 SAcLJ 136 at 139–52; Keith Mason, 'Deconstructing constructive trusts in Australia' (2010) 4 J Eq 98.

2138. *Bailey v. Angove's Pty Ltd* [2016] UKSC 47; [2016] 1 WLR 3179 at [27].

2139. *See Ching Mun Fong v. Liu Cho Chit* [2001] SGCA 36; [2001] 3 SLR 10 at [36] and more recently, *Wee Chiaw Sek Anna v. Ng Li-Ann Genevieve (sole executrix of the estate of Ng Hock Seng, deceased)* [2013] SGCA 36; [2013] 3 SLR 801. *Cf Sumoi Paramesvaeri v. Fleury, Jeffrey Gerard* [2016] SGHC 181; [2016] 5 SLR 302 at [61]. In *Sumoi*, Abdullah JC, however, took the view that Singapore law does not presently recognise remedial constructive trust.

2140. [1996] AC 669 at 714–15.

2141. [2013] SGHC 249 at [140].

2142. [1996] AC 669 at 714–15.

2143. *Guy Neale v. Nine Squares Pty Ltd* [2015] SGCA 64; [2015] 1 SLR 1097 at [124].

2144. A constructive trust arising over a mistaken payment in circumstances where the recipient has knowledge of the transferor's mistake: see *Wee Chiaw Sek Anna v. Ng Li-Ann Genevieve (sole executrix of the estate of Ng Hock Seng, deceased)* [2013] SGCA 36; [2013] 3 SLR 801.

2145. *See* Tang Hang Wu, 'The Constructive Trust in Singapore: Five Persistent Puzzles' (2012) 22 SAcLJ 136 at 148.

B. Constructive Trust and Constructive Trusteeship

1110. The language of 'constructive trustee' has caused some confusion in the past, particularly in the area concerning limitation periods. The expression has been used in the proprietary sense as well as non-proprietary sense: to describe both a trustee of a constructive trust as well as someone who is being made to account as if he/she is a trustee (but he/she is not).[2146] The label 'constructive trustee', in its non-proprietary sense, has been commonly applied to describe: (a) *a trustee de son tort*; (b) a defendant who dishonestly assists a breach of trust or fiduciary duty; and (c) a knowing recipient of trust property. The non-proprietary usage – essentially to denote personal equitable relief – is unhelpful and should be corrected. In *Williams v. Central Bank of Nigeria*, a dispute concerning limitation periods, the UK Supreme Court clarified that dishonest assistants and knowing recipients are not constructive trustees.[2147]

1111. The aforesaid terminological conflation, even until recently, is evident in Singapore case law. The courts have described knowing recipients and dishonest assistants as constructive trustees.[2148] In fact, the terminological conflation has led to conceptual confusion in *Comboni Vincenzo v. Shankar's Emporium (Pte) Ltd.* In that case, Kan Ting Chiu J's process of reasoning clearly intermingled requirements for establishing liability for knowing receipt and the requirements for the award of a remedial constructive trust.[2149]

§2. Different Categories of Institutional Constructive Trusts (A Selection)

1112. In this section, we will consider the different circumstances in which an institutional constructive trust arises. Owing to space constraint, however, we will focus on a selection, particularly those that have undergone recent developments or remain contentious under Singapore law.

2146. *See Dubai Aluminium Co Ltd v. Salaam* [2002] UKHL 48; [2003] 2 AC 366 at [142] (Lord Millett). *See also* Lionel Smith, 'Constructive Trusts and Constructive Trustees' (1999) 58 CLJ 294.

2147. [2014] UKSC 10; [2014] 2 WLR 355, noted James Lee, 'Constructing and limiting liability in equity' (2015) 131 LQR 39. *Cf* Charles Mitchell and Stephen Watterson, 'Remedies for Knowing Receipt' in Charles Mitchell (ed.), *Constructive and Resulting Trusts* (Hart Publishing, 2010) Chapter 4 at 129. Mitchell and Watterson are of the view that a knowing recipient is under 'a distinctive, primary, custodial liability, which closely resembles the liability of express trustees to account for the trust property with which they are charged'.

2148. *Caltong (Australia) Pty Ltd v. Tong Tien See Construction Pte Ltd* [2002] SGCA 28; [2002] 2 SLR(R) 94 at [31]; *Comboni Vincenzo v. Shankar's Emporium (Pte) Ltd* [2007] SGHC 55; [2007] 2 SLR(R) 1020 at [64]; *George Raymond Zage III v. Ho Chi Kwong* [2010] SGCA 4; [2010] 2 SLR 589.

2149. *See* a probing analysis of the case in Yeo Tiong Min, 'Restitution' (2007) 8 SAL Annual Review at 377–81 at [20.44]–[20.56]; Tang Hang Wu, 'The Constructive Trust in Singapore: Five Persistent Puzzles' (2010) 22 SAcLJ 136 at 144–47.

I. Mistaken Payment

1113. In *Chase Manhattan Bank NA v. Israel-British Bank (London) Ltd,*[2150] the claimant bank had mistakenly paid the defendant bank a sum of money. By the time proceedings were brought by the claimant to recover the mistaken payment, the defendant had become insolvent. It became therefore necessary for the claimant, desirous of significant recoupment, to trace and assert proprietary claim over the assets that could be traced. As equitable tracing is subject to the prerequisite of a fiduciary relationship,[2151] it was crucial for the claimant to show that the money was held on trust for them before the defendant's insolvency. Goulding J held that 'a person who pays money to another under a factual mistake retains an equitable property in it and the conscience of the other is subjected to a fiduciary duty to respect his proprietary rights'.[2152] In *Westdeutsche*, however, Lord Browne-Wilkinson commented that the trust in *Chase Manhattan* could arise at the point when the defendant bank had knowledge of the mistake and not at the earlier point of receipt, as the defendant's conscience could not be said to have been affected at the time.[2153] More recently, the UK Supreme Court in *Bailey* affirmed in obiter, without mention of Lord Browne-Wilkinson's comments in *Westdeutsche* or further elaboration, that a constructive trust may arise over a payment made pursuant to a fundamental mistake.[2154]

1114. The UK Supreme Court's brief obiter in *Bailey* is, however, unlikely to be accepted under Singapore law, in light of the local courts' views on the availability of a remedial constructive trust. In *Ching Mun Fong v. Liu Cho Chit*, as affirmed later in *Wee Chiaw Sek Anna v. Ng Li-Ann Genevieve (sole executrix of the estate of Ng Hock Seng, deceased)*,[2155] the Singapore Court of Appeal said:

> A remedial constructive trust is a restitutionary remedy which the court, in appropriate circumstances, gives by way of equitable relief. In order for a remedial constructive trust to arise, the payee's conscience must have been affected, while the moneys in question still remain with him.[2156]

1115. Accordingly, it would be contradictory, on present authorities and without further clarification from the Singapore Court of Appeal, to say that an institutional constructive trust may arise under Singapore law over a mistaken payment.

2150. [1981] Ch 105.
2151. *In re Diplock* [1948] Ch 465.
2152. [1981] Ch 105 at 119.
2153. [1996] AC 669 at 714–15.
2154. [2016] UKSC 47; [2016] 1 WLR 3179 at [30].
2155. [2013] SGCA 36; [2013] 3 SLR 801 at [171] and [182].
2156. [2001] SGCA 36; [2001] 1 SLR(R) 856 at [36].

II. *Pallant v. Morgan* Equity

1116. The *Pallant v. Morgan* equity[2157] was coined and formulated as a new category of constructive trust in *Banner Homes Group plc v. Luff Developments.*[2158] The key principles of the *Pallant v. Morgan* equity were enunciated by Chadwick LJ in *Banner Homes*:[2159]

(i) A *pre-acquisition* arrangement between the parties that one of them would acquire a property and the non-acquiring party would have some interest in it.
(ii) The arrangement need not be and is usually not contractually enforceable.
(iii) At no time before the acquisition (or before it was too late to restore the parties to the no-advantage or no-detriment position) did the acquiring party inform the non-acquiring party that it did not wish to proceed on the basis of the arrangement.
(iv) In reliance on the pre-acquisition arrangement, the non-acquiring party must have either conferred an advantage on the acquiring party in relation to the acquisition or suffered a detriment to its ability to acquire the property on equal terms. In many cases, the non-acquiring party's abstention from bidding for the property will constitute both an advantage to the other party and a detriment to itself.
(v) The advantage conferred or the detriment suffered in reliance on the pre-acquisition agreement renders it unconscionable for the acquiring party to act inconsistently with the pre-acquisition agreement after acquiring the property, for example, by retaining the property for itself.

1117. Under English law, as a result of Chadwick LJ's judgment in *Banner Homes*, the *Pallant v. Morgan* equity was traditionally conceived as a type of common intention constructive trust. This characterisation has, however, come under challenge recently. In *Crossco No 4 Unlimited v. Jolan Ltd*,[2160] Etherton LJ, in light of the developments of the common intention constructive trust in the domestic context,[2161] commented that the *Pallant v. Morgan* equity should be recharacterised as a constructive trust arising in response to a breach of fiduciary duty. Arden and McFarlane LJJ, on the other hand, did not think the court could depart from *Banner Homes*. Nevertheless, Arden LJ acknowledged that Etherton LJ's interpretation has the merits of restricting the situations in which the *Pallant v. Morgan* equity may arise and ensuring consistency with the developments in the law of proprietary estoppel.[2162] The debate on characterisation remains unresolved under English

2157. The name was derived from the case of *Pallant v. Morgan* [1953] Ch 43.
2158. [2000] Ch 372.
2159. [2000] Ch 372 at 396–99.
2160. [2011] EWCA Civ 1619; [2012] 2 All ER 754.
2161. *See Stack v. Dowden* [2007] UKHL; [2007] 2 WLR 831; *Jones v. Kernott* [2011] UKSC 53; [2012] 1 AC 776.
2162. *Crossco No 4 Unlimited v. Jolan Ltd* [2011] EWCA Civ 1619; [2012] 2 All ER 754 at [133].

law,[2163] as the courts in subsequent disputes were content with applying the *Banner Homes* principles. Nor did these cases require the debate to be resolved.[2164]

1118. Singapore law recognises the *Pallant v. Morgan* equity, although there has yet to be an opportunity for the Singapore courts to seriously consider its jurisprudential basis.[2165] Relevantly, Singapore law has, for good reasons,[2166] declined to follow the *Stack v. Dowden* line of developments.[2167] To the contrary, the Singapore Court of Appeal in *Chan Yuan Lan v. See Fong Mun* wholeheartedly endorsed Lord Neuberger's minority judgment in *Stack v. Dowden,*[2168] taking the view that there is no reason why a common intention constructive trust cannot arise in the commercial context.[2169]

III. Constructive Trust over Stolen Money

1119. In *Westdeutsche*, Lord Browne-Wilkinson suggested that an institutional constructive trust arises over stolen monies as soon as the theft has occurred.[2170] However, a thief merely gets possessory title to the stolen money (in tangible form), as opposed to ownership title.[2171] It has also been acknowledged that the thief's possessory title is good against the whole world except the victim of the theft (who has the superior possessory title).[2172] In *Shalson v. Russo*, a case on tracing, Rimer J thus said that such a type of constructive trust is untenable. As he explained:

> [A] thief ordinarily acquires no property in what he steals and cannot give a title to it even to a good faith purchaser: both the thief and the purchaser are vulnerable to claims by the true owner to recover his property. If the thief has no title in the property, I cannot see how he can become a trustee of it for the true owner: the owner retains the legal and beneficial title.[2173]

2163. For academic literature addressing this debate: see Man Yip, 'The *Pallant v. Morgan* equity reconsidered' (2013) 33 LS 549; Julius A.W. Grower, 'Explaining the *Pallant v. Morgan* equity' [2016] Conv 434.
2164. *See*, for example, *Achom v. Lalic* [2014] EWHC 1888 (Ch); *Generator Developments LLP v. LIDL (UK) GmbH* [2016] EWHC 816 (Ch).
2165. *See Ong Heng Chuan v. Ong Boon Chuan* [2002] SGHC 285; [2003] 2 SLR(R) 469; *Peh Kan Chan v. Tan Chong Realty (Pte) Ltd* [2016] SGHC 135.
2166. [2014] 3 SLR 1048 at [151]–[152].
2167. *See* further Man Yip, 'The Presumptions of Resulting Trust and Advancement under Singapore Law: Localisation, Nationalism and Beyond' in Andrew Robertson and Michael Tilbury (eds), *Divergences in Private Law* (Hart Publishing, 2016) Chapter 13.
2168. [2014] SGCA 36; [2014] 3 SLR 1048 at [153]–[159].
2169. [2014] SGCA 36; [2014] 3 SLR 1048 at [157].
2170. [1996] AC 669 at 715–16.
2171. *Costello v. Chief Constable of Derbyshire* [2001] EWCA Civ 381; [2001] 3 All ER 150.
2172. *Islamic Republic of Iran v. Barakat Galleries Ltd* [2007] EWCA Civ 1374; [2009] QB 22 at [15] (Lord Phillips).
2173. [2003] EWHC 1637 (Ch); [2005] Ch 281 at [110].

1120. Under Australian law, by contrast, it is well established that a constructive trust arises over stolen money.[2174] The established legal position does not obviate the need to resolve the conceptual difficulty aforementioned. In this connection, Tarrant suggests that it is the thief's possessory title (and not the stolen money itself) that is held on a constructive trust.[2175] But Tarrant makes clear that his account can only explain the theft of money in its tangible form, [2176] as money in its intangible form is a chose in action and cannot be stolen[2177] or converted.[2178] Building on Tarrant's analysis, Virgo further argues that the victim of theft has a choice between relying on his or her legal proprietary title or equitable possessory title in claiming against the thief or a subsequent possessor.[2179] The equitable possessory title offers the victim the advantage of being able to trace through mixtures for a claim to be made.

1121. This issue has yet to be considered by the Singapore courts. The further complexity under Singapore jurisprudence is whether such a constructive trust, if recognised at all, should be institutional or remedial in nature. If the stolen money constructive trust is recognised as an institutional constructive trust, Singapore law will have to grapple with the conceptual problem discussed above. But depending on how Singapore law defines the requirement of 'fault' for purpose of a remedial constructive trust, it is possible for the stolen money constructive trust to be remedial in nature.[2180] Under a remedial conceptualisation, the Singapore courts need not deal with the conceptual problem discussed above because a remedial constructive trust is awarded pursuant to the court's exercise of discretion. In other words, the court may order that such an event would lead to the separation of the legal title from the equitable title.

2174. *Black v. Freedman* (1910) 12 CLR 105.
2175. John Tarrant, 'Property Rights to Stolen Money' (2005) 32 U Western Australia L Rev 234; John Tarrant, 'Thieves as Trustees: In Defence of the Thief Principle' (2009) 3 J Eq 170. *Cf* Susan Barkehall-Thomas, 'Thieves as Trustees: The Enduring Legacy of *Black v. S Freedman & Co Ltd*' (2009) 3 J Eq 52; Robert Chambers, 'Trust and theft' in Elise Bant and Matthew Harding (eds), *Exploring Private Law* (CUP, 2010) Chapter 10.
2176. John Tarrant, 'Property Rights to Stolen Money' (2005) 32 U Western Australia L Rev 234 at 235–36.
2177. *R v. Preddy* [1996] AC 815. This decision prompted legislative amendment to the UK Theft Act 1968. Theft (Amendment) Act 1996 introduced an offence under section 15A of dishonestly obtaining a money transfer by deception.
2178. *OBG Ltd v. Allan* [2007] UKHL 21; [2005] 2 WLR 1174.
2179. Graham Virgo, *The Principles of Equity & Trusts*, 2nd edn (OUP, 2016) at 311–12.
2180. *See* further Man Yip, 'Singapore's remedial constructive trust: Lessons from Australia?' (2014) 8 J Eq 77 at 87–88.

IV. Constructive trust over unauthorised profits received in breach of fiduciary duty

1122. In *FHR European Ventures LLP v. Cedar Capital Partners LLC,*[2181] the UK Supreme Court resolved a long-standing controversy[2182] under English law by holding that a constructive trust arises over bribes and secret commissions received by fiduciary agents in breach of fiduciary duty. Notably, the *FHR* decision was arrived at by reason of Lord Neuberger's change of his views as previously held in *Sinclair Investments (UK) Ltd v. Versailles Trade Finance Ltd (in admin rec).*[2183] In *Sinclair Investments*, he laid down a controversial category-based test that required, in essence, some form of proprietary connection between the unauthorised benefits and the principal's assets (or assets that should properly belong to the principal) to justify proprietary relief.[2184] The *Sinclair Investments* categories ruled out proprietary relief in cases involving bribes and secret commissions as these unauthorised benefits are usually paid by third parties to the errant fiduciaries.

1123. By contrast, Singapore law has always taken the unrelenting position that an institutional constructive trust would arise over bribes received by a fiduciary in breach of his duty.[2185] This is consistent with the general attitude of Singapore law that a strongly deterrent approach is warranted in respect of breach of fiduciary duty.[2186] There is therefore little doubt that that the Singapore courts will maintain the approach in future disputes concerning the receipt of unauthorised benefits by fiduciaries. A more nuanced question is whether such a constructive trust should be recharacterised as a remedial constructive trust, especially in light of the fact that Australian law, which recognises a remedial constructive trust,[2187] regards a constructive trust arising over bribes as being remedial in nature.[2188] It is suggested that Singapore law is inclined towards taking a strongly deterrent approach to breaches

2181. [2014] UKSC 45; [2014] 3 WLR 535.
2182. *FHR European Ventures LLP v. Cedar Capital Partners LLC* [2014] UKSC 45; [2014] 3 WLR 535 at [1].
2183. [2011] EWCA Civ 347; [2011] 3 WLR 1153.
2184. [2011] EWCA Civ 347; [2011] 3 WLR 1153 at [88]. Essentially, a constructive trust would only arise over an asset received by a fiduciary in breach of fiduciary duty where the asset is or has been the beneficial property of the beneficiary (category 1) or it was acquired by taking an advantage of an opportunity or a right that properly belonged the beneficiary (category 2). The decision received mixed reviews: see, for e.g., David Hayton, 'Proprietary liability for secret profits' (2011) 127 LQR 487; Roy Goode, 'Proprietary liability for secret profits: a reply' (2011) 127 LQR 493; Graham Virgo, 'Profits obtained in breach of fiduciary duty: personal and proprietary claim?' (2011) 70 CLJ 502.
2185. *Thahir Kartika Ratna v. PT Pertambangan Minyak dan Gas Bumi Negara (Pertamina)* [1994] SGCA 105; [1994] 3 SLR(R) 312.
2186. *See* Yip Man and Goh Yihan, 'Navigating the Maze: Making Sense of Equitable Compensation and Account of Profits for Breach of Fiduciary Duty' (2016) 28 SAcLJ 884 at 890–92.
2187. The Australian model of remedial constructive trust, which is far more developed, does not appear to be identical to Singapore's framework. *See* further Man Yip, 'Singapore's remedial constructive trust: Lessons from Australia?' (2014) 8 J Eq 77.
2188. *Grimaldi v. Chameleon Mining NL (No 2)* (2012) 200 FCR 296 at [569]–[584].

involving the taking of bribes by agents. Accordingly, Singapore law would generally favour an institutional constructive trust approach.[2189]

V. Common Intention Constructive Trust (Domestic Context)

1124. Under English law, after the developments in *Stack v. Dowden* line of cases, the default starting point for domestic consumer cases (or at least where that is the primary purpose)[2190] is the common intention constructive trust framework laid down by the majority in *Stack v. Dowden*, and subsequently clarified in *Jones v. Kernott*. Notably, under English law, the *Stack v. Dowden* framework applies (as opposed to the presumption of advancement) even as between married couples during the subsistence of their marriage.[2191] There is some obiter suggestion in *Stack v. Dowden* that there may be a residual but very limited role for the resulting trust in domestic cases.[2192]

1125. The common intention constructive trust is undoubtedly recognised under Singapore law.[2193] Before the landmark ruling by the Singapore Court of Appeal in *Chan Yuen Lan v. See Fong Mun*,[2194] Singapore cases followed the pre-*Stack* approach endorsed by the House of Lords in *Lloyds Bank plc v. Rosset*.[2195]

1126. In *Chan Yuen Lan*, the Court of Appeal declined to follow the prevailing English approach as laid down by the majority in *Stack v. Dowden*. Instead, it endorsed Lord Neuberger's minority view in *Stack v. Dowden*. The Court of Appeal observed that the English developments were necessitated by the 'changing economic and social conditions in England', which included rises in both property

2189. *Cf* Alvin W-L See, 'Unauthorised Fiduciary Gains and the Constructive Trust' (2016) 28 SAcLJ 1014. See proposes an approach that considers the strength of the principal's interest on a case-by-case basis in determining whether an institutional or remedial constructive trust should be awarded. Where a principal's interest is not particularly strong, See argues that there is room for a remedial constructive trust which affords flexibility for the courts to take on board the legitimate interests of innocent third parties.

2190. *Laskar v. Laskar* [2008] EWCA Civ 347; [2008] 1 WLR 2695 at 2700. Cf *Marr v. Collie* [2017] UKPC 17; [2017] 3 WLR 1507, noted M George and B Sloan, 'Presuming too little about resulting and constructive trusts?' [2017] Conv 303. The Privy Council took a step back from the *Stack* developments and said that the overarching inquiry is focused on the parties' intentions.

2191. *Gibson v. Revenue and Customs Prosecution Office* [2008] EWCA Civ 645; [2009] 2 WLR 471 at [27].

2192. In *Stack v Dowden* [2007] UKHL 17; [2007] 2 AC 432 at [32], Lord Walker noted that the resulting trust 'may still have a useful function in cases where two people have lived and worked together in what has amounted to both an emotional and a commercial partnership'.

2193. *See*, e.g., *Tan Thiam Loke v. Woon Swee Kheng Christina* [1991] SGCA 32; [1991] 2 SLR(R) 595.

2194. [2014] 3 SLR 1048, noted Tang Hang Wu, 'A Dispute in Chancery Lane: Re-considering the Resulting and Common Intention Constructive Trust' (2015) 78 Conv 169.

2195. *Lloyds Bank plc v. Rosset* [1991] 1 AC 107. *Rosset* concerned a sole name case. Where joint names cases are concerned, the English law before *Stack* was not entirely clear; under Singapore law, see *Tan Thiam Loke v. Woon Swee Kheng Christina* [1991] SGCA 32; [1991] 2 SLR(R) 595.

prices and the number of unmarried cohabitees.[2196] Yet, there has been no legislative reform in England and Wales to deal with property disputes arising from such conditions. Further, the Court of Appeal was of the view that the diminished application of the presumption of advancement under English law was also a driver for the *Stack v. Dowden/Jones v. Kernott* developments, as the retention of the resulting trust alone would only put more emphasis on direct contributions to purchase price which the English courts consider to be restrictive.[2197] The Court of Appeal also considered that there are good reasons for not introducing the *Stack v. Dowden* framework into Singapore law.[2198] First, the *Stack v Dowden* analysis is productive of litigation because of the subjectivity and uncertainty inherent in the approach. The uncertainty would also lead to a risk of higher and disproportionate litigation costs. Second, the court pointed out that the domestic/commercial distinction, which determines the applicable tool of analysis, would not be straightforward to apply in some disputes.

1127. Lord Neuberger's approach,[2199] according to the Singapore Court of Appeal, avoids the rigid domestic/commercial classification. The court also agreed with Lord Neuberger's rejection of judicial imputation of intentions at the stage of quantification of interests, [2200] as this would prevent courts from employing the doctrine of common intentions constructive trust to achieve 'palm tree' justice. Further, Lord Neuberger's approach allows a consistent approach to be applied in both domestic and commercial contexts: the common intention constructive trust would apply in both instances to rebut the presumption of resulting trust. The Singapore Court of Appeal proceeded to lay down a six-step analytical framework for determining property ownership[2201] where there have been unequal contributions to the purchase price: [2202]

(a) Is there sufficient evidence of the parties' respective financial contributions to the purchase price of the property? If the answer is 'yes', it will be presumed that the parties hold the beneficial interest in the property in proportion to their respective contributions to the purchase price (*ie*, the presumption of resulting trust arises). If the answer is 'no', it will be presumed that the parties hold the beneficial interest in the same manner as that in which the legal interest is held.
(b) Regardless of whether the answer to (a) is 'yes' or 'no', is there sufficient evidence of an express or an inferred common intention that the parties should hold the beneficial interest in the property in a proportion which is different from that

2196. [2014] SGCA 36; [2014] 3 SLR 1048 at [127].
2197. [2014] SGCA 36; [2014] 3 SLR 1048 at [132].
2198. [2014] SGCA 36; [2014] 3 SLR 1048 at [152].
2199. [2014] SGCA 36; [2014] 3 SLR 1048 at [153]–[158].
2200. *See also Chia Kum Fatt Rolfston v. Lim Lay Choo* [1993] SGHC 203; [1993] 2 SLR(R) 793 in which the Singapore High Court held that parties' interests under a common intention constructive trust are commensurate with their financial contributions, rejecting non-financial contributions as being 'difficult to quantify' this could be read as rejecting an exercise of imputation of intention.
2201. *See* statutory presumptions prescribed in section 53 of the Land Titles Act (Cap. 157, 2004 Rev. Ed.) concerning the manner of holding in the absence of express stipulation.
2202. [2014] SGCA 36; [2014] 3 SLR 1048 at [160].

set out in (a)? If the answer is 'yes', the parties will hold the beneficial interest in accordance with that common intention instead, and not in the manner set out in (a). In this regard, the court may not impute a common intention to the parties where one did not in fact exist.

(c) If the answer to both (a) and (b) is 'no', the parties will hold the beneficial interest in the property in the same manner as the manner in which they hold the legal interest.

(d) If the answer to (a) is 'yes' but the answer to (b) is 'no', is there nevertheless sufficient evidence that the party who paid a larger part of the purchase price of the property (X) intended to benefit the other party (Y) with the entire amount which he or she paid? If the answer is 'yes', then X would be considered to have made a gift to Y of that larger sum and Y will be entitled to the entire beneficial interest in the property.

(e) If the answer to (d) is 'no', does the presumption of advancement nevertheless operate to rebut the presumption of resulting trust in (a)? If the answer is 'yes', then: (i) there will be no resulting trust on the facts where the property is registered in Y's sole name (*ie*, Y will be entitled to the property absolutely); and (ii) the parties will hold the beneficial interest in the property jointly where the property is registered in their joint names. If the answer is 'no', the parties will hold the beneficial interest in the property in proportion to their respective contributions to the purchase price.

(f) Notwithstanding the situation at the time the property was acquired, is there sufficient and compelling evidence of a subsequent express or inferred common intention that the parties should hold the beneficial interest in a proportion which is different from that in which the beneficial interest was held at the time of acquisition of the property? If the answer is 'yes', the parties will hold the beneficial interest in accordance with the subsequent altered proportion. If the answer is 'no', the parties will hold the beneficial interest in one of the modes set out at (b)–(e) above, depending on which is applicable.

1128. *Chan Yuen Lan* was resolved on the resulting trust analysis, as the parties to the dispute did not raise any argument based on the common intention constructive trust. Hence, the Court of Appeal did not go on to discuss the specifics of the recommended framework for resolving property disputes, or if refinements to the *Rosset* 'direct contributions' approach (where common intention constructive trust analysis is relevant) would be necessary, raising further issues for consideration.[2203] The *Chan Yuen Lan* framework has been applied and further developed in later cases. In particular, one obvious development in practice, as a result of the *Chan Yuen Lan* framework, is the greater awareness of the potential applicability of both

2203. One issue that needs to be resolved under Singapore law is the concept of common intention for establishing a common intention constructive trust. *See Sumoi Paramesvaeri v. Fleury, Jeffrey Gerard* [2016] SGHC 181; [2016] 5 SLR 302 at [62]; *Chia Hang Kiu (administratrix of the estate of Chia Chee Wah (alias Chay Ah Soo) deceased) v. Chia Kwok Yeo* [2016] SGHC 198.

resulting trust and common intention constructive trust doctrines in property ownership disputes and their interplay.[2204] In the subsequent case of *Ng So Hang v. Wong Sang Woo*, the High Court noted as follows:[2205]

> While the approach in *Chan Yuen Lan* starts its analysis with the purchase price resulting trust, in practice the foremost claim that is put forward is usually the common intention constructive trust, with an alternative basis relied upon of a proprietary estoppel; the resulting trust is usually the backdrop claim.

In *Ng So Hang*, the High Court did not adhere to the sequential order prescribed in the *Chan Yuen Lan* framework. Instead, it first dealt with the common intention constructive trust analysis, followed by the resulting trust analysis, and finally considered the claim based on proprietary estoppel.

2204. *See*, for e.g., *Su Emmanuel v. Emmanuel Priya Ethel Anne* [2016] SGCA 30; [2016] 3 SLR 1222; *Lai Hoon Woon (executor and trustee of the estate of Lai Thai Lok, deceased) v. Lai Foong Sin* [2016] SGHC 113.

2205. [2018] SGHC 162 at [24].

Chapter 7. Trustee's Duties

§1. Introduction

I. Trustee's Irreducible Core of Obligations

1129. The office of trusteeship is onerous as a trustee owes many kinds of duties, including both fiduciary and non-fiduciary duties. Fiduciary duties will be dealt with in the next chapter. The focus of the present chapter is on non-fiduciary duties, although it is acknowledged that there may be some degree of overlap between the two, in view of the controversy concerning the scope of peculiarly fiduciary duties.

1130. It is well established that a trustee owes an irreducible core of trustee obligations, a concept that was laid down by Millett LJ in *Armitage v. Nurse*:

> The duty of the trustees to perform the trusts honestly and in good faith for the benefit of the beneficiaries is the minimum necessary to give substance to the trusts.[2206]

1131. As the label 'irreducible core' suggests, the concept is concerned with the minimum content of trusteeship. At the fundamental level, the 'irreducible core' of trustee obligations thus serves to define or describe a trust relationship. A trustee is not properly a trustee if he/she does not owe the minimum duties that are characteristic of trusteeship, and the relationship is accordingly not a trust relationship.

1132. On a practical level, the 'irreducible core' concept performs a regulatory function. It prescribes the limit on duty exclusion and therefore significantly impacts the drafting of exclusion/exemption clauses. This was indeed the context in which the dispute in *Armitage v. Nurse* arose. The nub of the appeal before Millett LJ pertained to the permissible scope of a trust exemption clause under English law. According to Millett LJ, a trust exemption clause that purports to exempt liability for breach of the 'irreducible core' of trustee obligations is void.[2207] In principle, however, the exclusion of duties, to which the 'irreducible core' concept relates directly to, is distinct from the exoneration of liability. [2208] Simply put, that the duty exists and has been breached is different from the limitation/exoneration of the liability flowing from the breach.

1133. In *Tan Yok Koon v. Tan Choo Suan*, the Court of Appeal took the view that the duty to perform the trust 'honestly and in good faith for the benefit of the beneficiaries is perhaps more properly considered to be a fiduciary duty in the first place, and as constituting a subset of the obligation of loyalty'.[2209] Indeed, it would

---

2206. [1998] Ch 241 at 253–54.
2207. [1998] Ch 241 at 253–54.
2208. James Penner, 'Exemptions' in Peter Birks and Arianna Pretto (eds), *Breach of Trust* (Hart Publishing, 2002) 241.
2209. [2017] SGCA 1;3 [2017] 1 SLR 654 at [191].

be unreasonable to argue that the obligation of loyalty does not require good faith and honesty.[2210] In any event, trust is always considered to be the paradigmatic fiduciary relationship.

1134. However, Fox has forcefully challenged the utility of the 'irreducible core' concept. He argues that the concept cannot predict the enforceability of duty exclusion or modification clauses where the modification/exclusion in question is not extreme.[2211] It may serve the purpose of demarcating the 'outer limits of trust drafting'.[2212] Ultimately, it is a question of policy as to what are the limits of trust drafting and the answer to that question would vary depending on the policy concerns and national objectives of each jurisdiction.

II. Trustee's Duty of Care

A. *The Equitable Duty of Care*

1135. At general law, a trustee owes an equitable duty of care to exercise the same care as an ordinary, prudent business person would exercise in the conduct of his/her own affairs.[2213] Recent cases clarify that the duty of care ought to differentiate between the degrees of skill and experience possessed by different types of trustees. In *Bartlett v. Barclays Trust Co Ltd* said, Brightman J was of the view that a professional corporate trustee is required to exercise 'the special care and skill which it professes to have'.[2214] Finn J in *Australian Securities Commission v. AS Nominees Limited* was indeed prepared to hold trustee companies to a higher standard of care.[2215] As he observed, the traditional common law standard of care was 'settled a century ago and during a period when trust corporations were not used for the trading and investment purposes that are the commonplace in this country today'.[2216]

1136. A calibrated approach towards the trustee's equitable duty of care was endorsed in *Australian Securities and Investments Commission v. Drake (No 2).*[2217] As Edelman J explained, a trustee's equitable duty of care is ultimately founded upon the trustee's 'objective assumption or undertaking of responsibility in the trust deed or acceptance of trust duties arising from a declaration of trust'.[2218]

2210. Yip Man and Goh Yihan, 'Navigating the Maze: Making Sense of Equitable Compensation and Account of Profits for Breach of Fiduciary Duty' (2016) SAcLJ 884 at 889–90.
2211. Extreme duty exclusion or modification clauses may purport to exclude dishonest breaches or where all disputes arising under the trust are referred to the trustee for determination. *See* David Fox, 'Non-excludable trustee duties' (2011) 17 T&T 17 at 26.
2212. David Fox, 'Non-excludable trustee duties' (2011) 17 T&T 17 at 26.
2213. *Speight v. Gaunt* (1883) 22 Ch D 727 at 730.
2214. [1980] 1 WLR 430 at 444.
2215. (1995) 62 FCR 504 at 517–18.
2216. (1995) 62 FCR 504 at 517.
2217. [2016] FCA 1552 at [272]–[276].
2218. [2016] FCA 1552 at [274].

1137. Accordingly, under Australian law at least, the standard of care would vary between the different types of trustees. Singapore courts have yet to explicitly confirm that the same approach would be adopted under local law but there seems little reason for resisting it. After all, an objective approach – which would allow for having regard to the specific circumstances of the case – lies at the core of the duty of care.

1138. In the scenario where the trust assets comprise shares in a company, the trustee is to 'act in relation to the shares and to the controlling position which they conferred, in the same manner as a prudent man of business'.[2219] In this context, the 'prudent man of business' duty obliges the trustee to do more than merely receive information on the affairs of the company to which a shareholder is entitled. He/she is to supervise the progress of the affairs of the trust-owned company, and the discharge of this duty would require him/her have access to sufficient information, obtained through inquiry and consultation with the directors so that he/she may periodically consider whether the company's affairs are conducted as they should be. In extreme circumstances, he/she would be required to intervene by convening a general meeting to replace one or more of the directors. Where the trustees have controlling interest in a company, a convenient method of supervision is to appoint one or more of the trustees (or their nominee) as directors.[2220]

B. The Statutory Duty of Care

1139. Section 3A of the Trustees Act[2221] provides for the trustee's statutory of care. The provision reads as follows:

(1) In exercising any power, carrying out any duty or doing any act referred to in the First Schedule, a trustee shall exercise such care and skill as is reasonable in the circumstances, having regard in particular –
   (a) to any special knowledge or experience that he has or holds himself out as having; and
   (b) if he acts as trustee in the course of business or profession, to any special knowledge or experience that may reasonably be expected of a person acting in the course of that kind of business or profession.

(2) This section shall apply in relation to trusts whether created before, on or after 15th December 2004, except if, or in so far as, it appears from the trust instrument that the requirements of subsection (1) are not meant to apply.

2219. *Bartlett* [1980] 1 WLR 430 at 442.

2220. *Bartlett* [1980] 1 WLR 430 at 443. *See also In re Lucking's Will Trusts* [1968] 1 WLR 866, 874 (Cross J). *See* further Man Yip, 'Trust-owned companies: understanding the trustee's duties' (2018) 31 TLI 185.

2221. (Cap. 337, 2005 Rev. Ed.).

1140. The statutory duty of care applies to activities/functions set out in the First Schedule to the Trustees Act. In respect of non-scheduled functions or activities, the equitable duty of care shall apply.

1141. As is evident from the language, the standard of care under section 3A is calibrated based on the knowledge and experience of the trustee, differentiating between a lay trustee and a professional trustee and taking on board any knowledge or experience that the trustee (whether lay or professional) professes to have. Section 3A(2) further acknowledges that the statutory duty of care is subject to the terms of the trust instrument. In other words, as is consistent with the position at common law,[2222] the trust instrument may modify or exclude the statutory duty of care.

1142. It has been queried if there are any differences between the standard of care required under the equitable duty of care on the one hand and the statutory duty of care on the other.[2223] In light of the discussion above, unless Singapore law chooses to depart from Australian developments, there appears to be practically no difference between the standards required under the equitable duty of care and statutory duty of care.

§2. Specific Duties Relating to the Administration of Trust (A Selection)

I. Duties on Accepting Office of Trusteeship

1143. On their appointment, according to *Hallows v. Lloyd*, trustees are obliged to make inquiries as to what constitutes the trust property, inspect trust documents and ascertain matters affecting the trust, such as encumbrances.[2224]

1144. A replacement trustee, on appointment, must make reasonable inquiries as to whether his/her predecessor had committed any breach of trust.[2225]

II. Duty to Safeguard the Trust Assets

1145. The trustees are under a stringent duty to safeguard trust assets.[2226] Where there are debts being owed to the trust, trustees are obliged to take reasonable steps, including commencing legal proceedings where necessary, to recover the debt.[2227] Trustees may only be excused for not pursuing litigation to enforce the repayment

2222. *See Armitage v. Nurse* [1980] 1 WLR 430; *Australian Securities and Investments Commission v. Drake (No 2)* [2016] FCA 1552 at [285].
2223. Graham Virgo, *The Principles of Equity & Trusts*, 2nd edn (OUP, 2016) at 449.
2224. (1888) Ch 686 at 691.
2225. *Re Lucking's Will Trusts* [1968] 1 WLR 866.
2226. *Re Miller's Deed Trust* (1978) 75 LS Gaz 454.
2227. *Re Brogden* (1888) 38 Ch D 546.

of the debt if they could show that it is their well-founded belief that legal action would 'result in failure and be fruitless'.[2228]

III. Duty to Act Unanimously

1146. Save in cases involving charitable trusts, trustees must act unanimously.[2229] Trust property are to be held in the joint names of the trustees. In *Lewis v. Nobbs*, the trustees divided the investments between themselves, such that each held one-half of the bonds.[2230] One of the trustees committed a breach of trust by improperly dealing with the bonds in his possession. The other trustee was held liable for the loss.

IV. Duties Relating to Investment

1147. Unless the trust instrument specifies otherwise, a trustee is not obliged to invest the trust fund. However, the trustee has a power to invest, either pursuant to an express provision in the trust instrument or section 4 of the Trustees Act which provides as follows:

> Subject to the provisions of this Act –
>
> (a) a trustee may make any kind of investment that he could make if he were absolutely entitled to the assets of the trust; and
> (b) without prejudice to the generality of paragraph (*a*), a trustee may –
>   (i) invest any funds in his hands, whether at the time in a state of investment or not, in any manner specified in Part I, II or III of the First Schedule in force immediately before 15th December 2004; and
>   (ii) from time to time vary any such investment.

1148. The Trustees Act does not define 'investment', save to provide in section 4(2) that '"investment" includes investment in assets that do not yield any income'. Such an approach avoids the need for frequent and successful legislative amendments to update the statutory meaning of 'investment', given the rapid pace of developments in the financial world. Further, what investment a trustee should make in the circumstances is not a question of the definition of 'investment'; rather, it is a question of the proper decision-making process of the trustee having regard to the terms and circumstances of the trust. As such, the regulatory focus should be on controlling the trustees' exercise of discretion, through a series of related duties. This is indeed the approach taken by the Trustees Act.

2228. *Re Brogden* (1888) 38 Ch D 546 at 574 (Lopes LJ).
2229. *Luke v. South Kensington Hotel* (1879) 11 Ch D 121. As was held in the case, the decision by a majority of the trustees would not bind the trust.
2230. (1878) LR 8 Ch D 591.

1149. Section 2(2) of the Trustees Act makes clear that the statutory powers, which include the general power of investment under section 4, apply to the extent that 'a contrary intention is not expressed in the instrument'. Accordingly, where the trust instrument specifies that the trustees are to make certain kinds of investments or that certain kinds of investments are prohibited, the trustees must abide by the terms.

1150. The statutory duty of care under section 3A of the Trustees Act, discussed above, is applicable to investment activities carried out by the trustees.[2231] Section 5(1) of the Trustees Act further provides that the trustees, in exercising any power of investment, are to have regard to the standard investment criteria set out in subsection (3):

(a) the *suitability* to the trust of investments of the same kind as any particular investment proposed to be made or retained and of that particular investment as an investment of that kind; and
(b) the need for *diversification* of investments of the trusts, in so far as is appropriate to the circumstances of the trust. (Emphasis added.)

1151. By way of illustration, for the criterion on suitability, it may not be suitable to invest trust funds in long-term investments if the trust property is to be distributed in the near term. For the criterion on diversification, this is reflective of the modern investment philosophy that one ought not to put all the eggs in one basket. Section 5(2) requires the trustees to periodically review the investments and consider the need for variation, having regard to the standard investment criteria. It is important to stress that the duty under section 5 is to exercise the power of investment and review the investments having regard to the standard investment criteria; it is not a duty to diversify.[2232]

1152. Section 6 of the Trustees Act requires trustees to 'obtain and consider proper advice', having regard to the standard investment criteria, on how the power of investment should be exercised,[2233] and in the course of period review, on whether investments should be varied.[2234] Section 6(4) clarifies that 'proper advice' refers to 'the advice of a person who is reasonably believed by the trustee to be qualified to give such advice by his ability in and practical experience of financial and other matters relating to the proposed investment'. According to section 6(3), a trustee need not seek proper advice under subsection (1) or (2) if he 'reasonably concludes that in all the circumstances it is unnecessary or inappropriate to do so'. It may be unnecessary for a trustee to seek proper advice if he has the requisite

2231. *See* First Schedule of the Trustees Act.
2232. *Gregyson v. HAE Trustees Ltd* [2009] Bus LR 1640 at [90].
2233. Trustees Act, section 6(1).
2234. Trustees Act, section 6(2).

expertise in relation to the proposed investment. It may be unnecessary and inappropriate for the trustee to seek proper advice where the proposed investment involves a very small sum of money and is secured.[2235]

1153. In the context of investment, generally speaking, the trustees are to exercise the power of investment to yield the best financial return for the beneficiaries, judged in relation to the investment risks in question.[2236] Trustees cannot take into account their own ethical preferences in considering the exercise of the power. Indeed, it was said in *Harris v. Church Commissioners of England* that trustees 'must not use property held by them for investment purposes as a means for making moral statements at the expense of' the trust.[2237] That said, 'the trust defines what the "best interests" are' and the trustee's obligation is to promote what the trust is created for.[2238] It follows that the benefits that the beneficiaries are intended to receive under the trust must be determined in light of that 'best interests' as defined by the trust.[2239]

V. Duty to Distribute

1154. Where beneficiaries are entitled to distribution from the trust fund, the trustees are obliged to locate the beneficiaries and pay them what is due to them, without the need for any demand from the beneficiaries.[2240] Indeed, the trustees are under the duty to inform the beneficiaries of a fixed trust of their interests in the trust property on their becoming entitled to it, for example, on attaining the age as specified in the trust deed.[2241]

VI. Duty to Keep Accounts and Provide Information to the Beneficiaries

1155. A core aspect of trusteeship is the trustee's duty to keep accounts of the trust and allow the beneficiaries to inspect them.[2242] Beneficiaries' access to information relating to the trust enables them to find out what the status of the trust fund is and what transactions have taken place, and to determine whether the trustees have committed any breaches of trust. The duty to furnish accounts is a continuing duty and is not based on a breach of trust or the allegation of the same.[2243]

2235. Jamie Glister and James Lee (eds), *Modern Equity*, 20th edn (Sweet & Maxwell, 2015) at [19-016].
2236. *Cowan v. Scargill* [1985] Ch 270 at 286–287.
2237. [1992] 1 WLR 1241 at [15]. *See* further Rosy Thornton, 'Ethical Investments: A Case of Disjointed Thinking' (2008) 67 CLJ 396.
2238. *Re Merchant Navy Ratings Pension Fund* [2015] EWHC 448 (Ch) at [229].
2239. *Re Merchant Navy Ratings Pension Fund* [2015] EWHC 448 (Ch) at [229].
2240. *Hawkesley v. May* [1956] 1 QB 304 at 325.
2241. *Hawkesley v. May* [1956] 1 QB 304 at 322.
2242. *Lalwani Shalini Gobind v. Lalwani Ashok Bherumal* [2017] SGHC 90 at [16].
2243. *Lalwani Shalini Gobind v. Lalwani Ashok Bherumal* [2017] SGHC 90 at [19]–[20].

1156. To discharge the duty to furnish accounts, a trustee must give proper, complete and accurate documentation as well as justification for his/her administration of the trust. He/she must furnish information as to the current status of the trust fund and the past transactions, including all receipts, disbursements and distribution.[2244] The High Court also makes clear in *Lalwani Shalini Gobind v. Lalwani Ashok Bherumal* that more will be expected of a professional trustee as compared with a non-professional trustee in the discharge of this duty.[2245] For a professional trustee, it may not be sufficient to provide 'some financial documents in relation to the trust'.[2246] A non-professional trustee, on the other hand, may be granted 'fair and reasonable allowances'.[2247]

1157. However, the trustees are not obliged to provide all information as requested by the beneficiaries. It is well established that trustees need not disclose the reasons for their exercise of discretions.[2248] This protects trustees from being subject to constant scrutiny, which may impede them from the proper exercise of discretions.[2249] Further, the Privy Council in *Schmidt v. Rosewood Trust Ltd* has clarified that the beneficiaries' claim for the disclosure of information is to be approached as an aspect of the court's inherent jurisdiction to supervise the administration of trusts.[2250] Essentially, the court, when faced with a claim by the beneficiaries for disclosure, will have to be engaged in a balancing exercise of the competing interests of the trustees, beneficiaries and third parties.[2251] The court may order for limited disclosure and for safeguards to be put in place, particularly where issues of confidentiality (personal or commercial) are engaged in a particular case.[2252] As such, there are no fixed excluded categories of information/documents. Indeed, a letter of wishes, which is a confidential document and which relates closely to the trustees' exercise of discretion, may be ordered for disclosure in exceptional circumstances.[2253]

1158. Schmidt v. Rosewood Trust Ltd has been recently cited by the High Court in *Chiang Shirley v. Chiang Dong Pheng*[2254] in considering a complaint against the executor for failing to provide information and accounts despite repeated requests.[2255] The High Court further commented that a trustee/executor's continuing duty to provide information and accounts must operate within reasonable limits:[2256]

2244. *Glazier Holdings Pty Ltd v. Australian Men's Health Pty Ltd (No 2)* [2001] NSWSC 6 at [38].
2245. [2017] SGHC 90 at [23].
2246. [2017] SGHC 90 at [23].
2247. [2017] SGHC 90 at [23].
2248. *Re Beloved Wilkes' Charity* (1851) 3 Mac & G 440.
2249. *Re Londonderry's Settlement* [1965] Ch 918 at 935–936.
2250. [2003] UKPC 26; [2003] 2 AC 709.
2251. [2003] UKPC 26; [2003] 2 AC 709 at 734.
2252. [2003] UKPC 26; [2003] 2 AC 709 at 734.
2253. *See Breakspear v. Ackland* [2008] 3 WLR 698.
2254. [2015] SGHC 98; [2015] 3 SLR 770 at [87].
2255. Although the High Court did not explicitly affirm that the approach under *Schmidt v. Rosewood Trust Ltd* would be adopted under Singapore law, the better reading is that Singapore law would

In my view, it is common sense that there must be reasonable intervals between the demands and a trustee/personal representative should not be considered to be in breach of trust simply because he does not always supply the documents and information immediately upon the beneficiary's demand. Whether the trustee/personal representative has complied with his duty to supply documents and information is a fact-sensitive exercise in every case.

---

follow the approach. The High Court said (at [87]) that a number of the principles that may be distilled from the Privy Council decision are relevant to the dispute before it.

2256. *Chiang Shirley v. Chiang Dong Pheng* [2015] SGHC 98; [2015] 3 SLR 770 at [89]; affirmed in *Lalwani Shalini Gobind v. Lalwani Ashok Bherumal* [2017] SGHC 90 at [21].

Chapter 8. Fiduciary Duties

§1. Trustees as Fiduciaries

I. Express Trustees

1159. This chapter is focused on fiduciary duties in the context of trusteeship. As Millett LJ explained in *Bristol & West Building Society v. Mothew*, a fiduciary is someone who has 'undertaken to act for or on behalf of another in a particular matter in circumstances which give rise to a relationship of trust and confidence'.[2257]

1160. By conventional wisdom, there are two approaches to finding that a particular actor owes fiduciary duties. The first and traditional approach is to focus on the 'status' of the actor. For example, trustees, directors, solicitors, agents and partners are considered fiduciaries *per se*.[2258] A status-based approach has, however, been criticised for lacking sufficient explanatory power.[2259] The second approach is to determine whether fiduciary duties have arisen based on the circumstances of the case – that is, on an *ad hoc* basis.[2260] Following this approach, fiduciary relationships have been found to arise in circumstances beyond the recognised categories. Courts will look for 'peculiar vulnerability of a party to be affected by an abuse of a power or duty that has been entrusted to another'.[2261]

1161. In *Tan Yok Koon v. Tan Choo Suan*, the Court of Appeal affirmed the principle that 'fiduciary obligations are voluntarily undertaken'.[2262] In the court's view, that someone owes fiduciary obligations 'is a conclusion rather than a premise'.[2263] The court, however, clarified that the law is *not* looking for subjective willingness to undertake fiduciary obligations; rather, 'the fiduciary *voluntarily places himself* in a position where the law can *objectively* impute an intention on his or her party to undertake those obligations'.[2264] The court cited Justice Edelman's extrajudicial writing, 'The Role of Status in the Law of Obligations: Common Callings, Implied Terms, and Lessons for Fiduciary Duties' in Andrew S. Gold and Paul B. Miller (eds), *Philosophical Foundations of Fiduciary Law* (OUP, 2014), chapter 1. In that chapter, Justice Edelman makes the point that modern analysis of fiduciary law

---

2257. [1998] Ch 1 at 18. *See also Hospital Products Ltd v. United States Surgical Corporation* [1984] HCA 64; (1984) 156 CLR 41 at 96–97.
2258. *Ng Eng Ghee v. Mamata Kapildev Dave (Horizon Partners Pte Ltd, intervener)* [2009] SGCA 14; [2009] 3 SLR(R) 109 at [108].
2259. James Edelman, 'When do fiduciary duties arise?' (2010) 126 LQR 302 at 304-305
2260. *See*, for example, *SM Trading Services (a firm) v. Intersanctuary Ltd. (Kek Kim Hok, third party)* [2006] SGHC 102; [2006] 3 SLR(R) 397 at [74] and [79].
2261. *Ng Eng Ghee v. Mamata Kapildev Dave (Horizon Partners Pte Ltd, intervener)* [2009] SGCA 14; [2009] 3 SLR(R) 109 at [110].
2262. *Tan Yok Koon v. Tan Choo Suan* [2017] SGCA 13; [2017] 1 SLR 654 at [194], noted Alvin W-L See, 'Transferor's Intention, Trustee's Undertaking and the Scope of Fiduciary Liability' (2018) TLI 50.
2263. [2017] SGCA 13; [2017] 1 SLR 654 at [193].
2264. [2017] SGCA 13; [2017] 1 SLR 654 at [194] (emphasis as in original text).

should not be intensely focused on status because it is 'only a factor in the process of construction or implication of terms of an undertaking'.[2265] In his view, therefore, not all express trustees will owe fiduciary duties.[2266]

1162. It is unclear whether the Court of Appeal in *Tan Yok Koon* would be prepared to go so far as to *completely abandon* a status-based approach, and to search for the voluntary undertaking to act for the benefit of another in every case, including cases involving traditionally recognised fiduciaries, for example the express trustee. But as Justice Edelman has acknowledged in his extrajudicial writing, such a voluntary undertaking can be implied in many instances of express trusteeship.[2267] In this connection, the Court of Appeal in *Tan Yok Koon* did affirm that the express trustee owes fiduciary duties, in particular the fiduciary duty to perform the trust in good faith and for the benefit of the beneficiaries.[2268] The court nevertheless iterated that the express trustee owes fiduciary duties not by reason of his/her status but as a result of his/her voluntary undertaking to manage the trust property for the benefit of the beneficiaries.[2269] It seems such a voluntary undertaking is *presumed* for express trustees, unless the facts of the case point to the contrary.

1163. More interestingly, it appears that the Court of Appeal dissociates the existence of fiduciary relationship from the imposition of fiduciary duties:

> It should be noted that the fact that a fiduciary duty may be imposed on a fact-specific basis ought not to be perceived as being arbitrary in any way. In addition to the perceptive observations by Prof Finn (see above at [193]), the observations by Justice Edelman (see above at [193]) might also be usefully noted – at least in so far as both observations suggest that the mere existence of a fiduciary *relationship, without more, would not necessarily give rise to fiduciary duties.* As we shall see in a moment, the ***facts and circumstances*** are *also of the first importance in order to ascertain whether or not a fiduciary* ***duty*** *ought to be imposed even where there already exists an established fiduciary* ***relationship*** *between the parties concerned.*[2270]

2265. The Honourable Justice James Edelman, 'The Role of Status in the Law of Obligations: Common Callings, Implied Terms, and Lessons for Fiduciary Duties' in Andrew S. Gold and Paul B. Miller (eds), *Philosophical Foundations of Fiduciary Law* (OUP, 2014) 21 at 37.
2266. The Honourable Justice James Edelman, 'The Role of Status in the Law of Obligations: Common Callings, Implied Terms, and Lessons for Fiduciary Duties' in Andrew S. Gold and Paul B. Miller (eds), *Philosophical Foundations of Fiduciary Law* (OUP, 2014) 21 at 37.
2267. The Honourable Justice James Edelman, 'The Role of Status in the Law of Obligations: Common Callings, Implied Terms, and Lessons for Fiduciary Duties' in Andrew S. Gold and Paul B. Miller (eds), *Philosophical Foundations of Fiduciary Law* (OUP, 2014) 21 at 37.
2268. [2017] SGCA 13; [2017] 1 SLR 654 at [205]. Nothing on the facts suggest that any further investigation as to voluntariness was necessary.
2269. [2017] SGCA 13; [2017] 1 SLR 654 at [205].
2270. [2017] SGCA 13; [2017] 1 SLR 654 at [208] (emphasis as in original).

The above comment leaves one to wonder if someone should be properly described as a fiduciary (for being in a fiduciary relationship) if he does not in fact owe any fiduciary duty. It is hoped that the Court of Appeal will clarify this point in the future.

1164. Finally, one matter that deserves closer scrutiny is the position of a bare trustee. Under a bare trust, which may arise as an express trust, the trustee has no discretion in the administration of the trust. His/her only duty is to hold the property for the benefit of the beneficiaries. For this reason, it has been said that a bare trustee does not owe fiduciary duties.[2271] However, the bare trustee holds legal title which provides opportunity for exploiting the trust property for his/her own interests.[2272] For example, the bare trustee may earn profits from letting out the trust property to a third party in breach of trust. As such, there is still scope for the imposition of fiduciary duties to ensure the proper performance of the duty to hold the property for the benefit of the beneficiaries.

II. Resulting and Constructive Trustees

1165. For resulting and constructive trustees, given that the trust arises by operation of law, it has been said that such trustees do not owe fiduciary duties. In *Giumelli v. Giumelli*, Gleeson CJ, McHugh, Gummow and Callinan JJ said:

> In the present case, the constructive trust is proprietary in nature. It attaches to the Dwellingup property. Such a trust does not necessarily impose upon the holder of the legal title the various administrative duties and fiduciary obligations which attend the settlement of property to be held by a trustee upon an express trust for successive interests.[2273]

1166. To a similar effect, Millett J said in *Lonrho plc v. Fayed (No 2)*:

> It is a [mistake] to suppose that in every situation in which a constructive trust arises the legal owner is necessarily subject to all the fiduciary obligations and disabilities of an express trustee.[2274]

1167. As the Court of Appeal in *Tan Yok Koon* highlighted, Millett J was making a limited proposition that not every constructive trustee owes fiduciary duties as

---

2271. *Financial Management Inc v. Associated Financial Planners Ltd* (2006) 367 WAC 70. *See also* Paul B Miller, 'The Fiduciary Relationship' in Andrew S. Gold and Paul B. Miller (eds), *Philosophical Foundations of Fiduciary Law* (OUP, 2014) 63 at 77.

2272. Robert Flannigan, 'Bare trustee—Fiduciary Obligation—Whether Bare Trustee can Have Fiduciary Duty: *Financial Management Inc v. Associated Financial Planners Ltd*' (2006-2007) 26 Est Tr & Pensions J 114.

2273. [1999] HCA 10; (1999) 196 CLR 101 at [5].

2274. [1992] 1 WLR 1 at 11H -12B.

undertaken by an express trustee.[2275] The court went on to hold that resulting trustees may exceptionally owe fiduciary duties. The legal question, according to the court, 'is whether, *objectively* speaking, the resulting trustee can be said to have undertaken (whether expressly or impliedly) to act in a particular way which is fiduciary in nature'.[2276] This is a fact-specific determination. The court explained that while knowledge that one does not hold the beneficial interest in the property is not a sufficient condition, it is a necessary condition in order that the resulting trustee' conscience is 'affected in a way that equity can take cognisance of'.[2277] The court considered that an express trustee who becomes a resulting trustees on the failure of the express trust may still owe fiduciary duties, as it would be difficult to say that the express trustee's fiduciary duties cease upon the failure of the express trust.[2278] This is one of the two bases upon which the court found that the resulting trustee in the case owed fiduciary duties.[2279] The court, however, acknowledged that a resulting trustee's duties that are owed to the beneficiary will 'almost invariably be narrower' than an express trustee's duties.[2280]

1168. In *Tan Yok Koon*, the court also considered the alternative analysis of a presumed resulting trust – that the transfer of property (shares) was made on a gratuitous basis.[2281] It found that the resulting trustee in the case owed fiduciary duties because the trustee knew that she was not the beneficial owner of the trust property (the company shares), although it should not be missed that the resulting trustee's case was precisely to the contrary – that she was the beneficial owner. *Tan Yok Koon* concerned, in part, a complex family dispute over the beneficial ownership of shares in a family company. The events which led to the dispute spanned over many years. The peculiar family context was relevant to understanding the intention behind the series of transfers of shares between the family members. The court observed that the deceased father was an 'autocratic patriarch who demanded and generally received utmost respect from [the children] and drew no distinction between the assets of his family members and those of his companies'.[2282] The deceased father caused a number of shares in the company to be transferred to his children and wife. Four of the five children worked for the family business as instructed by the father. Importantly, as instructed by the father, these four children later transferred their shares to the eldest sibling in preparation for the establishment of a family trust, which did not materialise ultimately. However, it was also found that the siblings' respect and deference to their father waned over the years. On reviewing all the available evidence, the court found that the younger siblings

2275. [2017] SGCA 13; [2017] 1 SLR 654 at [190].
2276. [2017] SGCA 13; [2017] 1 SLR 654 at [206] (emphasis in italics as original).
2277. [2017] SGCA 13; [2017] 1 SLR 654 at [206].
2278. [2017] SGCA 13; [2017] 1 SLR 654 at [205].
2279. [2017] SGCA 13; [2017] 1 SLR 654 at [213]-[214]. The case concerned transfer of shares. On one analysis, the Court considered that the transfer of shares was for a non-charitable purpose trust which subsequently failed (the proposed family trust), and the express trustee of that failed express trust would thus hold the shares on a resulting trust for the settlors.
2280. [2017] SGCA 13; [2017] 1 SLR 654 at [206].
2281. [2017] SGCA 13; [2017] 1 SLR 654 at [213]-[214]. *See also Lim Ah Leh v. Heng Fock Lin* [2018] SGHC 156 at [161].
2282. [2017] SGCA 13; [2017] 1 SLR 654 at [86].

did not intend to relinquish their beneficial ownership in the shares when they transferred them to the eldest sibling. As the eldest sibling provided no consideration, the court was satisfied that she held the shares on a resulting trust for her other siblings.

§2. Peculiarly Fiduciary Duties: Nature and Function

1169. In *Mothew*, Millett LJ has made clear that not all breaches of duties by a fiduciary are breaches of fiduciary duties:

> The expression 'fiduciary duty' is properly confined to those duties which are peculiar to fiduciaries and the breach of which attracts legal consequences differing from those consequent upon the breach of other duties. Unless the expression is so limited it is lacking in practical utility. In this sense it is obvious that not every breach of duty by a fiduciary is a breach of fiduciary duty.[2283]

1170. A distinction must thus be drawn between peculiarly fiduciary duties and non-peculiarly fiduciary duties,[2284] as the remedial consequences would differ between the breaches of the two sets of duties. However, the drawing of this distinction is no straightforward exercise. While there is general consensus that the no-conflict rule and the no-profit rule are peculiarly fiduciary duties, there is much debate as to whether other duties ought to be characterised as fiduciary duties. In particular, a core aspect of the debate is centred on whether the content of fiduciary obligation is exhausted by proscriptive duties[2285] or if it comprises prescriptive duties as well.[2286]

1171. The position is presently unclear under Singapore law. In *Tan Yok Koon*, the Court of Appeal, by citing *Mothew*,[2287] seemingly affirmed that fiduciary duties include prescriptive duties such as the duty to act in good faith.[2288] In fact, the court held that the duty to act honestly and in good faith for the benefit of the beneficiaries – which is conventionally known as the irreducible obligation of trusteeship – is a fiduciary obligation.[2289] Yet, within the same breath, the court also affirmed the contrary position that fiduciary obligations could be described as 'proscriptive and

2283. [1998] Ch 1 at 16.
2284. *See generally* Matthew Conaglen, *Fiduciary Loyalty: Protecting the Due Performance of Non-Fiduciary Duties* (Hart Publishing, 2011) Chapter 3.
2285. *See* Matthew Conaglen, 'The Nature and Function of Fiduciary Loyalty' (2005) 121 LQR 452; Robert Flannigan, 'The Adulteration of Fiduciary Doctrine in Corporate Law' (2006) 122 LQR 449.
2286. *See*, for example, *Westpac Banking Corp v. The Bell Group Ltd (in liq)* (2012) 270 FLR 1; *Item Software (UK) Ltd v. Fassihi* [2005] 2 BCLC 91 at [41].
2287. [1998] Ch 1 at 18.
2288. *See generally* Lusina Ho, 'Good faith and fiduciary duty in English law' (2010) 4 J Eq 29.
2289. [2017] SGCA 13; [2017] 1 SLR 654 at [191].

prophylactic'.[2290] Conaglen, a chief defender of the exclusively proscriptive view of fiduciary obligations, explains the meaning of the prophylactic operation of the Anglo-Australian fiduciary doctrine: it 'operates so as to increase the likelihood of the fiduciary's faithful adherence to duty … by protecting the fiduciary from influences that are likely to interfere with proper performance of the fiduciary's *non*-fiduciary duties'.[2291] 'Prophylactic', on Conaglen's view, goes beyond the strictness in the application of the fiduciary principles.[2292] On his account of fiduciary doctrine, the doctrine performs a 'subsidiary and prophylactic form of protection for non-fiduciary duties'.[2293]

1172. But the question of whether fiduciary duties are exclusively proscriptive is inextricably linked to the question of the function of the fiduciary duties, that is, whether they are prophylactic in nature.[2294] And these are complex questions of law. As we shall see below, the Singapore Court of Appeal has recently endorsed a prescriptive duty of disclosure, a position that contradicts the widely popular view that fiduciary obligations are exclusively fiduciary.

§3. The No-Conflict Rule

1173. As a fiduciary, the trustee must not place himself/herself in a position of potential or actual conflict of interest and duty or conflict between duties.[2295] There is a great overlap between the operation of the no-conflict rule and the no-profit rule in practice because many of the cases where unauthorised profits have been made are likely to be cases involving a potential or actual conflict of interest and duty. The advantage of invoking the no-profit rule, however, is that the plaintiff need not prove that a conflict has arisen in the circumstances. Conceptually, it has been a long-standing debate as to whether the two rules are distinct and to what degree.[2296]

2290. [2017] SGCA 13; [2017] 1 SLR 654 at [192]. *Cf* Rebecca Lee, 'In Search of the Nature and Function of Fiduciary Loyalty: Some Observations on Conaglen's Analysis' (2007) 27 OJLS 327.

2291. Matthew Conaglen, *Fiduciary Loyalty: Protecting the Due Performance of Non-Fiduciary Duties* (Hart Publishing, 2011) at 61.

2292. Matthew Conaglen, *Fiduciary Loyalty: Protecting the Due Performance of Non-Fiduciary Duties* (Hart Publishing, 2011) at 62.

2293. Matthew Conaglen, *Fiduciary Loyalty: Protecting the Due Performance of Non-Fiduciary Duties* (Hart Publishing, 2011) at 62. *Cf* Rebecca Lee, 'In Search of the Nature and Function of Fiduciary Loyalty: Some Observations on Conaglen's Analysis' (2007) 27 OJLS 327.

2294. Kelvin F.K. Low, 'Fiduciary duties: the case for prescription' (2016) 30 TLI 3 at 11.

2295. Under Australian jurisprudence, there is a debate whether the test should be framed as 'position of conflict' or 'pursuit of conflict': see *Agricultural land Management Ltd v. Jackson (No 2)* [2014] WASC 102 at [267]–[268]; *cf Re Colorado Products Pty Ltd (in prov liq)* [2014] NSWSC 780 at [340].

2296. *See generally* Matthew Conaglen, *Fiduciary Loyalty: Protecting the Due Performance of Non-Fiduciary Duties* (Hart Publishing, 2011) at 120-125. Conaglen considers that the no-profit rule is 'an outgrowth from the conflict principle' and is 'applied in related but slightly different circumstances'.

I. Test for Determining Conflict

1174. In *Ng Eng Ghee v. Mamata Kapildev Dave*,[2297] the Court of Appeal, in *obiter*, indicated a preference to follow the stricter test in determining conflict as enunciated by the majority in *Boardman v. Phipps*,[2298] which requires only a *mere possibility* of conflict. This is notwithstanding that Lord Upjohn's 'real sensible possibility' of conflict test – albeit a dissenting judgment in *Boardman v. Phipps* – prevailed in lower English courts subsequently.[2299] As Lord Upjohn said:

> The phrase 'possibly may conflict' requires consideration. In my view it means that the reasonable man looking at the relevant facts and circumstances of the particular case would think that there was a real sensible possibility of conflict; not that you could imagine some situation arising which might, in some conceivable possibility in events not contemplated as real sensible possibilities by any reasonable person, result in a conflict.[2300]

The primary reason for the Court of Appeal's adoption of the stricter test is the need to 'extinguish all possibility of temptation and to deter fiduciaries who may be tempted to abuse their positions'.[2301]

1175. In the subsequent case of *Higgins, Danial Patrick v. Mulacek, Philippe Emmanuel*, the High Court, without considering the Court of Appeal's obiter comments in *Ng Eng Ghee* or providing any specific justification, endorsed Lord Upjohn's test.[2302] While deterrence is a worthwhile policy goal to pursue,[2303] that does not necessarily translate into adopting the strictest measure possible in every stage of the legal analysis of the fiduciary doctrine. One possible justification for applying a less stringent test in determining whether conflicts have arisen is to consider the combined effect of the no-profit rule and the no-conflict rule. The no-profit rule addresses many situations involving conflicts where the fiduciary has made unauthorised profits. The rule could be brought into play without the need to prove a conflict; it may be said that the conflict is presumed in such cases. As such, the situations that fall outside of the ambit of the no-profit rule but fall within the scope

2297. [2009] SGCA 30; [2009] 3 SLR(R) 109 at [142]–[145].
2298. [1967] 2 AC 46.
2299. *See*, for example, *Re Bhullar* [2003] BCC 711 at [42] (Parker LJ).
2300. [1967] 2 AC 46 at 124.
2301. *Ng Eng Ghee v. Mamata Kapildev Dave* [2009] SGCA 30; [2009] 3 SLR(R) 109 at [143]. Other reasons offered by the court related to the general difficulty of determining the errant fiduciary's motives and detecting actual conflicts given that the fiduciary is often well placed to conceal them (see [2009] SGCA 30; [2009] 3 SLR(R) 109 at [144]–[145]).
2302. [2016] SGHC 205; [2016] 5 SLR 848 at [97].
2303. The effect of both specific and general deterrence has been doubted by scholars, though such doubts are generally expressed in the context of searching for an appropriate justification for awarding proprietary relief for breach of fiduciary duty. *See*, for example, Katy Barnett, 'Distributive justice and proprietary remedies over bribes' (2015) 35 LS 302 at 305–306.

of the no-conflict rule would most likely be cases where the conflict has led to a loss.[2304] Yet, it is difficult to envisage how a theoretical possibility of conflict could be the cause of the alleged losses.

II. The Self-Dealing Rule and the Fair-Dealing Rule

1176. The self-dealing rule is invoked where the trustee purchases trust property, thereby placing himself/herself on both ends of the transaction. Under this rule, a trustee's purchase of trust property is voidable.[2305] As Conaglen explains, the self-dealing rule is underlined by the no-conflict principle.[2306] In a case of the trustee purchasing trust property, his self-interest of obtaining the lowest price conflicts with his duty owed to the trust to obtain the highest price. Fairness of the transaction is irrelevant.[2307] However, the trustee may avoid the application of the self-dealing rule if he has obtained the court's sanction to become the purchaser or if he has obtained the beneficiaries' fully informed consent.[2308]

1177. The fair-dealing rule deals with the situation where the trustee is purchasing the beneficiary's beneficial title to the trust property. The transaction is not liable to be set aside if the trustee can show that he took 'no advantage of his position and that the beneficiary was fully informed and received full value'.[2309] On Conaglen's rationalisation of the fair-dealing rule being part of the no-conflict principle, he argues that the fairness of the transaction is relevant to the operation of the fair-dealing rule because it 'provides evidence as to whether the principal's consent to the transaction was fully informed'.[2310] As fully informed consent is the focal concern, it follows that a transaction at undervalue but which was entered into with fully informed consent from the beneficiaries – and such consent could be proved in the case – would be upheld.[2311]

2304. Of course, the aggrieved principal might be seeking other remedies, most notably, injunctive relief.
2305. *Campbell v. Walker* (1800) 5 Ves 678 at 680.
2306. Matthew Conaglen, 'A Re-Appraisal of the Fiduciary Self-Dealing and Fair-Dealing Rules' [2006] CLJ 366.
2307. *Mulvany v. Dillon* (1810) 1 Ball & Beatty 409 at 418 (LC).
2308. Matthew Conaglen, *Fiduciary Loyalty: Protecting the Due Performance of Non-Fiduciary Duties* (Hart Publishing, 2011) at 128.
2309. *Tito v. Waddell (No 2)* [1977] Ch 106 at 225.
2310. Matthew Conaglen, *Fiduciary Loyalty: Protecting the Due Performance of Non-Fiduciary Duties* (Hart Publishing, 2011) at 129.
2311. Matthew Conaglen, *Fiduciary Loyalty: Protecting the Due Performance of Non-Fiduciary Duties* (Hart Publishing, 2011) at 133.

III. Conflicts Between Inconsistent Duties

1178. The law on the conflict between inconsistent duties is not as well studied as the law on conflict between duty and personal interest.[2312] However, given the topic's practical significance, it deserves more attention than it currently receives. As affirmed by the Court of Appeal in *Ohm Pacific Sdn Bhd v. Ng Hwee Cheng Doreen*, the fact of multiple engagements is not by itself fatal.[2313] In the first place, the duties owed to the different principals may not be conflicting. Moreover, if the applicable test for conflict is the 'real sensible possibility' of conflict, that there is a theoretical possibility of conflict between the duties will not bring the no-conflict rule into play.

1179. In *Ohm Pacific*, the defendant was the director and shareholder of Company A. The defendant's law firm acted for both Company A and Company B in a bridging finance transaction under which the defendant was appointed as an attorney for Company B. In the circumstances, the Court of Appeal found that the defendant was in (a) a conflict of duty owed to Company A and her duty owed to Company B; and (b) a conflict of duty owed to Company B and her personal interest in Company A.[2314]

1180. On Conaglen's account, the rule to avoid potential conflicts is prophylactic in nature: 'the object is to avoid situations in which proper performance of the non-fiduciary duties is jeopardised'.[2315] Yet, it is also clear that potential conflicts may be tolerated if the principals to whom inconsistent duties are owed have given informed consent for the fiduciary to act for both of them.[2316] Lord Cozens-Hardy MR said in *Moody v. Cox and Hatt*:

> He ought before putting himself in that position to inform the client of his conflicting duties, and either obtain from that client an agreement that he should not perform his full duties of disclosure or say, which would be much better, 'I cannot accept this business'. [2317]

1181. Even if the fiduciary had obtained the informed consent of both principals to continue acting while occupying a position of potential conflict of duties, he

2312. *See generally* Matthew Conaglen, 'Fiduciary regulation of conflicts between duties' (2009) 125 LQR 111; Matthew Conaglen, 'Remedial ramifications of conflicts between a fiduciary's duties' (2010) 126 LQR 72.

2313. [1994] SGCA 85; [1994] 2 SLR(R) 633 at [20], citing *Farrington v. Rowe McBride & Partners* [1985] 1 NZLR 83 at 90 (Richardson J).

2314. [1994] SGCA 85; [1994] 2 SLR(R) 633 at [18].

2315. Matthew Conaglen, *Fiduciary Loyalty: Protecting the Due Performance of Non-Fiduciary Duties* (Hart Publishing, 2011) at 148.

2316. *Ohm Pacific* [1994] SGCA 85; [1994] 2 SLR(R) 633 at [20]–[22].

2317. [1917] 2 Ch 71 at 81 (emphasis added). Conaglen rationalised that the critical factor is informed consent and informed consent is more readily obtained in a transaction involving two parties (fair-dealing rule situation), as opposed to a transaction involving one party on both ends (self-dealing rule situation).

would not be absolved from the breach of fiduciary duty if, in the course of acting for both parties, he actually preferred the interests of one principal to another.[2318]

1182. However, if the authorised potential conflict matures into an actual conflict,[2319] it is said that the fiduciary cannot continue to act for both principals. In *Bristol and West Building Society v. Mothew*, Millett LJ made the following observations regarding the rule to avoid 'actual conflict' of duties:

> [T]he fiduciary must take care not to find himself in a position where there is an actual conflict of duty so that he cannot fulfill his obligations to one principal without failing in his obligations to the other ... If he does, he may have no alternative but to cease to act for at least one and preferably both. The fact that he cannot fulfill his obligations to one principal without being in breach of his obligations to the other will not absolve him from liability. [2320]

1183. What is less clear is why resignation is an appropriate response in the circumstances. Even less clear is whether resignation is always the appropriate response and if something more may be required (e.g., arranging for a replacement or asking the principal to seek independent advice), depending on the circumstances of the case. Low has argued that 'an early discharge from both offices, whilst leaving a fiduciary exposed to claims from both principals, may indeed be preferable as a matter of total liability to both'.[2321] The better view, therefore, is that resignation is an adequate form of response to an instance of actual conflict in many situations because it could effectively reduce losses (by stopping further done from being done) suffered by both principals.

1184. In a more straightforward situation where the fiduciary acts for both principals in a transaction with conflicting interests – such as where one principal is to purchase a property from another principal[2322] – the fiduciary is in a position of actual conflict and will be liable for breach of fiduciary duty.[2323] This is because in such situations, the performance of one set of duties will inevitably involve the

---

2318. Hinted at by the Court of Appeal in *Ohm Pacific* [1994] SGCA 85; [1994] 2 SLR(R) 633 at [22]: 'Even if the respondent had obtained the informed consent of the appellants, she would still be liable to the appellants if she had not discharged her duty to the appellants because of her interests in Pacific Navigation and her conflicting duty to Pacific Navigation.'

2319. It may not be easy to determine when the actual conflict has ripened: see *Sun Indalex Finance LLC v. United Steelworkers* [2013] 1 SCR 271. *See* further Paul B. Miller, 'Multiple Loyalties and the Conflicted Fiduciary' (2014) 40 Queen's LJ 301.

2320. [1996] Ch 1 at 19 (emphasis added).

2321. Kelvin F.K. Low, 'Fiduciary Duties: The Case for Prescription' [2016] 30 TLI 3 at 21.

2322. The purchaser would strive for the lowest price whereas the seller would strive for the highest price.

2323. *See Agricultural Land Management Ltd v. Jackson (No 2)* [2014] WASC 102.

breach of the other set of duties.[2324] What is not fully investigated is whether in principle, seeking the informed consent from both principals could authorise the fiduciary to continue to act for them. This question does not readily arise in practice because at least one of the principals or both would not authorise the fiduciary to continue to act in the transaction.

1185. More unusually, in *Re Colorado Products Pty Ltd (in prov liq),*[2325] the defendant fiduciary occupied various roles in different companies: she was the director of the importing Australian company known as Colorado, the controller of the manufacturing Chinese company which supplied the goods to Colorado, as well as the company which leased Colorado's business premises. Black J dismissed most of the allegations relating to breach of the no-conflict rule because the alleged breaches 'were contemplated by the arrangements between the parties' or were not established.[2326] The conflicts pre-existed the plaintiffs' acquisition of their respective interests in Colorado and the business structure put in place contemplated that the conflicts would persist post-acquisition.[2327] The corporate officers of the plaintiffs had knowledge of the defendant director's multiple roles in the different companies.[2328] Further, Colorado's constitution expressly allowed a director to contract with Colorado, subject to the disclosure of the relevant interest.[2329] *Re Colorado* may thus be an unusual case of tolerated actual conflict. On another view, however, one may say that the defendant's duties were significantly modified in the circumstances such that she did not owe any fiduciary obligations in respect of the performance of her functions that would otherwise give rise to inherent actual conflicts.

IV. Informed Consent

1186. We now turn to consider what amounts to fully informed consent. In *Ng Eng Ghee*, the Court of Appeal described the concept of informed consent as the 'duty of full disclosure'.[2330] With respect, this label may cause confusion as informed consent is not a duty which if unperformed amounts to a breach of duty attracting remedial consequences. Informed consent is an authorisation mechanism, which, if obtained, would absolve liability for the breach of fiduciary duties (such as the no-conflict rule or the no-profit rule).

1187. On what amounts to informed consent, the court said as follows:

2324. Matthew Conaglen, *Fiduciary Loyalty: Protecting the Due Performance of Non-Fiduciary Duties* (Hart Publishing, 2011) at 149.
2325. [2014] NSWSC 789 at [340].
2326. [2014] NSWSC 789 at [387]
2327. [2014] NSWSC 789 at [365]. *See* further Justice Ashley Black, 'Equitable and statutory regulation of conflicts of interests and duty' Presentation at University of New South Wales Law School (10 May 2016) at 8.
2328. [2014] NSWSC 789 at [365].
2329. [2014] NSWSC 789 at [362].
2330. [2009] SGCA 30; [2009] 3 SLR(R) 109 at [146].

> The fiduciary must disclose the personal interest as soon as a possible conflict arises, or as soon after as practicable. An 'interest' may be constituted by 'the presence of some personal concern of possible significant pecuniary value in a decision taken, or transaction effected, by a fiduciary' (*Fiduciary Obligations* at para 472). It may be an interest which is not yet fully realised …[2331]

1188. The burden of proving full disclosure rests with the fiduciary.[2332] A fiduciary merely disclosing that he has an interest or informally making statements that 'put a fiduciary on inquiry' would not suffice.[2333] In *Ohm Pacific*, the Court of Appeal held that the fact that the principal had knowledge of the fiduciary's interests in another company and her acting also for that company did not amount to informed consent from the principal.[2334] For there to be informed consent, the fiduciary was required to explain her 'dual responsibilities in those transactions and how the [principal] would or might be prejudiced by also engaging her as their solicitor'.[2335] Neither would showing that informed consent would have been given had the fiduciary sought it amount to informed consent.[2336]

§4. The No-Profit Rule

1189. Regarding the no-profit rule, Singapore law has generally followed the traditional English approach:[2337] a fiduciary may not, by the use of his position, earn an unauthorised profit,[2338] unless he has sought the principal's informed consent.[2339]

1190. Breach of the no-profit rule is strict.[2340] It does not matter that the fiduciary has acted in good faith; whether the profit would or should otherwise have gone to the principal; whether the conduct benefited the principal; whether the fiduciary is duty-bound to obtain the profit for the principal;[2341] whether the disgorgement would have resulted in a windfall to the plaintiff;[2342] or that it would have been

2331. *Ibid.*, at [147].
2332. *Ibid.* at [148].
2333. *Ibid.* at [148].
2334. [1994] SGCA 85; [1994] 2 SLR(R) 633 at [22].
2335. *Ibid.*
2336. *Ng Eng Ghee* [2009] SGCA 30; [2009] 3 SLR(R) 109 at [148], citing *Murad v. Al-Saraj* [2005] EWCA Civ 959.
2337. *Regal (Hastings) Ltd v. Gulliver* [1967] 2 AC 134.
2338. To be clear, the no-profit rule is directed at the making of *unauthorised* profits. By way of legislative reform, trustees are allowed to receive remuneration for their administration of trust. *See* Trustees Act (Cap. 337, 2005 Rev. Ed.), sections 41Q and 41R.
2339. *Lim Suat Hua v. Singapore HealthPartners Pte Ltd* [2012] SGHC 63; [2012] 2 SLR 805 at [90].
2340. *Regal (Hastings) Ltd v. Gulliver* [1967] 2 AC 134 at 145.
2341. *Ibid.*, *v.* at 144–45.
2342. *Mona Computer Systems (S) Pte Ltd v Singaravelu Murugan* [2013] SGCA 63; [2014] 1 SLR 847 at [13]–[16].

impossible to obtain the principal's informed consent on the facts of the case.[2343] The strictness of the rule may be justified by the fact that the court cannot carry out adequate investigation in most cases because 'the facts are generally difficult to ascertain or are solely within the knowledge of the person who is being charged'.[2344]

1191. As the High Court explains in *Higgins, Danial Patrick*, the no-profit rule is aimed at 'protecting the integrity of the fiduciary relationship from being tainted by the prospect of a conflict of interest, it is stringently applied and bites even where the company did not, or even could not, take up the opportunity'.[2345]

§5. An Independent Duty of Disclosure?

1192. The English Court of Appeal decision in *Item Software (UK) Ltd v. Fassihi*[2346] stirred debate as to whether there is an independent fiduciary duty to disclose one's misconduct or even more broadly, a duty to disclose matters which one in good faith considers to be in the benefit of the principal to know. In that case, the defendant was the sales director of the claimant company and he had encouraged the claimant company's managing director to take a hard line approach in the company's negotiations with the counter-contracting party to a distribution agreement. Unbeknownst to the company, while the negotiations were ongoing, the defendant unsuccessfully attempted to divert the opportunity to a corporate entity set up by him. The managing director's negotiation approach led to the termination of the agreement.

1193. In *Item Software*, Arden LJ maintained that there is no independent duty to disclose misconduct but the requirement to disclose is tied to the duty of loyalty:

> For my part, I do not consider that it is correct to infer from the cases to which I have referred that a fiduciary owes a separate and independent duty to disclose his own misconduct to his principal or more generally information of relevance and concern to it. So to hold would lead to a proliferation of duties and arguments about their breadth. I prefer to base my conclusion in this case on the fundamental duty to which a director is subject, that is the duty to act in what he in good faith considers to be the best interests of his company. This duty of loyalty is the 'time-honoured' rule … [O]n the facts of this case, there is no basis on which Mr Fassihi could reasonably have come to the conclusion that it was not in the interests of Item to know of his breach of duty. In my

2343. *Keech v. Sandford* (1726) Sel Cas Ch 61.
2344. *Regal (Hastings) Ltd v. Gulliver* [1967] 2 AC 134 at 154 (Lord Wright).
2345. *Higgins, Danial Patrick* [2016] SGHC 205; [2016] 5 SLR 848 at [96].
2346. [2004] EWCA Civ 1244; [2005] BCLC 91.

> judgment, he could not fulfil his duty of loyalty in this case except by telling Item about his setting up of RAMS, and his plan to acquire the Isograph contract for himself.[2347]

Accordingly, the defendant was found to have been in breach of his duty of loyalty for failing to disclose his past misconduct – his surreptitious approach to the counter-contracting party.

1194. The decision has been subject to fierce criticisms.[2348] Berg points out that notwithstanding Arden LJ's insistence that the disclosure requirement is not a free-standing fiduciary duty, 'it functioned in precisely that way', operating as 'a separate and additional source of liability'.[2349] Berg suggests that the effect of *Item Software* is that a fiduciary whose misconduct generates some liability (e.g., for breaching the no-conflict rule) would face additional liability for failing to disclose his misconduct.[2350]

1195. We now turn to consider the Singapore position. There were High Court decisions iterating that although there is no free-standing duty of disclosure, a failure to disclose relevant information in certain circumstances could amount to a breach of fiduciary duty. In *Griffin Travel Pte Ltd v. Nagender Rao Chilkuri*, Chan J said:

> … even in the context of the fiduciary duties of a director, there is no *free-standing* duty to disclose. Rather, it is founded on the director's duty 'to act in what he in good faith considers to be the best interests of his company' (*Ranson* at [52], citing *Item Software (UK) Ltd v. Fassihi* [2004] EWCA Civ 1244) … To conclude, Nagender and Leny did not owe free-standing duties of disclosure to the Plaintiff but that is very different from saying that a failure to disclose is *never* a breach of fiduciary duty. A director can hardly argue that he has upheld his general duty of single-minded loyalty if his failure to disclose was motivated by bad faith, such as where the director was aware that such non-disclosure would cause harm to the company.[2351]

1196. In Clearlab SG Pte Ltd v Ting Chong Chai, Lee J said to a similar effect:

> [I]t was alleged that Ting breached his fiduciary duties by failing to inform Clearlab of the existence of a competitor, Aquilus. But Ting was not even under

2347. [2004] EWCA Civ 1244; [2005] BCLC 91 at [41] and [44].

2348. *See*, in particular, *P & v. Industries Pty Ltd v. Porto* [2006] VSC 131. *C.f.* Lusina Ho and Pey-Woan Lee, 'A director's duty to confess: a matter of good faith?' (2007) 66 CLJ 348. Ho and Lee argue that the duty of disclosure may be 'justified as an application of a director's duty to refrain from acting with the intention to prejudice the company's interests, and that this duty is fiduciary in nature'.

2349. Alan Berg, 'Fiduciary duties: a director's duty to disclose his own misconduct' (2005) 121 LQR 213 at 220.

2350. *Ibid*''.

2351. [2014] SGHC 205 at [51]–[52].

a contractual obligation to disclose the existence of a competitor, much less a fiduciary one. It would be a better argument to say that Ting was under a fiduciary duty to disclose the existence of the competitor that he wrongfully assisted by using Clearlab's confidential information.[2352]

1197. However, in *Centre for Laser and Aesthetic Medicine Pte Ltd v. GPK Clinic (Orchard) Pte Ltd*,[2353] the Court of Appeal seemingly suggested directly that the duty of disclosure is a free-standing fiduciary duty. In that case, a fiduciary was found liable for breach of fiduciary duty for failing to report to the principal that another employee was diverting patients to a competing clinic set up by that employee.[2354] The court relied on the High Court's ruling in *ABB Holdings Pte Ltd v. Sher Hock Guan Charles*.[2355] In *ABB*, the High Court accepted that the following are fiduciary duties owed by an employee to its employer:

(a) a duty to act in good faith and in the best interests of the plaintiffs;
(b) a duty not to place himself in a position where his duty to the plaintiffs and his personal interests may conflict;
(c) a duty to disclose to the plaintiff's information which came to him and which was of concern to the plaintiffs and was relevant to the plaintiffs to know;
(d) a duty not to disclose information of concern to the plaintiffs and [which] was relevant for the plaintiffs to know to third parties;
(e) a duty to disclose to the plaintiffs any potential threat and/or competitive risk posed to their business; and
(f) a duty to inform the plaintiffs of any activity, actual or threatened, which could damage the plaintiffs' interests.[2356]

1198. It is noteworthy that the duty to disclose is not limited to past misconduct of the fiduciary but is pitched at a more general level: to disclose information which would be in in the interests of the principal to know. On further reflection, if such a fiduciary duty is accepted under Singapore law, it means that the Singapore fiduciary doctrine is not exclusively proscriptive in nature, a position that may be justified. It is hoped that the Court of Appeal would clarify the Singapore position, by reference to relevant decisions from major common law jurisdictions and Singapore High Court decisions in *Griffin Travel* and *Clearlab*, when the opportunity arises before it.

2352. [2014] SGHC 221; [2015] 1 SLR 163 at [281].
2353. [2017] SGCA 68; [2018] 1 SLR 180.
2354. *Centre for Laser and Aesthetic Medicine Pte Ltd* [2017] SGCA 68; [2018] 1 SLR 180 at [76]–[77].
2355. [2009] SGHC 157; [2009] 4 SLR(R) 111.
2356. [2009] SGHC 157; [2009] 4 SLR(R) 111 at [7] and [42].

Selected Bibliography

AG Guest, 'Accession and Confusion in the Law of Hire-Purchases' (1964) 27 MLR 505

A.J. McClean, 'The Common Law Life Estate and the Civil Law Usufruct: A Comparative Study' (1963) 12 ICLQ 649

A.J. Oakley, *Constructive Trusts* (Sweet & Maxwell, 1997)

A.L. Rhodes, 'The *Quistclose* Trust's Detrimental Effect on Commercial Transactions' (2013) 27 TLI 179

Aedit Abdullah, 'Repudiation of Leases' [1998] SJLS 438

Alain-Laurent Verbeke, Bart Verdickt and Dirk-Jan Maasland, 'The Many Faces of Usufruct' in Cornelius van der Merwe and Alain-Laurent Verbeke (eds), *Time-Limited Interests in Land* (Cambridge: CUP, 2012)

Alan Berg, 'Fiduciary duties: a director's duty to disclose his own misconduct' (2005) 121 LQR 213

Alistair Hudson, *Equity and Trusts*, 8th edn (Routledge, 2015)

Alvin W-L See, 'The *Quistclose* Trust in Singapore' (2014) 20 T&T 362

Alvin W-L See, 'Contract for the Grant of a Compliant Option to Purchase' [2015] SJLS 241

Alvin W-L See, 'Unauthorised Fiduciary Gains and the Constructive Trust' (2016) 28 SAcLJ 1014

Alvin W-L See, 'Transferor's Intention, Trustee's Undertaking and the Scope of Fiduciary Liability' (2018) 32 TLI 50

Andrew Burrows, 'We Do This at Common Law But That in Equity' (2002) 22 OJLS 1

Andrew Burrows, 'Illegality after Patel v Mirza' (2017) 70 CLP 55

Andrew Harding (ed), *The Common Law in Singapore and Malaysia* (Butterworths, 1985)

Andrew Phang *et al*, *The Law of Contract in Singapore* (Academy Publishing, 2012)

Andrew Robertson and Michael Tilbury (eds), *Divergences in Private Law* (Hart Publishing, 2016)

Andrew S. Gold and Paul B. Miller (eds), *Philosophical Foundations of Fiduciary Law* (OUP, 2014)

Brian Green, '*Grey, Oughtred and Vandervell* - A Contextual Reappraisal' (1984) 47 MLR 385

Barrie Lawrence Nathan, 'In Defence of The Primary Trust: *Quistclose* Revisited' (2012) 18 T&T 123

Barry C. Crown, 'Severance of a Joint Tenancy' [1998] SJLS 166
Barry C. Crown, 'Passing the Benefit and Burden of Restrictive Covenants Governing Land in Singapore' [1998] SJLS 98
Barry C. Crown, 'Partial Alienation by One Co-Owner of Land' [2000] SJLS 92
Barry C. Crown, 'Requirement of a Pre-Existing Interest to Support a Caveat Under the Land Titles Act' [2000] SJLS 341
Barry C. Crown, 'Equity Trumps the Torrens System' [2002] SJLS 409
Barry C. Crown, 'Developments in the Law of Co-Ownership' [2003] SJLS 116
Barry C. Crown, 'The Lease for Life and the Requirement of Certainty' [2004] SJLS 37
Barry C. Crown, 'Back to Basics: Indefeasibility of Title Under the Torrens System' [2007] SJLS 117
Barry C. Crown, 'Whiter Torrens Title in Singapore?' (2010) 22 SAcLJ 9
Barry C. Crown, 'En Bloc Sales and Joint Tenancy' [2011] SJLS 564
Barry C. Crown, 'Where There's a Will, There's a Way' (2015) 27 SAcLJ 222
Bartholomew G.W., 'The Singapore Statute Book' (1984) 26 *Malayan L Rev* 1
Ben McFarlane and Robert Stevens, 'The Nature of Equitable Property' (2010) 4 J Eq
Ben McFarlane, *The Structure of Property Law* (Hart Publishing, 2008)
Bryan Chew, Vincent Hoong, Tay Lee Koon and Manimegalai d/o Vellasamy, 'Compulsory Acquisition of Land in Singapore' (2010) 22 SAcLJ 166
C.H. Tham, 'Exploding the Myth that Bare Sub-trustees "Drop Out"' (2017) 31 TLI 76
C.T. Emery, 'The Most Hallowed Principle—Certainty of Beneficiaries of Trusts and Powers of Appointment' (1982) 98 LQR 55
Chan, Helena, *An Introduction to the Singapore Legal System* (Malayan Law Journal, 1986)
Charles Harpum, 'Overreaching, Trustees' Powers and the Reform of the 1925 Legislation' (1990) 49 CLJ 277
Charles Mitchell (ed), *Constructive and Resulting Trusts* (Hart Publishing, 2009)
Charles Mitchell (ed), *Constructive and Resulting Trusts* (Hart Publishing, 2010)
Charles Mitchell and Stephen Watterson, 'Remedies for Knowing Receipt' in Charles Mitchell (ed), *Constructive and Resulting Trusts* (Hart Publishing, 2010)
Charles Mitchell and Paul Mitchell (eds), *Landmark Cases in Equity* (Hart Publishing, 2012)
Christian Twigg-Flesner, Rick Canavan and Hector MacQueen, *Atiyah and Adam's Sale of Goods*, 13th edn (Pearson, 2016)
D.O. McGovney, 'Irrevocable Offers' (1914) 27 Harv L Rev 644
D.W.M. Waters, *The Constructive Trust* (Athlone Press, 1964)
David Hayton, 'Developing the Obligation Characteristic of the Trust' (2011) 117 LQR 96
David Hayton, 'Proprietary liability for secret profits' (2011) 127 LQR 487
David Fox, 'The Transfer of Legal Title to Money' [1996] RLR 60
David Fox, 'Relativity of Title in Law and at Equity' [2006] CLJ 330
David Fox, *Property Rights in Money* (OUP, 2008)
David Fox, 'Non-excludable trustee duties' (2011) 17 T&T 17
Duncan Sheehan, *The Principles of Personal Property Law*, 2nd edn (Hart, 2017)

Selected Bibliography

Earl C Arnold, 'Law of Accession of Personal Property' (1922) 22 Columbia L Rev 103
Elaine Chew, 'Digging Deep into the Ownership of Underground Space – Recent Changes in Respect of Subterranean Land Use' [2017] SJLS 1
Eric Descheemaeker (ed), *The Consequences of Possession* (Edinburg University Press, 2014)
Elise Bant and Matthew Harding (eds), *Exploring Private Law* (CUP, 2010)
Ernest G Lorenzen, 'Specification in the Civil Law' (1925) 35 Yale LJ 29
F.W. Maitland, *Equity: A Course of Lectures* (John Brunyate, 2nd rev edn) (CUP, 1936)
Frederick Pollock (ed), *Table Talk of John Selden* (Selden Society, 1927)
Gareth Jones, 'Section 53(1)(c) and (2) of the Law of Property Act 1925 - Recent Developments' [1966] CLJ 19
Gary Chan, *The Law of Torts in Singapore*, 2nd edn (Academy Publishing, 2015)
Gary Watt, *Trusts and Equity*, 2nd edn (OUP, 2006)
Gbolahan Elias, *Explaining Constructive Trusts* (Clarendon Press, 1990)
Gerard McCormack, 'Mixture of Goods' (1990) 10 LS 293
Gerard McCormack, 'Reservation of title – past, present and future' [1994] Conv 129
Giovanni Pugliese 'On Roman Usufruct' (1966) 40 Tulane L Rev 523
Goh Yihan, 'Tort Law in the Face of Land Scarcity in Singapore' (2009) 26 Arizona J Intl & Comp L 335
Goh Yihan and Yip Man, '*Marley v. Rawlings*: Reflections from Singapore' [2014] SJLS 218
Goh Yihan & Paul Tan (eds), *Singapore Law: 50 Years in the Making* (Academy Publishing, 2015)
Graham Battersby, 'Formalities for the Disposition of Equitable Interests Under Trust' [1979] Conv 17
Graham Virgo, 'Profits obtained in breach of fiduciary duty: personal and proprietary claim?' (2011) 70 CLJ 502
Graham Virgo, *The Principles of Equity and Trusts* (OUP, 2012)
Graham Virgo, '*Patel v. Mirza*: One Step Forward and Two steps back' (2016) 22 T&T 1090
H. Stowe, 'The "Unruly Horse" has bolted' (1994) 57 MLR 441
Halsbury's Laws of Singapore (Singapore: LexisNexis, 2012), vol. 9(3)
Howard Hunter, *The Law of Sales in Singapore* (Academy Publishing, 2017)
HW Tang, 'The Right of Lateral Support of Buildings from the Adjoining Land' (2002) Conv 237
I.M. Hardcastle, 'Administrative Unworkability – A Reassessment of an Abiding Problem' [1990] Conv 24
J.E. Martin, *Modern Equity*, 17th edn (London: Sweet & Maxwell, 2005)
J.D. Feltham, 'Informal Trusts and Third Parties' [1987] Conv 246; Austin Wakeman Scott, 'Conveyances Upon Trusts Not Property Declared' (1924) 37 Harv L Rev 653
J.W. Harris, 'The Case of the Slippery Equity' (1975) 38 MLR 557
J.W.A. Thornely, 'Trusts of Personalty–Disposition of Interests–Formality' (1960) 18 CLJ 31

James Barr Ames, 'Constructive Trusts Based Upon the Breach of an Express Oral Trust of Land' (1907) 20 Harv L Rev 549
James Edelman, 'A "Fusion Fallacy" Fallacy?' (2003) 119 LQR 375
James Edelman, 'When do fiduciary duties arise?' (2010) 126 LQR 302
James Goudkamp, 'The end of an era? Illegality in private law in the Supreme Court' (2017) 133 LQR 1
James Lee, 'Constructing and limiting liability in equity' (2015) 131 LQR 39
James Penner, 'Exemptions' in Peter Birks and Arianna Pretto (eds), *Breach of Trust* (Hart Publishing, 2002)
James Penner, 'Lord Millett's Analysis' in William Swadling (ed), *The Quistclose Trust: Critical Essays* (Hart Publishing, 2004)
Jamie Glister, 'Mutual Intention and *Quistclose* Trusts' (2012) 6 J Eq 221
Jamie Glister and Pauline Ridge (eds), *Fault Lines in Equity* (Hart Publishing, 2012)
Jamie Glister and James Lee (eds), *Hanbury & Martin: Modern Equity*, 20th edn (Sweet & Maxwell, 2015)
John Baalman, *The Singapore Torrens system: being a commentary on the Land Titles Ordinance 1956 of the State of Singapore* (Govt. Printer, 1961)
John G Sprankling, 'Owning the Center of the Earth' (2008) 55 UCLA L Rev 979
John McGhee (ed), *Snell's Equity*, 33rd edn (Sweet & Maxwell, 2015)
John Mee, 'Automatic Resulting Trusts: Retention, Restitution, or Reposing Trust?' in Charles Mitchell (ed), *Constructive and Resulting Trusts* (Hart Publishing, 2009)
John Mee, 'Presumed resulting trusts, intention and declaration' (2014) 73 CLJ 86
John Tarrant, 'Property Rights to Stolen Money' (2005) 32 U Western Australia L Rev 234
John Tarrant, 'Thieves as Trustees: In Defence of the Thief Principle' (2009) 3 J Eq 170
Julius A.W. Grower, 'Explaining the *Pallant v. Morgan* equity' [2016] Conv 434
Justice Ashley Black, 'Equitable and statutory regulation of conflicts of interests and duty' Presentation at University of New South Wales Law School (10 May 2016)
KS Teo, 'Right of Support for Buildings Revisited' (2004) 78 ALJ 20
Katy Barnett, 'Distributive justice and proprietary remedies over bribes' (2015) 35 LS 302
Keith Mason, 'Deconstructing constructive trusts in Australia' (2010) 4 J Eq 98
Kelry Loi, 'Mortgagees Exercising Power of Sale: Nonfeasance, Privilege, Trusteeship & Duty of Care' [2010] JBL 576
Kelry CF Loi, 'Tracing and the Future of *Romalpa* Clauses' [2008] RLR 76
Kelry CF Loi, '*Quistclose* Trusts and *Romalpa* Clauses: Substance and *Nemo Dat* in Corporate Insolvency' (2012) 128 LQR 412
Kelvin F.K. Low and Tan Sook Yee, 'Equity and Trust' (2002) 3 SAL Ann Rev 202
Kelvin FK Low, 'Apparent gifts: re-examining the equitable presumption' (2008) 124 LQR 369
Kelvin F.K. Low, 'The Nature of Torrens Indefeasibility: Understanding the Limits of Personal Equities' (2009) 33 Melb U L Rev 205
Kelvin F.K. Low, 'The Story of "Personal Equities" in Singapore: Thus Far and Beyond' [2009] SJLS 161

Kelvin F.K. Low, 'Informal Dealings with Land: Retaining the Knotty Apron Strings' (2010) 22 Sing Ac LJ 704
Kelvin F.K. Low, 'Fiduciary duties: the case for prescription' (2016) 30 TLI 3
Kelvin FK Low, 'Non-Charitable Purpose Trusts: The Missing Right to Forgo Enforcement' in Richard Nolan, Kelvin FK Low and Tang Hang Wu (eds), *Trusts and Modern Wealth Management* (Hart Publishing, 2018, forthcoming)
Kevin Gray, 'Property in Thin Air' (1991) 50 CLJ 252
Kevin Gray and Susan Francis Gray, *Elements of Land Law*, 5th edn (OUP, 2009)
Lee Eng Beng, 'Not Quite Unclogged' [1997] SJLS 597
Lee Eng Beng, 'Unsecured Creditor Versus Unregistered Charge' (1998) 10 SAcLJ 241
Lim Chin Joo, 'Compulsory Land Acquisition in Singapore' (1968) 10 Malaya L Rev 1
Lionel Smith, 'Constructive Trusts and Constructive Trustees' (1999) 58 CLJ 294
Loo Wee Ling, *Law of Credit and Security* (LexisNexis, 2012)
Lord Denning, 'The Need for a New Equity' (1950) 5 CLP 1
Lord Millett, 'Proprietary Restitution' in Simone Degeling and James Edelman (eds) *Equity in Commercial Law* (Law Book Co, 2005) 309
Lord Millett, 'The *Quistclose* trust — a reply' (2011) 17 T&T 7
Louise Gullifer, '"Sales" on retention of title terms: is the English law analysis broken?' (2017) 133 LQR 244
Lusina Ho and Pey-Woan Lee, 'A director's duty to confess: a matter of good faith?' (2007) 66 CLJ 348
Lusina Ho, 'Good faith and fiduciary duty in English law' (2010) 4 J Eq 29
Lye Lin Heng, *Landlord and Tenant* (Butterworths, 1990)
Lynton Tucker, Nicholas Le Poidevin and James Brightwell, *Lewin on Trusts*, 19th edn (Sweet & Maxwell, 2015)
M George and B Sloan, 'Presuming too little about resulting and constructive trusts?' [2017] Conv 303
Man Yip, 'The *Pallant v. Morgan* equity reconsidered' (2013) 33 LS 549
Man Yip, 'Singapore's remedial constructive trust: Lessons from Australia?' (2014) 8 J Eq 77
Man Yip, 'The Restitutionary Aftermath of Contractual Illegality' [2015] RLR 106
Man Yip, 'The Commercial Context in Trust Law' [2016] Conv 347
Man Yip, 'The Presumptions of Resulting Trust and Advancement Under Singapore Law: Localisation, Nationalism and Beyond' in Andrew Robertson and Michael Tilbury (eds), *Divergences in Private Law* (Hart Publishing, 2016)
Man Yip, 'Trust-owned companies: understanding the trustee's duties' (2018) 31 TLI 185
Mark Pawlowski, 'Tenant abandonment – damages for loss of future rent' (2010) 126 LQR 361
Martin Dixon, 'The Non-Proprietary Lease: The Rise of the Feudal Phoenix' (2000) 59 CLJ 25
Matthew Conaglen, 'The Nature and Function of Fiduciary Loyalty' (2005) 121 LQR 452
Matthew Conaglen, 'A Re-Appraisal of the Fiduciary Self-Dealing and Fair-Dealing Rules' [2006] CLJ 366

Matthew Conaglen, 'Fiduciary regulation of conflicts between duties' (2009) 125 LQR 111
Matthew Conaglen, 'Remedial ramifications of conflicts between a fiduciary's duties' (2010) 126 LQR 72
Matthew Conaglen, *Fiduciary Loyalty: Protecting the Due Performance of Non-Fiduciary Duties* (Hart Publishing, 2011)
Michael Bridge, *The Sale of Goods*, 3rd edn (OUP, 2014)
Michael Bridge (ed), *Benjamin's Sale of Goods*, 10th edn (Sweet & Maxwell, 2017)
Michael Bridge, 'Certainty, Identification and Intention in Personal Property Law' in Paul S. Davies and James Penner (eds), *Equity, Trusts and Commerce* (Hart Publishing, 2017)
Michael Bryan, 'Constructive Trusts: Understanding Remedialism' in Jamie Glister and Pauline Ridge (eds), *Fault Lines in Equity* (Hart Publishing, 2012)
Michael Smolyansky, 'Reining in the *Quistclose* Trust: a Response to *Twinsectra v. Yardley*' (2010) 16 T&T 558
N Khublall, Compulsory Land Acquisition—Singapore and Malaysia, 2nd edn (Butterworths, 1994)
Nicholas Strauss, 'Imperfect Gifts and the Law of Property Act 1925, s. 53(1)(c)' (1967) 30 MLR 461
P.G. Turner, 'The High Court of Australia on Contracts to Assign Equitable Rights' [2006] Conv 390
P Pillai, 'The Primacy of the Principle of Reciprocity in the Singapore Land Regime' (2001) SAcLJ 198
P V Baker, 'Case note on *Grey v. Inland Revenue Commissioners*' (1958) 74 LQR 180
Patricia Loughlan, 'The Historical Role of the Equitable Jurisdiction' in Patrick Parkinson (ed), *The Principles of Equity*, 2nd edn (Lawbook Co, 2003) 3
Patrick Parkinson, 'Reconceptualising the Express Trust' (2002) 61 CLJ 657
Patrick Parkinson (ed), *The Principles of Equity*, 2nd edn (Lawbook Co, 2003)
Paul B Miller, 'The Fiduciary Relationship' in Andrew S. Gold and Paul B. Miller (eds), *Philosophical Foundations of Fiduciary Law* (OUP, 2014)
Paul B. Miller, 'Multiple Loyalties and the Conflicted Fiduciary' (2014) 40 Queen's LJ 301
Paul S. Davies and James Penner (eds), *Equity, Trusts and Commerce* (Hart Publishing, 2017)
Peter Birks, *An Introduction to the Law of Restitution,* revised ed (Oxford, 1989)
Peter Birks, 'Restitution and Resulting Trusts' in Stephen R. Goldstein (ed), *Equity and Contemporary Legal Developments* (Humaccabi Press, 1992)
Peter Birks and Arianna Pretto (eds) *Breach of Trust* (Hart Publishing, 2002)
Peter Jaffey, 'Explaining the Trust' (2015) 131 LQR 377
Phang Andrew, 'Theoretical Conundrums and Practical Solutions in Singapore Commercial Law: A Review and Application of Section 5 of the Civil Law Act' (1988) 17 *Anglo-American L Rev* 251
Phang B.L. Andrew, *The Development of Singapore Law* (Singapore: Butterworths, 1990)
Phang Andrew, 'Cementing the Foundations: The *Singapore Application of English Law Act 1993*' (1994) 28 *U British Columbia L Rev* 205

Phang Andrew, *Cheshire, Fifoot and Furmston's Law of Contract*, 2nd Singapore and Malaysian edn (Butterworths Asia, 1998)
Prakash Pillai, 'The Primacy of the Principle of Reciprocity in the Singapore Land Regime' (2001) SAcLJ 198
R Braddell, 'Heirs and the Common Law' (1941) MLJ xlvii
R.A. Buckley, *Illegality and Public Policy*, 3rd edn (Sweet & Maxwell, 2013)
R.C. Nolan, '*Vandervell v. I.R.C.*: A Case of Overreaching' (2002) 61 CLJ 169
R.C. Nolan, 'Equitable Property' (2006) 122 LQR 232
Rachel Leow and Timothy Liau, 'Resulting trusts: a victory for unjust enrichment' (2014) 73 CLJ 500
Rebecca Lee, 'In Search of the Nature and Function of Fiduciary Loyalty: Some Observations on Conaglen's Analysis' (2007) 27 OJLS 327
Richard Nolan, Kelvin FK Low and Tang Hang Wu (eds), *Trusts and Modern Wealth Management* (Hart Publishing, 2018, forthcoming)
Robert Chambers, *Resulting Trusts* (OUP, 1997)
Robert Chambers, 'Restrictions on the Use of Money' in William Swadling (ed), *The Quistclose Trust: Critical Essays* (Hart Publishing, 2004)
Robert Chambers, 'The Importance of Specific Performance' in Simone Degeling and James Edelman (eds.), *Equity in Commercial Law* (Law Book, 2005)
Robert Chambers, 'Trust and theft' in Elise Bant and Matthew Harding (eds), *Exploring Private Law* (CUP, 2010)
Robert Flannigan, 'The Adulteration of Fiduciary Doctrine in Corporate Law' (2006) 122 LQR 449
Robert Flannigan, 'Bare trustee—Fiduciary Obligation—Whether Bare Trustee can Have Fiduciary Duty: *Financial Management Inc v. Associated Financial Planners Ltd*' (2006-2007) 26 Est Tr & Pensions J 114
Robin Hickey, *Property and the Law of Finders* (Hart Publishing, 2010)
Ronald Dworkin, *Taking Rights Seriously* (Harvard University Press, 1978)
Roscoe Pound, 'The Progress of the Law – Equity' (1920) 33 Harvard L Rev 420
Rosy Thornton, 'Ethical Investments: A Case of Disjointed Thinking' (2008) 67 CLJ 396
Roy Goode, 'Proprietary liability for secret profits: a reply' (2011) 127 LQR 493
S.F.C. Milsom, *Historical Foundations of the Common Law*, 2nd edn (OUP, 1981)
S.M. Spencer, 'Beneficiaries and Transferring Trustees' [1967] Conv 175
Sarah Worthington, 'Sorting Out Ownership Interests in a Bulk: Gifts, Sales and Trusts' [1999] JBL 1
Sjef van Erp and Bram Akkermans (eds), *Cases, Materials and Text on National, Supranational and International Property Law* (Oxford: Hart Publishing, 2012)
Shannon Lindsay, *Caveats Against Dealings in Australia and New Zealand* (Federation Press, 1995)
Simone Degeling and James Edelman (eds) *Equity in Commercial Law* (Law Book Co, 2005)
Simon Douglas, 'How to reform section 62 of the Law of Property Act 1925' [2015] Conv 13
Sir Terence Etherton, 'Constructive Trusts: A New Model for Equity and Unjust Enrichment' (2008) 67 CLJ 265.

Soon Choo Hock and Andrew Phang Boon Leong, 'Reception of English Commercial Law in Singapore – A Century of Uncertainty' in Andrew Harding (ed), *The Common Law in Singapore and Malaysia* (Butterworths, 1985)

Stephen R. Goldstein (ed), *Equity and Contemporary Legal Developments* (Humaccabi Press, 1992)

Susan Barkehall-Thomas, 'Thieves as Trustees: The Enduring Legacy of *Black v. S Freedman & Co Ltd*' (2009) 3 J Eq 52

Susan Bright, Leases, Exclusive Possession and Estates' (2000) 116 LQR 7

Susan Bright, 'The Third Party's Conscience in Land Law' [2000] Conv 398

T.G. Youdan, 'Formalities for Trusts of Land and the Doctrine in *Rochefoucauld v. Boustead*' (1984) 43 CLJ 306

T.G. Youdan, 'Informal Trusts and Third Parties: A Response' [1988] Conv 267

Tan Cheng Han, 'Springing Security Interests and Registration' (2001) SAcLJ 451

Tan Sook Yee, 'Of Chattels, Fixtures and Retention of Title' [1988] 3 MLJ xvii

Tan Sook Yee, 'Execution against Co-Owned Property' [2000] SJLS 52

Tan Sook Yee, 'Equitable Leases, Subdivision and Section 4, Planning Act' (2002) 14 SAcLJ 133

Tan Yock Lin, *Personal Property Law* (Academy Publishing, 2014)

Tang Hang Wu, 'The Right of Lateral Support of Buildings from the Adjoining Land' (2002) Conv 237

Tang Hang Wu, 'Beyond the Torrens Mirror: A Framework of the In Personam Exception to Indefeasibility (2008) 32 Melb U L Rev 672

Tang Hang Wu and Kelvin F.K. Low, *Tan Sook Yee's Principles of Singapore Land Law*, 3rd edn (LexisNexis, 2009)

Tang Hang Wu., 'The Constructive Trust in Singapore: Five Persistent Puzzles' (2010) 22 SAcLJ 136

Tang Hang Wu, 'A Dispute in Chancery Lane: Re-considering the Resulting and Common Intention Constructive Trust' (2015) 78 Conv 169

Teo Keng Sood, 'Right of Support for Buildings Revisited' (2004) 78 ALJ 20

Teo Keang Sood, *Strata Title in Singapore and Malaysia*, 5th edn (LexisNexis, 2015)

Teo Keang Sood, 'The Trust Statutory Exception to Indefeasibility in the Singapore Torrens System' [2017] SJLS 151

Ter Kah Leng, '*En Bloc* Sales in Singapore: Critical Developments in the Law' (2009) 21 SAcLJ 485

The Honourable Justice James Edelman, 'The Role of Status in the Law of Obligations: Common Callings, Implied Terms, and Lessons for Fiduciary Duties' in Andrew S. Gold and Paul B. Miller (eds), *Philosophical Foundations of Fiduciary Law* (OUP, 2014)

Thomas W Merill, 'Accession and Original Ownership' (2009) 1 J Legal Analysis 459

Tsuyoshi Kataka and David L Callies (eds), *Taking Land* (University of Hawaii Press, 2002)

TTB Koh, 'The Law of Compulsory Land Acquisition in Singapore' (1967) 2 Malayan LJ ix

Victor C.S. Yeo, 'No Security For the Unsecured Creditors' (2000) SAcLJ 218

W.J.M. Ricquier and Soon Choo Hock, 'The "Licence Coupled with Equity" in Singapore and Malaysia' (1981) 23 Malaya LR 123
WJM Ricquier, 'Compulsory Purchase in Singapore' in Tsuyoshi Kataka and David L Callies (eds), *Taking Land* (University of Hawaii Press, 2002)
W.J.M. Ricquier, *Land Law*, 5th edn (LexisNexis, 2017)
WW Buckland, 'The Conception of Usufruct in Classical Law' (1927) 43 LQR 326
Walter G. Hart, 'What is a Trust?' (1899) 15 LQR 294
Walter Woon, 'Mesne Profits, Double Rent and Double Value in Singapore' [1985] MLJ lxiv
Wee Meng Seng, 'Duties of a Mortgagee and a Receiver: Where Singapore Should and Should Not Follow English Law' (2008) 20 SAcLJ 559
Wee Meng Seng, 'The Avoidance of Unregistered Charge and Extension of Time to Register' (2014) 26 SAcLJ 750
William Blackstone, *Commentaries on the Laws of England*, Book 2 (Clarendon Press, 1765)
William R Johnston, 'Emphyteusis: A Roman "Perpetual" Tenure' (1940) 3 U Toronto LJ 323
William Swadling, 'A New Role for Resulting Trusts?' (1996) 16 LS 110
William. Swadling, 'Limitation' in Peter Birks and Arianna Pretto (eds) *Breach of Trust* (Hart Publishing, 2002) 319
William Swadling, 'Orthodoxy' in William Swadling (ed), *The Quistclose Trust: Critical Essays* (Hart Publishing, 2004)
William Swadling (ed), *The Quistclose Trust: Critical Essays* (Hart Publishing, 2004)
William Swadling, 'Explaining Resulting Trusts' (2008) 124 LQR 72
William Swadling, 'The Nature of the Trust in *Rochefoucauld v. Boustead*' in Charles Mitchell (ed), *Constructive and Resulting Trusts* (Hart Publishing, 2010)
William Swadling, 'The Fiction of the Constructive Trust' (2011) 64 CLP 1
Yeo Tiong Min, 'Restitution' (2007) 8 SAL Annual Review at 377–81
Ying Kai Liew, '*Rochefoucauld v. Boustead* (1897)' in Charles Mitchell and Paul Mitchell (eds), *Landmark Cases in Equity* (Hart Publishing, 2012)
Yip Man, 'Trusts and Equity: Dreaming and Building a Singapore Equitable Jurisdiction' in Goh Yihan & Paul Tan (eds), *Singapore Law: 50 Years in the Making* (Academy Publishing, 2015)
Yip Man and Goh Yihan, 'Navigating the Maze: Making Sense of Equitable Compensation and Account of Profits for Breach of Fiduciary Duty' (2016) 28 SAcLJ 884

Table of Cases

Table of Cases

Table of Statutes

Index

(The numbers here refer to paragraph numbers.)

www.ingramcontent.com/pod-product-compliance
Lightning Source LLC
Chambersburg PA
CBHW071409230926
51846CB00001B/38
* 9 7 8 9 4 0 3 5 0 8 8 4 9 *